PRIVATE INTERNATIONAL LAW AND COMPETITION LITIGATION IN A GLOBAL CONTEXT

This important book systematically analyses the private international law issues regarding private antitrust damages claims which arise out of transnational competition law infringements. It identifies those problems that need to be considered by injured parties, defendants, judges and policy-makers when dealing with cross-border private antitrust damages claims in a global context. It considers the post-Brexit landscape and the implications in cross-border private proceedings before the English courts and suggests how the legal landscape should be developed. It also sets out how private international law techniques could play an increasingly important role in private antitrust enforcement.

Comprehensive and rigorous, this is required reading for scholars of both competition litigation and private international law.

Volume 37 in the series Studies in Private International Law

Studies in Private International Law

Recent titles in the series

Rethinking Judicial Jurisdiction in Private International Law
Milana Karayanidi

Economic Sanctions in EU Private International Law
Tamás Szabados

Clawback Law in the Context of Succession
Jayne Holliday

Place of Performance: A Comparative Analysis
Chukwuma Okoli

Private International Law in Nigeria
Chukwuma Okoli and Richard Oppong

Planning the Future of Cross Border Families: A Path Through Coordination
Edited by Ilaria Viarengo and Francesca Villata

The Private International Law of Authentic Instruments
Jonathan Fitchen

The Hague Judgments Convention and Commonwealth Model Law: A Pragmatic Perspective
Abubakri Yekini

A Guide to Global Private International Law
Edited by Paul Beaumont and Jayne Holliday

Parental Child Abduction to Islamic Law Countries
Nazia Yaqub

The Application of Foreign Law in the British and German Courts
Alex Critchley

The HCCH 2019 Judgments Convention: Cornerstones, Prospects, Outlook
Edited by Matthias Weller, João Ribeiro-Bidaoui, Moritz Brinkmann and Nina Dethloff

Jurisdiction Over Non-EU Defendants: Should the Brussels Ia Regulation be Extended?
Edited by Tobias Lutzi, Ennio Piovesani and Dora Zgrabljic Rotar

Private International Law and Competition Litigation in a Global Context
Mihail Danov

Private International Law and Competition Litigation in a Global Context

Mihail Danov

•HART•
OXFORD • LONDON • NEW YORK • NEW DELHI • SYDNEY

HART PUBLISHING

Bloomsbury Publishing Plc

Kemp House, Chawley Park, Cumnor Hill, Oxford, OX2 9PH, UK

1385 Broadway, New York, NY 10018, USA

29 Earlsfort Terrace, Dublin 2, Ireland

First published in Great Britain 2023

A catalogue record for this book is available from the British Library.

A catalogue record for this book is available from the Library of Congress.

ISBN: HB: 978-1-50991-866-9
ePDF: 978-1-50991-868-3
ePub: 978-1-50991-867-6

Typeset by Compuscript Ltd, Shannon

To find out more about our authors and books visit www.hartpublishing.co.uk. Here you will find extracts, author information, details of forthcoming events and the option to sign up for our newsletters.

SERIES EDITOR'S PREFACE

This is a monograph written by a senior academic who has devoted his career to focusing on private international law, especially private international law of competition. It is written from the starting point of English law and jurisdiction but as the title suggests with a global perspective. It makes excellent use of EU and US sources – two of the leading systems for competition law. It builds on the writer's extensive work in the field.

There is much to learn here about post-Brexit England and Wales as it begins to redevelop its own competition law and its own private international law. One example of this is how the broader English and Welsh tort jurisdiction created by the UK Supreme Court in a non-competition case (*Brownlie*) might impact on the English and Welsh courts being able to adjudicate on damages claims caused by a breach of (foreign) competition law where the indirect damage occurred in England and Wales.

Mihail Danov examines the history of attempts to improve global cooperation in the public law and regulatory sphere of competition law which have come to nothing so far. He acknowledges the existence of bilateral cooperation agreements (including between the US and EU) on these public law aspects of competition law. The main drive of the book, however, is to come up with suggestions as to how judicial cooperation on the civil and commercial aspects of transnational competition law infringements can be developed. The author is concerned with how the key components of private international law (jurisdiction, applicable law, and recognition and enforcement of foreign judgments) can be used in a cooperative way (perhaps via soft law or the innovation of a leading jurisdiction like England and Wales) to make it easier for the victims of breaches of (cross-border) competition law to get redress.

As someone who was involved in the negotiations on the inclusion of judgments against participants in hard-core cartels within the scope of the Hague Judgments Convention 2019, I am very aware of how difficult it is to secure any hard law provisions relating to private international law of competition at the global level. Making this first small step away from complete exclusion of competition law (the rule in the Hague Choice of Court Convention 2005) was a very difficult one for many countries (particularly in Asia), only achieved by compromises at the end of the negotiations in the Diplomatic Session, see David Goddard and Paul Beaumont, 'Recognition and Enforcement of Judgments in Civil or Commercial Matters' in Paul Beaumont and Jayne Holliday (eds) *A Guide to Global Private International Law* (Hart, 2022) 407 at 417. Danov is right to note in this book the limited practical impact of this inclusion. However, it is a major conceptual breakthrough for some States to accept that there is an area of competition law where uniform private international law rules are appropriate because in that area there is broad consensus on the behaviour being anti-competitive and meriting compensation for private parties affected by it. Reaching consensus on this matter in The Hague in 2019 makes me optimistic that it may be possible, with a lot of hard work, to arrive at consensus in The Hague on some parallel or related proceedings concerning participants in hard-core cartels and their victims (see the Jurisdiction Project at https://www.hcch.net/en/projects/legislative-projects/jurisdiction-project).

This is a scholarly book where the writer has profited from visiting the latest scholarship and revisiting older scholarship. One small example is the very interesting discussion of the public policy exception to the recognition and enforcement of foreign judgments in chapter 12. Central to Danov's discussion is the wisdom of an article by John Collier in 1984. The article assists Danov in a careful analysis of what was decided in the relevant English case law on public policy. Danov is also able to quote Collier's wise conceptual conclusion in the same article that the fraud exception to the recognition and enforcement of foreign judgments applies when it 'is contrary to public policy' to enforce the judgment.

This is a major book on private international law of competition by a leading scholar in the field. I warmly commend it to you as a must read for anyone working in the field.

Paul Beaumont
University of Stirling

CONTENTS

1

Introduction – Private Antitrust Damages Claims and Private International Law

The regime for private antitrust enforcement and judicial cooperation in competition law matters is an area which is inevitably affected by the UK decision to withdraw from the European Union ('Brexit').[1] The Brexit impact in the area is twofold. First, EU competition law provisions and Council Regulation 1/2003, which lays down the rules for their implementation, are no longer directly applicable[2] in the UK. Secondly, the Brussels Ia Regulation – which is inter alia set to 'further enhances access to justice'[3] – is no longer to be relied upon by the English courts to assume jurisdiction[4] and avoid parallel and/or related proceedings[5] as well as to recognise and enforce judgments in relation to private antitrust actions.

An alternative model for judicial cooperation in competition law matters may need to be considered by the UK and EU policy-makers post-Brexit. The issues are important because given that many injured parties are still bringing follow-on private antitrust damages claims[6] in the UK by relying on EU Commission decisions[7] which are adopted in proceedings 'initiated before the end of the transition period',[8] there is a risk that

[1] See: Articles 1, 126 and 127 from the Agreement on the withdrawal of the United Kingdom of Great Britain and Northern Ireland from the European Union and the European Atomic Energy Community ('Withdrawal Agreement') [2019] Official Journal C3841/1.

[2] Article 288(2) TFEU. See also: Case C-106/77 *Amministrazione delle finanze dello Stato v Simmenthal* EU:C:1978:49 [14 and 15].

[3] Recital 1 from Regulation (EU) No 1215/2012 on jurisdiction and the recognition and enforcement of judgments in civil and commercial matters (recast) – the Brussels Ia Regulation.

[4] eg *Vatenfall AB v Prysmian* [2018] EWHC 1694 (Ch); *Toshiba Carrier UK Ltd and Other v KME Yorkshire Limited & Others* [2011] EWHC 2665 (Ch); *Toshiba Carrier UK Ltd and Other v KME Yorkshire Limited & Others* [2012] EWCA Civ 169; *Provimi Limited v Aventis Animal Nutrition SA and Others* [2003] EWHC 961 (Comm).

[5] *Cooper Tire & Rubber Company v Shell Chemicals UK Limited* [2009] EWHC 2609 (Comm); *Cooper Tire & Rubber Company Europe Limited & Others* [2010] EWCA Civ 864.
M Danov, *Jurisdiction and Judgments in Relation to EU Competition Law Claims* (Oxford, Hart Publishing, 2010), J Basedow, S Francq and L Idot (eds), *International Antitrust Litigation Conflict of Laws and Coordination* (Oxford, Hart Publishing, 2012); M Danov, F Becker and P Beaumont (eds), *Cross-border EU Competition Law Actions* (Oxford, Hart Publishing, 2013).

[6] Case No: 1339/7/7/20, *Mark McLaren Class Representative Ltd v MOL (Europe Africa) Ltd, Mitsui OSK Lines Ltd, Nissan Motor Car Carrier Co Ltd* [2022] CAT 10.

[7] Article 95 of the Withdrawal Agreement. Eg Case AT.40009, *Maritime Car Carriers – Commission Decision of 21.2.2018 relating to a proceeding under Article 101 of the Treaty on the Functioning of the European Union and Article 53 of the EEA Agreement* C(2018) 983 final.

[8] Article 92 of the Withdrawal Agreement.

multiple claims related to the same transnational competition law infringement may be issued before the English courts as well as before a number of EU and non-EU Member States' courts. Moreover, even more difficult private international law issues would arise in cases where different (public) competition laws would be applicable with regard to conduct which distorts the competition and which causes antitrust damages across the UK as well as across the EU.

This book offers a private international law (PIL) perspective on cross-border competition litigation, focusing on the issues of jurisdiction (including aspects concerning related proceedings), applicable law (broadly defined to cover applicable (public) competition laws),[9] recognition and enforcement of judgments in relation to private antitrust claims arising out of transnational infringements. It will be demonstrated that appropriate PIL mechanisms are necessary to set up a regime for judicial cooperation in related private antitrust damages claims which arise in relation to the same transnational competition law infringements, causing antitrust damages to injured parties in multiple jurisdictions. The book will further set out the way for PIL tools to be implemented with a view to improving injured parties' access to legal remedies in a global context.

I. UK Regulatory Landscape and Brexit Implications

Above all, it should be noted that an effective competition law regime is perceived to be central for facilitating market access and the 'establish[ment of] an internal market'[10] within the European Union. Prior to Brexit, the UK – through the European Communities Act 1972 – had conferred exclusive legislative competence onto the European Union to adopt 'the competition rules [which are] necessary for the functioning of the internal market'.[11] In order to regulate the competition law aspects of cross-border trade within the EU,[12] Articles 101 and 102 formed a major part of the Treaty on the Functioning of the European Union (TFEU).[13] Moreover, Articles 101 and 102 TFEU are directly effective[14] provisions across the EU.

The provisions of the UK Competition Act 1998 (the 1998 Act) are modelled on EU competition law. Section 2(1) of the 1998 Act 'prohibits agreements between undertakings, decisions by associations of undertakings or concerted practices which [...] *may affect trade within the United Kingdom*, and [...] have as their object or effect the prevention, restriction or distortion of *competition within the United Kingdom*'. Likewise, Article 101(1) TFEU was set to prohibit 'all agreements between undertakings, decisions by associations of undertakings and concerted practices *which may affect trade between Member States* and which have as their object or effect the prevention, restriction or distortion of *competition within the internal market*'.

[9] Chapters 9 and 10.
[10] Article 3(3) of the Treaty on European Union (TEU). See also: Article 26 of the Treaty on the Functioning of the European Union (TFEU).
[11] Article 3(1)(b) TFEU.
[12] Article 3(1)(b) TFEU.
[13] J Drexl, 'Competition law as part of the European Constitution' in A Bogdandy and J Bast, *Principles of European Constitutional Law* 2nd edn (Oxford, Hart Publishing, 2009) 659.
[14] Recital 3 from Directive 2014/104/EU. See also: Case C-26/62 *Van Gend en Loos v Administratie der Belastingen* EU:C:1963:1.

Article 101(3) TFEU states that certain agreements – which fall within the scope of Article 101(1) TFEU but promote 'economic efficiencies',[15] meeting strictly defined exemption conditions – are not to be prohibited. The UK Supreme Court held that:

> [A] party in breach of Article 101(1) [may seek] exemption by satisfying the requirements of Article 101(3). The following four conditions must be satisfied. First, the anti-competitive conduct must contribute to improving the production or distribution of goods or to promoting technical or economic progress. Secondly, consumers must be allowed a fair share of the resulting benefit. Thirdly, it must not impose on the participating undertakings any restrictions which are not indispensable to the attainment of these objectives. Fourthly, it must not afford them the possibility of eliminating competition in respect of a substantial part of the products in question.[16]

Similarly, Section 9(1) of the 1998 Act declares that '[a]n agreement is exempt from the Chapter I prohibition', provided that somewhat identical exemption conditions are being satisfied.

Section 18(1) of the 1998 Act states that 'any conduct on the part of one or more undertakings which amounts to the abuse of a dominant position in a market is prohibited if it *may affect trade within the United Kingdom*'; whilst Article 102 TFEU prohibits 'any abuse by one or more undertakings of a dominant position within the internal market or in a substantial part of it [...] in so far as it *may affect trade between Member States*'.

It is well established that, in order for various regulatory objectives[17] to be pursued by national competition law systems, competition laws should be (publicly and privately) enforced.[18] In other words, competition laws (broadly defined to include the UK Competition Act 1998 and Articles 101 and 102 TFEU) could be enforced by regulators (eg the UK Competition Markets Authority; EU Commission) in public enforcement proceedings as well as by national courts in private antitrust enforcement proceedings.

Prior to the UK withdrawal from the European Union, Articles 101 and 102 TFEU were directly applicable[19] and directly effective[20] in the UK. This meant that EU competition law inter alia forming part of English and Welsh law,[21] and the UK institutions (including the Competition and Markets Authority, UK Competition Appeal Tribunal and English and Welsh courts) had to apply Articles 101 and 102 TFEU which were a 'direct source of right and duties'[22] in the UK.

[15] Communication from the Commission, *Notice Guidelines on the application of Article 81(3) of the Treaty* [2004] *Official Journal* C101/08 [59].

[16] *Sainsbury's Supermarkets Ltd and others v Mastercard Incorporated and others* [2020] UKSC 24 [107].

[17] A Bradford et al, 'Competition Law Gone Global: Introducing the Comparative Competition Law and Enforcement Datasets' (2019) 16 *Journal of Empirical Legal Studies* 411, 418.

[18] K Huschelrath, 'Public enforcement of anti-cartel laws – theory and empirical evidence' in K Huschelrath and H Schwitzer (eds), *Public and Private Enforcement of Competition Law in Europe* (Berlin, Springer-Verlag, 2014) 9.

[19] Article 288(2) TFEU. See also: *Simmenthal* (n 2) [14 and 15].

[20] Recital 3 from Directive 2014/104/EU. See also: *Van Gend en Loos* (n 14); Case 127/73 *BRT v SABAM* EU:C:1974:6 [16]; Case C-282/95 P *Guérin Automobiles v Commission* EU:C:1997:159 [39]; Case C-453/99 *Courage Ltd v Bernard Crehan* [2001] EU:C:2001:465 [23].

[21] *Van Gend en Loos* (n 14) 12.

[22] *Simmenthal* (n 2) [15].

Many private antitrust damages claims[23] which are brought before the English and Welsh courts as well as before the UK Competition Appeal Tribunal are preceded by decisions of the EU Commission, establishing the competition law infringement.[24] The fact that the EU enforcement pattern as well as the UK enforcement pattern is of a hybrid character, blending public and private aspects, appeared to be a major feature of the competition litigation in England and Wales.[25]

The aspects concerning 'the "split" jurisdiction of regulator for infringement, tribunal for causation and assessment of damages'[26] have been noted, in the context of the UK Competition Act 1998, by the English and Welsh courts as well as, in the EU context, by the CJEU.[27] For example, in *Otis*,[28] the CJEU held that

> a civil action for damages, such as the action before the referring court, requires, as can be seen from the order for reference, not only that a harmful event be found to have occurred, but also that loss and a direct link between the loss and that harmful event be established. Whilst it is true that, because of its obligation not to take decisions running counter to a Commission decision finding an infringement of Article 101 TFEU, the national court is required to accept that a prohibited agreement or practice exists, the existence of loss and of a direct causal link between the loss and the agreement or practice in question remains, by contrast, a matter to be assessed by the national court.
>
> Indeed, even when the Commission has in its decision determined the precise effects of the infringement, it still falls to the national court to determine individually the loss caused to each of the persons to have brought an action for damages. Such an assessment is not contrary to Article 16 of Regulation No 1/2003.[29]

It should be noted that Council Regulation 1/2003 reiterates the importance of public and private antitrust enforcement.[30] Article 16 of Council Regulation 1/2003 has an important role to play with a view to ensuring that Articles 101 and 102 TFEU are consistently enforced in the UK as well as in the other Member States. It is well established that EU Member States' judges must not render judgments which are contrary to a decision of the European Commission which determines whether a particular conduct

[23] eg *Mastercard Incorporated and others v Walter Hugh Merricks CBE* [2020] UKSC 51; Case Nos: 1282/7/7/18 and 1289/7/7/18, *UK Trucks Claim Ltd v Stellantis and Ors & Road Haulage Association Ltd v MAN SE and Ors* [2022] CAT 25; *NTN Corporation v Stellantis N.V.* [2022] EWCA Civ 16.

[24] eg COMP/34.579 *MasterCard*; COMP/36.518 *EuroCommerce*; COMP/38.580 *Commercial Cards, Non-Confidential Version – Commission Decision of 19/XII/2007 relating to a proceeding under Article 81 of the EC Treaty and Article 53 of the EEA Agreement*; Case AT.39824, *Trucks – Commission Decision of 19.7.2016 relating to a proceeding under Article 101 of the Treaty on the Functioning of the European Union (the Treaty) and Article 53 of the EEA Agreement* C(2016) 4673 final; Case AT.39824, *Trucks – Commission Decision of 27.9.2017 relating to a proceeding under Article 101 of the Treaty on the Functioning of the European Union (the Treaty) and Article 53 of the EEA Agreement* C(2017) 6467 final; Case AT.39922, *Bearings – Commission Decision of 19.3.2014 relating to proceedings under Article 101 of the Treaty on the Functioning of the European Union and Article 53 of the EEA Agreement* C(2014) 1788 final.

[25] M Danov and S Dnes, 'Cross-border EU competition law actions: new evidence from England and Wales' in Danov, Becker and Beaumont (n 5), 33, 50–57.

[26] *Enron Coal Services Ltd (in liquidation) v English Welsh & Scottish Railway Ltd* [2011] EWCA Civ 2 [149].

[27] Case C-199/11 *Europese Gemeenschap v Otis NV and Others* EU:C:2012:684.

[28] Ibid.

[29] Ibid [65–66]. See Case Nos: 1284/5/7/18 and 1290-1295/5/7/18 (T), *Royal Mail Group v DAF Trucks* [2020] CAT 7 [67].

[30] Arts 5 and 6 of Regulation 1/2003.

is anti-competitive (as being in conflict with Articles 101 and/or 102 TFEU).[31] As Lord Hoffmann noted, in *Crehan*,[32] '[t]he law on the relationship between the Commission and the national courts was [...] codified by Article 16 of Council Regulation (EC) No 1/2003'.[33] More specifically, Article 16 states that:

1. When national courts rule on agreements, decisions or practices under Article 81 or Article 82 of the Treaty which are already the subject of a Commission decision, they cannot take decisions running counter to the decision adopted by the Commission. They must also avoid giving decisions which would conflict with a decision contemplated by the Commission in proceedings it has initiated. To that effect, the national court may assess whether it is necessary to stay its proceedings. This obligation is without prejudice to the rights and obligations under Article 234 of the Treaty.
2. When competition authorities of the Member States rule on agreements, decisions or practices under Article 81 or Article 82 of the Treaty which are already the subject of a Commission decision, they cannot take decisions which would run counter to the decision adopted by the Commission.[34]

The EU policy-makers adopting Article 16 of Council Regulation 1/2003 appeared to have made the assumption that the EU Commission is the more appropriate forum to deal with EU-wide competition law infringements, with the national courts being bound by the EU Commission's decision and being expected to consider staying their proceedings to avoid inconsistent outcomes.[35]

Decisions of the EU Commission adopted in proceedings, 'which were initiated before the end of the transition period',[36] will continue to be 'binding on and in the UK'.[37] In this context, it should be pointed out that the binding nature of the *dispositif* (ie the operative part of the decision) and its legal effects (ie impacting on the legal positions of the addressees) is firmly established by the CJEU jurisprudence.[38] Likewise, the recitals which would lay down 'the essential basis'[39] of the regulator's decision are also binding for the national courts.[40] This means that in order for a national court to determine whether a particular recital is binding, they would need to consider whether its 'finding [...] is an essential basis or the necessary support for a determination in the operative part, or necessary to understand the scope of the operative part'.[41]

[31] Case C-234/89 *Stergios Delimitis v Henninger Bräu AG* EU:C:1991:91; Case C-344/98 *Masterfoods v HB Ice Cream*, EU:C:2000:689 [57].

[32] *Interpreneur Pub Company v Crehan* [2006] UKHL 38.

[33] Ibid [63].

[34] Article 16 of Council Regulation 1/2003.

[35] *Commission Notice on the co-operation between the Commission and the courts of the EU Member States in the application of Articles 81 and 82 EC* [2004] Official Journal C101/54 [12–14]. See more: Chapter 10.

[36] Article 92 of the Withdrawal Agreement.

[37] Article 95 of the Withdrawal Agreement.

[38] Case T-138/89, *NBV and NVB v Commission*, EU:T:1992:95 [31]. See more: Section 10.5 below.

[39] *BritNed Development v ABB* [2018] EWHC 2616 (Ch) [67.6.b]. Case C-164/02, *Netherlands v Commission*, EU:C:2004:54 [21]. See also: *Royal Mail Group* (n 29) [40].

[40] *BritNed* (n 39) [67.6.b]. See also: Article 58A of the UK Competition Act 1998; Article 16 of Council Regulation 1/2003.

[41] *Royal Mail Group* (n 29) [68].

It is well settled that any injured party (including multiple injured parties)[42] could bring a private antitrust claim against a person (be it an individual or legal entity whose conduct is in conflict (or allegedly in conflict) with UK competition law or EU competition law). It is widely acknowledged that, 'in order to establish a claim [for antitrust damages], it is necessary [for the injured parties] to show (i) an infringement of competition law, and (ii) actionable harm or damage caused by that infringement'.[43]

II. Private Enforcement of Competition Law in the UK and EU

The EU/UK model for competition law enforcement meant that private antitrust damages claims were classified into two broad categories: *follow-on* claims for antitrust damages were preceded by a prior regulatory decision establishing the infringement; and *stand-alone* claims in which the injured parties were not able to rely on such a prior regulatory decision which was binding in the UK.[44]

Mr Justice Flaux (as he then was) classified another category of claims as being *hybrid* in which injured parties 'advance a case which goes beyond the findings of fact of the (EU) Commission and seek to prove a more extensive infringement'.[45] In other words, it seems that a hybrid enforcement model[46] (blending public and private enforcement) encourages hybrid private antitrust damages claims. Such hybrid claims should enable claimants to go beyond the geographical and temporal scope of regulators' decisions by seeking antitrust damages in relation to different geographical areas and time periods.[47]

The fact that, initially, some EU Member States were attracting more competition law claims in comparison to other Member States[48] may well be explained by the principle of procedural autonomy,[49] leaving no doubt that the procedural and evidential rules – which vary in the different Member States – would impact on the outcome of a competition law dispute.[50] Since many EU competition law infringements are likely to

[42] *Allianz Global Investors GmbH And Others v Barclays Bank plc and Others* [2021] EWHC 399 (Comm).

[43] *BritNed* (n 39) [28]; Case Nos: 1284/5/7/18 (T) and 1290/5/7/18 (T) *Royal Mail Group Ltd v DAF Trucks Ltd and others* [2023] CAT 6 [168].

[44] eg Case No: 1382/7/7/21 *Consumers' Association v Qualcomm Inc* [2022] CAT 20; Case No: 1403/7/7/21, *Dr Rachael Kent v Apple* [2022] CAT 28; Case No: 1408/7/7/21 *Elizabeth Helen Coll v Alphabet Inc and Others* [2022] CAT 39.

[45] *Bord Na Mona Horticulture Limited, Bord Na Mona Plc v British Polythene Industries Plc, Combipac BV, Bischof + Klein GmbH & Co KG, FLS Plast A/S* [2012] EWHC 3346 (Comm) [42].

[46] Danov and Dnes (n 25) 50–57.

[47] eg *Deutsche Bahn AG & Others v MasterCard Incorporated* [2018] EWHC 412 (Ch).

[48] Commission Staff Working Document, *Impact Assessment Report – Damages actions for breach of the EU antitrust rules (Accompanying the proposal for a Directive on certain rules governing actions for damages under national law for infringements of the competition law provisions of the Member States and of the European Union (Text with EEA relevance))* COM(2013) 404 final / SWD(2013) 204 final [52].

[49] Case C-33/76 *Rewe-Zentralfinanz eG and Rewe-Zentral AG v Landwirtschaftskammer für das Saarland* EU:C:1976:188 [5–6]; Case C-261/95 *Rosalba Palmisani v Istituto nazionale della previdenza sociale (INPS)* EU:C:1997:351 [27]; Joined Cases C-295/04-298/04 *Manfredi v Lloyd Adriatico Assicurazioni SpA* EU:C:2006:461. See also Case C-126/97 *Eco Swiss China Time Ltd v Benetton International NV* EU:C:1999:269 [43]–[48]. See more: F Becker, 'Application of Community law by Member States' public authorities: between autonomy and effectiveness' (2007) 44 *CML Rev* 1035.

[50] *Wall v Mutuelle de Poitiers Assurances* [2013] EWHC 53 (QB) [16–17].

be cross-border in nature, the claimants appeared to be somewhat strategic,[51] considering the procedural advantages which they would derive by bringing their claim in one jurisdiction rather than another. Larger purchasers, having access to finance, could afford to be selective.[52]

The Antitrust Damages Directive was adopted to improve the injured parties' access to effective legal remedies. The legislative intervention at EU level (rather than at EU Member States level)[53] was justified by the fact that there are many 'large-scale infringements of competition law [which] often have a cross-border element'.[54] As part of this process of approximation of national laws, the EU policy-makers dealt with some important procedural issues. For example, the disclosure of evidence[55] was regarded as an important issue which had to be addressed, not least because 'competition law litigation is characterised by an information asymmetry, [which required for the EU policy makers] to ensure that claimants are afforded the right to obtain the disclosure of evidence relevant to their claim'.[56]

It is now settled that, in order for the courts to effectively deal with competition law claims, it is highly likely for the parties to require 'extensive disclosure, factual and expert evidence'.[57] This is particularly important because the UK experience in handling private antitrust damages claims strongly indicates that these cases raise fairly complex issues in relation to 'liability'[58] and 'quantum'.[59] The quantification of damages would be intertwined with the need for an appropriate methodology.[60] The issues are particularly important because it is now well established that:

> An overcharge is a concept that compares two prices: the price in fact charged during a cartel episode and the 'counterfactual' price that would have been charged but for the illegal cartel. Subtracting the second number from the first number gives the estimated overcharge. The skill and effort in overcharge cases goes into calculating the 'counterfactual' price. However, in a claim for aggregate damages across a class, it is also necessary to calculate the aggregate volume of commerce affected, to which the estimated percentage of overcharge can then be applied. That further task accordingly arises in the UKTC action but not in the RHA action where it would be necessary to determine the value of commerce only at an individual level, which might be provided by the individual class members rather than by an expert estimation.[61]

The level of complexity in quantifying damages in cross-border cases would inflate the litigation costs[62] which could impede the injured parties' access to legal remedies unless appropriate funding arrangements were being put in place.[63]

[51] J Lawrence and A Morfey, 'Tactical Manoeuvres in UK Cartel Damages Litigation' in Danov, Becker and Beaumont (n 5) 149.

[52] Danov and Dnes (n 25).

[53] Compare: 'the principle of subsidiarity' – Article 5(3) from the Treaty on European Union.

[54] Recital 9 of Directive 2014/104/EU.

[55] Articles 5, 6 and 7 of Directive 2014/104/EU.

[56] Recital 15 of Directive 2014/104/EU.

[57] *Dune Group* (n 58) [11.5].

[58] Case Nos: 1306-1325/5/7/19 (T) et al, *Dune Group Limited & Ors v MasterCard Incorporated & Ors* [2022] CAT 14 [11.4].

[59] Ibid [11.5].

[60] *Road Haulage Association* (n 23) [117–57].

[61] Ibid [117].

[62] *Merricks* (n 23) [74].

[63] Case Nos: 1329/7/7/19 and 1336/7/7/19 *Michael O'Higgins FX Class Representative Ltd v Barclays Bank Plc & Ors* [2022] CAT 16 [323].

III. Private International Law and Private Antitrust Enforcement

The issues concerning access to justice in private antitrust damages claims are important because many competition law infringements would be cross-border in nature, involving multinational groups of companies (which enjoy significant market power, if not a dominant position) whose anti-competitive practices would cause harm to multiple consumers and businesses who would be based in different jurisdictions.[64]

A number of PIL issues may arise in cross-border competition law claims. For example, several national courts may assume jurisdiction in related claims which arise out of the same transnational competition law infringement. The difficulties in relation to quantification of antitrust damages could be exacerbated in cases where the courts must apply foreign laws.[65] Moreover, it is well established that many national competition laws would apply extra-territorially.[66] The transnational nature of competition law infringements taken together with the extra-territorial application of national competition laws cumulatively indicate that private international law should have an important role to play with a view to improving the multiple injured parties' access to legal remedies in cross-border cases.

There is a strong argument that, in a global context, PIL mechanisms could be used to promote a level of judicial cooperation which should ensure that any common issues arising in related private antitrust damages claims are consistently dealt with by national courts, factoring in a diverse range of competition laws[67] and giving effect to any relevant foreign judgments. Such a mode of governance should improve injured parties' access to legal remedies in cross-border competition law cases which arise in a global context. In order to single out the PIL issues, the applicable UK PIL rules, as well as the EU PIL rules, which were applicable in the UK pre-Brexit, will be analysed and compared.

A. Pre-Brexit – The PIL Issues – Forum Selection

The EU experience with private antitrust enforcement has shown that the judicial cooperation in civil and commercial matters is essential with a view to allocating jurisdiction,

[64] Chapter 7.

[65] *Road Haulage Association* (n 23) [175–80]. See more: Chapter 10.

[66] eg *The LCD Appeals* [2018] EWCA Civ 220; Case C-413/14 P *Intel v Commission* EU:C:2017:632 [49] (Judgment of the Court (Grand Chamber) of 6 September 2017); Joined Cases 89/85, 104/85, 114/85, 116–17/85, and 125–29/85 *Ahlstrom v Commission* EU:C:1988:447 (*Wood Pulp Cartel Case*); *Timberline Lumber v Bank of America* 549 F 2d 597 (9th Cir 1976). See also Restatement of the Law (Third), The Foreign Relations Law of the United States (1987) [403]. J Adolphsen, 'The conflict of laws in cartel matters in a globalised world: Alternatives to the effects doctrine' (2005) *Journal of Private International Law* 151; V Pavic, *Extra-territoriality in the Matters of Antitrust* (European Press Academic Publishing, 2001); WS Dodge, 'Extraterritoriality and Conflict-of-Laws Theory: An argument for judicial unilateralism' (1998) *Harvard International Law Journal* 101; M Waelbroeck, 'The European Community Approach' in CJ Omstead (ed), *Extra-territorial Application of Laws and Responses Thereto* (International Law Association in association with ESC Publishing Limited, 1984) 74. See more: Chapter 9.

[67] Chapter 10.

avoiding parallel and related proceedings, and ensuring the recognition and enforcement of judgments in relation to cross-border competition law claims.[68]

A research project conducted between 2010–2012,[69] appeared to indicate that the various procedural aspects (eg disclosure and discovery of evidence) and the speed of procedure appear to have a major impact on the injured parties' decisions if and where to issue their private antitrust damages claim. In other words, PIL rules may well perform a governance function, promoting a level of adjudicatory competition and facilitating injured parties' access to legal remedies. The jurisdictional rules would be very important in so far as various procedural issues concerning evidence-gathering process (eg disclosure), opt-out or opt-in collective redress proceedings, costs and litigation funding (including the availability of contingency fees) would often depend on the place of litigation.[70]

The level of variation in the EU Member States' procedural rules meant that there were to be advantages (and/or disadvantages) for parties to have their private disputes determined in one jurisdiction (where a particular set of procedural rules and funding arrangements would be available) rather than another. This might explain why some EU Member States appeared to attract more follow-on private antitrust damages claims in comparison with others. The point was set out in the Impact Assessment Report that accompanied the EU proposal for Antitrust Damages Directive which stated that:

> [T]he vast majority of large antitrust damages actions are currently being brought in 3 European jurisdictions – namely in the UK, followed by Germany and the Netherlands – indicates that the rules applicable in these Member States are considered by claimants to be much more suitable for effectively bringing such claims than in other Member States.[71]

It is not only the jurisdictional rules which the parties would consider before bringing their cross-border claims, the choice-of-law rules would also be important to ascertain the national substantive law/s which would apply to the issues of causation and quantification. Strategic claimants might well consider such substantive law issues as limitation periods,[72] the amount of pass-through,[73] and compound interest,[74] when deciding if and where to issue proceedings in so far as – even in the EU where some rules are harmonised – different laws may apply over the span of the cartel agreement.[75]

Pre-Brexit, it was demonstrated that the level of complexity in competition law cases and the diverse set of procedural rules meant that establishing jurisdiction in one EU Member State rather than another might impact on the outcome of disputes, which might in turn promote a level of adjudicatory competition.[76] The place where the parties

[68] Danov (n 5); Basedow, Francq and Idot (n 5).

[69] Danov, Becker and Beaumont (n 5).

[70] Lawrence and Morfey (n 51) 149. See more: Danov, Becker and Beaumont (n 5).

[71] *Impact Assessment Report* (n 48) [52].

[72] Lawrence and Morfey (n 51) 152-4. See also: *Gemalto Holding BV v Infineon Technologies AG* [2022] EWCA Civ 782.

[73] Compare: Directive 2014/104/EU on certain rules governing actions for damages under national law for infringements of the competition law provisions of the Member States and of the European Union; *Illinois Brick Co v Illinois* 97 S.Ct. 2061 (1977).

[74] G Monti, 'EU law and interest on damages for infringements of competition law – A comparative report' (2016) EUI Working Paper LAW 2016/11, https://cadmus.eui.eu/bitstream/handle/1814/40464/LAW_2016_11.pdf?sequence=3&isAllowed=y.

[75] *Deutsche Bahn* (n 47).

[76] Danov, Becker and Beaumont (n 5).

litigate may be even more important post-Brexit, not the least because EU competition law is no longer directly applicable in the UK and the EU institutions have no jurisdiction in the UK. As a result, the aspects concerning the regulatory jurisdiction would need to be more systematically considered because competition law rules could gradually diverge.

Thus, the Brexit developments would inevitably impact on aspects concerning adjudicatory jurisdiction of the national courts in so far as the regime for judicial cooperation between the UK courts and EU Member State courts appears to be rapidly changing, with Brussels Ia no longer applicable in the UK. Governing related court proceedings, which arise out of the same transnational competition law infringement, would be a major governance issue which requires a PIL solution.[77] The issues are increasingly important because the transnational nature of the competition law infringements leave no doubt that there would be multiple injured parties (consumers; large and small businesses) in different jurisdictions.

B. Post-Brexit: Some PIL Issues and Challenges

The European Union (Withdrawal) Act 2018 repealed the European Communities Act 1972[78] and states that – with regard to 'retained EU law'[79] – '[a] court or tribunal [...] is not bound by any principles laid down, or any decisions made, on or after exit day by the European Court'.[80] A major problem is that the UK/EU Trade and Cooperation Agreement[81] sets the foundation for administrative cooperation between the competition regulators,[82] without providing a regime for judicial cooperation in competition law matters. The 2018 Act might have some important implications in so far as a competition law infringement may span a period of time which starts prior to Brexit and continues after Brexit.

Some of the 2018 Act implications and some important PIL issues were considered by the English and Welsh High Court in its judgment in *JJH Enterprises Ltd (trading as ValueLicensing) v Microsoft*.[83] In this case, ValueLicensing claimed that Microsoft infringed EU competition law by initiating a campaign which actively discouraged its

[77] Chapters 7, 8, 9 and 10 below. See also: *Road Haulage Association* (n 23) [5–6]; Case C-819/19 *Stichting Cartel Compensation, Equilib Netherlands BV v Koninklijke Luchtvaart Maatschappij NV* EU:C:2021:373 (AG Bobek) [97]. *Emerald Supplies Ltd v British Airways Plc* [2017] EWHC 2420 (Ch), *La Gaitana Farms SA & Ors v British Airways Plc* [2019] EWCA Civ 37; Case COMP/F/38.899 – *Gas Insulated Switchgear*, Commission Decision of 24.01.2007 relating to a proceeding pursuant to Article 81 of the EC Treaty and Article 53 of the EEA Agreement C(2006) 6762 final. *National Grid Electricity Transmission Plc v ABB Ltd and others* [2013] EWHC 822 (Ch). *National Grid Electricity Transmission Plc v ABB Ltd and others* [2014] EWHC 1555 (Ch).

[78] Section 1 of the European Union (Withdrawal) Act 2018. See also: Section 1 and 1A of the European Union (Withdrawal) Act 2020.

[79] Section 6(7) of the European Union (Withdrawal) Act 2018.

[80] Section 6(1) of the European Union (Withdrawal) Act 2018.

[81] Trade and Cooperation Agreement between the European Union and the European Atomic Energy Community, of the one part, and the United Kingdom of Great Britain and Northern Ireland, of the other part [2021] OJ L149/10.

[82] Art 361 of the UK/EU Trade and Cooperation Agreement.

[83] *JJH Enterprises Ltd (trading as ValueLicensing) v Microsoft* [2022] EWHC 929 (Comm).

customers to 'sell their perpetual licenses'.[84] Microsoft's conduct allegedly caused harm to ValueLicensing, whose main economic activities included re-sell of 'pre-owned perpetual licenses'[85] in relation to inter alia various Microsoft products.

In order for the English court to determine whether it had jurisdiction, the following questions had to be addressed: was UK competition law and/or EU competition law applicable? Was the English court an appropriate forum to hear and determine the stand-alone claim for damages? Since the claim concerned events which started before and after the end of the implementation period which was set out in the Withdrawal Agreement, an important preliminary issue concerned the applicable law with a view to ascertaining whether there was a restriction of competition. ValueLicensing issued a stand-alone claim for breach of Article 102 TFEU as well as Article 101 TFEU, seeking to recover antitrust damages in excess of £250 million.

The issues concerning the applicable (public) competition laws are important because any restriction of competition would raise important regulatory issues.[86] There could be multiple competition law systems[87] which may be applied by the national judges to determine whether the conduct amounts to an act 'restricting competition'[88] (eg anti-competitive agreement; abuse of dominant position). This means that the following issues need to be addressed, post-Brexit: is the concept of restriction of competition for the purposes of the retained Rome II Regulation to be narrowly defined to cover only restrictions of competition law under UK competition law?[89] Or should the concept in question be broadly defined to allow the English courts to apply any national competition law, in order to determine whether there is a restriction of competition law?[90]

An analysis of the judgment of the High Court in *JJH Enterprises Ltd (trading as ValueLicensing) v Microsoft*[91] appears to indicate that some major PIL issues might need to be addressed in cases where English judges are dealing with stand-alone antitrust claims issued after the implementation period had expired but concern conduct which occurred before 31 December 2020. Mr Justice Picken considered the implications of Article 6(1) of the European Union (Withdrawal) Act 2018 with a view to determining whether the English courts were bound by a judgment of the CJEU which was rendered on 6 October 2021 (ie after the UK withdrew from the European Union).[92] According to Mr Justice Picken:

> [T]here is at least a realistic possibility that s. 6(1) of the 2018 Act does not apply to the interpretation of Articles 101 and 102 of the TFEU insofar as ValueLicensing relies on them (as part of English law) in its claims for the pre-Brexit period. This is an issue which was the subject of a recent Article by Jack Williams, *'Accrued EU law rights: a guide for the perplexed'*, *EU Relations Law*, 5 January 2022 (https://eurelationslaw.com/blog/accrued-eu-law-rights-a-guide-for-the-perplexed); it is not an issue which is suitable for summary determination.

[84] Ibid [5].
[85] Ibid [5].
[86] See more: Chapter 9.
[87] Chapters 8, 9 and 10.
[88] Article 6(3) – Rome II Regulation.
[89] Compare: Section 11 of the Law Applicable to Contractual Obligations and Non-Contractual Obligations (Amendment etc.) (EU Exit) Regulations 2019.
[90] Chapters 10 and 11.
[91] *ValueLicensing* (n 83).
[92] Case C-882/19 *Sumal v Mercedes Benz Trucks España* EU:C:2021:800.

> However, in essence, the argument is that, insofar as ValueLicensing seeks to rely directly on Articles 101 and 102 in respect of the pre-Brexit period, those are rights which are to be regarded as having arisen under s. 2(1) of the European Communities Act 1972 (and, during the implementation period, s. 1A of the 2018 Act). The 1972 Act having now been repealed, then, pursuant to s. 16 of the Interpretation Act 1978, the rights that ValueLicensing had under the 1972 Act, whilst it was in force, fall to be treated as having now been accrued, so as to mean that ValueLicensing's claims for the pre-Brexit period are to be determined by reference to EU authority, whenever that authority is decided, since nothing in the Brexit legislation evinces a '*contrary intention*' and s. 6 of the 2018 Act is concerned only with the interpretation of '*retained EU law*' (i.e. such EU law as was incorporated, prospectively, into UK law on Brexit). If that is right, then, Microsoft UK cannot avoid *Sumal* for this further reason.[93]

Hence, Articles 101 and 102 TFEU, despite no longer being part of English law, had been directly applicable/effective in the UK until 31 December 2020. Mr Justice Picken made excellent points about the scope of Section 6(1) of the European Union (Withdrawal) Act 2018, but it is yet to be seen how the English courts should exercise their *forum non conveniens* discretion in stand-alone claims in which EU competition laws were to be applicable under Rome II, without being directly applicable and directly effective in the UK when the infringement occurred.

There are another set of important PIL issues which need to be addressed, post-Brexit. How should a group of companies that forms an undertaking which is a single economic unit be classified for PIL purposes?[94] What connecting factors should be used to allocate jurisdiction in such cases? The lack of appropriate PIL classification of a group of companies[95] which is a single economic unit was exposed in *JJH Enterprises Ltd (trading as ValueLicensing) v Microsoft*.[96]

IV. International Cooperation – Gaps in the Existing Regulatory Framework and Relevant Literature[97]

A level of judicial cooperation might need to be advanced for multiple competent national courts to consistently deal with the identical or common factual and substantive law issues in related claims arising in relation to the same conduct which restrict competition law/s. A major challenge is that there is no international convention which facilitates cooperation between the national courts that deal with related competition law claims in a global context.[98]

[93] *ValueLicensing* (n 83) [46].

[94] Chapters 3 and 6.

[95] *Adams v Cape Industries Plc* [1990] Ch. 433, 476.

[96] *ValueLicensing* (n 83).

[97] See more: M Danov, 'Global Competition Law Framework: A Private International Law Solution Needed' (2016) 12 *Journal of Private International Law* 77–105; M Danov and C Otero, 'Competition Law Enforcement: Private International Law and Access to Effective Legal Remedies in Cross-Border Cases' in P Beaumont and J Holliday (eds) *Guide to Global Private International Law* (Oxford, Hart Publishing, 2022) 233–46.

[98] Compare: Convention of 2 July 2019 on the Recognition and Enforcement of Foreign Judgments in Civil or Commercial Matters (Not yet in force). See more: Danov and Otero (n 97).

Attaining a level of judicial cooperation in cross-border cases presupposes the adoption of an international convention or the advancement of certain soft law mechanisms for judicial cooperation which address the difficult PIL issues in relation to the application of different applicable (public) competition laws (expressing diverse regulatory/public interests) as well as of diverse sets of procedural and substantive (private) laws which apply in relation to similar or identical issues in different jurisdictions. In order to outline the gap in the regulatory framework concerning international cooperation, a brief review of the existing collaborative arrangements is necessary.

A. International Cooperation: Lack of Framework for Judicial Cooperation

The idea of promoting a level of international cooperation with a view to effectively enforcing competition laws in a cross-border context[99] appears to be over 40 years old. It was 1980 when the United Nations agreed its Set of Principles and Rules on Competition (UNSPRC) which stated that: 'Collaboration between Governments at bilateral and multilateral levels should be established and, where such collaboration has been established, it should be improved to facilitate the control of restrictive business practices'.[100]

It could be argued that the advanced UN principles were, inter alia, designed to set the scene for future arrangements that would adequately improve cooperation among enforcers/adjudicators in cross-border cases. It seems that, in order to promote a level of international cooperation,[101] the EU Commission has entered into a number of bilateral agreements with non-EU countries.[102] An example of a major development in this context is the Agreement between the Government of the United States of America and the Commission of the European Communities regarding the application of their competition laws (US/EU Agreement).[103]

The US/EU Agreement was adopted to 'promote cooperation and coordination and lessen the possibility or impact of differences between the Parties in the application of their competition laws'.[104] The agreement contains specific provisions which aim to enable the US and EU institutions to notify their relevant enforcement activities;[105] share information which is necessary to ensure effective application of their competition laws, achieving an appropriately level of understanding about their enforcement activities;[106] and promote a level of 'cooperation and coordination in enforcement activities'.[107]

[99] Section F from the 'Set of Principles and Rules on Competition' (UNSPRC).
[100] Principle 2 from Section C of the UNSPRC.
[101] See European Commission, 'Facing the challenges of globalisation' http://ec.europa.eu/competition/international/bilateral/index.html.
[102] European Commission, 'Bilateral relations on competition issues' https://competition-policy.ec.europa.eu/international/bilateral-relations_en.
[103] [1995] OJ L95/47. See also *Agreement between the European Communities and the Government of the United States of America on the application of positive comity principles in the enforcement of their competition laws* (US/EU Agreement) [1998] OJ L173/26.
[104] See Article I(1) of the US/EU Agreement.
[105] See Article II of the US/EU Agreement.
[106] Article III of the US/EU Agreement.
[107] Article IV of the US/EU Agreement. See also: Article V of the US/EU Agreement.

The EU Commission[108] went further to make an argument for the advancement of an even more ambitious global competition law regime. More specifically, it was proposed that a multilateral legal instrument should be adopted under the auspices of the World Trade Organisation (WTO). It was felt that such a multilateral framework was necessary to safeguard the market access being an important aspect of cross-border trade, whilst avoiding 'conflic[t] of law[s] and jurisdiction[s] and to promote a gradual convergence of competition laws'.[109] According to the EU Commission, there was a major concern that the growing number of multinational companies and transnational economic activities could lead 'to an increase in cross-border anti-competitive practices [...]'.[110]

The EU initiative appeared to suggest that the cross-border nature of economic activities could lead to transnational competition law infringements which should call for an enhanced level of international cooperation with regard to enforcement of competition laws in cross-border cases.[111] The problem is that the subsequent developments left no doubt that it may be very difficult (if not impossible) to devise a global competition law regime.[112] In 2004, the WTO General Council decided that the issues concerning an enhanced level of cooperation between Contracting States with regard to competition law enforcement activities 'will not form part of the Work Programme set out in that Declaration and therefore no work towards negotiations on any of these issues will take place within the WTO during the Doha Round'.[113]

In 2001, the International Competition Network (ICN) was founded as informal network of competition authorities. In order to support less experienced national competition authorities, Horna[114] has made an argument that, through various international organisations, the international community could 'boost international cooperation and raise common interests in enforcement between mature and young agencies'.[115] Collaborative arrangements among regulators appear to have been considered in the 2014 *OECD Report on the Challenges of international co-operation in competition law enforcement*.[116] Such a conclusion could be strengthened by the results

[108] Communication From the Commission to the Council, *Towards an International Framework of Competition Rules*, COM(96) 284 final.
[109] Ibid 3.
[110] Ibid 3.
[111] Ibid.
[112] DK Tarullo, 'Competition policy for global markets' (1999) *Journal of International Economic Law* 445; EM Fox, 'Competition Law and the Millennium Round' (1999) *Journal of International Economic Law* 665; J Basedow, 'International Antitrust: From Extraterritorial Application to Harmonization' (2000) *Louisiana Law Review* 1037; AT Guzman, 'International Antitrust and the WTO: The Lesson from Intellectual property' (2003) 43 *Virginia Journal of International Law* 933; PB Stephan, 'Against International Cooperation' in RA Epstein and MS Greve (eds), *Competition Laws in Conflict: Antitrust Jurisdiction in the Global Economy* (AEI Press, 2004) 66; F Becker, 'International Competition Law between Unilateralism, Horizontalism and Globalism' in S Shao (ed), *Special Issues on International Law* (Renmin University Press, 2009) 296–341; J Malinauskaite, 'International competition law harmonisation and the WTO: past, present and future' in M Andenas and CB Andersen (eds), *Theory and Practice of Harmonisation* (Edward Elgar, 2011) 323, 338–51.
[113] Doha Work Programme, *Decision Adopted by the General Council on 1 August 2004*, WT/L/579, 2 August 2004, p 3.
[114] PM Horna, 'David & Goliath: How young competition agencies can succeed in fighting cross-border cartels' (2017) *The University of Oxford Centre for Competition Law and Policy*, Working Paper CCLP (L) 45.
[115] Ibid, 23.
[116] OECD, *Report on the Challenges of international co-operation in competition law enforcement* (2014). http://www.oecd.org/daf/competition/challenges-international-coop-competition-2014.htm.

of the survey among national competition authorities which was conducted by the ICN and the Organisation for Economic Co-operation and Development (OECD).[117] The regulators that responded appear to be reiterating the benefits of the cooperation among national competition authorities.[118] Its overall conclusion is that:

> Continuing and deepening the existing system of bilateral co-operation is important. However, making it work going forward will be increasingly complex, as business becomes more globalised, spanning more jurisdictions enforcing competition law. Governments may want to consider whether new approaches to international co-operation in enforcing competition law are required, in the face of this challenge. These might include, for instance, developing general standards designed to promote both convergence in substance and procedure as well as greater co-operation and co-ordination that could be applied in the context of differing national legal systems around the world.[119]

The issues concerning international cooperation appeared to be magnified in the digital era, with the foreword to the 2021 *Report*[120] – jointly produced by the OECD and ICN – acknowledging that '[t]he globalised and digitalised economy has created a highly interconnected world that has increased cross-border competition issues'.[121] It is worrying that a major finding of the 2021 *Report* is that a substantial amount of work is yet to be undertaken to address the challenges of attaining an enhanced level of cooperation in relation to coordination of related enforcement activities in cross-border cases.[122]

In 2021, the *Penrose Report* appeared to reiterate that international cooperation is needed, noting that 'Globalisation means plenty of competition investigations where [UK Competition and Markets Authority] needs to work in partnership with its equivalents in other countries, wherever international firms or supply chains span national boundaries'.[123] The deduction that international cooperation is much needed in a cross-border context is reflected in the 2022 DG Comp Management Plan, which strongly suggests that 'EU competition policy also strives to strengthening international cooperation in competition enforcement and making steps towards increased convergence of competition rules across different jurisdictions'.[124]

Likewise, the importance of furthering the international cooperation appears to be high on the agenda for the United Nations Commission for Trade and Development (UNCTAD).[125] The UNCTAD Guiding policies and procedures[126] for cooperation

[117] OECD/ICN, *Survey on International Competition Enforcement Co-operation* (2013) http://www.oecd.org/daf/competition/InternEnforcementCooperation2013.pdf.
[118] Ibid, 10.
[119] OECD Report (n 116) 54.
[120] OECD/ICN, *Report on International Co-operation in Competition Enforcement* (2021) https://www.oecd.org/daf/competition/OECD-ICN-Report-on-International-Co-operation-in-Competition-Enforcement.pdf.
[121] Foreword – ibid, 3.
[122] Ibid, 3.
[123] John Penrose MP, *Power to the people: independent report on competition policy* (February 2021) 17.
[124] European Competition – DG Comp, *Management Plan 2022* Ref. Ares(2022)778769 – 02/02/2022, p 3.
[125] 'Annex 2: Final version of the UNCTAD Survey Report' in Intergovernmental Group of Experts on Competition Law and Policy, *Report of the discussion group on international cooperation*, 17th Session 11–13 July 2017, para 19 – emphasis in the original).
[126] UNCTAD, *Guiding policies and procedures under Section F of the United Nations Set on Competition* (2021) UNCTAD/DITC/CPLP/MISC/2021/2.

between national competition authorities appeared to be advanced in 2021. A major principle is that any '[c]ooperation between authorities is based on mutual trust and is performed on a voluntary basis'.[127] The problem is that, whilst 'mutual trust'[128] appears to be fundamental for any form of cooperation, there is no definition of the concept of mutual trust, which might adversely affect the willingness of some competition authorities to cooperate with others by exercising their 'discretion whether to cooperate'.[129]

It would have been better, if the concept of mutual trust had been defined to cover certain major principles (such as certain procedural rights like the right to fair trial and hearing – due process) which are fundamental for the proper enforcement of competition law in cross-border cases. Analogies could have been made with the EU developments where 'mutual trust as a tool of EU governance results, to a certain extent, in a horizontal "unbundling" of the exercise of national authority and territoriality'.[130]

There is a major gap in the existing regulatory framework. There is no regime for judicial cooperation in competition law matters. This is a real issue because PIL techniques may well have been used to develop a system of judicial cooperation which factors foreign regulatory interests in.[131] The reluctance of the international community to advance such a mechanism for judicial cooperation is reflected in the narrow definition of enforcement activities to cover only proceedings before national regulators,[132] *excluding any cooperation in relation to private antitrust damages claims before national courts.*

The lack of a PIL mechanism which promotes a level of judicial cooperation in private antitrust damages claims might be due to the fact that private antitrust enforcement has been often seen as inferior to public enforcement of competition, especially in the EU.[133] Directive 2014/104/EU on antitrust damages claims, which entered in force on 27 December 2014, made a major impact on the way in which private antitrust enforcement is being perceived in the EU. It seems that '[a]ll Member States have now transposed the rules of the Directive'.[134] The cross-border nature of the economic activities which is borne out in the competition law infringements strongly indicates that the public and private international law aspects need to be thoroughly considered in a global context.

In spite of the evidently narrow scope of the existing framework for international cooperation, Terhechte[135] has submitted that 'it is possible in the field of the judiciary

[127] Ibid – principle 3.
[128] Ibid – recital 4 from the Preamble.
[129] Ibid – principle 3.
[130] C Rizcallah, 'The challenges to trust-based governance in the European Union: Assessing the use of mutual trust as a driver of EU integration' (2019) 25 *European Law Journal* 37, 39.
[131] Danov (n 97).
[132] eg Article I(2)(B) and 1(C) of the US/EU Agreement.
[133] WPJ Wils, 'Should Private Enforcement be Encouraged in Europe' (2003) 26 *World Competition* 473, 480–84.
[134] Transposition of the Directive in Member States, http://ec.europa.eu/competition/antitrust/actionsdamages/directive_en.html.
[135] JP Terhechte, *International Competition Enforcement Law Between Cooperation and Convergence* (Berlin, Springer, 2011).

to discern certain network formations',[136] citing as relevant the Association of European Competition Law Judges, International Association of Judges and American Judges Association.[137] That said, it is difficult to see how judges' associations could actively promote a level of judicial cooperation without an appropriate convention (or any other legislative instrument) in place to systematically deal with such issues as allocation of jurisdiction and related/parallel proceedings, which arise in relation to the same anti-competitive conduct deployed by the same multinational group/s of companies, in a global context.[138]

There is a level of scepticism as to whether the international community is interested in adopting a specific international convention which applies in competition law matters. The rather exceptional regulatory nature of competition law, expressing fundamental national interests, makes it somewhat difficult for the states to agree to attain a level of judicial cooperation. This appears to be deduced from the 2019 Convention on the Recognition and Enforcement of Foreign Judgments in Civil or Commercial Matters which states that:

> This Convention shall not apply to [...] anti-trust (competition) matters, except where the judgment is based on conduct that constitutes an anti-competitive agreement or concerted practice among actual or potential competitors to fix prices, make rigged bids, establish output restrictions or quotas, or divide markets by allocating customers, suppliers, territories or lines of commerce, and where such conduct and its effect both occurred in the State of origin.[139]

The 2019 Convention could only apply to judgments which are awarding damages arising out of anti-competition agreements (or practices) that restrict competition by their object. In other words, the 2019 Convention does not apply to abuses of dominant positions and agreements which may restrict competition by effect.[140] It is not only that a significant proportion of the competition law disputes are excluded, but it is also surprising to see that the Hague Convention would only apply with regard to judgments in relation to competition law infringements in cases where the 'conduct and its effect [on prices] both occurred in the State of origin'.[141] The restrictive wording and the narrow scope of the 2019 Hague Convention puts beyond any doubt that its provisions would have very limited (if any) impact on the injured parties' access to legal remedies in cross-border competition law cases.[142]

If both the conduct and its effect on prices had materialised in the same jurisdiction, then the defendant would most probably have assets in the State of origin (as long as this was the place where the infringement had been committed as well as the place where the damage was sustained).[143] It is difficult to see why the injured parties would need

[136] Ibid 16.
[137] Ibid.
[138] Compare: Brussels Ia.
[139] Article 2(1)(p) of the Hague Judgments Convention. See more: Danov and Otero (n 97).
[140] *Sainsbury's* (n 16). See also: *Commission Decision of 19/XII/2007* (n 24).
[141] Article 2(1)(p) of the Hague Judgments Convention.
[142] Danov and Otero (n 97).
[143] Compare: Chapter 4.

to recognise and enforce a judgment abroad, if the defendants had assets in the State of origin.[144]

More importantly, the issues concerning multiplicity of related claims, which arise out of transnational competition law infringements, appear to be exposed in the *Interchange Fees*[145] and *Trucks*[146] litigation. The lack of an international convention which promotes judicial cooperation between national courts in private antitrust cases means that various regulatory regimes (eg UK competition law; US antitrust laws; EU competition law) may be applied. Moreover, various substantive and procedural rules may also be applicable in relation to numerous competition law claims arising out of the same (or related) transnational infringements but issued before different national courts.

In view of this, it will be necessary to consider, in this book, to what extent a soft mechanism for judicial cooperation could allow for any identical issues to be somewhat consistently dealt with in related proceedings before the different national courts.

B. Gap in the Literature: Judicial Cooperation in Competition Law Matters

The governance aspects of global competition[147] as well as of the various competition laws across the globe[148] appear to have been discussed in the literature. Although the issues of applying national competition laws in a global context had been discussed by policy-makers[149] and commentators for some time,[150] the WTO failure to devise a

[144] Danov and Otero (n 97).

[145] Case Nos: 1517/11/7/22 (UM) and 1266/7/7/16, *The Merchant Interchange Fee Umbrella Proceedings* [2022] CAT 31.

[146] *Road Haulage Association* (n 23) [5–6].

[147] eg Epstein and Greve (n 112); O Budzinski, *The Governance of Global Competition: Competence Allocation in International Competition Policy* (Edward Elgar, 2008); EM Fox and MJ Trebilcock (eds), *The Design of Competition Law Institutions: Global Norms, Local Choices* (Oxford, OUP, 2012).

[148] E Elhauge and D Geradin, *Global Competition Law and Economics* 2nd edn (Oxford, Hart Publishing, 2011); A Ezrachi (ed), *Research Handbook on International Competition Law* (Edward Elgar, 2012).

[149] *Towards an International Framework of Competition Rules* (n 108). See also: European Commission, *XXVIth Report on Competition Policy 1996* (Published in conjunction with the 'General Report on the Activities of the European Union – 1996); The US Department of Justice – International Competition Policy Advisory Committee, *The Final Report to the Attorney General and Assistant Attorney General* http://www.justice.gov/atr/icpac/finalreport.html.

[150] DK Tarullo, 'Norms and institutions in global competition policy' (2000) *The American Journal of International Law* 478; EM Fox, 'Antitrust and Regulatory Federalism: Races Up, Down, and Sideways' (2000) 75 *New York University Law Review* 1781; Budzinski (n 147); EM Fox, 'Linked-In: Antitrust and the Virtues of a Virtual Network' (2009) *The International Lawyer* 151, 154; Tarullo (n 112); Fox (n 112); Basedow (n 112); Guzman (n 112); Stephan (n 112); Becker (n 112); Malinauskaite (n 112); EM Fox, 'Antitrust and Institutions: Design and Change' (2010) 41 *Loyola University Chicago Law Journal* 473, 486. See also: DA Crane, *The Institutional Structure of Antitrust Enforcement* (Oxford University Press, 2011); D Sokol, 'International Antitrust Institutions' in AT Guzman (ed), *Cooperation, Comity, and Competition Policy* (Oxford University Press, 2011) 187.

global competition law regime[151] strongly indicated that a different form of cooperation might be needed.[152]

The competition law literature predominantly addresses the questions concerning the advantages and disadvantages of public and private enforcement modes as well as with the relevant modes' interaction which would be central to the design of an optimal national enforcement regime.[153] There is a substantial amount of literature dealing with the issues concerning private antitrust enforcement in the US[154] and EU.[155]

However, a major gap in the literature remains: setting up a regime for judicial cooperation in antitrust matters that allows for the chosen (optimal and individual) national enforcement models (which may be advancing public and/or private enforcement modes) to interact with each other in cross-border cases with a view to improving the injured parties' access to legal remedies in related claims that arise out of the same transnational competition law infringement. Nonetheless, the issues concerning the allocation of jurisdiction, avoidance of parallel proceedings, applicable law and the recognition and enforcement of judgments in relation to competition law claims have been discussed in the private international law literature.[156]

There are a number of books[157] that have discussed the relevant developments in relation to private antitrust litigation in the EU, without sufficiently considering the PIL

[151] *Towards an International Framework of Competition Rules* (n 108). See also: *XXVIth Report on Competition Policy* (n 149) 95; *Singapore First WTO Ministerial Conference – Adopted 13 December 1996*, WT/MIN(96)/DEC, 18 December 1996 [20]; Report (1998) of the Working Group on the Interaction between Trade and Competition Policy to the General Council, WT/WGTCP/2, 8 December 1998; Working Group on the Interaction between Trade and Competition Policy, *Communication From the United States*, WT/WGTCP/W/35, 1 October 1997; Working Group on the Interaction between Trade and Competition Policy, *Submission by the European Community and its Member States*, WT/WGTCP/W/45, 24 November 1997; Doha WTO Ministerial 2001: Ministerial Declaration – Adopted on 14 November 2001, WT/MIN(01)/DEC/1, 20 November 2001, [23–25]; Doha Work Programme (n 113).

[152] See: Section V below.

[153] WF Schwartz, 'An Overview of the Economics of Antitrust Enforcement' (1980) 68 *Georgetown Law Journal* 1075; S Shavell, 'The Optimal Structure of Law Enforcement' (1993) 36 *Journal of Law and Economics* 255; RP McAfee, HM Mialon and SH Mialon, 'Private v. public antitrust enforcement: A strategic analysis' (2008) 92 *Journal of Public Economics* 1863; WPJ Wils, 'The relationship between public antitrust enforcement and private actions for damages' (2009) 32 *World Competition* 3, 18 – accessible at http://papers.ssrn.com/sol3/papers.cfm?abstract_id=1296458; K Huschelrath and S Peyer, 'Public and private enforcement of competition law: A differentiated approach' (2013) 36 *World Competition* 585.

[154] See: S Salop and L White, 'Private Antitrust Litigation: An Introduction and Framework' in L White (ed), Private Antitrust Litigation, New Evidence, New Learning (MIT Press, Cambridge, Mass 1988).

[155] WPJ Wils, *Principles of European Antitrust Enforcement*, (Oxford, Hart Publishing, 2005); J Basedow (ed), *Private Enforcement of EC Competition Law*, (Kluwer, 2007); A Komninos, *EC Private Antitrust Enforcement: Decentralised Application of EC Competition Law by National Courts*, (Oxford, Hart Publishing, 2008); J Basedow, JP Terhechte and L Tichy (eds), *Private Enforcement of Competition Law*, (Baden-Baden, Nomos, 2011); B Rodger (ed), *Competition Law: Comparative Private Enforcement and Collective Redress across the EU* (Kluwer, 2014); I Lianos, P Davis and P Nebbia, *Damages Claims for the Infringement of Competition Law* (OUP, 2015); M Ioannidou, *Consumer Involvement in Private EU Competition Law Enforcement* (OUP, 2015).

[156] Danov (n 5); Basedow, Francq and Idot (n 5); Danov, Becker and Beaumont (n 5).

[157] eg M Bergstrom, M Iacovides and M Strand (eds), *Harmonising EU Competition Litigation: The New Directive and Beyond* (Oxford, Bloomsbury, 2016); PL Parcu, G Monti and M Botta (eds), *Private Enforcement of EU Competition Law: The Impact of the Damages Directive* (Cheltenham, Edward Elgar Publishing, 2018); M Strand, VB Venegas and MC Iacovides (eds), *EU Competition Litigation: Transposition and First Experiences of the New Regime* (Oxford, Hart, 2019).

aspects which are central to facilitating injured parties' access to effective legal remedies in a global context. The issues concerning the interrelation between the regulatory and the adjudicatory jurisdiction have also been discussed in the private international law literature.[158] That said, there is a gap in the PIL literature, which does not sufficiently consider the governance aspects of related competition law claims that arise out of the same transnational competition law infringements and which are issued before different courts in a global context.

The PIL issues concerning related private antitrust damages claims need to be systematically addressed in a global context because many transnational competition law infringements will be raising difficult regulatory issues (ie public international law aspects, including various comity[159] considerations). Further, the judges in such cases will be dealing with complex PIL issues which would, inter alia, be concerning the jurisdiction of multiple national courts to deal with issues of causation and quantification of damages in related competition law claims, arising out of transnational infringements causing antitrust damages to multiple injured parties down a commercial chain of distribution.

Given the fact that competition law has a primary function to regulate economic activities, the notion of the territoriality needs to be factored in to a competition law system which is set to safeguard certain national objectives and legitimate regulatory interests.[160] Dealing with the issues concerning multiple regulatory interests,[161] which are reflected in the various national competition laws, is fairly difficult because:

> In the study of international law, a sharp distinction is usually drawn between public international law, concerned with the rights and obligations of states with respect to other states and individuals, and private international law, concerned with issues of jurisdiction, applicable law and the recognition and enforcement of foreign judgments in international private law disputes before national courts.[162]

These issues are at the crossroads of private international law and public international law. That said, there is a strong argument that the notion of territoriality needs to be systematically dealt with in any PIL mechanism which is set to promote judicial cooperation in cross-border competition law cases. Indeed, it is well established that '[t]he primary source of regulatory authority for states in public international law is considered to be territorial'.[163]

The regulatory nature of competition laws and their extra-territorial application raises major issues concerning the conflict of competition laws and governance of related private antitrust damages claims. Systematically addressing these issues through PIL

[158] Danov (n 97); Danov and Otero (n 97).

[159] See: OECD, Inventory of international co-operation agreements on competition, containing separate inventories: Provisions on negative comity – https://www.oecd.org/daf/competition/competition-inventory-provisions-negative-comity.pdf; Provisions on positive comity – https://www.oecd.org/daf/competition/competition-inventory-provisions-positive-comity.pdf.

[160] Bradford et al (n 17).

[161] T Hartley, 'Public Policy and Mandatory Provisions' in P Beaumont and J Holliday (eds), *A Guide to Global Private International Law* (Oxford, Hart, 2022) 75–87.

[162] A Mills, *The Confluence of Public and Private International Law: Justice, Pluralism, Subsidiarity in the International Constitutional Ordering of Private Law* (Cambridge, CUP, 2009) 1.

[163] Ibid 234.

mechanisms would be central to the effective governance of related private enforcement proceedings in cross-border competition law cases.[164] There is a strong argument that a suitably chosen private international law mode of governance could set the scene for a level of judicial cooperation which might be necessary to improve the injured parties' access to effective legal remedies in cross-border cases arising in a global context.[165]

A PIL approach to judicial cooperation should be key to addressing the complex regulatory issues which arise in competition law cases. If the regulatory jurisdiction (territorial scope of competition laws) were to overlap with the adjudicatory jurisdiction (territorial scope of the court's jurisdiction), then each national court would take a narrow view on the scope of their competition laws (ie regulatory jurisdiction) which will in turn affect their adjudicatory jurisdiction. The judges may even decline to apply foreign competition laws and exercise adjudicatory jurisdiction in relation to antitrust harm caused to businesses and consumers in other jurisdictions.[166] The point was put forward by the UK Competition Appeal Tribunal in *Dr Rachael Kent v Apple*:[167]

> [A]lthough there are a number of claims in the US which seeks redress against Apple on behalf of consumers, the US Sherman Act does not appear to apply extra-territorially so as to extend to claims of the present kind by UK consumers: see *Hoffmann-La Roche Ltd v Empagran S.A.* 542 US 155 (2004).[168]

In other words, since the regulatory jurisdiction (ie the scope of the US Sherman Act) would limit the adjudicatory jurisdiction of the US courts, both the UK and US courts would only have the adjudicatory jurisdiction to award damages arising out of anti-competitive practices which were either implemented within the jurisdiction or had qualified effects in the jurisdiction.[169] The important PIL questions which arise in such cases are: how are inconsistent outcomes to be avoided in related private damages claims arising out of the transnational competition law infringements[170] which may be issued in relation to the same infringement across the globe? To what extent should foreign regulatory and judicial findings be factored in by English and Welsh judges[171] with a view avoiding inconsistent outcomes?

Therefore, a balance must be struck between the aspects concerning regulatory jurisdiction[172] (ie which is intertwined with the territorial scope of competition law from a public international law perspective) and the issues in relation to adjudicatory jurisdiction[173] (ie having private international law inferences), whilst considering access to effective legal remedies in related competition law claims arising out of the same transnational infringement.[174] A transnational approach to judicial cooperation is necessary because these issues may be intertwined with the aspects concerning extra-territorial

[164] Chapters 7, 8, 9 and 10.
[165] S Sassen, *A Sociology of Globalization* (WW Norton & Company, London 2007) p 72.
[166] *F Hoffmann-La Roche Ltd v Empagran* (2004) 542 US 155, 165 and 167 (US Supreme Court).
[167] Case No: 1403/7/7/21, *Dr Rachael Kent v Apple* – Reasoned Order of the President (Service out of the jurisdiction), dated 26th May 2021.
[168] Ibid [6].
[169] Ibid. See also: *The LCD Appeals* (n 66).
[170] Chapters 7 and 8.
[171] Chapters 9 and 10.
[172] Chapter 9.
[173] Chapters 4, 5, 6 and 7.
[174] Chapter 2.

application of competition law provisions which may be enjoying a public policy character,[175] expressing the fundamental interests of the forum and being regarded as mandatory provisions for PIL purposes.[176]

V. Private Antitrust Damages Claims – PIL and Judicial Cooperation

International cooperation between public enforcers (ie regulators) appears to have been the focus of the existing legal framework in competition law matters. In other words, there is a regulatory gap in so far as there is no convention (or any arrangements) that promote judicial cooperation between national courts in a global context, governing issues in relation to private antitrust claims which arise out of transnational competition law infringements that cause antitrust damages to multiple injured parties in different jurisdictions.

Similarly, some scholars appear to regard the problems concerning international cooperation in competition law cases as falling within the ambit of public international law and/or global administrative law rather than private international law. This can be clearly deduced from Terhechte's conclusions that:

> International Competition Enforcement Law is drawn form a multitude of national regimes and the laws governing their cooperation, as well as basic legal principles, which appear at the level of *public international law* (i.e., the ban on intervention and the principle of state immunity), European law (e.g., from the principle of effet utile and the principle of harmonized implementation of community law and other regional legal systems (MERCOSUR, NAFTA, ASEAN, APEC, COMESA)). On this foundation convergence processes have also taken place in the area of procedural law to a considerable degree, which is apparent from the increasing penalization of competition law, the introduction of *Leniency*-programs or a reinforced application by private entities.
>
> The principle on which enforcement is based are of utmost significance not only for Competition Enforcement Law but also for new concepts of systematization beyond this legal area. This applies to administration in and by networks, as well as to approaches to a *Global Administrative Law (or International Administrative Law)*.[177]

This book will demonstrate that, whilst it is true that many of the relevant issues concerning governance would have public international law connotations, there are important private international law issues which may directly impact on injured parties' access to legal remedies in a global context. In order to fill the gap and set out PIL mechanisms which improve injured parties' access to legal remedies in related private antitrust damages claims arising out of cross-border competition law infringements, aspects of competition law as well as of the resolution of disputes with an international element need to be examined.

[175] Recital 1 of Directive 2014/104/EU on certain rules governing actions for damages under national law for infringements of the competition law provisions of the Member States and of the European Union [2014] Official Journal L349/1; *Eco Swiss* (n 49); Case C-38/98 *Régie nationale des usines Renault SA v Maxicar SpA and Orazio Formento* EU:C:2000:225.

[176] Articles 9 and 21 of Rome I; Articles 16 and 26 of Rome II. Chapter 10.

[177] Terhechte (n 135) 76–77 – the emphases added by the author.

A. International Cooperation: 'Mutual Trust'[178] – A Major Limitation

There may be some important institutional limitations that might adversely affect the effectiveness of any regime for international cooperation between regulators[179] which is based on the principle of 'mutual trust'.[180] A closely connected question concerns the level and extent of a national regulator's independence from their national governments in so far as such regulators (ie national competition authorities) often are administrative bodies.

A major issue, which may diminish the effectiveness of the existing framework for international cooperation, concerns the independence of national competition regulators. This is a long-standing issue, which has even been discussed by the CJEU in the EU context. In particular, in a case concerning the interpretation of the concept of 'court or tribunal' within the meaning of Article 267 TFEU, the following observations were made:

> [W]hilst it is true that the members of the Epitropi Antagonismou enjoy personal and operational independence and are bound in the exercise of their duties only by the law and their conscience within the meaning of Law No 703/1977, it nevertheless remains that there are no particular safeguards in respect of their dismissal or the termination of their appointment. That system does not appear to constitute an effective safeguard against undue intervention or pressure from the executive on the members of the Epitropi Antagonismou.[181]

In other words, the problem is that, if there are reservations about a regulator's independence, this might undermine any regime of international cooperation which is based on the principle of 'mutual trust'.[182] In other words, if a regulator's independence is questioned, then such regulators might often be mistrusted, which would negatively impact on the effects of regulators' decisions in other jurisdictions.

In a global context, this would pose an issue of institutional bias, which can be exported through a system for international cooperation. There is a view that any 'form of soft cooperation furthers the enforcement goals of regulators but does virtually nothing to address the over- and under-regulation of antitrust law at international level'.[183] There is a risk that some experienced and leading national competition authorities could potentially use such a form of cooperation to export their own 'policy bias'.[184] The regulatory literature has unequivocally suggested that '[t]he greater the policy bias of a national institution, the more biased will be any new form of global governance created by that institution'.[185]

[178] *Guiding policies and procedures* (n 126) principle 3.

[179] Danov and Dnes (n 25), 52–3.

[180] *Guiding policies and procedures* (n 126), principle 3.

[181] Case C-53/03 *Synetairismos Farmakopoion Aitolias & Akarnanias (Syfait) and Others v GlaxoSmithKline plc and GlaxoSmithKline* EU:C:2005:333 [31].

[182] *Guiding policies and procedures* (n 126) principle 3.

[183] A T Guzman, "The case for international antitrust" in Epstein and Greve (n 112) 99, 116.

[184] M Kahler and DA Lake, 'Economic integration and global governance: Why so little supranationalism?' in Mattli and N Woods (eds), *The Politics of Global Regulation* (Princeton University Press, Princeton 2009) 242, 255.

[185] Ibid 255 – emphasis in the original.

This strengthens the argument that, due to the 'interrelated nature of political and economic life in a world of global markets and local government',[186] a mechanism for judicial cooperation which is based on PIL rules may be much more trustworthy in so far as, for example, the independence of the UK judiciary could hardly be questioned.

B. An Argument for Judicial Cooperation

The deduction that attaining a level of judicial cooperation is central to improving access to justice in cross-border cases appears to be reflected in the Convention of 2 July 2019 on the Recognition and Enforcement of Foreign Judgments in Civil or Commercial Matters, which explicitly states that 'to promote effective access to justice for all and to facilitate rule-based multilateral trade and investment, and mobility, through judicial co-operation.'[187]

The issues must be considered as a matter of priority post-Brexit because, despite the fact that the UK made an 'application to accede'[188] to the Lugano Convention, the EU took the view that it should not 'give its consent to invite the United Kingdom to accede to the Lugano Convention.'[189] In a formal Communication[190] by the EU Commission to the EU Parliament and the EU Council, the rationale behind this approach appears to be as follows:

> [T]he Commission takes the view that the European Union should not give its consent to the accession of the United Kingdom to the 2007 Lugano Convention. For the European Union, the Lugano Convention is a flanking measure of the internal market and relates to the EU-EFTA/EEA context. In relation to all other third countries the consistent policy of the European Union is to promote cooperation within the framework of the multilateral Hague Conventions. The United Kingdom is a third country without a special link to the internal market. Therefore, there is no reason for the European Union to depart from its general approach in relation to the United Kingdom. Consequently, the Hague Conventions should provide the framework for future cooperation between the European Union and the United Kingdom in the field of civil judicial cooperation.[191]

As noted above,[192] the issues concerning judicial cooperation in competition law matters are important because the 2019 Hague Judgments Convention, which is yet to enter into force, can be regarded as being somewhat limited in its scope.[193] In particular, whilst the

[186] D Kennedy, 'Law and the Political Economy of the World' in G Burca, C Kilpatrick and J Scott (eds), *Critical Legal Perspectives on Global Governance* (Oxford, Bloomsbury, 2015) 65, 66.

[187] Preamble of the Convention of 2 July 2019 on the Recognition and Enforcement of Foreign Judgments in Civil or Commercial Matters.

[188] 612-04-04-01 – LUG 2/20, *Notification to the Parties of the Convention on Jurisdiction and the Recognition and Enforcement of Judgments in Civil and Commercial Matters, concluded at Lugano on 30 October 2007*, 14 April 2020.

[189] 612-04-04-01 – LUG 4/21, *Notification to the Parties of the Convention on Jurisdiction and the Recognition and Enforcement of Judgments in Civil and Commercial Matters, concluded at Lugano on 30 October 2007*, 1 July 2021.

[190] *Communication from the Commission to the European Parliament and the Council Assessment on the application of the United Kingdom of Great Britain and Northern Ireland to accede to the 2007 Lugano Convention* COM(2021) 222 final.

[191] Ibid, 4.

[192] See: Section IV.A above.

[193] See more: Danov and Otero (n 97).

Hague Conventions might work for the other civil and commercial disputes, the newly adopted Hague Convention appears to exclude antitrust matters[194] and may not be well suited to promote cooperation in cross-border competition law cases.[195]

Although a new model for judicial cooperation has recently been suggested,[196] the authors stopped short of singling out the specific private international law issues which are to be addressed (be it through an international convention and/or through soft mechanisms which facilitate judicial cooperation) with a view to improving the injured parties' access to justice in cross-border cases.[197] These issues are important because the cross-border nature of most competition law infringements, in which damages would often be suffered by businesses and consumers in a number of jurisdictions, poses challenges for litigants, adjudicators and policy-makers. In order for the EU and UK policy-makers to improve access to justice in claims arising out of cross-border competition law infringements, various PIL issues which address aspects of the regulatory and adjudicatory jurisdiction in related and parallel proceedings should be systematically dealt with in the post-Brexit era.[198]

The increase in the number of private antitrust damages claims in the UK in the years after the implementation of the EU Directive for Antitrust Damages and the non-application of the Brussels Ia/Lugano regime strongly suggest that there is a need for mechanisms for judicial cooperation in competition law matters which address the specific PIL issues that arise in these cases and which are set to improve the injured parties' access to legal remedies. It is a relatively safe proposition that the issues, which were identified more than 20 years ago by the EU Commission as justifications for setting out a global competition law regime, are even more relevant today.[199] Such a regime might be needed, not the least because global digital platforms such as Google, Facebook and Amazon are posing new challenges for enforcers in a global context.[200] More than 20 years ago, some major issues in this respect were set out by Richard Posner[201] who made the following insightful observation that:

> The mismatch between law time and new-economy real time is troubling in two respects. First, an antitrust case involving a new-economy firm may drag on for so long relative to the changing conditions of the industry as to become irrelevant, ineffectual. […]
>
> Second, even if the case is not made obsolete by passage of time, its pendency may cast a pall over parties to and affected by the litigation, making investment riskier and complicating business planning.

[194] Article 2(1)(p) of the Hague Judgments Convention. Prel Doc No 2 of December 2018, 'The possible exclusion of anti-trust matters from the Convention as reflected in Article 2(1)(p) of the 2018 draft Convention', 22nd Diplomatic Session of The Hague Conference on Private International Law.

[195] Danov and Otero (n 97).

[196] Ibid.

[197] See: Chapters 3 and 12 below.

[198] *The LCD Appeals* (n 66); *Media-Saturn Holding GmbH v Toshiba Information Systems (UK) Limited* [2019] EWHC 1095 (Ch).

[199] See: Section IV.A above.

[200] C Ducuing, 'When competition law and data protection law embrace: the German Competition Authority investigates Facebook' 9 January 2018 https://www.law.kuleuven.be/citip/blog/when-competition-law-and-data-protection-law-embrace-the-german-competition-authority-investigates-facebook/; G Sivinski, A Okuliar and L Kjolbye, 'Is big data a big deal? A competition law approach to big data' (2017) *European Competition Journal* 199.

[201] RA Posner, 'Antitrust in the New Economy' (2001) 68 *Antitrust LJ* 925.

> These problems are aggravated by the tendency of antitrust litigation to create multiple lawsuits out of a single dispute; call this the cluster-bomb effect. No sooner does the Antitrust Division bring a case, but the states, and now the European Union, are likely to join the fray, followed at a distance by the antitrust plaintiffs' class-action bar. The effect is to lengthen the original lawsuit, complicate settlement, magnify and protract the uncertainty engendered by the litigation, and increase litigation costs.[202]

This quotation captures the correlation between the issues concerning international cooperation and the aspects in relation to injured parties' access to timely legal remedies. This means that issues of growing legal uncertainty and increased litigation costs may be important in view of the fact that litigation might be perceived as an investment opportunity which, if there is no effectively functioning regime for judicial cooperation that provides injured parties with timely legal remedies, may become less attractive than desirable. The lack of a PIL regime which promotes judicial cooperation in competition law matters would affect the costs and length of the proceedings which might, in turn, impact on the willingness of parties to bring such claims and/or willingness of the litigation funders to finance claimants in such cases. A PIL regime for judicial cooperation might be necessary to enable multiple national courts to effectively and efficiently deal with related claims which are arising out of the same transnational competition law infringement, distorting the process of competition and causing damages to numerous injured parties across the globe.

Indeed, the failure of the WTO negotiations[203] may be regarded as an indication that a more flexible form of judicial cooperation is necessary to factor in different regulatory interests.[204] The need for such a softer form of cooperation was echoed in a speech by the former Director-General of the WTO, Mr Roberto Azevêdo, who noted that '[t]he lesson of [the WTO's subsequent and] recent successes is that the more open and flexible we are, the more likely we are to succeed'.[205]

An appropriate approach would be for the policy-makers to attain a level of judicial cooperation in competition law matters between the national courts (eg UK courts and the EU Member States' courts). This should allow for the courts to set out clear principles in relation to classification and assumption of jurisdiction as well as to enable judges to consider foreign competition laws or give due to regard to foreign regulatory findings.

VI. Purpose of this Book

This book is set to demonstrate that providing private parties with access to effective legal remedies presupposes a level of cooperation between national courts that may be dealing with related claims arising out of the same transnational conduct.

[202] Ibid 939–940.

[203] See Section IV.A above.

[204] Compare: Danov (n 97); H Muir-Watt, 'Governing Networks: A Global Challenge for Private International Law' (2015) *Maastricht Journal of European and Comparative Law* 352, 369.

[205] R Azevêdo, 'Remarks', *Opening Ceremony of the 11th WTO Ministerial Conference*, Buenos Aires, 10–13 December 2017, https://www.wto.org/english/news_e/spra_e/spra205_e.htm.

A regime of judicial cooperation in competition law matters which enables judges to factor in foreign regulatory interests and give due regard (or even effect) to foreign findings may be central to addressing the problems concerning the multiplicity of related proceedings. A PIL solution would make 'no room for the notion of territoriality in the conflict of laws which, on the contrary, permits and requires the application of whatever foreign law, statutory or common, public or private, its constituent rules refer to'.[206]

Given the global nature of many supply chains and competition law infringements,[207] it is more important than ever for an appropriate PIL mechanism to address the PIL problems concerning the coordination of related proceedings involving the same infringing undertakings in the European Union and in non-EU countries.[208] Such a form of cooperation should 'naturally bring about changes in the legal forms and institutional mechanisms of international governance'.[209]

A major challenge, which needs to be addressed in a cross-border context, concerns the fact that there would be multiple competent courts. This means that a PIL mechanism for judicial cooperation in antitrust matters would be necessary to address 'the problem of justice presented by multistate cases'[210] arising out of transnational competition law infringements which could distort the process of competition and cause antitrust damages in multiple jurisdictions. As part of this process, this book will draw on 'the principles of justice at the choice of law level',[211] whilst factoring the specific features of competition law claims.

The issues governing related competition law claims are very difficult because the (public) competition law rules as well as the substantive (private) laws concerning quantification of damages and procedural rules (articulating diverse legal traditions) could vary.[212] Appropriate PIL rules should ensure that national competition laws (which reflect different national interests) are effectively enforced in private antitrust proceedings before the national courts. It should be noted that since '[t]he regulation of globalisation is multilevel, as is legal globalisation itself',[213] private international law may be perceived as an appropriate mode of governance which could provide for a desired level of judicial cooperation in related competition law claims arising out of the same transnational infringement.

The problem, which this book addresses, concerns the PIL issues that arise in private antitrust damages claims. The issues concerning the interrelation between private international law and private antitrust enforcement have been considered by academic writers in some monographs[214] and edited volumes.[215] Although the existing academic

[206] FA Mann, *Conflict of Laws and Public Law, Recueil Des Cours: Collected Courses of the Hague Academy of International Law* (AW Sijtoff, 1971) 107, 190.

[207] Compare *Motorola Mobility LLC v AU Optronics Corp* 775 F3d 816 at 824 (7th Cir 2015) and *The LCD Appeals* (n 66).

[208] Danov and Otero (n 97).

[209] J-B Auby, *Globalisation, Law and State* (Oxford, Hart Publishing, 2017) 106–7.

[210] A T von Mehren, 'Conflict of Laws in a Federal System: Some Perspectives' (1969) 18 *International and Comparative Law Quarterly* 681.

[211] AJE Jaffey, *Topics in Choice of Law* (BIICL, London 1996) p 14.

[212] Danov (n 97).

[213] Auby (n 209) 151.

[214] Danov (n 5).

[215] Basedow, Francq and Idot (n 5); Danov, Becker and Beaumont (n 5).

literature somewhat incidentally touches upon the question of how the injured parties' access to appropriate legal remedies could be facilitated in cross-border cases arising in the EU context, the issues require a renewed attention and they need to be addressed systematically because there has been a marked increase in antitrust damages claims in England and Wales.[216]

Given the lack of an appropriate convention for judicial cooperation in competition law matters, it is worth considering responses to the following questions. Should/could a soft law mechanism of judicial cooperation be considered with a view to attaining a level of consistency in claims in relation to the same cross-border infringement? Might Brexit be an opportunity for the UK take a lead in devising a new mechanism for judicial cooperation (even if it were a soft law mechanism), balancing between different regulatory interests (eg USA/EU interests)? To what extent could a level of consistency be ensured in related proceedings in different jurisdictions which arise out of the same transnational infringements, and which involve different claimants and the same infringers?

In order to address these questions, this book will draw on the EU experience in governing private antitrust damages claims as well as on the UK experience in dealing with cross-border competition law claims issued before English courts. The purpose of this book is to set out the main aspects which need to be considered with a view to advancing a mechanism (even if it were to be a soft one) for judicial cooperation which improves the injured parties' access to legal remedies with regard to cross-border competition law infringements in a global context. A theoretical model will be set out to outline the relationship between the PIL rules and access to justice in cross-border competition law actions arising in a global context.[217] On that basis, doctrinal studies[218] will be undertaken. The book will engage with the reported case law, governmental and international organisations' reports and academic publications which will provide the author with the information which is necessary for him to identify how the current regime appears to be functioning, and what are the problems at the moment. This would be important with a view to putting forward a case for a regime of co-operation which is based on private international law principles, in order to make private antitrust enforcement more effective in a global context.[219]

Drawing on the EU/UK experience with private antitrust enforcement, this book aims to demonstrate that a level of judicial cooperation through PIL mechanisms is much needed because many competition law infringements would be transnational in nature (eg EU competition law infringements in particular would naturally 'affect trade between Member States').[220] Since such transnational infringements would affect consumers and businesses across borders, related private damages claims may

[216] eg *Mark McLaren Class Representative* (n 6); *Michael O'Higgins FX Class Representative* (n 63); *Road Haulage Association* (n 23); *BT Group PLC & Anr v Le Patourel* [2022] EWCA Civ 593.

[217] See: Chapter 2.

[218] R Cryer at al, *Research Methodologies in EU and International Law* (Oxford, Hart Publishing, 2011) pp 7–9.

[219] See also: J Basedow, *An economic analysis of private international law* (Mohr Siebeck, 2006); JE Calfee and R Craswell, 'Some effects of uncertainty on compliance with legal standards' (1984) 70 *Virginia Law Review* 965; R Craswell and JE Calfree, 'Deterrence and uncertain legal standards' (1986) 2 *Journal of Law, Economics and Organisation* 279; AM Polinsky and S Shavell, 'Legal error, litigation and the incentive to obey the law' (1989) 5 *Journal of Law, Economics and Organisation* 99.

[220] Articles 101 and 102 TFEU.

be issued in multiple jurisdictions. In other words, PIL mechanisms are necessary to govern related private antitrust damages which arise out of transnational competition law infringements.

A transnational approach to judicial cooperation should allow for any inconsistency between the outcomes in related proceedings to be minimised, ensuring that legitimate regulatory interests (eg UK and EU regulatory interests) are properly safeguarded. In order to propose a workable PIL solution, a distinction should be drawn between what the desirable framework for judicial cooperation is and what regime actually is achievable.[221] Although there is an argument that a PIL mechanism for judicial cooperation should be important in a global context, the major challenge in this respect concerns setting out an appropriate and achievable level of judicial cooperation which aims to improve injured parties' access to legal remedies in cross-border competition law cases, post-Brexit.

[221] J-PP Langlois and CC Langlois, 'Dispute Settlement Design for Unequal Partners: A Game Theoretic Perspective' (2007) 33 *International Interactions* 347, 362.

2

Theoretical Aspects – PIL and Access to Justice in Private Antitrust Damages Claims

I. Introduction: Some Specific Features – Private Antitrust Litigation

In this chapter, some specific features of a large proportion of private antitrust damages claims, which require specific private international law (PIL) solutions, will be briefly set out. With this in mind, a theoretical model will be set out in order to link some important PIL issues with the injured parties' entitlement to legal remedies and their access to legal remedies in private antitrust damages claims with an international element. Once this has been done, the author will start considering the PIL issues (eg regulatory breach; quantification of damages) which are relevant to the parties' *entitlement to legal remedies* as well the important PIL issues (eg jurisdiction and relevant procedural rules; avoiding related proceedings) which relate to the parties' *access to legal remedies*. Overall, the chapter aims to set the scene for a more in-depth analysis by outlining some important PIL issues which need to be considered in the following chapters.

A specific feature of many competition law infringements, and in particular the infringements established by the EU Commission, is that they have a cross-border character. PIL has traditionally been very important in private antitrust damages claims which often have an international element, involving transnational groups of companies[1] or causing harm to multiple injured parties.[2] More specifically, the PIL rules have been used to ascertain the set/s of substantive laws that will apply to the merits of the case (eg the type of competition law infringement,[3] limitation periods,[4] pass-through,[5] quantification of damages,[6] compound interest).[7] The choice-of-law rules – ascertaining

[1] Case C-882/19 *Sumal v Mercedes Benz Trucks España* EU:C:2021:800.

[2] Case Nos: 1517/11/7/22 (UM) and 1266/7/7/16, *The Merchant Interchange Fee Umbrella Proceedings* [2022] CAT 31.

[3] *JJH Enterprises Ltd (trading as ValueLicensing) v Microsoft* [2022] EWHC 929 (Comm).

[4] Case Nos: 1349-1350/5/7/20 (T) and 1383-1384/5/7/21 (T), *Westover Ltd v Mastercard* [2021] CAT 12.

[5] *The Merchant Interchange Fee Umbrella Proceedings* (n 2).

[6] Case No: 1241/5/7/15 (T), *Sainsbury's Supermarkets v MasterCard* [2016] CAT 11.

[7] G Monti, 'EU law and interest on damages for infringements of competition law – A comparative report' (2016) EUI Working Paper LAW 2016/11, http://cadmus.eui.eu/bitstream/handle/1814/40464/LAW_2016_11.pdf?sequence=3&isAllowed=y.

the applicable substantive laws – have been very important for national judges to assess damages in cross-border competition law claims. This means that the PIL rules would be important not least because the 'prospect of success'[8] of a competition law claim with an international element would depend on the choice-of-law rules[9] (as well as on the applicable competition law rules)[10] which may in turn impact on the jurisdiction of the English court under the Civil Procedure Rules or Competition Appeal Tribunal Rules.

Another specific feature of some transnational competition law infringements is that they have lasted for a significant period of time, which means that the evidential matters and in particular 'the disclosure [might] be hugely burdensome, not only because of the breadth of the documents and data involved but because it covers a period of 23 years (i.e. 276 months)'[11] in some cases. In order for the multiple injured parties to substantiate their competition claims, the rules concerning evidence and procedure have been fairly important.[12] Since the procedural rules are different in different jurisdictions, the place of litigation has been indicative of the procedural and evidential rules which would be applied by the national courts. The PIL rules,[13] which are used by national judges to assume jurisdiction in cross-border competition law claims, also have a bearing on the set of procedural rules which is to apply in private antitrust damages claims. In other words, the jurisdictional rules should allow sophisticated injured parties to establish jurisdiction before an appropriate forum where the procedural rules would enable them to substantiate their claims and quantify any antitrust damages with a view to attaining their desired legal remedies.[14]

Another characteristic attribute of competition litigation is that multiple competition law claims will arise out of the same transnational competition law infringement. Such claims may be issued by multiple injured parties, who are up or down a supply chain or chain of commerce, in different jurisdictions. This means not only that appropriate procedural rules and case-management mechanisms are necessary for national judges to avoid inconsistent outcomes in related claims which are issued in the same jurisdiction,[15] but it also suggests that appropriate PIL mechanisms for judicial cooperation may be necessary to avoid inconsistent outcomes in related claims issued in different jurisdictions.[16] A level of judicial cooperation may be needed to ensure a level of consistency in dealing with any common issues in multiple claims arising out of the same competition law infringements.

[8] The Competition Appeal Tribunal Rules 2015, r 31(2)(b).

[9] Chapters 10 and 11.

[10] Chapters 9 and 10.

[11] Case Nos: 1284-1290/5/7/18 (T), *Royal Mail Group Ltd v DAF Trucks Ltd* [2021] CAT 10 [11].

[12] *Bain v Whitehaven Rly Co* (1850) 3 HL Cas 1, 19 cited in P Torremans and J Fawcett, *Cheshire, North & Fawcett Private International Law* 15th edn (Oxford, OUP, 2017) 80.

[13] Chapters 4, 5 and 6.

[14] See also: *Provimi Limited v Aventis Animal Nutrition SA and Others* [2003] EWHC 961 (Comm); *Cooper Tire & Rubber Company v Shell Chemicals UK Limited* [2009] EWHC 2609 (Comm); *Cooper Tire & Rubber Company Europe Limited & Others* [2010] EWCA Civ 864; *Toshiba Carrier UK Ltd and Other v KME Yorkshire Limited & Others* [2011] EWHC 2665 (Ch); *Toshiba Carrier UK Ltd and Other v KME Yorkshire Limited & Others* [2012] EWCA Civ 169.

[15] *The Merchant Interchange Fee Umbrella Proceedings* (n 2). See more: Chapter 6.

[16] Case Nos: 1282/7/7/18 and 1289/7/7/18, *UK Trucks Claim Ltd v Stellantis and Ors & Road Haulage Association Ltd v MAN SE and Ors* [2022] CAT 25 [5–6]. See more: Chapters 7 and 8.

An added layer of complexity, which needs to be set out with a view to singling out an appropriate PIL solution, is that – in addition to any private antitrust enforcement proceedings – it is highly likely for regulatory proceedings in relation to the same conduct to be issued in different jurisdictions.[17] From a PIL perspective, it would be important to consider what the effects (if any) of foreign regulatory findings would be in England and Wales.[18] The issues are important because PIL rules would be equally relevant in follow-on claims[19] (where the parties are relying on a prior and binding decision of the EU Commission or another foreign regulator establishing the competition law infringement)[20] as well as in stand-alone claims.[21]

Therefore, there are several sets of PIL issues which need to be addressed by the courts of England and Wales in cross-border competition law claims. These include, for example: would the English courts have the jurisdiction to hear and determine competition law claims against a multinational group of companies? Which law/s should be applied to determine whether there is a competition law infringement? What would be the effects (if any) of any foreign proceedings and/or any foreign decisions/judgments in this respect? Would the English courts have the jurisdiction to hear and determine claims for damages caused in other jurisdictions or would its jurisdiction be rather limited to damages caused in England and Wales? Which law should be applied by the English courts when dealing with issues of causation and quantification?

II. Entitlement to Legal Remedies and Access to Legal Remedies

In order to systematically identify and address the PIL issues which arise in relation to PIL, a theoretical model is devised to link the choice-of-law rules with the aspects concerning the entitlement to legal remedies (ie substantive law matters which could impact on the outcome of the disputes). A rather complex aspect in this context is that, given the nature of competition laws which regulate economic activities, a number of private antitrust disputes might often be raising *regulatory issues* concerning the conduct which allegedly restricts competition as well as *private law issues* concerning various aspects of causation and quantification of damages in cross-border disputes. In view of this, the issues concerning classification would need to be systematically considered.[22] The theoretical model goes further to link the jurisdictional rules with the issues concerning access to legal remedies (eg jurisdiction; governance aspects of related claims in different jurisdictions; preclusive effects of foreign judgments).

[17] eg Case No: 1382/7/7/21 *Consumers' Association v Qualcomm Inc* [2022] CAT 20; Case No: 1403/7/7/21, *Dr Rachael Kent v Apple* [2022] CAT 28; Case No: 1408/7/7/21 *Elizabeth Helen Coll v Alphabet Inc and Others* [2022] CAT 39.

[18] Chapter 12.

[19] eg *Vatenfall AB v Prysmian* [2018] EWHC 1694 (Ch).

[20] Case AT.39610, *Power Cables – Commission Decision of 2 April 2014* C2014 2139 final.

[21] *ValueLicensing* (n 3).

[22] See: Chapter 3 below.

The main facet of the devised theoretical model is that it draws a distinction between the aspects governing the injured parties' entitlement to legal remedies and the aspects concerning their access to legal remedies. The proposed approach draws on the work of Dame Hazel Genn[23] who notes, in a domestic context, that '[t]he civil justice *system* is partly about substantive rights,[24] but perhaps more importantly it is about the provision that society makes for citizens and business to bring civil suits – the *right of action* and the *machinery to make good* that right'.[25] Indeed, it is well established that, in a domestic context, private law deals with rights and remedies for parties in civil and commercial disputes.[26] According to Professor Jaffey,[27] the private law theory distinguishes between the so-called primary private relationship (setting out the rights and obligations of the parties) and the 'remedy [which] serves to protect or fulfil the primary relation'.[28] The contemporary literature on remedies appears to advance a view that '[w]hen considering whether the legal system is currently fit for purpose, it is never enough to ask merely whether the substantive rules are fair; remedies are key'.[29]

In other words, in order to devise a theoretical model which is set to address the PIL issues and improve injured parties' access to legal remedies, a distinction should be drawn between the aspects in relation to entitlement to legal remedies (ie rights in cross-border cases) and the aspects in relation to access to justice (ie remedies in cross-border cases). Given that the EU has endeavoured to create a transnational justice system, a reference should be made to the EU Justice Agenda for 2020 which expressly noted that '[t]here are no rights without effective remedies'.[30] This signifies that the distinction between rights and remedies is important in a transnational context, being central to the functioning of the EU civil justice system which sets out the foundation of the EU PIL framework for judicial cooperation in civil and commercial matters.[31]

More importantly, the EU law literature[32] appears to advance the view that, in the context of private enforcement of EU law, a 'distinction [is often to be drawn] between right and remedy and in that connection between "constitutive" and "executive" remedial rules'.[33] In particular, Van Gerven tries to separate the 'constitutive'[34] or the substantive law element (ie the law establishing the right to damages for breach of EU competition law) from the 'executive'[35] component which concerns the conditions for bringing

[23] H Genn, *Judging Civil Justice* (Cambridge, CUP, 2010).

[24] JA Jolowicz 'On the nature and purpose of civil procedure law' in JA Jolowicz, *On Civil Procedure* (Cambridge University Press, 2005) cited in Genn (n 23) 11.

[25] Genn (n 23) 11.

[26] P Jaffey, *Private Law and Property Claims* (Oxford, Hart Publishing, 2007) 35–75.

[27] Ibid.

[28] Ibid, 57.

[29] S Hedley, 'Is remedies a subject?' in R Halson and D Campbell (eds) *Research Handbook on Remedies in Private Law* 2, 15.

[30] Communication from the Commission, *The EU Justice Agenda for 2020 – Strengthening Trust, Mobility and Growth within the Union*, COM(2014) 144 final, para 4.1(ii).

[31] See more: M Danov and P Beaumont, 'Measuring the Effectiveness of the EU Civil Justice Framework: Theoretical and Methodological Challenges' (2015/2016) 17 *Yearbook of Private International Law* 151.

[32] W Van Gerven, 'Of rights, remedies and procedures' (2000) 37 *Common Market Law Review* 501, 526.

[33] Ibid, 526.

[34] Ibid.

[35] Ibid.

private antitrust damages claims (ie standing to sue; extent and scope of liability, including heads of damages; burden and standard of proof; limitation periods).[36]

Van Gerven's approach to rights and remedies somewhat echoes the PIL approach which distinguishes between substantive law issues (ie *lex causae*) and procedural law issues (*lex fori*).[37] The PIL approach has been particularly relevant to tortious claims for damages[38] which is why this distinction is fairly relevant with regard to private antitrust damages that classify as tortious for PIL purposes.[39]

That said, Van Gerven's theoretical model, which was devised when analysing the issues concerning rights and remedies with regard to 'enforcement of [EU] law, in relation to claims brought by private parties before national courts',[40] does not fully reflect the post-2000 legislative developments through the Rome II Regulation and Antitrust Damages Directive which are particularly relevant in the context of competition law claims in a cross-border context.

In order to consider the extent to which the PIL rules improve the injured parties' access to legal remedies, this chapter will draw on the PIL literature[41] and the legislative developments by considering two major sets of issues. First, the relevant competition laws (and their territorial scope)[42] along with the substantive law issues[43] (eg burden of proof; limitation periods; causation and quantification of damages) will be examined as being central to the injured parties' *entitlement to legal remedies*. As a result, the issues concerning the injured parties' entitlement to damages will be governed by *lex causae*[44] and Rome II,[45] provided that it is broad enough to cover the applicable (public) competition law which is to determine whether the conduct is anti-competitive. The relevant PIL issues must be duly discussed with a view to improving injured parties' access to justice in cross-border competition law cases.

[36] Ibid, 525.

[37] R Garnett, 'Substance and Procedure' in P Beaumont and J Holliday (eds) *Guide to Global Private International Law* (Oxford, Hart Publishing, 2022) 119. See also: CM Schmitthoff, *The English Conflict of Laws* 3rd edn (London, Steven & Sons, 1954) 395. See also: A Scott, 'Substance and procedure and choice of law in torts' (2007) *Lloyd's Maritime and Commercial Law Quarterly* 44; M Illmer, 'Neutrality matters—some thoughts about the Rome Regulations and the so-called dichotomy of substance and procedure in European private international law' (2009) *Civil Justice Quarterly* 237; JM Carruthers, 'Substance and Procedure in the Conflict of Laws: A Continuing Debate in Relation to Damages' (2004) 53 *International & Comparative Law Quarterly* 691; P Beaumont and Z Tang, 'Classification of Delictual Damages – *Harding v Wealands* and the Rome II Regulation' (2008) 12 *Edinburgh L Rev* 131; M Danov, *Jurisdiction and Judgments in Relation to EU Competition Law Claims* (Oxford, Hart Publishing, 2010) Ch 5.

[38] Carruthers (n 37); Beaumont and Tang (n 37).

[39] See: Chapter 3 below.

[40] Van Gerven (n 32) 501.

[41] Schmitthoff (n 37) 395. See also: Scott (n 44); Illmer (n 37); Carruthers (n 37); Beaumont and Tang (n 37); Danov (n 37).

[42] See: Chapter 9.

[43] Article 15 of Regulation (EC) No 864/2007 of the European Parliament and of the Council of 11 July 2007 on the law applicable to non-contractual obligations (Rome II); The Law Applicable to Contractual Obligations and Non-Contractual Obligations (Amendment etc.) (EU Exit) Regulations 2019, Regulation 11.

[44] See M Danov, 'Data Analysis: Important Issues to be Considered in a Cross-Border Context' in P Beaumont, M Danov, K Trimmings & B Yuksel (eds), *Cross-Border Litigation in Europe* (Oxford, Hart Publishing, 2017).

[45] Article 15 of Rome II.

Second, the procedural law issues (eg case management of multiple related claims;[46] standard of proof; evidence and procedure) will be considered as affecting the injured parties' *access to legal remedies*. Since the procedural issues, which are governed by *lex fori*, are explicitly excluded from Rome II,[47] the relevant jurisdictional rules would pre-determine the procedural rules which would in turn impact on the outcome of a competition law claim with an international element. The correlation between the relevant procedural rules and the outcome of a private law dispute was captured by Mr Justice Tugendhat, who noted that: '[h]aving regard to the differences of procedure, it is not surprising that outcomes are different, even in those cases where there is no significant difference between the provisions of the substantive laws of the states in question'.[48] The procedural rules would not only have a bearing on the outcome of the dispute, but they would also affect the parties' exposure to the costs. The point was made by Lord Justice Jackson, who noted that '[t]he costs rules of each jurisdiction are linked to the evidential practices'.[49]

Hence, the jurisdictional rules would be important for the parties to issue proceedings before a court where the procedural rules are most appropriate for the resolution of the dispute, impacting on its outcome (by allowing parties to sufficiently substantiate their claims) as well as on the parties' exposure to costs.[50] For example, the injured parties' exercise of their rights to effective legal remedies may be dependent on establishing jurisdiction before a national court[51] whose procedural and evidential rules are sufficiently appropriate to enable the judges to certify the relevant claims[52] and assess any antitrust damages.[53] This is even more so in competition law cases where 'the boundary between issues as to the likely availability of data at trial [being closely connected with disclosure rules] and issues as to the merits [being closely connected with the quantification of damages] is by no means easy to define, or to identify in practice'.[54]

Therefore, in order to systematically analyse the PIL issues concerning access to justice in private antitrust damages claims, there are two sets of issues which should be considered in this book. First, the injured parties' *entitlement to legal remedies* would depend on establishing that there is a *restriction of competition law* (eg EU competition law; UK competition law) as well as on *causation and quantification* which must be dealt with by applying the applicable set of private law/s[55] (eg English tort law; German tort law). The choice-of-law rules would need to be considered in this context. Secondly, the injured parties' *access to legal remedies* would depend on the set of applicable procedural

[46] Article 1(3) of Rome II.

[47] Article 1(3) of Rome II. See more: Chapter 11.

[48] *Steven John Kilfoy Wall v Mutuelle De Poitiers Assurance* [2013] EWHC 53 (QB) [17].

[49] *Steven John Kilfoy Wall v Mutuelle De Poitiers Assurance* [2014] EWCA Civ 138 [43]–[44].

[50] J Lawrence and A Morfey, 'Tactical Manoeuvres in UK Cartel Damages Litigation' in M Danov, F Becker and P Beaumont (eds), *Cross-Border EU Competition Law Actions* (Oxford, Hart Publishing, 2013) 149.

[51] *Viking Line ABP v The International Transport Workers' Federation, The Finnish Seamen's Union* [2005] EWHC 1222 (Comm); *British Airways plc & Anor v Sindicato Espanol de Pilotos de Lineas Aereas & Anor* [2013] EWHC 1657 (Comm).

[52] eg *Mastercard Incorporated and others v Walter Hugh Merricks CBE* [2020] UKSC 51.

[53] Ibid. See also: *Sainsbury's Supermarkets Ltd v MasterCard Incorporated* [2020] UKSC 24; *BritNed Development v ABB AB and ABB* [2019] EWCA Civ 1840.

[54] *Merricks* (n 52) [75].

[55] *BritNed* (n 53) [28] and [29].

and evidential rules which must be applied by the national judges when determining whether an injured party (or any categories of injured parties) would be entitled to legal remedies. The jurisdictional rules (including the rules avoiding parallel and related proceedings[56] and the effects of any foreign regulatory/adjudicatory findings)[57] would be central in this context.

III. Entitlement to Remedies – Regulatory Jurisdiction and Regulatory Breach[58]

It is well established that '[c]ompetition law is one of the most commonly deployed instruments to regulate the operation of markets and is standard feature of economic policy in developed and developing countries'.[59] In view of the regulatory function of competition law, the issues concerning judicial cooperation are important because most competition laws would apply extraterritorially, which has been widely discussed by the courts.[60]

The extraterritorial application of competition laws (which must be applied by the forum as being mandatory) has public and private international law connotations. There is a view that 'in a world with extraterritorial application of antitrust laws, the most restrictive antitrust laws will govern business behaviour'.[61] In view of that, it is important to consider how to promote an appropriate PIL approach to judicial cooperation which enables judges to factor in the legitimate regulatory interests of all the countries concerned.[62]

A national judge dealing with a private damages claim should determine whether there is a competition law infringement in the first place. As part of this process, the existence of a regulatory breach (eg an anti-competitive agreement; fixing prices; an abuse of dominant position; foreclosing the market and/or harming the market structure) should be established by applying the applicable set of competition laws.[63]

[56] Chapters 7 and 8.

[57] Chapter 12.

[58] *BritNed* (n 53) [28]; *Enron Coal Services Ltd (In Liquidation) v English Welsh & Scottish Railway Ltd* [2011] EWCA Civ 2 [143], [149] and [150]. See more: Chapter 9.

[59] A Bradford et al, 'Competition Law Gone Global: Introducing the Comparative Competition Law and Enforcement Datasets' (2019) 16 *Journal of Empirical Legal Studies* 411.

[60] *The LCD Appeals* [2018] EWCA Civ 220; Case T-286/09T *Intel v Commission* EU:T:2014:547; Case C-413/14 P *Intel v Commission* EU:C:2017:632, Case C-231/14 P *InnoLux Corp v European Commission* EU:C:2015:451; Joined Cases 89/85, 104/85, 114/85, 116–17/85, and 125–29/85 *Ahlstrom v Commission* EU:C:1988:447 (Wood Pulp Cartel Case); Compare: A list of recent US cases *Re Extraterritoriality* – D Collins, 'Extraterritoriality' in *Applied Antitrust Law* (2018), http://www.appliedantitrust.com/26_extraterritoriality.html.

[61] JO McGinnis, 'The political economy of international antitrust harmonization' in RA Epstein and MS Greve (eds), *Competition Laws in Conflict: Antitrust Jurisdiction in the Global Economy* (AEI Press, 2004) 126 at 127.

[62] AT von Mehren, 'Special Substantive Rules for Multistate Problems: Their role and significance in contemporary choice of law methodology' (1974–75) *Harvard Law Review* 347; M Danov, 'Global Competition Law Framework: A Private International Law Solution Needed' (2016) 12 *Journal of Private International Law* 77.

[63] *The LCD Appeals* (n 60) [43].

In cross-border competition law cases, the 'jurisdiction to prescribe'[64] (ie 'legislative or regulatory jurisdiction, [which] is designed to explore the extent and limits of the reach of a nation's laws')[65] is interlinked with the court's jurisdiction to adjudicate.[66]

In a transnational context, the response to the question about the applicable competition laws may often raise a preliminary issue about the territorial scope of the relevant set of competition laws,[67] which are often intertwined with the regulatory jurisdiction.[68] In other words, there would often be important public international law[69] issues that need to be addressed when ascertaining the competition law rules which should determine whether there is a restriction of competition law. A national judge would, in fact, be regulating cross-border business activities by enforcing its national law. This poses a very important question about the scope of UK competition law and/or EU competition law, raising an issue about 'the authority of a state to make its law [extraterritorially] applicable to persons or activities'.[70] The response to this question is closely linked to the issue of adjudicatory jurisdiction which denotes the competence of a national judge to determine whether there is a competition law infringement in a cross-border context, awarding appropriate and effective legal remedies, as the case may be under the national legislation.

The issues are complex because there appear to be over 130 sets of national competition laws across the globe.[71] A difficult PIL issue is that, since the competition law infringements are transnational (involving multinational companies that enjoy significant market power), national competition laws have extra-territorial effects.[72] The point was encapsulated by Fox and Crane who submitted that:

> Acts and conspiracies in New York, Washington, Tokyo, Zurich, Frankfurt, Johannesburg, Bejing, Delhi, or Sao Paulo may affect people around the world. Nonetheless, the great body of antitrust law is national. Two mature – although always changing – bodies of antitrust law, European and American, are the most visible models.[73]

A PIL mechanism should be necessary for the national courts to deal with related private antitrust damages claims which arise out of the same transnational competition law infringement. An important PIL problem in this respect is that there could be

[64] AF Lowenfeld, *International Litigation and Arbitration* 2nd edn (West Group, 2002) 39. J Adolphsen, 'The conflict of laws in cartel matters in a globalised world: Alternatives to the effects doctrine' (2005) *Journal of Private International Law* 151, 155. See also: Opinion of Advocate General Darmon in Joined Cases 89/85, 104/85, 114/85, 116–17/85, and 125–29/85 *Ahlstrom v Commission* (Wood Pulp) EU:C:1988:258 [28].

[65] Lowenfeld (n 64) 39. See also: Adolphsen (n 64) 155.

[66] AT von Mehren and DT Trautman, 'A Jurisdiction to Adjudicate: A Suggested Analysis' (1966) *Harvard Law Review* 1121.

[67] *The LCD Appeals* (n 60) [61]–[107].

[68] Ibid.

[69] *Wood Pulp Cartel Case* (n 60); Case C-413/14 P *Intel v Commission*, EU:C:2017:632 [49].

[70] *Hartford Fire Insurance v California* (1993) 509 US 764, 813.

[71] Bradford et al (n 59); PM Horna, 'David & Goliath: How young competition agencies can succeed in fighting cross-border cartels' (2017) *The University of Oxford Centre for Competition Law and Policy*, Working Paper CCLP (L) 45 at 3; EM Fox and A Arena, 'The international institutions of competition law' in EM Fox and MJ Trebilcock (eds), *The Design of Competition Law Institutions: Global Norms, Local Choices* (Oxford University Press, 2012) 444.

[72] Chapter 9.

[73] EM Fox and DA Crane, *Global Issues in Antitrust and Competition Law* 2nd edn (West Academic Publishing, 2017) at 1.

a number of applicable substantive sets of national competition laws which may apply extra-territorially and which could be relied upon by national judges to determine whether the conduct in question is anti-competitive. Could PIL provide a solution in this respect?[74]

On the one hand, given that the various competition laws and competition cultures adopted and developed across the globe differ at certain points, there is a risk of a conflict of competition laws.[75] For example, certain problems appeared to be exposed by widely discussed *Google* proceedings in relation to its shopping comparison facility before the US Federal Trade Commission[76] and the European Commission.[77] The two major regulators took different views on whether Google's conduct in relation to administering the way its search engine directs traffic towards various shopping comparison web sites was anti-competitive.[78] Indeed, Elhauge and Geradin[79] make a case that there are real issues concerning conflicts of competition laws by submitting that:

> Although […] U.S. and EU doctrine [i.e. sets of competition law rules] are closer than they might appear and probably converging over time, there remain important differences. Those differences include divergent rules on: (1) excessive unilateral pricing; (2) above-cost predatory pricing; (3) a recoupment requirement for below-cost predatory pricing; (4) unilateral duties to deal; ([5]) loyalty and volume-based discounts; ([6]) vertical territorial restraints; and ([7]) vertical and conglomerate mergers. Moreover, even when the doctrines do not differ, their application can lead to conflicting conclusions if the courts or agencies in the U.S. and EU differ in their assessment of the facts of particular cases or how the law applies to those facts. And even when the U.S. and EU agree, other affected nations may not.[80]

On the other hand, a choice-of-law solution would not necessarily work in addressing the problem of conflict of competition laws. A major regulatory issue is that many national competition law provisions express the public policy of the forum and in particular fundamental national economic interests.[81] The various national policy-makers may legitimately pursue different objectives.[82] That said, in a global context, a major difficulty is that there would be multiple national competition laws which are intended to protect important national public interests, and, as a result, for the choice of

[74] Chapter 10.

[75] H Klodt, 'Conflicts and conflict resolution in international anti-trust: Do we need international competition rules?' (2005) *The World Economy* 877, 883. See also: RA Epstein and MS Greve (eds), *Competition Laws in Conflict: Antitrust Jurisdiction in the Global Economy* (The AEI Press, Washington 2004).

[76] Statement of the Federal Trade Commission Regarding Google's Search Practices In the Matter of Google Inc. FTC File Number 111-0163 –3 January 2013, https://www.ftc.gov/sites/default/files/documents/public_statements/statement-commission-regarding-googles-search-practices/130103brillgooglesearchstmt.pdf.

[77] Case AT.39740, *Google Search (Shopping)*, Antitrust Procedure – Council Regulation (EC) 1/2003 – Commission Decision of 27.6.2017 relating to proceedings under Article 102 of the Treaty on the Functioning of the European Union and Article 54 of the Agreement on the European Economic Area, C(2017) 4444 final [341].

[78] See more: Chapter 9.

[79] E Elhauge and D Geradin, *Global Competition Law and Economics* 2nd edn (Hart Publishing, 2011).

[80] Ibid, 1137.

[81] eg Case C-126/97 *Eco Swiss China Time Ltd v Benetton International NV* EU:C:1999:269; Case C-38/98 *Régie nationale des usines Renault SA v Maxicar SpA and Orazio Formento* EU:C:2000:225.

[82] See more: Chapter 10.

law purposes, competition law rules are regarded as 'overriding mandatory provisions'[83] which express the public policy of the forum.[84]

The problem is that, if each judge were to apply the competition laws of the forum,[85] it is highly likely that different sets of competition laws would apply and there would be inconsistent outcomes in the related private damages claims which are connected to the same transnational conduct and which are issued before different courts.[86] A PIL solution will be proposed for national judges to deal with the issues concerning conflict of competition laws.[87]

Brexit would potentially add another layer of complexity in so far as, when determining liability in competition law cases where the anti-competitive conduct occurred after the UK withdrawal from the EU, Articles 101 and 102 TFEU would no longer be directly applicable and directly effective in the UK. This means that one should clearly differentiate between the substantive law aspects which have a regulatory nature (ie determining whether there is a competition law infringement) and the substantive law aspects which have a private law character (being important for quantifying damages in such cases).[88]

The fact that Articles 101 and 102 TFEU no longer form part of UK competition law would have a major impact on the jurisdiction of the UK Competition Appeal Tribunal to deal with claims where a breach of EU competition law (rather than UK competition law) is pleaded;[89] which would, in turn, have implications for the ability of certain injured parties to put forward applications for collective proceedings orders[90] in cases where EU competition law is not directly applicable in the UK. A closer reading of Chapter 2 of Title XI from Part Two of the EU–UK Trade and Cooperation Agreement[91] strongly indicates that, whilst the changes to the UK/EU substantive competition laws would be minimal in the short-term, jurisdiction of the European Commission and the CJEU will inevitably change.

It is highly likely that the UK and EU will continue to share common interests which may justify an appropriate level of judicial cooperation in cross-border competition law cases, aiming to ensure the 'effective enforcement' of competition laws, post-Brexit.[92] The UK–EU Trade and Cooperation Agreement appears to acknowledge that by stating that, in order 'to enhance the effective enforcement of their respective competition law, the [UK and EU] recognise the importance of cooperation between their respective competition authorities with regard to developments in competition policy and

[83] Article 16 of Rome II.

[84] eg Recital 1 of Directive 2014/104/EU on certain rules governing actions for damages under national law for infringements of the competition law provisions of the Member States and of the European Union [2014] Official Journal L349/1; *Eco Swiss* (n 81); *Maxicar* (n 81). See more: Chapter 10.

[85] Article 16 of Rome II. See also: The Law Applicable to Contractual Obligations and Non-Contractual Obligations (Amendment etc.) (EU Exit) Regulations 2019.

[86] See more: Chapter 10.

[87] See: Chapters 10 and 13.

[88] *BritNed* (n 53) [10].

[89] Article 47A(2) of the Competition Act 1998.

[90] Article 47B of the Competition Act 1998.

[91] EU–UK Trade and Cooperation Agreement [2021] OJ L149/448.

[92] Article 361 of the EU–UK Trade and Cooperation Agreement [2021] OJ L149/448.

enforcement activities.'[93] Although an appropriate level of administrative cooperation between the UK CMA and the European Commission as well as the various national competition authorities appears to be envisaged the UK–EU Trade and Cooperation Agreement, there is a major gap in the regulatory framework which does not appear to promote judicial cooperation in competition law matters.

IV. PIL Issues – Quantification of Damages[94]

The EU legislator has acknowledged that '[t]he right in Union law to compensation for harm resulting from infringements of Union and national competition law requires each Member State to have procedural rules ensuring the effective exercise of that right'.[95] It is well established that the '[n]ational courts […] have an equally essential part to play in applying the competition rules [and] awarding damages to the victims of infringements'.[96]

Even more complex issues would arise for injured parties to whom the relevant interchange fees have caused damages in a number of different jurisdictions. One set of problems concerns the quantification of damages which are sustained in a number of jurisdictions. Some of the issues could be deduced from the judgment of the High Court of England and Wales in *Deutsche Bahn v MasterCard*.[97] In this case, the claimants involved seven groups of companies. They were doing business in eighteen different European jurisdictions. In order to identify the laws which were to be applied with a view to determining whether the claims 'were barred by limitation',[98] the English court had to rely on three different private international law regimes which were applicable in England and Wales over the relevant period of time.[99]

The PIL issues and the aspects concerning the length of the limitation periods may raise important preliminary issues which might have an impact on the parties' entitlement to legal remedies in cases where the court takes the view that some 'claims were *prima facie* time-barred'.[100] In this context, it should be noted that the basic principle concerning the applicable law in Rome II is that the PIL rules should 'designate the same national law irrespective of the country of the court in which an action is brought'.[101] This has been reflected in Article 6(3)(a) which indicates that, irrespective of where the parties litigate, 'the law of the country where the market is, or is likely to be, affected' should be applied to quantify the antitrust damages in cross-border competition law cases.

[93] Article 361 of the EU–UK Trade and Cooperation Agreement.
[94] *BritNed* (n 53) [28]; *Enron* (n 58) [143], [149] and 150]. See Chapters 10 and 11.
[95] Recital 4 of Directive 2014/104/EU.
[96] Recital 3 of Directive 2014/104/EU.
[97] *Deutsche Bahn v MasterCard* [2018] EWHC 412 (Ch).
[98] Ibid, [18]. See also: *DSG Retail Ltd and Dixons Retail Group Ltd v MasterCard Inc* [2020] EWCA Civ 671.
[99] *Deutsche Bahn* (n 97) [12].
[100] *Dixons* (n 98) [61].
[101] Recital 6 of Rome II.

That said, in cases where 'the market is, or is likely to be, affected in more than one country, the person seeking compensation for damage who sues in a court in a part of the United Kingdom, may instead choose to *base his or her claim on the law of the court seised*'.[102] If the necessary requirements are satisfied, certain categories of parties might be tempted to be somewhat selective when deciding where to bring their private antitrust damages claims. The fact that some parties may be strategic, aiming to derive certain substantive law and/or procedural advantages by issuing their claim in one jurisdiction rather than another, appears to be acknowledged in the Impact Assessment Report.[103]

As noted in chapter 1, an empirical study,[104] which was conducted around the time when the proposed Antitrust Damages Directive was drafted, indicated that – whilst the private international law rules will certainly have an important role to play when it comes to deciding if and where to litigate – various procedural aspects (eg disclosure and discovery of evidence) and the speed of procedure will have a major impact on the forum selection process in cross-border competition law cases. Since there were incentives for the parties to *forum shop*,[105] parties may often be involved in expensive jurisdictional battles[106] in so far as private parties' effective access to appropriate legal remedies may depend on the place where the competition law dispute is to be determined. This appears to be reflected in the EU Antitrust Damages Directive which suggests that parties' access to effective legal remedies in competition law cases is dependent on both substantive law rules (eg 'limitation periods';[107] 'joint and several liability';[108] 'passing-on defence';[109] a rebuttable presumption that 'cartel infringements cause harm')[110] and the procedural/disclosure rules[111] which should enable claimants to prove and quantify the specific damages which were caused to them.

There may be complex issues concerning the burden of proof and standard of proof in relation to the pass-on defence[112] as well as concerning '[t]he question of when the limitation period expires for individual claims by foreign members who might opt in to the class'.[113] As acknowledged by Judge Carl Wetter,[114] the EU Antitrust Damages Directive 'is an important step in the harmonisation of the rules governing private

[102] Article 6(3)(b) of Rome II – emphasis added by the author.

[103] Commission Staff Working Document, *Impact Assessment Report – Damages actions for breach of the EU antitrust rules Accompanying the proposal for a Directive on certain rules governing actions for damages under national law for infringements of the competition law provisions of the Member States and of the European Union* SWD(2013) 203 final [52]. See more: Chapter 1.

[104] Danov, Becker and Beaumont (n 50).

[105] G Ruhl, 'Methods and approaches in choice of law: An economic perspective' (2006) 24 *Berkeley Journal of International Law* 801, 811.

[106] *The LCD Appeals* (n 60) 220.

[107] Article 10 of Directive 2014/104/EU.

[108] Article 11 of Directive 2014/104/EU.

[109] Article 13 of Directive 2014/104/EU.

[110] Article 17(2) of Directive 2014/104/EU.

[111] Articles 5, 6 and 7 of Directive 2014/104/EU.

[112] *NTN v Stellantis NV* [2022] EWCA Civ 16 [33].

[113] Case Nos: 1282/7/7/18 and 1289/7/7/18, *UK Trucks Claim Ltd v Fiat Chrysler Automobile NV and Others, DAF Trucks NV and Others; Road Haulage Association Ltd v MAN SE and Others* [2019] CAT 15 [21].

[114] C Wetter, 'Foreword' in M Bergstrom, M Iacovides and M Strand (eds), *Harmonising EU Competition Litigation: The New Directive and Beyond* (Oxford, Hart Publishing, 2016) 1.

enforcement in the European Union',[115] but it is highly likely that the various procedural and evidential rules will still have a major impact on the parties' strategic decision to issue proceedings in one jurisdiction rather than another. The level of diversity[116] which remains in a global context may explain why the PIL rules allocating jurisdiction (ie predetermining procedural and evidential rules) as well as why the choice-of-law issues (ie ascertaining the substantive law rules) would be important with a view to allowing injured parties to strategically select where to issue their private antitrust damages claims. For example, it seems that a level of variation with regard to certain substantive law concerning interests remains in the EU.[117] More importantly, the Directive contains no requirement for the EU Member States 'to introduce collective redress mechanisms for the enforcement of Articles 101 and 102 TFEU'.[118] The adopted solutions may vary from country to country[119] and so would vary the effectiveness of the national private antitrust enforcement regimes.[120]

V. Access to Justice – Issues of Jurisdiction and Related Proceedings

The PIL rules, which are relied on by national courts to assume jurisdiction and avoid related claims, would be indicative as to which procedural rules would apply. The UK experience unequivocally demonstrates that an appropriate set of procedural mechanisms[121] and the experience of judges and legal practitioners would be important to parties' access to legal remedies. For example, the weaknesses in the functioning of the Brussels Ia regime for judicial cooperation were exposed by strategic parties who sought to generate a level of uncertainty and inflate litigation costs which may impede their opponents' access to legal remedies in these jurisdictions. This was notoriously demonstrated in *Cooper Tire*,[122] where Lord Justice Longmore partly defeated some of the defendants' delaying strategies by refusing to stay the English legal proceedings, noting that the delay in a foreign court may legitimately be a major consideration for a court to refuse to stay the legal proceedings.[123]

[115] Ibid.

[116] Recital 7 of the Directive on Antitrust Damages Actions.

[117] Monti (n 7) [76].

[118] Recital 13 of Directive 2014/104/EU.

[119] The Communication from the Commission, *Guidelines for national courts on how to estimate the share of overcharge which was passed on to the indirect purchaser* [2019] OJ C267/4 [34].

[120] Commission Staff Working Document on the implementation of Directive 2014/104/EU of the European Parliament and of the Council of 26 November 2014 on certain rules governing actions for damages under national law for infringements of the competition law provisions of the Member States and of the European Union SWD(2020) 338 final at 14.

[121] See: Competition Appeal Tribunal, Practice Direction 2/2022: *Umbrella Proceedings* – 6 June 2022.

[122] *Cooper Tire* EWHC (n 14) [117]–[118].

[123] *Cooper Tire* EWCA (n 14) [54]–[55]. See C Slothers, M Gardner and S Hinchliffe, 'Forum shopping and "Italian torpedoes" in competition litigation in the English courts' (2011) *Global Competition Litigation Review* 67. See more: Chapter 7.

The relevant points have nicely been set out by Lawrence and Morfey,[124] who have made the following observations:

> Many claimants favour bringing their claims in the UK, for a variety of reasons, including benefitting from the extensive disclosure requirements available in the English litigation, the 'loser-pays' costs rule, the development of modestly sized but developing claimant bar, and the increasing legal certainty around several issues as a result of previous cases having clarified various procedural and substantive issues from which new claimants can benefit.[125]

That said, the transnational nature of many competition law claims strongly indicates that multiple national courts may have jurisdiction over competition law claims arising out of the same set of cross-border economic activities which involve the same transnational group/s of companies.[126] The multiplicity of proceedings might pose questions about the preclusive effects (if any) of foreign regulatory findings and/or foreign judgments which deal with the same transnational infringements.[127] Dealing with these issues through PIL mechanisms may be important for different national courts to consistently deal with related claims arising out of the same transnational infringement/s.

The lack of a global regime for judicial cooperation to deal with the specific issues arising in cross-border competition law disputes[128] might impede injured parties' access to legal remedies. Post-Brexit, these issues require a renewed attention because, despite the fact that a Trade and Cooperation Agreement was negotiated between the UK and the EU, the UK is no longer part of the Brussels Ia/Lugano regime which is set to facilitate jurisdictional cooperation and avoid related and parallel proceedings in the EU/European Economic Area.

The PIL issues concerning the collective redress proceedings and the level of variation which appears to exist in this context are important because, given the temporal and territorial dimensions of the transnational competition law infringements, the aggregate damage which is caused to numerous injured parties across the globe would often be in the hundreds of millions[129] and even billions.[130] A major issue, which may need to be addressed in this context, is that the various classes of injured parties may be active across different levels of the supply chain. This means that some of the injured parties may be absorbing any illicit overcharge; whilst other injured parties may be, at least partly, pass it on down the chain of distribution.[131]

The problem is that, despite the high level of aggregate damage, the individual damages, which will often be absorbed by individual consumers in cases where they

[124] Lawrence and Morfey (n 50).

[125] Ibid, 149.

[126] Chapters 7 and 8.

[127] Chapter 12.

[128] See: the Opinion of Advocate General Jääskinen in Case C-352/13 *Cartel Damage Claims (CDC) Hydrogen Peroxide SA v Evonik Degussa GmbH* EU:C:2014:2443 [8]. See also Danov (n 37).

[129] *Qualcomm* (n 17). See also: Which?, 'UK 4G smartphone owners could be entitled to a £480 million payout' – *Press Release*, 25 Feb 2021, https://www.smartphoneclaim.co.uk/Content/Documents/Which%20Press%20Release%20-%2025%20February%202021.pdf.

[130] *Merricks* (n 52).

[131] M Danov, G Howells and D Fairgrieve, 'Collective redress antitrust proceedings: How to close the enforcement gap and provide redress for consumers' in Danov, Becker and Beaumont (n 50) 253–82.

are indirect purchasers, will be nominal or, at very least, insignificant in comparison to the litigation costs.[132] This means that, unless there are appropriate collective redress mechanisms, the availability of pass-on defence in cases where the claims are brought by direct purchasers mean that an enforcement gap may remain in certain jurisdictions.[133]

A level of judicial cooperation may be central to avoiding inconsistent outcomes in such related proceedings which involve direct[134] and indirect purchasers[135] and which are issued in different jurisdictions. The issues are indeed important and complex because, under the UK and EU law, 'compensation of harm can be claimed by anyone who suffered it, irrespective of whether they are direct or indirect purchasers from an infringer'.[136] The multiple sets of related proceedings may be issued in England by merchants as well as on behalf of consumers exposed the issues. For example, in *Sainsbury's v Mastercard*,[137] *Asda v Mastercard*[138] and *Sainsbury's v Visa*,[139] the various English judges took different views on whether the same type of agreement, setting out default interchange fees, was anti-competitive. The Court of Appeal of England and Wales[140] appeared to address some of the problem by allowing the Commission to make submissions[141] under Article 15(3) of Regulation 1/2003 as well as by 'tak[ing] the view that the three cases should, so far as possible, be heard by the same tribunal and at the same time'.[142]

However, since both direct and indirect purchasers may bring claims for competition law damages, there may be a level of uncertainty and complexity as to whether the injured party has 'passed on the whole or part of the overcharge resulting from the infringement of competition law'.[143] How would those issues be dealt with in a different jurisdiction? The issues are indeed complex because the illegal interchange fee may have a different impact on the prices in different sectors (and potentially different effects in different jurisdictions) which means that 'some gaps [in the available data] will be unbridgeable, so that nothing is recovered in relation to particular market sectors'.[144] This would in turn impact on the certification of the claimants' class[145] in different jurisdictions which may in turn impact on their access to legal remedies, if some of the

[132] *Sainsbury's* CAT (n 6) [481-2].

[133] Ibid 484.

[134] Ibid; *Asda Stores Ltd and others v MasterCard Inc* [2017] EWHC 93 (Comm); *Sainsbury's Supermarkets Ltd v Visa Europe Service LLC* [2017] EWHC 3047 (Comm).

[135] *Merricks* (n 52).

[136] See: Article 12(1) from Directive 2014/104/EU on certain rules governing actions for damages under national law for infringements of the competition law provisions of the Member States and of the European Union.

[137] *Sainsbury's* CAT (n 6).

[138] *Asda* (n 136).

[139] *Visa* (n 136).

[140] *Sainsbury's Supermarkets Ltd v MasterCard Inc* [2018] EWCA Civ 1536.

[141] European Commission's Written Observations of 21 February 2018, https://ec.europa.eu/competition/court/visa_mastercard_commission_observation1_en.pdf; European Commission's Written Observations on Article 101(3) issues dated 6 April 2018, https://ec.europa.eu/competition/court/visa_mastercard_commission_observation2_en.pdf.

[142] *Sainsbury's* EWCA (n 142) [363]. See also: *Sainsbury's* UKSC (n 53).

[143] Article 13 of the Directive on antitrust damages actions. *Devenish* [2008] EWCA Civ 1086 [151].

[144] *Merricks* (n 52) [74].

[145] Ibid [75].

related claims are not certified. On the contrary, if the claims are certified, then what would be the effect of the foreign factual findings which relate to the same transnational infringement?

VI. Concluding Remarks – Setting the Scene for Further Analysis of the Existing PIL Rules

As noted above, the long-lasting nature of competition law infringements and the high number of injured parties means that the aggregate value of the competition law claims would often be high, which has in turn impacted on the willingness of the litigation funders to finance such claims.[146] The EU model for administration of justice created by Brussels Ia offered the possibility for claimants to choose where to issue their competition law claims, with lawyers from different international law firms competing and promoting their own jurisdictions as venues of choice for high value claims.

As part of this process of adjudicatory competition, parties may factor in such attributes as: the value of the desired remedy (considering the relevant overcharge; pass-through); litigation costs and funding arrangements; procedural rules; experience of judges and lawyers; speed in achieving the desired result (which would be pre-determined by the procedural rules at the place of litigation as ascertained by the relevant jurisdictional rules). The UK experience in dealing with private antitrust damages claims and the EU legislative developments captures the correlation between the efficient procedural rules and effective substantive law provisions which will in turn both impact on the injured parties' access to justice as well as on the litigation funders' decision to finance litigation.

There may be even more complex issues in a global context. For example, standing may indeed be an issue[147] which might need to be more systematically considered from a PIL perspective in private antitrust damages claims involving non-EU jurisdictions. It is well established that, according to EU and UK competition law, any injured party (be they 'direct or indirect purchasers')[148] have standing to bring an antirust claim for damages before national courts.[149] That said, an entirely different approach to standing appears to be advanced in the USA where only direct purchasers could normally issue a private antitrust damages claim.[150] The prevailing view in the literature is that standing would be a substantive law matter for PIL purposes,[151] raising issues concerning injured parties' entitlement to legal remedies in cross-border competition law cases.

[146] Case No: 1266/7/7/16, *Walter Hugh Merricks CBE v MasterCard Inc* [2017] CAT 16 [96–137] and the Annex; Case No: 1339/7/7/20, *Mark McLaren Class Representative Ltd v MOL (Europe Africa) Ltd* [2022] CAT 10 [45]; Case Nos: 1329/7/7/19 and 1336/7/7/19 *Michael O'Higgins FX Class Representative Ltd v Barclays Bank Plc & Mr Philip Evans v Barclays Bank plc* [2022] CAT 16 [318–325]; *Road Haulage Association* (n 16) [224–230].

[147] *Sainsbury's* UKSC (n 53) [195–96].

[148] Article 12(1) of Directive 2014/104/EU. See *The Merchant Interchange Fee Umbrella Proceedings* (n 2).

[149] Article 3(1) of Directive 2014/104/EU.

[150] *Illinois Brick Co v Illinios* 431 US 730 (1977). See more: Danov, Howells and Fairgrieve (n 131) 260.

[151] D-PL Tzakaz, 'Collective Redress Proceedings: Specific Issues Regarding Jurisdiction and Choice of Law' in Danov, Becker and Beaumont (n 50) 223, 236.

More importantly, the indirect purchasers' standing to issue private antitrust damages appears to have major implication for the ability of defendants to raise a *pass-on* defence in the UK. The point was put forward by the UK Supreme Court, noting that:

> 195. In the United States, concerns about the complexity, uncertainty and cost of calculating the existence and effects of pass-on in federal anti-trust litigation have caused the US Supreme Court to exclude a defence of pass-on under federal law and to allow the claimant to use the amount of the overcharge as the basis of its claim in a treble-damage suit: *Hanover Shoe Inc v United Shoe Machinery Corpn* 392 US 481 (1968), 491-494 per White J.
>
> 196. By contrast, in the United Kingdom there is, as is well known, no entitlement to treble damages. Nor is there any exclusion of pass-on as an element in the calculation of damages and the normal rule of compensatory damages applies to claims for damages for breach of statutory duty [...].[152]

Therefore, the substantive law issues concerning standing may be closely linked to the availability[153] or non-availability[154] of the pass-on defence. The availability of the pass-on defence could increase the level complexity with regard to the quantification of damages which would in turn require appropriate procedural mechanisms for case-managing such claims as well as substantive law solutions with regard to assessment of damages. More importantly, the various national developments strongly indicate that even more complex issues would arise in cross-border competition law cases which arise in a global context, strengthening the argument for a transnational approach to judicial cooperation which facilitates injured parties' access to legal remedies in cross-border cases.

In order to systematically address the relevant PIL issues, the relevant classification issues, which should be important for judges to assume jurisdiction and/or ascertain the applicable law, will be considered. It will be demonstrated that competition law disputes with an international element may pose complex questions in various dimensions (eg contractual;[155] tortious;[156] company law;[157] regulatory) which all may be classified differently by different national judges. A national judge faced with a competition law claim would need to apply its own law to address any classification questions head-on.[158]

Once the classification issues have been briefly dealt with, the existing jurisdictional rules which apply in cross-border competition law cases before the English courts will be examined along with the relevant issues which would arise under the Brussels Ia/Lugano regime.[159] The PIL issues are important because – given the cross-border nature of competition law infringements – there would often be multiple injured parties across the globe. The specific private international law problems in respect of cross-border class actions and judgments in relation to antitrust infringements that have occurred

[152] *Sainsbury's* UKSC (n 53) [195–96].
[153] *Sainsbury's* UKSC (n 53) [197].
[154] *Hanover Shoe Co v Union Shoe Machinery Corporation*, 392 US 481 (1968).
[155] See: Chapter 5.
[156] See: Chapter 4.
[157] See: Chapters 3 and 6.
[158] See more: Chapter 3.
[159] Chapters 4 and 5.

in several countries are discussed in Chapter 6. The issues concerning related and parallel proceedings will be discussed in Chapters 7 and 8. Since the injured parties – up and down the chain of distribution – would involve large purchasers (which may include multinational companies and/or large national companies), SMEs, and individuals, diverse strategies may be deployed by various injured parties in the different jurisdictions.

In Chapters 9 and 10, it will be demonstrated that it is important to draw a distinction between the scope of the regulatory jurisdiction (ie applicable national/regional substantive competition laws) and the scope of the adjudicatory jurisdiction (ie the competence of national adjudicator/regulator) to hear and determine a cross-border competition law dispute.[160] The different regulatory objectives[161] – which may be legitimately pursued by the various competition law systems – strongly indicate that there would be a level of variation between the national substantive competition laws. This means that, if a national judge exclusively applies their national competition laws, then the question whether there is a competition law infringement would depend on the place where proceedings are taking place.

Since the 'conflict of laws provides a potentially useful framework for viewing disputes among multiple normative orders',[162] the choice of law issues that may arise before the English courts under Rome I[163] and Rome II will also be examined in Chapters 10 and 11. Indeed, the question as to which set of laws would apply to the merits of a competition law dispute denotes a choice-of-law problem in so far as such a dispute may essentially be regarded as a commercial dispute[164] which may be dealt with in the retained Rome II regulation, post-Brexit. Hence, private international law solutions might naturally work in cross-border competition law cases.

In Chapter 12, the issues concerning the recognition and enforcement of foreign judgments in relation to competition law claims will be discussed. Finally, it will be demonstrated that an effective private international law mode of governance – which factors in important public international law connotations – should enable national adjudicators to factor in legitimate foreign regulatory interests. This is important because the fact that diverse national legal orders may share different interests and pursue distinct objectives[165] appears to suggest that there may often be a conflict of competition laws. If these issues are factored in systematically, then it would be more likely for the English judgments to be recognised and enforced abroad (or, at very least, generate preclusive effects in other jurisdictions).

[160] Compare: The dissenting opinion of Justice Scalia in *Hartford Fire Insurance Co v California*, 113 S.Ct. 2891 at 2909 (1993). See more: Chapter 9.

[161] Bradford et al (n 59).

[162] PS Berman, *Global Legal Pluralism: A Jurisprudence of Law Beyond Borders* (Cambridge University Press, 2012) 192.

[163] Regulation (EC) 593/2008 on the law applicable to contractual obligations (Rome I); The Law Applicable to Contractual Obligations and Non-Contractual Obligations (Amendment etc.) (EU Exit) Regulations 2019, Regulation 10.

[164] eg Art 6 of Rome II.

[165] See: Bradford et al (n 59).

3

Transnational Competition Law Infringements – Some Classification Issues

I. Introduction and Some Preliminary Remarks

As noted above,[1] the free trade arrangements and the increasingly global nature of many economic activities (including through various digital platforms) have cumulatively led to an ever-growing number of transactions with an international element[2] and supply chains which are increasingly transnational.[3] Various cross-border transactions and transnational supply chains would often involve undertakings[4] which could consist of numerous subsidiaries incorporated in different jurisdictions.[5] It is highly likely that some of these multinational groups might enjoy market power in a number of jurisdictions.[6]

The PIL issues appear to be significant because some of these transnational economic activities could lead to 'cartels with international effects'[7] and/or 'international abuses of a dominant position'.[8] Since many 'cross-border anti-competitive practices'[9] would likely be 'implemented'[10] and/or have 'qualified effects'[11] in a number of jurisdictions, antitrust damages could be caused to consumers and businesses in multiple jurisdictions. This means that related private antitrust damages claims could

[1] Chapter 1.

[2] Communication From the Commission to the Council, *Towards an International Framework of Competition Rules*, COM(96) 284 final at p 3.

[3] *Motorola Mobility LLC v AU Optronics Corp* 775 F3d 816, 824 (7th Cir, 2015); *The LCD Appeals* [2018] EWCA Civ 220.

[4] *Towards an International Framework* (n 2) 3.

[5] eg Recitals 7, 13, 17 and 21 – Case AT.39824, *Trucks – Commission Decision relating to a proceeding under Article 101 of the Treaty on the Functioning of the European Union (the Treaty) and Article 53 of the EEA Agreement* – 19.7.2016, C(2016) 4673 final.

[6] FH Easterbrook, 'Limits of Antitrust' (1984) 63 *Texas Law Review* 1, 20. See also: Competition and Markets Authority, *OFT415 – Assessment of Market Power* (2004).

[7] *Towards an International Framework* (n 2) 3.

[8] Ibid. See more: M Danov and C Otero, 'Competition Law Enforcement: Private International Law and Access to Effective Legal Remedies in Cross-Border Cases' in P Beaumont and J Holliday (eds), *Guide to Global Private International Law* (Oxford, Hart Publishing, 2022) 233–46.

[9] *Towards an International Framework* (n 2) 3.

[10] *The LCD Appeals* (n 3) [70]. See also: Joined cases 89, 104, 114, 116, 117 and 125 to 129/85 *A Ahlström Osakeyhtiö and others v Commission of the European Communities* EU:C:1988:447 [16]; Case T-286/09 *Intel Corp. v European Commission* EU:T:2014:547 [232].

[11] *The LCD Appeals* (n 3) [89–95]; *Intel* (n 10) [250–296]; Case C-413/14 P *Intel Corp v European Commission* EU:C:2017:632 [45–61].

arise out of the same transnational competition law infringement. How would any classification issues be approached by the various national judges?

It appears that in cross-border competition law claims, the process of classification[12] is important for a national judge to categorise the competition law issue/s and identify the relevant connecting factors[13] which may be important, with a view to applying the jurisdictional and choice of law rules. PIL issues in relation to classification would be very important and need to be addressed head-on. Goetzke and Michaels[14] have recently submitted that:

> [T]he characterisation [or classification] is a core concern in private international law. Many judicial opinions in the field concern primarily the question how issues should be best characterised [classified]; much scholarly literature does the same. In addition, scholars ask more generally how characterisation [or classification] should be best achieved – according to the categorisation of the *lex fori* or of the *lex causae*, or in some other way – and what policy considerations matter.[15]

Accordingly, the PIL issues concerning classification are very important because, in order for the national courts to decide whether they have jurisdiction and ascertain the applicable law, it would be necessary to classify the legal category within which the claim falls in the first place. More specifically, a number of classification issues need to be considered by national judges with a view to assuming jurisdiction and ascertaining the applicable law in private antitrust damages claims.[16] Although the relevant classification issues will be duly considered throughout the book, the purpose of this chapter is to echo the importance of Lord Mance's 'internationalist'[17] approach to classification which should be further developed and used in cross-border competition law cases. There are three sets of preliminary classification issues which will be briefly considered in this chapter.

First, given the regulatory nature of competition laws – would private antitrust damages claims classify as 'administrative matters'[18] or 'civil and commercial matters'[19] for the purposes of the relevant multilateral international instruments? The classification issues might be important because stand-alone claims might be raising regulatory issues. For example, would the conduct in question classify as an act 'restricting competition'[20] (eg an anti-competitive agreement which restricts the competition by object;[21] or an agreement that has the effect of distorting the competition;[22] abuse of dominant position – eg excessive pricing;[23] exclusionary practices)?[24] The classification of the

[12] C Goetzke and R Michaels, 'Characterisation' in Beaumont and Holliday (n 8) 31.

[13] SL Gössl and R Lamont, 'Connecting Factors' in Beaumont and Holliday (n 8) 47.

[14] Goetzke and Michaels (n 12).

[15] Ibid 31.

[16] See more: Chapters 4, 5, 6, 10 and 11.

[17] *Raiffeisen Zentralbank Osterreich* (n 65) [26].

[18] Article 1(1) of Rome I; Article 1(1) of Rome II; Article 1(1) of Brussels Ia. Article 1(1) of Convention of 2 July 2019 on the Recognition and Enforcement of Foreign Judgments in Civil or Commercial Matters;.

[19] Article 1(1) of Rome I; Article 1(1) of Rome II; Art 1(1) of Brussels Ia. Compare: the notion of 'civil or commercial matter' – Article 1(1) of the 2019 Convention.

[20] Article 6(3) – Rome II Regulation.

[21] *Trucks – Commission Decision* (n 5) [80–82].

[22] *Sainsbury's Supermarkets v Mastercard* [2020] UKSC 24.

[23] eg Case No: 1403/7/7/21, *Dr Rachael Kent v Apple* [2022] CAT 28 [12.3]. See also: Case No: 1382/7/7/21, *Consumers' Association v Qualcomm Inc* [2022] CAT 20 [17].

[24] eg *Dr Rachel Kent* (n 23) [12.1–2].

relevant subject matter would have an impact on the applicable regulatory set of public competition laws which would in turn affect the court's adjudicatory jurisdiction[25] and the appropriateness of the court seised.[26]

Secondly, the private law aspects of a competition law claim might need to be classified. As with many disputes involving private parties, competition law claims may either classify as 'non-contractual obligations in civil and commercial matters'[27] (within the meaning of Rome II – eg damages for breach of statutory duty) or 'contractual obligations in civil and commercial matters'[28] (within the meaning of Rome I – eg claim for invalidity of a contract or contractual term which is in conflict with competition law).[29]

Thirdly, it is well established that 'an undertaking [was broadly defined to] encompass [for competition law purposes] every entity engaged in an economic activity, regardless of the legal status of the entity and the way in which it is financed'.[30] In other words, a transnational group of companies, which includes a number of wholly-owned subsidiaries,[31] should be 'classifie[d …] as "one economic unit [provided that the various] subsidiaries do not enjoy real autonomy in determining their course of action in the market"'[32] for competition law purposes. But how should a group of companies, which classifies as an 'undertaking'[33] for competition law purposes, be classified for the purposes of private international law?[34]

II. 'Administrative matters' and 'civil and commercial matters'[35]

A specific classification issue which might arise in competition law claims concerns the question of whether the claim is stand-alone[36] or follow-on.[37] Classifying the

[25] *The LCD Appeals* (n 3) [119–121]. See also: Article 33(1) of Brussels Ia.
[26] *The LCD Appeals* (n 3) [128–132].
[27] Article 1 of Rome II.
[28] Article 1 of Rome I.
[29] J Fitchen, 'Choice of law in international claims based on restriction of competition: Article 6(3) of the Rome II Regulation' (2009) 5 *Journal of Private International Law* 337, 346–47.
[30] Case C-41/90 *Klaus Höfner and Fritz Elser v Macrotron GmbH* EU:C:1991:161 [21].
[31] Case T-102/92 *Viho Europe BV v Commission of the European Communities* EU:T:1995:3.
[32] Ibid [49]. See also: *Provimi Limited v Aventis Animal Nutrition SA and Others* [2003] EWHC 961 (Comm) [30]; *Cooper Tire & Rubber Company Europe Limited & Others* [2010] EWCA Civ 864 [47].
[33] *Höfner* (n 30) [21].
[34] See below: Section IV. See: Chapter 4 (the proposed approach). See also: Chapter 6 (the current approach) *Cooper Tire & Rubber Company v Shell Chemicals UK Limited* [2009] EWHC 2609 (Comm); *Cooper Tire* – EWCA (n 32); *Toshiba Carrier UK Ltd and Other v KME Yorkshire Limited & Others* [2011] EWHC 2665 (Ch); *Toshiba Carrier UK Ltd and Other v KME Yorkshire Limited & Others* [2012] EWCA Civ 169; *Nokia Corporation v AU Optronics Corporation* [2012] EWHC 731 (Ch).
[35] See: Article 1 of Rome I; Article 1 of Rome II; Art 1 of Brussels Ia. Compare: the notion of "civil or commercial matter" – Article 1 of Convention of 2 July 2019 on the Recognition and Enforcement of Foreign Judgments in Civil or Commercial Matters (Global Judgments Convention); Article 1 of Council Regulation (EC) No 1206/2001 on cooperation between the courts of the Member States in the taking of evidence in civil or commercial matters (Evidence Regulation); Article 1 of Convention of 18 March 1970 on the Taking of Evidence Abroad in Civil or Commercial Matters (Evidence Convention).
[36] *Qualcomm* (n 23).
[37] Case Nos: 1329/7/7/19 and 1336/7/7/19 *Michael O'Higgins FX Class Representative Ltd v Barclays Bank Plc & Ors* [2022] CAT 16 [150–151].

claim as stand-alone or follow-on would have major implications for the issues of applicable substantive laws (broadly defined to cover the competition laws). In the latter context, there is a distinction between the regulatory aspects in relation to competition law infringements (which are to be addressed by applying the relevant set of public competition laws) and the private law aspects in relation to causation and quantification of damages (which are to be dealt with by applying the applicable set of national private laws).

It should be noted that, in the EU context, the important classification issues arising under the Brussels Ia were identified by Mr Justice Aikens in *Provimi*,[38] stating that:

> The nature of the cause of action, characterised according to English law, is that of a private law claim for damages for the tort of breach of statutory duty [...]. So the broad issue is: what are the ingredients of a cause of action (in English law) for damages for infringing [Article 101(1) TFEU]. It is clear that the cause of action is a mixture of EU Competition law and English 'domestic' law. Thus what is a breach of [Article 101(1) TFEU] is a matter of EU law. But a claim for breach can only be made against an entity recognised by English domestic law. That entity must be shown to have been in breach of [Article 101(1) TFEU]. And it must be shown, as a matter of English law, that the entity that is in breach of [Article 101 TFEU] is liable in damages to this particular claimant for that breach.[39]

Mr Justice Aikens's judgment[40] signifies the regulatory nature of the competition laws. In particular, the judge distinguishes the issues in relation to the infringement (arising under EU law) from the tortious issues (arising under English law).[41] In a pre-Brexit context, the distinction was only theoretical in so far Articles 101 and 102 TFEU were part of English law, being directly applicable[42] provisions which formed 'part of [each Member States'] legal heritage'.[43] The issues concerning classification would, however, be increasingly important, post-Brexit, and they will have major implications for the applicable (public) competition law/s and the issues concerning the jurisdiction of English courts.

The regulatory nature of public competition laws (which may be publicly and/or privately enforced)[44] strongly indicates that the issues concerning the classification of the relevant cause of action as a civil and/or commercial matter would be central to the scope of many private international law instruments[45] which are set to promote judicial cooperation and which may be broadly interpreted to be applicable with regard to the recognition and enforcement of judgments in relation to competition law claims.

Classification issues would often need to be addressed, in order to ascertain whether the subject matter is within the scope of some private international law instruments as well as to determine what the appropriate private international law provisions and relevant connecting factors are. In other words, a major issue is that, since many public

[38] *Provimi* (n 32).
[39] Ibid [25].
[40] Ibid.
[41] Ibid.
[42] Case C-106/77 *Amministrazione delle finanze dello Stato v Simmenthal* EU:C:1978:49 [14 and 15].
[43] Case 26-62 *NV Algemene Transport- en Expeditie Onderneming van Gend & Loos v Netherlands Inland Revenue Administration* EU:C:1963:1, at 12.
[44] Case Nos: 1377/5/7/20 and 1378/5/7/20 *Epic Games v Apple* [2021] CAT 4 [139].
[45] eg Rome I and II. See more: Chapter 10.

competition laws would have a regulatory nature, the question of whether a competition law claim is to be classified as 'civil and commercial matters'[46] will have an impact on the scope of many private international law instruments which were adopted to apply in a cross-border context.[47] This means that there would inevitably be preliminary disputes about the classification of competition law claims which may (or may not) be within the ambit of the concepts of 'anti-trust (competition) matters',[48] 'civil or commercial matters'[49] or 'administrative matters'.[50]

Some peculiar problems are bound to arise with regard to judicial cooperation in a global context because the existing Hague Conventions are not sufficiently tailored to promoting judicial cooperation in competition law matters.[51] The classification is important because the 'anti-trust (competition) matters'[52] are explicitly excluded from the scope of the Hague Convention on Choice of Court Agreements. A somewhat more nuanced approach appears to be advanced by the 2019 Hague Convention on the Recognition and Enforcement of Foreign Judgments in Civil or Commercial Matters. Although the competition law matters appear to be excluded from the scope of the 2019 Hague Convention, certain categories of competition law claims are within its ambit in so far as it states that:

> This Convention shall not apply to [...] anti-trust (competition) matters, except where the judgment is based on conduct that constitutes an anti-competitive agreement or concerted practice among actual or potential competitors to fix prices, make rigged bids, establish output restrictions or quotas, or divide markets by allocating customers, suppliers, territories or lines of commerce, and where such conduct and its effect both occurred in the State of origin.[53]

The wording of this provision strongly indicates that there would be specific classification issues concerning the question whether the claims are in respect of conduct which is to be classified as amounting to an anti-competitive agreement and/or abuse of dominant position. For example, there might be a classification issue which should be addressed by an adjudicator who should take a view on what 'constitutes an anti-competitive agreement'[54] within the meaning of the 2019 Hague Convention. If the private damages claims were to be arising out of an anti-competitive competitive agreement, then it seems clear that conduct which restricts competition by object would be within the scope of the 2019 Convention; but is an anti-competitive agreement which

[46] Article 1 of Rome I; Article 1 of Rome II; Article 1 of Brussels Ia.

[47] Compare: the notion of 'civil or commercial matter' – Article 1 of Convention of 2 July 2019 on the Recognition and Enforcement of Foreign Judgments in Civil or Commercial Matters (Global Judgments Convention); Article 1 of Council Regulation (EC) No 1206/2001 on cooperation between the courts of the Member States in the taking of evidence in civil or commercial matters (Evidence Regulation); Article 1 of Convention of 18 March 1970 on the Taking of Evidence Abroad in Civil or Commercial Matters (Evidence Convention).

[48] Article 2(1)(p) of the Hague Convention of 2 July 2019 on the Recognition and Enforcement of Foreign Judgments in Civil or Commercial Matters (the 2019 Hague Convention).

[49] Article 1(1) of the 2019 Hague Convention.

[50] Ibid.

[51] Danov and Otero (n 8).

[52] Article 2(1)(h) of the Hague Convention of 30 June 2005 on Choice of Court Agreements.

[53] Article 2(1)(p) of the 2019 Convention.

[54] Ibid.

classifies restricting competition by 'effect'[55] (rather than 'object')[56] likely to be outside of the exception?[57]

Although, it is well established that a private antitrust damage claim would classify as a 'civil and commercial matter'[58] for the purposes of Brussels Ia (and the Lugano Convention),[59] certain regulatory proceedings would likely be outside of its scope.[60] The issues are important because competition laws may be enforced in proceedings before the EU Commission (or national competition authorities) in the public interest[61] as well as in closely connected private proceedings before national courts.[62] As a result, there could potentially be related and parallel proceedings, generating a level of delay and uncertainty. In particular, Article 9 of Directive 2014/104/EU and Article 16 of Council Regulation 1/2003 both deal with the effects of the regulators' decisions findings on national court proceedings, but there is a regulatory gap and uncertainty as to the effects of the related and parallel proceedings (ie before the decision is reached). Article 1(1) states that:

> Th[e Brussels Ia] Regulation shall apply in civil and commercial matters whatever the nature of the court or tribunal. It shall not extend, in particular, to revenue, customs or administrative matters or to the liability of the State for acts and omissions in the exercise of State authority (*acta iure imperii*).[63]

The exclusion of 'administrative matters'[64] from the ambit of Brussels Ia means that the classification[65] of the competition law claim/s as administrative or civil and commercial matters would be important with a view to deciding whether proceedings are within the scope of Brussels Ia. There is an argument that Brussels Ia may not be suited to avoiding related and parallel proceedings before a national court based in one Member State and regulatory proceedings before a national competition authority in another Member State.[66] This point may be deduced from the opinion of Advocate General Kokott in *flyLAL-Lithuanian Airlines AS, in liquidation v Starptautiskā lidosta Rīga VAS and Air Baltic Corporation AS*.[67] In this case, AG Kokott took the view that 'the question of

[55] Competition Act 1998 s 2(1)(b); Article 101(1) TFEU.

[56] Competition Act 1998 s 2(1)(b); Article 101(1) TFEU.

[57] eg *Sainsbury's* – UKSC (n 22).

[58] Article 1(1) of Brussels Ia.

[59] See: Commission Notice on the co-operation between the Commission and the courts of the EU Member States in the application of Articles 81 and 82 [2004] OJ C101/04 [3]. See more: M Danov, 'EU Competition Law Enforcement: Is Brussels I suited to dealing with all the challenges?' (2012) 61 *International and Comparative Law Quarterly* 27–54.

[60] Compare: Danov (n 59).

[61] Case C-126/97 *Eco Swiss China Time Ltd v Benetton International NV* EU:C:1999:269; Case C-38/98 *Régie nationale des usines Renault SA v Maxicar SpA and Orazio Formento* EU:C:2000:225.

[62] Article 16 of Regulation 1/2003; Art 9 of Directive 2014/104/EU on certain rules governing actions for damages under national law for infringements of the competition law provisions of the Member States and of the European Union Text with EEA relevance.

[63] Article 1(1) of Brussels Ia.

[64] Article 1(1) of Brussels Ia.

[65] *Raiffeisen Zentralbank Osterreich AG v Five Star Trading LLC and others* [2001] EWCA Civ 68 [26] and [28].

[66] Danov (n 59).

[67] Case C-302/13 *flyLAL-Lithuanian Airlines AS, in liquidation v Starptautiskā lidosta Rīga VAS and Air Baltic Corporation AS* EU:C:2014:2319.

classification in the context of the subject-matter of the dispute'[68] was at the heart of the Court of Justice's preliminary ruling. In order to classify the subject-matter, the question – which must be addressed – is whether the proceedings between the parties concern the "exercise of public powers".[69]

The classification test is: *Does a party to the proceedings act in 'exercise of its public powers'?*[70] If the answer to this question is in the affirmative, then the competition law proceedings would be regarded as an administrative matter, being outside of the ambit of Brussels Ia.[71] If the answer is negative because, for example, the European Commission (or a national competition authority or another public authority)[72] sought to recover compensatory damages for being continuously supplied with certain products at an inflated price – for example, then the dispute would be classified as raising civil and commercial matters.

Therefore, the wording of the provisions setting out the scope of the applicable private international law instruments (ie 2019 Hague Convention; the 2007 Lugano Convention; the Brussels Ia Regulation) seems to suggest that there are compelling reasons for the concept of 'civil and commercial matters' to be narrowly defined in so far as public-administrative proceedings would be outside of its scope.

III. A Three-Step Test – Classification

Once the matter has been classified as falling within the ambit of civil and commercial matters, there will be another set of classification issues which are to be dealt with by the national courts. As part of this process, the national courts will have to classify whether a relevant competition law claim is raising contractual and/or tortious and/or company law and/or regulatory issues. There are real issues concerning classification in so far as a mixture of legal concepts would need to be classified in cross-border competition law claims. The specific issues could indeed be deduced by undertaking appropriate analysis of the relevant case law.

The classification issues and the relevant connecting factors which were to be dealt with for the jurisdiction purposes could be deduced from the High Court of England and Wales' judgment in *Provimi v Aventis Animal Nutrition*.[73] This was one of the first private antitrust damages claims which strongly indicated that private international law rules were to have a very important role to play for the effective enforcement of competition law in a cross-border cases.

In line with the prevailing enforcement pattern at the time, the competition law damages claim in *Provimi*[74] was preceded by an EU Commission decision[75] which

[68] See: Opinion of Advocate General Kokott in Case C-302/13 *flyLAL-Lithuanian Airlines AS, in liquidation v Starptautiskā lidosta Rīga VAS and Air Baltic Corporation AS* EU:C:2014:2046 [52].
[69] Ibid [31] and [32].
[70] Ibid [30].
[71] Article 16 of Council Regulation 1/2003. Article 9 of Directive 2014/104/EU.
[72] eg *Glasgow City Council v VFS Financial Services Ltd, AB Volvo & Others* [2020] CSOH 92.
[73] *Provimi* (n 32).
[74] Ibid.
[75] Case COMP/E-1/37.512, *Vitamins – Commission Decision of 21 November 2001 relating to a proceeding pursuant to Article 81 of the EC Treaty and Article 53 of the EEA Agreement* [2003] OJ L6/1.

established that a number of undertakings agreed and implemented certain price-fixing arrangements for various categories of vitamins which were contrary to Article 101 TFEU.[76] The infringement lasted for a period of over 10 years for some categories of vitamins.[77] The cross-border nature of the infringement was duly reflected in the EU Commission's findings that the relevant vitamins markets were 'at least EEA-wide. However, there are several indications that point to worldwide markets for each of the vitamin products'.[78] The latter point could be strengthened by noting that there were proceedings in the USA[79] and Canada.[80] The EU regulator established that major producers of vitamins have colluded to create a global cartel, allocating markets and fixing prices[81] which distorted the process of competition within the European Economic Area.

In a subsequent set of proceedings before the English court, the issue of classification was only briefly[82] addressed by Mr Justice Aikens:

> [T]here was no argument on 'characterisation' of the issue for the purpose of selecting the rule of conflicts of laws that lays down the connecting factor and then the appropriate system of law tied to the connecting factor: *cf Macmillan Inc v Bishopsgate Investment Trust plc (No 3)* [1996] 1 WLR 387 at 391–2 per Staughton LJ. The implicit assumption in argument was that the claim for breach of statutory duty should be characterised as a tort and, for present purposes, English law, including EU law, was the correct law to apply to the claims. This was even though the claimant is Trouw Germany, which presumably would have suffered damage in Germany rather than England. The position may be different for the periods before and after the *Private International Law (Miscellaneous Provisions) Act 1995* came into effect. But that point was not argued.[83]

The tortious[84] classification was reiterated by the Court of Appeal of England and Wales in *BritNed* that happened to be the first judgment 'in which damages have been awarded by an English court or tribunal after a trial for anti-competitive cartel conduct which infringes'[85] competition law. In this case, Mr Justice Marcus Smith sitting at the High Court of England and Wales – summarised the following principles:

> In English law, competition law infringements are vindicated as statutory torts. To establish a claim, two things must be shown: (i) an infringement of competition law; and (ii) actionable harm or damage, caused by that infringement. […] A breach of duty by the defendant is not enough. The cause of action will not accrue until actionable damage occurs. The damage is said to form the gist of the action.[86]

[76] Ibid [2].
[77] Ibid [700–711].
[78] Ibid [69]. See also: [673–677].
[79] Ibid [149–154].
[80] Ibid [155–157].
[81] Ibid [535].
[82] *Provimi* (n 32) [25, 107–113].
[83] See: the text in footnote 83 in *Provimi* (n 32).
[84] J Steiner, 'How to make the action suit the case: domestic remedies for breach of ECC law' (1987) *European Law Review* 102, 107–108; KM Stanton, 'New forms of the tort of breach of statutory duty' (2004) 120 *Law Quarterly Review* 324. See also: M Staines, 'The right to sue in Ireland for violation of the EEC rules on competition' (1977) 2 *Legal Issues of Eur Integration* 53. See also: CA Jones, *Private Enforcement of Antitrust Law in the EU, UK and USA* (Oxford, OUP, 1999) 146.
[85] *BritNed Development Limited v ABB AB and ABB Limited* [2019] EWCA Civ 1840 [13].
[86] *BritNed Development Limited v ABB AB and ABB Limited* [2018] EWHC 2616 (Ch) [10]; Case Nos: 1284/5/7/18 (T) and 1290/5/7/18 (T) *Royal Mail Group Ltd v DAF Trucks Ltd and others* [2023] CAT 6 [167 and 168].

The tortious classification of competition claims appears to find further support in the set of EU legislative acts which aimed to 'pave the way for decentralised application of the E[U] competition rules by national [...] courts'.[87] The decentralisation reform[88] of EU competition law enforcement culminated in the adoption of Council Regulation 1/2003 and Directive 2014/104/EU which aim to improve injured parties' access to justice. The latter legislative instrument clearly states that:

> 1. Member States shall ensure that any natural or legal person who has suffered harm caused by an infringement of competition law is able to claim and to obtain full compensation for that harm.
> 2. Full compensation shall place a person who has suffered harm in the position in which that person would have been had the infringement of competition law not been committed. It shall therefore cover the right to compensation for actual loss and for loss of profit, plus the payment of interest.[89]

The above quotation appears to reiterate the tortious classification in a transnational context.[90] An analysis of the judgment, in *Provimi*,[91] captures the classification issues which need to be addressed by the court with a view to assuming jurisdiction. In particular, the judge has set out several PIL issues, including those about the classification of a group of companies which will be considered further in the next section.

Before doing this, it should be noted that an 'internationalist'[92] approach as advanced by Lord Mance[93] would be much needed with regard to private antitrust damages claims arising out of transnational competition law infringements. The relevant principles are derived from the judgment of the Court of Appeal of England and Wales in *Macmillan Inc v Bishposgate Trust (No 3)*,[94] being repeatedly reiterated by different judges.[95] In *Raiffeisen Zentralbank Osterreich v Five Star Trading*,[96] Lord Justice Mance nicely summarised them as follows:

> 26 [...] the identification of the appropriate law may be viewed as involving a three-stage process: (1) characterisation of the relevant issue; (2) selection of the rule of conflict of laws which lays down a connecting factor for that issue; and (3) identification of the system of law which is tied by that connecting factor to that issue: see *Macmillan Inc v Bishopsgate*

[87] Ibid [13]. See also: Commission (EC), 'Damages actions for breach of EC antitrust rules' (Green Paper) COM (2005) 672 final; 'Damages Actions for Breach of the EC Antitrust Rules' (White Paper) COM (2008) 165 final; Commission Staff Working Paper accompanying the White Paper on damages actions for breach of EC rules SEC(2008) 404.

[88] Modernisation of the Rules Implementing Articles 85 and 86 of the EC Treaty' (White Paper) Commission Programme 99/027 COM (1999) 101 final [1999] OJ C132/1.

[89] Article 3(1) and (2) of Directive 2014/104/EU.

[90] *Provimi* (n 32) [25]. See also: *BritNed* – EWCA (n 85) [2, 20 and 21]. *Application des Gaz v Falks Veritas* [1974] Ch 381, 396; *Garden Cottage Foods v Milk Marketing Board* [1984] AC 130, 131. M Danov, *Jurisdiction and Judgments in relation to EU Competition Law Claims* (Oxford, Hart, 2010).

[91] *Provimi* (n 32).

[92] *Raiffeisen Zentralbank Osterreich* (n 65) [26]. See also: *Provimi* (n 32) [109].

[93] Ibid [26].

[94] *Macmillan Inc v Bishposgate Trust (No 3)* [1996] 1 WLR 387 (CA).

[95] *Secure Capital SA v Credit Suisse AG* [2015] EWHC 388 (Comm) [32] per Mr Justice Hamblen (as he then was); *Raiffeisen Zentralbank Osterreich* (n 65).

[96] *Raiffeisen Zentralbank Osterreich* (n 65) [26 and 28].

> *Investment Trust pic (No 3)* [1996] 1 WLR 387, 391-392 per Staughton LJ. The process falls to be undertaken in a broad internationalist spirit in accordance with the principles of conflict of laws of the forum, here England.
>
> [...]
>
> 28 The three-stage process identified by Staughton LJ cannot [...] be pursued by taking each step in turn and in isolation. As Auld LJ said in *Macmillan Inc v Bishopsgate Investment Trust pic (No 3)* [1996] 1 WLR 387,407:
>
> 'the proper approach is to look beyond the formulation of the claim and to identify according to the lex fori the true issue or issues thrown up by the claim and defence. *This requires a parallel exercise in classification of the relevant rule of law.* However, classification of an issue and rule of law for this purpose, the underlying principle of which is to strive for comity between competing legal systems, should not be constrained by particular notions or distinctions of the domestic law of the lex fori, or that of the competing system of law, which may have no counterpart in the other's system. Nor should the issue be denned too narrowly so that it attracts a particular domestic rule under the lex fori which may not be applicable under the other system ...' (Emphasis added.)[97]

The above quotation leaves no doubt that the relevant classification issues normally need to be considered with a view to ascertaining the applicable law.

The classification issues have been duly identified by Professor Fitchen,[98] who masterfully analysed the Rome II implications with regard to cross-border competition law disputes. He takes the view that it will be a two-step classification exercise which is to be undertaken under Rome II. First, the adjudicator needs to determine whether the competition law claim concerns 'non-contractual obligations in civil and commercial matters'[99] within the meaning of Rome II.[100] Secondly, another classification task will entail for the adjudicator to ascertain the appropriate rule which is to apply for the specific competition law claim.[101] Given that Professor Fitchen's analysis focussed on the application of an EU instrument which was applicable in the UK in the pre-Brexit era, the role of the Court of Justice of the European Union in ensuring 'uniform interpretation'[102] and proper classification of the relevant issues was duly outlined in his analysis.[103]

Professor Fitchen's suggestion,[104] however, blurs the distinction between the classification[105] (which is necessary to identify the PIL rule) and the relevant connecting factors[106] (which are necessary to ascertain the applicable law). A different approach to classification could be deduced from the CAT's judgment in *Westover Ltd v Mastercard.*[107]

[97] *Raiffeisen Zentralbank Osterreich* (n 65) [26 and 28].
[98] Fitchen (n 29) 346–347.
[99] Article 1 of Rome II.
[100] Ibid.
[101] Fitchen (n 29) 346.
[102] Case C-283/81 *CILFIT v Ministero della Sanità* EU:C:1982:335 [7].
[103] Fitchen (n 29) 346–347.
[104] Ibid 346–7 and 357.
[105] Gössl and Lamont (n 13).
[106] Goetzke and Michaels (n 12).
[107] Case Nos: 1349–1350/5/7/20 (T) and 1383–1384/5/7/21 (T), *Westover Ltd v Mastercard* [2021] CAT 12.

Although the UK CAT did not explicitly approach this preliminary dispute as raising classification issues for the purposes of Rome II, a closer analysis of the judgment along with the wording of Article 6(3) strongly indicates that the court has impliedly advanced an internationalist and rather pragmatic approach[108] to classification. In particular, a three-step test with regard to classification under Article 6(3) of the Rome II could be advanced. First, the non-contractual obligation (ie tortious liability for any 'overcharge damages'[109] and/or 'lost sales damages';[110] denying the claimant's access to a digital platform which is necessary for them to access their customers)[111] must be set out with a view to determining whether the claim is within the scope of Rome II as well as with a view to setting out the relevant rule/s and connecting factors.

Secondly, the restriction of competition law which gives rise to the competition law claim/s must be classified (eg default interchange fee; price-fixing arrangements; denying/suspending access to a digital platform). Thirdly, classifying the relevant restriction of the competition may be important for the court to classify the direct effects of the conduct with a view to ascertaining where the market is affected for the purposes of Article 6(3)(a).[112] If there are price-fixing arrangements, an increase in the price and/or loss of sales may classify as being such direct effect (ie direct damage).[113] If the claimant's access to a digital platform in Country A is barred, then the loss of sales in that country may classify as being the relevant effects.[114] Therefore, the UK CAT judgment in *Westover Ltd v Mastercard*[115] is a welcome development which should provide more clarity and certainty for the application of Article 6(3) of Rome II.

IV. A Group of Companies, Undertaking and 'Single Economic Unit'

The *Provimi*[116] case demonstrates that the tortious classification of the competition law restrictions would have significant implications for identifying the relevant connecting factors when determining the court's jurisdiction for the purposes of the Brussels Ia/Lugano Convention. The relevant points were duly outlined by the High Court of England and Wales in *Cooper Tire*, with Mr Justice Teare holding that: '[t]he tort alleged by the Claimants and as found by the Commission was, as submitted by the Claimants, a Europe-wide tort which crossed borders and was linked to numerous jurisdictions'.[117] In other words, the tortious classification and the act restricting competition appear to have an impact on how the relevant connecting factors are to apply for the purposes of establishing jurisdiction under the English Civil Procedure Rules and UK Competition Appeal Tribunal Rules as well as under the Brussels Ia regime.

[108] A Yekini and P Beaumont, 'Pragmatism and Private International Law' in Beaumont and Holliday (n 8) 17.
[109] Case No: 1241/5/7/15 (T), *Sainsbury's Supermarkets v MasterCard* [2016] CAT 11 [13.4–5].
[110] Ibid [13.4 and 13.6].
[111] *Unlockd Ltd v Google* [2018] EWHC 1363 (Ch). See more: Chapter 4.
[112] *Westover* (n 107) [53].
[113] See more: Chapter 11.
[114] *Unlockd Ltd v Google* [2018] EWHC 1363 (Ch). See more: Chapter 4.
[115] *Westover* (n 107).
[116] *Provimi* (n 32).
[117] *Cooper Tire* – EWHC (n 34) [115].

That said, the fact that antitrust damages may be suffered in different jurisdictions taken together with the somewhat limited territorial scope of the jurisdiction of the courts at the place where the damage occurred,[118] may explain why the injured parties often tried to invoke Article 8(1) of Brussels Ia in cases involving a group (or groups of companies) that have engaged in a transnational competition law infringement.[119] This poses the following questions: should a local subsidiary, forming part of a transnational group of companies, be classified as a separate legal entity? Or should it rather be classified as an 'association of […] legal persons' within the meaning of Article 63(1) of Brussels Ia?

The concept of undertaking is quite different from the concept of 'company or other legal person or association of natural or legal persons'[120] which is normally used for the private international law purposes.[121] Articles 101 and 102 TFEU as well as Chapters 1 and 2 of the Competition Act 1998 regulate relationships between *undertakings* which enjoy significant enough market power, being capable to affect trade in the UK and/or the EU, as the case may be. The concept of *undertaking* for the purposes of competition law is broadly defined to 'encompass […] every entity engaged in an economic activity, regardless of the legal status of the entity and the way in which it is financed'.[122] The major problem with regard to classification is that the competition law's concept of *undertaking* 'can embrace a number of legal entities, as long as they act as a single economic unit, and no legal entity acts independently for any relevant purpose'.[123]

Brexit might be an opportunity for the English courts to systematically deal with these issues under the Civil Procedure Rules, which might be impacting on the jurisprudence in the European Union. There are indeed important classification issues. The court should have rather considered whether a group of companies, which classifies as a single undertaking for competition law purposes, should be classified as an 'association of […] legal persons'[124] for purpose of Brussels Ia. The problem is that an analysis of the *Provimi*[125] case strongly indicates that, instead of the court addressing the classification issue head-on for jurisdictional purposes, the court rather dealt with the much more complex question concerning the liability of a group of companies which would be difficult to address before trial and which might need to be considered in private antitrust damages claims issued against a single 'undertaking'[126] (ie 'single economic unit').[127]

An argument for a rather different PIL approach to classification could be made by outlining the issues which would arise with regard to liability for transnational competition law infringements which are committed by a multinational group of companies. The issues were discussed in the *Shell*[128] case where the CJEU held that:

> [EU competition law] is aimed at economic units which consist of a unitary organization of personal, tangible and intangible elements which pursues a specific economic aim on a

[118] Case C-21/76 *Handelskwekerij Bier v Mines de Potasse d'Alsace* EU:C:1976:166 [21].
[119] See more: Chapter 6.
[120] Article 63(1) of Brussels Ia.
[121] *Adams v Cape Industries Plc* [1990] Ch 433.
[122] *Höfner* (n 30) [21].
[123] *Provimi* (n 32) [30]. See also Chapters 4 and 6. See *Cooper Tire* EWCA, above n 4, [47].
[124] Article 63(1) of Brussels Ia.
[125] *Provimi* (n 32).
[126] Ibid [30].
[127] Ibid [30].
[128] Case T-11/89 *Shell International Chemical Company Ltd v Commission of the European Communities* EU:T:1992:33.

> long-term basis and can contribute to the commission of an infringement of the kind referred to in that provision.
>
> The Court holds that Shell and the Shell group operating companies which produce and market chemical products constitute a single unitary organization of personal, tangible and intangible elements which pursues, on a long-term basis, the objective inter alia of producing and selling polypropylene with a view to maximizing profits, even, in some cases, to the detriment of the individual profits of its various components. In that organization, each company plays a specific role. The operating companies produce or sell polypropylene, while the applicant plays a stimulating and coordinating role between the various operating companies of the group. Consequently, Shell and the Shell group operating companies constitute a single undertaking.[129]

This example demonstrates that there would be particularly important classification issues which would need to be systematically addressed, for private international law purposes, in competition law cases against multinational groups of companies which are classified as single undertakings. In particular, there may be a number of preliminary issues and evidential hurdles because, as previously noted,[130] it may be far from clear 'which legal entities within a corporate group are liable for an infringement of Article 101(1) TFEU and to what extent'.[131] There might be an even higher level of complexity in cases where the relevant undertaking has modified its structure, so that the original infringer no longer exists.

> […] the concept of an 'undertaking', within the meaning of Article 101 TFEU covers any entity engaged in an economic activity, irrespective of its legal status and the way in which it is financed (judgment of 11 December 2007, *ETI and Others*, C-280/06, EU:C:2007:775, paragraph 38 and the case-law cited).
>
> 37 That concept, placed in that context, must be understood as designating an economic unit even if in law that economic unit consists of several persons, natural or legal (judgment of 27 April 2017, *Akzo Nobel and Others v Commission*, C-516/15 P, EU:C:2017:314, paragraph 48 and the case-law cited).
>
> 38 As regards the restructuring of an undertaking, such as that at issue in the main proceedings, in which the entity which committed the infringement of EU competition law has ceased to exist, it must be recalled that, when an entity that has committed an infringement of the competition rules is subject to a legal or organisational change, this change does not necessarily create a new undertaking free of liability for the conduct of its predecessor that infringed the competition rules, when, from an economic point of view, the two are identical (see, to that effect, judgments of 11 December 2007, *ETI and Others*, C-280/06, EU:C:2007:775, paragraph 42; of 5 December 2013, *SNIA v Commission*, C-448/11 P, not published, EU:C:2013:801, paragraph 22; and of 18 December 2014, *Commission v Parker Hannifin Manufacturing and Parker-Hannifin*, C-434/13 P, EU:C:2014:2456, paragraph 40).
>
> 39 It is therefore not contrary to the principle of individual liability to impute liability for an infringement to a company which has taken over the company which committed

[129] Ibid [311–312].

[130] M Danov, 'Jurisdiction in cross-border EU competition law cases: Some specific issues requiring some specific solutions' in M Danov, F Becker and P Beaumont (eds), *Cross-Border EU Competition Law Actions* (Oxford, Hart Publishing, 2013) 167.

[131] See: the reference request by Mr Rabinowitz in *Cooper Tire* – EWCA (n 32) [47].

> the infringement where the latter has ceased to exist (judgment of 5 December 2013, *SNIA v Commission*, C-448/11 P, not published, EU:C:2013:801, paragraph 23 and the case-law cited).[132]

The cross-border context within which various multinational groups of companies operate strongly indicates that there would be different national regimes setting out the conditions for establishing legal entities[133] within their territory. More importantly, it is highly likely that the groups of companies could well be classified differently for PIL purposes by the different judges, considering the relevant facts and applicable laws.

The argument that PIL rules would have an important role to play in cross-border competition law cases, involving groups of companies, on both sides, as claimants and defendants could be strengthened by making reference to the judgment of the US Court of Appeals for the Seventh Circuit in *Motorola*.[134] In particular, the problems in ascertaining individual liability could be exacerbated in cases where the injured parties are also groups of companies, with their relevant subsidiaries suffering direct harm in a number of different jurisdictions which in turn might impact on their standing to seek compensation in competition law disputes in certain jurisdictions.[135] The point about potentially different solutions (and potentially complex classification issues) was set out by Circuit Justice Posner, who made the following observations:

> Motorola wants us to treat it and all of its foreign subsidiaries as a single integrated enterprise, as if its subsidiaries were divisions rather than foreign corporations. But American law does not collapse parents and subsidiaries (or sister corporations) in that way. Some foreign nations, it is true, treat multinational enterprises as integrated units. […] But the United States and other developed countries refused to buy that theory. They insisted, and continue to insist, that corporate formalities should be respected unless one of the recognized justifications for piercing the veil, or otherwise deeming a parent and a subsidiary one, is present.[136]

The judgment appears to indicate that there are difficult policy choices to be made in this context, but the author feels that – for the private international law purposes – it would have been sufficient for the courts to classify a single undertaking – which consist of a number of legal entities/subsidiaries – as being an 'association of […] legal persons'[137] within the meaning of Brussels Ia.

The advantages of the proposed approach would be twofold. First, once a group of companies has been properly classified as an association of legal persons, then the relevant connecting factors should be used to determine where the relevant association of legal persons (ie infringing undertaking) is domiciled within the meaning of Brussels Ia or present within the jurisdiction for the purposes of the CPR or UK CAT rules which would 'entitle the courts of the country to take in personam jurisdiction'.[138] Further the aspects in relation to *forum non conveniens* would be systematically considered.[139]

[132] Case C-724/17 *Vantaan kaupunki v Skanska Industrial, Solutions Oy, NCC Industry Oy, Asfaltmix Oy*, EU:C:2019:204 [36–40].
[133] J Borg-Barthet, The Governing Law of Companies in EU Law (Hart Publishing, Oxford 2012).
[134] *Motorola Mobility* (n 3).
[135] Ibid 819–20.
[136] Ibid 820.
[137] Article 63(1) of Brussels Ia.
[138] *Adams* (n 121) 476.
[139] Chapter 7.

Secondly, if the English courts were to assume jurisdiction, the difficult issues concerning the liability of individual legal entities forming part of the same infringing undertakings would be properly dealt with by applying the relevant applicable laws during trial.

V. Concluding Remarks

This chapter demonstrates that competition law claims would give rise to many classification issues. A judge faced with a stand-alone claim for competition law damages would have to classify the anti-competitive conduct with a view to applying the relevant connecting factors 'in light of the offending conduct viewed as a whole'.[140] On that basis, the judges should be able to assume jurisdiction and/or ascertain the applicable regulatory regime as well as the applicable substantive law.

There would be some difficult questions to be dealt with when classifying the matter as 'civil and commercial'[141] or 'administrative'.[142] It seems that, if the proceedings were to be issued by a regulator in exercise of their regulatory powers, the matter would be classified as administrative – being outside the scope of Brussels Ia[143] as well as being outside the scope of Rome I and II. Although the above analysis strongly suggests that private antitrust damages claims would classify as tortious, it should be added that there would be some rather complex PIL issues which concern the classification of competition law claims, arising out of contracts which might include jurisdiction and/or arbitration agreements. These issues will be more systematically dealt with in the forthcoming chapters and Chapter 5 in particular.

Furthermore, there is an argument that the issues concerning the classification of an undertaking, which is a group of companies, should be more systematically dealt with for PIL purposes. It is beyond doubt that only after an undertaking/single economic unit is classified for private international law purposes, it would be possible for the English court to apply the relevant connecting factors and determine whether it should assume jurisdiction.[144] There is a strong argument that a multinational group of companies – which is regarded as an undertaking/single economic unit within the meaning of competition law – should be classified as an 'association of [...] legal persons'[145] for PIL purposes.[146] The current approach and a proposed new approach will be further examined in the subsequent chapters, not least because they may need to be systematically dealt with by judges, in order to categorise the restriction of competition and identify the appropriate connecting factors.

[140] *The LCD Appeals* (n 3) [98]. C Withers, 'Jurisdiction and Applicable Law in Antitrust Tort Claims' (2002) *Journal of Business Law* 250, 257–58.

[141] Article 1 of Rome I; Article 1 of Rome II; Article 1 of Brussels Ia.

[142] Article 1 of Rome I; Article 1 of Rome II; Article 1 of Brussels Ia. See more: section II and Chapter 7.II.B above.

[143] *flyLAL-Lithuanian Airlines* (n 67). See more: See Opinion of Advocate General Kokott in *flyLAL-Lithuanian Airlines* (n 68) [30–32 and 52].

[144] Chapters 4, 6, 7, 9 and 10.

[145] Article 63(1) of Brussels Ia.

[146] See more: Chapters 4 and 6.

The complexity of the transnational competition law infringements – which by definition will span across several jurisdictions – appears to suggest that a pragmatic[147] and internationalist[148] approach should be advanced by national judges when dealing with any classification questions. Given the lack of common transnational principles with regard to major issues concerning classification in cross-border competition law disputes, the following three-step test[149] will be suggested. First, the anticompetitive conduct which gives rise to tortious liability for breach of competition law should be classified. Secondly, the specific act restricting competition should be classified (eg excessive prices; access refusal). Thirdly, the direct effects of the act restricting competition should be classified – eg an illegal 'overcharge'[150] and/or 'lost sales'.[151]

The classification issues are important because, in order to determine whether there is a relevant jurisdictional basis for the English courts or for the UK Competition Appeal Tribunal to assume jurisdiction, the anticompetitive conduct – which has distorted competition and which was implemented and/or has qualified effects in England and Wales – a judge might need to ascertain the nature of the competition law infringement (eg being an agreement which has the object or effect of restricting competition). In this context, the anti-competitive conduct along with the act restricting competition should be set out and the relevant connecting factors applied.[152] For example, if a global platform[153] or if certain hi-tech giants[154] were to abuse their dominant positions, then the abusive anti-competitive conduct would need to be classified as being exclusionary abusive practice[155] (eg access refusal) and/or exploitative abusive practice (eg excessive or inflated prices)[156] which would in turn allow the court to apply the relevant connecting factors – assuming or declining jurisdiction. Likewise, in *DSG Retail v MasterCard*,[157] there were default 'multilateral interchange fees ("MIFs") [which were] arrived at by decisions of an association of undertakings'[158] and which were in conflict with Article 101 TFEU.[159] That said, the proceedings in this case[160] also demonstrate that there might be very complex choice-of-law issues concerning the limitation periods which would need to be dealt with separately.[161]

[147] Yekini and Beaumont (n 108).
[148] *Raiffeisen Zentralbank Osterreich* (n 65) [26].
[149] *Westover* (n 107); Article 6(3) of Rome II.
[150] *Sainsbury's* – CAT (n 109) [13.4–5].
[151] Ibid [13.4 and 13.6].
[152] Ibid [14 and 38].
[153] Case No: 1433/7/7/22, *Dr Liza Lovdahl Gormsen v Meta Platforms Inc, Meta Platforms Ireland Ltd, Facebook UK Ltd* – Reasoned Order, dated 15 March 2022.
[154] Case No: 1403/7/7/21, *Dr Rachael Kent v Apple Inc, Apple Distribution Int'l Ltd* – Reasoned Order – 26 May 2021; Case No: 1382/7/7/21, *Consumers' Association v Qualcomm Inc* – Reasoned Order – 15 March 2021.
[155] Case No: 1403/7/7/21, *Dr Rachael Kent v Apple Inc, Apple Distribution Int'l Ltd* [2022] CAT 28 [12.1–2].
[156] Ibid [12.3]. Case No: 1382/7/7/21, *Consumers' Association v Qualcomm Inc* [2022] CAT 20 [3]; Case No: 1433/7/7/22, *Dr Liza Lovdahl Gormsen v Meta Platforms Inc, Meta Platforms Ireland Ltd, Facebook UK Ltd* – Reasoned Order, dated 15 March 2022 [12].
[157] Case No: 1236/5/7/15, *DSG Retail Ltd, Dixons Retails Ltd v MasterCard Inc, MasterCard Int'l Inc, MasterCard Europe Sprl* [2015] CAT 7.
[158] Ibid [7].
[159] Case COMP/34.579 – *MasterCard, Case COMP/36.518 – EuroCommerce, Case COMP/38.580 – Commercial Cards, Non-Confidential Version of the Commission Decision relating to a proceeding under Article 81 of the EC Treaty and Article 53 of the EEA Agreement*, December 2007.
[160] *DSG Retail Ltd and Dixons Retail Group Ltd v MasterCard Inc* [2020] EWCA Civ 671.
[161] See more: Chapter 11.

4

Jurisdiction – Tortious Private Antitrust Damages Claims

I. Introduction – Cross-Border Private Antitrust Litigation

There is an increasingly growing number of competition law cases[1] where foreign defendants (eg foreign infringers based in EU countries and/or non-EU countries) could engage in transnational competition law infringements which may cause antitrust damages to claimants in England and Wales. Before addressing the relevant PIL issues, it should be noted that, in England and Wales, a competition law claim form may be issued before the High Court of England and Wales or before the UK Competition Appeal Tribunal (CAT). The Senior Courts Act 1981 sets out the general rules concerning the Divisions of the High Court.[2] The Competition Act 1998 (the 1998 Act) lays downs some important provisions which specify the jurisdiction of the Competition Appeal Tribunal. In particular, Section 47A specifies that the CAT will have jurisdiction to deal with claims by:

> "(2) [...] a person who has suffered loss or damage may make in civil proceedings brought in any part of the United Kingdom in respect of an infringement decision or an alleged infringement of –
>
> a) the Chapter I prohibition,
> b) the Chapter II prohibition,
>
> (3) The claims are –
>
> a) a claim for damages;
> b) any other claim for a sum of money;
> c) in proceedings in England and Wales or Northern Ireland, a claim for an injunction."[3]

[1] eg Case No: 1468/7/7/22, *Mr Justin Gutmann v Apple Inc, Apple Distribution International Limited, and Apple Retail UK Limited* – Reasoned Order of the Chair (Service out of the Jurisdiction) 26 July 2022; Case No: 1433/7/7/22, *Dr Liza Lovdahl Gormsen v Meta Platforms Inc, Meta Platforms Ireland Ltd, Facebook UK Ltd* – Reasoned Order of the President (Service out of the jurisdiction) – 15 March 2022; Case 1408/7/7/21, *Elizabeth Helen Coll v Alphabet Inc and Others* – Reasoned Order of the President (Service out of the jurisdiction) – 29 September 2021; Case No: 1403/7/7/21, *Dr Rachael Kent v Apple Inc and Apple Distribution International Ltd* – Reasoned Order of the President (Service out of the jurisdiction) 26/05/2021; Case No: 1382/7/7/21, *Consumers' Association v Qualcomm Inc* – Reasoned Order of the President (Service out of the jurisdiction) – 15 March 2021.

[2] Sections 5, 6 and 7.

[3] Section 47A(2) and (3) of the 1998 Act. See also: The Competition (Amendment etc.) (EU Exit) Regulations 2019.

In other words, the CAT, which is a specialist court dealing with competition law claims, would have jurisdiction to hear and determine private antitrust damages. In this context, the CAT could award damages and/or provide injured parties with injunctive relief (if there is a relevant basis for the court to assume jurisdiction).[4] That said, the UK CAT will not have the jurisdiction to issue 'a formal declaration that specified conduct constitutes a breach'.[5] If the desired legal remedy concerns declaratory relief, then the claim form should be issued before the High Court of England and Wales for that court to issue such declarations.

Nonetheless, it is important to outline that only the CAT would have the jurisdiction to issue a 'collective proceedings order'.[6] In other words, the CAT will be competent to deal with collective competition law claims which are issued by injured parties' representatives on behalf of multiple injured parties in the UK.[7] Since some of these collective redress proceedings will be issued on behalf of multiple consumers, it will be suggested that Section 15B of the Civil Jurisdiction and Judgment Act 1982 (the 1982 Act) and Section 47B of the 1998 Act be cumulatively constructed in a way which allows for the UK policy-makers' objectives to be effectively pursued in cross-border competition cases, safeguarding consumers' interests.[8]

In cases where the 1982 Act does not apply, the Civil Procedure Rules (CPR) and the Competition Appeal Tribunal Rules 2015 should be central to determining whether the English courts have jurisdiction over a private antitrust damages claim. In particular, Rule 31 of the UK Competition Appeal Tribunal Rules 2015[9] states that:

> (2) Where the permission of the Tribunal is required for service of the claim form on one or more foreign defendants out of the jurisdiction, the claimant shall make an application for permission verified by a statement of truth setting out—
>
> (a) the address of such foreign defendant or, if not known, in what place that defendant is, or is likely, to be found; and
>
> (b) that the claimant believes that the claim against any such foreign defendant has a reasonable prospect of success; and
>
> (c) if under rule 30(3)(b), the claimant contends that the proceedings are to be treated as taking place in England and Wales, which ground set out in paragraph 3.1 of Practice Direction 6B of the CPR is relied on; or
>
> (d) if under rule 30(3)(b), the claimant contends that the proceedings are to be treated as taking place in Scotland, which ground set out in Schedule 8 of the Civil Jurisdiction and Judgments Act 1982(a) is relied on; or
>
> [...]; and
>
> (f) any material facts relied on.
>
> (3) Where paragraph (2) applies, the Tribunal shall not give permission for service out of the jurisdiction unless satisfied that the Tribunal is the proper place in which to bring the claim.

[4] *Unlockd Ltd v Google* [2018] EWHC 1363 (Ch) [45] and [48]. Case Nos: 1377/5/7/20 and 1378/5/7/20, *Epic Games v Apple, Alphabet and Google* [2021] CAT 4 [91–98].

[5] *Epic Games* (n 4) [85].

[6] Competition Act 1998 s 47B(4).

[7] Competition Act 1998 s 47B(2) and (4).

[8] See: Chapter 6.

[9] UK Competition Appeal Tribunal Rules 2015 r 31(2)(d).

Since the purpose of this chapter is to consider the rules conferring jurisdiction on the English courts in private antitrust damages with an international element, the UK CAT rules will be examined along with the CPR, Practice Directions 6A and 6B. More specifically, given that the focus is on private antitrust damages claims, the tort and injunction grounds for jurisdiction as set out in para 3.1 of CPR PD 6B will be examined. As part of this process, the practice under Brussels Ia which was relied upon by the English courts to allocate jurisdiction prior to Brexit will also be considered 'by way of comparison'.[10]

The adopted approach in examining English jurisdiction rules and comparing them with the Brussels Ia rules appears to be in line with the practice of the UK Supreme Court.[11] Indeed, examining the jurisdictional grounds under the Brussels Ia regime might be necessary for, at least, two main reasons. First, many cross-border competition law cases were decided by the English courts under the Brussels Ia regime which means that the relevant jurisprudence might impact on the post-Brexit jurisprudence. This should enable the English judges to take a lead in advancing an internationalist approach to interpretation, influencing rather than following the CJEU jurisprudence in novel cases with an international element. Secondly, many of the grounds listed in Schedule 8 of the 1982 Act would be somewhat identical to the grounds which are set out in the Brussels Ia Regulation.

II. Service of a Claim Form within the Jurisdiction

Above all, it is well established that it will be possible for the English courts to assume jurisdiction in cases where the defendant is present in England and Wales and where the defendant is served with a claim form within the jurisdiction.[12] In other words, the presence of a company in England and Wales at the time of service should enable the courts to assume jurisdiction. This rule should not give rise to any specific difficulties in cross-border competition law claims.

That said, as noted above,[13] a specific feature of competition litigation is that many private antitrust damages claims would naturally be issued against companies[14] or indeed groups of companies[15] that engage in transnational economic activities. In view of this, it will be necessary to examine the rules concerning the service of a claim form on commercial companies along with the specific issues which arise in cases where the infringing undertaking is a group of companies that has penetrated the UK market

[10] *FS Cairo (Nile Plaza) LLC v Lady Brownlie* [2021] UKSC 45 [29].

[11] Ibid.

[12] L Collins and J Harris (eds) *Dicey, Morris and Collins on the Conflict of Laws* 16th edn (London, Sweet & Maxwell, 2022) Rule 32 – [11–038].

[13] See: Chapter 3 above.

[14] Case No: 1329/7/7/19, *Michael O'Higgins FX Class Representative Limited v Barclays Bank* – Order of the President (Service out of the jurisdiction) –16 August 2019; Case No: 1382/7/7/21, *Consumers' Association v Qualcomm Inc* [2022] CAT 20.

[15] *JJH Enterprises Ltd (trading as ValueLicensing) v Microsoft* [2022] EWHC 929 (Comm); Case No: 1403/7/7/21, *Dr Rachael Kent v Apple* [2022] CAT 28; *Dr Liza Lovdahl Gormsen* (n 1).

by setting up a wholly-owned subsidiary. Given the fact that the corporate structure of various entities – which enjoy sufficient market power to distort the process of competition – may vary, the territorial connection of an infringing company or the connection of a subsidiary that forms part of an infringing group of companies (or an infringing undertaking) with the forum might need to be considered in a greater detail.

There are two major issues which will be examined in this section. First, Section 1139 of the Companies Act 2006 as well as CPR Part 6 together with PD 6A will be examined as being relevant for a claim form to be served to a company which has engaged in anti-competitive activities and which is present in England and Wales.[16] Secondly, the specific aspects concerning the service of a claim form on a multinational group of a company which is regarded as a 'single economic unit'[17] and which has a subsidiary present in the jurisdiction.

A. Foreign Companies – Registered Office or Other Establishment

A competition law claim form may be served on a company whose registered office is in England and Wales by the methods set out in CPR Part 6 or those specified in the Companies Act 2006.[18] More specifically, the 'principal office of the company; or any place of business of the company within the jurisdiction which has a real connection with the claim'[19] would constitute major connecting factors for a company which is registered in England and Wales. Alternatively, a claim form may be served 'by leaving it at, or sending it by post to, the company's registered office'.[20] It is a requirement, under the Companies Act 2006, for a company to 'have a registered office to which all communications and notices may be addressed'.[21] There is an obvious tactical advantage for claimants to use these connecting factors because in cross-border competition law cases, where the defendant is present in England and Wales, '[n]o permission is needed to serve defendants in the jurisdiction'.[22]

These jurisdictional rules would be particularly important in cases where the competition law claims are issued against infringing entities that are present in the jurisdiction.[23] For example, some of the infringers (eg Barclays Bank; NatWest; Royal

[16] See: JJ Fawcett, 'A new approach to jurisdiction over companies in private international law' (1988) 37 *ICLQ* 645. See also P Rogerson, 'English court's jurisdiction over companies: How important is service of the claim form in England?' (2000) 3 *Company Financial and Insolvency Law Review* 272.
Case No: 1440/7/7/22 *Clare Mary Joan Spottiswoode CBE v Nexans France S.A.S. & Others* – Reasoned Order of the President (Service out of the Jurisdiction) 19 August 2022 [8].

[17] Case C-73/95 P *Viho v Commission* EU:C:1996:405 [16]. *ValueLicensing* (n 15).

[18] CPR 6.3(2). See more: *Dicey, Morris and Collins* (n 12) Rule 32 – [11–050].

[19] CPR 6.9(2).

[20] Companies Act 2006 s 1139(1).

[21] Companies Act 2006 s 86.

[22] *Epic Games* (n 4) [73]. See also: Civil Procedure Rules, Practice Direction 6A.

[23] eg *Michael O'Higgins* (n 14). See also: *Emerald Supplies & Another v British Airways* [2009] EWHC 741 (Ch); *Emerald Supplies & Sothern Glass House Produce v British Airways* [2010] EWCA Civ 1284.

Bank of Scotland; UBS AG[24]) may be addressees of the regulator's decisions[25] which establish competition law infringement and which are binding for the English courts. If the infringers (ie defendants) in question are present in the jurisdiction, then the claim form or indeed a collective proceedings claim form could be served on the defendants as being present within the jurisdiction.[26] Given the fact that London is a global financial and business centre, many multinational companies might be present in England which could in turn constitute a relevant basis for jurisdiction.

Moreover, the requirements concerning the assumption of jurisdiction in claims issued against an 'overseas company [which is defined as] a company incorporated outside the UK'[27] and which has a branch in England – might be even more important in some cross-border competition law claims. Such foreign companies are required to register certain information with the Registrar of Companies.[28] This includes 'particulars identifying every person resident in the United Kingdom authorised to accept service of documents on behalf of the company, or [making] a statement that there is no such person'.[29] This requirement is important because Section 1139(2) of the Companies Act 2006 states that:

> A document may be served on an overseas company whose particulars are registered under section 1046—
>
> (a) by leaving it at, or sending it by post to, the registered address of any person resident in the United Kingdom who is authorised to accept service of documents on the company's behalf, or
>
> (b) if there is no such person, or if any such person refuses service or service cannot for any other reason be effected, by leaving it at or sending by post to any place of business of the company in the United Kingdom.[30]

The provision was relied upon in *Clare Mary Joan Spottiswoode CBE v Nexans France*[31] where the President of the UK CAT reiterated that no permission was required for a claim form to be served overseas because the defendant could 'be served at the address of its UK establishment, pursuant to section 1139(2) of the Companies Act 2006'.[32] The rationale is for the English courts to be able to assume jurisdiction in a case where a foreign company is exercising economic activities by being present in the jurisdiction. This should allow, for example, an action to be brought in England and Wales against

[24] *Michael O'Higgins* (n 14) [2].

[25] Case AT.40135, *FOREX (Three Way Banana Split) – Commission Decision relating to a proceeding under Article 101 of the Treaty on the Functioning of the European Union and Article 53 of the EEA Agreement* – 16.5.2019, C(2019) 3631 final; CASE AT.40135 *FOREX (Essex Express) – Commission Decision relating to a proceeding under Article 101 of the Treaty on the Functioning of the European Union and Article 53 of the EEA Agreement* – 16.5.2019, C(2019) 3621 final.

[26] CPR Part 6 and CPR 7.5(1). See also: *Michael O'Higgins* (n 14) [2]; The Competition Appeal Tribunal Rules 2015 r 76(4). See more: *Dicey, Morris and Collins* (n 12) Rule 32 – [11–038]; A Zuckerman, 'New provision for service: a great improvement threaten by discretion' (2009) *Civil Justice Quarterly* 1.

[27] Companies Act 2006 s 1044.

[28] Companies Act 2006 s 1046.

[29] Companies Act 2006 s 1056.

[30] Companies Act 2006 s 1139(2).

[31] Case No: 1440/7/7/22 *Clare Mary Joan Spottiswoode CBE v Nexans France S.A.S. & Others* – Reasoned Order of the President (Service out of the Jurisdiction) 19 August 2022.

[32] Ibid [8].

a foreign company which forms part of a cartel (or enjoys a dominant position) and which markets a product (charging an inflated/excessive price, in breach of UK competition law) in England through its English branch and/or establishment.[33]

The problem is that, in most competition cases, the market would rather be penetrated through setting up a subsidiary which would have a separate legal personality, being different from a branch. It has been submitted that the '[subsidiary] normally acts for itself and not for the parent company'[34] which means that even a 'wholly-owned subsidiary'[35] would not classify as a branch for private international law purposes due to the fact that a subsidiary has a separate legal personality. The issues are important because the practice of the regulators is to address their decisions establishing the infringements to the parent company. The issues have been captured in *Emerson*[36] where the UK Competition Appeal Tribunal stated:

> the Commission's practice is not always to specify in the operative part all the legal entities which form the 'undertaking' which has been found to infringe. Where, for example, there is a corporate group with numerous subsidiaries, all of whom form a single infringing undertaking, he stated that the Commission's practice has been to specify the ultimate parent company or 'Topco', rather than listing in the operative part of the decision each and every subsidiary involved in the unlawful conduct. [Mr Jon Turner KC] submitted that where this occurs the legal person named in the operative part of the decision as the 'undertaking' will be a representative, and the finding of infringement is not limited to that entity.[37]

Therefore, the concept of 'undertaking', which – as noted above[38] – is a widely accepted classification for groups of companies for competition law purposes, indicates that there are some specific issues which may arise in cross-border competition law claims.

An important question may be whether a local subsidiary of a multinational group of companies (which constitutes a single undertaking for competition law purposes) could be classified as a branch for PIL purposes. If the response to this question is in the affirmative, then a claim form could be served on a foreign company which had penetrated the market by setting up an English subsidiary that is present in the jurisdiction.

B. Subsidiaries of Multinational Groups of Companies

As noted above, the PIL issues in cases involving multinational groups of companies are often dealt with by addressing the question of whether the corporate veil should be lifted, which may give rise to a considerable (and rather heated) debate before the

[33] Ibid [8, 19 and 22].

[34] Fawcett (n 16) 659. See also: WA Allwood, 'Art 5(5): Meaning of "branch, agency or other establishment"' (1988) 13 *EL Rev* 213; Case C-139/80 *Blanckaert & Willems PVBA v Luise Trost* EU:C:1981:70; Case C-218/86 *Sar Schotte GmbH v Parfums Rothschild SARL* EU:C:1987:536 [15].

[35] Companies Act 2006 s 1159(2).

[36] Case No: 1077/5/7/07, *Emerson Electric Co v Morgan Crucible Company PLC and Ors* [2011] CAT 4.

[37] Ibid [38].

[38] Chapter 3.

English courts.[39] The issues are important because, for example, an infringing undertaking may implement various anti-competitive practices by setting up a subsidiary that markets a cartelised product at an inflated price or provides certain services by charging excessive prices.

There is an argument that, given the wide scope of the concept of 'undertaking' for competition law purposes,[40] the question whether a multinational company is present in the jurisdiction may be approached rather differently. Classification problems might arise because its local subsidiary is not a branch, which means that a claim form could not be served to such a multinational group of companies within the jurisdiction. Indeed, the parent–subsidiary relationship within a multinational group of companies could give rise to complex issues in relation to classification for PIL purposes. In other words, the central PIL question should be: should a wholly-owned subsidiary of a multinational group of companies, which is a single undertaking/economic entity, classify as a branch for PIL purposes?

The response to this question matters because, as noted above, a common scenario in competition law cases is that they would involve multinational group/s of companies that may have numerous subsidiaries. On the one hand, it is doubtful whether a multinational group of companies can be regarded as having established a 'place of business [...] within the jurisdiction'[41] when it engages in economic activities in England and Wales through its local subsidiary which is a separate legal entity.

On the other hand, there are specific considerations which must be factored in to competition law cases. It is not only the specific concept of 'undertaking' which would be relevant, but it is also the fact that certain parent companies (which are subject to competition law) would have, by definition, the market 'power to behave to an appreciable extent independently of its competitors, customers and ultimately of its consumers'.[42] Should there be an assumption that since a parent company, which has market power, would control its subsidiaries,[43] a multinational group of companies is to be considered as a single (albeit transnational) unit for the purposes of assuming jurisdiction in private antitrust damages claims?

i. Article 7(5) of Brussels Ia

Schedule 8 of the Civil Jurisdiction and Judgments Act 1982 which stipulates that 'a person may also be sued – [...] as regards a dispute arising out of the operations of a branch, agency or other establishment, in the courts for the place in which the branch, agency or other establishment is situated'.[44] The latter provision appears to be identical

[39] *Adams v Cape Industries* [1990] ChD 433.

[40] Chapter 3.

[41] CPR6.9(2).

[42] Case 27/76 *United Brands Company and United Brands Continentaal BV v Commission of the European Communities* EU:C:1978:22 [65]. See also: Case 85/76 *Hoffmann-La Roche & Co AG v Commission of the European Communities* EU:C:1978:22 [38]; *Streetmap v Google* [2016] EWHC 253 (Ch).

[43] Compare: Case C-97/08 P *Akzo Nobel NV and Others v Commission of the European Communities* EU:C:2009:536 [60]; Joined Cases C-6/73 and C-7/73 *Istituto Chemioterapico Italiano SpA and Commercial Solvents Corp v Commission of the European Communities* EU:C:1974:5, 264 (AG Warner).

[44] Section 2(f) of Schedule 8 of the Civil Jurisdiction and Judgments Act 1982.

to the text of Article 7(5) which sets out 'the place in which the branch, agency or other establishment is situated'[45] as a major connecting factor.

There is a view that the subsidiary may be covered by the concept of branch under Article 7(5) in cases where it is 'acting as an extension of [a multinational] company'.[46] The economic realities and any specific circumstances should be considered 'even if, from the point of view of company law, the two companies are independent of each other'.[47] This sounds like a classification issue which should be addressed, in competition law cases, by determining whether the parent company (which enjoys significant market power) could influence the conduct of the subsidiary. In *De Bloos*, the CJEU took the view that 'when the grantee of an exclusive sales concession is subject neither to the control nor to the direction of the grantor, he cannot [classify] as being [...] a branch, agency or other establishment'.[48] The rationale in this judgment has been nicely summarised by AG Reischel:[49]

> characteristics of a branch are, on the one hand, a certain autonomy and, on the other, being subordinate to the parent company and subject to the control of that company. Particular characteristics are the absence of its own legal personality and the authority to act on behalf of the parent company. An agency is similar but its autonomy is certainly less marked.[50]

That said, a different approach to classification might well be adopted in competition cases whether a parent company exercise control over its subsidiaries' 'course of action in the market'.[51] Addressing this question head-on should be key to determining whether a multinational group of companies is to be regarded as a single undertaking for the purposes of competition law[52] which in turn might indicate that the local subsidiary should classify as a branch for the private international law purposes.

It is well established that the EU 'Commission may generally assume that a wholly-owned subsidiary essentially follows the instructions given to it by its parent company and thus does not determine autonomously its commercial policy'.[53] The EU Commission (or the UK Competition and Markets Authority), when establishing a competition law infringement, would normally be expected to 'define the undertaking that is to be held accountable for the infringement of [EU competition law] by identifying one or more

[45] Article 7(5) of Brussels Ia. See: Case C-14/76 *De Bloos v Bouyer* EU:C:1976:134; *Blanckaert* (n 34); *Sar Schotte* (n 34); Case C-439/93 *Lloyd's Register of Shipping v Société Campenon Bernard* EU:C:1995:104. See: P Torremans and JJ Fawcett, *Cheshire, North & Fawcett: Private International Law* 15th edn (Oxford, OUP, 2017) pp 279–83.

[46] *Sar Schotte* (n 34) [15].

[47] Ibid.

[48] *De Bloos* (n 45) [23]. See also: the opinion of AG Reischl in Case C-14/76 *De Bloos v Bouyer* – Opinion of Mr Advocate-General Reischl, Delivered on 15 September 1976 EU:C:1976:120, 1519.

[49] *De Bloos* (n 48).

[50] Ibid 1519.

[51] *Viho* (n 17) [16].

[52] Case C-48/69 *Imperial Chemical Industries Ltd v Commission of the European Communities* EU:C:1972:70 [134]; Case C-66/86 *Ahmed Saeed Flurgreisen v Zentrale zur Bekämpfung unlauteren Wettbewerbs* EU:C:1989:140 [35]. Case C-15/74 *Centrafarm v Sterling Drug* EU:C:1974:114 [41]; *Viho* (n 17). See also: *Provimi Limited v Aventis Animal Nutrition SA and Others* [2003] EWHC 961 (Comm) [31]. See more: J Faull and A Nikpay, *The EC Law of Competition* 2nd edn (Oxford, OUP, 2007) pp 206–08. Compare: *Adams* (n 39) 532.

[53] Case COMP/E-1/38.823, *PO/Elevators and Escalators – Commission Decision relating to a proceeding under Article 81 of the EC Treaty* C (2007) 512 final [604].

legal persons to represent the undertaking'.[54] Since it is quite common for an infringing undertaking to penetrate the various national markets through a transnational 'network of subsidiaries' (which would distort the process of competition and which would cause antitrust damages to multiple injured parties in different jurisdictions),[55] the regulator's approach appears to be in line with Articles 101 and 102 TFEU (as well as with the 1998 Act). The CJEU has held:

> In the specific case where a parent company has a 100% shareholding in a subsidiary which has infringed the Community competition rules, first, the parent company can exercise a decisive influence over the conduct of the subsidiary (see, to that effect, *Imperial Chemical Industries* v *Commission*, paragraphs 136 and 137) and, second, there is a rebuttable presumption that the parent company does in fact exercise a decisive influence over the conduct of its subsidiary (see, to that effect, *AEG-Telefunken* v *Commission*, paragraph 50, and *Stora*, paragraph 29).[56]

Addressing the classification question may be important because, if an infringement had been established by the EU Commission (or the UK Competition Markets Authority), then an important PIL question is whether an injured party can sue in England and Wales a local subsidiary that is not named in the EU Commission's decision which only refers to the parent company.[57]

Although the concept of 'undertaking' for the purposes of Articles 101 and 102 TFEU is different from the concept of 'persons'[58] for the purposes of establishing jurisdiction under Brussels Ia, a subsidiary forming part of a multinational group of companies may well classify as a branch for the purposes of Article 7(5) of Brussels Ia and Schedule 8 of the Jurisdiction and Judgments Act 1982. This would be particularly so in cases where the subsidiary is part of the same group of companies, being 'engaged in the same economic undertaking'.[59] The deduction could be strengthened by AG Werner's analysis of the parent–subsidiary relationship for the purposes of Articles 101 and 102 TFEU, setting out the following three principles:

> 1. that there is a presumption that a subsidiary will act in accordance with the wishes of its parent because according to common experience subsidiaries generally do so act;
> 2. that, unless that presumption is rebutted, it is proper for the parent and the subsidiary to be treated as a single undertaking for the purposes of [Articles 101 and 102 TFEU]; and
> 3. that the presumption can only be rebutted if it is shown affirmatively, by those concerned to rebut it, that the subsidiary in fact conducted its business autonomously. I confess that to my mind this must be a very difficult onus to discharge. […][60]

[54] Case COMP/F/38.620, *Hydrogen Peroxide and Perborate – Commission Decision relating to a proceeding pursuant to Article 81 of the EC Treaty and Article 53 of the EEA Agreement* C(2006) 1766 final [372].

[55] Ibid [88].

[56] *Akzo Nobel* (n 43) [60].

[57] *Cooper Tire & Rubber Company v Shell Chemicals UK Limited* [2009] EWHC 2609 (Comm); *Cooper Tire & Rubber Company Europe Limited & Others* [2010] EWCA Civ 864; *Toshiba Carrier UK Ltd and Other v KME Yorkshire Limited & Others* [2011] EWHC 2665 (Ch); *Toshiba Carrier UK Ltd and Other v KME Yorkshire Limited & Others* [2012] EWCA Civ 169; *Nokia Corporation v AU Optronics Corporation* [2012] EWHC 731 (Ch).

[58] *Commercial Solvents* (n 43) 263. See also: *Adams* (n 39) 535; Article 63(1) of Brussels Ia; CPR 2.3.

[59] *Toshiba Carrier* – EWHC (n 57) [49].

[60] *Commercial Solvents* (n 43) 264.

The proposed principles should be equally relevant when a group of companies, which constitutes a single undertaking, is being classified for PIL purposes. The proposed principles would be of relevance in cross-border competition law cases where a subsidiary implements a cartel agreement that is entered into by its parent and the parent's competitors as well as in cases where a subsidiary is being used by a multinational group which enjoys a dominant position to coordinate/implement its abusive practice in a particular territory.

However, the problem is that there is a significant limitation of the territorial scope of that court's jurisdiction under Article 7(5) in so far as there is a requirement that the competition law 'action must concern the operations of the branch, agency or other establishment'.[61] More specifically, the scope of that court's jurisdiction is limited to the local antitrust harm (as opposed to the antitrust damages which may have been caused in other jurisdictions). This means that, despite the fact that it might be advantageous for an antitrust claim to be issued against a parent company because the subsidiary may not be sufficiently solvent[62] and/or disclosure may be sought from the parent company, the well-advised claimants (who have suffered damages in a number of EU Member States) may rather rely on different provisions. Such claimants would rather try to establish jurisdiction by relying on Article 8(1) of Brussels Ia[63] which might also enable them to have all damages claims governed by *lex fori*.[64]

That said, in order for the classification issues to be systematically dealt with by judges and the jurisdiction to be allocated to an appropriate court under Brussels Ia, a very practical question is whether an infringing undertaking, which is a single economic unit that consists of number of legal entities (ie wholly-owned subsidiaries), should rather classify as an 'association of [...] legal persons' within the meaning of Article 63(1) of Brussels Ia.[65]

ii. Classification of Multinational Group of Companies – Post-Brexit

It is well settled that 'if the foreign company has a branch in England, it may be served in England under CPR, r 6.9 even if the claim has no connection with the branch or with England'.[66] Classifying a subsidiary of a foreign group of companies (which constitutes a single undertaking) as a branch might have significant implications for the jurisdiction of the English courts in competition law claims, post-Brexit. The presence of a subsidiary in the forum should be a sufficient basis for jurisdiction, allowing the English courts to assume jurisdiction over antitrust claims brought against a multinational group of companies which carries on business within the jurisdiction through its subsidiary. In other words, the foreign parent would be subject to jurisdiction by virtue of service of a claim form within the jurisdictions.

[61] Case 33/78 *Somafer v Saar-Ferngas* EU:C:1978:205 [13]. See: *Cheshire, North & Fawcett* (n 45) 282–83.
[62] *Metall und Rohstoff AG v Donaldson Lufkin & Jenrette Inc and Another* [1990] 1 QB 391.
[63] See: Chapter 6 below.
[64] Chapter 11 below.
[65] See: Chapter 3 above.
[66] *Dicey, Morris and Collins* (n 12) Rule 32 – [11–055].

In order to advance such an approach, post-Brexit, the English courts need to reconsider the issues concerning the classification and assumption of jurisdiction in competition law claims issued against multinational groups of companies that may be liable for breach of competition law. At present, the jurisprudence is far too reliant on the judgment of the High Court of England and Wales in *Adams v Cape Industries*.[67] In *Adams v Cape Industries*, the English court held that:

> The question whether the corporate veil should be lifted is more difficult. It is, I think, one which raises an issue of general importance. Is a parent company to be treated, for jurisdiction purposes, as resident in a country in which its wholly owned subsidiary is resident and carries on business? Should the answer be dependent on whether the subsidiary's business is associated with and, in a group sense, a part of the business of the parent company?[68]

Since *Adams v Cape Industries* was not a competition law case, the concept of 'single undertaking' was not considered. A signal that a different approach may be advanced in competition law cases may be deduced by the fact that the High Court of England and Wales made an obiter reference to the opinion of AG Warner, which was inter alia cited above[69] and which was submitted to the CJEU in *Commercial Solvents*,[70] stating that:

> [N]either Article [101 TFEU] nor Article [102 TFEU] anywhere refers to 'persons'. In both Articles the relevant prohibitions are directed to 'undertakings', a much wider and looser concept. This indeed is what one would expect, because it would be inappropriate to apply rigidly in the sphere of competition law the doctrine referred to by English lawyers as that of *Salomon v Salomon & Co. Ltd.* [1897] A.C. 22 – i.e. the doctrine that every company is a separate legal person that cannot be identified with its members. Basically that doctrine exists in order to preserve the principle of limited liability. It is concerned with the rights of creditors in the context of company law. It has been applied, with more or less happy results, in other spheres, such as those of conveyancing, of contracts and of liability for tort. But to export it blindly into branches of the law where it has little relevance, could, in my opinion, serve only to divorce the law from reality.[71]

The above quote, which was cited in *Adams v Cape Industries* by Mr Justice Scott, sitting in the High Court of England and Wales, might be interpreted as indicating that a different approach may be advanced in a competition law case against a multinational group of company which classifies as a single economic entity/'undertaking'[72] for jurisdictional purposes. In other words, classifying a multinational group of companies as a single undertaking may be central to determining that a multinational group, which engages in anti-competitive conduct and which penetrates the English market through a wholly-owned subsidiary, is present in the jurisdiction in private antitrust damages claims.

[67] *Adams* (n 39).
[68] Ibid 474–75.
[69] See: Section 4.II.B.i above.
[70] *Commercial Solvents* (n 43) 263.
[71] *Commercial Solvents* (n 43) 263 cited in *Adams* (n 39) 475.
[72] See: the judgment in Case C-41/90 *Klaus Höfner and Fritz Elser v Macrotron GmbH* EU:C:1991:161. See also: *Hydrogen Peroxide and Perborate* (n 54) [371].

The concept of the undertaking should strongly suggest that a parent company that enjoys significant market power (if not a dominant position) and its wholly-owned subsidiary would need to be broadly classified for jurisdictional purposes.[73] This means that, in competition law cases, the central question should be whether a multinational group which is liable to distort competition and which has implemented the anti-competitive conduct through its subsidiary should be regarded as being present within the jurisdiction. As part of this process, the judges should consider the anti-competitive (or allegedly anti-competitive) conduct which is deployed and the control which is exercised by the parent over the local subsidiary, in order to determine whether the multinational group (which constitutes a single undertaking) is to be regarded as being present in the jurisdiction.

Analogies could be made with the judgment of the US District Court for the Eastern District of New York in *Bulova Watch v Hattori*.[74] In this case, the claim, which inter alia raised issues of unfair competition, was issued against a Japanese company that penetrated the market by using local subsidiaries. The US federal court held that:

> Whether or not the court would pierce the corporate veil and impose liability on the parent for activities of the subsidiary is not the issue here. […]
>
> [The] subsidiaries almost by definition are doing for their parent what their parent would otherwise have to do on its own. The question to ask is not whether the American subsidiaries can formally accept orders for their parent, but rather whether, in the truest sense, the subsidiaries' presence substitutes for the presence of the parent.[75]

Therefore, an approach which allows for a multinational group of companies – which has penetrated the market through subsidiaries – to be classified as being present in the jurisdiction may enable the English court to assume jurisdiction on the basis of service of a claim form within the jurisdiction. There is a strong argument for a similar approach to be advanced by the English courts in cross-border competition law cases, post-Brexit. If such a classification were to evolve with a view to determining whether a multinational group is present in the jurisdiction, then the aspects concerning *forum non conveniens* would become central to assuming jurisdiction because the defendants could often 'disput[e] the Tribunal's jurisdiction'.[76]

The proposed approach should reflect the fact that it is increasingly common for transnational groups of companies to be formed, so that multinational undertakings that enjoy significant market power can penetrate global markets through a network of subsidiaries.[77] It remains to be seen whether such a classification will be adopted by the Court of Appeal in an appropriate case under the English CPR.[78]

[73] Compare: *Commercial Solvents* (n 43) 264.

[74] *Bulova Watch v Hattori* 508 F Supp 1322 (1981).

[75] Ibid 1342.

[76] The Competition Appeal Tribunal Rules 2015, r 34. See more: Chapter 6.

[77] Compare: the corporate structure of the Apple and Google groups in *Epic Games* (n 4) [29–35].

[78] A Mukarrum, 'Private international law and substantive liability issues in tort litigation against multinational companies in the English courts: recent UK Supreme Court decisions and post-Brexit implications' (2022) 18 *Journal of Private International Law* 56–82.

III. Defendant Not Being Present in the Jurisdiction

The purpose of this section is to briefly outline the main principles[79] and connecting factors which would be relevant for the English courts to assume jurisdiction in competition law claims which would arise out of transnational competition infringements. In cases where the infringing entity has no presence in England and Wales, a claimant may issue court proceedings against them by seeking a permission for the claim form to be served out of the jurisdiction.[80]

A. Domicile as a Connecting Factor

Before outlining the main principles for service of a competition law claim form out of the jurisdiction where the permission of the court is needed, it should be noted that a 'permission of the Tribunal is not required for service out of the jurisdiction'[81] in competition law 'proceedings whose subject-matter is a matter relating to a consumer contract where the consumer is domiciled in the United Kingdom'.[82] The consumer's domicile would be an important connecting factor which would need to be considered in competition law claims that arise out of consumer contracts.[83] In this context, the court will consider whether the consumer is residing in the UK, having 'a substantial connection with the United Kingdom'.[84]

Although Brussels Ia no longer applies in the UK, the Civil Jurisdiction and Judgments Act 1982 was amended to include new Section 15B which is modelled on Section 4 of Chapter II of the Brussels Ia Regulation.[85] The rationale is to improve consumers' access to legal remedies by allowing them to 'bring proceedings against the other party to the consumer contract [...] in the courts for the place where the consumer is domiciled (regardless of the domicile of the other party to the consumer contract)',[86] which is important if the other party (ie the defendant) is not domiciled in the UK.[87]

The facilitative regime would be applicable in cross-border cases where the consumer is domiciled in the UK[88] as long as the claimant classifies as a consumer (ie acting outside his trade or profession).[89] The specific aspects in relation to contracts concluded by consumers under Section 15B of the 1982 Act are dealt with in Chapter 5[90]

[79] A Arzandeh, '"Gateways" within the Civil Procedure Rules and the future of service-out jurisdiction in England' (2019) 15 *Journal of Private International Law* 516–540.
[80] The Competition Appeal Tribunal Rules 2015 r 31(2).
[81] Competition Appeal Tribunal Rules 2015 r 31(1).
[82] Civil Jurisdiction and Judgments Act 1982 s 15B(2).
[83] CPR 6.33(2).
[84] Civil Jurisdiction and Judgments Act 1982 s 41(2). See more: Section 5.IV and 6.II below.
[85] *Dicey, Morris and Collins* (n 12) Rule 31 – [11–027].
[86] Civil Jurisdiction and Judgments Act 1982 s 15B(2)(b).
[87] Civil Jurisdiction and Judgments Act 1982 s 15B(2)(a).
[88] Civil Jurisdiction and Judgments Act 1982 s 15B(1).
[89] See more: J Hill, *Cross-border Consumer Contracts* (OUP, Oxford, 2008) 88–97.
[90] Chapter 5.IV below.

which deals with competition law claims arising out of contracts as well as in Chapter 6[91] which addresses the problems in relation to competition law claims which are issued on behalf of multiple consumers.

The defendant's domicile remains relevant with a view to allocating jurisdiction within the UK.[92] These aspects would be particularly important in cases where 'the claimant contends that [the UK CAT] proceedings are to be treated as taking place in Scotland'.[93] The application of Section 1 of Sch 8 of the 1982 Act would be straightforward in cases where the competition law claim/s are issued in Scotland where the company (which had infringed competition law) has its 'registered office'[94] or 'statutory seat'[95] or 'central administration'[96] or 'place of business'.[97]

Jurisdictional challenges are less likely to be raised and succeed in cases where the '[d]efendants [being duly incorporated companies] are addressees of the Commission's decisions'[98] and they are domiciled at the place where the proceedings are issued.[99] As noted above,[100] there might be an argument that a multinational group, which consists of multiple subsidiaries and which is a single undertaking, should classify as an 'association'[101] which would in turn require the domicile of such a multinational group to be ascertained. However, it is yet to be seen whether a different approach would be advanced by the English courts, post-Brexit.

B. Main Principles – Service Out of the Jurisdiction

The important principles concerning the service of a claim form out of the jurisdiction have been thoroughly discussed in cross-border competition cases by the High Court of England and Wales in *JJH Enterprises Ltd (trading as ValueLicensing) v Microsoft*[102] as well as by the UK Competition Appeal Tribunal in *Epic Games Inc v Apple Inc.*[103]

There are three major requirements[104] which must be considered by a court in the context of an application by a claimant seeking permission to serve a claim form out of the jurisdiction: prospects of success; the territorial connection between the claim/desired legal remedy and the forum; and the level of appropriateness of English courts.[105] First, the claimant has to demonstrate that 'the claim against [the relevant] foreign

[91] Chapter 6.II below.
[92] Civil Jurisdiction and Judgments Act 1982, Schedule 4 and 8 s 1.
[93] Competition Appeal Tribunal Rules 2015 r 31(2)(d).
[94] Civil Jurisdiction and Judgments Act 1982, ss 42 and 42A.
[95] Article 63(1)(a) – Brussels Ia.
[96] Civil Jurisdiction and Judgments Act 1982, ss 42 and 42A. See also: Article 63(1)(b) – Brussels Ia.
[97] Civil Jurisdiction and Judgments Act 1982, ss 42 and 42A. See also: Article 63(1)(c) – Brussels Ia.
[98] *Allianz Global Investors GmbH And Others v Barclays Bank plc and Others* [2021] EWHC 399 (Comm) [2]. See also: Summary of Commission Decision of 16 May 2019 relating to a proceeding under Article 101 of the Treaty on the Functioning of the European Union and Article 53 of the EEA Agreement (Case AT.40135 – *Forex-Three Way Banana Split*) [2020] OJ C226/5.
[99] *Emerald Supplies Ltd & Others v British Airways v Air Canada & Others* [2014] EWHC 3513 (Ch).
[100] Chapter 3 above.
[101] Article 63(1) of Brussels Ia. See also: Civil Jurisdiction and Judgments Act 1982, s 42A.
[102] *ValueLicensing* (n 15). See also: *The LCD Appeals* [2018] EWCA Civ 220.
[103] *Epic Games* (n 4) 4.
[104] *Four Seasons Holdings Incorporated v Brownlie (Brownlie I)* [2017] UKSC 80 [3]; *Epic Games* (n 4) [78].
[105] *Brownlie I* (n 104) [66].

defendant [who is to be served out of the jurisdiction] has a reasonable prospect of success'.[106] This requirement is important to safeguard the interests of the defendant by requiring the claimant to substantiate 'the existence of [a] relevant cause of action [which] has been sufficiently established'.[107] As part of this process, the English judges would need to consider 'whether the inflated prices paid by the claimants as a result of the cartels constituted a foreseeable, immediate and substantial effect in the [United Kingdom] so as to bring the claim within the territorial scope of [UK competition law]',[108] taking a view on whether the claimant has reasonable prospects of success.[109]

Secondly, once the first requirement has been satisfied, a claimant has to satisfy the court that the claim falls within one of the gateways set out in paragraph 3.1 of Practice Direction B to Part 6 (PD 6B) of the CPR.[110] This requirement is duly reflected in the 2015 CAT Guide to Proceedings which states that:

> if the claimant states that the proceedings should be treated as taking place in England and Wales, the Tribunal will apply the approach of the High Court and the grounds for service out of the jurisdiction must satisfy one of the 'gateways' under paragraph 3.1 of CPR Practice Direction 6B. See *DSG Retail Ltd v MasterCard, Inc* [2015] CAT 7.[111]

Given the lack of special rules allocating jurisdiction in cross-border competition law claims, it is beyond doubt that CPR 6.36 which refers to para 3.1 of CPR PD 6B should both be relevant to identify an appropriate ground for a claim form to be served out of the jurisdiction with the permission of the court. This was clearly reiterated in *The LCD Appeals*, with Lord Justices Henderson and Asplin submitting that 'the principles upon which permission to serve out of the jurisdiction is granted are set out in CPR 6.36 and 6.37, read with paragraph 3.1 of Practice Direction 6B'.[112] Therefore, since there are no special gateways for the CAT to assume jurisdiction in cross-border competition law claims, the Tribunal 'will apply the same approach as that which applies to civil claims in the High Court'.[113]

There are several jurisdictional gateways which are set out in para 3.1 of CPR PD 6B and which would be relevant in competition law cases. More specifically, the following gateways could be relevant in respect of competition law claims: the tort gateway (para 3.1(9) of CPR PD 6B); the injunction gateway (para 3.1(2) of CPR PD 6B); the multi-defendant gateway[114] (para 3.1(3) of CPR PD 6B); the contract gateways[115] para 3.1(6) of CPR PD 6B which should be read along with gateways (4A) and (8) of CPR PD 6B). In order for the English court to assume jurisdiction, the claimant should demonstrate that there is a good arguable case their claim could be issued in the

[106] Competition Appeal Tribunal Rules 2015 r 31(2)(b).
[107] *Seaconsar v Bank Markazi* [1994] 1 AC 438 (CA) 452.
[108] *Unlockd* (n 4) [30] citing *The LCD Appeals* (n 102).
[109] See: Section IV below.
[110] CPR 6.37(1)(a).
[111] Competition Appeal Tribunal, Guide to Proceedings (2015) [5.43].
[112] *The LCD Appeals* (n 102) [40].
[113] Case No: 1236/5/7/15 *DSG Retail Limited and Another v MasterCard Incorporated and Others* [2015] CAT 7 [18]. See also: *Epic Games* (n 4) [77].
[114] See: Chapter 6 below.
[115] See: Chapter 5 below.

jurisdiction on the ground/s set out in para 3.1 of CPR PD 6B. This is set to ensure that the claims have 'relevant connections with England'.[116]

The required territorial connections may be satisfied, if the claimant – relying on the injunction gateway – sought an order for the defendant to do something (eg provide access to a digital platform)[117] and/or to refrain from doing certain acts (eg 'restricting the download'[118] of their competitor's products) in England and Wales.[119] In other cases, the competition claims may be within the ambit of certain gateways because the claimant is able to demonstrate that there are 'some jurisdictional fact[s]'[120] which provide sufficient connection between the dispute and the forum. For example, antitrust damages which had been sustained in the jurisdiction, would constitute a relevant connecting factor.[121] The requirement would be satisfied, if the claimant/s were to show that a competition law infringement, which causes antitrust damage or will cause such damage, was committed in England and Wales.[122] Likewise, a patent transfer agreement which was made within the jurisdiction may contain terms which are unfair and discriminatory, being in conflict with competition law.[123]

The required evidential standard, which needs to be satisfied when considering whether a competition claim comes with the ambit of para 3.1 of PD 6B is '"good arguable case" [which] reflects in [an interlocutory] context that one side has a much better argument on the material available'.[124] The test has been recently re-considered by the UK Supreme Court in *Brownlie I*, where the Supreme Court judges took the view that:

> The reference to 'a much better argument on the material available' is not a reversion to the civil burden of proof which the House of Lords had rejected in *Vitkovice*. What is meant is (i) that the claimant must supply a plausible evidential basis for the application of a relevant jurisdictional gateway; (ii) that if there is an issue of fact about it, or some other reason for doubting whether it applies, the Court must take a view on the material available if it can reliably do so; but (iii) the nature of the issue and the limitations of the material available at the interlocutory stage may be such that no reliable assessment can be made, in which case there is a good arguable case for the application of the gateway if there is a plausible (albeit contested) evidential basis for it. I do not believe that anything is gained by the word 'much', which suggests a superior standard of conviction that is both uncertain and unwarranted in this context.[125]

This quotation unequivocally suggests that the claimant must have 'the better of the argument on whether their claim comes within the gateway(s)'[126] which are set out in para 3.1 of PD 6B.

Thirdly, the UK Competition Appeal Tribunal and English courts will not give permission for service of a claim form out of jurisdiction unless satisfied that England

[116] *Brownlie I* (n 104) [31].
[117] *Unlockd* (n 4) [45].
[118] *Epic Games* (n 4) [93d].
[119] *Brownlie I* (n 104) [4]. See: para 3.1(2) of CPR PD 6B.
[120] *Brownlie I* (n 104) [4].
[121] *Dr Rachael Kent* (n 1) [5]; *Qualcomm* (n 1) [2–4].
[122] *Michael O'Higgins* (n 14).
[123] *Samsung Electronics v Huawei Technologies* [2016] EWCA Civ 489 [2].
[124] *Canada Trust Co and Others v Stolzenberg and Others (No 2)* [1998] 1 WLR 547, 555.
[125] *Brownlie I* (n 104) [7].
[126] *Epic Games* (n 4) [78b].

is 'the proper place in which to bring the claim'.[127] The claimant has 'the burden of proof [...] to persuade the court that England is the appropriate forum for the trial of the action, [and] that this is clearly so'.[128] The '[a]pplications for permission need not be served on the defendants'[129] which signifies that such an application would be separate from the claim form.[130] The practice of the UK Competition Appeal Tribunal is for applications seeking the Tribunal's permission to serve a claim form out of the jurisdiction to be 'determined on papers'.[131] Thus, a specific procedural feature is that the Tribunal takes a view on whether such an application is to be granted without hearing any submissions by defendants.[132] If a permission were to be granted by the Tribunal, the service must be effected in accordance with the English CPR.[133]

The defendants' rights to a fair trial and hearing will be safeguarded by allowing them to make an application which seeks 'to set aside that decision on the basis that the Tribunal does not have jurisdiction or that such jurisdiction should not be exercised'.[134] As part of this process, the Competition Appeal Tribunal reiterated that 'hearings concerning the issue of appropriate forum should not involve masses of documents, long witness statements, detailed analysis of the issues, and long argument'.[135] If the CAT were to declare that 'the Tribunal has no jurisdiction or will not exercise its jurisdiction may also make further provision as to the disposal or stay of the proceedings'.[136]

Having set out the main requirements for service of a claim form out of the jurisdiction, the specific issues, which need to be considered in private antitrust damages claims, will be set out below.

IV. Reasonable Prospects of Success

As noted above, in order for a claim form to be served out of the jurisdiction, a claimant has to demonstrate that their competition law 'claim against [a] foreign defendant has a reasonable prospect of success'[137] within the meaning of CPR 6.37(1)(b). In *Epic Games v Apple*, the UK CAT held that the claimants must demonstrate that:

> There is a serious issue to be tried on the merits of the claim: i.e. that there is a real as opposed to fanciful prospect of success on the claim. This is the same test as would be applied if the claimant were resisting a summary judgment application by the defendant: *AK Investment CJSC v Kyrgyz Mobile Tel Ltd* [2011] UKPC 7 at [71].[138]

[127] CPR 6.37(3); r 31(3) of the Competition Appeal Tribunal Rules 2015 (SI 2015/1648).
[128] See: *Spiliada Maritime v Cansulex* [1987] AC 460, 481. See also: CPR 6.37(3).
[129] Competition Appeal Tribunal, Guide to Proceedings (2015) [5.44].
[130] Ibid [5.42].
[131] Ibid [5.44]. *Epic Games* (n 4) [2].
[132] Ibid [5.44].
[133] Civil Procedure Rules – Part 6 – Service of Documents.
[134] *Epic Games* (n 4) [3].
[135] *VTB Capital plc v Nutritek International* [2013] UKSC 5 [82] cited in *Epic Games* (n 4) [3]. See also: *Okpabi v Royal Dutch Shell plc* [2021] UKSC 3 at [20].
[136] Rule 31(6) of the Competition Appeal Tribunal Rules 2015 (SI 2015/1648).
[137] Competition Appeal Tribunal Rules 2015 r 31(2)(b).
[138] *Epic Games* (n 4) [78a].

An important deduction, which could be drawn from Mr Justice Roth's judgment, is that the UK CAT follows Lord Collins's approach[139] in aligning the reasonable prospects test for the services out of the jurisdiction with the 'test [...] for summary judgment'.[140] More importantly, this appears to be in line with the test for the required standard of proof which needs to be satisfied for a competition law claim to proceed to trial, which appeared to be set out by the UK Competition Appeal Tribunal as follows:

> The test is whether there is a realistic prospect of the plea succeeding at trial, the same test as that which applies on a summary judgment application. A realistic chance is one that carries some degree of conviction and is more than merely arguable [...]. However, the court must take into account evidence that can reasonably be expected to be available at trial, as well as the evidence before it, and should be wary of deciding difficult or new points of law in the absence of real facts [...].[141]

That said, the test might need to be adjusted in cases where the claimant pleads causation between the competition law infringement and the antitrust damages caused (or likely to be caused) in England and Wales for the purposes of para 3.1(9)(a) of PD 6B. Given the evidential difficulties in competition cases, 'all that [may be] required is a broad brush and theoretical averment, devoid of fact or particularisation about the causative link'.[142] Drawing analogies with the Court of Appeal of England and Wales's judgment in *NTN Corporation v Stellantis NV*,[143] the suggested test should be used for PIL purposes in competition law cases where a claimant seeks to serve a claim form out of the jurisdiction under para 3.1(9)(a) of PD 6B. In particular, such a claimant should be required to demonstrate that:

> (a) that there is a legal and proximate, causal, connection between the [anti-competitive conduct / act and the antitrust damages sustained in the jurisdiction]; and (b), that this connection is '*realistic*' or '*plausible*' (the two phrases being interchangeable) and carries some '*degree of conviction*'; and (c) that the evidence is more than merely '*arguable*'. The assessment will be fact and context specific and, to foreshadow a point I refer to later, may depend upon the characteristics of the industry or sector in question.[144]

This approach is consistent with the one advanced in *Seaconsar*[145] where it was held that 'the standard of proof in respect of the cause of action can broadly be stated to be whether, on the affidavit evidence before the court, there is a serious question to be tried'.[146] The same standard of proof would be equally relevant in cases where

[139] *AK Investment CJSC v Kyrgyz Mobil Tel Limited and Others* [2011] UKPC 7.

[140] Ibid [71].

[141] Case Nos: 1284–1290/5/7/18 (T), *Royal Mail Group Ltd v DAF Trucks Ltd* [2021] CAT 10 [22] – citations omitted. *NTN Corporation v Stellantis N.V.* [2022] EWCA Civ 16 [22]. Compare: *Viskovice Horni v Korner* [1951] AC 869 (HL) 889.

[142] *Stellantis* (n 141) [22]. See also: Section 11.VII below.

[143] Ibid.

[144] Ibid [33].

[145] *Seaconsar* (n 107).

[146] Ibid 452.

injunctive relief is being sought. The point was made in *Adidas v Draper*[147] where the Chancellor of the High Court held:

> In this case it is also, in my judgment, appropriate to have some regard to the strength of the parties' cases. I cannot forecast how the facts will be found at trial. But given the evidence before me I am satisfied that there is a serious issue to be tried based on evidence of substance. If the facts alleged are proved the prospects of success at trial, in addition to all the other matters to which I have referred, in my judgment, justify the grant now of the interlocutory relief sought.[148]

Since a specific feature of competition law claims is that a claimant would have limited evidence *before disclosure* in so far as most of the evidence (concerning pricing and any overcharge) will be with the defendant, the pleadings will be very important for claimants 'to articulate with proper particularity a necessary element of [the] claimant's cause of action'[149] in cross-border competition law cases. Indeed, a specific feature of competition law cases is that claimants' pleadings might draw on foreign regulatory findings and/or court proceedings.[150] As part of this process, the territorial scope of UK competition law would be duly considered.[151]

V. Tortious Gateway

As already noted above,[152] competition law claims for damages which are caused to injured parties would classify as tortious for the PIL purposes. The first major CPR requirement is for the claimant to demonstrate that the competition law 'claim is made in tort'.[153] The tortious gateway sets out the connecting factors:

> A claim is made in tort where –
>
> (a) ***damage*** was sustained, or will be sustained, within the jurisdiction; or
> (b) ***damage*** which has been or will be sustained results from an act committed, or likely to be committed, within the jurisdiction.[154]

It seems to be clear that, in order for the English courts to assume jurisdiction, the judges must be satisfied that either the damage was sustained within the jurisdiction or the damage resulted from an act committed within the jurisdiction. In this context, the court would need to consider 'whether the links between [the infringer/s and/or

[147] *Adidas-Salomon AG v Roger Draper and Derek Paul Howorth sued on behalf of themselves and the members of the Lawn Tennis Association* [2006] EWHC 1318 (Ch).

[148] Ibid [86].

[149] Case Nos: 1329/7/7/19 and 1336/7/7/19, *Michael O'Higgins FX Class Representative Limited v Barclays Bank* [2022] CAT 16 [208].

[150] *Dr Rachael Kent* (n 1) [4]. See more: Chapter 12.

[151] See: Chapter 9.

[152] See: Chapter 3.

[153] Para 3.1(9) – CPR PD 6B.

[154] Ibid – emphases added by the author.

the infringer's conduct] and the English forum are such as to justify [them] being brought'[155] in England and Wales.

Nonetheless, it is now well established that it is not necessary for a claimant to sustain damages, in order for their competition law claim to come within the tortious gateway, provided that the desired remedy is an injunction.[156] Although the aspects concerning any 'overcharge damages'[157] and/or 'lost sales damages'[158] may need to be considered as an important element for damages to have been sustained, the wording of the tortious gateway should allow for an antitrust claim to fall within it in cases where the claimant seeks an injunction that would restrain anti-competitive conduct which will cause damages.[159]

There are two sets of classification issues which need to be considered. First, the 'nature'[160] of the competition law infringement must be clearly outlined in the pleading.[161] For example, the English courts would need to consider whether there is an anti-competitive agreement within the meaning of Chapter I of the 1998 Act (or Article 101 TFEU in cases where it was directly applicable in the UK)[162] between competitors or whether a single undertaking has abused its dominant position within the meaning of Chapter II of the 1998 Act (or Article 102 TFEU, if directly applicable in the UK).[163] These questions are raising regulatory issues which may often be addressed by the UK and/or foreign regulators whose decisions might be relied upon in claimants' pleadings.[164] A claim for competition law damages would classify as tortious irrespective of whether there are incidental regulatory issues (ie including pending regulatory proceeding seeking to establish that there is a competition law infringement)[165] and/or whether there are 'incidental issue[s] of contract'[166] (eg the validity of contract or certain contractual terms that are in conflict with competition law).[167]

Secondly, the relevant 'elements'[168] of the pleaded tort, which causes antitrust damages to the claimant, should be set out. The 'necessary elements'[169] of private antitrust damages claims were set out by the UK CAT in *Michael O'Higgins FX Class Representative Ltd v Barclays Bank*[170] as follows: '*(i)* an infringement of competition law must be shown, which *(ii)* has resulted in actionable harm or damage suffered by the

[155] *Metall und Rohstoff* (n 62) 437.
[156] *Epic Games* (n 4) [117]. See more: below.
[157] Case No: 1241/5/7/15 (T), *Sainsbury's Supermarkets v MasterCard* [2016] CAT 11 [13.4-5].
[158] Ibid [13.4 and 13.6].
[159] *Epic Games* (n 4) [117].
[160] *Metall und Rohstoff* (n 62) 444, 469, 471, 472.
[161] Ibid 471 and 472.
[162] *ValueLicensing* (n 15) [46].
[163] Ibid.
[164] *Qualcomm* (n 14) [18–25].
[165] *Dr Rachael Kent* (n 1) [4 and 5].
[166] P Kaye, *Civil Jurisdiction and Enforcement of Foreign Judgments* (Oxford, Professional Books, 1987) 570. See also: *Matthews v Kuwait Bechtel Corporation* [1959] 2 QB 57 (CA); *Coupland v Arabian Gulf Oil* [1983] 1 WLR 1136 (CA); *Base Metal Trading v Shamurin* [2003] EWHC 2419 (Comm); [2004] ILPr 5; a'ffd *Base Metal Trading v Shamurin* [2004] EWCA Civ 1316 (CA).
[167] *Dr Liza Lovdahl Gormsen* (n 1) [12a and 12a]; Case C-59/19 *Wikingerhof GmbH & Co KG v Booking.com BV* EU:C:2020:950.
[168] *Metall und Rohstoff* (n 62) 402, 444, 472 and 473.
[169] *Michael O'Higgins FX Class Representative* (n 149) [172].
[170] Ibid.

claimant or class, [...] *(iii)* caused by that infringement'.[171] This means that the English courts would need to consider how the anti-competitive conduct of the defendant (be it through price-fixing arrangements; or be it through an abuse of a dominant position as classified above) has affected the prices of the products which the claimant was purchasing and/or the services they were using.[172]

The above aspects are important because '[d]amages (actual or apprehended) are [...] a necessary element of the cause of action'.[173] Since it is well settled that 'in order to recover damages for the infringement, it is necessary for the claimant to show [...] that it has suffered actionable harm or damage caused by the infringement',[174] damages would be a necessary element for a competition law claim to classify as tortious. On that basis, the English courts should determine whether there is a sufficient connection between the anticompetitive conduct of the infringer (eg, defendant) and England.

Hence, an important consideration is whether the English courts should advance a wider approach to the interpretation of the relevant connecting factors in cases where antitrust damages were sustained in different jurisdictions or the anti-competitive act which restricts competition law was committed in multiple jurisdictions.[175] The issue needs renewed attention, post-Brexit, because the wording of paragraph 3.1(9) was modified 'in 1987 to ensure that English law is consistent with [...] the Brussels [Ia/Lugano regime]'.[176] It should be noted that the tortious ground for the allocation of jurisdiction in cases where the defendant is domiciled within the EU is to be found in Article 7(2) of Brussels Ia. A private antitrust damages claim would fall within the ambit of Article 7(2) of Brussels Ia which states that:

> A person domiciled in a Member State may be sued in another Member State [...] in matters relating to tort, delict or quasi-delict, in the courts for the place where the harmful event occurred or may occur.

The latter provision is indeed identical to Section 2(c) of Sch 8 of the 1982 Act which states that 'a person may also be sued [...] in matters relating to delict or quasi-delict, in the courts for the place where the harmful event occurred or may occur' and which is to apply, if 'the proceedings are to be treated as taking place in Scotland'.[177]

The provision should be purposively interpreted in the light of the Brussels Ia recitals which set out the relevant policy objectives.[178] The expression 'matters relating to tort' 'covers all actions which seek to establish the liability of a defendant and which are not related to a "contract" within the meaning of [Article 7(1) of Brussels Ia]'.[179] Although the 'place where the harmful event occurred'[180] appears to be a different connecting

[171] Ibid [169] citing *BritNed Development Ltd v ABB AB* [2018] EWHC 2616 (Ch) [10] aff'd *BritNed Development Ltd v ABB AB* [2019] EWCA Civ 1840.

[172] *AB Volvo v Ryder Ltd* [2020] EWCA Civ 1475 [83]; *Stellantis* (n 141).

[173] *Unlockd* (n 4) [40].

[174] Case No: 1298/5/7/18, *Achilles Information Ltd v Network Rail Infrastructure Ltd* [2022] CAT 9 [5.1].

[175] Compare: *Cooper Tire* – EWHC (n 57).

[176] *ABCI v Banque Franco-Tunisienne* [2003] EWCA Civ 205 [42].

[177] UK Competition Appeal Tribunal Rules 2015 r 31(2)(c).

[178] Case C-189/87 *Athanasios Kalfelis v Bankhaus Schröder* EU:C:1988:459; Case C-51/97 *Réunion Européenne v Spliethoff's Bevrachtingskantoor* EU:C:1998:509.

[179] *Kalfelis* (n 178) [17].

[180] Case C-21/76 *Handelskwekerij GJ Bier BV v Mines de potasse d'Alsace SA* EU:C:1976:166 [19].

factor in comparison to those specified in para 3.1(9) of PD 6B, the CJEU has broadly interpreted Article 7(2) to encompass two separate connecting factors: 'the place where the damage occurred'[181] and 'the place of the event giving rise to it'.[182]

The CJEU's interpretation was set to ensure that 'the place where the damage occurred'[183] could be used as an alternative connecting factor which may enable the claimant to issue proceedings in a jurisdiction that is different from the one where the defendant is domiciled. It is not only that, in some cases, there might be an overlap between 'the place of event giving rise to the damage'[184] and the place of the defendant's domicile,[185] but also 'the place where the damage occurred'[186] would normally ensure that there is a sufficient connection between the claim and the court.[187]

The same approach appears to be followed in cross-border competition cases. In *Cartel Damage Claims (CDC) Hydrogen Peroxide v Akzo Nobel*,[188] the CJEU clearly stated that the two connecting factors should provide the claimant with a choice in deciding to issue proceedings against the defendant 'in the courts for either of those places'.[189] Therefore, both connecting factors (ie the place of the event giving rise to damages; the place where the damage occurred) should provide a sufficient level of proximity, which would be central to 'the efficacious conduct of proceedings'[190] and ease of taking evidence.[191] How should the relevant connecting factors, which are set out in para 3.1(9) of PD 6B, be interpreted by the English court? Should the Brussels Ia approach be followed? Or should the English court rather advance a new approach to interpretation and assumption of jurisdiction in so far as there is an increasingly compelling view that 'the Brussels I Regulation […] is not fully geared towards […] "private enforcement"'?[192]

A. 'Damage was Sustained, or will be Sustained, within the Jurisdiction'[193]

As already noted above, in order for an English court to assume jurisdiction in cross-border competition law claims, the claimant would need to demonstrate that there

[181] Ibid.
[182] Ibid.
[183] Ibid [19].
[184] ibid [21].
[185] Ibid.
[186] Ibid.
[187] Case C-68/93 *Shevill and Others v Presse Alliance* EU:C:1995:61 [23] and [33]. See also Recital 16 of Brussels Ia; *Cheshire, North & Fawcett* (n 45) 270–2. Compare: Case C-68/93 *Shevill and Others v Presse Alliance* EU:C:1994:303, 425–26 (AG Darmon).
[188] Case C-352/13 *Cartel Damage Claims (CDC) Hydrogen Peroxide SA v Akzo Nobel NV* EU:C:2015:335.
[189] Ibid [38].
[190] *Bier* (n 180) [11].
[191] Ibid [17]; Case C-220/88 *Dumez France and Others v Hessische Landesbank and Others* EU:C:1990:8 [17]; *Shevill* (n 187) [19]; Case C-364/93 *Antonio Marinari v Lloyds Bank plc and Zubaidi Trading Company* EU:C:1995:289 [10]; Case C-167/00 *Verein für Konsumenteninformation v Karl Heinz Henkel* EU:C:2002:555 [46].
[192] See: the Opinion of Advocate General Jääskinen in Case C-352/13 *Cartel Damage Claims (CDC) Hydrogen Peroxide SA v Evonik Degussa GmbH* EU:C:2014:2443 [8].
[193] Para 3.1(9)(a) PD 6B.

is a good arguable case that antitrust damage, which is caused by a competition law infringement, is sustained in England and Wales.[194] There are two big sets of questions concerning the interpretation of this connecting factor which would have implications for the value of a private antitrust damage which is issued before the English courts: how is damage to be defined for a competition law claim to come within the tortious gateway, considering the required standard of proof and the interlocutory stage of the proceedings?[195] What will be the territorial scope of the court's jurisdiction, if antitrust damages were to be sustained in multiple jurisdictions?

In many private competition law claims, the claimants would normally seek to recover antitrust damages which in turn means that the desired legal remedies would be financial/monetary.[196] Since the English court would naturally consider 'the nature of the acts by which the damage is done'[197] when assessing damages in competition law claims, it makes sense for the judges to consider the relevant anti-competitive conduct with a view to ascertaining whether any damage was sustained in the jurisdiction. In other words, ascertaining whether any damage was sustained in England and Wales presupposes the courts will classify the relevant restriction of competition (eg fixing prices; sharing markets; tying two products together) which may (or may not) be pre-established by a regulator. The deduction could be strengthened by the CJEU judgment in *flyLAL-Lithunian Airlines*[198] where it was held that:

> [T]he alleged anticompetitive conduct of the defendants in the main proceedings related to the market for flights to and from Vilnius Airport and, according to flyLAL, resulted in distortion of competition in that market. In addition, that conduct allegedly caused damage to flyLAL.
>
> In the present case, which concerns losses incurred by an airline on flights operated to and from the capital of the Member State where that company is established, the main market affected must be considered to be that of the Member State in which that company conducts the main part of its sales activities relating to such flights, namely the Lithuanian market.[199]

That said, in order to ascertain the place where the antitrust damage was sustained *in some cases*, the issues concerning any overcharge which may have been paid by the claimants may be considered along with *the issues in relation to pass-on*. A specific feature in many competition law claims, which are issued by large purchasers, is that the defendant would have a defence that claimants incurred no loss because the overcharge was passed onto its customers which in turn might mean that no damage was

[194] *Apple Retail UK Ltd v Qualcomm (UK) Ltd* [2018] EWHC 1188 (Pat) [93].

[195] See above.

[196] C Withers, 'Jurisdiction and applicable law in antitrust tort claims' (2002) *Journal of Business Law* 250, 255; A Komninos, *EC Private Antitrust Enforcement: Decentralised Application of EC Competition Law by National Courts* (Oxford, Hart Publishing, 2008) 210–11. See more: KM Stanton, 'New forms of the tort of breach of statutory duty' (2004) 120 *LQR* 324, 332, 333 and 334. See also: Oxera and multi-jurisdictional team of lawyers led by Dr A Komninos, *Quantifying antitrust damages: towards non-binding guidance for courts – Study prepared for the European Commission* http://ec.europa.eu/competition/antitrust/actionsdamages/quantification_study.pdf.

[197] *Achilles* (n 174) [5.4].

[198] Case C-27/17 *AB 'flyLAL-Lithunian Airlines' v Starptautiskā lidosta 'Rīga' VAS and 'Air Baltic Corporation' AS* EU:C:2018:533.

[199] Ibid 38–39.

sustained in the jurisdiction. The point was put forward by Mr Justice Morgan in *Apple v Qualcomm* where the judge noted that:

> This is a case of an alleged overcharge being made by the Second Defendant. The first person who might suffer a loss as the result of there being an overcharge is the person who pays the overcharge on buying the relevant goods. That person's loss would seem to be the amount of the overcharge, absent any other considerations. If the first person to pay the overcharge sells the goods on and passes on the overcharge to his buyer then absent any other considerations, the first person does not suffer a loss by paying the overcharge but might conceivably suffer a loss if selling the goods at a price, which includes the overcharge, results in lost sales.[200]

This poses the question how 'damage' should be defined for the purposes of para 3.1(9) of PD 6B. Should it be narrowly defined to cover only the 'direct damage'[201] which would normally be the 'immediate consequence of [a competition law] infringement'[202] in line with the EU approach? Or should it be broadly defined, moving away from the EU approach, with a view to determining whether the antitrust damage is sustained in the jurisdiction?[203]

i. EU Approach: A Narrow Definition of Damage and Narrow Scope of Jurisdiction of the Court at 'the Place where the Damage Occurred'[204]

The practice within the Brussels Ia regime appears to suggest that the limited scope of the adjudicatory jurisdiction is linked with the fact that the connecting factor – 'the place where the damage occurred'[205] – is narrowly interpreted to allocate jurisdiction to the courts where the *direct damage* occurred. The *Dumez* case[206] concerned the location of damages suffered by a multinational group of companies. The CJEU had to determine whether the parent company could rely on Article 7(2) of Brussels Ia to issue proceedings in France, as being the place where the damage occurred, provided that the initial damage was rather suffered by its subsidiary in Germany.[207] The CJEU held the place where the damage occurred is to be narrowly interpreted as being the 'place where the event giving rise to the damage, and entailing tortious, delictual or quasi-delictual liability, directly produced its harmful effects upon the person who is the immediate victim'.[208] The narrow interpretation was reiterated in *Marinari*,[209] where the CJEU held that Article 7(2) of Brussels Ia cannot be 'construed so extensively as to encompass any place where the adverse consequences can be felt of an event which has already caused damage actually arising elsewhere'.[210]

[200] *Apple Retail* (n 194) [95].
[201] Case C-451/18 *Tibor-Trans Fuvarozó és Kereskedelmi Kft. v DAF Trucks NV* EU:C:2019:635 [31].
[202] Ibid [31].
[203] Para 3.1(9)(b) PD 6B.
[204] *Bier* (n 180) [21].
[205] Ibid [19].
[206] *Dumez* (n 191).
[207] Ibid [4].
[208] Ibid [20].
[209] See: *Marinari* (n 191) [14]–[15].
[210] Ibid [14].

Jurisdiction issues[211] may arise in cross-border competition law cases because the courts may be expected to localise the infringer's anticompetitive conduct (ie the injured party's damage could be sustained in multiple jurisdictions). The first step in the process of allocation of jurisdiction would be for the judges to classify the conduct which distorts competition as being, for example, the conclusion of certain 'cartel agreements'[212] which are in conflict with competition law. As part of this process, 'the place of the conclusion of the cartel'[213] could be ascertained as an important connecting factor in some cases. Likewise, if the 'loss consisting in additional costs incurred because of artificially high prices'[214] were to constitute the 'direct damage'[215] for PIL purposes, then classifying the relevant anti-competitive conduct would be important for the courts to ascertain the place where the damage occurred in certain cases. The points were implicitly made by the CJEU in the *Tibor-Trans* case where it was stated that:

> the damage alleged by Tibor-Trans consists of additional costs incurred because of artificially high prices applied to trucks following collusive arrangements constituting a single and continuous infringement of Article 101 TFEU which had been effective throughout the EEA between 17 January 1997 and 18 January 2011 and in which fifteen international truck manufacturers, including DAF Trucks, had participated. [... T]he damage alleged in the case in the main proceedings results essentially from the additional costs incurred because of artificially high prices and, therefore, appears to be the immediate consequence of an infringement pursuant to Article 101 TFEU and thus constitutes direct damage which, in principle, provides a basis for the jurisdiction of the courts of the Member State in which it occurred.[216]

Hence, the relevant anti-competitive conduct and its 'immediate consequence[s]'[217] should be ascertained for jurisdictional purposes. More specifically, the CJEU went on to state that the Member State 'where the market [is] affected by the anticompetitive conduct [...] must be regarded as the place where the damage occurred'.[218] The CJEU appears to clearly indicate that the relevant restriction of competition is the cartel agreement that appears to have an effect on the prices which would have been artificially inflated in the jurisdictions where the market was affected.[219] On that basis, it appears to be clear that the direct damage occurs at the place where the injured party purchases the goods (ie paying the overcharge).[220]

The problem is that the *narrow definition of damage* along with the *limited scope of the relevant court jurisdiction* would make 'the place where the damage occurred'[221] a less appropriate connecting factor than desirable in cases where the claimant purchased

[211] See: Withers (n 196) 250; See also: BJ Rodger, 'Competition law in a Scottish forum' (2003) *Juridical Review* 247.
[212] *Cartel Damage Claims* (n 188) [12].
[213] Ibid [44].
[214] Ibid [52].
[215] *Tibor-Trans* (n 201) [31].
[216] Ibid [30–31].
[217] Ibid [31].
[218] Ibid [33].
[219] Ibid [37].
[220] *Apple Retail* (n 194) [98]; Case C-30/20 *RH v AB Volvo* EU:C:2021:604 [42].
[221] *Bier* (n 180) [19].

the cartelised product from multiple locations. The problems were exposed in *RH v AB Volvo*[222] where the court dealt with some issues concerning international and territorial jurisdiction by holding that:

> In the case of purchases made in several places, to confer jurisdiction on the courts for the place where the undertaking harmed has its registered office is consistent with the requirement of predictability referred to in paragraph 38 above, since the defendants, members of the cartel, cannot be unaware of the fact that the purchasers of the goods in question are established within the market affected by the collusive practices. In addition, that conferral of jurisdiction is consistent with the objective of proximity, and the place of the registered office of the undertaking harmed fully guarantees the efficacious conduct of potential proceedings [...].
>
> [...] Article 7(2) of Regulation No 1215/2012 must be interpreted as meaning that, within the market affected by collusive arrangements on the fixing and increase in the prices of goods, either the court within whose jurisdiction the undertaking claiming to be harmed purchased the goods affected by those arrangements or, in the case of purchases made by that undertaking in several places, the court within whose jurisdiction that *undertaking's registered office* is situated, has *international and territorial jurisdiction*, in terms of the place where the damage occurred, over an action for compensation for the damage caused by those arrangements contrary to Article 101 TFEU.[223]

There are two problems with this ruling. First, it is difficult to see how a *direct damage* – which would be caused to an individual claimant – would be 'identifiable [...] at that victim's registered office'[224] in cases where the cartelised product was purchased in one EU Member State and the purchaser's registered office was based in another EU Member State. Nonetheless, it should be noted that, in *RH v AB Volvo*, all the transactions concerning the sale of trucks at an inflated price occurred in a single EU Member States,[225] so that ruling might simply be relevant in such cases. Would the same principles and connecting factors apply if damages were to be suffered in several Member States (rather than a single Member State)?

Secondly, it is welcome to see that the CJEU appears to be setting out the place of the 'undertaking's registered office'[226] as a new connecting factor in cases where the antitrust damage occurred in several places. Is the concept of the undertaking for these purposes broad enough to cover a multinational group of companies that has been engaged in transnational economic activities by setting up subsidiaries and suffering loss in different jurisdictions? If yes, where is the registered office of an undertaking which consists of multiple wholly-owned subsidiaries? These are open questions which need to be addressed by the CJEU in due course, which raises the level of uncertainty, indicating that Article 7(2) Brussels Ia (and Section 2(c) of Sch 8 of the 1982 Act) may not be effectively allocating jurisdiction in competition law claims which arise out of transnational competition law infringements.

[222] *AB Volvo* (n 220).
[223] Ibid [41 and 42].
[224] Ibid [41].
[225] Ibid.
[226] Ibid [42].

A major problem, which the CJEU appeared inter alia to try to address by introducing the 'undertaking's registered office'[227] as a new connecting factor in multiple locality cases, is the limited territorial jurisdiction at the court where the damage occurred. The point was clearly made by the English High Court in *SanDisk v Koninklijke Philips Electronics*[228] where Mr Justice Pumfrey observed that the scope of the territorial jurisdiction at the courts where the damage occurred would be limited to the damages sustained in the jurisdiction, submitting that '[t]he jurisdiction based upon the place of the harmful event will be international, while the jurisdiction based upon the relevant harm will be restricted to England and Wales'.[229] In other words, the Member State's court at the place where the damage occurred will have jurisdiction to award compensatory damages only in respect of the claimant's loss which is incurred in the jurisdiction in question.[230] This would be a major limitation in competition law claims issued by large purchasers of a cartelised product as they are likely to have purchased the product in several Member States. The legal implications for such claimants were set out by Mr Justice Teare in *Cooper Tire*:

> I consider that the Claimants can only rely on the place where the damage occurred. It is common ground that some damage occurred in England because some [Butadiene Rubber] and [Emulsion Styrene Butadiene Rubber] was sold here. However, *it is also common ground that if jurisdiction is established on that basis it is only established in respect of the damage which occurred in England. That is, I understand, a very small part of the whole.*[231]

The fact that, under Brussels Ia, 'a court having jurisdiction [on that basis] *only* has jurisdiction in respect of damage, if any, actually suffered in that territory'[232] meant that the claimants that are groups of companies would rather try to establish jurisdiction by relying on alternative bases of jurisdiction under Brussels Ia.[233] Indeed, as already noted above, an added layer of complexity, which is linked to the narrow definition of *the damage* for the purposes of Brussels Ia, is that such claimants would normally need to deal with the pass-on arguments in competition law claims. The issues with a narrow definition of damage, which covers only *direct damage*, were set out by the UK CAT in *Deutsche Bahn AG & Others v Morgan Crucible Company*.[234] In this case, it was noted that there are particularly difficult issues which would need to be dealt with at an interlocutory stage in competition law cases, where the direct and indirect purchasers are based in different jurisdictions. The CAT held that:

> We consider that it is extremely debatable whether this is truly a case where the UK Claimants are seeking to recover for the indirect consequences of harm initially suffered by others. The nature of passing on is that loss is <u>either</u> suffered by the direct purchaser from the Cartel <u>or</u>

[227] Ibid [42].
[228] *SanDisk v Koninklijke Philips Electronics* [2007] EWHC 332 (Ch).
[229] Ibid [25]. See also: *Shevill* (n 187).
[230] J Basedow, 'Jurisdiction and choice of law in the private enforcement of EC competition law' in J Basedow (ed), *Private Enforcement of EC Competition Law* (The Hague, Kluwer Law International, 2007) 229, 234.
[231] *Cooper Tire* – EWHC (n 57) [65] – emphasis added by the author.
[232] Case No: 1173/5/7/10, *Deutsche Bahn AG & Others v Morgan Crucible Company PLC & Others* [2013] CAT 18 [29].
[233] Ibid [46].
[234] *Deutsche Bahn* (n 232).

> it is suffered by the indirect purchaser. The same damage is not suffered by both. Of course, there may be a partial passing on by the direct purchaser, in which case some damage will be sustained by the direct purchaser and some by the indirect purchaser. But these losses will, nevertheless, be distinct. [...]
>
> We are also wary of regarding this as a case of 'indirect' loss within the *Dumez* principle. In a case where the direct purchasers and the indirect purchasers were situated in different jurisdictions, we can see that extremely difficult questions might arise.[235]

The implications of the narrow interpretation are significant because, even though the national court at 'the place where the damage occurred'[236] may well be competent, it will only have jurisdiction to award compensatory damages with regard to the local harm[237] caused by an international cartel. Hence, the narrow definition of direct damage along with the limited scope of the jurisdiction strongly suggested that Article 7(2) of Brussels Ia was not suited to allocate jurisdiction in cross-border competition law cases arising out of transnational infringements. Nonetheless, the limited territorial scope of jurisdiction of the court at the place where the antitrust damage occurred was confirmed by the CJEU in *CDC*,[238] ruling that:

> the jurisdiction of the court seised of the matter by virtue of the place where the loss occurred is limited to the loss suffered by the undertaking whose registered office is located in its jurisdiction, an applicant such as CDC, who has consolidated several undertakings' potential claims for damages, would therefore (...) need to bring separate actions for the loss suffered by each of those undertakings before the courts with jurisdiction for their respective registered offices.[239]

Thus, a major question is: could the foregoing problems be addressed by the English courts by advancing a broad definition of damage for the purposes of para 3.1(9) of PD 6B as well as by broadening the territorial scope of the jurisdiction in cases where damage was sustained in England and Wales as well as in other jurisdictions?

ii. Damage Sustained in England – The Broader the Definition of Damage, the Broader the Territorial Scope of Jurisdiction

It is important to bear in mind that 'the interpretation of a connecting factor [...] will, by an English court, always be answered in accordance with English law'.[240] The latter point could be strengthened by the judgment of the UK Supreme Court in *Brownlie I*[241] which inter alia addressed the question as to how the relevant connecting factors should be interpreted, following the UK withdrawal from the EU. In particular, Lord Sumption questioned whether 'Rome II has any bearing on the construction of the jurisdictional

[235] Ibid [44.3.ii and iii] – emphases in the original.
[236] *Bier* (n 180) [19].
[237] *SanDisk* (n 228) [25]. See also: *Shevill* (n 187).
[238] *Cartel Damage Claims* (n 188) [55].
[239] Ibid [55]. See also *Cooper Tire* – EWHC (n 57) [65].
[240] L Collins (ed), *Dicey and Morris on the Conflict of Laws* 11th edn (London, Sweet & Maxwell, 1987) 1382–1383 cited in *Metall und Rohstoff* (n 62) 441. *Dicey, Morris and Collins* (n 12) [11–181].
[241] *Brownlie I* (n 104) [60].

gateways in the Practice Direction',[242] strongly suggesting that English law should rather apply in this context.

There is a very strong case that the tortious gateway which is set out in PD 6B should be more broadly interpreted than the Brussels I rules in so far as 'the natural construction of [the English] rules indicates a wider gateway to service out of the jurisdiction'.[243] There are two major reasons for the English courts to advance a broader definition of damages for CPR purposes. First, drawing certain analogies with the judgments of Mr Teare KC in *Margaret Booth v Peter Phillips*[244] and Mr Justice Haddon-Cave in *Michael Wink v Croatio Osiguranje DD*,[245] the wording of the two sets of provisions is different.[246] Whilst Article 7(2) uses the words 'the harmful event' which is interpreted to cover 'the place where *the damage* occurred',[247] para 3.1(9) of PD 6B is broader by using the word 'damage', which signifies that 'some damage (not all of the damage) [needs to be] sustained within the jurisdiction'.[248]

Secondly and more importantly, it is well established that, under the English CPR, the aspects concerning procedural[249] and evidential matters,[250] which are more closely linked with the 'practicalities of litigation',[251] are being more systematically considered as part of the broader *forum conveniens* discretionary powers.[252] Indeed, it has been submitted that '[t]he case law of the Court of Justice ("CJEU") on [Article 7(2) of Brussels Ia] is not relevant to the construction of Ground 9(a) because the two schemes are fundamentally different in structure and policy'.[253] The latter point was echoed by Lady Hale, making the following observations:

> It is also necessary to bear in mind the difference between the two schemes. The European scheme deliberately eschews any discretion in favour of clear and certain rules, in the context of a scheme which governs, not only jurisdiction, but also recognition and enforcement of the resulting judgments. No doubt that is why the Court of Justice was anxious to restrict the scope of the *Bier* decision by drawing the direct/indirect distinction. That is not a feature of the English scheme, which retains the 'valuable safety valve' of discretion, a discretion which need not be limited to the *Spiliada* principles, but can concentrate on the real question, which is 'the proper place for the resolution of the dispute' (as Professor Briggs puts it).[254]

With this in mind, there are indeed compelling reasons for the English courts to advance a different approach to the interpretation of 'damage'[255] which, according to Lord Lloyd-Jones, reflects the fundamentally different objectives which are pursued by the Brussels Ia and the English CPR.[256]

[242] Ibid [22].
[243] Ibid [61].
[244] *Margaret Booth v Peter Phillips* [2004] EWHC 1437 (Admlty).
[245] *Michael Wink v Croatio Osiguranje DD* [2013] EWHC 1118 (QB).
[246] *Brownlie I* (n 104) [50].
[247] *Bier* (n 180) [19].
[248] *Margaret Booth* (n 244) [36]. See also: *Michael Wink* (n 245) [27]. *Brownlie I* (n 104) [50].
[249] *Bier* (n 180) [11].
[250] *Bier* (n 180) [17]; *Dumez* (n 191) [17]; *Shevill* (n 187) [19]; *Marinari* (n 191) [10]; *Henkel* (n 191) [46].
[251] *Brownlie I* (n 104) [31] (Lord Sumption).
[252] *Brownlie I* (n 104) [66] (Lord Wilson).
[253] *Michael Wink* (n 245) [41]. See also: *Brownlie I* (n 104) [44].
[254] *Brownlie I* (n 104) [51].
[255] *Lady Brownlie* (n 10) [48–51].
[256] Ibid [55].

On the one hand, the Brussels Ia jurisdictional rules form part of a wider regime for judicial cooperation which is set to facilitate the free circulation of judgments across the EU. This presupposes for any special jurisdiction rules – which allocate jurisdiction to a national court that is different from the one where the defendant is domiciled – to be narrowly interpreted. The rationale is for the EU jurisdictional rules to provide for legal certainty, whilst limiting the national judges' discretionary powers.[257] In this context, the 'notion of direct damage'[258] has a very important role to play with a view to ensuring that a 'particular kind of loss sustained has sufficient connection'[259] with the court which has adjudicatory jurisdiction, so that it can be regarded as sufficiently appropriate to hear and determine the claim/s.

On the other hand, the notion of *damage* which is set out in para 3.1(9) of PD 6B is only set to ensure that there is a sufficient territorial connection, 'link[ing] the wrongdoing with a particular jurisdiction'.[260] Indeed, a major distinctive feature of the English jurisdictional rules is that the enquiry whether England and Wales is 'the appropriate jurisdiction is not performed simply by the breadth of the gateway but in addition by the forum non conveniens discretion'[261] which does not exist under Brussels Ia.

Hence, a different approach may be necessary to reflect the distinction between the EU PIL rules and the English jurisdictional rules as well as to provide a broad definition of damage which is necessary for the English courts where there is a sufficient territorial connection with the pleaded tortious act and England and Wales. Lord Lloyd-Jones took the view that there is no compelling reason for damage within the meaning of para 3.1(9) of PD 6B to be limited to direct damage by holding:

> In my view, therefore, there is no reason to read 'damage' in paragraph 3.1(9)(a) as limited to the damage which violates the claimant's right and which completes the cause of action. On the contrary, the word in its ordinary and natural meaning and when considered in the light of the purpose of the provision extends to the physical and financial damage caused by the wrongdoing, considerations which are apt to link a tort to the jurisdiction where such damage is suffered. Moreover, this reading is supported by the omission of the definite article in the current article of the rule, an amendment which was intended to reflect the decision in *Metall und Rohstoff* that it is sufficient that some significant damage has been sustained in the jurisdiction.
>
> [...]
>
> For the reasons set out above, I consider that there is no sound reason to limit 'damage' in gateway 9(a) to damage which completes a cause of action. Furthermore, I can see no reason to apply within English domestic rules the distinction between direct and indirect damage which has now developed in the Brussels system. To my mind, the word 'damage' in paragraph 3.1(9)(a) of Practice Direction 6B simply refers to actionable harm, direct or indirect, caused by the wrongful act alleged. This reading reflects the ordinary and natural meaning of the word and is in accordance with the purpose of the provision and with principle. There is no need to limit its scope to direct as opposed to indirect damage, a distinction which in any event I consider

[257] Ibid.
[258] Ibid.
[259] Ibid.
[260] Ibid [51].
[261] Ibid [55].

> obscure and likely to give rise to difficulty in its application. Furthermore, the Court of Appeal in *Metall und Rohstoff* was clearly correct in holding that a claimant may suffer damage within the meaning of the domestic tort gateway in more than one place.[262]

The advanced broad definition of *damage* may have major implications for competition law damages claims. A particular feature of cross-border competition law claims is that they may involve transnational groups of companies not only as defendants (ie infringing undertakings), but also as claimants. The point can be illustrated by making reference to the High Court of England and Wales's judgment in *Apple v Qualcomm*.[263] In this case, the claimants, who were five companies from the Apple group of companies, issued, inter alia, a competition law claim. The claimants sought a declaration that two defendants from the Qualcomm group abused their dominant position[264] by charging excessive royalties[265] as well as damages for the overcharge[266] they paid and loss of sales.[267] There are difficult issues as to where the various direct and indirect damages may have been suffered as well as whether any damage has been sustained in the jurisdiction, if the claimant has passed on the overcharge down the chain of distribution. Mr Justice Morgan submitted that:

> If a claimant puts forward the case that it has suffered a loss by buying in this jurisdiction and paying an overcharge, then it will be open to a defendant to say that that claimant did not suffer that loss because it passed on the overcharge. The burden of showing that the overcharge has been passed on is on the defendant and that will have to be reflected when the court considers whether there is a plausible, albeit contested, basis for the allegation that the claimant has suffered loss within the jurisdiction.
>
> As to where any such losses might be made, if the loss is paying an overcharge when buying the goods, the loss would seem to be made where the goods are bought. If the loss comes from reduced sales then the loss would seem to be in the market where the seller suffers the loss of sales.[268]

Therefore, a broad definition of damage to include both direct and indirect damages which may be sustained in the jurisdiction should provide for a sufficient connection between the infringement and England as a place where significant damage occurred.

The latter point could be strengthened further by looking at the competition law claims which was issued by Epic Games against Apple.[269] Epic Games develops software products and apps. In order for their products to run on any Apple device, Epic Games needs access to iOS. The parties entered into a 'Developer Program License Agreement (DPLA)' through which Epic Games obtained an Apple Developer account.[270] Epic Games alleged that Apple abused its dominant position 'by terminating Epic 84 Apple

[262] Ibid [51 & 81].
[263] *Apple Retail* (n 194).
[264] Ibid [16].
[265] Para 129 of the Draft Amended Particulars of the Claim cited in *Apple Retail* (n 194) [105].
[266] Ibid.
[267] Ibid.
[268] *Apple Retail* (n 194) [98–99].
[269] *Epic Games* (n 4).
[270] Ibid [36].

Developer Account and/or threatening to terminate all of Epic's access to Apple software'[271] as well as by charging excessive prices. There was, inter alia, a claim which was issued by Epic Games in relation to its 'Unreal Engine' which was special software 'create[ing] realistic 3D-content'.[272] In considering whether damages were sustained in England and Wales for the purposes of an application to serve the claim form out of the jurisdiction, Mr Justice Roth held that:

> A large part of the work on the Unreal Engine is carried out by [Epic Games UK Ltd ('E3')] in England. Accordingly, the alleged threat to cease supplying access to iOS software necessary for the development of Unreal Engine undoubtedly would cause significant damage to E3 in England. That software is supplied under the DPLA with [Apple Inc ('A1')] held by [Epic Games International S.à.r.l. ('E2')]. But as Unreal Engine is also developed by [Epic Games Inc ('E1')], the damage to development work by E3 would harm E1's product which, as I understand it, E1 supplies to app developers in the UK. If indirect damage is sufficient for gateway 9(a), then it seems E3 would suffer damage in England and E1 would suffer damage to its product in England. I think they have a good argument that this constitutes significant damage in England.[273]

The foregoing examples demonstrate how a broad interpretation of damage may enable the English courts to address some of the weaknesses of the Brussels Ia regime with a view to more systematically determining the requirements for territorial connection and proximity between the private antitrust damages claim and England. The UK Supreme Court decision to adopt a broad definition of 'damage' for the purposes of para 3.1(9) of PD 6B should allow the English courts to establish that there is sufficient territorial connection between the competition law infringement and England in cases were 'some significant damage has been sustained in England'.[274] The advantages for the English courts to advance this were reflected in the reasoned order of Mr Justice Roth in *Consumers' Association v Qualcomm*,[275] where the President of the UK CAT held that:

> On the basis that *indirect damage is sufficient for the tort gateway under PD6B paragraph 3.1(9)*, I am also satisfied that there is an arguable case that the alleged losses suffered by the proposed class members were sustained or will be sustained within the UK. The claimants comprising the class on whose behalf the Proposed Class Representative seeks to bring these proceedings are final consumers who have made purchases (other than second-hand purchases) of LTE-enabled Apple and Samsung smartphones in the UK.[276]

The advanced approach should enable the English courts to 'swiftly and efficiently [determine their jurisdiction] at the outset of proceedings, and such determinations [w]ould, so far as possible, avoid pre-judging the substantive issues [in relation to pass-on] that will arise at trial'.[277] It is to be anticipated for the English courts to confirm that, if 'some significant [antitrust] damage has been sustained in England',[278] they would

[271] Para 122c of the Claim Form cited in *Epic Games* (n 4) [49].
[272] *Epic Games* (n 4) [23].
[273] Ibid [126].
[274] *Metall und Rohstoff* (n 62) 437. *Lady Brownlie* (n 10) [51].
[275] *Qualcomm* (n 1).
[276] Ibid [5].
[277] *Deutsche Bahn* (n 232) [44.3.i].
[278] *Metall und Rohstoff* (n 62) 437. *Lady Brownlie* (n 10) [51].

also have jurisdiction to award compensatory damages in relation to the loss which the claimants have sustained in other jurisdictions. More importantly, the judgment of the UK CAT in *Epic Games* further demonstrates that, even after a competition law had passed through the jurisdictional gateway, the English courts could still refuse to exercise their jurisdiction on *forum conveniens* grounds.[279]

B. 'Act Committed, or Likely to be Committed, within the Jurisdiction'[280]

The claimant would also be able to demonstrate that there is a territorial connection between the competition law infringement and England if they were to demonstrate that '[d]amage which has been or will be sustained results from an act committed, or likely to be committed, within the jurisdiction'.[281] In other words, a claimant would need to demonstrate that a competition law infringement was committed in England and Wales. As part of this process, the following two aspects must be considered:

> First, in deciding whether an alleged tort has been committed in this country or in some other country, our courts will look back over the series of events constituting it and ask themselves 'Where in substance did this cause of action arise?' Secondly, in answering this question, the courts will apply exclusively English law.[282]

If the relevant antitrust damages which were to be sustained were classified as 'overcharge damages'[283] and/or 'lost sales damages',[284] then the court would need to classify the competition law infringement which had an effect on the prices and/or adversely affected the claimants' sales. In other words, a judge would need first to classify the alleged competition law restriction (eg cartel agreement; abuse of dominant position). Once this had been done, the judge would set out the relevant elements of the infringement and ascertain whether the act was committed in England and Wales.

An example of a competition law infringement, which was committed in England and Wales and which gave rise to multiple claims, is *FOREX*.[285] In this case, the collusive conduct, which was in conflict with Article 101 TFEU, related to the banks' 'alleged illegal manipulation of the FX markets [which] took place in around 200 chat rooms and was also orchestrated by email, telephone, text and WhatsApp messages and in person meetings'.[286] Significant damage was caused to multiple claimants who 'bought currency at a higher price and sold it at a lower price than they would in the absence of the anti-competitive behaviour found'.[287] Since the traders who illegitimately exchanged the

[279] Ibid [132–141].
[280] Para 3.1(9)(b) PD 6B.
[281] Ibid.
[282] *Metall und Rohstoff* (n 62) 443.
[283] *Sainsbury's Supermarkets* (n 157) [13.4–5]. *Epic Games* (n 4) [119].
[284] *Sainsbury's Supermarkets* (n 157) [13.4 and 13.6]. *Epic Games* (n 4) [124].
[285] *Three Way Banana Split* (n 25); *Essex Express* (n 25).
[286] *Allianz Global* (n 98) [1].
[287] *Michael O'Higgins FX Class Representative* (n 149) [186].

information through various communication channels were employed by some major banks in London,[288] Mr Justice Roth took the view that the competition law infringement was committed in England and Wales.[289]

That said, the 'difficult[ies] to localise'[290] the elements of the competition law infringements were outlined by Mr Justice Pumfrey in *SanDisk v Koninklijke Philips Electronics*.[291] In this case, the claimant alleged that the defendant had abused its 'dominant position in the market for the licensing of patents essential to the production, sale and importation into the EEA of MP3 players and MP3-compliant memory cards'.[292] A number of exclusionary and exploitative abusive practices were pleaded, including 'refus[al] deal',[293] 'tying practices'[294] and 'excessive royalties'.[295] SanDisk relied on a written offer of a licence which contained certain restrictive terms,[296] which was classified as an abuse of a dominant position.[297]

On that basis, the court held that the infringements which were to give rise to damages did not take place in England. It was held that 'a tortious act is not complete until a statement has been both made and understood, the relevant location is that where the statement was made'.[298] A better approach might have been for an offer of a licence to be regarded as prima facie evidence that the defendant's conduct could constitute abuse of a dominant position (rather than an abuse in itself). That said, the problem in localising the infringement would still remain. For example, if the offer of a licence agreement (which contains restrictive terms) were to be regarded as a 'refusal to contract on reasonable terms',[299] would the court at the place where the market is affected/foreclosed (or likely to be affected/foreclosed) have jurisdiction?

The aspects in relation to the question of where the competition law infringement is committed are likely to be somewhat identical to those that the English courts had to consider with a view to ascertaining 'the place of event giving rise to the damage'[300] for the purposes of Article 7(2) of Brussels Ia. The advantage is that the court at that place would have international jurisdiction, under Brussels Ia, to award damages in respect of the loss which is caused worldwide.[301] The disadvantage is that the place where a transnational competition infringement is committed may be very difficult, if not impossible, to ascertain in some cases, as can be deduced by the in-depth analysis undertaken by Mr Justice Teare in *Cooper Tire*:

> In the present case the act complained of is a 'complex single and continuous infringement' of [Article 101 TFEU] by agreeing price targets, sharing customers by non-aggression

[288] Ibid [162].
[289] *Michael O'Higgins* (n 14) [2].
[290] *SanDisk* (n 228) [22].
[291] Ibid.
[292] Ibid [14].
[293] Ibid [15.i].
[294] Ibid [15.ii. and iii].
[295] Ibid [15.iv].
[296] Ibid [16].
[297] *SanDisk* (n 228) [22].
[298] Ibid.
[299] Opinion of AG Jacobs in Case C-7/97 *Oscar Bronner GmbH & Co KG v Mediaprint Zeitungs- und Zeitschriftenverlag GmbH & Co KG and Others* EU:C:1998:264 [47].
[300] *Bier* (n 180) [21].
[301] *Cooper Tire* – EWHC (n 57) [65]. See below.

> agreements and exchanging sensitive commercial information relating to prices, competitors and customers. The meetings which gave rise to it took place in a number of locations including Milan, Vienna, Amsterdam, Brussels, Richmond-on-Thames, Frankfurt, Grosse Leder, and Prague. The cartel was ended at a meeting in London. I consider that this is a case where it is, at the very least, difficult to say where the event which gave rise to the damage occurred. It was suggested that the cartel was set in motion in England over the period 28-30 August 1995 and that that is sufficient to show that the place where the harmful event occurred was in England; see *Sandisk Corporation v Koninklijke Philips Electronics NV* [2007] EWHC 332 (Ch) at paragraphs 25 and 41. I have, I confess, a sense of unease, in concluding, in the context of a Europe-wide cartel orchestrated at meetings in several countries, that the place where the harmful event occurred is England because that is where the first meeting took place. That seems to me to be unrealistic. In truth the harmful events occurred in several countries.[302]

The difficulties for claimants to ascertain the place where a transnational competition law infringement, which may amount to a transnational cartel, is carried out were reiterated by the UK CAT in *Deutsche Bahn v Morgan Crucible Company*.[303] Furthermore, the difficulties to ascertain 'the place of the conclusion of the cartel'[304] were acknowledged by the CJEU in *Cartel Damage Claims (CDC) Hydrogen Peroxide SA v Akzo Nobel*[305] where the Court held that 'it is not possible to identify a single place where the cartel […] was concluded since the cartel consisted of a number of collusive agreements concluded during various meetings and discussions which took place in various places'.[306]

The foregoing examples clearly demonstrate that ascertaining the place where an act which causes antitrust damages is committed may be a fairly difficult task in cases where there is a transnational competition infringement that involves a multinational group of companies (and/or multinational groups of companies). Given the increasingly transnational nature of economic activities and various supply chains, it is highly likely for many transnational competition law infringements to be committed partly within and partly outside the jurisdiction. This will often be the case where a cartel may consist of multiple anti-competitive agreements[307] which might well be negotiated during meetings in several countries.[308]

In order to address the weaknesses of the EU regime in relation to the allocation of jurisdiction under Article 7(2) of Brussels Ia which were highlighted in this section, it will be appropriate for the English court to assume jurisdiction over a competition law claim, even if not all acts have been committed within the jurisdiction.[309] The test might be: has the antitrust damage 'resulted from substantial and efficacious acts committed within the jurisdiction (whether or not other substantial and efficacious acts have been committed elsewhere)?'[310] It seems to the author that, if this test were to be applied by Mr Justice Teare in *Cooper Tire*, the English court could have assumed jurisdiction

[302] *Cooper Tire* – EWHC (n 57) [65].
[303] *Deutsche Bahn* (n 232) [27].
[304] Ibid [44].
[305] *Cartel Damage Claims* (n 188).
[306] Ibid [45].
[307] Ibid.
[308] *Cooper Tire* – EWHC (n 57) [65].
[309] *Metall und Rohstoff* (n 62) 437.
[310] Ibid.

on the basis that the cartel were initiated in England which would in turn be a strong indication that the competition law infringement was committed in the jurisdiction (rather than on the basis of Article 8(1) of Brussels Ia).

VI. Injunction Gateways

According to Lord Wilberforce, 'there can be no doubt that the primary remedy against a prohibited act is an injunction against continuance of it'.[311] A claim form may be served out of the jurisdiction in cases where the desired legal remedy is 'an injunction [...] ordering the defendant to do or refrain from doing an act within the jurisdiction'.[312] That said, para 3.1(5) of PD 6B that allows for '[a] claim [to be] made for an interim remedy under section 25(1) of the Civil Jurisdiction and Judgments Act 1982' – which provided a basis for jurisdiction to grant provisional measures in support of foreign competition law proceedings which are within the scope of Brussels Ia – would no longer be relevant in competition cases. Since Section 25(1) of the 1982 Act requires the subject matter of the proceedings to be within the ambit of the 2005 Hague Convention, it will not be relevant to competition law claims which are explicitly excluded from the 2005 Convention.[313]

Nonetheless, it is well established that, under para 3.1(2) of PD 6B, a claimant may seek an injunction restraining foreign undertakings and/or associations of undertakings from continuing to engage in any anti-competitive conduct which would be implemented and/or could have qualified effects in England.[314] A claim for an injunction could often be brought together with a tortious claim for private antitrust damages.[315] It should be noted that the injunction gateway 'includes an interlocutory injunction'[316] which are central to facilitating injured parties' timely access to effective legal remedies. It is well settled now that:

> The right to obtain an interlocutory injunction is merely ancillary and incidental to the pre-existing cause of action. It is granted to preserve the status quo pending the ascertainment by the court of the rights of the parties and the grant to the plaintiff of the relief to which his cause of action entitles him, which may or may not include a final injunction.[317]

The importance of interlocutory injunctions for injured parties to obtain timely access to effective legal remedies in cross-border competition law cases was revealed in *Adidas-Salomon v Draper*.[318] In this case, the Grand Slam Committee (GSC) which includes representatives of all defendants, Grand Slam Tournaments, and the International Tennis Federation (ITF) modified their dress code. The dress code was set

[311] *Garden Cottage Foods v Milk Marketing Board* [1984] 1 AC 130, 152 (per Lord Wilberforce – dissenting).
[312] Para 3.1(2) PD 6B.
[313] Article 2(2)(h) of the Convention of 30 June 2005 on Choice of Court Agreements.
[314] *Adidas-Salomon* (n 147); *Garden Cottage Foods* (n 311).
[315] *Unlockd* (n 4) [18 and 19]. See also: *Garden Cottage Foods* (n 311).
[316] *Siskina v Distos Compania Naviera SA* [1979] AC 210, 256.
[317] Ibid.
[318] *Adidas-Salomon* (n 147).

to limit on-court advertising on tennis players' clothing, setting out particular requirements in relation to the size and placement of the various manufacturers' logos.

The claimant's argument was the defendants had 'singled out Adidas and indicated that the revised interpretation [of the dress code] would be applied to its 3-Stripes motif'.[319] In order to protect their rights derived from Articles 101 and 102 TFEU (which were directly applicable and directly effective in the UK), Adidas issued court proceedings, seeking declaratory and injunctive relief. Their central argument was that Grand Slam Tournaments abused their collective 'dominant position on the market for the provision and promotion of premium international tennis tournaments for individuals'[320] by setting out a dress code which was enforced in a discriminatory manner. In dealing with the issue of jurisdiction, the Chancellor of the High Court took the view:

> In the case of [Tennis Australia] and [United States Tennis Association] their Grand Slam tournaments do not take place within the European [Union]. In the case of the ITF some of the tournaments or parts of them take place outside the European [Union]. But each of them is a party to the GSC decision and ITF made the ITF decision. Each of those decisions affects the Tennis Championships at Wimbledon. In my view that is sufficient to confer jurisdiction on this court to apply [Articles 101 and 102 TFEU] to each of those decisions. Whether or not that jurisdiction should be exercised by granting injunctions against [Tennis Australia] and [United States Tennis Association] in relation to their own Grand Slam tournaments in Australia and the United States is another matter.[321]

The fact that the decision was implemented in England meant that English courts had jurisdiction because there was a required level of territorial connection between the forum and the act that was to be restrained in England.

The necessary territorial link[322] was further considered in *Unlockd v Google*.[323] The companies, Unlockd Group were software developers, devising various apps for 'smartphones operating on the Android operating system (OS)'.[324] They entered into contractual arrangements with companies from the Google group. Unlockd had a 'direct account with Google for the supply of ads and receipt of revenue through the AdMob service as follows: [...] a) for Tesco Mobile Xtras: C2; b) for Boost Dealz: Unlockd Media Inc; c) for flybuys: Unlockd AU'.[325] In March 2018, Google barred their access to its network, removing their apps from its Play Store. Unlockd claimed that Google's conduct was anti-competitive and issued legal proceedings, seeking damages and an injunction. In considering jurisdiction, Mr Justice Roth held that:

> As regards the injunction gateway, it is clear that the acts within the jurisdiction do not include the suspension/refusal of access to the Play Store and AdMob as regards the Boost Dealz app in the US or the flybuys app in Australia. Although I have accepted, and it is indeed now conceded, that the Claimants can obtain jurisdiction over [Google LLC] on the basis of access to the Tesco Mobile app in England and Wales, and their claim for an injunction in that

[319] Ibid [41].
[320] Ibid [18].
[321] Ibid [48].
[322] *SanDisk* (n 228) [49–51]. See also: *Credit Suisse Trust SA v Cuoghi* [1998] QB 818, 827 (per Millett LJ).
[323] *Unlockd* (n 4).
[324] Ibid [4].
[325] Ibid [10].

> regard, that does not mean that [Google LLC] thereby comes within the jurisdiction of this court for a claim for an injunction which also orders the defendant to do an act elsewhere.[326]

Mr Justice Roth's judgment strongly indicates that the requirement in para 3.1(2) of PD 6B for the act to be performed within the jurisdiction would mean that the injunction gateway will not be particularly helpful in cases where the anti-competitive conduct was carried out in another jurisdiction. This poses the questions: what if the claimants seek to restrain anti-competitive conduct and/or acts which are committed in another jurisdiction, but cause damages in England? In other words, it is important to consider whether (and to what extent) a competition law claim for injunctive relief will fall within para 3.1(9) of PD 6B in cases where foreign anti-competitive conduct causes (or is likely to cause) anti-trust damage in England and Wales. The possibility for English judges to do so was discussed in *Epic Games v Apple*[327] where Mr Justice Roth took the view that:

> The tort gateway [...] encompasses two alternatives. Both are framed in terms of the damage that has been or will be sustained. It is somewhat unusual to found jurisdiction on that gateway in proceedings where no damages are claimed. However, I do not regard that as an obstacle: although the permissible claims are only for injunctive relief, *if those injunctions seek to restrain tortious conduct which causes damage*, there is no reason, in my view, why it is not open to the Claimants to rely on the tort gateway.[328]

Mr Justice Roth's interpretation of the tortious gateway is welcome. Indeed, the foregoing examples strongly suggest that the need for a party to obtain injunctive relief was outlined as being particularly important in abuse of dominant position cases[329] (which may inter alia be raising issues of collective dominance[330] and anti-competitive agreements)[331] in so far as these infringements may adversely affect a claimant's economic activities by driving them out of business and causing them 'what is called "irreparable" damage'.[332] That said, it is well established that a central question which judges may need to address in competition law cases is 'whether there is a serious question to be tried'.[333]

VII. Discretion

As noted above, the English courts would not give permission for a claim form to be served out of the jurisdiction unless persuaded that England and Wales was the appropriate forum for the competition law claims to be heard and determined.[334] In other words, the objective is for the court to determine whether 'England and Wales is the

[326] Ibid [45]. See also: *Epic Games* (n 4) [96].
[327] *Epic Games* (n 4).
[328] Ibid [117].
[329] *Garden Cottage Foods* (n 311); *Epic Games* (n 4).
[330] *Adidas-Salomon* (n 147).
[331] *Unlockd* (n 4).
[332] *Garden Cottage Foods* (n 311) 153 (per Lord Wilberforce – dissenting).
[333] Ibid 141 (per Lord Diplock). See also: *Adidas-Salomon* (n 147) [86]; *Unlockd* (n 4) [22].
[334] *Spiliada* (n 128) 481. See also: JJ Fawcett, 'Trial in England or Abroad: The underlying policy considerations' (1989) 9 *OJLS* 205; A Briggs, 'Forum non conveniens – the last word?' (1987) *Lloyd's Maritime and Commercial Law Quarterly* 1.

proper place in which to bring the claim'.[335] Although Lord Briggs observed that the very same concept 'has previously been labelled forum conveniens and appropriate forum',[336] he went to acknowledge that the 'fundamental principle'[337] remains unchanged.[338]

A central question which needs to be addressed in this context is the court 'where the case may be tried "suitably for the interests of all the parties and for the ends of justice"'.[339] The factors which are to be considered in this context can be deduced from the UK Supreme Court judgment in *Brownlie I*, where Lord Wilson reiterated the broader scope of the enquiry.[340] More specifically, a somewhat narrow view appeared to be taken by Lord Sumption, who noted that:

> The discretion as to *forum conveniens* authorises the court to decline a jurisdiction which it possesses as a matter of law, because the dispute, although sufficiently connected with England to permit the exercise of jurisdiction, could be more appropriately resolved elsewhere. The main determining factor in the exercise of the discretion on *forum conveniens* grounds is not the relationship between the cause of action and England but ***the practicalities of litigation***.[341]

In this context, Lord Wilson[342] broadly listed the factors that need to be factored in by drawing on Lord Wilberforce's speech in *Amin Rasheed Shipping v Kuwait Insurance*[343] which was cited by Lord Goff in *Spiliada*.[344] According to Lord Wilberforce,[345] in order to determine whether England and Wales is the *proper place* for the purposes of CPR 6.37(3), 'the court must take into account the nature of the dispute, the legal and practical issues involved, such questions as local knowledge, availability of witnesses and their evidence and expense'.[346]

Following this line of reasoning, a number of factors may be considered by judges when exercising their discretion in cross-border competition law cases, but the main thrust of the judges' enquiry should be on the nature of the dispute and the appropriateness for the courts in terms of dealing with the relevant competition law issues (ie establishing a regulatory breach)[347] as well as with the aspects concerning causation and quantification of damages (which may be intertwined with disclosure of data and complex data analyses, involving expert witnesses).[348]

As part of this process, the court may take into consideration who the parties to the dispute are. Is the competition law claim issued by a foreign company against another

[335] CPR 6.37(3); Competition Appeal Tribunal Rules 2015 r 31(3).
[336] *Vedanta Resources Plc and another v Lungowe and others* [2019] UKSC 20 [66] (per Lord Briggs).
[337] *Spiliada* (n 128) 482. *Epic Games* (n 4) [132].
[338] *Vedanta* (n 336) [66].
[339] *Spiliada* (n 128) 482. *Vedanta* (n 336) [66]; *AK Investment* (n 139) [88].
[340] *Brownlie I* (n 104) [66] (per Lord Wilson).
[341] *Brownlie I* (n 104) [31] (per Lord Sumption) – emphasis added.
[342] *Brownlie I* (n 104) [66] (per Lord Wilson).
[343] *Amin Rasheed Shipping Corporation v Kuwait Insurance Co* [1984] AC 50.
[344] *Spiliada* (n 128) 478–9.
[345] *Amin Rasheed* (n 343) 72 (Lord Wilberforce).
[346] Ibid 72 cited by *Spiliada* (n 128) 478–9. See also: *Ilyssia Compania Naviera SA v Ahmed Abdul-Qawi Bamaodah (The Elli 2)* [1985] 1 Lloyd's Rep 107, 113 (Ackner LJ) cited in *Spiliada* (n 128) 480.
[347] Chapter 9 and 10.
[348] Chapter 2.

foreign company? For example, if the claim involves two US companies as claimants and defendants, it is likely that the majority of the 'factual witnesses'[349] may be in the US, which would make it the proper place for the parties to bring their claim. On the contrary, if the proceedings involve two English companies with significant damages having been caused in England, then England might be considered to be the appropriate forum.[350]

That said, if a representative action were to be brought on behalf of millions of consumers (who were domiciled in the UK),[351] then, even if there were to be a class action in the US, it is unlikely that the US court would award remedies to the UK consumers. In other words, the fact that there might not be a mechanism for the UK consumers to attain remedies in the foreign competition law proceedings could be a major factor which would make the UK CAT the appropriate forum.[352]

Finally, it should be noted that analogies could be drawn between the determination of properness of the English courts and the doctrine of *forum non conveniens*. According to Professor Fawcett:

> *Forum conveniens* can be defined as a court taking jurisdiction on the ground that the local forum is the appropriate forum (or an appropriate forum) for trial or that the forum abroad is inappropriate. It is a positive doctrine, unlike the doctrine of *forum non conveniens*, which is a negative doctrine concerned with declining jurisdiction.[353]

The parallel and/or related proceedings which are pending abroad (in relation to the very same transnational infringement) may be a major factor which is to be considered when the English courts are deciding whether to exercise their *forum non conveniens* discretion.[354]

VIII. Some Conclusions

The common law rules for the assumption of jurisdiction should work reasonably well in cross-border competition law claims. The issues concerning the narrow interpretation of the connecting factor, 'the place where the damage occurred',[355] which allocates jurisdiction to the courts where the *direct damage* occurred[356] under Brussels Ia will not arise under para 3.1(9) of PD 6B. In particular, the UK Supreme Court has broadly interpreted the requirement for 'damage [to be] sustained [...] within the jurisdiction'[357] to cover both direct and indirect damage.[358] This should not only address the weaknesses

[349] *Epic Games* (n 4) [134].
[350] *DSG Retail* (n 113) [41].
[351] *Dr Liza Lovdahl Gormsen* (n 1) [5].
[352] Ibid [17].
[353] JJ Fawcett, 'General Report' in JJ Fawcett (ed), *Declining Jurisdiction in Private International Law – Reports to the XIVth Congress of the International Academy of Comparative Law, Athens, August 1994* (Oxford, OUP, 1995) 1, 6.
[354] See more: Chapter 7 below.
[355] *Bier* (n 180) [19].
[356] Chapter 4.
[357] Para 3.1(9) PD 6B.
[358] *Lady Brownlie* (n 10) [51 & 81].

of the Brussels Ia regime, but it should also allow the English courts to establish that there is sufficient territorial connection between the competition law infringement and England in cases where indirect damage has been sustained in England.[359]

Moreover, the requirement for the claimant to demonstrate that their claim has a 'reasonable prospect of success'[360] would nicely align with the 'test […] for summary judgment'[361] and/or strike-out application which competition lawyers will be familiar with. The broad definition damage[362] for the purposes of para 3.1(9) of PD 6B should enable the English courts to have jurisdiction to award compensatory damages in relation to the loss which the claimants have sustained in other jurisdictions, provided that 'some significant [antitrust] damage has been sustained in England'.[363] In other words, the jurisdiction of the English courts under para 3.1(9) of PD 6B should not be limited to local harm. Finally, the fact that the English courts or 'the Tribunal shall not give permission for service out of the jurisdiction unless satisfied that [England and Wales or] the Tribunal is the proper place in which to bring the claim'[364] should allow the English courts to have more flexibility when deciding whether to assume jurisdiction, considering aspects in relation to regulatory jurisdiction and related/parallel proceedings.

Nonetheless, the fact that the EU Member State court could have jurisdiction under Article 7(2) of Brussels I and the English courts could have jurisdiction under para 3.1(9) of PD 6B strongly indicates that antitrust damages may be sustained by multiple injured parties in different jurisdictions which would inevitably lead to related proceedings. Furthermore, a specific issue which needs to be considered in cross-border competition law claims concerns the question of how a multinational group of companies, which are considered as a single undertaking, should classify for PIL purposes.[365]

Although the private antitrust damages claims would normally classify as tortious,[366] infringing undertakings that engage in anti-competitive conduct would naturally aim to maximise their profits by imposing certain restrictive terms and/or charging excessive prices. In other words, such undertakings would naturally enter into numerous contractual arrangements (including jurisdiction/arbitration agreements) with their customers (which may be consumers and/or businesses). If and when their customers realise that they are (or they have been) subject to contracts restricting competition, they might issue competition law claims and seek declaratory/injunctive/monetary relief. How would competition law claims arising out of contracts classify for jurisdictional purposes?

[359] *Qualcomm* (n 1) [5].

[360] Civil Procedure Rules 6.37(1)(b); Competition Appeal Tribunal Rules 2015 r 31(2)(b).

[361] *AK Investment* (n 139) [71].

[362] *Lady Brownlie* (n 10) [51 & 81].

[363] *Metall und Rohstoff* (n 62) 437. *Lady Brownlie* (n 10) [51].

[364] Competition Appeal Tribunal Rules 2015 r 31(3); Civil Procedure Rules 6.37(3).

[365] See: Chapter 6.

[366] eg *BritNed* – EWHC (n 171) [10]; *BritNed* (n 171) – EWCA [2]; *Michael O'Higgins FX Class Representative* (n 149) [168–175]; *DSG Retail* (n 113).

5

Jurisdiction in Competition Law Cases – Contractual Relationships between the Parties

I. Introduction

As noted above,[1] some specific classification issues need to be addressed with regard to competition law claims that arise out of injured parties' contractual relationships which involve cartelists or undertakings that may be abusing their dominant positions.[2] A major classification problem is that the same set of facts gives rise to claims/remedies which may be contractual claims (concerning invalidity/validity of the contract or certain terms of the contract; or entitlement to an adjusted and/or discounted price) as well as tortious claims for antitrust damages caused by a competition law breach.[3] There is a fine line between a competition law claim which classifies as contractual (ie coming within the contract gateways of PD 6B of the Civil Procedure Rules 1998 or the concept of 'matters relating to contract'[4] of Sch 8 of the Competition Act 1998) and a competition law claim which classifies as tortious (ie coming within the tort gateway of PD 6B or 'matters relating to delict'[5] of Sch 8 of the 1998 Act).

The classification issues need to be addressed because a contract that is in conflict with Chapter 1 of the Competition Act 1998 (and/or Article 101 TFEU) is 'automatically void'.[6] The 'nullity referred to [in Section 2(4) of the 1998 Act (or/and Article 101(2) TFEU)] is absolute'.[7] 'An agreement which is null and void by virtue of this provision has no effect as between the contracting parties and cannot be [held] against third parties'.[8] One notable difference is that Article 102 TFEU and the Chapter 2 prohibition do not include a provision equivalent to Article 101(2) TFEU and Section 2(4) of the 1998 Act, which automatically nullifies any agreements prohibited by Article 101(1) TFEU and Chapter 1

[1] Chapter 4.

[2] Compare: *Ryanair Limited v Esso Italiana Srl* [2013] EWCA Civ 1450 [33] and [41].

[3] Ibid. *Microsoft Mobile Ltd v Sony Europe Ltd and Others* [2017] EWHC 374 (Ch). See more: Section III.B below.

[4] Compare: Article 7(1)(a) of Brussels Ia.

[5] Compare: Article 7(2) of Brussels Ia.

[6] Case C-453/99 *Courage Ltd v Bernard Crehan and Bernard Crehan v Courage Ltd and Others* EU:C:2001:465 [21 and 22]. See also: HG Beale and others (eds), *Chitty on Contracts* vol 1, 34th edn (London, Sweet & Maxwell, 2022) [18–088].

[7] Case C-22/71 *Béguelin Import Co v SAGL Import Export* EU:C:1971:113 [29]. Case C-48/72 *SA Brasserie de Haecht v Wilkin-Janssen* EU:C:1973:11 [25]–[27]; *Gibbs Mew v Gemmell* [1998] EuLR 588 (CA).

[8] *Béguelin Import* (n 7) [29].

of the 1998 Act. Nonetheless, it should be noted that the CJEU has stated that an agreement in conflict with Article 102 TFEU should also invalidate any anti-competitive contractual arrangements (and any restrictive contractual terms) which are agreed by the parties.[9]

Given that the cartelists' anti-competitive agreements which are in conflict with Chapter 1 of the 1998 Act (and/or Article 101 TFEU) would be invalidated,[10] there would be important questions about the effects of the anti-competitive conduct on the contractual arrangements (which might also include choice-of-court agreements) between the infringing undertakings and the injured parties.[11] Once the classification issues have been dealt with (ie any related competition law claim has duly been classified), the relevant set of jurisdictional rules and connecting factors will be applied by the English courts with a view to deciding whether to assume or decline jurisdiction.

The purpose of this chapter is to address the difficult issues concerning the assumption of jurisdiction in relation to cross-border competition law claims arising out of contracts between infringing undertakings and their customers (eg consumers; businesses).

II. Jurisdiction Rules – Competition Law Claims

There are several major sets of jurisdiction rules which would be relevant with regard to cross-border competition law claims which arise out of contractual relationships between the infringing undertakings and their customers.

A. Service Out – No Permission Required

Competition law claims arising out of consumer contracts. Section 15B of the 1982 Act is set to safeguard the rights of the UK consumers by allowing them to 'serve the claim form on a defendant out of the United Kingdom',[12] without any permission of the court being required in consumer claims which are falling within its ambit.[13] In particular, Section 15B of the Civil Jurisdiction and Judgments Act 1982 addresses the issues concerning the jurisdiction in disputes 'whose subject-matter is a matter relating to a consumer contract where the consumer is domiciled in the United Kingdom'.[14] The 1982 Act goes further to state that:

> The consumer may bring proceedings against the other party to the consumer contract —
>
> a) where the other party to the consumer contract is domiciled in the United Kingdom, in the courts of the part of the United Kingdom in which the other party to the consumer contract is domiciled, or

[9] Case C-127/73 *BRT v SABAM* EU:C:1974:25 [2 and 14]. See also: U Bernitz, 'The sanction of voidness under Articles 82 EC and its relation to the right to damages' in A Ezrachi (ed), *Article 82 EC: Reflection on its Recent Evolution* (Oxford, Hart Publishing, 2009) 187, 188–89.

[10] See: Article 101 TFEU; Section 2(4) of the Competition Act 1998.

[11] *Esso Italiana* (n 2) [40 and 50].

[12] Civil Procedure Rules r 6.33(2).

[13] Ibid. See also: The Competition Appeal Tribunal Rules 2015 r 31(2).

[14] Civil Jurisdiction and Judgments Act 1982 s 15B(1).

> b) in the courts for the place where the consumer is domiciled (regardless of the domicile of the other party to the consumer contract).
>
> Proceedings may be brought against the consumer by the other party to the consumer contract only in the courts of the part of the United Kingdom in which the consumer is domiciled.[15]

The consumer's domicile appears to be an important connecting factor in cross-border competition law cases involving consumers. That said, there are major PIL issues which need to be addressed in the context of competition law claims arising out of consumer contracts.[16] In particular, given the tortious classification of private antitrust damages claims, a central question may be: should a tortious claim for antitrust damages, which are caused to a consumer – who has entered into contractual arrangement with an infringing undertaking, be within the scope of s 15B of the 1998 Act? This question will be addressed head-on in this chapter.

Competition law claims and contracts which contain jurisdiction agreements. Another set of closely connected problems which need to be examined in this chapter concerns the scope of the jurisdiction agreements/clauses which form part of contracts between an infringing undertaking and its customers. These contracts might sometimes include jurisdiction agreements. This means that questions about whether certain competition law claims are within the scope of the dispute resolution agreements could be common in some cases. In this context, it should be noted that a new rule was incorporated into the CPR which is set to expedite the resolution of disputes arising out of contracts that include jurisdiction agreements. CPR 6.33(2B) states that:

> The claimant may serve the claim form on a defendant outside the United Kingdom where, for each claim made against the defendant to be served and included in the claim form—
>
> (a) the court has power to determine that claim under the 2005 Hague Convention and the defendant is a party to an exclusive choice of court agreement conferring jurisdiction on that court within the meaning of Article 3 of the 2005 Hague Convention; or
>
> (b) a contract contains a term to the effect that the court shall have jurisdiction to determine that claim.

Although the 2005 Hague Convention does not apply with regard to competition law matters, jurisdictional agreements might confer jurisdiction on certain national courts to deal with competition law claims.[17] This means that, if a competition law claim were to be within the scope of jurisdictional agreement, a claim form may be served out of jurisdiction – without a permission of the court being required. In other words, ascertaining the scope of a choice-of-court agreement presupposes for a judge to classify the relevant competition law claim/s as being contractual or tortious.

Hence, it is important for this chapter to consider how competition law claims arising out of contracts would be classified and whether the so classified claims would be within the scope of the relevant jurisdiction agreements/clauses. The existing case law[18] strongly indicates that there are particularly difficult classification issues which are

[15] Civil Jurisdiction and Judgments Act 1982 s 15B(1) and (2).

[16] See: Chapter 8 below.

[17] Case C-595/17 *Apple Sales International and Others v MJA* EU:C:2018:854.

[18] eg *Esso Italiana* (n 2); Case C-352/13 *Cartel Damage Claims (CDC) Hydrogen Peroxide SA v Evonik Degussa GmbH and Others* EU:C:2015:335.

linked to a national court's decision on *whether a competition law claim arising out of a contract* is within the scope of a choice-of-court agreement. The issues are important because, in some cases, it might be difficult to distinguish between the competition law claims which are to be classified as contractual and the competition law claims which are to be classified as tortious. It is likely that all these 'question[s] of interpretation [would be] a matter for the national court to resolve',[19] so that – even if there were to be a framework for judicial cooperation through PIL mechanisms – the English courts would have to systematically address these questions.

B. Service Out – Permission Required

As already noted above,[20] in cases where the permission of the court is required for a claim form to be served out of the jurisdiction, there are three requirements which should be satisfied. First, the claimant should substantiate their competition claim. The required standard of proof is 'reasonable prospect of success'.[21] In order to satisfy the test, the claimant would need to show that 'there is a real as opposed to fanciful prospect of success on the claim'.[22] As noted above,[23] the advantage of this approach is that it is aligning the reasonable prospects test for the services out of the jurisdiction with the 'test […] for a summary judgment application'[24] on which there is a growing body of judgments in relation to competition law claims brought before the English courts. The UK Competition Appeal Tribunal has clarified that '[a] realistic chance is one that carries some degree of conviction and is more than merely arguable'.[25] As part of this process, the claimant would need to demonstrate that the anti-competitive conduct had either been implemented or had qualified effects in the UK, so that UK competition law is infringed (see Chapters 3 and 9).

Secondly, if the UK CAT 'proceedings are to be treated as taking place in England and Wales',[26] a claimant has to make a good arguable case that their competition law claim is within one of the gateways set out in para 3.1 of PD 6B.[27] There are four separate gateways that may be relevant with regard to contractual disputes – para (6) (ie contract was concluded in England; made by an agent in England; governed by English law; included an English jurisdiction clause/agreement), para (7) (breach of contract committed in England), para (8) (non-validity declaration) and (8A) (unlawfully causing breach of contract).

[19] Case C-214/89 *Powell Duffryn plc v Wolfgang Petereit* EU:C:1992:115 [33].
[20] Chapter 4.
[21] Civil Procedure Rules 6.37(1)(b); Competition Appeal Tribunal Rules 2015 r 31(2)(b).
[22] Case Nos: 1377/5/7/20 and 1378/5/7/20 *Epic Games Inc v Apple Inc* [2021] CAT 4 [78a].
[23] See more: Chapter 4.IV above.
[24] *Royal Mail Group* (n 25) [22].
[25] Case Nos: 1284–1290/5/7/18 (T), *Royal Mail Group Ltd V DAF Trucks Ltd* [2021] CAT 10 [22]. *NTN Corporation v Stellantis NV* [2022] EWCA Civ 16 [22]. Compare: *Viskovice Horni v Korner* [1951] AC 869 (HL) 889.
[26] Competition Appeal Tribunal Rules 2015 r 31(2)(c).
[27] Ibid. See also: Civil Procedure Rules 6.37(1)(a).

Alternatively, if the UK CAT 'proceedings are to be treated as taking place in Scotland',[28] a claimant has to demonstrate that their claim comes within one of the relevant grounds as set out in Sch 8 to the 1982 Act.[29] There are two provisions which may be relevant. Section 2(b) of Sch 8 to the 1982 Act would apply in cases where there is no choice-of-court agreement between the parties. According to Section 2(b): 'a person may also be sued [...] in matters relating to a contract, in the courts for the place of performance of the obligation in question'.[30] In other words, the competition law claim is to be classified as contractual in the first place, and then the jurisdiction should be assumed by the court at the place of performance of the contractual obligation that allegedly distorts competition.[31]

In cases where there is a choice-of-court agreement that covers the competition law claims, Section 6 of Sch 8 to the 1982 Act (which is modelled on Article 25 of Brussels Ia) should apply. Section 6 states that:

> (1) If the parties have agreed that a court is to have jurisdiction to settle any disputes which have arisen or which may arise in connection with a particular legal relationship, that court shall have jurisdiction.
> (2) Such an agreement conferring jurisdiction shall be either –
>   (a) in writing or evidenced in writing; or
>   (b) in a form which accords with practices which the parties have established between themselves; or
>   (c) in international trade or commerce, in a form which accords with a usage of which the parties are or ought to have been aware and which in such trade or commerce is widely known to, and regularly observed by, parties to contracts of the type involved in the particular trade or commerce concerned.
> (3) Any communication by electronic means which provides a durable record of the agreement shall be equivalent to 'writing'.

The existing case law[32] strongly indicates that there would be complex issues which need to be addressed by the court with a view to determining whether a specific competition law claim is within the scope of a jurisdiction agreement. Would the fact that there is a prior contractual relationship – from which the competition law claim is arising – impact on the classification of the claims and the relevant connecting factors which are set out in the specific gateways that are to be used to establish jurisdiction? Would any competition law claim arising out of such a contractual relationship, involving the infringing undertaking and their customer who is an injured party suffering antitrust damages, be classified as tortious or contractual? If there was a jurisdiction (or arbitration) agreement between the parties, would the so classified claim be within the ambit of the parties' agreement?

Thirdly, the English courts or 'the Tribunal shall not give permission for service out of the jurisdiction unless satisfied that [England and Wales or] the Tribunal is the

[28] Competition Appeal Tribunal Rules 2015 r 31(2)(d).
[29] Ibid.
[30] Compare: Article 7(1) of Brussels Ia.
[31] Compare: *Boss Group v Boss France* [1996] 4 All ER 970, 975 (per Saville LJ). See more: Danov (n 70).
[32] eg *Esso Italiana* (n 2); Case C-352/13 *Cartel Damage Claims (CDC) Hydrogen Peroxide SA v Evonik Degussa GmbH and Others* EU:C:2015:335; *Apple Sales International* (n 17).

proper place in which to bring the claim'.[33] As already noted above, in order to determine whether England and Wales is the appropriate place for the competition law claims to be heard and determined, the English judges should consider the nature of the competition law infringement and any related regulatory and/or judicial proceedings in the UK or abroad.

The act distorting the process of competition (eg specific cartel arrangements; specific abuses of a dominant position) should be ascertained. In other words, the relevant elements of the specific prohibited practices or anti-competitive conduct should be set out. On that basis, it will be important to consider the extent to which the UK market is affected and the applicability (or territorial scope) of UK competition law. The practical issues concerning the claimants' access to evidence, access to litigation funding and the expert witnesses should also be duly factored in.[34]

Since the aspects concerning the standard of proof and the factors concerning exercise of discretion have already been discussed above,[35] the purpose of this chapter is to examine what the requirements are for the English courts to assume jurisdiction in competition law claims arising out of contracts. As part of this process, it will be considered how the contract gateways should apply in competition law claims that are brought by contracting parties.

III. Classification Issues – Contract and Tort

The classification issues are important because a competition law infringement may have several important legal implications. First, certain contracts or contractual arrangements between the parties may be necessary for a party to gain access to certain products or services which are offered by dominant undertakings.[36] Secondly, since antitrust damages may have been caused to a particular injured party and/or even to a class of injured parties (eg consumers), there may be specific issues in relation to consumers who may have accepted certain terms and conditions[37] and who may be entitled to antitrust damages. Thirdly, different issues may need to be addressed as the anti-competitive conduct may vary (eg cartels; abuses of dominant position) which might in turn have an impact on the classification process.

There may be additional aspects in so far as the desired legal remedies (ie contractual; tortious) may impact on the classification process.[38] Since the anticompetitive conduct is prohibited, an injured party may be entitled to obtain injunctive relief[39] which may

[33] Competition Appeal Tribunal Rules 2015 r 31(3); Civil Procedure Rules 6.37(3).

[34] *Amin Rasheed Shipping Corporation v Kuwait Insurance Co* [1984] AC 50, 72 (Lord Wilberforce) cited in *Spiliada Maritime v Cansulex* [1987] AC 460, 478–9 (per Lord Goff). See also: *Ilyssia Compania Naviera SA v Ahmed Abdul-Qawi Bamaodah (The Elli 2)* [1985] 1 Lloyd's Rep 107, 113 (Ackner LJ) cited in *Spiliada Maritime v Cansulex* [1987] AC 460 (HL) 480 (per Lord Goff).

[35] See: Chapter 4.

[36] *Epic Games* (n 22) [15 and 36].

[37] eg Case No: 1433/7/7/22, *Dr Liza Lovdahl Gormsen v Meta Platforms Inc, Meta Platforms Ireland Ltd, Facebook UK Ltd* – Reasoned Order, dated 15 March 2022.

[38] Chapter 3.

[39] Ibid; Case C-59/19 *Wikingerhof GmbH & Co KG v Booking.com BV* EU:C:2020:950; *Purple Parking v Heathrow Airport Limited* [2011] EWHC 987 (Ch).

be necessary for certain claimants to continue to do business by, for example, gaining access to a certain category of customers through the defendant's digital platform. The need for the judges to provide a declaratory/injunctive/compensatory relief for injured parties should be reiterated. For example, in *Epic Games*, Mr Justice Roth submitted that 'when the Tribunal reaches a decision to grant an injunction or, indeed, to award damages, that will be based on findings that the defendant is in certain respects infringing competition law'.[40] But, this is an entirely different legal remedy in comparison to the one which will take the form of declaratory relief, with the court formally taking the view that there is an infringement not the least because such '[a] declaration by a court or Tribunal carries particular status',[41] having major consequences for the infringing undertakings in cross-border competition law disputes. To what should these aspects concerning desired legal remedies be factored into the classification process?

Moreover, different issues might arise when the classification exercise is conducted under PD 6B as opposed to Section 15B and Sch 8 of the 1982 Act in so far as the latter sets of jurisdiction provisions appear to be modelled on the Brussels Ia regime. The specific classification issues which may be arising under the Brussels Ia/Lugano regime were identified by the UK Supreme Court in *Canada Trust Co v Stolzenberg (No 2)*[42] where Lord Steyn stated:

> The problem inherent in the application of the concepts of the [Brussels Ia Regulation] in national legal systems requires a twofold classificatory inquiry. In the first place it is necessary to interpret a particular concept used in the [Regulation] independently by reference to the language, structure, system and objectives of the [Regulation]. Secondly, recognising that a concept of the [Regulation] may have a different content in various national legal systems, it is necessary to apply it to the procedural regime of the particular legal system.[43]

Lord Steyn's opinion strongly suggests that a peculiar set of classification issues are bound to arise when national judges apply multilateral PIL instruments which allocate jurisdiction in cross-border cases. In this chapter, the above identified classification issues will be examined by considering the relevant aspects in relation to anti-competitive agreements and abuses of dominant positions.

A. Private Antitrust Damages Claims Issued by Contracting Parties

The classification problems[44] are bound to arise in cases where the competition law claims arise out of contracts between an infringing undertaking and its customer/s. The issues are important because, in order for some anti-competitive practices (eg illegal price-fixing)[45] to be implemented, it is often necessary for such undertakings to enter

[40] *Epic Games* (n 22) [85].
[41] Ibid.
[42] *Canada Trust Co v Stolzenberg (No 2)* [2002] 1 AC 1. The case was also cited in *Provimi Limited v Aventis Animal Nutrition SA and Others* [2003] EWHC 961 (Comm).
[43] *Canada Trust* (n 42) 8.
[44] *Wikingerhof* (n 39).
[45] eg Case AT.39824, *Trucks – Commission Decision relating to a proceeding under Article 101 of the Treaty on the Functioning of the European Union (the Treaty) and Article 53 of the EEA Agreement* – 19.7.2016,

into contractual arrangements with their customers, selling their products at an inflated price over a number of years.[46]

There are bound to be complex issues concerning classification and interpretation in cross-border competition law cases, where there are contractual arrangements between an infringing undertaking and an injured party who may have suffered antitrust damages. Professors Francq and Wurmnest have submitted:

> [D]amages claims by indirect purchasers directed against a producer who conspired with other producers to fix prices may be considered as non-contractual obligations as the overcharge is not rooted in the contract itself but in the *ex ante* coordination of the pricing by the cartel.[47]

This quotation captures the importance of the tortious classification with regard to private antitrust damages claims issued by an indirect purchaser. One should go a step further and argue that the tortious classification should prevail even in cases where the claims are issued by direct purchasers. This is widely accepted by the English courts.[48] The approach may be justified by the fact that, as noted above,[49] there are several major elements of a claim for competition law damages.[50] Claimants should prove that there is 'an infringement of competition law'[51] which has affected the prices. On that basis, they would need to establish that there is an 'actionable harm or damage, caused by that infringement'.[52]

An appropriate way to deal with difficult classification issues, which arise in competition law claims issued by contracting parties, appears to be put forward in Daniel Beard KC's 'powerful submissions'[53] which were nicely summarised by Lord Justice Rix as follows:

> [A]rticle 101 [TFEU] does not operate by either invalidating contractual arrangements with customers of cartel operators or by requiring the prices charged to such customers to be adjusted to some new and acceptable norm. A cartel in breach of article 101 [TFEU] does not render any price or fee specified in a customer contract unlawful. On the contrary, article 101 [TFEU] operates by invalidating the arrangements *between* the cartel parties, and it gives their customers a remedy not in the form of adjusted contractual prices but in the form of damages for losses created by the cartel parties' breach of statutory duty. Those damages are to be quantified not necessarily by any uplift beyond some other hypothetical price, but by what the customer has lost. That might depend on many factors, including the degree to which the

C(2016) 4673 final; Case AT.39824, *Trucks – Commission Decision relating to a proceeding under Article 101 of the Treaty on the Functioning of the European Union and Article 53 of the EEA Agreement* – 27.9.2017, C(2017) 6467 final.

46 *Royal Mail Group Ltd v DAF Trucks* – High Court (Ch) – Directions Order – 13 June 2018 [15].

47 S Francq and W Wurmnest, 'International Antitrust Claims under the Rome II Regulation' in J Basedow, S Francq and L Idot (eds), *International Antitrust Litigation: Conflict of Laws and Coordination* (Oxford, Hart Publishing, 2012) 91, 97.

48 *Provimi* (n 42) [25; 114–125].

49 Chapter 3.

50 *BritNed Development Ltd v ABB AB* [2018] EWHC 2616 (Ch) [10].

51 Ibid [10].

52 Ibid.

53 *Esso Italiana* (n 2) [40].

> price can be said to have been inflated, such as whether the customer has been able to pass on the inflated price to its customers in turn (who themselves may therefore have a claim against the cartel parties for breach of statutory duty), or whether the customer has lost out on further sales that it might have made if it had been charged a lower price.[54]

In other words, as Daniel Beard KC noted in *Ryanair v Esso Italiana*,[55] and with whom Lord Justice Rix agreed,[56] it is the cartelists' anti-competitive agreement which is null and void. The effect of a prohibited anti-competitive agreement, which is nullified, on the series of related contracts with the infringing undertakings' customers is an entirely different matter. If such customers were to issue private antitrust damages claims, their competition law claims should be classified as tortious,[57] which would be important with a view to determining whether the claim is within the scope of the tortious gateway for the purposes of PD 6B.[58] Would the classification be different if the desired legal remedy was an injunction[59] or declaration rather than damages?

The appropriate and effective legal remedies which are desired by the parties may need to be considered with a view to classifying competition law claims as contractual or tortious. According to Lord Justice Rix, 'it would make nonsense for the party affected by any requirement for an adjusted price lower than the cartel engendered inflated price (ie on this hypothesis Esso Italiana) to have a right to cancel the contract'.[60] In spite of the tortious classification of antitrust damages claims, other legal remedies (rather than damages) may be sought by the injured parties. Such claimants could be entitled to damages as a remedy (eg any overcharge; loss of sales), but they could also be entitled to invalidate / terminate the contract or seek an 'adjusted price'[61] or even discounted price. If the parties felt that the latter set of remedies in contract would be more desirable and appropriate in the circumstances, then this could potentially lead to a different classification.

Would the classification issues be different in cases involving contracting parties, provided that the relevant anti-competitive conduct is classified as an 'abuse of dominant position'? The difficult classification issues, which arise in abuse of dominant position cases, were identified by the Court of Justice of the European Union in *Wikingerhof GmbH v Booking.com & Co BV*.[62] In this case, a German company, Wikingerhof, was providing hotel services in Germany. In order to promote its services and gain access to customers in the digital era, the claimant entered into certain contractual arrangements with the defendant, a Netherlands-based company, Booking.com. It was standard contract which made a reference to the defendant's terms and conditions which were periodically reviewed and amended by the defendant.

[54] Ibid [29].
[55] Ibid [40].
[56] Ibid [28].
[57] Case No: 1339/7/7/20 *Mark McLaren Class Representative Ltd v MOL (Europe Africa) Ltd* – Order – 30 March 2020 [4]; Case No: 1329/7/7/19 *Michael O'Higgins FX Class Representative Ltd v Barclays Bank Plc and Others* – Order – 16 August 2019 [2].
[58] See: Chapter 4.
[59] Compare: *Epic Games* (n 22).
[60] *Esso Italiana* (n 2) [30].
[61] Ibid.
[62] *Wikingerhof* (n 39) [30].

Booking.com is a well-known digital platform which, inter alia, has contractual arrangements with hotel service providers whose services are offered on Booking.com's platform in return for certain commission fees. The dispute arose after the terms of conditions were modified. With this in mind, the following questions might be important in cross-border competition law cases, post-Brexit: is a competition law claim to be classified as contractual simply because a dominant undertaking and its customer have a contractual relationship, and the claim/s will be arising out of the contract? Can a claimant overlook the existence of contract and base their claim solely on the tortious gateway – para 3.1(9) of PD 6B? According to Professors Francq and Wurmnest:

> More difficult to [classify] are claims in the field of refusals to supply by dominant undertakings. […] In such cases, the litigants often have a prior business relationship which is ended unilaterally in one or the other way by one party. Even though a rule of law requiring the supplier (even fully contrary to his will) to enter into a new contract with the plaintiff is not an obligation freely assumed in the strict sense, many commentators argue that claims against parties who are under a duty to deal must be regarded as a contractual matter under the Brussels I Regulation as such claims aim at the conclusion of a contract.[63]

A different approach to addressing classification issues appeared to be advanced by the CJEU in *Wikingerhof GmbH v Booking.com & Co BV*.[64] In this case, the claimant issued competition law claims against the defendant before the German courts. The claimant alleged that the defendant abused its dominant position by imposing certain restrictions on the claimant as well as by charging them an excessive commission fee.[65] The legal remedy, which the claimant sought to attain, was an injunction. Since there was a Dutch jurisdiction clause, there were several PIL issues which the German judges had to deal with. After the German courts held that the Dutch jurisdiction clause was not valid as it did not fulfil the Brussels Ia requirements, the issue whether the competition law claims were to be classified as contractual or tortious was central for the German courts to ascertain whether they have jurisdiction under Brussels Ia.[66] The classification issues were indeed addressed head-on by AG Henrik Saugmandsgaard Øe who noted:

> the action at issue in the present case has the particular feature that it is between the parties to a contract and that the alleged anticompetitive conduct of which Wikingerhof complains against Booking.com occurs within their contractual relationship, since it consists in the fact that Booking.com imposes, in the context of that relationship, unfair trading terms on Wikingerhof. It is possible, moreover, that some, or indeed all, […] of those contested practices are covered by the provisions of the general terms and conditions applicable to the contract in question. It therefore falls to be ascertained whether, in such circumstances, the classification 'relating to a contract' prevails over the classification 'relating to tort' for the purposes of the Brussels I bis Regulation.
>
> The Bundesgerichtshof (Federal Court of Justice) considers that that question should be answered in the negative. Like Wikingerhof and the Commission, I share that view. The opposite stance taken by Booking.com and by the Czech Government reflects, in my view, the

[63] Francq and Wurmnest (n 47) 97.

[64] *Wikingerhof* (n 39) [30].

[65] Case C-59/19 *Wikingerhof GmbH & Co KG v Booking.com BV* EU:C:2020:688 – the opinion of AG Henrik Saugmandsgaard Øe [9–12].

[66] Ibid [3].

> uncertainties surrounding, in the Court's case-law, the dividing line between 'matters relating to a contract' and 'matters relating to tort'.[67]

Addressing systematically the PIL issues is important with a view to advancing an 'internationalist'[68] approach to classification, post-Brexit. The judgment of the CJEU in *Kafelis*[69] might have been interpreted as strongly indicating that different national judges might share different views on the classification of private antitrust damages claims issued by one contracting party against the other.[70] On the one hand, AG Darmon took the view that that 'an action based on tort and contract […] is governed exclusively by the rules laid down for contractual matters in [Article 7(1) of Brussels Ia]',[71] indicating that contractual classification of private antitrust damages should prevail.[72]

On the other hand, the CJEU did not follow AG Darmon's suggestion, holding that 'all actions which seek to establish the liability of a defendant and which are not related to a "contract" within the meaning of [Article 7(1) of Brussels Ia]'[73] should classify as tortious. The UK Supreme Court has interpreted the CJEU jurisprudence as defining claims under Article 7(1) and (2) of Brussels Ia as being 'mutually exclusive'.[74] The matter has to be classified as either one relating to a tort or as one relating to a contract, but not both.[75] AG Henrik Saugmandsgaard Øe[76] appeared to summarise all these principles and went to state that:

> *[A] claim must be classified in the light of the principal question of law raised therein. The existence of a mere preliminary or interlocutory issue of a contractual nature, which the court must resolve in order to determine that claim, is not decisive for the purposes of the classification of that claim.* […] Otherwise, that would amount to conferring jurisdiction on the court with jurisdiction in respect of the contract to adjudicate on a claim which does not essentially raise questions of a contractual nature and which therefore does not have a particularly close link with that court.[77]

On that basis, the CJEU took the view a that the competition law claim which was issued by Wikingerhof should classify as tortious because 'the legal issue at the heart of the case in the main proceedings is whether Booking.com committed an abuse of a dominant position within the meaning of German competition law'.[78] The CJEU

[67] Ibid [26–27].

[68] *Raiffeisen Zentralbank Osterreich AG v Five Star Trading LLC and others* [2001] EWCA Civ 68 [26]. See also: *Provimi* (n 42) [109].

[69] Case C-189/87 *Kalfelis v Schröder and Others* EU:C:1988:459.

[70] M Danov, *Jurisdiction and Judgments in relation to EU Competition Law Claims* (Oxford, Hart Publishing, 2011) 34.

[71] Case C-189/87 *Kalfelis v Schröder and Others* EU:C:1988:312 [31] opinion of AG Darmon. See also: *Kleinwort Benson v Glasgow City Council* [1999] 1 AC 153, 166–67 (Lord Goff), 183–84 (Lord Clyde).

[72] *Kalfelis* – AG Darmon (n 71) [31]. See also: C Castronovo, 'Private law remedies for antitrust violations – a point of view from Italy' in J Basedow, *Private Enforcement of EC Competition Law* (The Hague, Kluwer Law International, 2008) 107, 117.

[73] *Kalfelis* (n 69) [18].

[74] *Agnew and Others v Länsforsäkringsbolagens AB* [2001] 1 AC 223, 267. See also: *Kalfelis* (n 69) [19].

[75] P Torremans and JJ Fawcett, *Cheshire, North & Fawcett: Private International Law* 15th edn (Oxford, OUP, 2017) 264–66.

[76] *Wikingerhof* – opinion AG (n 65) [58–63].

[77] Ibid [104].

[78] *Wikingerhof* (n 39) [35].

ruling appears to be closely aligned with Kaye's view[79] that, 'when the principal subject matter of the proceedings concerns the existence or not of liability in tort, the matter in dispute should be regarded as tortious for the purposes of application of [Article 7(2) of Brussels Ia], notwithstanding the existence of the incidental issue of contract'.[80]

Therefore, the CJEU approach seems to be in line with the English jurisprudence.[81] In other words, a competition law claim – which is issued by a contracting party and which seeks antitrust damages – should classify as tortious.[82]

B. Same Facts – Breach of Contract and Antitrust Damages

Although the classification of Wikingerhof's competition law claim as tortious is welcome, a closer look at the CJEU judgment appears to indicate that thrust of the CJEU's reasoning is on the fact that 'it is not indispensable [for the court] to interpret the contract between the parties to the main proceedings'[83] with a view to determining whether the defendant's conduct was anti-competitive.

The problem is that test – whether the interpretation of the contract (or any contractual arrangements) is (or is not) necessary for the court to determine if there is a competition infringement – would be very difficult to apply in practice.[84] The flaws were indeed identified by AG Henrik Saugmandsgaard Øe who noted:

> Admittedly, since the various practices complained of by Wikingerhof against Booking.com [...] take place in the context of their contractual relationship, it will be necessary to determine the precise content of their commitments in order to establish the reality of those practices. I observe, in that respect, that Wikingerhof claims, inter alia, that, when Booking.com displays the prices for its hotel as being more advantageous, there is no valid contractual basis for that practice. Since the parties disagree on that point, [...] the court will have to interpret Booking.com's general terms and conditions in order to establish their precise wording, which will undeniably constitute a question of contract law, coming within the *lex contractus*.[85]

The AG's analysis appears to indicate that the interpretation of contractual terms would indeed be necessary for the court to ascertain whether there is a competition law infringement. The advanced *classification* test – concerning the *indispensability of the relevant contract's interpretation for the court's determination whether there is a competition law infringement* – would work even less satisfactorily in competition law cases where the same fact (eg non-delivery of raw materials by a dominant undertaking which are due under a contract) were to give rise to a claim for specific performance

[79] P Kaye, *Civil Jurisdiction and Enforcement of Foreign Judgments* (Oxford, Professional Books, 1987).

[80] ibid p 570. See also: C Kessedjian, 'Competition' in C McLachlan and P Nygh (eds) *Transnational Tort Litigation: Jurisdictional Principles* (Oxford, Clarendon Press, 1996) 171, 174.

[81] See: *Matthews v Kuwait Bechtel Corporation* [1959] 2 QB 57 (CA); *Coupland v Arabian Gulf Oil* [1983] 1 WLR 1136 (CA); *Base Metal Trading v Shamurin* [2003] EWHC 2419 (Comm); [2004] ILPr 5; a'ffd *Base Metal Trading v Shamurin* [2004] EWCA Civ 1316 (CA).

[82] *Wikingerhof* (n 39) [38].

[83] Ibid [35].

[84] *Wikingerhof* – opinion AG (n 65) [97].

[85] Ibid [123].

under the contract as well as to a competition law claim for abuse of dominant position (ie refusal to supply).[86]

In other words, there may be cross-border competition law cases where the same set of facts gives rise to contractual claims in which the claimant seeks a 'contractual remedy'[87] (eg specific performance under the contract; termination of the contract) as well as competition law claims in which the claimant seeks competition law remedies – a declaration that there is a competition law infringement; an injunction for the defendant to restore supplies; damages in relation to loss of sales and/or any other 'financial loss was caused […] by a breach of contract'.[88] This reiterates the point that, since a competition law infringement 'brings with it its own remedy',[89] it makes sense for any classification test to factor the desired legal remedies in. The deduction could be strengthened by the judgment in *Marc Brogsitter*,[90] where the CJEU held that:

> [T]he mere fact that one contracting party brings a civil liability claim against the other is not sufficient to consider that the claim [would classify as contractual].
>
> That is the case only where the conduct complained of may be considered a breach of contract, which may be established by taking into account the purpose of the contract.
>
> That will a priori be the case where the interpretation of the contract which links the defendant to the applicant is indispensable to establish the lawful or, on the contrary, unlawful nature of the conduct complained of against the former by the latter.
>
> It is therefore for the referring court to determine whether *the purpose of the claims* brought by the applicant in the case in the main proceedings is to *seek damages*, the legal basis for which can reasonably be regarded as a breach of the rights and obligations set out in the contract which binds the parties in the main proceedings, which would make its taking into account indispensable in deciding the action.[91]

Hence, in order for the courts to systematically classify the competition law claims as tortious and/or contractual, a two-step test could be suggested. First, do the claimant's pleadings raise concerns about the anti-competitive nature of the defendant's conduct? Secondly, if the answer is in affirmative, then the court will need to examine whether the contract is simply a means for the defendant to implement their anti-competitive strategy – affecting prices and/or sales of the infringing undertaking's contracting parties – or rather whether the contract includes certain contractual terms (which have the effect to distort competition).[92] In the latter context, the questions would be: what are the legal remedies which the injured parties seek to attain?[93] Does the contracting party seek any financial and/or injunctive relief? Or does the contracting party simply seek a declaration that a contract or contractual term is in conflict with competition law and, thus, void?

[86] See: the example provided by the UK CAT in *Royal Mail* (n 25) [32]. See also: *Wikingerhof* – opinion AG (n 65) [54].

[87] *Esso Italiana* (n 2) [39].

[88] *Royal Mail* (n 25) [32].

[89] *Esso Italiana* (n 2) [39].

[90] Case C-548/12 *Marc Brogsitter v Fabrication de Montres Normandes EURL and Karsten Fräßdorf* EU:C:2014:148.

[91] Ibid [23–26].

[92] *Esso Italiana* (n 2) [28 and 29].

[93] Ibid [30 and 39].

A classification test that considers remedies may be particularly important in cross-border competition law cases before the English courts. The inherent difficulty is that the since there may be certain acts (eg refusal to supply by a dominant undertaking; prices not being 'negotiate[d] in good faith')[94] could classify as a breach of a contract and a competition law infringement, a contracting party may seek remedies in both contract and tort.

There appear to be entirely different approaches with regard to the scope of the contract and tort grounds for the allocation of jurisdiction under Brussels Ia and the scope of the relevant gateways under the English common law. As noted above, for the purposes of Brussels Ia, a competition law claim has to classify as contractual or tortious,[95] with the so-classified claim falling either under Article 7(1) or Article 7(2) of Brussels Ia which are both 'mutually exclusive'.[96] The common law approach is somewhat more flexible. It is widely accepted that '[i]f the claimant has alternative remedies in contract and tort upon the same facts, [they] can choose [their] remedy'[97] when deciding upon the gateway which could be relied on to serve a claim form out of the jurisdiction.

In order to sustain their proposition that the claimant may have a choice whether to base their claim on the tortious or contractual gateway, the editors of *Dicey, Morris and Collins*[98] cite *Matthews v Kuwait Bechtel.*[99] In this case, the claimant was an employee who had sustained personal injuries in the course of their employment in Kuwait. Since the tort was committed in Kuwait, the claimant could not rely on the tort gateway to serve the claim form onto their employer out of the jurisdiction;[100] so that the claimant alleged that the defendant had infringed their contractual duty to provide 'safe premises, plant and equipment',[101] which allowed for the claim to fall within the contractual gateway and serve the claim form out of the jurisdiction. Whilst both parties agreed that there was a duty for the defendant to provide safe working conditions, they disagreed whether the claim should classify as contractual or tortious for PIL purposes. In order to address the classification question, Lord Justice Sellers[102] drew on the opinion of Lord Radcliff in *Lister v Romford Ice and Cold Storage*[103] where it was held that:

> The existence of the duty arising out of the relationship between employer and employed was recognized by the law without the institution of an analytical inquiry whether the duty was in essence contractual or tortious. What mattered was that the duty was there. A duty may exist by contract, express or implied. Since, in any event, the duty in question is one which exists by imputation or implication of law and not by virtue of any express negotiation between the parties, I should be inclined to say that there is no real distinction between the two possible sources of obligation. […] It is a familiar position in our law that the same wrongful act may

[94] *Microsoft Mobile* (n 3) [60].
[95] *Wikingerhof* – opinion AG (n 65).
[96] *Agnew* (n 74) 267. See also: *Kalfelis* (n 69) [19].
[97] L Collins and J Harris (eds), *Dicey, Morris and Collins on the Conflict of Laws* 16th edn (London, Sweet & Maxwell, 2022) Rule 35 [11–157].
[98] Ibid.
[99] *Matthews* (n 81).
[100] Ibid 61.
[101] Ibid 62.
[102] Ibid 65–6.
[103] *Lister v Romford Ice and Cold Storage Co Ltd* [1957] AC 555.

> be made the subject of an action either in contract or in tort at the election of the claimant, and, although the course chosen may produce certain incidental consequences which would not have followed had the other course been adopted, it is a mistake to regard the two kinds of liability as themselves necessarily exclusive of each other.[104]

Whilst the approach seems diametrically different from the one advanced under Brussels Ia, Lord Sellers[105] took the view that the same broad interpretation should be followed for the purposes of PD 6B.

Mr Justice Marcus Smith's judgment in *Microsoft Mobile v Sony Europe*[106] appears to suggest that Lord Sellers' approach might also be followed in certain cross-border competition law cases where there is a breach of a contract which would also amount to a restriction of competition law. In this case, the defendants appeared to advance an argument that any price-fixing arrangements, which were in conflict with competition law, would also be in conflict with the contractual requirements for the parties to act in good faith. On that basis, it was argued the dispute could be regarded as being within the scope of the arbitration agreement because any cartel which were to fix prices would naturally mean that the prices were negotiated in bad faith, with an illegal surcharge being added.[107] Mr Justice Marcus Smith held that:

> It is irrelevant that a contractual claim has not been pleaded by Microsoft Mobile. Microsoft Mobile stressed that its claims were pleaded entirely in tort, and of course that is right. However, the mere fact that a claim in contract has not been pleaded is, to my mind, irrelevant. Were the manner in which a case was actually pleaded to matter, instead of how a case could have been pleaded, it would be easy for a claimant to circumvent the scope of an arbitration or jurisdiction clause by selectively pleading or not pleading certain causes of action. It would be an extraordinary outcome were a claimant successfully to be able to contend that, because a contractual claim had not been pleaded, a 'parallel' claim in tort arising out of exactly the same facts and with a scope defined by that contract fell outside the scope of such a provision. The proposition only has to be stated to be rejected.[108]

Therefore, in order to determine whether the competition law claim was within the scope of the arbitration agreement, Mr Justice Marcus Smith considered whether there was any genuine overlap between a *contractual claim* for the price negotiations to be carried out in good faith (allowing the injured party to recover any damages caused by a cartel member who breached their duty) and a *tortious claim* for antitrust damages which would allow the injured party to recover the difference between the price paid and the price which would have been paid, if there were no price-fixing arrangements.[109] Might one go a step further and argue that there is an 'implied term [for the parties] to comply with EU competition law'?[110] Should such 'a term […] be implied in […] contract[s with undertakings that enjoy market power] in order to give [them] business efficacy'?[111]

[104] Ibid 587.
[105] *Matthews* (n 81) 67-8.
[106] *Microsoft Mobile* (n 3).
[107] Ibid [70].
[108] Ibid [72ii].
[109] Ibid.
[110] PJ Kirby KC, 'Staying competition claims: a consideration of Microsoft v Sony', *Arbitration Blog*, Thomson Reuters, 20 March 2017.
[111] *Lister* (n 103) 576.

It would be more appropriate for the court to consider the terms of the contracts, classify the act restricting competition and take account of the parties' desired legal remedy with a view to deciding whether the competition law claim should classify as contractual or tortious. That said, it seems clear that there may be cases where a jurisdictional clause (or arbitration agreement) may cover not only competition law claims which classify as contractual, but also any related tortious claims for antitrust damages. These issues will be dealt with separately in section VI below.

C. Non-Validity Declarations and Counterclaims

There may be contractual terms which restrict competition,[112] with the parties seeking declaratory relief.[113] For example, a contracting party may claim that the contract or certain contractual terms would be in conflict with UK competition law. The desired remedy may be a non-validity declaration in respect of the whole contract[114] or, alternatively, the inclusion into the contract of such anti-competitive terms could raise a separate set of contractual issues as to how the principle of severance is to affect the nature of the parties' contractual arrangements.[115] It is well established that '[t]he question of severance arises where a particular provision is unlawful or void, and the choice is between invalidity of the whole agreement or of just the particular provision'.[116]

There may well be many competition law claims which would classify as contractual. For example, an association of undertakings[117] that is a holder of certain IP rights may grant a licence to its customers that requires them 'not to supply decoding devices enabling access to the protected subject-matter with a view to their use outside the territory covered by the licence agreement'.[118] If its customers[119] were to seek a declaration that the term in question is void,[120] then the competition law claim would classify as contractual. That said, given the fact that the party who is subject to a contract that is in conflict in competition law may simply refuse to comply with the term/s which restrict competition, many of the competition law claims – which seek a declaration of invalidity of certain contractual terms – may be raised as a defence in proceedings which are issued by the undertaking which may try to enforce the allegedly anti-competitive term or contract.[121]

Likewise, the opinion of AG Henrik Saugmandsgaard Øe leaves it beyond any doubt that a competition law claim which seeks a declaration that a contractual term or contract is invalid as being in conflict with competition law would classify as a matter relating to

[112] Case C-403/08 *Football Association Premier League Ltd and Others v QC Leisure and Others* EU:C:2011:631.
[113] *The Football Association Premier League Ltd v QC Leisure & ors* [2008] EWHC 44 (Ch).
[114] *English Welsh & Scottish Railway Ltd v E. On UK plc* [2007] EWHC 599 (Comm).
[115] R Whish and D Bailey, *Competition Law* 10th edn (Oxford, OUP, 2021) pp 344–5.
[116] *Courage Ltd v Crehan (No 1)* [1999] ECC 455 [154].
[117] *Football Association Premier League* – CJEU (n 112).
[118] Ibid [141 and 146].
[119] *Football Association Premier League* – EWHC (n 113). Compare: *Crehan (No.1)* (n 116).
[120] *Football Association Premier League* – EWHC (n 113) [17].
[121] Ibid.

a contract within the meaning of Article 7(1) of Brussels Ia and/or Section 2(c) of Sch 8 to the 1982 Act.[122] Following this line of reasoning, it can be suggested that the court at the place of performance of the contractual obligation that allegedly distorts competition would have jurisdiction to determine whether the parties' contract is compliant with competition law.[123]

If an undertaking were to try to enforce a contract (or a contractual term) which was in conflict with competition law and the anti-competitive conduct were to cause damages (or to result in damages being caused in future), the other party to the contract might even bring a counterclaim seeking damages and/or injunctive relief. The English court would have jurisdiction to hear and determine such competition law counterclaims because it is well established that a claimant who issues proceedings in England and Wales submits to the jurisdiction.[124] According to *Dicey, Morris and Collins*,[125] the following principles would be relevant in this context:

> A claimant who begins proceedings in general gives the court jurisdiction to entertain a counterclaim against the claimant which may extend to cases in which, if separate proceedings were to be brought, permission to serve process under CPR, r.6.36 and PD6B, para.3.1, i.e. Rule 35, might not be obtainable.[...] Although it is sometimes said that it is not necessary that the counterclaim be related to the claim,[...] the true principle is that a counterclaim is allowed so that justice can be done as between the parties.[...] In English law this principle is given effect by the rule that the court may require a counterclaim to be disposed of separately.[126]

In other words, there might even be a tactical advantage in certain cases for injured parties to refuse to comply with any anti-competitive terms and wait for the infringing undertaking to try to enforce such terms or contracts, so that counterclaims for antitrust damages could be also brought in England.

Somewhat similar principles would apply under Section 2(o)(iii) of the 1982 Act, which would be relevant if the UK CAT proceedings were to be treated as taking place in Scotland. That said, the 1982 Act appears to lay down the requirement for the 'counterclaim [to] aris[e] from the same contract or facts on which the original claim was based'.[127] This requirement is identical to the one which is set out in Article 8(3) of Brussels Ia. It seems clear that a counterclaim for private antitrust damages will satisfy this requirement as long as the counterclaim relates to the same agreement that is alleged to distort competition. There would be a factual connection between a claim for enforcement of a contract (or contractual term) and a counterclaim for antitrust damages which have been sustained by the restrictive terms of the very same agreement. In view of that, it seems that again the dispute over the compliance of the agreement

[122] *Wikingerhof* – opinion AG (n 65) [135]. Case C-38/81 *Effer v Kantner* [1982] ECR 825.

[123] Compare: *Boss Group* (n 31) 975. See *Kleinwort Benson* (n 71) 182; *Agnew* (n 74) 258. See also: A Briggs, 'Decisions of British courts during 1996: private international law' (1996) 67 *British Yearbook of International Law* 577, 583 (supporting the decision).

[124] *AK Investment CJSC v Kyrgyz Mobil Tel Limited and Others* [2011] UKPC 7 [72].

[125] *Dicey, Morris and Collins* (n 97).

[126] Ibid – Rule 33–[11–064].

[127] Section 2(o)(iii) of the 1982 Act.

with competition law and its terms' effect on the prices of volume of sales will be at the heart of the argument between the parties.

Accordingly, the requirement of Section 2(o)(iii) of the 1982 Act and Article 8(3) of Brussels Ia[128] that the claim and the counterclaim arise out of 'the same contract or facts'[129] will be easily satisfied as the application of competition law is largely a fact-based assessment. Moreover, there is no doubt that a private antitrust law damages claim would involve a separate judgment and could be distinguished from a pure defence.[130] Based on that, it can be stated that a claim for damages arising out of a contract that infringes competition law can be brought as a counterclaim on the basis of Section 2(o)(iii) of the 1982 and Article 8(3) of Brussels Ia.[131]

Therefore, there are two major sets of questions for the English courts to consider in order to systematically classify the issued competition law claims as tortious and/or contractual. The author would suggest a two-step test. First, the competition law infringement and the anti-competitive nature of the defendant's conduct should be set out. Secondly, the desired legal remedies which the parties seek to attain would also affect the classification of the competition law claims.[132] That said, different classification issues could arise depending on whether the competition law claim is issued by the consumer[133] (or on behalf of consumers)[134] and/or whether the parties' agreement includes a jurisdiction clause.[135]

IV. Consumer Claims – Some Specific Issues

As noted above, Section 15B of the 1982 Act is set to improve consumers' access to legal remedies in cross-border cases. The provision should have major implications for the jurisdiction of English courts in competition law cases where the claims are issued by consumers which are broadly defined to cover claims by 'a person who concludes the contract for a purpose which can be regarded as being outside the person's trade or profession'.[136] In this context, Section 15E(1) of the 1982 Act states that:

> 'consumer contract' means—
>
> (a) a contract for the sale of goods on instalment credit terms,
>
> (b) a contract for a loan repayable by instalments, or for any other form of credit, made to finance the sale of goods, or

[128] See Case C-341/93 *Danværn Production A/S v Schuhfabriken Otterbeck GmbH & Co* EU:C:1995:139 [7] (opinion of the AG Leger).

[129] Case VIII ZR 110/92 *Re A Counterclaim under Italian Law* [1995] ILPr 133 (Federal Supreme Court, Germany); *Cha Cha Denmark v Commercial Textiles* [2002] ILPr 53 (Danish Supreme Court); Case VIII ZR 263/00 *Re The Assertion of a Set-off and Counter Claim* [2003] ILPr 543 (Federal Supreme Court, Germany).

[130] Case C-341/93 *Danværn Production A/S v Schuhfabriken Otterbeck GmbH & Co* EU:C:1995:239 [12], [15], [16] and [18]. See also: A Briggs, 'Brussels Convention' (1995) 15 *YBEL* 498; T Hartley, 'Article 6(3): Counterclaims' (1996) 21 *ELR* 166.

[131] Compare: *Wikingerhof* – opinion AG (n 65) [137].

[132] Ibid [30 and 39].

[133] Section IV.

[134] Chapter 6.

[135] See: Section V below.

[136] Civil Jurisdiction and Judgments Act 1982 s 15E(1).

(c) a contract which has been concluded with a person who—
  (i) pursues commercial or professional activities in the part of the United Kingdom in which the consumer is domiciled, or
  (ii) by any means, directs such activities to that part or to other parts of the United Kingdom including that part,

and which falls within the scope of such activities,

but it does not include a contract of transport other than a contract which, for an inclusive price, provides for a combination of travel and accommodation or a contract of insurance.

Provided that the consumers' claims arise out of consumer contracts, they should be within the ambit of Section 15B of the 1982 Act. If the service users – who are consumers for the purposes of the 1982 Act – were to issue private antitrust damages claims, would such claims which naturally classify as tortious be within the scope of Section 15B of the 1982 Act? The fact that the response to this question has major practical implications was reflected in the UK CAT's reasoned order in *Dr Liza Lovdahl Gormsen v Meta Platforms.*[137]

It is increasingly common for claimants to issue proceedings against hi-tech giants that enjoy dominant positions.[138] For example, a dominant undertaking[139] may be imposing 'Unfair Data Requirement [that may be] contained in [its] Terms of Service'[140] which may also contain some 'unfair trading conditions'.[141] It should be noted that Section 15B of the 1982 Act is modelled on Section 4 of Brussels Ia, which strongly indicates that the CJEU jurisprudence rendered in this context should be persuasive.

In spite of the fact that Article 17 of Brussels Ia seems similar to Article 7(1) of Brussels Ia as both are using the expression 'matters relating to contract', the provisions are not identical – not least because the former has a specific purpose to protect the interests of consumers. Nonetheless, there is a view that the Court's 'interpretations [of] "matters relating to contract" in [Article 7(1) of Brussels Ia] have to be taken into account in interpreting the similar provisions of [Article 17 of Brussels Ia]'.[142] Notwithstanding, the more persuasive view is that '[Article 17 of Brussels Ia] constitutes a *lex specialis* in relation to [Article 7(1) of Brussels Ia]'.[143] The expression 'matters relating to contract' within the meaning of Article 17 of the Brussels Ia Regulation should be broadly interpreted to cover private antitrust damages claims that arise out of consumer contracts,[144] which should be in line with the spirit of consumer protection.

The interests of the consumers who have sustained antitrust damages would be more appropriately safeguarded if Section 15B of the 1982 Act were to be applicable with

[137] *Dr Liza Lovdahl Gormsen* (n 37) [5, 9 and 10]. See more: Chapter 6.

[138] Case No: 1408/7/7/21 *Elizabeth Helen Coll v Alphabet Inc* [2022] CAT 39; Case No: 1403/7/7/21, *Dr Rachael Kent v Apple* [2022] CAT 28; Case No: 1382/7/7/21, *Consumers' Association v Qualcomm Inc* [2022] CAT 20; *Dr Liza Lovdahl Gormsen* (n 37).

[139] *Dr Liza Lovdahl Gormsen* (n 37).

[140] Ibid [12a].

[141] Ibid [12c].

[142] Case C-89/91 *Shearson Lehmann Hutton v TVB Treuhandgesellschaft für Vermögensverwaltung und Beteiligungen* EU:C:1993:15 [87] of the opinion of AG Darmon.

[143] Case C-27/02 *Petra Engler v Janus Versand GmbH* EU:C:2005:33 [32].

[144] Compare: Case C-96/00 *Rudolf Gabriel* [2002] EU:C:2002:436 [49]; Case C-334/00 *Fonderie Officine Meccaniche Tacconi v Heinrich Wagner Sinto Maschinenfabrik* EU:C:2002:499 [23].

regard to all claims arising out of the contract. This would allow for a higher level of '"centralization" of jurisdiction'[145] at the court of the consumer's domicile. This might reasonably be attained by endorsing a 'one-stop method of adjudication'[146] in respect of all claims (including claims for private antitrust damages) arising out of consumer contracts.[147] The purpose of Articles 17 and 18 of Brussels Ia, which could reasonably and legitimately be pursued by Section 15B of the 1982 Act, is to enable the consumer to bring all claims arising out a contract before the same court. This would be important for the courts 'avoid, in so far as possible, creating a situation in which a number of courts had jurisdiction in respect of one and the same contract'.[148] Indeed, in *Reliantco Investment*,[149] the CJEU took the view that:

> In view of the fact that a multiplicity of courts having jurisdiction risks placing at a particular disadvantage a party deemed to be weak, such as a consumer, it is in the interest of the proper administration of justice that the latter should be able to bring before one and the same court all of the difficulties that are likely to arise from a contract which the consumer has allegedly been induced to conclude by reason of the professional's use of forms of wording liable to mislead the other contracting party (see, to that effect, judgment of 11 July 2002, *Gabriel*, C-96/00, EU:C:2002:436, paragraph 58).
>
> [... F]or the purposes of determining the courts having jurisdiction, an action in tort brought by a consumer comes under Chapter II, Section 4, of that regulation if it is indissociably linked to a contract actually concluded between that consumer and the seller or supplier, which is a matter for the national court to verify.[150]

A case for a broader interpretation of Section 15B of the 1982 Act to cover private antitrust damages claims arising out of consumer contracts may be further justified as follows.[151] First, the wording of Section 15B of the 1982 Act leaves no doubt that the provision is meant to cover all claims arising out of a contract concluded by a consumer.[152] This deduction can be strengthened by reading Section 15B(2) of the 1982 Act, which determines jurisdiction in such disputes by stating that '[a] consumer may bring proceedings against the other party to a contract' without limiting such proceedings to be concerned with contractual claims only. Indeed, Section 4 of Chapter II in Brussels Ia is without prejudice to Article 6 and Article 7(5) only, so that the courts' jurisdiction to hear and determine a private antitrust damages claim arising out of a consumer contract and closely related to the consumer contract in question could not be precluded by reference to Article 7(2) of Brussels Ia. In other words, Section 4 of Chapter II in the Brussels Ia

[145] Case C-89/91 *Shearson Lehmann Hutton v TVB Treuhandgesellschaft für Vermögensverwaltung und Beteiligungen* EU:C:1993:15 [108] (AG Darmon). Compare: *Premium Nafta Products Ltd v Fili Shipping* [2007] UKHL 40; *The Playa Larga* [1983] 2 Lloyd's Rep 171 (CA) 183; *The 'Angelic Grace'* [1995] 1 Lloyd's Rep 87, 89.

[146] *Premium Nafta Products Ltd v Fili Shipping* [2007] UKHL 40 [27].

[147] Compare Case C-180/06 *Renate Ilsinger v Martin Dreschers* EU:C:2009:303 [51].

[148] Case C-180/06 *Renate Ilsinger v Martin Dreschers* EU:C:2009:303 [44].

[149] Case C-500/18 *Reliantco Investment and Reliantco Investment Limassol Sucursala București* EU:C:2020:264.

[150] Ibid [63 and 73].

[151] See more: M Danov, 'The Brussels I Regulation: cross-border collective redress proceedings and judgments' (2010) 6 *Journal of Private International Law* 359; Danov (n 70) – s 2.2.5.

[152] Case C-27/02 *Petra Engler v Janus Versand GmbH* EU:C:2005:33 [34]. See more: J Hill, *Cross-border Consumer Contracts* (Oxford, OUP, 2008) 86–87.

Regulation would confer jurisdiction over contractual claims and closely related private antitrust damages claims arising out of such consumer contracts.

Secondly, the jurisdiction of courts over claims related to consumer contracts is special and is meant to strengthen consumer protection in the UK. Such jurisdiction should not be limited by the narrow interpretation defining claims under Article 7(1) under Brussels Ia which no longer applies in the UK.[153] A similar approach may be advanced within the EU where the proposal of AG Darmon in *Kalfelis* that 'an action based on tort and contract [...] is governed exclusively by the rules laid down for contractual matters'[154] is to be followed in respect of competition law claims brought by consumers under Section 4 of Chapter II of Brussels Ia. Such a deduction can be further strengthened by pointing out that:

> 'centralisation' of jurisdiction, which seemed to me necessary in the context of matters relating to a contract, referred to in [Article 7 of Brussels Ia], is even more necessary [with regard to] contracts concluded by a consumer, [who could suffer particular harm by reason of] the multiplication of bases of jurisdiction [...].[155]

This would certainly be a very strong argument in cases where there is a sufficiently close connection between a private antitrust damages claim and a consumer contract.[156] Thus, there are very strong legal and policy reasons indicating that Section 15B of the 1982 Act and Section 4 of Chapter II of Brussels Ia should both cover private antitrust damages claims that are closely connected with consumer contracts. This deduction could be strengthened by noting that '[c]onsumer litigation both publicizes abusive marketing practices and can play a role in deterring such practices being used in the future'.[157]

Therefore, there are very strong and persuasive arguments that Section 15B of the 1982 Act is set to enable the English courts to assume jurisdiction in claims for antitrust damages, which arise out of consumer contracts. It is an entirely separate question whether the scope of Section 15B of the 1982 Act should be broad enough to cover collective redress proceedings issues on behalf of multiple consumers under Section 47B of the Competition Act 1998.[158]

V. Jurisdiction Agreements

As already noted above, it would be common for infringing undertakings to enter into a number of contractual arrangements with their customers; such contracts may contain

[153] eg *Kalfelis* (n 69); Case C-334/00 *Fonderie Officine Meccaniche Tacconi v Heinrich Wagner Sinto Maschinenfabrik* EU:C:2002:499 [23]; Case C-96/00 *Rudolf Gabriel* [2002] EU:C:2002:436 [49].

[154] *Kalfelis* – AG Darmon (n 71) [31]. See also: Case C-89/91 *Shearson Lehmann Hutton v TVB Treuhandgesellschaft für Vermögensverwaltung und Beteiligungen* EU:C:1993:15 [111] (AG Darmon).

[155] Case C-89/91 *Shearson Lehmann Hutton v TVB Treuhandgesellschaft für Vermögensverwaltung und Beteiligungen* EU:C:1992:410 [108] (AG Darmon).

[156] This would be certainly so with regard to competition law claims which would raise a contractual claim (is the whole contract invalid, or is only part of it?) and a tortious claim (is there a breach of statutory duty and damages?). See more: Section 5.III above.

[157] Hill (n 152) 87.

[158] The question will be addressed in Chapter 6, which is set to address the specific issues in cases involving multiple claimants.

anti-competitive terms – charging excessive prices and/or imposing certain restrictions on the contracting parties. A closely connected issue, which was identified by Mr Justice Marcus Smith, concerns the fact that many undertakings that enjoy market power may wish to include jurisdiction agreements into the contracts with their customers. In other words, the issue is that certain agreements (which may, in whole or in part, have the effect of restricting competition and/or have an effect on prices of certain products) might also include jurisdiction and/or arbitration agreements.[159] There may even be 'exclusive jurisdiction clause[s] in the[ir] Terms of Service'.[160]

If competition law claims were to be issued in relation to these contracts, would the competition law claims be within the scope of the jurisdictional clause/agreement? The case law[161] appears to indicate that the issues concerning the scope of the jurisdiction clause are intertwined with the problems of classification of the competition law claims (which may arise in cases where there is a contract that includes a jurisdiction agreement between an infringing undertaking and its customer) as well as with the issues concerning the classification of the relevant anti-competitive conduct (considering its effects on the process of competition and/or prices). It will be demonstrated that these issues might need to be systematically addressed, in order for the English to take a lead in advancing an 'internationalist'[162] approach to classification with a view to minimising – as far as possible in a cross-border context – the risk for other national judges to classify certain claims arising out of the same contracts differently.

In order to determine whether a particular competition law claim falls within the scope of a choice-of-court agreement between the contractual parties,[163] there are two major steps to be followed. As noted above,[164] the first step is to classify the competition law claims as being contractual and/or tortious (which must be addressed in line with the case law discussed above). Secondly, the scope of the jurisdiction clause must be ascertained with a view to determining whether the so-classified competition law is within its scope. As part of this process, it would be necessary for a national judge to also classify the nature of the competition law infringement (ie the act restricting competition), considering its effect on the process of competition as well as on the prices, along with the desired legal remedies.

A. Scope – Competition Law Claims (Contractual v Tortious)

The difficult issues concerning the scope of jurisdiction and arbitration agreements and the issues concerning the classification of cross-border competition law claims arising out of contracts can be easily demonstrated by looking at the relevant case law.

[159] eg *Microsoft Mobile* (n 3); *Esso Italiana* (n 2) 1450.

[160] *Dr Liza Lovdahl Gormsen* (n 37) [15].

[161] eg Case C-352/13 *Cartel Damage Claims (CDC) Hydrogen Peroxide SA v Akzo Nobel NV* EU:C:2015:335; *Apple Sales International* (n 17); *Provimi* (n 42).

[162] *Raiffeisen* (n 68) [26]. See also: *Provimi* (n 42) [109].

[163] Case C-352/13 *Cartel Damage Claims (CDC) Hydrogen Peroxide SA v Akzo Nobel NV* EU:C:2015:335 [67]. See also: Case C-214/89 *Powell Duffryn plc v Wolfgang Petereit* EU:C:1992:115 [37]; *Case C-269/95 Francesco Benincasa v Dentalkit Srl* EU:C:1997:337 [31].

[164] See: Section III above.

The relevant issues may be deduced by considering the judgments of the Court of Appeal of England and Wales in *Ryanair Limited v Esso Italiana Srl*[165] and the High Court judgment in *Microsoft Mobile*[166] as well as the judgment of the Court of Justice of the European Union in *Apple Sales International v MJA*.[167]

As already noted above, the aspects concerning the classification of the relevant claims and the legal remedies desired by the claimant appear to be central to determining whether the dispute was within the scope of the jurisdictional clause. The issue concerning the classification of the nature of a competition law claim arising out of contract was further addressed under English law in *Ryanair Limited v Esso Italiana Srl*.[168] In this case, there was a contractual relationship between the parties; an interesting fact was that the competition law infringement was established by the Italian Competition Authority.[169] More specifically, the Italian regulator took the view that a cartel agreement had the effect to 'set up barriers to entry and distort and inflate the price of jet fuel supplied at various Italian airports'.[170] Esso Italiana along with other oil companies were parties to the anti-competitive agreement. In order to implement the agreement in question, the cartelists entered into individual contracts with various air companies, charging them excessive prices. One such contract was concluded between Ryanair and Esso Italiana.

The parties' contract included a 'non-exclusive English jurisdiction clause'.[171] Ryanair issued proceedings in England, relying on the parties' jurisdictional agreement, submitting the tortious claim for private antitrust damages was closely related to a contractual claim in relation to the relevant price arrangements between the parties.[172] Mr Justice Eder, sitting at the High Court of England and Wales, appeared to agree with Ryanair's argument in relation to the classification of the relevant contractual and tortious claims, which was important for him to ascertain whether the tortious claim was closely connected with the contractual claim.[173]

However, an appeal was allowed by the Court of Appeal of England and Wales. In particular, Lord Justice Rix held that 'there is no prospect of Ryanair having a contractual claim under [the contract] such as would give a remedy, albeit limited to goods supplied under the contract itself, which reduplicated the effect of a statutory duty pursuant to article 101 [TFEU]'.[174] Nonetheless, certain tortious claims may well be within the scope of the jurisdiction/arbitration agreement. In other words, the classification of a competition law claim as tortious does not necessarily mean that the claim is outside of the scope of the jurisdiction/arbitration agreement; the pleaded legal remedies and the nature of the infringement should be considered as well.

[165] *Esso Italiana* (n 2).
[166] *Microsoft Mobile* (n 3).
[167] *Apple Sales International* (n 17).
[168] *Esso Italiana* (n 2).
[169] Ibid [5].
[170] Ibid.
[171] Ibid [10].
[172] Ibid.
[173] Ibid [13–15].
[174] Ibid [41].

The importance for the English courts to 'uphold and enforce the parties' contractual bargain as set out in the arbitration agreement'[175] may also be factored in by the English courts. The relevant points could be derived from the judgment of the High Court of England and Wales in *Microsoft Mobile v Sony Europe*[176] which was briefly discussed above.[177] In this case, the competition law infringement appeared to be established by the EU Commission.[178] In order to classify the competition law claim – ascertaining the desired legal remedies and the scope of the jurisdiction agreement, the relevant anticompetitive conduct had to be set out.

More specifically, the claim concerned prohibited price-fixing arrangements which amounted to anti-competitive conduct within Article 101 TFEU.[179] 'There were, originally, six defendants'[180] which included Sony Europe and Sony Corporation which 'were [allegedly formed] part of a single economic unit, and so an "undertaking" for the purposes of EU and EEA competition law'.[181] Since Sony Europe was domiciled in England, the English courts were to have jurisdiction under Article 4 of Brussels Ia (which was directly applicable at the time).[182] That said, the fact that the 'other Defendants [we]re all companies domiciled in Japan and the Republic of Korea'[183] meant that, in order for the English courts to assume jurisdiction, the requirement for the service of claim form out of the jurisdiction had to be satisfied.[184] Such an order was duly rendered.[185]

Sony Europe (and Sony Corporation) sought a stay of the legal proceedings, relying on an arbitration clause[186] which formed part of the contracts that were binding for them. A specific feature of the parties' agreement is that it contained an express term for the product prices to be 'mutually agreed in writing and negotiated in good faith'.[187] Mr Justice Marcus Smith held that:

> There may be many reasons why a change in price might not be negotiated by SELLER in good faith, and so amount to a breach of [contract]. No doubt some of these might require consideration only of the conduct of SELLER, unrelated to SELLER's interactions with third parties. But, equally, SELLER's failure to act in good faith may [...] have been actuated by SELLER's dealings with third parties, in the form of a cartel or other (illegal) combination. In such a case, the overlap between the contractual claim, the cartel claim and the combination claim will be considerable.[188]

[175] *Enka Insaat Ve Sanayi AS v OOO Insurance Company Chubb* [2020] UKSC 38 [177].
[176] *Microsoft Mobile* (n 3).
[177] See: Section III.B above.
[178] CASE AT.39904, *Rechargeable Batteries – Commission Decision of 12.12.2016 relating to a proceeding under Article 101 of the Treaty on the Functioning of the European Union and Article 53 of the EEA Agreement* C(2016) 8456 final.
[179] *Microsoft Mobile* (n 3) [5, 6 and 10–15].
[180] Ibid [7].
[181] Ibid [8].
[182] Ibid [22 and 32].
[183] Ibid [24].
[184] Practice Direction 6B.
[185] *Microsoft Mobile* (n 3) [26].
[186] Ibid [35].
[187] Ibid [59].
[188] Ibid [72.vi].

If the arbitration clause was broad enough to cover the contractual claim that the prices were not negotiated in good faith, the tortious claim for antitrust damages would also be within its ambit.[189] Similarly, the English High Court had previously found that, despite the fact that claims for breach of competition law do raise regulatory concerns which are distinct from other tortious claims, the issues they raised in the particular dispute between the parties may be within the scope of an arbitration agreement.[190] Thus, the foregoing examples show that systematically ascertaining the question about the nature of the competition law claim/s and the desired legal remedies would be central to properly ascertaining whether competition law claims are within the scope of the arbitration agreement.

More importantly, Mr Justice Marcus Smith's judgment appeared to draw on the opinion of AG Jääskinen[191] and the CJEU judgment in *Cartel Damage Claims (CDC) Hydrogen Peroxide*[192] with a view to reiterating that it is for the national court to ascertain the scope the relevant arbitration/jurisdiction clause.[193] In particular, the CJEU held that:

> 68 A jurisdiction clause can concern only disputes which have arisen or which may arise in connection with a particular legal relationship, which limits the scope of an agreement conferring jurisdiction solely to disputes which arise from the legal relationship in connection with which the agreement was entered into. The purpose of that requirement is to avoid a party being taken by surprise by the assignment of jurisdiction to a given forum as regards all disputes which may arise out of its relationship with the other party to the contract and stem from a relationship other than that in connection with which the agreement conferring jurisdiction was made […].
>
> 69 In the light of that purpose, the referring court must, in particular, regard a clause which abstractly refers to all disputes arising from contractual relationships as not extending to a dispute relating to the tortious liability that one party allegedly incurred as a result of its participation in an unlawful cartel.[194]

As part of this process, it is important to draw a distinction between the PIL aspects in relation to the classification of the relevant competition law claims and the issues concerning the scope of the jurisdiction clauses (which may be broad enough to cover private antitrust damages claims). With this in mind, it should be noted that the act restricting competition and its effects on the process of competition and/or prices need to be set out. On that basis, the competition law claims are to be classified by the national judges with a view to determining whether they are within the scope of the jurisdiction agreement (or arbitration agreement).[195] For example, if there was an unlawful cartel between infringing undertakings that had the object of distorting the process of

[189] See more: below.

[190] *ET Plus SA & Ors v Welter & Ors [2005]* EWHC 2115 (Comm) [46 and 51].

[191] Case C-352/13 *Cartel Damage Claims (CDC) Hydrogen Peroxide SA v Evonik Degussa GmbH and Others* EU:C:2014:2443 – AG Jääskinen.

[192] Case C-352/13 *Cartel Damage Claims (CDC) Hydrogen Peroxide SA v Evonik Degussa GmbH and Others* EU:C:2015:335.

[193] *Microsoft Mobile* (n 3) [80–81].

[194] Case C-352/13 *Cartel Damage Claims (CDC) Hydrogen Peroxide SA v Evonik Degussa GmbH and Others* EU:C:2015:335 [68–69].

[195] *Provimi* (n 42) [57].

competition in so far as the antitrust harm would be caused by the unlawful cartel,[196] then any subsequent contract between the members of the cartel and their customers would only be implementing the unlawful cartel (ie imposing a cartel induced overcharge), affecting the prices which injured parties should be entitled to recover. These aspects should be thoroughly considered when ascertaining the scope of the jurisdiction agreement and parties' intentions.

B. Scope – Act/s Restricting Competition and Legal Remedies

The fact that Rome I explicitly states that jurisdiction agreements are excluded from its scope[197] appears to suggest that the law governing the jurisdiction clause or the arbitration agreement would apply to determine their validity as well as to ascertain whether they are broad enough to cover any competition law claims.[198] As far as the scope of the jurisdiction clauses is concerned, the English court's approach appears to be aligned with the one under Brussels Ia[199] and potentially Sch 8 to the 1982 Act.

Since the 'issue [of scope of jurisdiction clause] is to be determined by the "applicable law"',[200] the law governing the jurisdiction clause or arbitration agreements[201] must be ascertained in the first place. This means that interpreting the scope of jurisdiction agreements presupposes both the relevant restrictions of competition law (ie cartel agreements; abuses of dominant position) and the competition claims (ie contractual; tortious nature) to be systematically classified with a view to determining whether the dispute is within the scope of the jurisdiction agreement. The relevant issues were highlighted in *Provimi* where Mr Justice Aikens considered Swiss law,[202] French law[203] and German law[204] in order to determine whether the parties' claims for antitrust damages were within the scope of the parties' choice-of-court agreements governed by those laws.[205]

A closer look at the expert witnesses' submissions demonstrates that competition law claims arising out of contract, which implements certain anti-competitive arrangements, might be classified differently by various experts, giving evidence about their national laws. For example, despite the fact that the High Court of England and Wales classified the competition law claims as being tortious in nature, Mr Justice Aikens noted that:

> whilst both Professor Lécuyer and Professor Gaudemet-Tallon have said that the key issue is the nature of the claim, neither has analysed the claim by reference to the pleadings in the

[196] Compare: Case C-352/13 *Cartel Damage Claims (CDC) Hydrogen Peroxide SA v Evonik Degussa GmbH and Others* EU:C:2015:335.

[197] Article 1(2)(e) of the Rome I Regulation.

[198] *Dicey, Morris and Collins* (n 97) – Rule 42 [12–076].

[199] *Provimi* (n 42) [61]. See also: Case C-269/95 *Francesco Benincasa v Dentalkit Srl* EU:C:1997:337 [31].

[200] *Provimi* (n 42) [61]. *Dicey, Morris and Collins* (n 97) – Rule 42 [12-076]. Compare: O Kahn-Freud, 'Jurisdiction agreements: some reflections' (1977) 26 *ICLQ* 825, 828–829.

[201] *Enka Insaat Ve Sanayi AS v OOO Insurance Company Chubb* [2020] UKSC 38 [140].

[202] *Provimi* (n 42) [57–66].

[203] Ibid [103–125].

[204] Ibid [84–102].

[205] Ibid.

> Aventis actions. Moreover, neither expert has pointed to any Articles in the French Civil Code or other general doctrine of French law which might assist me in ascertaining the principles on which a French court would proceed when characterising the present claim. Effectively each has simply argued that a French court would regard the claim as either tortious or contractual in nature.[206]

The above quote captures that classifying a competition law claim may be quite a complex issue which presupposes an analysis of the claim in the light of the specific competition law restriction. Indeed, Mr Justice Aikens considered that Professor Gaudemet-Tallon failed to make a distinction between 'a case where the price was fixed unilaterally after the conclusion of a valid contract'[207] and a case where the price was fixed by infringing undertakings which participated in a cartel.

It was concluded that a widely drafted jurisdiction clause may not cover private antitrust damages claims under the laws of Switzerland, Germany and France. The deduction may be justified by the fact that, since the competition law claims were in relation to a secret and illegal cartel which had affected the prices, causing damages to the claimants, the scope of the jurisdiction agreements was not broad enough to cover the private antitrust damages claims in so far as the parties could not have intended to confer jurisdiction with regard to these claims to the chosen court.[208] In other words, it seems that the tortious classification along with the fact that the existence of an unlawful cartel (which may have had an effect on the prices of the cartelised product) have both been factored in when ascertaining the scope of the jurisdiction clauses. This conclusion could be strengthened by the CJEU judgment in *CDC*.[209]

That said, had there been a different act restricting competition (eg abuse of dominant position) and had there been a different competition law claim which classifies as contractual, the scope of the jurisdiction agreement could have been interpreted differently. For example, if the desired remedies were contractual in nature in so far as the parties may be seeking a declaration that certain contractual terms were invalid, then there would have been a contractual dispute of how the principle of severance of illegal provisions from otherwise lawful agreements would affect the parties' contract.[210] The level of complexity may be higher in cases where the restriction of competition is classified as abuse of dominant position,[211] with the relevant infringement being directly caused by the agreement between the dominant undertaking and the claimant parties which appears to have the effect of distorting competition.[212] For example, if a dominant undertaking is allegedly abusing its dominant position by imposing certain restrictive

[206] Ibid [116].
[207] Ibid [117].
[208] See more about the scope of the German jurisdiction clause, *Provimi* (n 42) [104]; the scope of the French jurisdiction clause [127]; the scope of the Swiss jurisdiction clause, *Provimi* (n 42) [67–68]. See also: Decision 16013/2001 *Re The Termination of a Distribution Contract* [2003] ILPr 633 (Multi-Member First Instance Court, Thessaloniki).
[209] Case C-352/13 *Cartel Damage Claims (CDC) Hydrogen Peroxide SA v Evonik Degussa GmbH and Others* EU:C:2015:335. See also: Tim Reher, 'Specific Issues in Cross-Border EU Competition Law Actions Brought by Multiple Claimants in a German Context' in M Danov, F Becker and P Beaumont (eds), *Cross-border EU Competition Law Actions* (Oxford, Hart Publishing, 2013).
[210] R Whish and D Bailey, *Competition Law* 10th edn (Oxford, OUP, 2021) pp 344–5.
[211] Francq and Wurmnest (n 47) 97.
[212] Compare: *Apple Sales International* (n 17) [17].

terms which are in conflict with Chapter 2 of the 1998 Act and/or Article 102 TFEU, then the competition law claims arising out of such contracts might classify differently.

Some important aspects concerning competition law claims arising out of contractual relationship between the parties were dealt with by the CJEU in the *Apple* case.[213] In this case, there was a semi-exclusive distributorship agreement between Apple Sales International and eBizcuss. The parties' contract included a choice-of-court agreement. In 2012, eBizcuss issued proceedings against Apple Sales International in France, submitting the defendant, inter alia, abused its dominant position. There was no prior decision of a competent regulator. The defendant challenged the jurisdiction of the French courts, invoking an Irish jurisdiction clause. This posed the question whether the advanced competition law claim was within the scope of the parties' choice of court agreement. The matter reached the CJEU, which took the view that:

> while the anti-competitive conduct covered by Article 101 TFEU, namely an unlawful cartel, is in principle not directly linked to the contractual relationship between a member of that cartel and a third party which is affected by the cartel, the anti-competitive conduct covered by Article 102 TFEU, namely the abuse of a dominant position, can materialise in contractual relations that an undertaking in a dominant position establishes and by means of contractual terms.[214]

In other words, the CJEU judgment in the *Apple* case[215] appears to indicate that the test is: does the relevant anti-competitive conduct directly materialise in the particular contractual relationship between the parties? In other words, do the terms of the agreement have a restrictive effect on the process of competition? If the answer were to be in the affirmative, then is the primary remedy contractual (ie declaratory relief)? If 'yes', then the claim would classify as a competition law claim which was connected to the contract and which might be within the scope of the jurisdiction agreement. For example, if there were terms of the contract which a dominant undertaking directly imposed certain restrictions on its customers, then the terms in question would constitute the actual anti-competitive conduct which would cause the relevant antitrust harm; and the primary remedy might be declaratory relief and/or injunction. If the answer were to be in the negative, then the question would be: does the anti-competitive conduct have an effect on the prices and/or the volume of sales? Are private antitrust damages the primary remedy which the parties seek to attain? If yes, then the competition law claim would classify as tortious.

The Court of Justice appears to take the view that 'a prior finding by a competition authority of an infringement of competition rules'[216] should not be seen as 'a prerequisite for the application of a jurisdiction clause':[217]

> 33 As the Advocate General observed in point 83 of his Opinion, the existence or absence of a prior finding by a competition authority of an infringement of competition rules has no connection with the considerations that must prevail when determining whether a jurisdiction clause is to apply in an action for damages allegedly suffered as a result of an infringement of competition rules.

[213] Ibid.
[214] Ibid [28].
[215] Ibid.
[216] Ibid [33 and 34].
[217] Ibid [36].

> 34 In the context of Article 23 of Regulation No 44/2001 [now Article 25 of Brussels Ia], a distinction dependent on the existence or absence of a prior finding by a competition authority of an infringement of competition law would also be contrary to the objective of foreseeability which underpins that provision.
>
> 35 Moreover, [...] the right of any person that considers himself or herself prejudiced by an infringement of competition law rules to seek compensation for the harm suffered is independent of the prior finding of such an infringement by a competition authority.[218]

That said, the CJEU failed to consider that if the regulatory breach had been established, the relevant contractual terms would have been invalidated; and the relevant competition law claim could have been classified as being tortious, with the primary remedy being antitrust damages. This would have meant that the jurisdictional clause could not have been broad enough to cover the competition law claim in question.

In other words, a prior regulatory decision establishing a competition law infringement might mean that the parties might desire different legal remedies. The desired legal remedies would in turn impact on the classification of a competition law claim as tortious or contractual which may in turn be determinative for the scope of the jurisdictional agreement.[219] In other words, if a competition law infringement had been established, then a competition law claim might reasonably seek entirely different primary legal remedies, which would have a bearing on the classification of the relevant claims.[220]

C. Specific Aspects for Consumer Contracts and Separability

As already noted, in order to invoke an exclusive jurisdiction agreement (or an arbitration agreement), the party would need to demonstrate not only that the competition law claims are within its scope, but also that the jurisdictional agreement (or arbitration agreement) is valid and enforceable. A specific feature of Section 15B of the 1982 Act is that it sets out some important requirements for jurisdictional clauses/agreements which are to be invoked in disputes against consumers. In particular, Section 15B(6) of the 1982 Act states that the rule allocating jurisdiction to the courts of the consumer's domicile

> may be departed only by an agreement -
>
> (a) which is entered into after the dispute has arisen,
>
> (b) which allows the consumer to bring proceedings in courts other than those indicated in this section, or
>
> (c) which is entered into by the consumer and the other party to the contract, both of whom are at the time of conclusion of the contract domiciled or habitually resident in the United Kingdom and in the same part of the United Kingdom, and which confers jurisdiction on the courts of that part of the United Kingdom, provided that such an agreement is not contrary to the law of that part of the United Kingdom.

218 Ibid [33–35].
219 See: Chapter 7.
220 Compare: *Epic Games* (n 22).

In other words, the effect of Section 15B of the 1982 Act is that jurisdiction clauses that do not comply with the above conditions would not be enforceable.[221] The rationale behind such a restrictive rule is that the UK domiciled consumers' access to effective legal remedies was facilitated by the introduction of more effective and efficient collective redress mechanisms which may be issued on an opt-in or opt-out basis under Section 47B of the 1998 Act.[222] Indeed, whilst consumers may be reluctant to litigate a competition law claim abroad where they would incur higher costs and would have to manage cross-border litigation risks,[223] they could access generous litigation funding in this country in appropriate cases.[224]

The position under Section 15B of the 1982 Act is closely aligned with the one under Section 4 of the Brussels Ia Regulation. In line with Article 19(1) of Brussels Ia, an infringing undertaking would not be able to rely on a jurisdiction agreement which formed part of a consumer contract unless the jurisdiction agreement was entered into after the dispute had arisen; or at the time of the conclusion of the contract the consumer and the infringing undertaking were domiciled or habitually resided in the same Member State and agreed to the jurisdiction of the courts of that Member State.[225] This would be the case irrespective of whether the jurisdictional agreement was in respect of a Member State court or a non-Member State court.[226]

Finally, it should be noted that the doctrine of separability will have an important role to play in cases where it is alleged that the contract (and incorporated jurisdictional clause) were void *ab initio* under the applicable substantive competition laws. The rationale behind the separability principles was summarised by the UK Supreme Court as follows:

> Under the separability doctrine, an arbitration agreement is viewed for certain purposes, both at common law and under section 7 of the Arbitration Act 1996, as a separate contract from the main contract. The reason for that is in order to ensure that the arbitration agreement is effective despite the non-existence, invalidity, termination or rescission of the main contract. In other words, it stops the argument that the parties have not agreed to arbitration to deal with disputes about the non-existence, invalidity or initial ineffectiveness of the main contract; and it also stops the argument that the arbitration agreement cannot deal with disputes once the main contract has been terminated or rescinded.[227]

It is now well established that the doctrine of separability is applicable not only in relation to arbitration agreements, but also with regard to 'jurisdiction clauses at common law, at least where the jurisdiction agreement is governed by English law'.[228] The doctrine of separability appears to be also advanced in respect to jurisdiction agreements[229]

[221] *Dicey, Morris and Collins* (n 97) – Rule 42 [12–071].
[222] See more: Chapter 6.
[223] Hill (n 152) 196–197.
[224] eg *Qualcomm* (n 138); *Dr Liza Lovdahl Gormsen* (n 37).
[225] Article 19(3) of the Brussels Ia Regulation. See more: Hill (n 152) 196–200.
[226] Compare: *Samengo-Turner v March & McLennan (Services) Ltd* [2007] EWCA Civ 723, [2008] ICR 18 (CA).
[227] *Enka Insaat Ve Sanayi AS v OOO Insurance Company Chubb* [2020] UKSC 38 [232].
[228] *Dicey, Morris and Collins* (n 97) – Rule 42 [12-079].
[229] Case C-214/89 *Powell Duffryn v Peteriet* EU:C:1992:115 [14]. See also: Case C-269/95 *Benincasa v Dentalkit* EU:C:1997:78 [73] opinion of AG R-J Colomer.

which come with the Brussels Ia regime, with the CJEU drawing a distinction between the 'jurisdiction clause and the substantive' terms of the parties' agreement because 'the jurisdiction clause [...] serves a procedural purpose [so it is to be] governed by the provisions of the [Brussels Ia Regulation]'.[230]

The relevance of the doctrine of separability with regard to jurisdiction agreements was explicitly confirmed by the English Court of Appeal in *Deutsche Bank AG v Asia Pacific Broadband Wireless Communications*[231] where Lord Justice Longmore held that:

> It is only if the jurisdiction clause is itself under some specific attack that a question can arise whether it is right to invoke the jurisdiction clause. Examples of this might be fraud or duress alleged in relation specifically to the jurisdiction clause. Another example might be if the signatures to the agreement were alleged to be forgeries, although no authority has so far so stated. Even in such a case someone has to decide whether the signatures were in fact forged. It might well be thought that a mere allegation to that effect could not have the effect of rendering a jurisdiction clause inapplicable.[232]

Therefore, the doctrine of separability might have some implications for certain competition claims where there is a dispute about the validity of the contract between an infringing undertaking and its customer in so far as such a dispute would normally be within the scope of the jurisdictional clause.

VI. Service Out of the Jurisdiction – Contractual Competition Law Claims

As noted above,[233] there would be two major sets of competition law claims which would classify as contractual and which would fall within the ambit of the contractual gateways of PD 6B. First, it is now established that 'an action for a declaration that a contract is null and void'[234] would classify as contractual. Although it is possible for the whole contract to be invalidated,[235] it is often possible that there may be a genuine contractual dispute about the extent to which a contractual term which is in conflict with UK competition would entail the invalidity of the whole contract.[236]

Secondly, the English common law appears to indicate there may be a category of competition law claims which would arise out of a breach of a contract (ie a specific product not being supplied) that also constitutes a competition law infringement (ie refusal to supply). Also, the obligation for an undertaking which enjoys market power to set out its prices 'in good faith'[237] might be an express[238] or implied

[230] *Benincasa* (n 163) [24–25].
[231] *Deutsche Bank AG and Others v Asia Pacific Broadband Wireless Communications Inc and Another* [2008] EWCA Civ 1091 [24].
[232] Ibid [24].
[233] See: Section III above.
[234] *Wikingerhof* – opinion AG (n 65) [135].
[235] *English Welsh & Scottish Railway Ltd v E. On UK plc* [2007] EWHC 599 (Comm) [29]–[30].
[236] Ibid. See also: *Courage Ltd v Crehan (No 1)* [1999] ECC 455 [154]. See more: R Whish and D Bailey, *Competition Law* 10th edn (Oxford, OUP, 2021) pp 344–5.
[237] *Microsoft Mobile* (n 3) [59].
[238] Ibid.

contractual term;[239] and it is also a statutory duty for such an undertaking to be compliant with UK competition law.[240]

It should be noted that para 3.1(6) of PD 6B enables a claimant to 'serve a claim form out of the jurisdiction with the permission of the court under rule 6.36 where':[241]

> A claim is made in respect of a contract where the contract –
>
> (a) was (i) made within the jurisdiction or (ii) concluded by the acceptance of an offer, which offer was received within the jurisdiction;
> (b) was made by or through an agent trading or residing within the jurisdiction or
> (c) is governed by the law of England and Wales.

Although the wording of the above gateway appears to indicate that a non-validity declaration may not come within its ambit of para 3.1(6) of PD 6B, a claim seeking a declaration that a contract is invalid under UK competition law would come within para 3.1(8) of PD 6B. More specifically, the latter gateway allows for a claim to be 'made for a declaration that no contract exists where, if the contract was found to exist, it would comply with the conditions set out in paragraph (6)'.[242] The primary issue which the court would deal with in such a case would be whether the specific contract as a whole or certain terms of the contract would be in a conflict with competition law. The desired legal remedy would be for the claimant to obtain a declaratory relief. Para 3.1(8) of PD 6B must be read and interpreted together with para 3.1(6) of PD 6B.

A very important ground which may be relied upon in cross-border competition law cases is para 3.1(6)(c) of PD 6B. The rule allows for a claim form to be served out of the jurisdiction in cases where a claimant makes a good arguable case that 'the contract is governed by the law of England and Wales'. The Rome I Regulation is to be applied[243] to determine whether a contract by its terms or by implication is governed by English law for jurisdictional purposes.[244] If English law was applicable, then the 1998 Act should apply and the required territorial connection between the forum and the defendant's conduct/act restricting competition would be sufficient for the claim form to be served out of the jurisdiction.

It should also be noted that choice-of-law rules cannot restrict the application of the provisions which cannot be derogated within the meaning of Article 3(3) of Rome I and the overriding mandatory provisions of the forum under Article 9(2) of Rome I.[245] If the UK mandatory provisions were applicable to determine whether a contract was valid under UK competition law and another law were to govern the other contractual matters,[246] then different laws could govern different contractual claims.[247] If a claimant

[239] Kirby (n 110).
[240] *Lister* (n 103) 587.
[241] Para 3.1 of PD 6B.
[242] Civil Procedure Rules para 3.1(8) PD 6B.
[243] Statutory Instruments 2019 No 834 *Exiting the European Union Private International Law – The Law Applicable to Contractual Obligations and Non-Contractual Obligations (Amendment etc.) (EU Exit) Regulations 2019*; *Bank of Baroda v Vysya Bank* [1994] 2 Lloyd's Report 87 (QBD (Comm)); *Egon Oldendorff v Liberia Corporation* [1995] 2 Lloyd's Rep 64 (Comm).
[244] *Dicey, Morris and Collins* (n 97) Rule 35 [11-156]; See also: JJ Fawcett, 'The interrelationship of jurisdiction and choice of law in private international law' (1991) 44 *CLP* 39.
[245] Chapter 10.
[246] Compare: *Lyle & Scott Ltd v American Eagle Outfitters* [2021] EWHC 90 (Ch) [77].
[247] WLM Reese, 'Dépeçage: A Common phenomenon in Choice of Law' [1973] 73 *Colum L Rev* 58.

were to make a case that – regardless of the applicable law under Rome I – the claimants had reasonable prospects of success in establishing that the anti-competitive conduct was *implemented* in England or had *qualified effects* in the UK,[248] then, given the public policy nature of UK competition law, UK competition law should be applied to determine whether the contract was valid. The requirements for anti-competitive practice to be 'implemented' or to have 'qualified effects' in the UK market should discourage claimants from raising frivolous competition law claims in purely contractual disputes in order to have their disputes litigated in England.

The importance of the UK competition law – which should enjoy the status of overriding mandatory provisions for the purposes of Rome I – means that the requirement for the contract to be governed by English law for the purposes of para 3.1(6) of PD 6B would be satisfied in cases where a contracting party makes a claim for a declaration that the contract is void as being in conflict with UK competition law. Indeed, according to the editors of *Dicey, Morris and Collins*:[249]

> where an issue of English public policy arises in relation to a contract which is (or may be) governed by English law, it is desirable that it should be decided by the English court; [...] conversely, where the foreign court may apply its own public policy to defeat a claim based on a contract governed by English law, that too is a reason for the English court taking jurisdiction.[250]

Therefore, there are strong arguments suggesting that the fact that UK competition law would be applicable to the contractual competition law about the validity of contract or contractual terms would be sufficient to satisfy the requirement concerning the territorial connection between the forum and the defendant's competition law infringement. Hence, the fact that the UK competition law and indeed English public policy is at stake should suffice for the purposes of PD 6B, provided that there is a reasonable prospect for the claimant to establish that the 'implementation' test and/or the 'qualified effects' test[251] were satisfied, indicating that UK competition law must apply.

In addition, a claim form in relation to competition law claims which classify as contractual may be served out of the jurisdiction in cases where the contract that contains terms that are in conflict with competition law 'was made within the jurisdiction'[252] or in cases where the 'contract was made by or through an agent trading or residing within the jurisdiction'.[253] The question whether the contract was made 'by or through' a local agent would be a question of fact and there are no particular difficulties in applying this rule to competition law claims, but given the nature of competition law cases, which often involve sophisticated multinational companies enjoying market power and penetrating the markets through their subsidiaries, it is unlikely for this to be often relevant in competition law cases.

More importantly, there might be competition law cases where it could be difficult to determine the place where the contract was made for the purposes of para 3.1(6)(a)

[248] *Epic Games* (n 22) [88]. See also: *The LCD Appeals* [2018] EWCA Civ 220.
[249] *Dicey, Morris and Collins* (n 97) Rule 35.
[250] Ibid [11-157].
[251] *The LCD Appeals* [2018] EWCA Civ 220.
[252] Civil Procedure Rules para 3.1(6)(a) of PD 6B.
[253] Civil Procedure Rules para 3.1(6)(b) of PD 6B.

of PD 6B. In such cases, the relevant place might be 'determined by reference the provisions of English domestic law on the conclusion of contracts'.[254] The rules appear to be derived from the judgment in *Entores v Miles Far East Corporation*[255] where Lord Denning held:

> When a contract is made by post it is clear law throughout the common law countries that the acceptance is complete as soon as the letter is put into the post box, and that is the place where the contract is made. […]
>
> [T]he rule about instantaneous communications between the parties is different from the rule about the post. The contract is only complete when the acceptance is received by the offeror: and the contract is made at the place where the acceptance is received. In a matter of this kind, however, it is very important that the countries of the world should have the same rule.[256]

It has been suggested that the place where 'the acceptance is received by the offeror'[257] should be the relevant connecting factor which should be considered by the courts to determine where a contract is concluded by emails.[258] The rule might be difficult to apply in some competition cases where multiple contracts might be concluded with different subsidiaries which are based in different countries and which form part of the same multinational group of companies.[259] Nonetheless, the claimant in competition law cases would normally be able to invoke the unique character of competition laws as governing the competition law claim for the purposes of para 3.1(6)(c) PD 6B, provided the conduct is within the territorial scope of 1998 Act. In such cases, the contract gateway should work reasonably well as long as the competition law claims classify as contractual and the desired legal remedies are also contractual (eg non-validity declaration).

The above deduction could be strengthened by noting the important role which paras 3.1(7) and (8A) of PD 6B as well as para 3.1(4A) of PD 6B could play in some cases. First, paras 3.1(7) and (8A) of PD 6B allow the English courts to assume jurisdiction in cases where the claim is made in respect of a breach of a contract committed within the jurisdiction. This might be relevant in cases where there is an overlap between a *contractual claim* seeking specific performance or damages for a breach of contractual obligation to set the prices in good faith[260] and a *tortious claim* for antitrust damages. Such a broad interpretation would be in line with Lord Sellers's broad interpretation of PD 6B in *Matthews v Kuwait Bechtel Corporation*.[261]

Secondly, para 3.1(4A)(c) of PD 6B was introduced to allow for a claim form to be served out of the jurisdiction in cases where 'a claim is made against the defendant which […] falls within [para 3.1(6) of PD 6B], and a further claim is made against the same defendant which arises out of the same or closely connected facts'.[262] The central question concerns the extent to which the facts are required to be identical and/or

[254] *Dicey, Morris and Collins* (n 97) [11-150].
[255] See *Entores LD v Miles Far East Corporation* [1955] 2 QB 327.
[256] Ibid 332–4.
[257] Ibid 333.
[258] *Dicey, Morris and Collins* (n 97) [11-150].
[259] Compare: *Four Seasons Holdings Incorporated v Brownlie* [2017] UKSC 80 [16].
[260] *Microsoft Mobile* (n 3).
[261] *Matthews* (n 81) 67–8. See also: *Dicey, Morris and Collins* (n 97) Rule 35 [11-157].
[262] Civil Procedure Rules para 3.1(4A)(c) of PD 6B.

connected for the further claim to be regarded as being within the scope of para 4A. In *Eli Lilly v Genentech*,[263] Mr Justice Birss took the view that:

> The purpose of gateway (4A) is to allow the joinder of a further claim against the same defendant based on the same or closely connected facts so as to further the interests of justice, including taking into account practical considerations such as procedural economy and an avoidance of inconsistent results.
>
> If facts unique to the second claim include disputed matters of primary fact and would require extensive cross-examination and disclosure resolve, then that would support a conclusion that the connection between the facts is not sufficiently close to justify service out. But if the key factual issues in the second claim are facts it has in common with the anchor claim and the difference in the relevant facts is only on matters which are undisputed or which can readily be dealt with without substantial disclosure and little or no cross-examination, then the factual connection may be sufficiently close to justify service out.[264]

The above test appears to indicate that the claimant's pleadings need to carefully consider the aspects concerning the relevant facts and the necessary evidence which is required to substantiate the specific competition law claims. Since the wording of para 3.1(4A)(c) of PD 6B 'make it clear that the facts need not be the same provided that they are closely connected',[265] it could be argued that a contractual claim that certain terms which have the effect to distort competition are invalid could be closely connected with a tortious claim that the contractual terms in question affected the prices or the volume of claimant's sales.

VII. Some Conclusions

It is well established that private antitrust damages claims would classify as tortious[266] irrespective of whether they arise out of contract and irrespective of whether they raise incidental contractual issues.

More difficult issues would arise with regard to competition law claims which are issued by contracting parties who have entered into contractual arrangements with undertakings whose conduct is anti-competitive. A two-step test could be suggested in a scenario where the same facts give rise to contractual and tortious claims. Do the claimant's pleadings raise concerns that certain contractual terms have the effect of restricting competition? If yes, what are the legal remedies which the injured parties seek to attain?[267] Does the contracting party seek any financial and/or injunctive relief? Or do they simply seek a declaration that a contract or contractual term is in conflict with competition law and, thus, void?

There might also be difficult issues that would arise in cases where the parties' contracts include jurisdiction (or arbitration) clauses. In such a scenario, a common

[263] *Eli Lilly & Co v Genentech Inc* [2017] EWHC 3104 (Pat).
[264] Ibid [32 and 33].
[265] *Apple v Qualcomm* [2018] EWHC 1188 (Pat) [84].
[266] See: Chapters 3 and 4.
[267] *Esso Italiana* (n 2) [30 and 39].

question would be whether a competition law claim is within the scope of the choice-of-court agreement. The current jurisprudence appears to indicate that the test is: does the relevant anti-competitive conduct directly materialise in the particular contractual relationship between the parties? In other words, do the terms of the agreement have a restrictive effect on the process of competition? That said, there are specific rules with regard to consumer contracts. A choice-of-court agreement would be binding for a consumer, only if the parties had agreed upon it after the dispute had arisen.[268] Indeed, it is well settled that private antitrust damages claims arising out of consumer contracts should be within the scope of Section 15B of the 1982 Act which is set to safeguard the rights of the UK consumers and which allows them to issue their competition law claims before the courts of their domicile.

Finally, having considered the contract and tort[269] gateways which are set out in para 3.1 of PD 6B, it should be noted that it is doubtful whether a multinational group of companies can be regarded as having established a 'place of business [...] within the jurisdiction'[270] when it engages in economic activities in England and Wales through its local subsidiary which is a separate legal entity. The classification problems might arise because a local subsidiary is not a branch, which means that a claim form could not be served to its parent company within the jurisdiction.

The issues are important because many competition law infringements would involve a multinational group of companies that may have numerous subsidiaries, causing damages to multiple injured parties in different jurisdictions. For example, an infringing undertaking may implement various anti-competitive practices by setting up a subsidiary or an exclusive distributor that markets a cartelised product at an inflated price or provides certain services by charging excessive prices (ie abusing its dominant position). Therefore, the parent–subsidiary relationship within a multinational group of companies could give rise to complex issues in relation to classification for private international law purposes. An important question is: to what extent should a multinational group of companies, which is used to reflect the specific economic realities and which is reflected in the broad competition law concept of undertaking, be considered as a single (albeit transnational) unit for the purposes of assuming jurisdiction against a multinational group of companies that carries its economic activities by setting up a subsidiary in England and Wales?

[268] Article 19(3) of the Brussels Ia Regulation. See more: Hill (n 152) 196–200.
[269] Chapter 4 above.
[270] CPR 6.9(2).

6

Multiple Claimants and/or Multiple Defendants

I. Introduction – Multiple Injured Parties and/or Multiple Infringers

The complex PIL issues that surface in relation to antitrust claims arising out of anticompetitive agreements appeared to be signalled in the *CDC*[1] case, which happened to be the first private antitrust damages claim that raised PIL issues and reached the CJEU. It should be noted that the private antitrust damages claims were preceded by an EU Commission decision[2] which established a transnational competition law infringement. This might explain why the jurisdictional issues were in relation to 'claims for damages [involving] 32 undertakings domiciled in 13 different Member States of the European Union or of the European Economic Area'.[3] The CJEU proceedings clearly demonstrated that complex jurisdictional issues had to be systematically dealt with because the anti-competitive conduct appeared to cause antitrust damages to a number of businesses in different EU Member States.

The transnational nature of competition law infringements strongly indicates that antitrust damages could be caused by multinational groups of companies to multiple injured parties (ie consumers, SMEs, large companies) in different jurisdictions. There would be at least two major issues that would need to be dealt with through PIL rules that promote judicial cooperation in competition law matters. First, it is common for judges to deal with multiple private antitrust damages claims, which would often involve groups of companies, sustaining/causing antitrust damages in multiple jurisdictions.[4] Secondly, it is increasingly common to have collective redress claims which are issued on behalf of multiple injured parties, and in particular consumers,[5]

[1] Case C-352/13 *Cartel Damage Claims (CDC) Hydrogen Peroxide SA v Evonik Degussa GmbH and Others* EU:C:2015:335.

[2] Case COMP/F/38.620, *Hydrogen Peroxide and Perborate – Commission Decision relating to a proceeding pursuant to Article 81 of the EC Treaty and Article 53 of the EEA Agreement* C(2006) 1766 final.

[3] *Cartel Damage Claims* (n 1) [11].

[4] eg *Cooper Tire & Rubber Company v Shell Chemicals UK Limited* [2009] EWHC 2609 (Comm); *Motorola Mobility LLC v AU Optronics Corp* 775 F3d 816 (7th Cir, 2015).

[5] eg Case No: 1433/7/7/22, *Dr Liza Lovdahl Gormsen v Meta Platforms Inc, Meta Platforms Ireland Ltd, Facebook UK Ltd* – Reasoned Order, dated 15 March 2022 [17]. See also: Case No: 1403/7/7/21, *Dr Rachael Kent v Apple Inc. Apple Distribution Int'l Ltd* [2022] CAT 28 [6]; Case No: 1408/7/7/21, *Elizabeth Helen Coll v Alphabet Inc* – Reasoned order of the President – Service out of the jurisdiction – 29 September 2021 [11].

against multinational groups of companies that enjoy significant market power in numerous jurisdictions.

There are two sets of jurisdictional rules which should be used by the English courts to assume jurisdiction in cases involving multiple claimants (ie various injured parties) and/or multiple defendants (ie several infringing undertakings or a number of separate legal entities forming part of the same infringing undertaking). The first set of rules is to be found in Section 15B of the Civil Jurisdiction and Judgments Act 1982. As already noted, it is well settled now that the scope of the latter provision is broad enough to cover private antitrust damages claims which are issued by consumers.[6] That said, it is important to ascertain whether Section 15B of the 1982 Act could be relied upon by 'a person [who is authorised] to act as the representative in collective proceedings'[7] brought on behalf of consumers.

The second set of jurisdictional rules which will be examined in this chapter are the Civil Procedure Rules, which would be applicable in relation to private antitrust damages claims which are issued against multiple defendants. It is well established that if competition law damages are sustained in England and Wales, multiple claimants could issue private antitrust damages claims against multiple defendants by relying on para 3.1(9) of PD 6B.[8] In order to outline the important issues which need to be addressed in a post-Brexit context, this chapter will examine para 3.1(3) of PD 6B, which along with para 3.1(9) of PD 6B, both would often be cumulatively invoked as 'alternative bases for jurisdiction'[9] in competition law cases which involve multiple defendants.[10]

II. Multiple Consumers – Section 15B of the 1982 Act

As noted in the previous chapter, Section 15B of the 1982 Act has been modelled on Section 4 of Brussels Ia. In view of this it might be thought that the question about its scope and appropriateness to cover private antitrust damages claims issued on behalf of multiple consumers might need to be considered in light of the relevant case law advanced by the CJEU.

In the EU context, it has been submitted that the answer to the question about the scope of Section 4 of Brussels Ia would depend on the nature of the legal remedies which are being sought on behalf of consumers.[11] For example, the CJEU has taken the view

[6] See: Chapter 5.IV above.

[7] Competition Act 1998 s 47B(8).

[8] JJ Fawcett, 'Multi-party Litigation in Private International Law' (1995) 44 *ICLQ* 744, 745. See more: *Elizabeth Helen Coll* (n 5) [9–10]; *Dr Liza Lovdahl Gormsen* (n 5).

[9] Fawcett (n 8) 745.

[10] Case No: 1377/5/7/20, *Epic Games v Apple and Google* [2021] CAT 4 [89]; Case No: 1468/7/7/22 *Mr Justin Gutmann v Apple* – Reasoned Order (Service out of the jurisdiction) – 26 July 2022 [14]; Case No: 1437/7/7/22 *Elisabetta Sciallis v Fender Musical Instruments Europe Ltd* – Order (Service out of the jurisdiction) – 17 June 2022 [18–19]; *JJH Enterprises Ltd (ValueLicensing) v Microsoft Corp* [2022] EWHC 929 (Comm); Case No: 1440/7/7/22, *Clare Mary Joan Spottiswoode CBE v Nexans France S.A.S. & Others* – Reasoned Order of the President (Service out of the Jurisdiction) 19 August 2022 [19–21].

[11] M Danov, 'The Brussels I Regulation: cross-border collective redress proceedings and judgments' (2010) 6 *Journal of Private International Law* 359.
M Danov, *Jurisdiction and Judgments in Relation to EU Competition Law Claims* (Oxford, Hart Publishing, 2010).

that competition law proceedings are not within the scope of Section 4 of Brussels Ia in cases where the claims are issued in the public interest by a consumer association in respect of allegedly anticompetitive conduct *notwithstanding the absence of damage.*[12] The author, however, thinks that Section 4 of Brussels Ia may be invoked by a consumer representative who has issued collective redress proceedings seeking antitrust damages caused by a transnational competition law infringement on behalf of identified (or identifiable) consumers.

Notwithstanding, the question about the scope of Section 4 of Brussels Ia has received a renewed attention in the EU context.[13] The EU debate has been fostered by the adoption of Directive (EU) 2020/1828 on representative actions for the protection of the collective interests of consumers.[14] There are several qualifications to be made in this context. First, it should be noted that Directive (EU) 2020/1828 does not extend to collective redress antitrust proceedings. It is a major surprise that infringements of Articles 101 and 102 TFEU do not appear among the 'collective interests'[15] which the Directive is set to safeguard.

Secondly, whilst it makes sense for the interpretation of the Brussels Ia regime to be aligned[16] with the collective redress mechanisms that are devised by the EU and EU Member States in order for them 'to bring unlawful practices to an end and to obtain redress for consumers',[17] there is a strong argument that the interpretation of Section 15B of the 1982 Act should rather be brought it into line with Section 47B of the Competition Act 1998 which is set to improve UK consumers' access to legal remedies in competition law cases.[18] Hence, Section 15B of 1982 Act and Section 47B of the 1998 Act should be consistently interpreted.

Thirdly, it is essential to outline that, when interpreting Section 15B of the 1982 Act, it may be very important for judges to give 'further consideration [...] to the use of third party funding as a last resort means of providing access to justice'.[19] The latter point is also reflected in Lord Justice Henderson's judgment in *Paccar Inc v Road Haulage Association Ltd and UK Trucks Claim Ltd*[20] where the judge noted that '[t]hird party litigation funding is now a substantial industry which, although driven by commercial motives, is widely acknowledged to play a valuable role in furthering access to justice'.[21] In this context, the judge made a reference to Lord Justice Jackson's *Review of Civil*

[12] Case 167/00 *Verein für Konsumenteninformation v Karl Heinz Henkel* EU:C:2002:555 [32–33].

[13] F Rielaender, 'Aligning the Brussels Regime with the Representative Actions Directive' (2022) 71 *ICLQ* 107–138; A Pato, *Jurisdiction and Cross-Border Collective Redress: A European Private International Law Perspective* (Oxford, Hart Publishing, 2019) 153–55.

[14] Directive (EU) 2020/1828 *on representative actions for the protection of the collective interests of consumers* [2020] Official Journal L409.

[15] Article 2(1) of Directive (EU) 2020/1828.

[16] Rielaender (n 13).

[17] Recital 1 of Directive (EU) 2020/1828.

[18] Competition Act 1998 s 47B(11)(b).

[19] Recommendation 13 – M Napier, P Hurst, R Musgrove and J Peysner, *'Improved Access to Justice – Funding Options & Proportionate Costs' Report & Recommendations* at 12, https://www.judiciary.uk/wp-content/uploads/JCO/Documents/CJC/Publications/CJC+papers/CJC+Improved+access+to+Justice+-Funding+options+and+proportionate+costs.pdf.

[20] *Paccar Inc v Road Haulage Association Ltd and UK Trucks Claim Ltd* [2021] EWCA Civ 299.

[21] Ibid [5].

Litigation Costs: Final Report[22] which in turn indicates that facilitating injured parties' access to finance should improve their access to legal remedies in cross-border competition law cases.

The point that consumers' access to legal remedies might be dependent on their access to finance is reflected in Directive (EU) 2020/1828, which noted that the litigation costs may be financed by 'traders or hedge funds, including in the event of funding by third parties'.[23] In other words, it seems that the correlation between the injured parties' access to justice and their access to finance is now universally accepted; and these aspects may also need to be considered by the English courts when interpreting the scope of Section 15B of the 1982 Act with regard to private antitrust damages claims issued before the UK Competition Appeal Tribunal.

A. Access to Justice

It is now well settled that a specific feature of transnational competition law infringements is that they would involve multinational groups of companies that enjoy significant market power and whose anti-competitive conduct could cause damages to multiple consumers. This means that Section 15B of the 1982 might play an important role in claims which are issued on behalf of consumers who are domiciled in the UK.[24]

The Explanatory Memorandum to the Civil Jurisdiction and Judgments (Amendment) (EU Exit) Regulations 2019[25] clearly sets out that the UK is set to continue to protect consumers by safeguarding certain procedural rights which had been conferred onto them by Section 4 of Chapter II of Brussels Ia. In particular, it has been stated that the 1982 Act is amended to include:

> a right to be sued in relation to a consumer […] dispute only in the part of the UK in which they are domiciled (regardless of the domicile of the other party), and a right to sue the other party in such a dispute in parts of the UK with relevant connections – all of which largely obviates the need for the consumer […] to sue abroad in such cases (with the attendant expense and difficulty for this category of economically weaker parties which having to sue outside their own forum brings). These rules operate both as between the different parts of the UK (England and Wales, Northern Ireland, Scotland) and where the dispute has an international connection.[26]

As already noted above, it is now well established that Section 15B of the 1982 Act – which is modelled on Section 4 of Chapter II of Brussels Ia – should be broad enough to cover tortious claims for antitrust damages as long as the competition law claim is 'indissociably linked to a contract actually concluded between that consumer'[27] and the

[22] The Right Honourable Lord Justice Jackson, *Review of Civil Litigation Costs: Final Report* December 2009, https://www.judiciary.uk/wp-content/uploads/JCO/Documents/Reports/jackson-final-report-140110.pdf. The *Final Report* was cited in *Paccar* (n 20) [5].

[23] Recital 25 of Directive (EU) 2020/1828.

[24] Chapters 4 and 5.

[25] UK Statutory Instrument 2019 No. 479.

[26] Ibid [2.6].

[27] Case C-500/18 *Reliantco Investment and Reliantco Investment Limassol Sucursala București* EU:C:2020:264 [73].

infringing undertaking. On that basis, it may be argued that an English court would have jurisdiction under Section 15B of the 1982 Act over a collective redress proceeding issued on behalf of consumers under Section 47B of the 1998 Act in so far as the resolution of any competition law claims which classify as contractual is necessary for the court to deal with the tortious claims for antitrust damages, or if the private antitrust damages claims which classify as tortious are closely connected and arise from the same consumer contract.[28]

However, a difficult issue is whether a proposed consumer representative 'who is [to be] authorised by a collective proceedings order to bring collective proceedings'[29] could still rely on the protective regime which allows the UK CAT to assume jurisdiction in claims issued on behalf of consumers under Section 15B of the 1982 Act. In the EU jurisprudence, there is a view that the regime 'protects the consumer only in so far as he personally is the plaintiff or defendant in proceedings'.[30] It has been submitted that 'it is [...] implicit that one of the parties to the litigation must be a consumer in order for Section 4 to apply'.[31] In a recent paper,[32] Rielaender has claimed that:

> While several scholars have argued for a more expansive interpretation of Articles 17–19 Brussels Ia according to which a representative consumer claimant should be entitled to bring proceedings against a trader with respect to claims arising from a multitude of consumer contracts in the courts of the place where any one of the consumers concerned is domiciled, [...] it is by now widely accepted that the special protective jurisdiction granted to consumers in Title II, Section 4, Brussels Ia, is generally inapplicable to legal persons, be they consumer associations or private companies. [...] Any other conclusion could hardly be reconciled with the wording, let alone the logic, of the provisions on consumer contracts that are specifically designed to offset the presumed structural imbalance between the parties to the contract.[33]

It is difficult to see why the legal status of the consumer representative should impact on the response to the question whether a collective redress claim on behalf of consumers is within the scope of Section 4 of Chapter II of Brussels Ia. Although consumer associations[34] and 'a special purpose vehicle, incorporated [...] for the specific purpose of pursuing the proposed collective proceedings'[35] may well be consumer

[28] Analogy can be made with the judgments of English courts in the context of interpreting the scope of arbitration agreements – eg *The Playa Larga* [1983] 2 Lloyd's Rep 171 (CA) 183; *The 'Angelic Grace'* [1995] 1 Lloyd's Rep 87 (CA) 89; *Premium Nafta Products Ltd v Fili Shipping* [2007] UKHL 40, concerned with one-stop adjudication.

[29] Competition Act 1998 s 59(1).

[30] Case C-89/91 *Shearson Lehmann Hutton Inc v TVB Treuhandgesellschaft für Vermögensverwaltung und Beteiligungen mbH* EU:C:1993:15 [23].

[31] J Hill, *Cross-border Consumer Contracts* (Oxford, OUP, 2008) 97. See also: Case C-89/91 *Shearson Lehmann Hutton Inc v TVB Treuhandgesellschaft für Vermögensverwaltung und Beteiligungen mbH* EU:C:1992:410 [35] (AG Darmon).

[32] Rielaender (n 13).

[33] Ibid 118 – citations omitted.

[34] eg Case No: 1382/7/7/21, *Consumers' Association v Qualcomm Inc* [2022] CAT 20.

[35] Case No: 1527/7/7/22 *Alex Neill Class Representative Ltd v Sony Interactive Entertainment Europe Ltd* – Summary of collective proceedings claim form – 21 September 2022; Case Nos: 1282/7/7/18 and 1289/7/7/18 *UK Trucks Claim Ltd v Stellantis and Ors & Road Haulage Association Ltd v MAN SE and Ors* [2022] CAT 25; Case No: 1329/7/7/19, *Michael O'Higgins FX Class Representative Ltd v Barclays Bank Plc* – Order – 16 August 2019.

representatives, collective redress proceedings on behalf of consumers may also be issued by individuals.[36]

In order to substantiate his argument, Rielaender[37] makes, inter alia, reference to *Henkel*.[38] In this case, the proceedings were issued by an Austrian consumers association. The desired legal remedy was an injunction, which was necessary to prevent Henkel from continuing to use certain unfair terms in their contracts with consumers in Austria. A specific feature of the proceedings was that the action was brought on behalf of 'the entire class of consumers'.[39] In view of the fact that the consumers association was not a party to a consumer contract, but was rather pursuing its 'legitimate interest under national law in protecting consumers',[40] the CJEU held that such a claim would not fall within the ambit of Section 4 of Chapter II of Brussels Ia, and it would classify as tortious rather than contractual.[41]

The *Henkel*[42] approach should be distinguished. An entirely different interpretation should be advanced in relation to claims in collective proceedings which are issued on behalf of identified (or identifiable) consumers, who are party to consumer contracts. In such cases, the defendants would have engaged in anti-competitive conduct which had the effect of distorting competition and which had affected UK prices, causing antitrust damages to multiple and identifiable UK consumers (who had actually purchased those products). One should not forget that the rationale behind promoting collective redress proceedings is to make 'possible litigation that would not be in the courts at all if individual actions were required'.[43] The issues concerning access to justice appear to be duly considered by judges as part of the certification process, with the UK Supreme Court judges holding that '[c]ollective proceedings are a special form of civil procedure for the vindication of private rights, designed to provide access to justice for that purpose where the ordinary forms of individual civil claim have proved inadequate for the purpose'.[44]

The question of who is a party to litigation does not arise for the purposes of allocating jurisdiction under Section 15B of the 1982 Act. The wording of Section 15B of the 1982 Act leaves no doubt that the proceedings *may* be brought by consumers, but they *may* equally be issued by a consumer representative on behalf of consumers. The fact that 'any offer to settle by a defendant in the collective proceedings shall be made to the class representative'[45] who had issued the proceedings[46] would not impact on the scope of Section 15B of the 1982 Act in so far as such a dispute would be primarily concerned with substantive rights of identified (or identifiable) consumers.

[36] eg *Elizabeth Helen Coll* (n 5) [9–10]; *Dr Liza Lovdahl Gormsen* (n 5); *Mr Justin Gutmann* (n 10).

[37] Rielaender (n 13).

[38] *Henkel* (n 12).

[39] ibid [25]. See also the opinion of AG Jacob – Case C-167/00 *Verein für Konsumenteninformation v Karl Heinz Henkel* EU:C:2002:171 [10] and [12].

[40] *Henkel* (n 12) [9.2].

[41] Ibid [33, 40 and 50].

[42] Ibid.

[43] KW Dam, 'Class actions: efficiency, compensation, deterrence, and conflict of interest' (1975) 4 *Journal of Legal Studies* 47, 49. See also: C Hodges, 'From class actions to collective redress: a resolution in approach to compensation' (2009) *Civil Justice Quarterly* 41.

[44] *Mastercard Incorporated and others v Walter Hugh Merricks CBE* [2020] UKSC 51 [45].

[45] Competition Appeal Tribunal Rules 2015 r 94(2).

[46] Competition Act 1998 s 47B(2).

The President of the UK CAT in his reasoned order which was made in *Dr Liza Lovdahl Gormsen v Meta Platforms* appears to suggest that Section 15B of the 1982 Act should be broad enough to cover private antitrust damages claims issued on behalf of multiple consumers under Section 47B of the 1998 Act.[47] In this case, the claimants made an application for service of a collective redress claim form out of the jurisdiction by inter alia relying on Section 15B of the 1982 Act. The President of the UK CAT appeared to take the view that the provision should allow the Tribunal to assume jurisdiction in a collective redress claim for private antitrust damages arising out of consumer contracts,[48] holding that:

> In relation to Facebook Ireland, the Proposed Class Representative's primary position in the Rule 31 Application is that permission is not required to serve the claim form on Facebook Ireland out of the jurisdiction pursuant to rule 6.33(2) CPR in conjunction with section 15B of the Civil Jurisdiction and Judgments Act 1982 ('the 1982 Act') […] and that the Tribunal has jurisdiction concerning consumer claims in the UK. […]
>
> The Rule 31 Application contends that a proposed class member is a 'consumer' and the Terms of Service constitute a 'consumer contract' within the meaning of the 1982 Act because at all material times, Facebook pursued and/or directed commercial or professional activities in the UK.
>
> Expressly without prejudice to the rights of Meta and Facebook Ireland to apply pursuant to Rule 34 of the Tribunal Rules to dispute the Tribunal's jurisdiction, I have concluded (on the basis of the materials before me) that a proposed class member is a 'consumer' and that the Terms of Service properly constitute a 'consumer contract' for the purposes of the 1982 Act. If this is right, permission is not required to serve the Second Proposed Defendant out of the jurisdiction […].[49]

There is indeed a strong argument that the collective redress proceedings issued by consumer representatives and seeking damages on behalf of consumers would be within the scope of Section 15B of the 1982 Act. Mr Justice Marcus Smith's approach should allow for the interpretation of Section 15B of the 1982 Act taken together with Section 47B of the 1998 Act to lay down the consumer's domicile[50] a major connecting factor in collective redress antitrust proceedings that are issued before the UK CAT.

Nonetheless, had the consumer's rights been assigned, then an entirely different approach may be advanced. It is now settled that Section 4 Chapter II of Brussels Ia would not be broad enough to cover collective redress proceedings issued by 'a consumer to whom the claims of other consumers have been assigned'[51] and/or by a commercial company to whom that person had assigned his rights.[52] Putting this scenario aside, there are very strong legal and policy considerations indicating that UK consumers should be allowed to bring their collective actions in the UK CAT by relying on Section 15B of the 1982 Act.[53]

[47] *Dr Liza Lovdahl Gormsen* (n 5) [5, 9 and 10].

[48] Compare Case C-189/87 *Kalfelis v Schröder and Others* EU:C:1988:312 [31] (AG Darmon).

[49] *Dr Liza Lovdahl Gormsen* (n 5) [5, 9 and 10].

[50] R Mulheron, 'Asserting personal jurisdiction over non-resident class members: comparative insights for the United Kingdom' (2019) 15 *Journal of Private International Law* 445.

[51] Case C-498/16 *Maximilian Schrems v Facebook Ireland Ltd* EU:C:2018:37 [44].

[52] *Shearson* (n 30).

[53] M Danov, 'The Brussels I Regulation: Cross-Border Collective Redress Proceedings and Judgments' (2010) 6 *Journal of Private International Law* 359.

The reasoned order in *Dr Liza Lovdahl Gormsen v Meta Platforms*[54] strongly indicates that Section 15B of the 1982 Act may play a very important role in facilitating opt-out collective proceedings to be issued on behalf of millions of UK consumers. Such an interpretation would mean that Section 15B of the 1982 Act would allow for a cross-border collective redress claim for private antitrust damages to be issued on behalf of millions of consumers as long as they are 'domiciled in the United Kingdom on the domicile date and ha[ve] not opted out of opt-out collective proceedings'.[55] The consumer's domicile is determined by Section 41(2) of the Civil Jurisdiction and Judgments Act 1982 which states that:

> An individual is domiciled in the United Kingdom if and only if—
> (a) he is resident in the United Kingdom; and
> (b) the nature and circumstances of his residence indicate that he has a substantial connection with the United Kingdom.[56]

The points concerning the consumer's domicile and the relevant domicile date were also addressed by the UK Competition Appeal Tribunal in *Merricks*.[57] A common approach to the interpretation of Section 15B of the 1982 Act and Section 47B of the 1998 Act should safeguard the interests of the UK consumers. This should improve UK consumers' access to legal remedies; they would avoid any cross-border litigation risks, somewhat minimising the level of uncertainty and litigation costs which might ensue if they were to litigate abroad.[58]

B. Access to Finance

The purpose of this section is to make an argument that a specific feature of many competition law proceedings is that they would inevitably involve multiple claimants. There is a strong argument that a purposive interpretation of Section 15B of the 1982 Act presupposes for the English courts to consider the rationale of Section 47B of the 1998 Act. A purposive interpretation would be particularly necessary because there are important public policy objectives to 'introduce an opt-out collective actions regime and an opt-out collective settlement regime'[59] in the UK. The UK experience appears to demonstrate that appropriate procedural mechanisms that are intended to provide collective redress for injured parties may be important to incentivise litigation funders to finance such claims, which would in turn improve multiple injured parties' access to legal remedies.

The proposed purposive interpretation of Section 15B of the 1982 Act to cover private antitrust claims issued on behalf of multiple consumers (irrespective of whether the consumer representatives are individuals or legal entities) could be strengthened by considering the high litigation costs that may be disproportionate to the damage suffered by individual consumers. Since it is well established that '[t]he costs rules of

[54] *Dr Liza Lovdahl Gormsen* (n 5) [5–10].
[55] Competition Appeal Tribunal Rules 2015 r 73(2)(b). See also: Competition Act 1998 s 59(1).
[56] Civil Jurisdiction and Judgments Act 1982 s 41(2).
[57] See Case No: 1266/7/7/16, *Merricks v MasterCard* [2021] CAT 28 [58].
[58] Danov (n 53).
[59] Consumer Rights Act 2015, *Explanatory Notes* [434].

each jurisdiction are linked to the evidential practices',[60] the availability of third-party litigation funding[61] along with appropriate legislative interventions which allowed for collective proceedings to be issued on behalf of multiple injured parties may make a real impact on the willingness of claimants to issue proceedings in England and Wales.

In view of this, it would be important for such collective redress proceedings to be initiated on behalf of identified (or identifiable) UK consumers against foreign defendants whose conduct has affected the prices of relevant products/services in the UK market,[62] distorting competition in the UK.[63]

The correlation between the available litigation funding and the injured parties' 'access to justice'[64] appeared to be further considered by the Competition Appeal Tribunal in *Michael O'Higgins FX Class Representative v Barclays Bank*.[65] A particularly important aspect was put forward by Mr Paul Lomas who, in his dissenting judgment, went further to note that:

> In creating an opt-in class, it would be necessary to establish a critical mass of core claimants to make such a claim viable as an action. The (formidable) costs of bringing this action are not materially dependent on the size of the class. However, the total size of the damages claim is critical because it supports the funding to pursue the claim. That is a function of the number of class members and the size of their claims. In essence, that total likely damages claim has to be large enough for the economics of bringing the claim, with its costs and risks, to be rational. [...]
>
> The evidence from the funders establishes, not surprisingly, that the current funding packages would not be applicable to an opt-in [collective proceedings order 'CPO'] (having been designed for an opt-out arrangement) and the current funders have no commitment to any arrangements for an opt-in CPO. Of course, those arrangements could be renegotiated or other funders approached, but the evidence also points to real difficulties, given the changed economics, in creating a viable new funding package on an opt-in basis.[66]

Setting up an effective collective redress mechanism which incentivise litigation funders to finance consumer claims may be a major aspect which is to be duly considered by English judges when interpreting the scope of Section 15B of the 1982 Act. The point appears to be also captured by Lord Justice Green, who noted that '[i]t is self-evident that in many large-scale consumer based collective actions the availability or non-availability of third party funding might be dispositive of whether the claim ever gets off the ground'.[67] Indeed, a collective redress regime that operates on an *opt-out* basis[68] would be more likely to attract litigation funding[69] which would in turn improve access to justice.

The Consumer Rights Act 2015 introduced a collective redress mechanism which allowed the Competition Appeal Tribunal to deal with multiple competition law claims

[60] *Steven Wall v Mutuelle De Pointiers Assurances* [2014] EWCA Civ 138 [44].
[61] Section 58B of the Courts and Legal Services Act 1990.
[62] See: Chapter 11.
[63] Chapters 9 and 10.
[64] *Merricks* (n 44) [45].
[65] Case Nos: 1329/7/7/19 and 1336/7/7/19, *Michael O'Higgins FX Class Representative Ltd v Barclays Bank Plc & Ors* [2022] CAT 16 [37, 95, 96, 286, 372.2 and 432].
[66] Ibid [436 and 439].
[67] Ibid [77].
[68] Section 47B(11) of the Competition Act 1998.
[69] *BT Group Plc v Justin Le Patourel* [2022] EWCA Civ 593 [76]–[77].

which 'raise the same, similar or related issues of fact or law and are suitable to be brought in collective proceedings'.[70] This turned out to be a major development, which appears to be central for the UK to improve access to legal remedies in private antitrust damages claims and may be another argument to justify a broad interpretation of Section 15B of the 1982 Act. The collective proceedings order in *Merricks* strongly indicates that the effective functioning of the collective redress regime appeared to be dependent on how the *suitability*[71] requirement was to be interpreted and applied by the judges when ascertaining whether the claims are 'eligible for inclusion in collective proceedings'.[72]

The majority of the UK Supreme Court judges indicated that competition law claims which 'disclose no reasonable cause of action'[73] will not proceed before the UK CAT, but they went on to state that 'the certification process is not about, and does not involve, a merits test'.[74] This approach is set to ensure that claimants are required to demonstrate that they have 'a triable cause of action'[75] without imposing 'an inappropriately high merits threshold'[76] onto them. A number of collective redress proceedings appeared to be certified by the CAT.[77] In this context, the CAT judges took opportunity to clarify that 'the relative test of suitability does not require a determination that it is impossible to try the claims individually but that it is more suitable to try the claims collectively, having regard to a multi-factorial evaluation'.[78]

Given the fact that competition law infringements would last for a number of years and cause harm to multiple injured parties, the Supreme Court judges acknowledged that there is a fine line 'between issues as to the likely availability of data [which would be key to the assessment of damages] at trial and issues as to the merits'[79] of private antitrust damages claims. The aspects concerning methodology would be considered in so far as 'claims cannot be suitable for aggregate damages if there is no credible methodology for calculating those damages or basis on which such a methodology could fairly be applied, i.e. the Microsoft test'.[80]

Therefore, there are a number of broader policy considerations which provide strong arguments for Section 15B of the 1982 Act to be broadly interpreted to cover representative claims issued on behalf of consumers. Although such a broad interpretation would bring Section 15B of the 1982 Act in line with Section 47B of the 1998 Act and incentivise litigation funders to finance such claims, the lack of a framework of judicial cooperation would mean that multiple related collective redress proceedings would be bound to arise in different jurisdictions. This means that an alternative approach to judicial cooperation must be considered in a global context.[81]

[70] Section 47B(6) of the Competition Act 1998.

[71] Section 47B(6); *Michael O'Higgins FX Class Representative* (n 65) [68]. Compare: *Merricks* (n 44) [75]; *Road Haulage Association* (n 35) [158–186].

[72] Section 47B(5)(b) of the Competition Act 1998.

[73] *Merricks* (n 44) [26].

[74] Ibid [59]; *Michael O'Higgins FX Class Representative* (n 65) [67]. Compare: *Merricks* (n 44) [113–114].

[75] *Merricks* (n 44) [74].

[76] Ibid [75].

[77] Case Nos: 1304/7/7/19 and 1305/7/7/19, *Justin Gutmann v First MTR South Western Trains Ltd* [2021] CAT 31; Case No: 1339/7/7/20, *Mark McLaren Class Representative v MOL (Europe Africa) Ltd* [2022] CAT 10; *Road Haulage Association* (n 35) [168]; *BT Group* (n 69); *Qualcomm* (n 34).

[78] *Road Haulage Association* (n 35) [168].

[79] *Merricks* (n 44) [75].

[80] *Gutmann* (n 77) [180].

[81] Chapters 7, 8, 12 and 13.

III. Multiple Defendants

It is not only that there would be multiple injured parties (ie claimants), but the case law also strongly indicates that there would be multiple infringers (ie defendants).[82] As already noted above,[83] the CPR rules and para 3.1 of PD 6B, which sets out the rule for the assumption of jurisdiction in cases that involve multiple defendants, would equally be applicable in cross-border competition law claims.

A. Service Out of the Jurisdiction

In order for a claim form to be served out of the jurisdiction, three major requirements must be satisfied by the relevant claimant/s. First, the competition law claim must be substantiated, with the claimant demonstrating that their claim has 'a reasonable prospect of success'.[84] As part of this process, the claimant would need to demonstrate that the allegedly anti-competitive conduct has either been 'implemented' or had 'qualified effects' in the UK, so that UK competition law is applicable.[85]

The claimant/s might often rely on foreign regulatory decisions/proceedings[86] and/or foreign private enforcement proceedings[87] with a view to demonstrating that their claim meets the required standard of proof. These aspects were reflected in the Mr Justice Roth's reasoned order for the service of claim form out of the jurisdiction in *Elizabeth Helen Coll v Alphabet*, where the President of the UK CAT held:

> Abuse is alleged essentially on two alternative bases, as summarised in Mr Streatfeild's evidence: (a) the contractual and technical restrictions imposed (i) on manufacturers of Android smartphones and tablets ('GMS devices') and (ii) on developers of Apps that are to be available on GMS devices, including the requirement that all payments to download such Apps or make in-App purchases are made using Google's Play Store payment processing system; and (b) the charging of unfair and excessive prices in the form of commission on such purchases. I consider that insofar as this conduct may have taken place either in the US or partly in the US and partly in Ireland, it is well arguable that it was foreseeable in each case that it would have an immediate and substantial effect in the EU and the UK (among other places). On that basis, it will satisfy the 'qualified effects' test for substantive jurisdiction. I think it is seriously arguable that the matters relied on and alleged constitute abusive conduct and, given the prominence of GMS devices in the EU and the UK, I think it is clear that alleged anti-competitive conduct will have an appreciable effect on trade between Member States of the EU (before 31 December 2020) and within the UK: see *Epic Games* at [88]. Accordingly, I think there is a serious issue to be tried on the merits of the case against Alphabet, Google LLC and Google Ireland.[88]

[82] eg *Cartel Damage Claims* (n 1); *Cooper Tire* – EWHC (n 4); *Cooper Tire & Rubber Company Europe Limited & Others* [2010] EWCA Civ 864; *Toshiba Carrier UK Ltd and Other v KME Yorkshire Limited & Others* [2011] EWHC 2665 (Ch).

[83] Chapters 4 and 5.

[84] Civil Procedure Rules 6.37(1)(b); Competition Appeal Tribunal Rules 2015 r 31(2)(b).

[85] See more: Chapters 4 and 9.

[86] Case No: 1408/7/7/21, *Elizabeth Helen Coll v Alphabet Inc and Others* [2022] CAT 39 [4].

[87] Ibid [5].

[88] *Elizabeth Helen Coll* (n 5) [6].

Secondly, if the proceedings were to be taking place in England and Wales for the purposes of the UK CAT rules, then the claimant would need to demonstrate that their claim comes within one of the gateways which could be used to issue proceedings against multiple defendants. In particular, para 3.1(3) of PD 6B states that:

> A claim is made against a person ('the defendant') on whom the claim form has been or will be served (otherwise than in reliance on this paragraph) and –
>
> (a) there is between the claimant and the defendant a real issue which it is reasonable for the court to try; and
>
> (b) the claimant wishes to serve the claim form on another person who is a necessary or proper party to that claim.

The quoted text strongly indicates that several requirements must be satisfied for a competition law claim to come within the multi-defendant gateway. It must be demonstrated that there is a real issue between the claimant and an anchor defendant that is based in England. The requirement will be duly considered in cases against multiple defendants where the strike-out applications may often be brought by the defendants, alleging that there is no real issue to be tried between the claimant/s and the anchor defendant.[89] This would be particularly so where the defendant is a wholly-owned subsidiary forming part of an infringing undertaking.[90] The requirement is set to safeguard the interests of foreign defendants by making sure that a claimant may not tactically issue a claim against an anchor defendant with a view to strategically bringing a claim against the foreign defendants.[91] This is reinforced by requiring the claimant to demonstrate that the foreign defendant is a 'necessary or proper party' to the competition claim against the anchor defendant, which should in turn ensure that there is a territorial connection between the English court jurisdiction and the claim against the foreign defendant.

Finally, the courts would not give their permission for a claim form to be served out of the jurisdiction unless satisfied that England and Wales or the UK CAT is 'the forum in which the case can be suitably tried for the interests of all the parties and for the ends of justice'.[92] The relevant principles that may be relevant for cases involving multiple claimants and defendants were summarised in *Mr Justin Gutmann v Apple*[93] where it was held:

> I find that in all the circumstances England and Wales is clearly the appropriate forum for the trial and that the Tribunal ought to exercise it discretion to permit service out of the jurisdiction. In particular I rely upon the fact that the proposed class is resident or domiciled in the UK and will have suffered damage in the UK. I also place reliance upon the fact that the claim relates to UK and EU competition law.
>
> Altogether, I therefore consider that the UK (and this Tribunal) is clearly and distinctly the appropriate forum for the trial of this action.[94]

In this context, the judges should factor in such aspects as: where the anti-competitive conduct is deployed;[95] whether the documents or 'the preponderance of

[89] *ValueLicensing* (n 10) [42–54].
[90] Ibid [42–54].
[91] Fawcett (n 8) 747.
[92] *Clare Mary Joan Spottiswoode CBE* (n 10) [24].
[93] *Mr Justin Gutmann* (n 10).
[94] Ibid [15–16].
[95] *Clare Mary Joan Spottiswoode CBE* (n 10) [24].

relevant documents'[96] are located in the jurisdiction along with any expert witnesses;[97] the number of injured parties;[98] any English jurisdiction agreements;[99] any foreign proceedings and the territorial scope of the foreign competition laws.[100] Since the aspects concerning the reasonable prospects of success and *forum conveniens* have already been dealt with above,[101] the focus of this section will be on the jurisdictional rules allocating jurisdiction in competition law cases involving multiple claimants and defendants.

B. The *Provimi*[102] Approach

The cross-border nature of competition law infringements causing antitrust harm in a number of jurisdictions means that many competition law disputes would often involve not a single claimant and a single defendant, but rather several groups of companies on each side.[103]

The High Court of England and Wales's judgment in *Provimi*[104] made a major contribution to the jurisprudential developments with regard to the allocation of jurisdiction in cross-border competition law actions against groups of companies within the EU. In this case, the claimants were 'two English companies and a German company. Those companies were all direct purchasers of vitamins from companies within the Roche and Aventis groups'.[105] The claimants were direct purchasers of vitamins (ie the cartelised product). They were getting their supplies from various members of three infringing undertakings (which were groups of companies). As a result of the cartel (which had an effect on the prices of various vitamins), they appeared to sustain antitrust damages in both England and Germany.

The claimants appeared to strategically issue their private antitrust damages claims in England.[106] They inter alia relied on Article 8(1) of Brussels Ia, which is indeed identical to Section 2(o)(i) of Sch 8 to the 1982 Act. According to this provision:

> A person domiciled in a Member State may also be sued [...] where he is one of a number of defendants, in the courts of the place where any one of them is domiciled, provided the claims

[96] Case No: 1518/5/7/22, *London Array Limited & Others v Nexans France SAS & Others* – Reasoned Order of the President (Service out of the Jurisdiction)–19 August 2022 [26].

[97] Ibid.

[98] *Elizabeth Helen Coll* (n 5) [11].

[99] Ibid.

[100] Ibid.

[101] See: Chapter 4.

[102] *Provimi Limited v Aventis Animal Nutrition SA and Others* [2003] EWHC 961 (Comm). See: M Danov, 'Jurisdiction in cross-border EU competition law cases: Some specific issues requiring some specific solutions' in M Danov, F Becker and P Beaumont (eds), *Cross-border EU Competition Law Actions* (Oxford, Hart Publishing, 2013) 167–196.

[103] Case Number 1357/5/7/20 (T), *Stellantis NV (formerly Fiat Chrysler Automobiles NV) & Others v NTN Corporation & Others* [2021] CAT 14. See also: *Cooper Tire* – EWHC (n 4); *Cooper Tire* – EWCA (n 82); *Toshiba Carrier* – EWHC (n 82).

[104] *Provimi* (n 102).

[105] Ibid [3].

[106] J Lawrence and A Morfey, 'Tactical Manoeuvres in UK Cartel Damages Litigation' in Danov, Becker and Beaumont (n 102) 149, 150.

> are so closely connected that it is expedient to hear and determine them together to avoid the risk of irreconcilable judgments resulting from separate proceedings.[107]

It was beyond any doubt that the above provision would be particularly important in cases where a claimant wishes to pursue a competition law claim against two or more defendants. Its rationale is to centralise litigation against all defendants in one Member State and avoid the risk of (potentially) irreconcilable judgments, if the different actions were brought in different Member States.[108] Ultimately, the CJEU held that:

> Article [8(1) Brussels Ia] must be interpreted as meaning that the rule on centralisation of jurisdiction in the case of several defendants, as established in that provision, can apply in the case of an action for damages, and for disclosure in that regard, brought jointly against *undertakings* which have participated in different places and at different times in a single and continuous infringement, which has been established by a decision of the Commission, of the prohibition of anti-competitive agreements, decisions and concerted practices provided for under EU law, even where the applicant has withdrawn its action against the sole co-defendant domiciled in the same State as the court seised.[109]

The proposed approach was adopted to facilitate claimants' access to effective legal remedies in cross-border competition law disputes. For example, if one of those companies is domiciled in one EU Member State and another one is domiciled in another EU Member State, then the claimant would be able to proceed against both companies in either jurisdiction.

That said, it was not quite clear how this provision would apply in competition law cases where the infringing undertakings are multinational groups of companies. In other words, as already noted above,[110] there are particularly difficult classification issues to be addressed in competition law cases, not least because the concept of 'undertaking' for competition law purposes is broadly defined to cover a corporate group with numerous subsidiaries.[111] The broad definition of 'undertaking' echoes the transnational model for corporate governance of companies that engage in cross-border trade currently, which in turn reflects the fact that the European Union has promoted an advanced level of economic integration which is facilitated by freedom of establishment (as well as by the free movement of capital, goods and service) across the EU and the European Economic Area.

In order to establish jurisdiction in England by relying on the above provision in *Provimi*,[112] the claimants issued proceedings against an English company, Roche Products Limited, which was strategically identified as the anchor defendant for the purposes of Article 8(1) of Brussels Ia. After establishing jurisdiction against the local subsidiary in England, the claimants sought to join Vitamine Europa AG and F Hoffmann-La Roche AG with a view to strategically suing multiple defendants

[107] Compare: s 2(o)(i) of Sch 8 of the 1982 Act.
[108] *Cartel Damage Claims* (n 1).
[109] Ibid [33] (emphasis added by the author).
[110] Chapter 3.
[111] Case C-41/90 *Klaus Höfner and Fritz Elser v Macrotron GmbH* EU:C:1991:161 [21].
[112] *Provimi* (n 102).

in England. Since no contractual relationship existed between the German claimant and the anchor defendant, Roche Products Ltd, the classification issues were fairly important. It should be noted that in the claim form:

> it is not alleged that Trouw UK purchased any products from Roche Germany or that Trouw Germany purchased any products from Roche UK during the relevant period. It is alleged that the defendants were part of one 'undertaking' and were, for [the] competition law purposes, 'one economic entity'.[113]

In spite of the fact that the local subsidiary and its parent company were separate legal entities, they were regarded as being part of the 'same economic unit'[114] for competition law purposes. The fact that the whole group of companies (being a single undertaking) was found to infringe competition law was sufficient for the judge to conclude that there was a real issue between the claimants and the local subsidiary, which was the anchor defendant for the purposes of Article 8(1) of Brussels Ia. More specifically, in *Provimi*, Mr Justice Aikens stated that:

> there is a tension between English law and EU Competition law concepts. In English law the separate identity of corporations is respected and knowledge of one corporation will not be readily imputed to another. But EU Competition law maintains the concept of an 'undertaking', which is more flexible than a legal entity. It can embrace a number of legal entities, so long as they act as a single economic unit and no legal entity acts independently for any relevant purpose.
>
> It seems to me to be arguable that where two corporate entities are part of an 'undertaking' (call it 'Undertaking A') and one of those entities has entered into an infringing agreement with other, independent, 'undertakings', then if another corporate entity which is part of Undertaking A then implements that infringing agreement, it is also infringing [Article 101 TFEU].[115]

The High Court assumed jurisdiction because, according to Mr Justice Aikens, '[e]ach entity would have contributed to a situation where it took part in the cartel, upheld the cartel prices and so (arguably) caused loss'.[116] Therefore it was concluded that 'there was a "real issue" [...] as between [the German company and the two English companies]'.[117]

The somewhat broad interpretation of the English court in *Provimi*[118] and the fact that many infringing undertakings would be transnational groups of companies meant that Article 8(1) of Brussels Ia naturally turned out to be a major provision, which was often invoked in competition law cases.[119] It was indeed advantageous for claimants to base their claim on Article 8(1) of Brussels Ia because such claimants were not required to demonstrate that the actions relating to the various defendants must have the same basis (eg tort or contract) in so far as the provision was set to cover competition law

[113] Ibid [18].
[114] Case C-73/95 P *Viho v Commission* EU:C:1996:405.
[115] *Provimi* (n 102) [30–31]. See also: *Cooper Tire* – EWCA (n 82) [47].
[116] *Provimi* (n 102) [40].
[117] Ibid [42].
[118] *Provimi* (n 102).
[119] Lawrence and Morfey (n 106) 150.

claims which classify as contractual and/or tortious.[120] This was reflected in the legal literature, with Wilderspin[121] arguing that:

> there can be little doubt that, for a claimant who envisages bringing actions against several defendants in a single forum, which will often be the case in actions arising from competition law infringements, in particular cartels, [Article 8(1) of Brussels Ia] is among the most important provisions of the Regulation.[122]

The importance of *Provimi*[123] for a claimant to establish that 'there is between the[m] and the defendant a real issue which it is reasonable for the court to try'[124] could be deduced from the decisions of the English courts in *Media-Saturn v Toshiba Information Systems (UK)*[125] and *ValueLicensing v Microsoft*.[126] More specifically, in the former case, Mr Justice Barling held:

> The *Provimi* Ground claim, as I understand it, is not that liability passes up one corporate chain from [MT Picture Display Co Ltd] to [Toshiba Corporation] and then down a different corporate chain from [Toshiba Corporation] to [Toshiba Information Systems (U.K.) Limited]. It is rather that [Toshiba Corporation], [MT Picture Display Co Ltd], [Toshiba Information Systems (U.K.) Limited], and the other Toshiba Defendants formed a single economic unit or 'undertaking' which (along with PC and others) infringed Article 101, and whose knowledge is 'one and the same'. To the extent that any one or more of those entities in some way participated in and/or implemented the cartel in question, that entity is *ex hypothesi* liable, regardless of its knowledge of the cartel. […]
>
> Therefore, provided that there is also an arguable case (1) that the relevant 'undertaking' existed, (2) that the entity in question [Toshiba Information Systems (U.K.) Limited] was a member of it, and (3) that there was some participation/implementation by [Toshiba Information Systems (U.K.) Limited], this basis of liability is unfit for summary disposal. Elements (1) and (2) are conceded for present purposes (at least insofar as [Toshiba Corporation] and [Toshiba Information Systems (U.K.) Limited] are concerned), and I consider (3) to be clearly arguable on the basis of the largely uncontroversial facts relating to [Toshiba Information Systems (U.K.) Limited's] role and activities.[127]

Although this statement was made in the context of Article 8(1) of Brussels Ia, which was applicable in the pre-Brexit era, the *Provimi*[128] approach was endorsed by the English court in *ValueLicensing v Microsoft*,[129] where Mr Justice Picken drew on the above quote endorsing the *Provimi* point in cases falling under para 3.1(3) of PD 6B.[130]

[120] Case C-98/06 *Freeport plc v Olle Arnoldsson* EU:C:2007:595 [38–41]. See also: Opinion of AG Mengozzi – Case C-98/06 *Freeport plc v Olle Arnoldsson* EU:C:2007:302 [45].

[121] M Wilderspin, 'Jurisdiction issues: Brussels I Regulation Articles 6(1), 23, 27 and 28' in J Basedow, S Francq and L Idot (eds), *International Antitrust Litigation Conflict of Laws and Coordination* (Oxford, Hart Publishing, 2012) 41, 57.

[122] Ibid 52.

[123] *Provimi* (n 102).

[124] Paragraph 3.1(3)(a) of PD 6B.

[125] *Media-Saturn Holding GmbH & Ors v Toshiba Information Systems (UK) Ltd & Ors* [2019] EWHC 1095 (Ch).

[126] *ValueLicensing* (n 10).

[127] *Media-Saturn Holding* (n 125) [155 and 157]. See also: *ValueLicensing* (n 10) [67 and 68].

[128] *Provimi* (n 102).

[129] *ValueLicensing* (n 10).

[130] Ibid [67 and 68].

Post-Brexit, an alternative approach which could be developed is to rather classify the parent company and its local subsidiary as a single economic unit for private international law purposes.[131] If the local subsidiary were to classify as a branch for jurisdictional purposes, then a claim form could be served on the multinational group of companies within the jurisdiction. This approach would mean that no permission would be required for the claim form to be served out of the jurisdiction in such cases,[132] but it is yet to be seen whether such an approach would be advanced under the English CPR, post-Brexit.

In the meantime, since the focus of this chapter is on the current practice, which was developed by the English courts, the case law, which appears to be heavily influenced by *Provimi*,[133] the jurisprudence under Brussels Ia will be inter alia examined.

C. 'A real issue which is reasonable for the court to try'[134]

An argument for examining the jurisprudence of the English courts as developed under Article 8(1) of Brussels Ia could be strengthened by noting that English judges have systematically advanced 'an additional requirement'[135] which – whilst not clearly set out in Brussels Ia – mirrors para 3.1(3)(a) of PD 6B. Lord Justice Leggatt held that the multi-defendants' ground for the allocation of jurisdiction under Brussels Ia is 'analogous with'[136] para 3.1(3) of PD 6B in so far as the claimant is expected to demonstrate that 'there is a real issue that the plaintiffs may reasonably ask the court to try'.[137]

Lord Justice Leggatt's judgment was duly cited in *Provimi*[138] which might explain why the same approach appears to be followed in *ValueLicensing v Microsoft*[139] in the context of para 3.1(3) of PD 6B. More specifically, it seems that under both sets of jurisdictional rules, Brussels Ia and para 3.1(3) of PD 6B, it is important for a claimant to establish that there is 'a real issue which is reasonable for the court to try'[140] against an anchor defendant on whom the claim form has been or will be served. As Mr Justice Roth put it:

> it is first necessary to examine the claim against the so-called 'anchor' defendant(s) in isolation. If, on analysis, there is no real issue to be tried against the anchor defendant(s) which it is reasonable for the Tribunal to try, this head of jurisdiction is not made out.[141]

[131] See: Chapter 4.
[132] Compare: Paragraph 1A of PD 6B.
[133] *Provimi* (n 102).
[134] Paragraph 3.1(3)(a) of PD 6B.
[135] Fawcett (n 8) 752.
[136] *Owners of Cargo Lately Laden on Board the Rewia v Caribbean Liners (Caribtainer) Ltd* [1993] ILPr 507 [8].
[137] Ibid.
[138] *Provimi* (n 102) [42].
[139] *ValueLicensing* (n 10).
[140] Paragraph 3.1(3)(a) of PD 6B.
[141] *Epic Games* (n 10) [100].

The above deduction could be strengthened by making reference to the judgments in *Epic Games*[142] and *ValueLicensing v Microsoft*,[143] which reiterate that a common approach is being advanced for the purposes of para 3.1(3)(a) as well as for the purposes of Article 8(1) of Brussels Ia in so far as under both jurisdictional rules it must be shown that 'there is a real issue between the Claimants and one of the Anchor Defendants, that is, an issue which cannot be struck out.'[144]

Under Civil Procedure Rules, rule 3.4,[145] the court may strike out a competition law claim[146] if 'the statement of case discloses no reasonable grounds for bringing or defending the claim'.[147] This means that if the competition law claim against the anchor defendant is struck out, there would not be a sufficient territorial connection between the claim and foreign defendant (who should have been a necessary or proper party to the claim which had been struck out); as a result, the English courts would not have jurisdiction over the claim against a foreign defendant, which might be a parent company of a transnational group of companies (abusing its dominant position), or which might be another member of a transnational cartel.

It should indeed be noted that the strike-out applications appear to be quite common in cases where the anchor defendants would be subsidiaries forming part of a corporate group which had engaged in certain anti-competitive activities. The strike-out test was clearly set out in *Stellantis v NTN Corporation*[148] where the CAT took the view that:

> the present [strike-out] application is to be determined by applying the same test […] as [the one which] was applied by Tribunal in Royal Mail at [22]: i.e. whether there is a realistic prospect of the new plea [to] succeed[…] at trial. A realistic prospect is one that carries some degree of conviction and is more than merely arguable. However, the court must take into account evidence that can reasonably be expected to be available at trial, as well as the evidence before it, and should be wary of deciding difficult or new points of law in the absence of real facts.[149]

One should note that this test is identical with the one which should be advanced when the court is evaluating whether 'the claim has a reasonable prospect of success'[150] within the meaning of the Civil Procedure Rules as well as within the meaning of the Competition Appeal Tribunal Rules 2015. A level of alignment in relation of the standard of proof at this interlocutory stage (ie prior to disclosure) should be welcome for the courts to swiftly deal with any jurisdiction issues.

The case law shows that there may be some complex issues to be addressed by the courts at the jurisdiction stage in cases involving transnational groups of companies that enjoy market power and have numerous subsidiaries across the globe. The cases before the English courts strongly indicate that the questions of liability may be difficult,

[142] Ibid.
[143] *ValueLicensing* (n 10).
[144] *Cooper Tire* – EWHC (n 4) [37]. See also: *FKI Engineering v Dewind Holdings* [2007] EWHC (Comm) [32].
[145] Civil Procedure Rules, Part 3, The Court's Case Management Powers, http://www.justice.gov.uk/courts/procedure-rules/civil/rules/part03.
[146] See: Glossary – Civil Procedure Rules, http://www.justice.gov.uk/courts/procedure-rules/civil/glossary.
[147] Civil Procedure Rules r 3.4(2)(a).
[148] *Stellantis* (n 103).
[149] Ibid [13].
[150] See: Civil Procedure Rules r 6.37(1)(b). See also: Competition Appeal Tribunal Rules 2015 r 31(2)(b).

not least because, as noted in chapter 3, it may be far from clear 'which legal entities within a corporate group are liable for an infringement of [competition law] and to what extent'.[151]

There are two aspects which the courts and policy makers should be aware of. First, the injured parties may be strategically issuing proceedings against a local subsidiary (ie an anchor defendant) with a view to involving multiple defendants. Second, addressing the issues concerning the prospects of success of a claim, at an interlocutory stage, against a local subsidiary, is adding a level of complexity. A court faced with the difficult question of ascertaining the prospect of success of a claim issued against a local subsidiary may be tempted to rely on the *single undertaking* concept at an interlocutory stage, with a view to determining whether the claim should be struck out.[152]

This means that an important question in cross-border cases is to what extent para 3.1(3) of PD 6B (or Article 8(1) of Brussels Ia) may be relied upon in a claim against a local subsidiary of a transnational group which consists of multiple subsidiaries who may not have any knowledge of the arrangement between the cartelist, for example. In *Cooper Tire*,[153] Mr Justice Teare held:

> An undertaking in European competition law is an economic unit. That unit is engaged in an economic activity. [...] An undertaking may act by or through those legal entities which constitute the undertaking. Whilst the infringement of [Article 101 TFEU or Chapter 1 of the 1998 Act] is that of the undertaking, liability for the resulting fine or damages must be attached to a legal person. Where a subsidiary is personally involved in the infringement by implementing the offending agreement there is no need to enquire into whether or not the subsidiary is involved by having decisive influence over another legal entity. Since the legal entity which makes the offending agreement plainly has knowledge of it, a rational consequence of the concept of an undertaking as a single economic entity, made up of its constituent legal entities, is that the undertaking has knowledge of the offending agreement. There is therefore no need, before attaching liability to a legal entity which is part of that undertaking and has implemented the offending agreement, to allege and prove that that legal entity had knowledge of the offending agreement. It is sufficient that the undertaking had such knowledge.[154]

The High Court of England and Wales appears to indicate that if one legal entity that forms part of a transnational group of companies that constitutes a single undertaking has knowledge about the anti-competitive arrangements among the cartelists, then this would suffice to deduce that all legal entities that form part of the infringing undertaking would have had such knowledge. This is line with *Provimi*, which appears to indicate that any wholly-owned subsidiary that formed part of an undertaking may be liable for damages which were caused by the anti-competitive conduct of the transnational group of companies.[155] The *Provimi* point, however, was revisited by the Court of Appeal. Lord Justice Longmore took the view that:

> 45. As to the Provimi point, we can readily agree that, as Aikens J said, it is 'arguable'. We would, however, add that it is also arguable the other way. Although one can see that a parent

[151] See the reference request by Mr Rabinowitz in *Cooper Tire* – EWCA (n 82) [47].

[152] *ValueLicensing* (n 10) [54]. See also: Case C-882/19 *Sumal v Mercedes Benz Trucks España* EU:C:2021:800 [14–15 and 67].

[153] *Cooper Tire* – EWHC (n 4).

[154] Ibid [50].

[155] *Provimi* (n 102) [40].

> company should be liable for what its subsidiary has done on the basis that a parent company is presumed to be able to exercise (and actually exercise) decisive influence over a subsidiary, it is by no means obvious even in an [Article 101 TFEU or Chapter 1 of the 1998 Act] context that a subsidiary should be liable for what its parent does, let alone for what another subsidiary does. Nor does the Provimi point sit comfortably with the apparent practice of the Commission, when it exercises its power to fine, to single out those who are primarily responsible or their parent companies rather than to impose a fine on all the entities of the relevant undertaking. If, moreover, liability can extend to any subsidiary company which is part of an undertaking, would such liability accrue to a subsidiary which did not deal in rubber at all, but another product entirely? These and other difficulties have been ventilated by Mr Nicholas Khan in the 2003 volume of European Lawyer page 16 and Mr Brian Kennelly in the May 2010 issue of the CPI Anti-Trust Journal.
>
> 46. If it had been necessary to address the Provimi point, we would have been inclined to say that it would be necessary to make a reference to the ECJ before coming to a conclusion on jurisdiction. It would be possible to say that, because a claimant only has to show that he has a case against an anchor defendant which cannot be struck out, the fact that the Provimi point is arguable should not deter the English court from assuming jurisdiction. But that would mean that the Provimi point could never be decided in a jurisdiction (and possibly, therefore, in any other) context. That would not be a satisfactory state of affairs.[156]

The '*Provimi* point' further reappeared before the English courts in *Toshiba Carrier and others v KME Yorkshire and others.*[157] In this case, the claimants sought damages against the defendants, which were members of the *Industrial Tubes* cartel.[158] None of the companies that were named in the Commission decision was domiciled in England. The claimants, however, decided to issue their claim in England against UK-domiciled anchor defendants, KME Yorkshire (a company in the KME group) as well as against Nemco and WW (UK) (companies in the Wieland-Werke group). It has been argued that 'the claims [against the UK-defendants] have only been brought against them in order to secure jurisdiction in relation to the non-domiciled defendants'[159] which included addressees of the European Commission decision establishing the infringement.[160]

The Chancellor of the High Court took the view that the *Provimi* approach was not 'plainly wrong'.[161] It was concluded that there was a real issue between the claimant and the local subsidiary, and the defendant's strike-out application was dismissed.[162] On that basis, the Chancellor of the High Court went on to state that the English court had the jurisdiction to hear and determine the competition law claimant against the foreign defendants. The defendants appealed. The application for permission to appeal was granted. After hearing the appeal, the Court of Appeal held that there was a seriously arguable *stand-alone* claim against KME UK for an infringement of Article 101 TFEU.[163]

[156] *Cooper Tire* – EWCA (n 82) [45–46].
[157] *Toshiba Carrier* – EWHC (n 82).
[158] Case COMP/E-1/38.240 *Industrial tubes – Commission Decision of 16 December 2003 relating to a proceeding pursuant to Article 81 of the EC Treaty and Article 53 of the EEA Agreement* C(2002) 4820 Final CORR.
[159] *KME Yorkshire Ltd v Toshiba Carrier* [2012] EWCA Civ 169 [42].
[160] *Toshiba Carrier* – EWHC (n 82) [16–17].
[161] *Toshiba Carrier* – EWHC (n 82) [42].
[162] *Toshiba Carrier* – EWHC (n 82) [45].
[163] *KME Yorkshire Ltd v Toshiba Carrier* [2012] EWCA Civ 1190 [29–32].

Given that the respondents had made a stand-alone claim, the Court stated that the *Provimi* point did not arise in the present case.[164] Although the claim had been preceded by a decision of the EU Commission establishing an infringement by the KME group of companies, the claimant had to change its claim from a follow-on claim to a stand-alone claim in view of the fact that the defendant, a company from the KME group, was not named in the EU Commission decision as an infringing legal entity.[165] The stand-alone claim was that the defendant, KME UK, participated in, and implemented, the cartel arrangements with *knowledge of the cartel agreement*. In other words, it was accepted by the litigants that the claimants 'must prove KME UK's knowledge of the cartel agreement and practices'.[166]

Likewise, the *Provimi* point reappeared in *Nokia Corporation v AU Optronics Corporation*,[167] where Mr Justice Sales (as he then was) took the view that:

> In my view, it is well arguable that as a matter of EU law a civil law damages claim can be maintained by a person who has suffered loss as a result of paying inflated prices by reason of cartel arrangements in breach of Article 101 against a member of a participating undertaking which implemented the arrangements, albeit without knowledge of the cartel – at least where there is some significant element of influence or control by a member of the undertaking which does have knowledge of the cartel over the activities of the implementing member of the undertaking (control within the relevant undertakings is pleaded in this case).[168]

On that basis, the strike-out application was dismissed, which signified the approach under Brussels Ia. Post-Brexit, the issues concerning the requirements for the English courts to assume jurisdiction in cross-border competition law claims issued against a group of companies was dealt with in *JJH Enterprises Ltd (trading as ValueLicensing) v Microsoft*.[169] In this case, the private antitrust claim was issued against three defendants – Microsoft UK, Microsoft US and Microsoft Ireland – which formed part of the Microsoft group of companies that sells Microsoft software products and provides services to Mircrosoft customers across the globe. Since Microsoft Corporation is a US company, it appeared that the claimant had strategically issued their stand-alone claim against a local subsidiary which could be used as an anchor defendant 'on whom the claim form has been or will be served'[170] with a view to serving the claim form to Microsoft US and Ireland as being 'necessary or proper part[ies]'.[171]

In spite of the fact that the claimant might have tactically issued proceedings in England (rather than in the USA or Ireland), it seems clear that the claimant appeared to perceive the defendants as a 'single economic unit'. This could be clearly deduced from the claim form, in which the claimant failed to set out how each of the three separate legal entities (ie defendants) were involved in the alleged EU competition law infringement. The point was captured by the defendants' counsel, Mr O'Donoghue KC, who

[164] Ibid [37].
[165] Ibid [22]. See also: *Toshiba Carrier* – EWHC (n 82).
[166] *Toshiba Carrier* – EWCA (n 163) [37].
[167] *Nokia Corporation v AU Optronics Corporation* [2012] EWHC 731 (Ch).
[168] Ibid [82].
[169] *ValueLicensing* (n 10).
[170] Paragraph 3.1(3) of the CPR Practice Direction 6B, Service out of the jurisdiction.
[171] Ibid.

noted that 'the central allegations in the Particulars of Claim are made compendiously against "*Microsoft*" (defined in paragraph 1 as meaning "*the Defendants*"), without distinguishing between Microsoft US, Microsoft UK and Microsoft Ireland'.[172]

The defendants tried to challenge the jurisdiction of the English court by making an attempt to strike out the claim against Microsoft UK. As part of their jurisdictional challenge, the defendants unsuccessfully tried to put forward a strong argument that Microsoft UK (being a separate legal entity) was not engaging in any anti-competitive conduct.[173] The issue of liability of a group of companies, which consists of a parent company and subsidiaries that form a *single economic unit* for the purposes of EU competition law, was considered by the CJEU in *Sumal*.[174] In this case the CJEU took the view that:

> the victim of an anticompetitive practice by an undertaking may bring an action for damages, without distinction, either against a parent company who has been punished by the Commission for that practice in a decision or against a subsidiary of that company which is not referred to in that decision, where those companies together constitute a single economic unit. The subsidiary company concerned must be able effectively to rely on its rights of the defence in order to show that it does not belong to that undertaking and, where no decision has been adopted by the Commission under Article 101 TFEU, it is also entitled to dispute the very existence of the conduct alleged to amount to an infringement.[175]

On that basis, the English court held that the stand-alone competition law claim against Microsoft UK had 'reasonable prospects of success',[176] so that it could not be struck out. It was held that 'there is no requirement that ValueLicensing should have to plead infringements of the competition rules by Microsoft UK itself. It is sufficient that ValueLicensing has alleged that Microsoft UK is a member of an infringing undertaking'.[177] In other words, the fact that it was pleaded that Microsoft UK, Microsoft Ireland and Microsoft US were part of the same economic unit was sufficient for the claimants to demonstrate 'there is between [ValueLicensing] and [Microsoft UK] a real issue which it is reasonable for the court to try'[178] for jurisdictional purposes.

There are some fairly important issues concerning the assumption of jurisdiction in cases where the claim is issued against a UK-based subsidiary that forms part of a multinational group of companies that is to be regarded as a single economic unit for the purposes of EU competition law. In other words, it seems that the same jurisdictional issues which were identified in *Provimi* reappeared under the English PIL rules. The *Provimi* approach has been rightly criticised by Professor Fitchen who felt that it was 'translat[ing] the widest application of the undertaking concept into a parasitic private law claim'.[179] Whilst the stand-alone competition law claim may well be legitimate

[172] *ValueLicensing* (n 10) [14].
[173] *ValueLicensing* (n 10) [10, 27–28, 32].
[174] *Sumal* (n 152) [14–15].
[175] Ibid [67].
[176] *ValueLicensing* (n 10) [54].
[177] Ibid.
[178] Paragraph 3.1(3) of the CPR Practice Direction 6B, Service out of the jurisdiction.
[179] J Fitchen, 'Allocating jurisdiction in private competition law claims within the EU' (2006) 13 *Maastricht Journal of European and Comparative Law* 381, 395.

(rather than parasitic), Mr O'Donoghue KC also submitted that '*Provimi* was wrongly decided'.[180] In this context, Mr Justice Picken held that:

> I do not consider the *Provimi* point to be suitable for summary determination. As previously explained when addressing *Sumal*, I consider it inappropriate, when dealing with applications such as the present, for the Court to decide on a summary basis that UK competition rules should henceforth diverge from (pre-Brexit, established) EU rules. It is telling, indeed, that in two important respects (*Sumal* and *Provimi*) and despite the summary nature of the application(s), Microsoft UK urges the Court to depart from authority (CJEU and High Court respectively) in a significant way.[181]

The problem with the advanced approach is that Mr Justice Picken appears to indicate that because the claim against Microsoft UK which forms part of a single economic unit was not struck out, it was possible for 'ValueLicensing to invoke the "necessary or proper party" jurisdictional gateway contained in paragraph 3.1(3) of PD 6B to the CPR in order to establish jurisdiction as against Microsoft US and Microsoft Ireland'.[182]

But if the Microsoft UK, Microsoft US and Microsoft Ireland constitute a single economic unit for the purposes of competition law, then why should they be classified as separate parties in a competition law claim issued against them for PIL purposes? In other words, if the parent companies and subsidiaries, forming part of a multinational group of companies (ie an infringing undertaking for competition law purposes), were to classify as a single economic unit for the purposes of para 3.1(3)(a) of PD 6B, then *why should the parent company be regarded as a separate (be it a necessary or proper) party under para 3.1(3)(b) of PD 6B?* They are either a single economic unit or separate parties, but not both, for the purposes of para 3.1(3) of PD 6B.

As noted above, an alternative approach would be to classify the parent company and its local subsidiary as a single economic unit for PIL purposes. On that basis, their local subsidiary could classify as a branch for CPR purposes.[183] If the proposed alternative approach was advanced, then Microsoft UK (ie the English subsidiary of Microsoft Inc) could have been regarded as its branch of Microsoft for CPR purposes in so far it forms part of a single economic undertaking (indicating that it has no operative autonomy, being controlled by the parent company).[184] This means that, if Microsoft were to classify as a single economic unit, then a claim form could have be served on Microsoft within the jurisdiction, with no permission being required for the claim form to be served out of the jurisdiction in cases where the claim form can be served in the jurisdiction.[185]

[180] *ValueLicensing* (n 10) [31] – emphasis in the original.
[181] Ibid [68] – emphasis in the original.
[182] Ibid [70].
[183] See: Chapter 4 above.
[184] *Viho* (n 114) [16]. Case COMP/E-1/38.823, PO/Elevators and Escalators – Commission Decision relating to a proceeding under Article 81 of the EC Treaty C (2007) 512 final [604]. Compare: Case C-14/76 *De Bloos v Bouyer – Opinion of Mr Advocate-General Reischl, Delivered on 15 September 1976* EU:C:1976:120 at 1519.
[185] Paragraph 1A of PD 6B.

D. 'Necessary or Proper Party'[186]

The current practice is for para 3.1(3)(a) of PD 6B to be interpreted broadly to allow the claimant to issue a claim not only against a foreign infringing undertaking that has an establishment in the UK and sue other foreign undertakings,[187] but also against a local subsidiary (eg Apple UK) that forms part of an infringing undertaking, in order to join their parent company (eg Apple Inc) that is regarded as 'a necessary [or] proper party'[188] within the meaning of PD 6B.

It is well established that '[i]n determining whether a defendant is a necessary or proper party the courts are very much influenced by English procedural rules on joinder of parties',[189] which means that CPR 19.2(2) would be relevant. The prevailing approach at the moment[190] is for claimants to invoke para 3.1(3) of PD 6B in cases where 'the Proposed Defendants are all members of the same corporate group and [...] they would probably be regarded as part of the same economic entity [....] for the purpose of competition law'.[191]

The practice under para 3.1(3) of PD 6B is in line with the practice of the English courts under Article 8(1) of Brussels Ia. In competition law claims, the 'necessary or proper party'[192] requirement (as well as the need to 'avoid the risk of irreconcilable judgments resulting from separate proceedings')[193] would be easily satisfied, if the claims are issued against legal entities that form part of the same transnational group of companies and are regarded as a single undertaking, which allegedly abuses its dominant position.[194] This would also be clearly so in competition law cases where a claimant seeks to add a parent company as being a necessary and a proper party in a claim against a subsidiary implementing a cartel agreement. The joinder should enable the court to address all issues which would naturally involve common questions of fact (eg amount of overcharge; pass through) and law (eg regulatory infringement; quantification of damages), including the relationship between the parent and the subsidiary.

Likewise, the requirement for the foreign defendant to be a necessary or proper party against an English anchor defendant should be easily satisfied in cases where the claimant/s would issue competition law claims which arise out of the same competition law infringement and involve common questions of fact. This would be particularly so if the claimants wanted to sue several cartelists that are jointly and severally liable.

It should also be noted that, even if the claimant is suing a sole member of a transnational cartel, the judgments in the *Emerald*[195] and *IMI*[196] cases strongly indicate that the original defendant may bring additional claims against the other cartelist, so that

[186] Paragraph 3.1(3)(b) of PD 6B.
[187] *Clare Mary Joan Spottiswoode CBE* (n 10) [19–20].
[188] Case No: 1377/5/7/20, *Epic Games, Inc and Others v Apple Inc and Another* – Transcript of hearing (Service out of the jurisdiction) 21/01/2021 Page 78, lines 6–9.
[189] Fawcett (n 8) 747 and 748.
[190] *Elizabeth Helen Coll* (n 5); *ValueLicensing* (n 10); *Mr Justin Gutmann* (n 10) [14].
[191] *Elizabeth Helen Coll* (n 5) [5].
[192] Paragraph 3.1(3)(b) of PD 6B.
[193] Article 8(1) of Brussels Ia.
[194] *Elizabeth Helen Coll* (n 5); *ValueLicensing* (n 10); *Mr Justin Gutmann* (n 10).
[195] *Emerald Supplies Ltd & Others v British Airways v Air Canada & Others* [2014] EWHC 3513 (Ch).
[196] *IMI PLC and another v Delta Ltd and another* [2015] EWHC 1676 (Ch).

para 3.1(4) of PD 6B would equally be relevant in such cases. In this context, it should be noted that a claim form may be served out of the jurisdiction, if there was a competition law claim which 'is an additional claim under Part 20 and the person to be served is a necessary or proper party to the claim or additional claim'.[197]

IV. Conclusion

There is a strong argument that Section 15B of the 1982 Act, which is modelled on Section 4 of Brussels Ia, should be interpreted broadly to cover collective redress claims for damages issued on behalf of consumers.[198] The interpretation of Section 15B of the 1982 Act should rather be aligned with the UK regime, which is set to improve the injured parties' access to legal remedies in competition law cases.[199] Therefore, Section 15B of 1982 Act should be consistently interpreted considering Section 47B of the 1998 Act, which both cumulatively make the domicile of the claimants an important connecting factor. More importantly, a 'further consideration should be given to the use of third-party funding as a last resort means of providing access to justice'[200] and bundling claims together may be important for litigation funders.

Another important consideration is that there may be many competition law cases where several undertakings took part in a cartel (upholding the cartel induced overcharge, causing loss). In such a scenario, each infringing entity could be liable for damages.[201] In other words, there may be multiple defendants that 'are jointly and severally liable for loss suffered in the UK by [multiple] class members'.[202] As a result there would not be only cases where a claimant brings a private antitrust damages claimant against a defendant, but there would also be a number of multi-claimant and multi-defendant cases, involving groups of companies.[203] This may be explained by the fact that multiple consumers and/or multiple businesses (ie SMEs and large purchasers; indirect and direct purchasers) may be adversely affected by an anti-competitive practice or conduct.

A closer look at some of the pending collective redress proceedings strongly indicates that there is a number of related proceedings issued against hi-tech giants which would normally enjoy dominant positions.[204] These cases are potentially raising complex issues about the existence of a transnational competition law infringement (ie abuses of dominant positions)[205] and quantification of damages. There might be two sets of PIL issues in cases in relation to transnational competition law infringements.

[197] Paragraph 3.1(4) of PD 6B.
[198] *Dr Liza Lovdahl Gormsen* (n 5) [5, 9 and 10].
[199] Competition Act 1998 s 47B(11)(b).
[200] Recommendation 13 – *Improved Access to Justice* (n 19).
[201] See: *Provimi* (n 102) [38].
[202] *Michael O'Higgins* (n 35) [2].
[203] eg *Road Haulage Association* (n 35).
[204] *Dr Rachael Kent* (n 5); *Qualcomm* (n 34); *Elizabeth Helen Coll* (n 5); *Dr Liza Lovdahl Gormsen* (n 5); *Mr Justin Gutmann* (n 10); Case No: 1523/7/7/22, *BSV Claims Limited v Bittylicious Limited & Others* – Summary of collective proceedings claim form 13 September 2022.
[205] S Francq and W Wurmnest, 'International Antitrust Claims under the Rome II Regulation' in Basedow, Francq and Idot (n 121) 91, 97.

First, one set of PIL problems (concerning causation) could arise in cases where there is a prior regulatory decision that is binding in the UK and has established that there is a transnational competition law infringement.[206] In this scenario, the English courts would have to deal with the issues of causation and quantification.[207] Secondly, an entirely different set of PIL issues could arise in competition law cases in stand-alone claims in which there would not be a prior regulatory decision that was binding for the UK courts. In the latter scenario, the English courts would also have to consider the aspects concerning the regulatory jurisdiction, which might well impact on their adjudicatory jurisdiction.[208]

Therefore, the wide bases for the assumption of jurisdiction under English law[209] as well as for the allocation of jurisdiction under Brussels Ia,[210] strongly indicate that there would often be related proceedings that arise out of same transnational competition law infringement. An added layer of complexity is that the related private antitrust damages proceedings will involve various injured parties (be they consumers or businesses) who are at different levels of the commercial chain or the chain for distribution and who are based in the UK as well as in different EU Member States. More importantly, the different injured parties will be suing the same groups of companies (ie infringing undertakings) in different jurisdictions, bringing claims in relation to identical anti-competitive conduct. This presents a major governance challenge: how would different national judges attain consistent outcomes in related and parallel competition law claims which arise out of transnational competition law infringements?

Indeed, difficult issues in relation to related and parallel proceedings would need to be carefully considered in cross-border competition law disputes.[211] New forms of judicial cooperation and/or case management mechanisms are necessary to enable judges to more effectively and efficiently deal with multiple related claims.[212] The argument that the issues concerning the governance and coordination of related damages claims arising out of transnational competition law infringements should be more systematically considered may be strengthened by noting that the Brussels/Lugano regime does not apply to proceedings issued in the UK after the end of the transition period (ie 31 December 2020).[213] In spite of the UK's formal request[214] to join the Lugano

[206] Case AT.39824, *Trucks – Commission Decision relating to a proceeding under Article 101 of the Treaty on the Functioning of the European Union (the Treaty) and Article 53 of the EEA Agreement* – 19.7.2016, C(2016) 4673 final; Case AT.39824, *Trucks – Commission Decision relating to a proceeding under Article 101 of the Treaty on the Functioning of the European Union and Article 53 of the EEA Agreement* – 27.9.2017, C(2017) 6467 final.

[207] Chapter 11.

[208] Chapters 9 and 10.

[209] Chapters 4 and 5.

[210] Chapters 4 and 5.

[211] See: Chapters 7 and 8 below.

[212] Case Nos: 1517/11/7/22 (UM) and 1266/7/7/16, *The Merchant Interchange Fee Umbrella Proceedings* [2022] CAT 31.

[213] Article 67 of the Withdrawal Agreement. See also: Communication from the European Commission to the European Parliament and the Council, *Assessment on the application of the United Kingdom of Great Britain and Northern Ireland to accede to the 2007 Lugano Convention* COM(2021) 222 final.

[214] 612-04-04-01 – LUG 3/20, *Notification to the Parties of the Convention on Jurisdiction and the Recognition and Enforcement of Judgments in Civil and Commercial Matters, concluded at Lugano on 30 October 2007* – Bern, 22 May 2020.

Convention, which provides for judicial cooperation in civil and commercial matters (broadly defined to cover antitrust matters), the EU took the view that it is 'not [...] in a position to give its consent to invite the United Kingdom to accede to the Lugano Convention'.[215]

The lack of a 'global legal system'[216] and/or an international convention means that a soft law mechanism might be needed to attain an appropriate level of judicial cooperation in related antitrust damages claims arising in a global context. This would be important in order to ensure that any related/common issues are being somewhat consistently dealt with by different national judges. The questions are: how are multiple and related competition law damages claims, raising similar issues, to be coordinated, with a view to consistently determining issues in relation to liability and quantification of damages in cross-border competition law cases? How should national judges take account of the relevant competition laws of all the jurisdictions that have legitimate interests to regulate the relevant economic activities?

[215] 612-04-04-01 – LUG 4/21, *Notification to the Parties of the Convention on Jurisdiction and the Recognition and Enforcement of Judgments in Civil and Commercial Matters, concluded at Lugano on 30 October 2007 –* Bern, 1 July 2021.

[216] A-M Slaughter, *A New World Order* (Princeton University Press, 2004) 85.

7

Related and Parallel Proceedings Arising Out of Transnational Competition Law Infringements

I. Introduction

The transnational nature of various economic activities, which are pursued by multinational groups of companies being active in global markets,[1] means that private antitrust damages in relation to the same transnational competition law infringement would be sustained by injured parties in multiple jurisdictions. If those injured parties were to issue their claims before the courts where the damage was sustained, then there is a risk that the multiple courts would not be able to consistently deal with any common issues arising in related private antitrust damages claims that arose out of the same transnational competition law infringement/s. The issues are even more important in a global context, not least because national judges would often be applying their own national competition laws which may have mandatory character, expressing their public policy.[2]

Competition law claims may be issued on behalf of consumers or businesses; they can include contracting parties; they might involve transnational groups of companies that enjoy market power. The English courts' adjudicatory jurisdiction could be derived from paras 3.1(2), (3), (6) or (9) of PD 6B as long as the competition law claim has reasonable prospects of success and England is the proper place for the competition law claims to be heard and determined. Likewise, various EU Member States' courts may have jurisdiction under Articles 4, 7 and 8(1) of Brussels Ia. This means that multiple related competition law claims arising out of the same transnational competition law infringement may be issued in different jurisdictions.

The lack of an international convention to promote judicial cooperation in competition law matters strongly suggests that related and parallel proceedings, which arise out of the same transnational competition law infringement, may hardly be avoided in a global context. For example, the wide scope of para 3.1(3) of PD 6B and Article 8(1) of Brussels Ia, taken together with the fact that many competition law infringements

[1] Compare: *Motorola Mobility LLC v AU Optronics Corp* 775 F 3d 816 at 824 (7th Cir 2015) and *The LCD Appeals* [2018] EWCA Civ 220.

[2] Chapters 9 and 10.

would involve multinational groups of companies with numerous subsidiaries, should leave no doubt that some injured parties would often have a choice between two or more forums, where they could issue their private antitrust damages claims.[3]

The purpose of this chapter is to consider how parallel and related proceedings arising out of the same competition law infringement are coordinated with a view to avoiding inconsistent outcomes. In theory, one way to achieve a desired level of consistency is by consolidating proceedings and centralising litigation against multiple defendants in cross-border competition actions.[4] Centralising litigation in claims which involve multiple claimants and multiple defendants would minimise the level of inconsistency that would ensue if there were separate proceedings in relation to the same transnational competition law.[5] In the EU context it has been suggested[6] that appropriate jurisdictional rule/s should be adopted in order to allow for cross-border competition litigation against a multinational group (or rather multinational groups) of companies to be centralised before an appropriate court.

The problem is that there is no mechanism which allows for related private antitrust damages against such infringing undertakings to be consolidated before an appropriate forum either in the EU or in the global context. PIL issues are more and more important in cross-border competition law cases because the UK is no longer part of the Brussels Ia/Lugano framework for judicial cooperation. In spite the fact that, post-Brexit, there is no longer a regime for judicial cooperation between the UK and the EU,[7] many private antitrust damages claims would arise of competition law infringements which have affected the prices of various products/services in the UK as well as in the EU.

The PIL literature suggests that an appropriate way to avoid related and parallel proceedings (which may arise out of transnational competition law infringements) is through PIL mechanisms which allow national judges to decline jurisdiction on *forum non conveniens*[8] or *lis pendens* grounds.[9] Another way to avoid such parallel proceedings might be to restrain the parties from continuing with their competition law claims abroad in cases where the 'failure to restrain will result in inconsistent judgments in England and abroad'.[10] The anti-suit injunctions may be granted by the English court, but such anti-suit injunctions would fly in the face of the principle of mutual trust, which meant that they were incompatible with the Brussels Ia/Lugano regime.[11]

[3] See: Chapter 6.

[4] M Danov, F Becker and P Beaumont, (eds) *Cross-border EU Competition Law Actions* (Oxford, Hart Publishing, 2013).

[5] Ibid; M Danov, *Jurisdiction and Judgments in Relation to EU Competition Law Claims* (Oxford, Hart Publishing, 2010).

[6] M Danov, 'Jurisdiction in cross-border EU competition law cases: Some specific issues requiring some specific solutions' in Danov, Becker and Beaumont (n 4) 167–96.

[7] *FS Cairo (Nile Plaza) LLC v Lady Brownlie* [2021] UKSC 45 [29].

[8] A Arzandeh, 'Should the *Spiliada* Test Be Revised?' (2014) 10 *Journal of Private International Law* 89–112.

[9] JJ Fawcett, 'General Report' in JJ Fawcett (ed), *Declining Jurisdiction in Private International Law – Reports to the XIVth Congress of the International Academy of Comparative Law, Athens, August 1994* (OUP, Oxford 1995) 1, 2.

[10] Ibid 40.

[11] Case C-159/02 *Gregory Paul Turner v Felix Fareed Ismail Grovit, Harada Ltd and Changepoint SA* EU:C:2004:228; Case C-185/07 *Allianz SpA and Generali Assicurazioni Generali SpA v West Tankers Inc* EU:C:2009:69.

The aspects concerning declining jurisdiction and avoidance of related and parallel proceedings have been examined in a comparative context by some leading PIL scholars in their reports submitted to the XIVth Congress of the International Academy of Comparative Law.[12] In this context, Professor Fawcett noted that:

> The phrase 'declining jurisdiction' refers to the situation where a court which has jurisdiction refuses to exercise it. This is a situation with which lawyers from both common law and civil law jurisdictions are familiar. [...] It is to be distinguished from the situation where the rules on jurisdiction are not satisfied and a court therefore dismisses the action on the basis that it has no jurisdiction. Of course, in both situations, the result is the same: the court refuses to try the action.
>
> It is well known that in many States a court may decline to exercise jurisdiction / or assert that it has no jurisdiction on the basis of *forum non conveniens* (i.e. the appropriate forum for trial is abroad or the local forum is inappropriate) or *lis pendens* (i.e. parallel proceedings involving the same parties and cause of action are continuing in two different States at the same time).[13]

It should be further noted that the doctrine of *forum non conveniens*[14] is deployed under the English PIL regime, whilst the *lis pendens* approach is advanced within the EU. For the purposes of this book, the author will also consider the issues concerning 'related actions'[15] which would arise in relation the same anti-competitive conduct that may be put into operation by the same dominant undertaking or may be implemented by the same cartelists in different jurisdictions.

In order to consider how parallel and related proceedings arising out of the same competition law infringement should be coordinated, the author will examine the doctrine of *forum non conveniens* along with the possibility for the English courts to award anti-suit injunctions. In addition, the EU regime, which is set to avoid parallel proceedings within the European Union, will be considered, in order for the author to evaluate whether it is feasible for a similar regime to be advanced in a global context. On that basis, the important PIL issues will be examined with a view to advancing a theoretical model[16] that should be used to set the scene for judicial cooperation, which would be important to avoid inconsistent outcomes in related competition law claims arising out of the same transnational competition law infringement.

II. Some Major Issues – Avoiding Inconsistent Outcomes

The wide bases for jurisdiction, which were discussed in the previous chapters,[17] strongly indicate that there would be fairly complex issues in multiple related claims arising out of the same transnational competition law infringement.

[12] Fawcett– *Reports to the XIVth Congress* (n 9).
[13] Fawcett – General Report (n 9) 2.
[14] A Arzandeh, 'The origins of the Scottish forum non-conveniens doctrine' (2017) 13 *Journal of Private International Law* 130–151.
[15] Fawcett – General Report (n 9) 43.
[16] See: Chapter 8.
[17] See: Chapters 4, 5 and 6.

The problems, which need to be considered under the Brussels Ia Regulation, were exposed in the follow-on claims in relation to the *Trucks* cartel.[18] More specifically, the transnational competition law infringement in question concerned price-fixing arrangements between the manufacturers of medium and heavy trucks.[19] The cartel operated for approximately 14 years,[20] with the cartel members having an 'aggregate market share in the European Economic Area (EEA) [of] approximately 90%'.[21] The relevant volume of commerce and the size of the market seem to suggest that the cartel may have caused a significant amount of damage to multiple injured parties.

The issues could be deduced from the collective redress proceedings which were issued by the Road Haulage Association (RHA) and the UK Trucks Cartel (UKTC).[22] More specifically, the UK CAT noted that:

> The RHA application states that the average price of a truck over the relevant period was £50,000 and gives what it acknowledges is only a crude estimate of the potential cartel overcharge at 25%. On that basis, the average damages per truck are £10,000 plus interest. The UKTC application states that Dr Lilico's very preliminary rough estimate is that the damages are £21,000 per truck, including compound interest.[23]

The high value of the cartel induced (estimate) overcharge and the prospects of success (in view of the EU Commission's findings) meant that a significant proportion of the injured parties are likely to bring their private antitrust damages claims before the national courts. In particular, many of the injured parties were prepared to issue proceedings[24] or to opt in to a set of collective redress proceedings.[25] In other words, the high value of the follow-on claims might incentivise injured parties to bring damages claims (and litigation funders to assist them with costs) which in turn would result in multiple sets of related proceedings in the UK as well as in different EU Member States.[26]

The lack of a multilateral mechanism which ensures that inconsistent findings in related proceedings, arising out of the same cross-border competition law infringement, are avoided means that an alternative mechanism for judicial cooperation may be central to improving the injured parties' access to legal remedies in cross-border competition law cases, post-Brexit. The point may be strengthened by considering

[18] Case AT.39824, *Trucks – Commission Decision relating to a proceeding under Article 101 of the Treaty on the Functioning of the European Union (the Treaty) and Article 53 of the EEA Agreement* – 19.7.2016, C(2016) 4673 final; Case AT.39824, *Trucks – Commission Decision relating to a proceeding under Article 101 of the Treaty on the Functioning of the European Union and Article 53 of the EEA Agreement* – 27.9.2017, C(2017) 6467 final.

[19] *Trucks – Commission Decision* – 19.7.2016 (n 18) [5].

[20] Ibid [62–63].

[21] Ibid [24].

[22] Case No: 1517/11/7/22 (UM) and 1266/7/7/16, *UK Trucks Claim Ltd v Stellantis and Road Haulage Association Ltd v MAN SE & Ors* [2022] CAT 25.

[23] Ibid [164].

[24] eg Case Nos: 1284/5/7/18 (T) and 1290–1295/5/7/18 (T), *Royal Mail Group Ltd v DAF Trucks Ltd & Others, BT Group Plc & Others v DAF Trucks Ltd & Others, Ryder Ltd & Another v MAN SE & Others, Suez Groupe SAS & Others v Fiat Chrysler Automobiles NV & Others, Veolia Environment SA & Others v Fiat Chrysler Automobiles NV & Others, Wolseley UK Ltd 7 Others v Fiat Chrysler Automobiles NV & Others, Dawsongroup Plc & Others v DAF Trucks NV & Others* [2018] CAT 19.

[25] *Road Haulage Association* (n 22).

[26] Ibid [5–6].

the problems which were exposed in the *MasterCard* follow-on litigation in the UK.[27] In this case, the EU Commission took the view that the default multilateral interchange fee (MIF) was in conflict with Article 101 TFEU.[28] Since the prohibited MIF formed a substantial part of the Merchant Service Charge which was paid by merchants who participated in MasterCard & Visa schemes, antitrust damages were caused to many merchants and millions of consumers.

But how were the private antitrust damages to be quantified, if there were related claims that arose out of the same transnational infringement and that were issued by consumers and merchants in different jurisdictions? The issues were indeed complex because Merricks's claim was initially issued on behalf of 'all UK resident adult consumers of goods and services purchased in the UK [...]. The size of the represented class was estimated in the claim form to be 46.2m people'.[29] Moreover, multiple claims were issued by retailers[30] as well as on behalf of 'councils, local authorities and universities'.[31] The significant number of multiple and related claims reflected the fact there was a long commercial chain, with different injured parties passing through and/or absorbing any antitrust damage down the chain of commerce.[32] On that basis, the defendants sought to introduce a pass-on defence, arguing that certain categories of claimants (eg various merchants) had passed on the relevant overcharge down the chain and had not suffered any loss.[33] The difficult issues were set out by the UK CAT:

> One of the issues that gives rise to clear differences between the parties is that of 'pass on'. Where there has been a competition law infringement by infringer *A*, and as a result party *B* has paid more for a good or service than *B* would, but for the infringement, have paid, then prima facie it appears to be the case that *B* has a claim, against *A*, for the amount of the overcharge. However, *A* may contend that the *prima facie* case does not hold, in that *B* has passed on the loss (sustained by *B*), in whole or in part, to party *C*. *C* could be someone who bought a good or service from *B* where the price paid by *C* to *B* included, in whole or in part, the overcharge which was originally paid by *B* to *A*. Matters are complicated by the fact that if the overcharge was indeed passed on by *B* to *C*, then *C* has a self-standing claim against *A*, as the party who has in fact borne the loss arising out of *A*'s infringement.[34]

In order to avoid the inconsistent factual findings, the multiple related claims should be consolidated as far as possible.[35] This means that any relevant jurisdictional rules should be interpreted in a way which allows for centralisation of related claims, minimising

[27] Case Nos: 1517/11/7/22 (UM) and 1266/7/7/16, *The Merchant Interchange Fee Umbrella Proceedings* [2022] CAT 31. See also: *Sainsbury's Supermarkets Ltd v MasterCard Incorporated and others* [2020] UKSC 24; *Mastercard Incorporated and others v Walter Hugh Merricks CBE* [2020] UKSC 51.

[28] Case COMP/34.579 – *MasterCard*, Case COMP/36.518 – *EuroCommerce*, Case COMP/38.580 – *Commercial Cards*, Non-Confidential Version of the Commission Decision relating to a proceeding under Article 81 of the EC Treaty and Article 53 of the EEA Agreement, December 2007.

[29] *Merricks* (n 27) [11].

[30] eg *Sainsbury's* (n 27); Schedule of 'Host Cases', as updated on 19 August 2022, to the Umbrella Proceedings Order – dated 4 July 2022.

[31] *The Merchant Interchange Fee Umbrella Proceedings* (n 27) [51].

[32] M Danov, G Howells and D Fairgrieve, 'Collective redress antitrust proceedings: How to close the enforcement gap and provide redress for consumers' in Danov, Becker and Beaumont (n 4) 253 at 280.

[33] *The Merchant Interchange Fee Umbrella Proceedings* (n 27) [34].

[34] Ibid [3].

[35] Ibid [13].

'the perils of bilateral dispute resolution'.[36] These specific aspects should inevitably impact on the way in which any *forum conveniens* discretion would be exercised.

The above CAT's judgment strongly indicates that, in a single jurisdiction, the case management of the related claims would be central for the contentious issues to be clearly set out, which should in turn enable the UK CAT to give clear guidance to the parties as to what evidence should be collected for the UK CAT to address the issues:

> Pleadings in competition cases are exceedingly important, given the very difficult issues that arise for determination in such cases. [...] In particular, pleadings serve the very important purpose – at least in competition cases – of not only defining the issues that arise for determination, but the way in which those issues are going to be proved. [...]
>
> The Tribunal [...] can control the evidence that it receives in order to determine the issues that arise for determination in the cases before it.[37]

A case management mechanism in a single jurisdiction may be central for the judges to ensure an appropriate sample is selected and the type of required evidence (eg econometric evidence) is clearly set out.[38] But what if the related claims are issued in different jurisdictions, indicating that there is a risk that various national judges potentially reach divergent outcomes? The level of complexity would indeed multiply in cases where multiple private antitrust damages claims are issued on behalf of different classes of injured parties before different national courts. The problem is that any related proceedings may lead to inconsistent outcomes in so far as the different 'claims will have to be determined in each case on the basis of the pleadings and the evidence adduced'[39] in different jurisdictions.

Might a soft mechanism for judicial cooperation (eg cooperation between lawyers with a view to discussing their pleadings in different jurisdictions) enable judges to somewhat more consistently quantify the damages in follow-on damages claims? If the findings of the English judges were to be considered in other jurisdictions, then a level of consistency might potentially be attained.[40] The question is whether, in the absence of an international convention to promote judicial cooperation, the existing *forum non conveniens* rules along with a soft law mechanism for judicial cooperation could be relied upon to avoid inconsistent outcomes in related competition law claims arising out of the same transnational competition law infringement.

III. *Forum Non Conveniens* and Anti-Suit Injunctions

The problem with parallel and related proceedings that are linked to the same transnational infringement is that the UK judge and the foreign judges might both need to deal with common issues such as: is the conduct in question anti-competitive (eg exchange

[36] Ibid.
[37] Ibid [59 and 60].
[38] Ibid [61].
[39] *Sainsbury's* (n 27) [246].
[40] See: Chapter 12.

of information on the prices; excessive prices); has this particular infringement caused damages (affecting the prices); how are the damages to be quantified? If there are multiple related claims arising out of the same transnational competition law infringement, then there is a risk that various national judges may take different views on any of the common issues (eg the existence of regulatory breach; causation; the amount of overcharge). In other words, there is a risk that various common issues could be inconsistently dealt with by the different national judges unless a level of judicial cooperation in antitrust matters is attained.

The challenge is how to govern cross-border proceedings with a view to attaining consistent outcomes in cases where the related claims are issued in different jurisdictions, so that the inconsistent outcomes in related multiple competition law claims arising out of the same transnational competition law infringement are minimised as far as possible. The specific question is whether the doctrine of *forum non conveniens* along with anti-suit injunctions would enable the English courts 'to solve the problems of parallel proceedings by encouraging the parties early on to opt for trial in the appropriate forum, and discontinue proceedings in other fora'.[41]

A. *Forum Non Conveniens*

As noted above,[42] a claimant's application for service of a claim form out of the jurisdiction would normally be 'heard *ex parte*, without submissions from the Defendants'.[43] This means that any order for service of a claim form out of the jurisdiction will be made 'without prejudice to the rights of [the defendants] to apply pursuant to Rule 34 of the Tribunal Rules to dispute the Tribunal's jurisdiction'.[44] In particular, r 34(1) states that:

> A defendant who wishes to —
>
> (a) dispute the Tribunal's jurisdiction to hear the claim; or
> (b) argue that the Tribunal should not exercise its jurisdiction,
>
> may apply to the Tribunal for an order declaring that it has no such jurisdiction or should not exercise any jurisdiction which it might have.

As part of such jurisdictional challenges, the defendant/s would normally seek to substantiate that 'there is some other available forum, having competent jurisdiction, which is the appropriate forum for the trial of the action'.[45] On that basis, the English proceedings could be stayed, so that the parties would have all their claims determined in the foreign court rather that engage in two sets of private antitrust proceedings arising out of transnational competition law infringement.

[41] Fawcett – General Report (n 9) 42.
[42] Chapter 4.
[43] Case Nos: 1377/5/7/20 and 1378/5/7/20, *Epic Games v Apple, Alphabet and Google* [2021] CAT 4 [3].
[44] Case No: 1433/7/7/22, *Dr Liza Lovdahl Gormsencv Meta Platforms and Others*, Reasoned Order of the President – Service out of the jurisdiction – 15 March 2022 [10]. See also: Case No: 1440/7/7/22 *Clare Mary Joan Spottiswoode CBE v Nexans France SAS Nexans SA and Others* – Reasoned Order of the President – Service out of the jurisdiction – 19 August 2022 [2].
[45] *Spiliada Maritime v Cansulex* [1987] AC 460, 476.

Having one set of competition law proceedings (rather than two sets) may be important for some parties to centralise their litigation proceedings, reducing the level of inconsistency and minimising their costs and any delay. The relevant issues, which may be reasonably associated with being involved in the two sets of proceedings, could be deduced from the judgment of the High Court of England and Wales in *Federal Deposit Insurance Corporation v Barclays Bank*[46] as well as from the judgment of the US Court of Appeals (Second Circuit) in *Schwab Short-Term Bond Market v Lloyds Banking*.[47] Both sets of proceedings were in relation to some major banks' collusive practice to manipulate the LIBOR rate, which was allegedly in conflict with UK competition law as well as in conflict with US antitrust law, causing damages to multiple parties in the United States.[48]

The first set of proceedings were commenced in the US in 2014, with the claimants seeking inter alia damages for breach of US antitrust law.[49] It is worth noting that the US proceedings, which were case-managed through the US multi-district litigation procedure, involved more claimants and defendants in comparison to the UK proceedings. The issue concerning parallel proceedings, however, was important because the claimants and defendants in the English proceedings were also parties to the US proceedings.

The proceedings in England were commenced after the defendants successfully challenged the jurisdiction of the US courts to hear and determine the claims against the foreign defendants (ie UK banks).[50] In view of this, the US claimants were quick to issue proceedings in England before any limitation periods had elapsed.[51] However, the subsequent developments and the US court judgment in *Schwab Short-Term Bond Market v Lloyds Banking*[52] meant that there was a possibility for the US courts to have jurisdiction, so that the claimants could continue to engage with the US proceedings. In view of these developments in the US, the claimants made a request for a stay of the English proceedings.

In this context, Mr Justice Mann summarised the main issues which might be important for the parties to streamline or consolidate the proceedings (and minimise their cost) as far as possible rather than have two sets of proceedings running in parallel:

> If there were no stay then [the Claimants' counsel, Ms Prevezer KC,] said there would be a risk of a serious waste of costs here, mainly on the disclosure process, if it transpired that the US proceedings were to continue and these proceedings were not. The bank defendants have given a first round of disclosure, so the next step would be likely to be some more request-driven disclosure. The claimant has given a large amount of disclosure already, but is working on further disclosure which it will have to give if the proceedings carry on here. It has already done 9 months work, and the current estimate is that it will take another 9 months, with commensurately very high costs. Those costs might well be wasted if there were no stay.

[46] Ibid.

[47] *Schwab Short-Term Bond Market v Lloyds Banking* 22 F 4th 103 (2nd Cir 2021).

[48] *Federal Deposit Insurance Corporation as Receiver of Amcore Bank NA and Others v Barclays Bank Plc and Others* [2022] EWHC 391 (Ch) [2].

[49] Ibid [3].

[50] Ibid [3–4].

[51] Ibid [5]. See also: *Federal Deposit Insurance Corporation as Receiver of Amcore Bank NA and Others v Barclays Bank Plc and Others* [2020] EWHC 2001 (Ch) [16–21].

[52] *Schwab Short* (n 47).

> The BBA defendants have not yet given disclosure, but they have given some details of the number of documents which have to be reviewed, and Ms Prevezer's estimate of those costs is in the region of £2.6m if not more (the BBA defendants have not themselves given a figure).[53]

This quotation nicely captures the additional delay and costs which the parties would incur if the parallel and related proceedings were to be running in several jurisdictions; but, more importantly, the judgment appears to indicate that 'the US requirements on disclosure were different and the English disclosure could not just be ported into the US proceedings'.[54] This raises an issue of 'inconvenience'[55] as opposed to convenience which is at the heart of the court's determination whether England/UK CAT is 'the proper place in which to bring the claim'.[56] There is a view that 'multiple private litigation regarding the same agreement or network of agreements [...] can lead to inconsistent outcomes'[57] which is a risk that might need to be better governed in cross-border cases. The point could be deduced from the UK CAT judgment in *Allianz Global Investors v Deutsche Bank*,[58] where the following observations were put forward by Mr Justice Jacobs:

> I accept the Claimants' submission that it is appropriate for (or at least predictable that the Tribunal will want) both sets of proceedings to be subject to sensible joint case management, potentially up to and including having them consolidated or heard together.
>
> The alternative approach, of the two cases proceeding independently and on separate tracks – including being subject to two separate trials in close proximity – would potentially lead to duplication of the work required by the Tribunal and inconsistent findings in the two sets of proceedings. This is a result which, if reasonably possible, should be avoided, not least because consistency of outcome is a very desirable objective [...]. Furthermore, the rationale behind the CAT's *Practice Direction 2/2022: Umbrella Proceedings* is that the resources of the CAT should be deployed efficiently, and with a view to avoiding duplication and inconsistent findings. That rationale applies, perhaps with even greater force, to cases such as the present, where the allegation against all the various Defendants concerns the same underlying conduct. I accept Ms Demetriou's submission that it is likely to be a 'nightmare scenario' for there to be entirely separate trials involving the two groups of Defendants.[59]

It seems clear that the judges and parties in England would endeavour to avoid related and parallel proceedings, in a domestic context, by appropriately case-managing and consolidating competition law claims arising out of the same transnational competition law infringements.

That said, avoiding the 'nightmare scenario'[60] which concerns parallel and related proceedings (which would in turn result in multiple trials) in different jurisdictions would be a much more complex task in cross-border cases. It is beyond any doubt that

[53] *Federal Deposit Insurance* (n 48) [15].
[54] Ibid.
[55] Fawcett – General Report (n 9) 41.
[56] Competition Appeal Tribunal Rules 2015, r 31(3). See also: Civil Procedure Rules, r 6.37(3).
[57] S Brammer, *Co-operation between National Competition Agencies in the Enforcement of EC Competition Law* (Oxford, Hart Publishing, 2009) 27.
[58] *Allianz Global Investors Gmbh and Other v Deutsche Bank AG London* [2022] CAT 44.
[59] Ibid [47–48].
[60] Ibid [48].

a key question which national courts would need to address in cross-border competition law cases is how to deal with the issues concerning related/parallel competition law proceedings,[61] whilst ensuring that like issues are being dealt with alike[62] in cases where the CAT has taken the view that the UK proceedings will not be stayed and will continue along with the foreign proceedings.[63]

Indeed, it is well settled that the 'multiplicity of proceedings',[64] including any related 'parallel proceedings',[65] which could potentially lead to 'inconsistent findings'[66] and higher litigation costs, would be another factor to be weighed up in this context. There is a risk of 'duplication if [a claimant] had to claim for the element of its loss caused by the MSC in each country in the court of that country instead of as part of a single set of proceedings'.[67] Since the victims of cross-border infringements would often be at a different level of the supply chain and they would often be based in different jurisdictions, parallel and/or related proceedings in different jurisdictions might need to be avoided to minimise any inconsistencies, where possible, as part of the *forum non conveniens* discretion.

In *Epic Games v Apple*,[68] the CAT took the view that the following factors should be considered by the courts when exercising their discretion:

> The governing approach to determination of whether England is clearly the appropriate forum derives from Lord Goff's classic speech in *The Spiliada* [1987] AC 460. Lord Goff there emphasised that the fundamental consideration is the interests of all the parties and the ends of justice. As numerous judgments have subsequently shown, a range of factors may therefore be taken into account, including (i) the residence or place of business of the parties; (ii) the location of likely witnesses; (iii) the existence of parallel proceedings; (iv) the applicable law (v) the cost and delay; (vi) a legitimate personal or juridical advantage; and (vii) the jurisdictional gateway relied on. See note 6.37.16 in *Civil Procedure 2020 (the 'White Book')*, However, this is not an exhaustive list, and the relevance and importance of any factor will vary significantly from one case to another in the 'evaluative or balancing exercise' which the court or tribunal has to carry out: per Lord Neuberger in *VTB Capital* at [97].[69]

The non-exhaustive list of factors enables the judges to strike a balance between multiple factors which are relevant to ascertaining an appropriate forum for the related claims to be determined. The rationale is for the judges to factor in a 'wide, indeed unlimited, range of considerations which come within the themes of appropriateness and justice'.[70] Therefore, the judgments of Lord Goff in *Spiliada*[71] and Lord Wilberforce in *Amin Rasheed*[72] should be applied when determining whether competition law claims should

[61] Brammer (n 57) 25.
[62] *The Merchant Interchange Fee Umbrella Proceedings* (n 27) [15].
[63] Fawcett – General Report (n 9) 41.
[64] *Spiliada* (n 45) 470.
[65] *Epic Games* (n 43) [132].
[66] *JJH Enterprises Ltd (trading as ValueLicensing) v Microsoft* [2022] EWHC 929 (Comm) [76].
[67] Case Nos: 1236/5/7/15, *DSG Retail Ltd, Dixons Retail Ltd v MasterCard* [2015] CAT 7 [41].
[68] *Epic Games* (n 43).
[69] Ibid [132].
[70] Fawcett – General Report (n 9) 20.
[71] *Spiliada* (n 45) 478–9.
[72] *Amin Rasheed Shipping Corporation v Kuwait Insurance Co* [1984] AC 50, 72 (Lord Wilberforce).

be heard and determined in England and Wales. This means that the English courts would need to consider the specific features of the competition law claim along with the transnational character of any competition law infringement (including any regulatory findings).

Moreover, the courts should also factor in the aspects concerning evidence and disclosure, the expertise of their legal teams and appropriately qualified expert witnesses, the availability of litigation funding and conditional fee arrangements.[73]

B. Natural Forum – Remedies and Applicable Laws

As noted in chapter 4, the *forum conveniens* doctrine would work reasonably well in cases where England and Wales or the UK CAT is '"the natural forum" [– the one] with which the action had the most real and substantial connection'.[74] For example, the CAT would be the natural forum in a follow-on competition law case where the products, which were bought at an inflated price, were marketed in the UK; the claimant/s (or the class of claimants) were domiciled in England; the regulatory breach were established by the UK CMA.[75] The relevant factors were set out by the CAT in *Elisabetta Sciallis v Fender*:[76]

> the products to which these proceedings relate were marketed and sold in the UK. The damage occurred in this jurisdiction. Fender Europe is a company incorporated in England, and has its registered office here. Fender Europe will be sued in England as of right. The claims are in part follow-on claims from a Decision of the CMA based on a breach of competition rules as applied in the UK.[77]

However, there might be cases where the CAT is not *the natural forum*. In particular, there might be cases where there might be a foreign forum which has a 'real and close connection [with] the dispute'.[78] It has been submitted that '[t]his factor may be linked to the convenience of the parties in that it focuses on the place where the parties' dispute is centred, and this is often where one or both of the parties reside'.[79] For example, this was duly considered as an important factor in *Epic Games v Apple*,[80] where the parties were large North American corporations.[81] However, this was not the sole factor, but it was considered along with the availability of witnesses, the level of overlap between any parallel and related proceeding and any additional costs which would impact on the convenience of litigating in one jurisdiction rather than another. In other words, the proper place for the injured parties to bring their competition law claims may be abroad, if it were to be more cost-efficient for the parties to join the foreign

[73] See: Chapter 4.
[74] *The Abidin Daver* [1984] 1 AC 398, 415.
[75] Case No: 1437/7/7/22, *Elisabetta Sciallis v Fender Musical Instruments Europe Ltd & Fender Musical Instruments Corp* – Reasoned Order of the Chair (Service out of the jurisdiction)–17 June 2022.
[76] Ibid.
[77] Ibid [20].
[78] P Beaumont, 'Great Britain' in Fawcett – *Reports to the XIVth Congress* (n 9) 207, 218.
[79] Ibid.
[80] *Epic Games* (n 43).
[81] Ibid [134].

proceedings which should in turn allow the English court to avoid parallel/related proceedings. In *Epic Games v Apple*,[82] the UK CAT took the view that:

> The factual and economic evidence, including expert economic evidence, that would have to be given on such issues in [this] action under UK competition law therefore substantially overlaps with the evidence that will be given in the US proceedings. The additional cost if this action proceeded in the Tribunal in addition to the US proceedings is accordingly, in my view, very significant even allowing for the cost of presenting expert evidence of English law to the US court.[83]

That said, a closer look at the *Epic Games v Apple* case strongly suggests that 'the unavailability of appropriate remedies in the *prima facie* more appropriate forum would appear to give more discretion to English courts to retain jurisdiction on grounds of justice'.[84] It seems clear that the ability of the parties to attain effective legal remedies in the foreign legal proceedings would be a major consideration which would be factored in by the English courts with a view to determining whether the CAT is the proper place for the parties to bring their competition law claim. The relevance of this factor was reiterated in *Epic Games v Apple*[85] where the CAT noted that:

> If it was the Claimants' case that their claims under UK competition law were not justiciable in the US or that the US courts would not grant injunctive relief extending to the UK, that would in my judgment be a powerful factor in favour of holding that this country is clearly or distinctly the appropriate forum.[86]

The availability of damages in foreign parallel and related proceedings appeared to be considered by the CAT in a number of cases which appeared to be issued on behalf of consumers. This has been particularly the case where the foreign proceedings are pending before the US courts. Since it is now established that US antitrust law would not apply extra-territorially in cases where the anti-competitive conduct has not had qualified effects in the US,[87] it could be difficult for UK consumers to access effective legal remedies in the U.S. private antitrust enforcement proceedings. For example, in *Dr Liza Lovdahl Gormsen v Meta Platforms*, Mr Justice Marcus Smith held:

> "although there is a similar class action in the US which seeks redress against Meta on behalf of consumers, the US Sherman Act does not appear to apply extra-territorially so as to extend to claims of the present kind by UK consumers: see *Hoffmann-La Roche Ltd v Empagran S.A.* 542 US 4 155 (2004) and it appears that the US action is limited to '*persons in the United States*'."[88]

[82] *Epic Games* (n 43).
[83] Ibid [136].
[84] Beaumont (n 78) 211.
[85] *Epic Games* (n 43).
[86] Ibid [139].
[87] *F Hoffmann-La Roche Ltd v Empagran* (2004) 542 US 155 at 165; 124 SCt 2359 (Sup Ct (US)); See also E Wind, 'Remedies and Sanctions in Article 82 of the EC Treaty' (2005) 26 *European Competition Law Review*, 659, 667. See more: Chapter 9.
[88] *Dr Liza Lovdahl Gormsen* (n 44) [17]. See also: Case No: 1403/7/7/21, *Dr Rachael Kent v Apple Inc. Apple Distribution Int'l Ltd* [2022] CAT 28 [6]; Case No: 1382/7/7/21, *Consumers' Association v Qualcomm Inc* – Reasoned Order of the President (Service out of the jurisdiction), 15 March 2021 [6]; Case No: 1408/7/7/21, *Elizabeth Helen Coll v Alphabet Inc* – Reasoned order of the President – Service out of the jurisdiction – 29 September 2021 [11].

The quotation strongly suggests that the applicable competition laws, which would express English public policy, may be another important factor which the judges would consider when exercising their discretion.[89]

Given the regulatory nature of national competition laws, it is highly likely that the aspects concerning the applicable regulatory competition regime[90] will be taken into account by the English courts when exercising their discretion to assume jurisdiction or stay their legal proceedings. As part of this process, the English courts may ascertain the extent to which the UK market is affected,[91] considering whether there is any prior regulatory decision/s rendered by the UK CAT or whether foreign courts/regulators should not be more appropriate to safeguard foreign regulatory interests. The latter point was set out by Mr Justice Roth, holding:

> Where allegedly anti-competitive conduct concerns the Australian market, that is a matter for Australian competition law, and similarly where it concerns the US market, that is a matter for US Federal or State antitrust law. Indeed, I note that on 21 March 2018 well-known Australian lawyers instructed by Unlockd Media Pty Ltd sent a letter before action to Google alleging a breach of Australian competition law and threatening to seek an interim injunction in the Federal Court of Australia. And on the same day, a leading US law firm wrote on behalf of the same company to Google, threatening an antitrust claim for damages and a complaint to the relevant US antitrust authorities.
>
> I recognise that when a global company pursues an allegedly anti-competitive international strategy which may affect its competitors in many different markets across the world, it is much more convenient if such an adversely affected competitor could bring its complaint against that conduct in one forum. *But mere convenience is not a basis to extend further the extraterritorial reach of EU competition law, still less does it make it appropriate for the English court to assume the role of competition policeman of the world.*[92]

The territorial scope of UK competition law, which 'reflects a public policy to protect the interests of UK consumers and businesses against anti-competitive conduct and arrangements',[93] as well as various comity considerations, might be equally perceived as important factors which could impact on the judges' willingness to exercise their discretion[94] by deciding that England and Wales is not the appropriate place for the parties to litigate. This would be particularly so in competition cases which are raising regulatory concerns in some developed competition law jurisdictions which are capable enough to safeguard their own regulatory interests. These aspects may be considered along with the fact that, if EU competition law were to be applicable, the English courts may no longer have the power to make preliminary references to the CJEU[95] or seek assistance from the EU Commission.[96]

Another important feature of private antitrust damages claims, which was set out in Lord Wilberforce's dissenting judgment in *Garden Cottage v Milk Board*,[97] concerns the

[89] Beaumont (n 78) 212–4 and 220.
[90] *ValueLicensing* (n 66) [78].
[91] Ibid [72].
[92] *Unlockd Ltd v Google* [2018] EWHC 1363 (Ch) [50 and 51].
[93] *Epic Games* (n 43) [139].
[94] Compare: *The LCD Appeals* (n 1).
[95] *ValueLicensing* (n 66) [79].
[96] See: Article 15 of Regulation 1/2003.
[97] *Garden Cottage Foods v Milk Marketing Board* [1984] 1 AC 130, 147 (per Lord Wilberforce – dissenting).

fact that, 'even assuming that the [claimant] company is held entitled to damages, the *quantum* must be *wholly uncertain*'.[98] The application and implementation of the various substantive and procedural principles concerning the quantification of damages may be fairly complex because 'quantification is a complex process, usually involving difficult economic, econometric and statistical evidence'.[99] This means that the experience of legal teams and their '[p]leadings in competition cases are exceedingly important',[100] as well as the experience of the expert witnesses,[101] and may be key for the claims to satisfy the standard of proof for a claim and/or plea to proceed to trial[102] and beyond (ie judgment on the merits; settlement). This may be another major factor to be considered when evaluating the appropriateness of the court.

Finally, the aspects in relation to 'substantial justice'[103] need to be considered with a view to evaluating the appropriateness of the foreign forum. An English court may need to go a step further and determine whether substantial justice will be provided by the foreign court, if the claims were to be brought there. If there were to be a real risk that this will not be the case, the court may take the view that England and Wales is the proper place for the claim to be heard and determined.[104] The relevant principles were summarised by Lord Briggs as follows:

> Even if the court concludes (as I would have in the present case) that a foreign jurisdiction is the proper place in which the case should be tried, the court may nonetheless permit (or refuse to set aside) service of English proceedings on the foreign defendant if satisfied, by cogent evidence, that there is a real risk that substantial justice will not be obtainable in that foreign jurisdiction. The same test was, prior to *Owusu v Jackson*, applicable in the context of an application for a stay of English proceedings against a defendant served within the jurisdiction. The question whether there is a real risk that substantial justice will be unobtainable is generally treated as separate and distinct from the balancing of the connecting factors which lies at the heart of the issue as to proper place, but that is more because it calls for a separate and careful analysis of distinctly different evidence than because it is an inherently different question. If there is a real risk of the denial of substantial justice in a particular jurisdiction, then it seems to me obvious that it is unlikely to be a forum in which the case can be tried most suitably for the interests of the parties and the ends of justice.[105]

In such a case, 'the burden of proof shifts to the [claimant]'[106] to persuade the court that, despite the fact that the natural forum is abroad, the UK CAT or the English courts will not be staying their proceedings. The issues concerning access to justice in competition law cases are intertwined with the issues concerning the injured parties' access to finance, costs[107] and litigation funding.[108] As already noted above, a specific feature of

[98] Ibid [154] – emphasis added by the author.

[99] Case Nos: 1329/7/7/19 and 1336/7/7/19 *Michael O'Higgins FX Class Rep v Barclays Bank plc* [2022] CAT 16 [173]. See also: *The Merchant Interchange Fee Umbrella Proceedings* (n 27).

[100] *The Merchant Interchange Fee Umbrella Proceedings* (n 27) [59].

[101] *Spiliada* (n 45) 470–1.

[102] Case Nos: 1284–1290/5/7/18 (T), *Royal Mail Group Ltd v DAF Trucks Ltd & Others, BT Group Plc & Others v DAF Trucks Ltd & Others* [2021] CAT 10 [22].

[103] *Vedanta Resources PLC and another v Lungowe and others* [2019] UKSC 20 [89].

[104] *Spiliada* (n 45) 482.

[105] *Vedanta Resources* (n 103) [66].

[106] *Spiliada* (n 45) 478; *The Abidin Daver* (n 74) 411 (Lord Diplock).

[107] *Epic Games* (n 43) [132].

[108] *Vedanta Resources* (n 103) [90].

private antitrust damages claims is that there is a high level of complexity and uncertainty in relation to quantum,[109] which in turn requires experienced legal teams and expert witnesses. Since in some competition law cases '[t]he likely cost and burden of disclosure may well require skilled case management',[110] for any common issues in cases involving multiple injured parties to be effectively and efficiently dealt with, an appropriate case-management mechanism may be central for the judges to be able to dispense justice in cross-border competition law cases.

The UK experience in implementing the EU policy, which was set to encourage private antitrust enforcement,[111] shows that appropriate procedural mechanisms might incentivise third party litigation funding.[112] Such litigation funders may provide funding in some jurisdictions, but not in others, which may foster a process of adjudicatory competition. A claimant could argue that, if they were to litigate abroad, their access to finance would be impeded which would in turn deprive from access to justice.

The above analysis appears to indicate the doctrine of *forum non conveniens* should help the English judges to avoid parallel and/or related proceedings in cases where there is only one natural forum, which is abroad. However, a real difficulty in competition law cases is that there may be cases 'where no particular forum can be described as the natural forum for the trial of the action [and] where there can be pointers to a number of different jurisdictions'.[113]

The problems in identifying a natural forum in competition law cases are bound to arise because there are multiple competition laws,[114] and it is highly likely for the anti-competitive conduct to be implemented in a number of jurisdictions[115] and cause damages to multiple injured parties.[116] This means that English or CAT proceedings as well as any foreign proceedings may often continue to run in parallel – raising concerns concern about consistency and leading to increased expenses and a higher level of legal uncertainty,[117] which may well have an impact on settlement dynamics and injured parties' access to legal remedies.

C. Anti-Suit Injunctions

The greater the number of multiple and related competition law claims that are issued in different jurisdictions and that arise out of the same transnational infringement, the

[109] *Garden Cottage Foods* (n 97) 154 (per Lord Wilberforce – dissenting).

[110] *Merricks* (n 27) [74].

[111] White Paper on Damages actions for breach of the EC antitrust rules COM(2008) 165 final; Directive 2014/104/EU of the European Parliament and of the Council of 26 November 2014 on certain rules governing actions for damages under national law for infringements of the competition law provisions of the Member States and of the European Union Text with EEA relevance.

[112] *BT Group PLC & Anr v Le Patourel* [2022] EWCA Civ 593.

[113] *Spiliada* (n 45) 477.

[114] A Bradford et al, 'Competition Law Gone Global: Introducing the Comparative Competition Law and Enforcement Datasets' (2019) 16 *Journal of Empirical Legal Studies* 411.

[115] *Trucks – Commission Decision* – 19.7.2016 (n 18); *Trucks – Commission Decision* – 27.9.2017 (n 18). See also: *Cooper Tire & Rubber Company v Shell Chemicals UK Limited* [2009] EWHC 2609 (Comm).

[116] *Road Haulage Association* (n 22) [5–6].

[117] Fawcett – General Report (n 9) 41.

greater the risk for judges to inconsistently deal with any common issues (eg relevant market; effects on competition; causation; overcharge; pass-on). The issue, which is also reflected in the relevant literature, is that if parallel and related proceedings are not effectively governed there is a risk that the parties may be forced to deal with issues of 'injustice, delay, increased expense, and inconsistent findings'[118] with regard to competition law claims arising out of the same competition law infringement. Could the English courts or the UK CAT solve the problems in relation to parallel proceedings arising out of the same transnational infringement by exercising their jurisdiction to grant anti-suit injunctions?

The answer to this question is important because, whilst the anti-suit injunctions could be awarded to restrain certain litigants from continuing with their private antitrust enforcement proceedings abroad, it may be inappropriate to grant such injunctions in cross-border competition law cases. It was established that:

> An anti-suit injunction is an order of the court requiring the injunction defendant [...] not to commence, or to cease to pursue, or not to advance particular claims within, or to take steps to terminate or suspend, [...] court or arbitration [...] proceedings in a foreign country, or court proceedings [...] elsewhere in England. The order is addressed to, and binds, the actual or potential litigants in the other proceedings, and is not addressed to, and has no effect on, the other court.[119]

In spite of the fact that, in theory, the anti-suit injunctions may play an important role in avoiding parallel and/or related proceedings, such injunctions presuppose a degree of 'caution because [granting them] involves indirect interference with the process of the foreign court concerned'.[120] This is particularly so in competition law claims arising out of transnational competition law infringements which, by definition, would mean that multiple legal orders would have regulatory jurisdiction to safeguard their own regulatory interests.

It may be inappropriate for the English courts to exercise their jurisdiction to grant such injunctions in cases where foreign courts may have legitimate regulatory interests to apply their own competition laws. An alternative solution may be necessary because the English legal literature[121] strongly suggests that 'judicial chauvinism has been replaced by judicial comity'.[122] Indeed, it is now widely accepted that '[a]nti-suit injunctions may result in interference in foreign proceedings in breach of comity'.[123] A case for an alternative solution may be strengthened by noting that anti-suit injunctions would be incompatible with principle of mutual trust which is central to the effectiveness of the Brussels Ia/Lugano regime.[124]

[118] L Collins and M G Droz, *Second Commission – The principles for determining when the use of the doctrine of forum non conveniens and anti-suit injunctions is appropriate* (Institut De Droit International, Session de Bruges 2003) para 'd' from the Preamble. See also: C McLachlan, 'Lis Pendens' in *International Litigation* (Leiden/Boston, Martinus Nijhoff Publishers, 2009) 23.

[119] T Raphael, *The Anti-Suit Injunctions* (Oxford, OUP, 2008) [1.05].

[120] *South Carolina v Assurantie Maatshapij* [1987] AC 24, 40. See also: Raphael (n 119) 110–118.

[121] Raphael (n 119) 110–118; L Collins, 'Comity in Modern Private International Law' in JJ Fawcett (ed), *Reform and Development of Private International Law – Essays in Honour of Sir Peter North* (Oxford, OUP, 2002) 89.

[122] *The Abidin Daver* (n 74) 411.

[123] Collins and Droz (n 118) para 'f' from the Preamble.

[124] *West Tankers* (n 11); Opinion of Advocate General Kokott in Case C-185/07 *Allianz SpA v West Tankers Inc*, EU:C:2008:466; *Grovit* (n 11). A Briggs, 'Anti-suit injunction and utopian ideals' (2004) 120 *LQR* 529.

The relevance of anti-suit injunctions with regard to antitrust law disputes can be illustrated by the *Laker Airways*[125] litigation. The case may be regarded as a good example demonstrating how conflicting, but legitimate, regulatory interests may be difficult to balance in related proceedings in England and Wales[126] as well as in the US.[127] The US court identified the reason for the lack of a desired level of judicial cooperation in antitrust matters by submitting that: 'At the root of the conflict are the fundamentally opposed policies of the United States and Great Britain regarding the desirability, scope, and implementation of legislation controlling anticompetitive and restrictive business practices'.[128]

The latter point concerning the regulatory jurisdiction and the territorial scope of the US antitrust laws could be strengthened by considering the UK Supreme Court judgment, discharging the injunction which was granted by the Court of Appeal.[129] It was held that:

> by obtaining an air transport licence from C.A.A. to operate scheduled services on routes between the United Kingdom and the United States as British airlines designated by the United Kingdom government under Bermuda 2, B.A., B.C. and Laker alike voluntarily submitted themselves to a regulatory regime which, so far as their operations within the territorial jurisdiction of the United States were concerned, required that each of them should become subject to American domestic law including American antitrust laws. In the circumstances as I have outlined them, it seems to me to be impossible to argue plausibly either that Laker by submitting itself to such a regime precluded itself from relying upon any cause of. action against B.A. or B.C. that might accrue to it under American antitrust laws as a result of what these airlines subsequently did within the territorial jurisdiction of the United States; or that there was anything so unconscionable or unjust in Laker's conduct in pursuing such cause of action in a U.S. court that an English judge, in the proper exercise of a judicial discretion, would be entitled to grant an injunction to prevent Laker from doing so.[130]

More importantly, the *Laker Airways* litigation strongly suggests that the 'extraterritorial application'[131] of competition laws along with the legitimate interests of the US legal order to regulate the antitrust aspects of the conduct is at the heart of the problem. One should go a step further and investigate whether a desired level of judicial cooperation in cross-border competition law cases could be achieved by encouraging national judges to be more systematically dealing with (regulatory and adjudicatory) jurisdictional issues. Might it be possible for a PIL approach to the issues of adjudicatory jurisdiction and regulatory jurisdictions, to allow for the national courts to factor in any relevant national regulatory interest irrespective of where the parties litigate? Might such a private international law mechanism, which draws on the notion of comity and

See also: J Mance, 'Exclusive Jurisdiction Agreements and European Ideals' (2004) 120 *LQR* 357; TC Hartley, 'The Brussels I Regulation and Arbitration', 63 *International and Comparative Law Quarterly* (2014) 843; Case C-536/13 *Gazprom v Lietuvos Resublika*, EU:C:2015:316.

[125] *British Airways Board v Laker Airways* [1984] 1 QB 142; *Laker Airways Limited v Sabena* 731 F 2d 909 (DC Circuit, 1984).

[126] *British Airways* (n 125).

[127] *Laker Airways Limited v Sabena* 731 F 2d 909 (1984), US Court of Appeals DC.

[128] Ibid 955.

[129] *British Airways v Laker Airways* [1985] AC 58.

[130] Ibid 84.

[131] L Collins, 'Comity in Modern Private International Law' in Fawcett (n 121) 89, 105.

which addresses the issues concerning regulatory and adjudicatory jurisdiction, be even more important in cases where there is a conflict of competition laws?[132]

Prior to advancing a theoretical model which might be necessary to promote a level of judicial cooperation through a set of soft mechanisms, it will be necessary to examine how effectively the Brussels Ia/Lugano regime is capable of avoiding parallel and/or related competition law cases. In this context, it should be noted that a specific feature of the Brussels Ia/Lugano regime is that it has created a multilateral framework for judicial cooperation in civil and commercial matters that is broad enough to cover private antitrust claims, but excludes public enforcement proceedings.[133] The so-created regime for judicial cooperation is directly applicable,[134] forming an important part of the legal order of a significant number of EU Member States as well as jurisdictions from the European Economic Area (EEA).[135]

IV. Multilateral Solution (Brussels Ia/Lugano)

One of the key objectives of the Brussels Ia/Lugano regime is to create 'a clear and effective mechanism for resolving cases of *lis pendens* and related actions'.[136] The rationale is for the EU Member States to 'minimise the possibility of concurrent proceedings and to ensure that irreconcilable judgments will not be given in different Member States'.[137] Indeed, it is now well established that Articles 29 and 30 of Brussels Ia are 'intended to prevent parallel proceedings before the courts of different [Member States] and to avoid conflicts between decisions which might result therefrom',[138] which is in turn central to ensuring that the rendered judgments would be recognised and enforced across the EU/EEA.[139]

It seems that Article 29 (*lis pendens*) and Article 30 (related actions) along with Article 8(1) of Brussels Ia may cumulatively be interpreted as aiming to attain a level of 'centralisation of jurisdiction and procedural efficiency'[140] in cross-border competition cases. These objectives appear to be very important in the context of private antitrust litigation so far as many of the relevant infringements, which would be established by the EU Commission, would be transnational in nature, causing antitrust harm to businesses and consumers in a number of EU Member States. The problem is that, as acknowledged by Advocate General Jääskinen,[141] the Brussels Ia/Lugano regime is not sufficiently suited to attain these objectives in relation to cross-border private antitrust claims.

[132] Chapters 8, 9, 10 and 12.

[133] See: Chapter 3 above.

[134] Case C-106/77 *Amministrazione delle finanze dello Stato v Simmenthal* EU:C:1978:49; Case C-6/64 *Costa v E.N.E.L.* EU:C:1964:66.

[135] Case C-26/62 *Van Gend en Loos v Administratie der Belastingen* EU:C:1963:1.

[136] Recital 21 – Brussels Ia.

[137] Ibid.

[138] Case C-144/86 *Gubisch Maschinenfabrik v Palumbo* EU:C:1987:528 [8].

[139] Ibid.

[140] Opinion of Advocate General Jääskinen in Case C-352/13 *Cartel Damage Claims (CDC) Hydrogen Peroxide SA v Evonik Degussa GmbH* EU:C:2014:2443 [107].

[141] Ibid [8].

An analysis of jurisdictional rules and their application in EU competition law cases will demonstrate that it may be very difficult for claimants to centralise competition litigation, which would mean that there would be a higher level of legal uncertainty, delay and costs. The absence of a pan-EU collective redress mechanism means that many claimants (eg SMEs and consumers in particular) may prefer to sue for the local damage before the courts in their home state. More specifically, since consumers could issue proceedings at the place of their domicile,[142] particularly difficult issues would arise in cases where the consumers are domiciled in different EU Member States. The problems for claimants to centralise collective representative proceedings in the EU have been set out by Pato:[143]

> concentration of proceedings would be difficult [if] consumers are domiciled in different Member States or in different locations within the same national territory: in which forum should all claims be centralised and according to which criteria? […] On the one hand, centralising claims in the domicile of one consumer is difficult to achieve, as courts of this domicile could hardly have jurisdiction over consumers located in a different place. […] On the other hand, bundling claims in the domicile of the representative entity is difficult to justify, as this forum is not expressly mentioned in section 4 [of Chapter 2 of Brussels Ia].[144]

This quotation appears to suggest that the lack of appropriate jurisdictional rules would mean that follow-on related and parallel competition law proceedings[145] would be bound to arise in the EU context. The problems would be exacerbated in cases where various injured parties (eg consumers; SMEs; large purchasers) had issued court proceedings against various members of the same group/s of companies (representing one or more infringing undertakings) in different EU Member States. With this in mind, there are three sets of provisions which will be examined in this section. First, Article 29(1) and (3) of Brussels Ia states that:

> [W]here proceedings involving the same cause of action and between the same parties are brought in the courts of different Member States, any court other than the court first seised shall of its own motion stay its proceedings until such time as the jurisdiction of the court first seised is established.
>
> […]
>
> Where the jurisdiction of the court first seised is established, any court other than the court first seised shall decline jurisdiction in favour of that court.

This provision is intended to deal with the problem of *lis pendens*.[146] In particular, Article 29 is concerned with the situation where the same parties (ie injured parties; infringing undertakings) have been involved in private antitrust enforcement proceedings which concern the same cause of action (ie liability for private antitrust damages), with at least two sets of proceedings being issued in two different EU Member States.

[142] See: Chapter 5.

[143] A Pato, *Jurisdiction and Cross-Border Collective Redress: A European Private International Law Perspective* (Oxford, Hart Publishing, 2019).

[144] Ibid 155.

[145] See: Brammer (n 57) 25.

[146] C McLachlan, 'Lis Pendens' in *International Litigation* (Martinus Nijhoff Publishers, Leiden/Boston, 2009).

In such cases, there is an obligation for the court second seised (as opposed to the court first seised) to stay its proceedings.

Article 30(1) and (2) of Brussels Ia goes further to deal with related competition law claims. The provision is question states that:

> Where related actions are pending in the courts of different Member States, any court other than the court first seised may stay its proceedings.
>
> Where the action in the court first seised is pending at first instance, any other court may also, on the application of one of the parties, decline jurisdiction if the court first seised has jurisdiction over the actions in question and its law permits the consolidation thereof.

This provision is broader in comparison to Article 29 in so far it does not require for the disputes to be in relation to the same cause of action, involving the same parties. In view of this, the court second seised *may* (rather than must) stay its proceedings, which is a form of a discretionary stay for the purposes of the Brussels Ia/Lugano regime. It is now well established that the court second seised with the claim is not entitled to 'examine the jurisdiction of the court first seised',[147] even if the court first seised has not decided the question of its jurisdiction 'within a reasonable time'.[148] Therefore, Articles 29 and 30 of Brussels Ia enable national courts to stay and/or decline their proceedings, giving priority to the court first seised[149] in competition cases where the parallel or related proceedings are before the EU Member State courts.

Article 33 of Brussels Ia is set to deal with the situation where the parallel proceedings are before an EU Member State court (eg The Netherlands) and a non-EU Member State court. More specifically, an EU Member States' court has discretionary powers to stay its proceedings in competition law cases where *parallel* (rather than related) proceedings are pending before 'a court in a Member State [which] is seised of an action involving the same cause of action and between the same parties as the proceedings in the [UK CAT, for example]'.[150] In such cases, according to Article 33(1):

> the court of the Member State may stay the proceedings if:
>
> (a) it is expected that the court of the third State will give a judgment capable of recognition and, where applicable, of enforcement in that Member State; and
>
> (b) the court of the Member State is satisfied that a stay is necessary for the proper administration of justice.

Article 34 goes further to address the problems which would arise in cases where the proceedings are related. The broad concept of 'proper administration of justice',[151] which is advanced in Articles 33 and 34, might be associated with the common law requirements for the courts to ascertain an appropriate forum, considering 'the interests of all the parties and the ends of justice'.[152] In view of this, one could argue that this is

[147] Case C-116/02 *Erich Gasser v MISAT* EU:C:2003:657 [44].

[148] Ibid [63, 68–69]. See for criticism of this ruling, TC Hartley, 'The European Union and the Systematic Dismantling of the Common Law of Conflict of Laws' (2005) 54 *ICLQ* 813, 820–21.

[149] P Herzog, 'Brussels or Lugano, Should you race to the Courthouse or race for a judgement?' (1995) 43 *American Journal of Comparative Law* 379, 381–84.

[150] Article 33 of Brussels Ia.

[151] Ibid.

[152] *Spiliada* (n 45) 476.

a broader form of discretion in comparison with the one provided under Article 30(2) of Brussels Ia. Another distinctive feature of Articles 33 and 34 of Brussels Ia is that any court (regardless of whether it is the court first seised or the court second seised) may stay its proceedings. As part of this process, the EU Member States courts would need to ascertain the territorial scope of EU competition laws. This might be an important factor in cross-border competition law cases which may in turn have an impact on EU Member State courts' adjudicatory jurisdiction (ie assuming or declining jurisdiction).[153]

A. Article 29 – Competition Law Cases[154]

The effect of Article 29 of Brussels I is that any court other than the court first seised must first stay its proceedings, and then decline to exercise jurisdiction, provided that the court first seised had assumed jurisdiction. Article 29 has been interpreted as requiring the national courts to consider whether the 'actions are between the *same parties* and involve the *same cause of action* and the *same subject-matter*'.[155]

The phrase 'same cause of action' may not be easily interpreted in cross-border competition law cases where various companies that form part of infringing undertakings might bring pre-emptive claims for negative declarations in relation to their liability to certain injured parties.[156] The CJEU jurisprudence appears to suggest that there are two major aspects for the court second seised to consider when ascertaining whether it should stay its proceedings. First, the judges should consider whether 'the "cause of action" comprises the facts and the rule of law relied on as the basis of the action'.[157] Secondly, the judges should set out what 'the object of the action'[158] is by considering the desired outcome of the claims which are issued.[159] More specifically, the CJEU took the view that:

> The question accordingly arises whether two actions have the same object when the first seeks a declaration that the [claimant] is not liable for damage as claimed by the defendants, while the second, commenced subsequently by those defendants, seeks on the contrary to have the [claimant] in the first action held liable for causing loss and ordered to pay damages.
>
> As to liability, the second action has the same object as the first, since the issue of liability is central to both actions. The fact that the [claimant's] pleadings are couched in negative terms in the first action whereas in the second action they are couched in positive terms by the defendant, who has become [claimant], does not make the object of the dispute different.[160]

Nonetheless, it may be far from clear whether the parallel proceedings would have the same cause of action, if a negative declaration concerning liability for damages sustained

[153] See: Chapter 9.
[154] See more: Danov (n 6).
[155] *Gubisch Maschinenfabrik* (n 138) [14] – emphases added by the author.
[156] Case 1346/5/7/20 *Volvo Car AB and Volvo Personvagnar AB v MOL (Europe Africa) Ltd and Others* – Order of the President – Service out of the jurisdiction – 20 May 2020 [6].
[157] Case C-406/92 *The owners of the cargo lately laden on board the ship 'Tatry' v The owners of the ship 'Maciej Rataj'* EU:C:1994:400 [39].
[158] Ibid [41].
[159] Ibid.
[160] Ibid [42–43].

is sought in one EU Member State and a private antitrust damages claim is issued in another EU Member State. The question was considered by the UK CAT in *Volvo v MOL (Europe Africa)*.[161] In this case, a private antitrust damages claim was issued by companies from the Volvo group. The claim in England was issued against ten defendants: MOL (Europa Africa) Ltd; Wallenius Wilhelmsen ASA; Walleniusrederna AB; Wallenius Wilhlmsen Ocean AS; Wallenius Logistigs AB; Wilhelmsen Ships Holding Malta Ltd; Eukor Car Carriers Inc; Kawasaki Kisen Kaisha Ltd; Nippon Yusen Kabushiki Kaisha; Compania Sudamamerica De Vapores SA. The private antitrust damages claims were preceded by a decision of the EU Commission, establishing that the parties were operating a cartel.[162]

However, prior to the English proceedings, six of the defendants in the English proceedings: Wallenius Wilhelmsen ASA; Walleniusrederna AB; Wallenius Wilhlmsen Ocean AS; Wallenius Logistigs AB; Wilhelmsen Ships Holding Malta Ltd; Eukor Car Carriers Inc, had started proceedings seeking a non-liability declaration in Sweden. The Swedish claim was issued against the companies from the Volvo group that were claimants in the UK CAT proceedings. In this context, Mr Justice Roth stated:

> I note that on 9 January 2020 [some of the] Defendants commenced proceedings against the Claimants in the Swedish Patent and Market Court (the 'Swedish Court') for a negative declaration as to their liability to the Claimants arising from infringements of Article 101 TFEU and/or Article 53 EEA Agreement. On 22 April 2020 the Swedish Court issued a decision that it had jurisdiction over the proceedings. That decision has not become binding as it is under appeal. The present claim is [...] said by the Claimants not to be based on the same cause of action as the proceedings before the Swedish Court for the purpose of Article 29 of Regulation (EU) No. 1215/2012 and Article 27 of the Lugano Convention, even for those parties which are common to the proceedings before the Tribunal and the Swedish Court. This is said to be because, despite similarities between the claims, the matters of law and fact involved in each will be different.[163]

The point was not further argued because the claim appeared to have subsequently settled. Hence, the following questions remain open: is the cause of action and subject matter the same if, for example, the English proceedings concern damages for breach of competition law (effects on prices) in England, and the Swedish proceedings involve damages caused by a breach of competition law in Sweden?

The argument that Article 29 may not be suited to apply in competition law cases could be strengthened by making reference to the proceedings in *Cooper Tire*.[164] In this case, there were two sets of proceedings in Italy and England. The Italian proceedings were issued by Eni SpA, Polimeri Europa SpA (collectively 'Enichem'). They were addressees of a Commission decision[165] that preceded the private antitrust dispute and that established an infringement of EU competition law. The first claim was issued against 28 defendants by Enichem in Italy. They claimed that the cartel had no effect on

[161] *Volvo Car and Volvo Personvagnar* (n 156).

[162] Case AT.40009 – *Maritime Car Carriers – Commission Decision relating to a proceeding under Article 101 of the Treaty on the Functioning of the European Union and Article 53 of the EEA Agreement* C(2018) 983 final.

[163] *Volvo Car and Volvo Personvagnar* (n 156) [6]. Compare: *Cooper Tire* – EWHC (n 115) [81].

[164] *Cooper Tire* – EWHC (115).

[165] Case COMP/F/38.638 – *Butadiene Rubber and Emulsion Styrene Butadiene Rubber.*

the price of Butadiene Rubber (BR) and Emulsion Styrene Butadiene Rubber (ESBR), and, as a result, the defendants suffered no damages. All defendants were tyre manufacturers – companies in the Pirelli, Michelin, Continental, Goodyear, Bridgestone and Cooper groups.[166]

In England, a few months later, 26 companies of the same groups of tyre manufacturers issued private antitrust damages claims against 23 defendants. All of the defendants were producers and sellers of BR and ESBR. Therefore, the parallel EU competition law actions involved not one claimant and one defendant but several groups of companies on each side. In particular, the 'same parties' requirement appears to give rise to specific difficulties in EU competition law cases, which could involve different companies from the different groups of companies liable for the EU competition law infringement, which could be regarded as tortfeasors, being jointly and severally liable for private antitrust damages. In this context, Mr Justice Teare observed:

> The Claimants in the English proceedings are in essence the same as the defendants in the Italian proceedings. There was no dispute that they could be regarded as the same parties. The difficulty arose with the Claimants in the Italian proceedings, Enichem, and the Defendants in the English proceedings, all the producers of BR and ESBR save Enichem. Debate was joined on the issue whether they were the same parties.[167]

After carefully considering the degree of identify between the parties, and their interests, the judge held that Enichem and the defendants in England were not the same parties. Thus, the application for a mandatory stay under Article 29 of Brussels Ia was rejected.

Cooper Tire clearly demonstrates that the 'same parties' requirement would be difficult to satisfy in most competition scenarios.[168] For example, proceedings in England against the French subsidiary of a German manufacturing company would not affect proceedings in Italy against the Italian subsidiary of the same German manufacturing company. Similarly, proceedings in France as to the validity of an anti-competitive agreement between a company and its French distributor would have little effect on the proceedings against its German distributor in Germany on a virtually identical contract which is arguably in conflict with EU competition law. There is little doubt that German proceedings would not be stayed. Moreover, 'a judgment in France as to the validity of the agreement with one's French distributor will not have effect when suing its German distributor in Germany on a virtually identical contract'.[169] The argument for an alternative form of judicial cooperation in antitrust matters may be strengthened by noting that it is not only that Article 29 is not suited to deal with the problem of problem of parallel proceedings arising out of the same infringement, but it is also that Article 30 of Brussels Ia may not be very useful either.

[166] *Cooper Tire* – EWHC (n 115) [68].
[167] Ibid [69].
[168] Danov (n 5).
[169] V Korah, *An Introductory Guide to EC Competition Law and Practice* 9th edn (Oxford, Hart Publishing, 2007) 221. See also: J Bourgeois and C Humpe, 'The Commission's Draft "New Regulation 17"' (2002) 23 *European Competition Law Review* 43, 46–47; Brammer (n 57) 27.

B. Article 30 – Competition Law Cases[170]

As already mentioned, if antitrust actions are not identical within the meaning of Article 29, but related, then Article 30 may be applied. In other words, Article 30(1) of Brussels Ia is designed to deal with related competition law proceedings, allowing the court second seised to stay its proceedings. In particular, Article 30 contains no requirement about the same cause of action or same parties in the two proceedings. If the court first seised has jurisdiction over the cross-border competition law actions and its law permits for the relevant proceedings to consolidated (ie avoiding related proceedings), Article 30(2) allows for the court second seised to decline to exercise jurisdiction. It should be clearly noted, however, that the discretion derived from Article 30 is different from the *forum non conveniens* discretion under common law. It has been submitted that 'the question: "which court would be the more convenient or the more appropriate?" does not arise'[171] under Article 30 of Brussels Ia.

The primary consideration would be whether the competition law claims 'are so closely connected that it is expedient to hear and determine them together to avoid the risk of irreconcilable judgments resulting from separate proceedings'.[172] If so, then a stay should be granted with a view to avoiding the identified risks. In other words, the degree of risk of irreconcilable judgments should be a fairly important factor which must be considered by the court. The considerations which were put forward in *Provimi*[173] in the context of 'irreconcilable judgments' within the meaning of Article 8(1) would be equally relevant here:

> [T]he law on the scope for making claims of this type is very undeveloped. I was not shown any French or German case law on this topic. […] So I have no idea how German or French courts might approach the issue of when or how a company within an 'undertaking' would infringe [Article 101 TFEU]; nor the circumstances in which a claimant could recover damages for an infringement. In particular I have no idea how those courts might approach the key issue of 'knowledge' which I have discussed above. Therefore it seems to me that it is highly arguable that different courts would take different approaches to these issues and that those different approaches could result in irreconcilable judgments.
>
> [T]herefore, I think that it must follow that it is expedient to hear and determine all these claims together to avoid the risk of irreconcilable judgments. Ultimately the question of when and how an infringement of [Article 101 TFEU] takes place and the circumstances in which a private law claim for damages can be maintained may need to be considered by the European Court. But it does not seem sensible to me that, in the meantime, there should be different views from different national courts which are given in relation to the same factual background and the same cartels, simply because the different defendants are of different domiciles.[174]

[170] See more: Danov (n 6).
[171] *The 'Linda'* [1988] 1 Lloyd's Rep 175 (QBD (Admlty)) 179 (Sheen J).
[172] Article 30(3) of Brussels Ia.
[173] *Provimi Ltd v Aventis Animal Nutrition SA* [2003] EWHC 961 (Comm).
[174] Ibid [48–49].

It is beyond doubt that there would be a risk of irreconcilable judgments if a cartel agreement (or abusive practice) had been implemented in several EU Member States and private antitrust damages claims in relation to that cartel (or abusive practice) are pending in two of those states.

Therefore, the application of Article 30 of Brussels Ia presupposes for the court second seised to determine whether the antitrust actions are related and, if so, whether to exercise its discretionary power to stay its proceedings. Both issues were addressed in *Cooper Tire* in which an application for a stay was put forward by Dow and Bayer defendants. In this case, the court clearly established that a claim, brought by a cartelist in Italy for a declaration that no damage was caused by the cartel, and a private antitrust damages claim in England against some cartelists, 'cover the same ground [...] save that the Italian court is not asked to assess the quantum of damage suffered by each purchaser of BR and ESBR'.[175] Since the English and Italian courts were considering broadly the same question,[176] it was held that 'the extent of relatedness and the risk of inconsistent decisions is substantial'.[177]

Having confirmed that the actions in Italy and England were related, the judge went on to consider whether the court should exercise its discretion. Although some defendants had submitted to the jurisdiction of the English courts and made no application for a stay, Mr Justice Teare accepted that the English court was entitled to stay the proceedings with a view to attaining the objectives of Articles 29 and 30 of Brussels Ia, holding that:

> It seems to me that a particularly good reason would be required to justify a stay in such circumstances [i.e. some defendants submitted to the jurisdiction and made no application for a stay] and the Defendants in question would surely be entitled to be heard on the question. I do not consider that there is such a reason in circumstances where the Italian Court has dismissed the proceedings before it and accordingly (a) the prospect of a decision on the merits in Italy is contingent upon a successful appeal in Italy and (b) the English Court will ultimately have to exercise its own jurisdiction.
>
> The stage reached in England is that the proceedings have been commenced and Particulars of Claim have been served. In Italy, the proceedings have been commenced but have been dismissed at first instance on jurisdictional and other grounds without consideration of the merits. The decision at first instance is now under appeal. If the appeal succeeds the Italian Court of Appeal will determine the merits.
>
> [...] It is agreed that a decision on the merits in Italy is not likely until September 2013–2014 [...].[178]

This quotation clearly shows that the stage which the proceedings had reached, as well as the potential delay of the Italian courts, were significant factors that were taken into account by the judge in exercising his discretion.[179] Was the judge wrong to factor in the time necessary for the Italian court to render a decision in Italy? Lord Justice Longmore,

[175] *Cooper Tire* – EWHC (n 115) [81].
[176] Ibid [106].
[177] Ibid [106].
[178] Ibid [111, 112 and 114].
[179] Ibid [117–118].

sitting in the Court of Appeal, held the delay may indeed be an important factor to be taken into account by the court when exercising its discretionary power pursuant to Article 30 of Brussels Ia. In particular, the judge stated:

> 54. The only substantive argument of Mr Rabinowitz which needs to be addressed is his submission that the judge was wrong to take into account the time when a decision was likely to be reached, in considering the stage which the proceedings had reached at the time of the application to the English court. He submitted that the judge was impliedly criticising the Italian court system by saying that it was unlikely a decision would be reached until September 2012. (In fact we now know that the next hearing in the appeal on the outright dismissal of the claim will not occur until January 2014).
>
> 55. But there is no such implied criticism. The fact that it may take different periods of time for similar proceedings to come to a conclusion in different jurisdictions, for whatever reasons, is not a criticism; it is merely a fact of life to which a judge cannot be expected to close his eyes.[180]

Indeed, by taking account of the delay factor when exercising their discretion, the judge partly considered the *strategic nature* of Enichem's claim for a negative declaration in Italy. It is well established that a claimant who intends to delay settlement of a future substantive antitrust law dispute may deliberately commence pre-emptive proceedings before a court that is not appropriately placed to deal with an EU competition law case.[181] This was noted by some of the commentators who submitted that:

> The discretionary nature of [Article 30 of Brussels Ia] limits the risk of proceedings being delayed by torpedoes, as the courts second seised of related (but not identical) actions can always choose to proceed with those actions.[182]

Does this really solve the problem? Although under the current framework the court can choose not to stay its proceeding by exercising its discretionary power to proceed with the action, this is not an entirely satisfactory solution.[183] The claimants in the English proceedings would remain defendants in the Italian proceedings. As a result, the litigants would have to engage in two sets of proceedings, generating a higher level of uncertainty which would entail a greater delay and higher litigation costs.

In other words, there would potentially be major problems concerning consistent outcomes in such related proceedings arising in relation to the same EU competition law claims which could impact on the settlement dynamics. More importantly, complex issues may arise at the recognition and enforcement stage[184] – the question '[w]hether joint tortfeasors have a sufficient privity of interest that might lead to the application of *res judicata* is not the subject of clear authority'.[185] The issues would multiply, post-Brexit,

[180] *Cooper Tire & Rubber Company Europe Ltd & Others* [2010] EWCA Civ 864 [54–55].

[181] Case C-116/02 *Erich Gasser GmbH v MISAT Srl* EU:C:2003:436, Opinion of AG Philip Leger [68]. Compare *Cooper Tire* – EWCA (n 180). See also TC Hartley, 'The European Union and the Systematic Dismantling of the Common Law of Conflict of Laws' (2005) 54 *ICLQ* 813, 820–21; P de Vareilles-Sommieres (ed), *Forum Shopping in the European Judicial Area* (Hart Publishing, 2007); Danov (n 5).

[182] C Slothers, M Gardner and S Hinchliffe, 'Forum shopping and "Italian torpedoes" in competition litigation in the English courts' (2011) *Global Competition Litigation Review* 67, 69.

[183] Fawcett – General Report (n 9) 41.

[184] See Chapter 12 below.

[185] *Cooper Tire* – EWHC (115) [80].

because there is risk that the UK and EU judges might start sharing divergent regulatory interests, which would reinforce the argument for a new approach to judicial cooperation in competition law matters.

C. Articles 33 and 34 – Competition Law Cases

Given the limited territorial scope of EU competition law (ie the regulatory jurisdiction), there would be parallel proceedings which may involve non-EU Member State courts. The point was captured by Article 33 of Brussels Ia which, as noted above, is set to deal with a situation where 'a court in a Member State [which] is seised of an action involving the same cause of action and between the same parties as the proceedings in the court of [a] third State'.[186] A major feature of such parallel competition law proceedings as well as of any related proceedings falling within the ambit of Article 34 is that there would potentially be different sets of public competition laws which could be applicable by the EU Member States courts and non-EU Member States courts.

As already noted above,[187] the point about the regulatory nature of EU competition law was captured by Mr Justice Aikens in *Provimi*.[188] Mr Justice Aikens's judgment[189] explicitly distinguishes the regulatory issues[190] (arising under EU law) from the private law issues (arising under English law).[191] Given the different regulatory regimes, the cause of action and subject matter may not be the same if, for example, the UK CAT proceedings concern damages for breach of UK competition law (effects on prices) in the UK, whilst the Dutch proceedings involve damages caused by a breach of EU competition law in the Netherlands, France and Germany. There is a strong argument that, in a Brussels Ia context, ascertaining the applicable regulatory set of public competition laws[192] would impact on the decision of a Member State court to decide whether to stay its proceedings under Brussels Ia.

Given the cross-border nature of many competition law infringements and given the fact that Articles 101 and 102 TFEU are to be regarded as 'overriding mandatory provisions'[193] for PIL purposes, the response to the question of how a national judge's discretion should be exercised under Articles 33(1) and 34(1) of Brussels Ia is important. Since EU competition law rules are 'necessary for the functioning of the internal market'[194] and express the fundamental interests of the EU,[195] their potential application

[186] Article 33 of Brussels Ia.

[187] See Section III.B above.

[188] *Provimi* (n 173).

[189] Ibid.

[190] Case COMP/E-1/37.512, *Vitamins* – Commission Decision of 21 November 2001 relating to a proceeding pursuant to Article 81 of the EC Treaty and Article 53 of the EEA Agreement (Case COMP/E-1/37.512 – Vitamins) (notified under document number C(2001) 3695) (Text with EEA [2003] Official Journal L6/1–89 [772–3].

[191] *Provimi* (n 173) [25]. See more: Chapters 10 and 11.

[192] Joined Cases 89/85, 104/85, 114/85, 116–17/85, and 125–29/85 *Ahlstrom v Commission* EU:C:1988:447, Case T-286/09 *Intel Corp v Commission* EU:T:2014:547 and Case C-413/14 P *Intel v Commission* EU:C:2017:632.

[193] Articles 9 and 21 of Rome I; Articles 16 and 26 of Rome II.

[194] Article 3(1) TFEU.

[195] Case C-126/97 *Eco Swiss China Time Ltd v Benetton International NV* EU:C:1999:269; Case C-38/98 *Régie nationale des usines Renault SA v Maxicar SpA and Orazio Formento* EU:C:2000:225.

as 'overriding mandatory provisions'[196] of the forum might impact on the adjudicatory jurisdiction of national courts[197] in so far as this would potentially affect the judges' willingness to exercise their discretion under Brussels Ia.

Therefore, it would be highly unlikely for an EU Member State court to decide that its proceedings – in which EU competition law is at stake – should be stayed under Articles 33(1) and 34(1) of Brussels Ia. The problem is that, if national judges were not to factor in foreign regulatory interests, multiple related proceedings would be bound to arise, which would in turn generate delay, inconsistencies and uncertainties. In other words, if each national competition law regime were to be exclusively applied by national judges, parallel and/or related proceedings would not be avoided. Hence, a more sophisticated regime of judicial cooperation in competition law matters is needed in a global context.[198]

The issues are important because an anti-competitive practice may be agreed between infringing undertakings (that may often be groups of companies with a number of wholly-owned subsidiaries) which may be implementing their anti-competitive arrangements/practices across the globe.[199] It is not only that the infringing undertakings' representatives may meet on a number of occasions in different capital cities,[200] but also the anti-competitive conduct, which could be implemented through various digital platforms, would cause damages to multiple injured parties across the globe. Articles 33 and 34 of Brussels Ia would not be able to solve the problems in competition law cases where EU competition law was at stake. It is unlikely for an EU Member State to stay its legal proceedings where the EU has legitimate interests to regulate the competition law of cross-border economic activities.

The narrow scope of Brussels Ia (in so far as it does not cover public enforcement proceedings) and the fact that the issues concerning regulatory jurisdiction are not systematically dealt with in the Brussels Ia regulation cumulatively indicate that there is a significant gap in the regulatory framework for judicial cooperation in competition law matters.

V. Some Preliminary Conclusions – Problems and Solutions

There are major PIL issues which need to be addressed with regard to related claims that may be issued on behalf of multiple injured parties. There is a strong argument that a high level of complexity and multiplicity of related proceedings in other jurisdictions would be characteristic features of many competition law claims. It is a relatively

[196] eg Article 16 of Rome II. See more Chapter 10.

[197] Compare: Article 33(1) and (2) of Brussels Ia. See also: *The LCD Appeals* (n 1).

[198] M Danov and C Otero, 'Competition Law Enforcement: Private International Law and Access to Effective Legal Remedies in Cross-Border Cases' P Beaumont and J Holliday (eds), *Guide to Global Private International Law* (Oxford, Hart Publishing, 2022).

[199] *Dr Liza Lovdahl Gormsen* (n 44) [17]. See also: *Dr Rachael Kent* (n 88) [6]; *Qualcomm Inc* (n 88) [6]; *Elizabeth Helen Coll* (n 88) [11].

[200] *Cooper Tire* – EWHC (n 115); *Cooper Tire* – EWCA (n 180).

safe assumption that, unless there are appropriate jurisdictional rules and effective case management mechanisms, the litigation costs[201] and level of uncertainty could impede the injured parties' access to legal remedies.

The issues concerning parallel and related private antitrust damages claims arising out of the same anti-competitive conduct need to be addressed in cross-border cases. The related claims would often involve different injured parties issuing claims against the same infringing undertakings. It is not only that different procedural rules may be applicable, but also there may be different (and sometimes conflicting) substantive (public) competition laws which may be applicable worldwide.[202] Since the various national judges could apply different sets of competition laws with a view to determining whether the conduct is anti-competitive, there is a real risk for them to reach irreconcilable judgments in any related competition law proceedings.

The wide bases for assumption of jurisdiction under the English common law along with the wide bases for the allocation of jurisdiction under the Brussels Ia Regulation strongly indicate that parallel proceedings are bound to arise. The issue would be exacerbated by the fact that both EU competition law and UK competition law would apply extra-territorially. There is a strong argument that a level of judicial cooperation – through PIL rules – in competition law matters be necessary with a view to improving the injured parties' access to legal remedies in cross-border competition law cases. More specifically, PIL rules may be central to ascertaining whether the injured parties would be entitled to legal remedies. PIL rules may also be important for the injured parties to establish jurisdiction before an appropriate forum where the procedural rules would allow them to substantiate their claim, whilst avoiding inconsistent outcomes in competition law claims arising out of transnational infringements.

A major challenge is: to what extent (if at all) could jurisdiction rules be relied upon to avoid inconsistent outcomes in related claims arising out of the same transnational infringement, without advancing an international convention which promotes judicial cooperation – dealing with issues of jurisdiction and applicable law/s in cross-border competition law? The efficient resolution of various preliminary issues (regulatory jurisdiction; scope of adjudicatory jurisdiction; applicable competition laws) – which may inevitably impact on the outcome of many cross-border competition law disputes – may be important to minimise the length of the relevant proceedings, whilst also reducing costs. Therefore, whilst there is a strong case that a private international law mode of governance would be necessary for the international community to effectively deal with cross-border competition law infringements, it is important to consider whether a softer form (rather than an international convention) should be advanced.

A. Lessons to be Learnt from Brussels Ia

The existing jurisdictional rules in Articles 4, 7 and 8 are not capable of putting an end to the multiplications of courts able to hear and determine private antitrust damages

[201] See: the Table 3: Proposed future expenditure – *Michael O'Higgins* (n 99) [323].
[202] Chapters 9 and 10.

claims arising out of the same transnational competition law infringement. The issues are exacerbated by the fact that Articles 29, 30 and 33 of the Brussels Ia are not capable of avoiding related and parallel proceedings arising out of the same transnational infringements.

The weaknesses of the Brussels Ia/Lugano regime were exposed in the proceedings which followed on from the *Truck* cartel.[203] The transnational nature of the cartel meant that there were inevitably multiple sets of related proceedings to be issued before the English courts as well as before some EU Member States' courts. The issues were set out in *UK Trucks Claim Ltd v Stellantis & Road Haulage Association Ltd v MAN*,[204] where the claimants sought a collective proceedings order, which was necessary for the UK Competition Appeal Tribunal to certify a collective redress claim which was issued on behalf of multiple injured parties. In this context, the CAT made some interesting observations, which signified the fact that multiple claims[205] may be issued in a number of different jurisdictions:

> A significant number of claims have been brought in the UK seeking damages from one or more [original equipment manufacturers, 'OEMs']. Seven of those actions, brought by major purchasers, have been case managed together and have now been set down for a series of trials. The first, a joint trial of claims by Royal Mail Group and by BT Group against DAF, is currently being heard. The second, a joint trial of claims by two major truck rental groups, Ryder and Dawsongroup, against four of the OEMs is due to commence on 13 March 2023. And the third, a joint trial of test claimants drawn from three actions by companies in, inter alia, the Suez, Veolia and Wolseley groups, is due to start on 9 April 2024. The various other proceedings are much less far advanced.
>
> *The claims brought in the UK are among several thousand claims against the OEMs brought in various European jurisdictions.*[206]

This example demonstrates that it is highly likely that the transnational competition law infringements would cause damages to different injured parties (eg large purchasers; SMEs; consumers) that may be up or down the supply chain. More importantly, such claims would often be issued in different jurisdictions against the same infringing undertaking/s which may often be groups of companies, having wholly-owned subsidiaries across the globe. This means that various national judges would need to determine some important and common issues which concern causation and various elements of quantification of damages – 'volume of commerce',[207] 'overcharge percentages'[208] and the 'level of pass-through'.[209]

[203] *Trucks – Commission Decision –* 19.7.2016 (n 18). See also: MS Ferro, 'The Playful State of Antitrust Damages Claims in the EU' *Competition Policy International* – 11 September 2019, https://www.competitionpolicyinternational.com/the-playful-state-of-antitrust-damages-claims-in-the-eu/.

[204] Fero (n 203).

[205] Case Nos: 1284–1290/5/7/18 (T), *Royal Mail v DAF Trucks* [2021] CAT 10; Case No: 1417/5/7/21 (T) *Dan Ryan Truck Rental Limited & Others v DAF Truck Limited & Others* Schedule of Claimants, *Road Haulage Association* (n 22).

[206] *Road Haulage Association* (n 22) [5–6] – emphasis added by the author.

[207] Case No: 1266/7/7/16, *Merricks v MasterCard Inc* [2017] CAT 16 [29–30].

[208] Ibid [31–38].

[209] Ibid [39–44].

Moreover, the Brussels Ia regime does not enable one EU Member State court (that is competent to hear and determine a competition law claim) to make a request for transfer of the case to another EU Member State court. Should there be a possibility for a second seised court to stay its proceedings[210] or make a request to transfer the proceedings to a court which is better placed to provide effective and timely legal remedies to all injured parties?[211] This should allow for the requested EU Member State court to assume jurisdiction as being more appropriate to safeguard the interests of all injured parties and facilitate their access to legal remedies.[212] In addition, given the scope of the Brussels Ia/Lugano regime, it would not avoid related proceedings before national courts in one EU Member State and public-administrative proceedings in another Member State, which may be pending in respect of the same transnational competition law infringement. How to deal with these problems in a global context?

B. A Proposed Solution – A Soft Law Mechanism

The issues concerning related and parallel proceedings are difficult to deal with, if there is no international convention which systematically deals with the issues concerning regulatory and adjudicatory jurisdiction. However, the Brexit developments strongly indicate that it may be arduous for the international community to agree upon such an international convention.

Since the issues concerning private law matters (ie assessment of damages caused to multiple injured parties and liability of infringing undertakings) are intertwined with the regulatory issues in cross-border competition law cases, there is a strong argument that a level of consistency between various related proceedings might best be attained through a soft mechanism for judicial cooperation in competition law matters. An argument for more effectively governing related competition law proceedings could be strengthened by the policy challenges which appeared to be identified by the UK CAT judgment in the context of the *Interchange Fees*[213] litigation. More specifically, the Tribunal appeared to strongly indicate that case-managing related competition law claims is a major policy challenge which must be addressed in a domestic context:

> re-litigation is to be avoided, or at least restricted, in relation to similar claims or issues brought by current claimants; and […] that future claimants should – so far as is appropriate and possible – also be bound by decisions in relation to similar claims or issues, or at the very least be strongly assisted towards the resolution of their claims by the Tribunal's earlier decisions.[214]

[210] Recital 44 of Directive 2014/104/EU and Article 15 of Directive 2014/104/EU; Danov (n 5) 138–139. See also: M Wilderspin, 'Jurisdiction issues: Brussels I Regulation Articles 6(1), 23, 27 and 28 in Antitrust Litigation' in in J Basedow, S Francq and L Idot (eds), *International Antitrust Litigation: Conflict of Laws and Coordination* (Oxford, Hart Publishing, 2012) 41, 59.

[211] Compare: Article 15 of Brussels IIa.

[212] Article 15 of Brussels II bis Regulation. See also: *In the Matter of E (A Child)* [2014] EWHC 6 (Fam) [35].

[213] *The Merchant Interchange Fee Umbrella Proceedings* (n 27).

[214] Case Nos: 1306-1325/5/7/19 (T) et al, *Dune Group Ltd & Ors v MasterCard* [2022] CAT 14 [14].

It is challenging enough to attain the desired level of consistency, if the related claims are being issued in the same jurisdiction;[215] and it is even more challenging to 'strive[e] for consistency of outcome in the broader sense of deciding like cases alike',[216] if the cases are issued in different jurisdictions. The deduction that there are some important aspects concerning the governance of parallel and related proceedings could be strengthened by noting that there are competition law cases which are pending before the UK CAT[217] and the High Court of England and Wales[218] in which the anti-competitive conduct is also investigated in foreign public and/or private enforcement proceedings.

Various important issues (ie the relevant market definition and the defendant's market power in a global context;[219] the anti-competitive nature of the conduct;[220] 'some elements of quantum [which] might be viewed as generic'),[221] which could impact on the claimants' entitlement to remedies and on the defendants' exposure to damages, may have been – at least partly – considered by foreign regulators/courts. For example, the UK Competition Appeal Tribunal in *Royal Mail v DAF*[222] appears to be considering major aspects concerning 'Overcharge and Value of Commerce'.[223] The same issues may well be relevant in another set of private antitrust enforcement proceedings which, whilst involving different claimants/defendants in different jurisdictions, may be related to the same anti-competitive conduct. If an English court judgment were to carry a degree of persuasiveness[224] in a cross-border context, one can see how a level of consistency between the decisions of various adjudicators on these issues might foster 'the settlement of other claims of a similar or identical nature'[225] in different jurisdictions.

Advancing an approach that goes some way towards addressing these challenges in cross-border cases should facilitate the resolution of cross-border competition law disputes. A level of judicial cooperation in competition law matters should ensure that national judges are somewhat consistently dealing with related/common issues arising out of cross-border competition law infringements. This should be important with a view to ensuring that like issues are treated alike,[226] which could in turn increase the level of legal certainty, improving the injured parties' access to legal remedies. In other words, a level of judicial cooperation is important to ensure that effective legal remedies are being awarded to multiple injured parties (ie consumers, businesses, SMEs) based in different jurisdictions.

Moreover, the case for an alternative (and softer) form of judicial cooperation could be strengthened by noting that the Brussels Ia Regulation in its current version does not

[215] *The Merchant Interchange Fee Umbrella Proceedings* (n 27).

[216] Ibid [15].

[217] eg *Road Haulage Association* (n 22); *Dr Rachael Kent* (n 88); Case No: 1382/7/7/21, *Consumers' Association v Qualcomm Inc* [2022] CAT 20; *Dr Liza Lovdahl Gormsen* (n 44).

[218] eg *Federal Deposit Insurance* (n 48).

[219] *Qualcomm* (n 217) [24].

[220] Ibid [25].

[221] *Dune Group* (n 214) [20] – emphasis in the original.

[222] Case Nos: 1284/5/7/18 (T) and 1290/5/7/18 (T), *Royal Mail Group v DAF, BT Group v DAF*, Order – Pre-trial Review – 22 March 2022.

[223] Ibid [4].

[224] Compare: *Dune Group* (n 214) [21].

[225] Ibid [21].

[226] *The Merchant Interchange Fee Umbrella Proceedings* (n 27) [15].

deal satisfactorily with the problem of parallel and related antitrust proceedings arising in a global context. It seems that the courts and the legal practitioners in some global cities (eg London, New York, Amsterdam, Frankfurt) could play a more prominent role in providing private parties with access to legal remedies in cross-border cases. The higher the level of transnational economic activities, the more important the role of global cities in governing these activities. A new model for international co-operation would be central to effectively co-ordinating multiple (public-administrative and private proceedings) in cross-border cases.

The problem is that if the different national judges were to continue to exclusively apply their own competition laws, which would often apply extra-territorially[227] as a matter of forum's public policy,[228] without considering any foreign regulatory interests and/or foreign findings, then it is a relatively safe prediction that inconsistent outcomes would be commonplace in such cases. Might the English judges also advance mechanisms which enable them to factor in foreign regulatory interests?

[227] Chapter 9.
[228] eg Recital 1 of Regulation 1/2003.

8

Theoretical Aspects – Improving Access to Justice – Judicial Cooperation

I. Introduction – Globalisation – Competition Law – Judicial Cooperation

The growing level of 'trade liberalization worldwide'[1] along with technological developments indicate that 'the possible range of agreements restraining competition between companies has grown as well'.[2] The problem is that, despite the continuous growth in the transnational economic activities facilitated by various inter-governmental organisations,[3] there is no global competition law regime,[4] which indicates that the competition law pluralism[5] is a major feature of the regulatory landscape in a global context.

The argument in this book is that private international law mechanisms should play an important role in balancing foreign regulatory interests.[6] In particular, the analysis in the previous chapter strongly indicates that PIL solutions are necessary to promote judicial cooperation in competition law matters. The effective private antitrust enforcement mechanisms, along with mechanisms for judicial cooperation, are more important (than ever) with a view to facilitating injured parties' access to legal remedies. A real PIL issue is how to govern related competition law claims which arise out of the same transnational competition law infringement and which cause damages to multiple injured parties in different jurisdictions.

In this chapter, the author will consider the theoretical aspects that will need to be addressed with a view to devising a private international law framework that promotes a level of judicial cooperation in competition law matters. It will be demonstrated that

[1] Q Wu, *Competition Laws, Globalization and Legal Pluralism* (Oxford, Hart Publishing, 2013) 2.

[2] JP Terhchte, *International Competition Enforcement Law Between Cooperation and Convergence* (Berlin, Springer, 2011) 12.

[3] eg World Trade Organisation, European Union.

[4] Chapter 1.

[5] Wu (n 1) 1–3.

[6] M Danov, 'Global Competition Law Framework: A Private International Law Solution Needed' (2016) 12 *Journal of Private International Law* 77–105; M Lehmann, 'Regulation, global governance and private international law: squaring the triangle' (2020) 16 *Journal of Private International Law* 1; M Danov and C Otero, 'Competition Law Enforcement: Private International Law and Access to Effective Legal Remedies in Cross-Border Cases' in P Beaumont and J Holliday (eds), *Guide to Global Private International Law* (Oxford, Hart Publishing, 2022) 233–246. See more: Chapters 9, 10 and 11.

PIL techniques would be central to reducing the risk of inconsistent outcomes in related private antitrust damages claims that relate to the same anti-competitive conduct, which should in turn improve injured parties' access to legal remedies.

II. Major Challenges – Related and Parallel Proceedings

An appropriate framework for judicial cooperation through PIL mechanisms is necessary to improve injured parties' access to legal remedies in a global context. It will be demonstrated that there are at least two major sets of challenges which need to be addressed in this context.

First, it is highly likely that, given the cross-border nature of many competition law infringements, there would be multiple applicable substantive (public) competition laws which would apply to ascertain whether the conduct is anti-competitive. The problem is that different competition laws, which legitimately pursue different economic interests,[7] could be applicable. There would not only be complex regulatory issues (ie applicable competition laws)[8] and specific IT issues,[9] but there would also be difficult substantive law issues concerning causation and quantification of damages[10] that are intertwined with the disclosure rules[11] and appropriate case management of multiple and related claims, which are issued on behalf of millions of injured parties.[12]

Secondly, there may be related and/or parallel proceedings in which different judges may be asked to determine whether the same conduct would be compliant with the applicable sets of competition laws.[13] The problem is that national enforcement systems across the globe may be constructed differently, reflecting the specific features of the national competition law cultures and legal heritages.[14] Although the aims of any competition law enforcement policy could be broadly similar, the means for attaining the objectives, through public and/or private enforcement modes, would vary. As a result, there would be a diverse set of multiple national competition law enforcement regimes which may be (more or less) effective than others; the level of experience and ability to deal with complex cross-border competition law disputes may be different in developed countries and developing countries, for example.[15]

In the light of the increasingly transnational nature of economic activities, it is important for PIL rules to be used to promote a level of judicial cooperation with a view to ensuring that the various chosen (optimal and national) enforcement models

[7] A Bradford et al, 'Competition Law Gone Global: Introducing the Comparative Competition Law and Enforcement Datasets' (2019) 16 *Journal of Empirical Legal Studies* 411.

[8] Chapter 9.

[9] RA Posner, 'Antitrust in the New Economy' (2001) 68 *Antitrust LJ* 925.

[10] Chapters 2 and 10.

[11] *Allianz Global Investors Gmbh and Other v Deutsche Bank AG London* [2022] CAT 44 [48–49].

[12] Case Nos: 1517/11/7/22 (UM) and 1266/7/7/16, *The Merchant Interchange Fee Umbrella Proceedings* [2022] CAT 31.

[13] Chapters 9 and 10.

[14] EM Fox and DA Crane, *Global Issues in Antitrust and Competition Law* 2nd edn (West Academic Publishing, 2017 – Kindle edition) 483.

[15] PM Horna, 'David & Goliath: How young competition agencies can succeed in fighting cross-border cartels' (2017) *The University of Oxford Centre for Competition Law and Policy*, Working Paper CCLP (L) 45.

as well as the various national regulatory objectives could be factored in by English judges dealing with private antitrust damages claims in a global context. In other words, a major objective, which is to be pursued with the proposed pragmatic model for judicial cooperation, is to enable the English judges to factor in foreign regulatory interests and effectively deal with competition law claims which arise out of transnational competition law infringements. The issues are increasingly important, with Professor Lehmann[16] submitting that:

> Private international lawyers need to engage more with foreign regulation. This is necessary in light of protecting global and national interests in the age of growing integration and interdependence between countries. While cooperation and coordination are increasingly prevalent among administrations of different countries, private international lawyers still are reluctant to give effect to foreign regulation. This must change.[17]

In order to devise a private international law mechanism – even if it were to be a soft law one, which promotes judicial cooperation in competition law matters – several related aspects need to be dealt with. A PIL mechanism should enable judges to factor in foreign regulatory interests with a view to addressing the governance aspects that would be key to attaining consistent outcomes in related claims. This should in turn improve injured parties' access to legal remedies in cross-border competition law cases.[18]

There is a strong argument that a new approach to judicial cooperation in competition law matters is indeed necessary to reflect the fact that the free trade arrangements[19] which are agreed among nations have set the scene for the increasingly cross-border economic activities. As a result, multinational companies have become part of transnational supply chains which may be central to the functioning of national economies. These issues were discussed in *Motorola Mobility LLC v AU Optronics Corp*[20] where the US court inter alia noted that '[n]othing is more common nowadays than for products imported to the United States to include components that the producers bought from foreign manufacturers',[21] with Circuit Judge Posner making the following observations that:

> Even [the claimant –] Motorola acknowledges 'that a substantial percentage of U.S. manufacturers utilize global supply chains and foreign subsidiaries to effectively compete in the global economy.' Some of those foreign manufacturers are located in countries that do not have or, more commonly, do not enforce antitrust laws consistently or uniformly, or whose antitrust laws are more lenient than ours, especially when it comes to remedies, notably punitive damages [...]. As a result, the prices of many products exported to the United States doubtless are elevated to some extent by price fixing or other anticompetitive acts that would be punished in proceedings under the Sherman Act if committed in the United States.[22]

[16] Lehmann (n 6).
[17] Ibid 29.
[18] Ibid 29–30.
[19] eg Trade and Cooperation Agreement between the European Union and the European Atomic Energy Community, of the one part, and the United Kingdom of Great Britain and Northern Ireland, of the other part [2021] OJ L149/10; Marrakesh Agreement establishing the World Trade Organization (with final act, annexes and protocol). Concluded at Marrakesh on 15 April 1994.
[20] *Motorola Mobility LLC v AU Optronics Corp* 775 F 3d 816 (7th Cir 2015).
[21] Ibid 824.
[22] Ibid 824.

This means that a cartelised product may be incorporated into another product (or various cartelised products may be assembled together) which would have an effect on the prices of the finished products and cause antitrust damages across the globe. The increasingly global nature of the supply chains means that an ineffective private antitrust enforcement regime in one country (or in a number of countries) may have a significant impact on a large proportion of end consumers and businesses across the globe. The issues concerning judicial cooperation in competition law matters are important because, whilst the competition law infringements are cross-border in nature, involving multinational companies that are engaging in transnational economic activities, the territorial scope of the relevant sets of competition laws is national.[23]

In other words, an enhanced level of international cooperation that promotes market access across the globe,[24] without sufficiently considering issues concerning judicial cooperation in related claims that arise out of the same transnational infringements or the same anti-competitive conduct, strongly suggests that the injured parties' access to legal remedies in cross-border competition law claims would be costly and time consuming. The scope of the regulatory jurisdiction[25] may limit the adjudicatory jurisdiction[26] in so far as judges in some jurisdictions may decline to exercise their adjudicatory jurisdiction in cases where the harm is caused to foreign consumers, limiting the scope of their claims to antitrust damages that are caused to local consumers.[27] This strongly indicates that related proceedings that arise out of the same transnational competition law infringement may be difficult (if not impossible) to avoid, so that the judges would rather need to consider how to attain somewhat consistent outcomes (giving effect to foreign regulatory findings).[28]

Since '[c]ompetition policies have not been able to keep pace with the globalization',[29] a soft form of judicial cooperation through PIL mechanisms may be necessary to improve injured parties' access to legal remedies whilst considering various legitimate regulatory interests and whilst considering any relevant findings which may be made in foreign and related regulatory and/or judicial proceedings. The latter aspects are particularly important because there is a view that:

> Regarding legal pluralism and globalization, the theory argues that the fragmentation of world society creates of form of global law that is apolitical and autopoietic yet cannot be measured by positive law standards. It suffers from the underdevelopment of political and institutional support at the global level, and is dependent on other social processes, such as

[23] Communication From the Commission to the Council, *Towards an International Framework of Competition Rules*, COM(96) 284 final, 18 June 1996, 3–4.

[24] Terhchte (n 2) 12.

[25] Chapter 9.

[26] Chapter 7.

[27] *Hoffmann-La Roche Ltd v Empagran SA* 542 US 4 155 (2004) cited in Case No: 1433/7/7/22, *Dr Liza Lovdahl Gormsen v Meta Platforms Inc, Meta Platforms Ireland Ltd, Facebook UK Ltd* – Reasoned Order, dated 15 March 2022 [17]. See also: Case No: 1403/7/7/21, *Dr Rachael Kent v Apple Inc. Apple Distribution Int'l Ltd* [2022] CAT 28 [6]; Case No: 1382/7/7/21, *Consumers' Association v Qualcomm Inc* – Reasoned Order of the President (Service out of the jurisdiction), 15 March 2021 [6]; Case No: 1408/7/7/21, *Elizabeth Helen Coll v Alphabet Inc* – Reasoned order of the President – Service out of the jurisdiction – 29 September 2021 [11].

[28] Chapter 12.

[29] Terhchte (n 2) 13.

> economic and social transactions in globalization. However, it is these economic and social transactions which would eventually serve as the premise for the politicization of these laws decentred from the state.[30]

An argument concerning a new framework for judicial cooperation could be strengthened, if one considers the enforcement challenges which characterise the digital markets. There is a strong view that the digital developments may foster globalisation by impacting on the way society interacts, using global platforms such as Google and Facebook.[31] Indeed, it appears that a growing number of claims for antitrust damages are issued against hi-tech giants before the UK CAT.[32] A specific feature of these cases is that they are subject to regulatory proceedings in other jurisdictions.[33]

The fact that multi-national companies use global capital[34] and deploy business strategies that are often global in nature[35] calls for a new model for judicial cooperation in cross-border competition law cases. The argument for such a pragmatic model for judicial cooperation could be strengthened by the lack of an international convention that promotes judicial cooperation in competition law matters.

III. Regulatory Aspects – Multiple and Diverse National Competition Laws

Given the regulatory function of competition laws, there is a strong case that PIL may have an important role to play with a view to advancing an appropriate model for judicial cooperation in cross-border competition law cases.[36] It will be demonstrated that, in a cross-border context, there are a number of challenges which are linked to the questions: to what extent could a balance be struck between the different regulatory objectives pursued by national competition law systems with a view to attaining a level of judicial cooperation?[37] How could a level of consistency be attained between related proceedings that are taking place in different jurisdictions and relate to the same conduct?[38]

[30] Wu (n 1) 3.

[31] C Ducuing, 'When competition law and data protection law embrace: the German Competition Authority investigates Facebook' (2018), https://www.law.kuleuven.be/citip/blog/when-competition-law-and-data-protection-law-embrace-the-german-competition-authority-investigates-facebook/. G Sivinski, A Okuliar and L Kjolbye, 'Is big data a big deal? A competition law approach to big data' (2017) *European Competition Journal* 199.

[32] eg *Dr Rachael Kent* (n 27); Case Number 1382/7/7/21, *Consumers' Association v Qualcomm Inc* [2022] CAT 20; *Elizabeth Helen Coll* (n 27); *Dr Liza Lovdahl Gormsen* (n 27).

[33] *Qualcomm* (n 32).

[34] R Wilson and W Dissanayake, 'Introduction: Tracking the Global/Local' in R Wilson (ed), *Global/Local: Cultural Production and the Transnational Imaginary* (Duke University Press 1996) 1. See also: F Jameson and M Miyoshi, *The Cultures of Globalization* (Duke University Press, 1998).

[35] Report on the functioning of Regulation 1/2003, COM(2009) 206 final [22].

[36] Danov (n 6); Lehmann (n 6); Danov and Otero (n 6).

[37] Chapter 10.

[38] Chapters 11 and 12.

The issues concerning international cooperation with regard to cross-border competition law infringements are complex in so far as various national regulators could legitimately pursue different regulatory objectives. As noted elsewhere,[39] the International Competition Network's (ICN) Survey on Competition Culture strongly indicates that national competition culture across the globe may vary, not the least because 'each jurisdiction is situated differently with respect to public policies that promote market competition or cooperation'.[40]

The existing level of diversity in this context has been clearly captured by academics[41] from Columbia Law School and Chicago Law School, who have compiled datasets that cover 131 competition law systems, 'provid[ing] a detailed coding of competition laws and their enforcement around the world'.[42] The comparative competition law datasets clearly shows that the competition law objectives could vary (being one major variable).[43] More importantly, it seems 'that roughly half of jurisdictions (49 percent) with a competition law include at least one partial or complete industry exemption'.[44] The difference in the substantive competition law provisions appears to indicate that each legal order may legitimately protect from competition certain sectors that are central to the functioning of the various national economies. In order to reflect the fact that individual countries may share different sectoral priorities, a PIL mechanism – which is sufficiently flexible and necessarily dynamic – is necessary to accommodate the national differences.

An analysis of the devised datasets[45] might strengthen the argument for promoting judicial cooperation in related private antitrust damages claims with a view to avoiding inconsistent outcomes. In particular, the comparative dataset provides conclusive evidence the resources in individual jurisdictions may vary significantly, which means that some of the national regulators (in particular those based in the developing countries)[46] would not have the resources to investigate cross-border competition law infringements. More specifically, the following observations were made:

> The countries that were best resourced are not particularly surprising – instead, staff sizes and budgets appear to correlate strongly with market size. With respect to staff size, the United States had the greatest number of staff in 2010 with a combined 1,320 people working in antitrust enforcement at the Department of Justice and Federal Trade Commission. Japan had the second highest staff numbers, with 791 people working on competition law in 2010, followed by the European Union, Brazil, and Canada with 590, 425, and 420 staffers working in each agency, respectively.[…] With respect to budget, the United States also dedicated the most resources to competition law enforcement. The combined Department of Justice and Federal

[39] Danov (n 6).

[40] ICN Advocacy Working Group, *Competition Culture Project*, 14th ICN Annual Conference, Sydney, 29 April–1 May 2015 p 9, https://www.internationalcompetitionnetwork.org/wp-content/uploads/2018/09/AWG_CompetitionCultureReport2015.pdf.

[41] Bradford et al (n 7).

[42] Ibid 412.

[43] Ibid. 418 and 421.

[44] Ibid 422.

[45] Bradford et al (n 7).

[46] Horna (n 15); EM Fox, 'Competition Law and the Millennium Round' (1999) *Journal of International Economic Law* 665.

Trade Commission budget for competition enforcement was 288 million USD in 2010. China established its three competition agencies in 2008 and immediately vested them with significant budgets. In fact, in 2010, the combined budget of Chinese agencies was 220 million USD, which was the second highest budget held by any jurisdiction. Following the United States and China, the next highest budgetary resources in 2010 were found in Japan (96 million USD), the United Kingdom (73 million USD), and Australia (59 million USD). These can be compared to a median agency budget of 3.3 million USD in 2010.[47]

If some national regulators were not to have the resources to investigate cross-border competition law infringements, then there is a real risk that an enforcement gap will widen unless their judges were somewhat or somehow able to rely on foreign regulatory and/or judicial findings. If there were no such model for judicial cooperation, then there would be a risk that the end consumers would absorb the antitrust harm in the jurisdictions where the enforcement framework was not functioning effectively.

Furthermore, the comparative competition law datasets strongly suggest that there would be different remedies available for competition law infringements.[48] In this context, it has been submitted that 'in 1950, just seven jurisdictions had a private right of action in their competition law, but by 2010 that number had increased to 72'.[49] The increase of the number of jurisdictions which provide for private antitrust enforcement leave no doubt that judicial co-operation is much needed. Indeed, there appear to be particular issues for cross-border competition law infringements, with the authors identifying 'the United States, the European Union, Brazil, Germany, and South Korea [as] regional leaders that undertake cases that often have an impact far beyond their own jurisdiction'.[50] It is not likely for many of the other enforcers to be dealing with very many cross-border infringements which might in turn impact on injured parties' access to effective legal remedies in cross-border cases.

Although their journal article is entitled 'Competition Law Gone Global […]',[51] an important conclusion drawn by its authors is 'that, despite the vast proliferation of competition law agencies around the world, most enforcement activities are carried out by a small number of jurisdictions'.[52] More importantly, the existence of very many national and diverse competition law regimes rather appears to suggest that, whilst the economic activities have – to a significant extent – gone global, the competition law regimes remain national.

There is a strong argument for devising an appropriate regime for judicial cooperation which should reflect the transnational nature of economic activities. The problem is that, whilst the economic activities are transnational, there is a significant number of national competition laws which may legitimately pursue different regulatory objectives. A PIL solution would be for English judges to factor in foreign competition laws.[53]

[47] Bradford et al (n 7) 432–434.
[48] Ibid 423.
[49] Ibid 424.
[50] Ibid 434.
[51] Ibid.
[52] Ibid 413.
[53] See: Chapters 9 and 10.

IV. Governance Aspects – Related Proceedings

The governance of related proceedings, which are connected to the same competition law infringement and which may be pending before different national courts, would pose issues concerning a conflict of competition laws[54] (broadly defined to cover issues concerning the regulatory breach as well as about causation and quantification of damages). As noted above, the question is whether, in the absence of an international convention, there is an argument for English judges to give effect to foreign regulatory findings (or to give effect to foreign judgments) establishing competition law infringements.[55] Might the willingness of English judges to do so, along with a soft PIL mechanism for judicial cooperation, enable the English courts to more systematically deal with related claims (raising identical or similar issues) in relation to the same conduct, avoiding inconsistencies with foreign proceedings and expanding their influences?

A. International Cooperation

The governance literature appears to suggest that new forms of international cooperation should be at 'the heart of the liberal democratic order',[56] with reliance being placed on the notion of 'positive comity'[57] as opposed to 'negative comity'.[58] In the latter context, the OECD *Inventory of Co-operation Agreements* provides the following definition:

> 'Positive comity' allows one party (requesting) to request the other party (requested) to take appropriate enforcement actions with respect to anti-competitive activities occurring in the territory of the requested party that adversely affect important interests of the requesting party. It is aimed at effective allocation of enforcement resources by allowing the better-placed party to deal with the problem (for example, it avoids difficulties of obtaining evidence in a foreign jurisdiction) and minimises conflicts between jurisdictions that may be caused by enforcement actions against activities occurring in another jurisdiction.[59]

The need for judicial cooperation in competition law matters may be particularly important in cases which concern transnational competition law infringements in relation to digital markets. The issues were exposed in *Infederation v Google*.[60] In this case, Google used its horizontal search engine to promote its own shopping comparison

[54] H Klodt, "Conflicts and conflict resolution in international anti-trust: Do we need international competition rules?" (2005) *The World Economy* 877, 883. See also: RA Epstein and MS Greve (eds), *Competition Laws in Conflict: Antitrust Jurisdiction in the Global Economy* (The AEI Press, Washington 2004).

[55] Chapter 12.

[56] A-M Slaughter, 'Government networks: the heart of the liberal democratic order' in GH Fox and BR Roth (eds), *Democratic Governance and International Law* (CUP, Cambridge 2000) 199.

[57] Ibid 215.

[58] OECD Competition co-operation and enforcement, 'Provisions on Negative Comity' in *Inventory of Co-operation Agreements* (2021), https://www.oecd.org/daf/competition/competition-inventory-provisions-negative-comity.pdf.

[59] Ibid 1.

[60] *Infederation v Google* [2013] EWHC 2295 (Ch). See also: Case AT.39740, *Google Search (Shopping) – Commission Decision relating to proceedings under Article 102 of the Treaty on the Functioning of the European Union and Article 54 of the Agreement on the European Economic Area*, C(2017) 4444 final. See also: Case T-612/17 *Google and Alphabet v Commission (Google Shopping)* EU:T:2021:763.

facility – which operated at vertical level – by using certain algorithms to direct internet traffic accordingly. As a result, Google's conduct adversely affected the economic activities of various undertakings which operated such vertical search engines.[61] Would this business conduct be regarded as anti-competitive? Or would it rather be regarded as an entirely legitimate business practice?

The dispute reached the EU[62] Commission and the US Federal Trade Commission.[63] The conduct was condemned as anti-competitive (entailing a penalty of several billion EUR under EU competition law).[64] That said, the identical conduct was perceived as legitimate under US law.[65] The relevant issues will be discussed in Chapter 9,[66] but – for the purposes of this chapter – it should be noted that the irreconcilable outcomes may well be explained by the fact that the relevant sets of competition laws were indeed different and the regulators could legitimately pursue different regulatory objectives.[67]

Some commentators have singled out the legal uncertainty[68] as the major issue, submitting 'Google has been fined for a novel abuse, or at least a novel interpretation of an existing abuse'.[69] Although the regulatory literature suggests that 'competition rules cannot provide the same degree of certainty as sector-specific rules',[70] there would always be some novel infringements. In view of this, the real issue is how to create a PIL mechanism which, whilst accepting that national regulators may legitimately take different views on the anticompetitive nature of the conduct, enables English judges to strike a fair balance between these interests in private antitrust damages arising out of transnational competition law infringements.[71]

It seems clear that the current PIL framework does not effectively deal with the issues concerning conflicting competition laws which may need to apply in private antitrust damages claims arising out of transnational competition law infringement. The multinational groups of companies may strategically exploit this regulatory gap and an ambiguity. For example, if Google's conduct was considered to amount to 'competition on the merits'[72] by one of the most influential enforcers in the world, this would inevitably make any dispute in another jurisdiction highly contentious and costly.

The issues could be significant because the *Google* case undoubtedly suggests that the outcome of the dispute may be different depending on where the proceedings are taking place. If the courts were to continue to be biased in applying their own competition laws (reflecting their own national public policy),[73] the outcomes in cross-border

[61] *Infederation v Google* [2013] EWHC 2295 (Ch) [3–4].

[62] *Google Search (Shopping) – Commission Decision* (n 60).

[63] FTC File Number 111-0163, 'Statement of the Federal Trade Commission Regarding Google's Search Practices' *In the Matter of Google Inc.* – 3 January 2013.

[64] *Google Search (Shopping) – Commission Decision* (n 60). See also: *Google and Alphabet* (n 60).

[65] Statement of the Federal Trade Commission (n 63).

[66] See: Chapter 9.IV.

[67] Compare: *Competition Culture Project* (n 40) 9.

[68] M Eben, 'Fining Google: a missed opportunity for legal certainty?' (2018) 14 *European Competition Journal* 129.

[69] Ibid 151.

[70] A Ottow, *Market and Competition Authorities: Good Agency Principles* (Oxford, OUP, 2015) 30.

[71] Chapter 10, 11, 12 and 13.

[72] Statement of the Federal Trade Commission (n 63) 2.

[73] Chapter 10 and 12.

competition law disputes could be diametrically opposed in cases where there is a conflict of competition laws. This is a PIL problem which needs to be dealt with by a PIL solution.

Therefore there is an argument that, from a private international law perspective, a regime for judicial cooperation is necessary for judges to factor in foreign regulatory interests.[74] The author's argument is that the fact that various legal orders may legitimately take different views as to whether there is a competition law infringement (or not) means that such a PIL regime would be necessary for the English judges to strike a balance between different regulatory interests which may reasonably be factored in to private antitrust damages claims arising out of transnational competition law infringements.

B. Access to Effective Legal Remedies

The issues which injured parties face in accessing effective legal remedies in such disputes may be deduced by considering how the proceedings evolved in the *Google Search (Shopping)* case.[75] It has been widely reported[76] that the complaint against Google was submitted by Foundem (which is a small enterprise).[77] A salient feature of the *Google Search (Shopping)*[78] dispute was the length of the proceedings. This was identified as a potentially major concern, which the policy-makers need to address, in cases against hi-tech giants over 20 years ago.[79] Indeed, it has been a long-lasting dispute, with the first complaint lodged on 3 November 2009 (and subsequently amended) on 2 February 2010.[80] Multiple-complaints against Google were subsequently brought forward by various complainants (eg Streetmap, Expedia, TripAdvisor, Deutsche Telecom – to name but a few). It took some years for the EU Commission to render its prohibition decision on 27 June 2017, with a confidential version being published on 18 December 2017. That said, it should be noted that the dispute is far from over. Although the General Court upheld the EU Commission's decision,[81] Google has made an appeal and the proceedings are still pending before the CJEU.[82]

Interestingly, the first publicly available judgment on preliminary issues in relation to the relevant private proceedings appears to have been rendered on 26 July 2013 by the High Court of England and Wales in *Infederation Ltd v Google*.[83] This claim poses interesting questions about the coordination of such complex proceedings, involving multiple injured parties from different countries. In view of the ongoing public-administrative proceedings before the European Commission, Mr Justice Roth temporarily stayed the private proceedings in England and Wales. Mr Justice Roth went further to order

[74] Chapter 10.
[75] *Google Search (Shopping) – Commission Decision* (n 60).
[76] R Manthorpe, 'Google's nemesis: meet the British couple who took on a giant, won … and cost it £2.1 billion' Wired UK – 14 February 2018, https://www.wired.co.uk/article/steve-king-black-swan-ai-data.
[77] Ibid.
[78] *Google Search (Shopping) – Commission Decision* (n 60).
[79] Posner (n 9) 939.
[80] *Google Search (Shopping) – Commission Decision* (n 60) [39].
[81] *Google and Alphabet* (n 60).
[82] Case C-48/22 P *Google and Alphabet v Commission (Google Shopping)* – still pending.
[83] *Infederation* (n 61).

limited disclosure by noting the difficulties that need to be factored in by policy-makers with a view to effectively enforcing competition laws in such competition law disputes. The following observation was put forward:

> Effective case management by the court is important in all major litigation. However, intensive case management is particularly appropriate in competition litigation where the range and complexity of issues can notoriously give rise to very substantial costs. Moreover, in an abuse of dominance claim the allegedly dominant defendant is usually significantly larger than the claimant, creating a real issue of inequality of arms as regards their respective financial positions to fund the litigation.[84]

In compliance with Mr Roth's disclosure order, 'Google disclosed 678 documents, almost all of which were derived from the pool of documents that had been provided by them to the Commission'.[85] Following a review of the documents, Foundem compiled an analysis which it wanted to share with the relevant regulator, the EU Commission. Google objected. The dispute on this preliminary issue was dealt with again by Mr Justice Roth. The judge held:

> the reality is that Foundem is indeed in a different position from other complainants as it has started and pursued proceedings before a national court. The result is that Foundem has had an opportunity to see the documents which other complainants in the European forum have not seen. But there is no suggestion that Foundem commenced these domestic proceedings for an improper purpose, or purely to gain some advantage with respect to the Commission's investigations. In my view, the fact that other complainants may not have seen these documents does not in any way lessen the important public policy that the proceedings before the national court should be consistent with the proceedings before the Commission. Such consistency means that the Commission should not be prevented from hearing arguments based on consideration of the same evidence.[86]

Mr Justice Roth took the view that Foundem's request for disclosure of its analysis to the EU Commission should be granted. However, more importantly, the High Court judgment reinforces the need for effective coordination of proceedings in cases where antitrust harm has been caused to multiple injured parties in a global context. Such disputes – involving many injured parties and the same infringing undertaking/s, deploying the same conduct – would inevitably be raising similar questions of fact and law, which indicate that a new mechanism for judicial cooperation in such cases is needed.

The binary nature of the argument as to what would be an effective legal remedy for injured parties in *Google Search (Shopping)*[87] may be demonstrated by making reference to the views of some of the lawyers representing Google, Vesterdorf and Fountoukakos,[88] who appear to believe that:

> Google is required to treat rival comparison shopping services and its own comparison shopping service equally. In the authors' view, Google has done so by putting in place a

[84] Ibid [33].
[85] *Infederation Ltd v Google Inc, Google Ireland Ltd, Google UK Ltd* [2015] EWHC 3705 (Ch) [7].
[86] Ibid [21].
[87] *Google Search (Shopping) – Commission Decision* (n 60).
[88] B Vesterdorf and K Fountoukakos, 'An Appraisal of the Remedy in the Commission's Google Search (Shopping) Decision and a Guide to its Interpretation in Light of an Analytical Reading of the Case Law' (2018) 9 *Journal of European Competition Law & Practice* 3.

> non-discriminatory auction mechanism by which rivals and Google Shopping compete for access to the Shopping Unit on equal terms. The Decision provides that Google cannot charge rivals a fee that has the same or equivalent object or effect as the infringement. That does not prevent Google from charging for access per se; instead, it amounts to no more than a requirement to treat rivals non-discriminatorily, which is exactly what Google's remedy does.[89]

An entirely different view is shared by one of the lawyers representing the interest of the Google rivals – Mr Gary Reback who made the point that the process of competition may have been irreversibly and adversely affected. He went further to note that '[w]hat the commission does not get is the network effect on the market – when competition is gone, it's gone and it's not coming back'.[90] The point was clearly made in the *Financial Times*,[91] by Mr Richard Stables, an executive at Google's rival, who reportedly submitted that '[t]he main beneficiary of Google's new way of doing things is, shockingly, Google'.[92] Therefore the real issue with this case is that the long-lasting proceedings made it increasingly difficult for injured parties to access effective legal remedies as well as for the adjudicators to swiftly award such remedies.[93] Instead of addressing this question head-on, Professor Akman[94] has argued that:

> The potential lack of an appropriate remedy should prompt the [EU] Commission to reconsider whether there is an infringement in the first place. It has indeed been remarked that at this stage in Google Search, it is difficult to imagine a remedy that would benefit consumers more than the 'do nothing' option.[95]

Nonetheless, it is difficult to see how the non-availability of an effective remedy for injured parties could be regarded as an argument that the regulators should 'do nothing'.[96] The access to justice must clearly be an issue in such cases.[97] With this in mind, an argument may be made that the courts rather than regulators might be better placed to award timely and effective remedies – potentially factoring multiple regulatory concerns. Indeed, some of the parties appear to have issued private antitrust damages claims in England and Wales.[98]

More importantly, the above analyses clearly demonstrate that PIL techniques may justifiably be used to deal with the problems concerning conflicting competition laws, not least because injured parties' timely access to legal remedies might be a real issue in cases where there is a conflict of competition laws. A particularly complex issue that

[89] Ibid 18.

[90] G Reback cited by R Toplensky and M Acton, 'Google antitrust remedy delivers few changes for rivals', *Financial Times* 27 October 2017.

[91] Toplensky and Acton (n 90).

[92] R Stables cited by Toplensky and Acton (n 90). See also: A Raff and S Raff, 'Game Over? What Google's Latest Behind-the-Scenes Manoeuvres Reveal About its Brazenly Non-Compliant "Remedy" in the Google Search (Comparison Shopping) Case', http://www.foundem.com/The_Google_SpendMatch_Debacle.pdf, 1, 5.

[93] Posner (n 9) 939–940.

[94] P Akman, 'The Theory of Abuse in Google Search: A Positive and Normative Assessment under EU Competition Law' (2017) University of Illinois Journal of Law, Tech & Policy 301.

[95] Ibid 370.

[96] Ibid.

[97] Posner (n 9) 939–940.

[98] *Kelkoo v Google* [2021] EWHC 1687 (Ch). See also: 1424/5/7/21 (T) *Kelkoo.com (UK) Limited & Others v Google UK Limited & Others* – pending before the UK CAT.

must be addressed in this context is how a private antitrust enforcement regime could operate globally, striking a balance between the legitimate regulatory interests of various national competition laws.[99]

C. 'Double Recovery'[100] and 'Double Jeopardy'[101]

There is another issue which needs to be considered with a view to setting out an appropriate PIL solution. In theory, it is well established that the related and/or parallel proceedings in relation to the same infringement could lead to 'double recovery'[102] and 'double jeopardy'[103] in cross-border competition law competition law cases.

The problem is that, since competition law infringements would cause damages to multiple injured parties who may be at different levels of the chain of distribution, there is a 'double recovery'[104] risk. The difficult issues which would arise in cases where the merchants have passed on part of the illegal overcharge down the chain of distribution were captured by the UK Supreme Court in *Sainsbury's v Mastercard*,[105] where it was held that:

> There are sound reasons for taking account of pass-on in the calculation of damages for breach of competition law. Not only is it required by the compensatory principle but also there are cases where there is a need to avoid double recovery through claims in respect of the same overcharge by a direct purchaser and by subsequent purchasers in a chain, to whom an overcharge has been passed on in whole or in part.[106]

Since both direct and indirect purchasers could sue for damages, the multiple set of proceedings which are related to the same infringement could lead to double recovery unless the 'share of overcharge which was passed on to the indirect purchaser'[107] was ascertained. Indeed, a highly complex issue in *Interchange Fees*[108] was whether the merchants had passed on (or absorbed in full or in part, to say the least) the anti-competitive MIFs. The difficulties in dealing with this question in separate sets proceedings were set out by the Competition Appeal Tribunal, noting that:

> [T]he courts [...] will seek to avoid inconsistency of outcome by consolidating related proceedings or hearing them together. But that may not always be possible: [A merchant] may commence proceedings in one jurisdiction, and [a consumer] in another. Of course, courts of differing jurisdictions will conscientiously apply their own laws, but it is important that the

[99] PB Stephan, 'Global Governance, Antitrust, and the Limits of International Cooperation' (2005) 38 *Cornell International Law Journal* 173, 182–186.

[100] *Sainsbury's Supermarkets Ltd and others v MasterCard Incorporated and others* [2020] UKSC 24 [197]; *The LCD Appeals* [2018] EWCA Civ 220 [97 and 99].

[101] *The LCD Appeals* (n 100) [97 and 99].

[102] *Sainsbury's* (n 100) [197]; *The LCD Appeals* (n 100) [97].

[103] *The LCD Appeals* (n 100) [97 and 99].

[104] *Sainsbury's* (n 100) [197].

[105] Ibid.

[106] Ibid [197].

[107] Communication from the Commission, *Guidelines for national courts on how to estimate the share of overcharge which was passed on to the indirect purchaser* [2019] OJ C267/4.

[108] *The Merchant Interchange Fee Umbrella Proceedings* (n 12).

> principles by which this jurisdiction at least operates be articulated, so as to assist (if no more than that) in achieving consistency of outcome. Equally, it may be that [the merchant's] claim and [the consumer's] claim are commenced in the same jurisdiction, but so far apart in time that it is not practically possible to hear both claims together.[109]

The quote clearly shows that appropriate procedural mechanisms (including collective redress proceedings on an opt-out basis)[110] may encourage injured parties to issue such claims. There might also be incentives for various litigation funders to fund those claims.[111] In spite of the fact that devising an appropriate case-management mechanism may allow for these cases to be efficiently dealt with in England and Wales, an open question is: how would a consistent outcome be attained in related proceedings pending before different national courts? In other words, a 'broad axe'[112] approach to quantification of damages along with case-management mechanisms could allow for antitrust damages to be quantified 'at a proportionate cost'[113] in a single jurisdiction, but a regime for judicial cooperation is necessary for related claims in relation to the same transnational infringement to be dealt with in a global context.

The problems would be exacerbated in cases where multiple proceedings are pending before the national courts in different jurisdictions, with various competition laws being applicable. The point about 'double recovery by those who had suffered from the cartel, and double jeopardy for the defendants'[114] was raised by the defendants in *LCD Appeals*.[115] Although the Court of Appeal dismissed the defendants' argument,[116] it went on to subsequently note, with regard to appropriateness of the English courts, that:

> it would not be satisfactory if the claimants were forced to sue some of the defendants in England and Wales (because they were served here as of right) and others in the Far East. They would then have to try to prove their case at two different trials, would be at risk of inconsistent findings of fact, and the courts of Taiwan or Japan would have to apply EU law as a foreign law. As we have already mentioned, both trials would involve the same or substantially the same issues and substantially the same witnesses and experts (if any).[117]

Therefore, multiple sets of related proceedings in different jurisdictions would entail a higher risk of inconsistent outcomes, which might impact on the parties' exposure to costs and damages,[118] which might generate delay and affect their access to legal remedies. Could there be a soft law mechanism for judicial cooperation with regard

[109] Ibid [13].
[110] Section 47B of the Competition Act 1998. See also: *Mastercard Incorporated and others v Walter Hugh Merricks CBE* [2020] UKSC 51.
[111] Case No: 1266/7/7/16, *Walter Hugh Merricks CBE v MasterCard Inc* [2017] CAT 16 [96–137] and the Annex; *UK Trucks Claim Ltd v Stellantis and Ors & Road Haulage Association Ltd v MAN SE and Ors* [2022] CAT 25 [224–230].
[112] *Sainsbury's* (n 100) [197–226]. See also: footnote 39 from the Communication from the Commission, *Guidelines for national courts on how to estimate the share of overcharge which was passed on to the indirect purchaser* [2019] OJ C267/4.
[113] *Sainsbury's* (n 100) [217].
[114] *The LCD Appeals* (n 100) [97].
[115] Ibid.
[116] Ibid 99.
[117] Ibid 130.
[118] *Sainsbury's* (n 100) [217].

to private antitrust damages claims? To what extent could a PIL mechanism be used to preserve the diverse national competition law traditions and ensure there is a level of consistency with regard to related cross-border competition law proceedings arising in a global context?[119]

V. Effects of Foreign Regulatory Proceedings/Findings[120]

It is difficult for the international community to agree upon an international convention because competition laws are enforced through public enforcement actions before national (or regional) regulators[121] as well as through private actions before national courts.[122] This means that the question whether a particular conduct is anti-competitive may be determined in legal proceedings before a national court *in one country*, but the very same question might be dealt with in related public-administrative proceedings before a regulator *in another jurisdiction*.[123]

In the EU context, Nazzini[124] submits that '[t]he multiplicity of sanctions and remedies for breaches of competition law entails that the same matter may be dealt with concurrently in different sets of proceedings before different administrative bodies or courts either in parallel or sequentially'.[125] Governing public and private proceedings which are dealt with by national courts as well as by competition law regulators in different jurisdictions may be an even bigger issue in a global context. Indeed, it is now well established that the 'private enforcement of the [competition] law can complement public enforcement'.[126]

It should be noted that, in the EU context, the issues are dealt with by Regulation 1/2003 (rather than Brussels Ia/Lugano regime). More specifically, Regulation 1/2003 inter alia aimed to minimise the risk of inconsistent outcomes in related private antitrust proceedings before the UK courts and any related public enforcement proceedings before the EU Commission. There was indeed a duty for the English courts to sincerely cooperate with the EU Commission.[127] This was reinforced by Article 16 of Regulation 1/2003, which imposed an obligation on the English courts to take every effort to avoid judgments which are irreconcilable with the EU Commission's decisions (be they actually rendered or 'contemplated by the Commission in proceedings it has initiated').[128] This reflects

[119] Compare: the 2019 Hague Judgments Convention. Danov and Otero (n 6).
[120] See more: Chapters 10, 12 and 13 below.
[121] Competition Act 1998, Chapter III. See also: Articles 4 and 5 of Council Regulation 1/2003.
[122] Competition Act 1998, Chapter IV. See also: Article 6 of Council Regulation 1/2003.
[123] M Danov, 'EU Competition Law Enforcement: Is Brussels I suited to dealing with all the challenges?' (2012) 61 *International and Comparative Law Quarterly* 27.
[124] R Nazzini, *Competition Enforcement and Procedure* 2nd edn (Oxford, OUP, 2016).
[125] Ibid at 3.
[126] Case Nos: 1377/5/7/20 and 1378/5/7/20, *Epic Games v Apple, Alphabet and Google* [2021] CAT 4 [139].
[127] Article 4(3) TEU. See also Case C-344/98 *Masterfoods Ltd v HB Ice Cream Ltd* EU:C:2000:689 [27].
[128] Article 16(1) of Regulation 1/2003. *Masterfoods* (n 127) [38, 51 and 52]; *Interpreneur Pub Company v Crehan* [2006] UKHL 38 [64–66].

the jurisprudence of the Court of Justice of the European Union as developed in *Delimitis*[129] and *Masterfoods.*[130] In the latter cases, the CJEU held that:

> When the outcome of the dispute before the national court depends on the validity of the Commission decision, it follows from the obligation of sincere cooperation that the national court should, in order to avoid reaching a decision that runs counter to that of the Commission, stay its proceedings pending final judgment in the action for annulment by the Community Courts, unless it considers that, in the circumstances of the case, a reference to the Court of Justice for a preliminary ruling on the validity of the Commission decision is warranted.[131]

Devising a multilateral PIL mechanism that somehow manages to govern related public enforcement proceedings before a regulator in one jurisdiction and private enforcement proceedings before national courts in another[132] is a major hurdle which must be overcome with a view to advancing a PIL mechanism for judicial cooperation in competition law matters. These difficulties might explain why there is a lack of an appropriate legal framework which facilitates judicial cooperation in competition law matters in a global context (as opposed to the existence of such a framework within the EU).[133] Nonetheless, the analysis in the previous chapters appears to suggest that, in a global context, the governance of related claims arising out of the same transnational competition law infringement is a major PIL issue which should be addressed with a view to improving the injured parties' access to legal remedies.

The private international law theory has thoroughly dealt with the problems concerning 'related actions'[134] in cross-border cases where the proceedings are exclusively before national courts. One potential solution is for one of the several competent courts to stay its proceedings, so that the related actions could be consolidated by strongly encouraging some judges to consider staying their proceedings or declining jurisdiction, which should allow the parties to centralise litigation before a forum which is appropriate to determine whether there is a competition law infringement and then deal with the issues of causation and quantification.[135] However, there are two major aspects which strongly indicate that this solution is unlikely to work in competition law cases. First, PIL mechanisms would normally not extend to cover regulatory proceedings.[136] Secondly, since national competition laws are set to safeguard public policy interests,[137] the national courts would often be reluctant to stay their proceedings.[138]

An alternative approach must be considered. Given that private antitrust enforcement 'reflects a public policy to protect the interests of UK consumers and businesses

[129] Case C-234/89 *Stergios Delimitis v Henninger Bräu AG* EU:C:1991:91.
[130] *Masterfoods* (n 127) [49].
[131] Ibid [57].
[132] Danov (123); Danov and Otero (n 6).
[133] Compare: Article 16 of Regulation 1/2003; Article 9 of Directive 2014/104/EU; Articles 29 and 30 of Brussels Ia.
[134] JJ Fawcett, 'General Report' in JJ Fawcett (ed), *Declining Jurisdiction in Private International Law – Reports to the XIVth Congress of the International Academy of Comparative Law, Athens, August 1994* (Oxford, OUP, 1995) 1, 43.
[135] Ibid 42–44.
[136] Danov (123).
[137] Chapters 10 and 12.
[138] Chapters 7 and 9.

against anti-competitive conduct and arrangements',[139] there is a strong argument for the English courts to take a lead in advancing such a PIL mechanism through positive comity and a series of soft law mechanisms. The issues are important because the judicial cooperation between the EU regulators and the UK courts is an area where the UK withdrawal from the EU is likely to generate an impact. The post-Brexit impact will be twofold. First, a European Commission's decision – which does not fall within the ambit of Article 95 of the Withdrawal Agreement[140] – will not be binding in the UK. Secondly, the UK courts would no longer be expected to stay their proceedings with a view to giving priority to any public enforcement proceedings before the European Commission.

The Brexit implications could inter alia impact on private antitrust enforcement patterns in England and Wales. On the one hand, since a previous study[141] has shown that the majority of private damages claims are preceded by a regulator's decision establishing a competition law infringement,[142] this might lead to a lower number of follow-on claims being issued in England, which might be perceived as a potential disadvantage. On the other hand, since stand-alone actions are possible in theory,[143] a potential advantage may be that injured parties would not need to wait for a public authority to establish a competition law infringement, which might adversely affect their timely access to effective legal remedies. Indeed, most recently, a number of stand-alone actions have been issued in England and Wales.[144]

The fact that the English courts are no longer required to stay their legal proceedings might allow them to factor in multiple regulatory interests and take a lead in devising a soft mechanism for judicial cooperation. In the UK, the problems regarding the functioning of institutional framework were exposed in *Enron Coal Services Ltd (In Liquidation) v English Welsh & Scottish Railway Ltd*[145] where Lord Justice Jacob took the view that 'the "split" jurisdiction of regulator for infringement, tribunal for causation and assessment of damages also needs some reconsideration'.[146] In a pre-Brexit context, Mr Lasok KC felt that:

> *Enron* [2011] EWCA Civ 2 is an example of a follow-on action in which the defendant's opportunity, to re-run before a court evidence considered by the competition authority, undermined the court's confidence in the relevance and/or strength of passages in the competition authority's decision. A rather different problem arises where, in the infringement decision, the

[139] *Epic Games* (n 126) [139].

[140] Agreement on the withdrawal of the United Kingdom of Great Britain and Northern Ireland from the European Union and the European Atomic Energy Community ('Withdrawal Agreement') [2019] Official Journal C3841/1.

[141] M Danov, F Becker and P Beaumont, (eds) *Cross-border EU Competition Law Actions* (Oxford, Hart Publishing, 2013).

[142] Ibid. See also: Article 16 of Regulation 1/2003).

[143] *Purple Parking Ltd and Meteor Parking Ltd v Heathrow Airport Ltd* [2011] EWHC 987 (Ch); *Streetmap.EU Ltd v Google* [2016] EWHC 253 (Ch).

[144] *JJH Enterprises Ltd (trading as ValueLicensing) v Microsoft* [2022] EWHC 929 (Comm); Case No: 1381/7/7/21 *Justin Le Patourel v BT Group PLC* [2021] CAT 30; Case Nos: 1304/7/7/19 & 1305/7/7/19, *Justin Gutmann v First MTR South Western Trains Ltd* [2021] CAT 31; *Qualcomm* (n 32).

[145] *Enron Coal Services Ltd (In Liquidation) v English Welsh & Scottish Railway Ltd* [2011] EWCA Civ 2.

[146] Ibid [149].

> competition authority is using the facts found by it to drive a particular theory, which may cause difficulties in a follow-on action if it becomes necessary to link the infringement to the facts of the case and, more particularly, the facts relating to causation and loss.[147]

Although Brexit might have been perceived as an opportunity for public and private enforcement proceedings to be consolidated before the UK CAT, the Penrose report[148] strongly indicates that a different enforcement model, which moves away from the one advanced by the EU Commission, does not appear to be a viable alternative for the UK policy-makers in the short-term or medium-term, to say the least. Nonetheless, the Penrose report leaves no doubt that an appropriate 'process redesign',[149] which involves 'an end-to-end review and redesign of procedures and case management in CMA and CAT',[150] is on the UK policy-makers' agenda.

Most specifically, there is strong case that 'a faster, tighter, cheaper and more efficient end-to-end case process'[151] is needed. Hence, the Penrose report takes the view that some appropriate procedural rules may be used to improve the injured parties' access to timely remedies in competition law cases.[152] Such legislative amendments would be welcome because it is well established that '[d]elays can render the judicial protection of the rights ineffectual, reduce the value of the rights, adversely affect economic activity and lead to economic distortions'.[153] The level of delay may be even more of an issue in cross-border cases, involving the hi-tech giants.[154]

It is suggested that, in addition to the procedural issues which are being addressed, a regime for judicial cooperation (which addresses the issues concerning related proceedings in a cross-border context) would need to be advanced for the related claims to be efficiently and effectively dealt with by English judges. There are complex issues (concerning avoidance of parallel and related proceedings) because, given the regulatory function of competition laws,[155] it is highly likely that in cases where there are transnational competition law infringements there would be a conflict of competition laws.[156] Since such transnational infringements would affect the process of competition as well as consumers' welfare in a number of countries, there would be multiple competition laws which would be applicable to determine whether there was a transnational competition law infringement.

Appropriately governing related proceedings, which arise out of the same transnational infringement and which are pending before different national courts, would be central to the injured parties' access to legal remedies. Since it is highly likely that in

[147] KPE Lasok, 'Some Procedural Aspects and How Could They Could/Should be Reformed' in Danov, Becker and Beaumont (n 141) 207, 209.

[148] J Penrose, *Power to the People: Stronger Consumer Choice And Competition So Markets Work for People, Not The Other Way Around*, February 2021.

[149] Ibid 18.

[150] Ibid 19 – emphasis in the original.

[151] Ibid.

[152] Compare: A Zuckerman, 'Justice in crisis: Comparative dimensions of civil procedure' in A Zuckerman (ed), *Civil Justice in Crisis: Comparative perspectives of Civil Procedure* (Oxford, OUP, 1999) 3, 10–11.

[153] Ibid 12. Posner (n 9).

[154] Posner (n 9) 939–40.

[155] A Shleifer, 'Understanding Regulation' (2005) 11 *European Financial Management*, 439.

[156] Bradford et al (n 7) 418 – '*Figure 3*: Comparative Competition Law Dataset – main variables'.

many competition law cases the related 'sets of proceedings [would often be] allowed to continue, the[n any] risk of irreconcilable judgments [or inconsistent outcomes] can be dealt with by the use of the doctrine of *res judicata*'[157] and positive comity considerations.[158] More importantly, the English courts could take a lead in advancing a soft law solution which allows for them to draw on foreign regulatory findings. Therefore, a comprehensive mechanism for judicial cooperation in competition law matters presupposes for policy-makers to systematically address the question about the effects of the foreign regulatory decisions in the UK.[159]

VI. Transnational Infringements, PIL and Global Cities

A level of judicial cooperation, through a PIL mechanism, is important in relation to antitrust damages claims because the '[g]lobal governance is not a matter of regulating states the way states regulate their citizens, but rather of addressing the issues and resolving the problems that result from the citizens going global'.[160] As already noted above,[161] the problem is that a review of the existing regulatory framework for international cooperation shows that the cooperation is limited to collaborative arrangements between competition authorities that engage in public enforcement activities in different jurisdictions. In other words, there is a major regulatory gap in relation to judicial cooperation. The PIL issues must be addressed with a view to improving injured parties' access to effective legal remedies in cross-border cases.

PIL techniques and some positive comity considerations may be successfully relied upon to preserve the inherent characteristics of the diverse competition law cultures across the globe.[162] The failure of the EU Commission 1996 initiative[163] for achieving an appropriate level of harmonisation and the failure of the subsequent negotiations within the WTO framework[164] have unequivocally demonstrated that a level of diversity of competition laws across the globe is highly likely to continue to exist in the foreseeable

[157] Fawcett (n 134) 41.
[158] Chapters 10 and 12.
[159] Chapters 10, 11 and 12.
[160] A-M Slaughter, *A New World Order* (Princeton, Princeton University Press, 2004) p 16.
[161] See: Chapter 1.
[162] H Muir Watt, 'Integration and diversity: The conflict of laws as a regulatory tool', in F Cafaggi (ed), *The Institutional Framework of European Private Law* (OUP, 2006) 107; L Tichy, 'A new role for private international law and procedural law in European Integration? A critical comment', in R Brownsword et al (eds), *The Foundations of European Private Law* (Hart Publishing, 2011) 393–412.
[163] *Towards an International Framework of Competition Rules* (n 23). See also: European Commission, *XXVIth Report on Competition Policy 1996* (Published in conjunction with the 'General Report on the Activities of the European Union – 1996) 95.
[164] Doha Work Programme, *Decision Adopted by the General Council on 1 August 2004*, WT/L/579, 2 August 2004, p 3. Compare: Doha WTO Ministerial 2001: Ministerial Declaration – Adopted on 14 November 2001, WT/MIN(01)/DEC/1, 20 November 2001, [23–25]. See also: Working Group on the Interaction between Trade and Competition Policy, *Communication From the United States*, WT/WGTCP/W/35, 1 October 1997; Working Group on the Interaction between Trade and Competition Policy, *Submission by the European Community and its Member States*, WT/WGTCP/W/45, 24 November 1997. See more: Chapter 1.

future and a PIL solution is much needed. That said, it may not be appropriate to rely on a PIL approach which presupposes 'the selection of a single governing law for resolution of multistate disputes'.[165] Applying one national set of competition law rules in cross-border competition cases may not produce satisfactory results in a global context, not least because different public interests would be at stake in the different jurisdictions in which the anti-competitive conduct has been implemented. The lack of an international convention strongly indicates that an alternative soft law mechanism should be considered.

In this book, the author puts forward an argument for a new approach to judicial cooperation which may be developed in the global cities where some major international law firms have their offices.[166] To this end, the issues concerning trans-governmentalism will need to be briefly set out. On that basis, it will be argued that informal transnational networks of law firms, which cooperate in cross-border cases pending before different national courts, would be central to improving injured parties' access to legal remedies. Such networks should set the scene for judicial cooperation with a view to minimising the inconsistencies and expenses, whilst attaining consistent outcomes in parallel competition law proceedings. This would be particularly important in relation to transnational competition law infringements which are committed through various digital platforms that would naturally have a global dimension.

A. Trans-National Networks and International Cooperation

Given the increasingly complex nature of competition law infringements, a softer form of 'institutionalized transgovernmentalism as a mode of international governance'[167] might somehow be advanced to promote a level of judicial cooperation in related competition law cases arising out of the same transnational competition law infringement. It will be argued that, in addition to positive comity, which may be actively advanced by national judges, transnational networks should play an increasingly important role with a view to minimising inconsistencies, 'expense and inconvenience to the parties of parallel proceedings'[168] in related competition law claims arising out of the same transnational competition law infringement.

The importance of transnational networks appears to be set out in the political science literature, suggesting that:

> What has been largely overlooked [...] is the emergence of a transgovernmental: a dense web of relations among domestic government institutions – courts, regulatory agencies, executives, and even legislatures.[...] A new generation of international problems [...] provide the incentives for such relations.[169]

[165] AT von Mehren, 'Special substantive rules for multistate problems: Their role and significance in contemporary choice of law methodology' (1974) *Harvard Law Review* 347, 353.
[166] See more: Chapter 13.
[167] Slaughter (n 56) 200.
[168] Fawcett (n 134) 41.
[169] Slaughter (n 56) 200.

In the area of competition law, a notable example would be the International Competition Network ('ICN')[170] as well as the European Competition Network[171] which has a particularly important role in the EU. At present, the ICN is an 'informal network of 141 competition authorities from 129 jurisdictions',[172] covering a variety of experience, competition cultures and legal traditions. The success of such a form of voluntary and informal cooperation between national regulators (ie competition authorities) has been widely acknowledged by various commentators.[173] Fox and Arena[174] explained the reasons for the success of this form of cooperation by submitting that:

> The ICN, now more than ten years old, is normally regarded as a success in moving law and process towards convergence. Its success is in large part attributed to the fact that it is comprised of the competition law community, not the trade community, and that, since it has no formal powers, little seems to be at stake in agreeing to (for example) recommended practices or principles. Moreover, because the agencies' agreements in ICN do not bind their governments, no higher governmental organization is needed, thus facilitating agreement.[175]

One could hardly deny the achievements of the ICN in this respect. However, it is difficult to see how the ICN could be used to reduce the risk of inconsistent outcomes resulting from parallel and related private antitrust enforcement proceedings arising out of the same transnational competition law infringement, which would inevitably result in duplication of work (public and private costs).[176] There is no possibility for all the related proceedings before different regulators to factor in multiple foreign regulatory interests, not least because regulators would be reluctant to positively apply foreign competition laws (which would naturally be safeguarding foreign regulatory interests). The issues have nicely been summarised by Capobianco and Nagy,[177] who submitted:

> In order to reduce the substantial transaction costs associated with uncoordinated parallel antitrust proceedings, jurisdictions should consider new and more advanced ways in which authorities could cooperate more effectively, including adopting lead jurisdiction models where one authority is designated to investigate and make a decision on a cross-border case on behalf of all other affected jurisdictions.
>
> The basic idea of 'lead jurisdiction' models is to identify the jurisdiction which is better placed to investigate a particular cross-border case and to designate it to handle the case and decide on behalf of all affected jurisdictions. [...] The investigation and decision-making will be made under the laws and procedures of the lead jurisdiction. The lead jurisdiction should have a substantial interest in the case and the necessary skills, competence, and resources to

[170] *ICN Factsheet and key messages*, 'ICN at A Glance' – April 2022, https://www.internationalcompetitionnetwork.org/wp-content/uploads/2022/08/Factsheet-2022.pdf.

[171] Commission Notice on cooperation within the Network of Competition Authorities [2004] OJ C101/43.

[172] *ICN Factsheet and key messages*, 'ICN at A Glance' – April 2022 at 1.

[173] See more: EM Fox and A Arena, 'The international institutions of competition law' in EM Fox and MJ Trebilcock (eds), *The Design of Competition Law Institutions: Global Norms, Local Choices* (Oxford University Press, 2012) 444, 481–84.

[174] Ibid.

[175] Ibid, 482–83.

[176] Compare: *Allianz Global Investors* (n 11) [48–49].

[177] A Capobianco and A Nagy, 'Developments in International Enforcement Co-operation in the Competition Field' (2016) 7 *Journal of European Competition Law & Practice* 566.

> lead the investigation with the assistance of the other jurisdictions, to co-ordinate the views of all relevant jurisdictions, and to decide on the case taking into account the interests of all the jurisdictions affected by the case.[178]

The idea of establishing a lead regulator, which is to investigate, whilst considering the various national regulatory interests, with a view to determining whether there is a competition law infringement in cross-border cases, is to be commended. But the problem is that if each regulator exclusively applies its own competition laws (which may be different, not least because, for example, developed and developing countries may be sharing different interests), there would be an issue of irreconcilable decisions. More importantly, the proposed model would increase the risk for some of the leading regulators (eg the EU and US regulators) to biasedly promote their own regulatory interests (rather than positively advance foreign regulatory interests). This would be an issue because, as noted above, some national regulators would not have the resources and/or the expertise to effectively enforce their competition law in cross-border cases.[179]

Once a regulatory decision establishing a competition law infringement had been rendered, its effects in other jurisdictions might be questioned.[180] Might an alternative approach, which promotes a level of judicial cooperation on the basis of PIL mechanisms and positive 'comity [considerations] be an ideal tool for global governance'?[181] Such an approach would provide benefits for other states in so far as their legitimate regulatory interests would be factored in,[182] but it would also provide benefits for the English and Welsh courts, which should be able to expand their influence and enhance their reputation by being able to deal with highly complex disputes. But, how could such an approach be advanced with a view to minimising the risks of inconsistent findings by various regulators that may legitimately pursue different competition policy objectives[183] as well as with a view to facilitating injured parties' access to legal remedies?

B. Global Cities and Law Firms Networks[184]

The proposed/alternative approach, which promotes a softer form of judicial cooperation, could be developed, if one considers the sociological aspects of globalisation.[185] The global cities appear to play an increasingly important in the functioning of the global economy.[186] Indeed, the case for advancing a mechanism for judicial cooperation may be strengthened by a number of collective redress proceedings which are issued against some hi-tech giants before the UK CAT.[187] The issue had been identified by

[178] Ibid 579.
[179] Bradford et al (n 7) 434; *Motorola Mobility* (n 20) at 820–21.
[180] Capobianco and Nagy (n 177) 576–77.
[181] Lehmann (n 6) 18.
[182] Ibid 19.
[183] Bradford et al (n 7); Klodt (n 54) 883; Epstein and Greve (n 54).
[184] See more: Chapter 13.
[185] S Sassen, *A Sociology of Globalization* (WW Norton & Company, London 2007) 111.
[186] Ibid 111–12.
[187] eg Case No: 1408/7/7/21 *Elizabeth Helen Coll v Alphabet Inc and Others* [2022] CAT 39; *Dr Liza Lovdahl Gormsen* (n 27); *Qualcomm* (n 32).

the relevant literature, with Professor Ezrachi submitting that '[e]xploitation through profiling, discrimination, use of asymmetric information and asymmetric bargaining powers, may give rise to novel forms of harm that adversely affect consumers and may necessitate intervention'.[188]

An argument for the English courts to take a lead in advancing a soft law mechanism for judicial cooperation in competition law matters could be strengthened by the digital developments as well as by the high level of market integration which is reflected in the existing transnational supply chains.[189] These developments indicate that various multinational companies may coordinate their anti-competitive practices from the various financial and business centres, which are based in global cities[190] such as London, Brussels, New York, Amsterdam, Paris, Frankfurt, Shanghai, Hong Kong. The higher the level of transnational economic activities, the more important the role of the global cities in governing these activities. Indeed, the possibility for transnational networks to play an increasingly important role with a view to enforcing competition laws in cross-border cases could be strengthened by reference to the political science literature.[191]

The important role that global cities and IT developments may play in coordinating anticompetitive practice may be, for example, demonstrated by the Forex Cartel Litigation.[192] In this case, the cartel members colluded and manipulated the Spot Foreign Exchange (FX Spot) market by electronically communicating with each other in specifically designated chat rooms. The scale of the transnational competition law infringement was significant. In related US proceedings, the Plea Agreement states that:

> The FX Spot Market is a global market in which participants buy and sell currencies. In the FX Spot Market, currencies are traded against one another in pairs. The EUR/USD currency pair is the most traded currency pair by volume, with a worldwide trading volume that can exceed $500 billion per day, in a market involving the exchange of currencies valued at approximately $2 trillion a day during the Relevant Period [of December 2007 – January 2013].[193]

The relevant electronic communications – through the chat rooms – enabled the infringing undertakings to coordinate their anti-competitive conduct in a global context. More specifically, a number of international banks based in London (Barclays, The Royal Bank of Scotland, Citigroup, JPMorgan and MUFG Bank) have been found to be 'taking part in two cartels in the Spot Foreign Exchange market for 11 currencies – Euro, British Pound, Japanese Yen, Swiss Franc, US, Canadian, New Zealand and Australian Dollars, and Danish, Swedish and Norwegian crowns'.[194] Subsequently, the

[188] A Ezrachi, 'EU Competition Law Goals and the Digital Economy' *Oxford Legal Studies Research Paper No. 17/2018*, https://papers.ssrn.com/sol3/papers.cfm?abstract_id=3191766, p 7.

[189] *Motorola Mobility* (n 20) 824.

[190] Sassen (n 185) 111–12.

[191] Slaughter (n 56) 200.

[192] *Allianz Global Investors GmbH And Others Claimants v Barclays Bank plc* [2021] EWHC 399 (Comm) appealed *Allianz Global Investors GmbH And Others Claimants v Barclays Bank plc* [2022] EWCA Civ 353; Case Nos: 1329/7/7/19 and 1336/7/7/19 *Michael O'Higgins FX Class Representative Ltd v Barclays Bank Plc & Mr Philip Evans v Barclays Bank plc* [2022] CAT 16 [372.2 and 432].

[193] *United States of America v Barclays Plc, Plea Agreement* (United States District Court, District of Connecticut) [4b], https://www.justice.gov/atr/file/838001/download.

[194] European Commission – Press release, 'Antitrust: Commission fines Barclays, RBS, Citigroup, JPMorgan and MUFG €1.07 billion for participating in foreign exchange spot trading cartel' – Brussels, 16 May 2019.

European Commission rendered two settlement decisions,[195] establishing that the banks had engaged in anti-competitive conduct. In 2019, the Financial Times reported that, '[i]n December [2018], law firm Quinn Emanuel filed a claim for damages in London in a 200-page document against RBS, UBS, HSBC, Barclays, Citigroup and JPMorgan, alleging that they manipulated the currencies markets'.[196] Indeed, a number of private antitrust damages claims appear to be issued in the UK.[197]

The example clearly shows how multi-national companies, doing business in certain global cities, could effectively and efficiently coordinate anti-competitive business practices which could cause antitrust harm to multiple injured parties in a global context. Another such example is the *LIBOR Fixing*[198] case. In this case the claimants' pleadings were informed by:

> i) regulatory findings and admissions in relation to LIBOR manipulation by individual Panel Banks which first began to be published in June 2012 in respect of Barclays, and were published by the [Financial Services Authority ('FSA')] in the UK, the Commodity Futures Trading Commission ('CFTC') and Department of Justice ('DOJ') in the US, and the Swiss Financial Market Supervisory Authority ('FINMA') in respect of UBS on 19 December 2012; and
> ii) evidence from criminal trials of traders and brokers concerning manipulation of LIBOR which began to come into the public domain in 2015.[199]

More importantly, the multiple regulatory proceedings may explain why 'in parallel with [the English court] proceedings there are proceedings in the United States, which had started earlier in March 2014'.[200] Indeed, it was only after the defendants in the US proceedings successfully challenged the US court's jurisdiction to deal with the claims issued by the foreign claimants that the English proceedings were issued.[201] More importantly, a closer look at an English court judgment shows that a skilful case management could allow for national courts proceedings to be stayed which would in turn allow 'allow for clarification of the position in parallel US proceedings',[202] minimising the risk of inconsistencies due to the multiplicity of proceedings in different jurisdictions.

An argument for judicial cooperation could be made by re-iterating that many cross-border competition law infringements would be committed by multinational

[195] Case AT.40135, *FOREX (Three Way Banana Split) – Commission Decision relating to a proceeding under Article 101 of the Treaty on the Functioning of the European Union and Article 53 of the EEA Agreement –* 16.5.2019, C(2019) 3631 final; CASE AT.40135 *FOREX (Essex Express) – Commission Decision relating to a proceeding under Article 101 of the Treaty on the Functioning of the European Union and Article 53 of the EEA Agreement* – 16.5.2019, C(2019) 3621 final.

[196] R Toplensky, S Morris and E Szalay, 'EU fines five banks €1bn over foreign exchange cartel', *Financial Times* – 16 May 2019.

[197] *Allianz Global Investors* (n 192) appealed *Allianz Global Investors* (n 192); Case Nos: 1329/7/7/19 and 1336/7/7/19 *Michael O'Higgins FX Class Representative Ltd v Barclays Bank Plc & Mr Philip Evans v Barclays Bank plc* [2022] CAT 16 [372.2 and 432].

[198] *The Federal Deposit Insurance Corporation (as receiver for Amcore Bank NA and others) Claimant v Barclays Bank Plc* [2020] EWHC 2001 (Ch).

[199] Ibid [20].

[200] *Federal Deposit Insurance Corporation as Receiver of Amcore Bank NA and Others v Barclays Bank Plc* [2022] EWHC 391 (Ch) [3].

[201] Ibid [4].

[202] Ibid [1].

groups of companies that enjoy market power in geographical markets that are transnational.[203] There would inevitably be multiple related competition law claims, which arise out of the same transnational infringements. Such infringements would naturally cause harm to multiple injured parties: consumers,[204] large retailers[205] and some other small and medium-sized enterprises (SMEs)[206] in different jurisdictions.

A soft law mechanism for judicial cooperation might need to be advanced to ensure that a national court decision on certain preliminary issues (eg regulatory infringement; quantum) may carry a degree of persuasiveness about the anti-competitive nature of the conduct, for example. Such a soft law mechanism for judicial cooperation might be important to ensure that, despite the fact that 'the outcome of a trial is usually only binding on the actual parties to the trial',[207] a judgment/decision in relation to certain anti-competitive activities rendered in one jurisdiction could be regarded as 'persuasive'[208] in another jurisdiction in proceedings involving different parties. The proposed approach night be similar to the one advanced by the Antitrust Damages Directive in relation to decisions of other EU Member States' national competition authorities.[209] Might the law firms based in the global cities be the catalyst for a more flexible regime for judicial cooperation which may improve the injured parties' access to appropriate legal remedies in cross-border cases? Should this approach allow for proceedings – which appear to be arising out of transnational infringements – to be coordinated more effectively?[210]

VII. Concluding Remarks

The foregoing analysis strongly suggests that multiple sets of related proceedings may be a real issue, posing difficult questions as to how a level of consistency could be attained in cross-border competition law claims. If the existing mechanisms for judicial cooperation do not allow for all the related follow-on damages to be centralised before an appropriate national court, there would be a risk that common issues may not be consistently dealt with, which would increase the level of uncertainty. This would mean that a different mechanism for judicial cooperation would be necessary.

Given that the transnational anti-competitive activities would, by definition, be organised by multinational companies to distort the process of competition across borders, it could be argued that transnational networks of law firms would be required to coordinate injured parties' strategies (and potentially defendants' strategies) in cases

[203] Case AT.39824, *Trucks – Commission Decision relating to a proceeding under Article 101 of the Treaty on the Functioning of the European Union (the Treaty) and Article 53 of the EEA Agreement* – 19.7.2016, C(2016) 4673 final – Recitals 61, 85 and 108.

[204] *Merricks* (n 111).

[205] *Sainsbury's* (n 100).

[206] Schedule of 'Host Cases', as updated on 19 August 2022, to the Umbrella Proceedings Order – dated 4 July 2022.

[207] Case Nos: 1306–1325/5/7/19 (T) et al, *Dune Group Ltd & Ors v MasterCard* [2022] CAT 14 [21].

[208] Ibid [21].

[209] Article 9(2) of Directive 2014/104/EU.

[210] See more: Chapter 13.

against multinational groups of companies. More specifically, transnational networks of the international law firms, which act for claimants in private antitrust damages claims, could set the scene for judicial cooperation in private antitrust matters.

In other words, transnational networks of law firms may set the scene for a higher level of judicial cooperation in related private antitrust damages claims which arise out of the same of transnational competition law infringements. If the foreign regulatory/court proceedings were to inform the parties' pleadings,[211] this should facilitate courts' decision-making in so far as the pleadings would provide 'some plausible factual foundation for the application of the broad economic theory'[212] which would be central for the courts to effectively and efficiently deal with these cases, whilst attaining a level of consistency in a cross-border context.

This cooperation could be facilitated by PIL rules which enable the English courts to assume adjudicatory jurisdiction – whilst considering – as part of the *forum conveniens* discretion – any foreign regulatory interests/proceedings and aspects in relation to access to justice. As part of this process, the following factors could be considered: how closely the competition law dispute is connected with the other legal order; how appropriately the adjudicators in the other country could deal with the case, factoring in any third countries' regulatory interests; whether the adjudicators in the other country could provide effective legal remedies to injured parties, safeguarding the procedural rights of the relevant defendants.[213] In order to set the scene for devising such a soft law mechanism for judicial cooperation, the author will consider, in Chapter 9, the issues regarding regulatory jurisdiction (ie determining whether there is a regulatory breach) and adjudicatory jurisdiction (ie having the competence to deal with a competition law claim) are central to the effective coordination of parallel proceedings.

Once the jurisdiction had been assumed, the judges would consider to what extent foreign regulatory interests should be factored in with a view to minimising any inconsistencies with foreign related proceedings[214] and ensuring that any rendered judgment would be recognised and enforced abroad.[215] How to achieve a level of judicial cooperation in competition law cases where a foreign regulator has taken the view that the conduct is anti-competitive? In other words, an important issue, which is to be considered in Chapters 10 and 11, concerns the extent to which the local and foreign applicable competition law/s should be considered by adjudicators at the stage when they are deciding whether to assume jurisdiction or not.[216] The question of whether foreign regulatory decisions may be relied on in proceedings before national courts[217] will be considered in Chapters 11 and 12.

[211] See more: Chapters 9 and 13.

[212] Case Nos: 1284–1290/5/7/18 (T), *Royal Mail Group Ltd v DAF Trucks Ltd & Other, BT Group Plc & Others v DAF Trucks Ltd & Others* [2021] CAT 10 [43].

[213] *G, A (Children: Habitual Residence and Article 15 transfer)* [2015] EWFC B41, 2015 WL 1651353 [41].

[214] Chapters 10 and 11.

[215] Chapters 11 and 12.

[216] AT von Mehren and DT Trautman, 'A Jurisdiction to Adjudicate: A Suggested Analysis' (1966) *Harvard Law Review* 1121, 1128.

[217] Compare: Article 16 of Council Regulation 1/2003; Article 9(2) of Directive 2014/104/EU.

9

Regulatory Jurisdiction and Adjudicatory Jurisdiction – Balancing Different Regulatory Interests

I. Introduction – Regulatory and Adjudicatory Jurisdiction

As already noted above,[1] the jurisdiction of a national court to adjudicate[2] over a private antitrust damages claim would presuppose for the judge to determine whether there is a competition law infringement.[3] To this end, a national judge would need to apply the relevant (public) competition law rules and determine whether the conduct is anti-competitive. The response to the latter question is closely connected with the issues concerning the territorial scope of the relevant competition laws to regulate cross-border economic activities.[4] The problem is that, since the anti-competitive conduct would often relate to transnational economic activities, there would be multiple competition laws[5] which might regulate the matter.

It is well established that the issues concerning the regulatory jurisdiction as well as the aspects in relation to '[t]he application by the [European] Union of its competition rules is governed by the territoriality principle as universally recognised principle of international law'.[6] That said, the analysis in Chapter 7 and 8 appears to indicate that governing related private antitrust damages claims arising out of the same transnational competition law infringement (ie the same anti-competitive conduct) would be a major issue, which needs to be addressed in a global context.

Setting out an appropriate PIL solution may be extra difficult because many competition law provisions would have extra-territorial effects. This may be a problem because, '[w]ith the extraterritorial law [which is] intended to penalize companies [...], [a national legal order can give] legal globalization a characteristic aspect of a territorial

[1] Chapter 2.

[2] AT von Mehren and DT Trautman, 'A Jurisdiction to Adjudicate: A Suggested Analysis' (1966) *Harvard Law Review* 1121.

[3] *BritNed Development v ABB AB and ABB* [2019] EWCA Civ 1840 [28] and [29].

[4] *The LCD Appeals* [2018] EWCA Civ 220 [91].

[5] A Bradford et al, 'Competition Law Gone Global: Introducing the Comparative Competition Law and Enforcement Datasets' (2019) 16 *Journal of Empirical Legal Studies* 411.

[6] COMP/39.309, *LCD (Liquid Crystal Displays) – Commission Decision relating to a proceeding under Article 101 Treaty on the Functioning of the European Union and Article 53 of the Agreement on the European Economic Area*, C(2010) 8761 final – Brussels – 8 December 2010 [230].

or extraterritorial law reflecting nothing but its political will'.[7] The extra-territorial application of national competition law provisions may be legitimately justified in so far as the anti-competitive conduct of undertakings based in one jurisdiction might adversely affect the process of competition and prices in another jurisdiction.[8] The importance of extra-territoriality in cross-border competition law cases is duly reflected in the comparative law datasets which were compiled by Bradford et al.[9] The relevant research data strongly suggests that, in 2010, the national competition laws would apply extra-territorially in over 60 jurisdictions.[10] There is a strong case that the *effects doctrine*,[11] which is closely associated with the 'territorial scope'[12] of the applicable competition laws, has public international law (rather than private international law) connotations.

Given that international cooperation at present appears to be limited to collaboration in relation to enforcement activities of various regulators (ie competition authorities) in different jurisdictions,[13] there is a need to for a level of judicial cooperation which, through PIL mechanisms and positive comity considerations, encourages judges to factor in foreign competition laws (ie foreign regulatory interests). In this chapter (as well as in Chapter 10), it will be argued that a private international law solution is needed to address the problems concerning the inclination of the national judges to extra-territorially apply their national competition laws, without systematically factoring in foreign competition laws.

There are two parts of the problem that require a PIL solution. One part of this problem is that the various national competition law systems may pursue different (or even conflicting) national regulatory interests, which would be reflected in the specified competition law objectives.[14] Another part of the problem is that national judges would naturally apply their own competition law, which would have a mandatory character (reflecting their public policy interests).[15] The PIL issues are important because, if the national competition laws enjoy a public policy character,[16] then the relevant laws must be applied by the national courts. Although there is no comparative data to specify how many competition laws would classify as mandatory provisions of the forum for private international law purposes,[17] the public policy nature of competition laws could well be seen as reflecting their regulatory nature and mandatory character. In other words,

[7] J-B Auby, *Globalisation, Law and State* (Oxford, Hart Publishing, 2017) 139–140.

[8] EM Fox, 'Linked-In: Antitrust and the Virtues of a Virtual Network' (2009) *The International Lawyer* 151, 154; FW Papp, 'Competition law and extraterritoriality' in A Ezrachi (ed), *Research Handbook on International Competition Law* (Edward Elgar, 2012) 21, 22.

[9] Bradford (n 5).

[10] Ibid 423.

[11] See below.

[12] *The LCD Appeals* (n 4) [61–100].

[13] See: Chapter 1.

[14] Bradford (n 5) 418.

[15] T Hartley, 'Public Policy and Mandatory Provisions' in P Beaumont and J Holliday (eds), *A Guide to Global Private International Law* (Oxford, Hart, 2022) 75–87.

[16] Recital 1 of Directive 2014/104/EU on certain rules governing actions for damages under national law for infringements of the competition law provisions of the Member States and of the European Union [2014] Official Journal L349/1; Case C-126/97 *Eco Swiss China Time Ltd v Benetton International NV* EU:C:1999:269; Case C-38/98 *Régie nationale des usines Renault SA v Maxicar SpA and Orazio Formento* EU:C:2000:225. See more: Chapter 10.

[17] Compare: Rome I and Rome II. See: Chapter 10.

a major private international law issue with this approach is that the national courts would simply apply their national competition law as long as the *qualified effects*[18] test was satisfied.[19]

According to Professor Mills, '[s]ometimes the effects doctrine is considered a separate basis for jurisdiction, although it is probably better viewed as a particular type of territorial connection'[20] for public international law purposes.[21] This means that the regulatory jurisdiction is set to reflect the territorial scope of the relevant competition laws that may apply extra-territorially.[22] The extra-territorial application of the competition laws of the *forum* would mean that there would be multiple (public) competition laws which may be applicable with regard to related private antitrust damages claims which arise out of the same transnational infringements and which are issued in different countries. The fact that different competition laws may be applicable to such related claims would clearly be a PIL issue which would need to be addressed head-on in a global context.[23]

Before advancing an appropriate PIL solution in Chapter 10 (ie a transnational approach to applicable competition laws) which may be used to promote judicial cooperation in cross-border competition law disputes, this chapter is set to demonstrate that the territoriality principles, as developed by the US and EU jurisprudence, are no longer suited to the resolution of multiple and related private antitrust damages claims, which increasingly relate to transnational infringements causing harm to multiple injured parties. With this in mind, the author will consider aspects in relation to extra-territoriality, conflict of competition laws and access to legal remedies in private antitrust damages claims with an international element.

II. The EU/UK Approach to Extra-Territorial Application of Competition Law

It is well established that UK competition law[24] and EU competition law may apply extra-territorially.[25] The problem of extra-territorial application of EU competition law was duly acknowledged in *InnoLux v European Commission*.[26] In this case, AG Wathelet noted that 'a broad interpretation of the territorial scope of EU competition law would entail the risk of conflicts of jurisdiction with foreign competition authorities and of double penalties for undertakings'.[27]

[18] *The LCD Appeals* (n 4).

[19] eg *The LCD Appeals* (n 4); Case C-413/14 P *Intel v Commission*, EU:C:2017:632 [49].

[20] A Mills, *The Confluence of Public and Private International Law: Justice, Pluralism, Subsidiarity in the International Constitutional Ordering of Private Law* (Cambridge, CUP, 2009) 235.

[21] Ibid 234–36.

[22] *The LCD Appeals* (n 4).

[23] See more: Chapter 13.

[24] Section 2(3) of the Competition Act 1998; Digital Markets, Competition and Consumers Bill s 117.

[25] Joined Cases 89/85, 104/85, 114/85, 116–17/85, and 125–29/85 *Ahlstrom v Commission* EU:C:1988:447 (*Wood Pulp*). See also: Case T-102/96 *Gencor Ltd v Commission* [1999] ECR II-753. See also Case No IV/M.619 *Gencor/Lonrho* [1997] OJ L11/30; Case T-210/01 *General Electric v Commission* [2005] ECR II-5575.

[26] Opinion of AG Wathelet in C-231/14 P *InnoLux Corp v European Commission* EU:C:2015:292.

[27] Ibid [42].

The author will argue that a PIL approach to the issues of regulatory and adjudicatory jurisdiction would be central to systematically addressing the issues concerning conflict of competition laws and related parallel proceedings in different jurisdictions with a view to improving the injured parties' access to legal remedies. It will be suggested that, in order to set out a PIL mechanism for judicial cooperation in competition law matters, it would be necessary for national judges to factor in foreign regulatory interests with a view to determining whether a particular transnational conduct is anti-competitive.[28] More specifically, the author will demonstrate that a PIL approach to issues of regulatory and adjudicatory jurisdiction would allow for a national court to consider the compatibility of transnational economic activities with the laws of multiple competition law systems which may have legitimate interests to *regulate* the allegedly anti-competitive conduct.[29] Once the scope of the competition law claim/s had been ascertained, the national courts would *adjudicate*[30] and determine whether there is a competition law infringement by applying (and/or factoring in) the relevant competition law/s[31] (ie foreign regulatory interests) as well as by quantifying the antitrust damages[32] which may have been caused to multiple injured parties in different jurisdictions.

A. Public Enforcement – Regulatory Jurisdiction and Territorial Scope

An important case, which sets out the EU approach in relation to extra-territorial application of EU competition law, is *Wood Pulp*.[33] In this case, the EU Commission investigated the conduct of the wood pulp manufacturers.[34] The relevant product market was the one for 'bleached sulphate pulp, as used in paper manufacturing and which is offered on the open market (so-called market pulp)'.[35] The issues concerning the regulatory jurisdiction and the territorial scope of EU competition law were central to determining whether the conduct was to be regarded as anti-competitive. Whereas the defendants' conduct was in conflict with EU competition law, the US Webb-Pomerene Act allegedly expressed the US legitimate regulatory interests to promote exports by exempting any export cartel agreements from the prohibitions laid down in the US antitrust laws.[36]

The jurisdictional issues were important because, whilst the major pulp manufactures were from Canada, the US, Sweden and Finland, a significant proportion of pulp was imported within the EU.[37] This posed the question whether there was a sufficient

[28] See more: Chapters 10, 11, 12 and 13.
[29] AT von Mehren, 'Special substantive rules for multistate problems: Their role and significance in contemporary choice of law methodology' (1974) *Harvard Law Review* 347.
[30] Chapters 3, 4, 5 and 6.
[31] See more: Chapter 10.
[32] See more: Chapter 11.
[33] *Wood Pulp* (n 25). See also: IV/29.725, *Wood Pulp*, Commission Decision of 19 December 1984 relating to a proceeding under Article 101 TFEU [1985] *Official Journal* L85/1.
[34] Recital 1 – *Wood Pulp* – Commission Decision (n 33).
[35] Ibid – Recital 2.
[36] Ibid [7].
[37] Ibid – Recitals 5–11.

territorial connection with the EU for the European Commission to exercise its regulatory jurisdiction and apply Article 101 TFEU in public enforcement proceedings against the pulp manufacturers. The EU Commission took the view that it had the jurisdiction to do so because:

> the addressees of this Decision were during the period of the infringement exporting directly to or doing business within the [EU]. Some of them had branches, subsidiaries, agencies or other establishments within the [EU]. The concertation on prices, the exchange of sensitive information relative to prices, and the clauses prohibiting export or resale all concerned shipments made directly to buyers in the [EU] or sales made in the [EU] to buyers there. The shipments affected by these agreements and practices amounted to about two-thirds of total shipments of bleached sulphate wood pulp to the [EU] and some 60 % of [EU] consumption. The agreements and practices appear to have applied to at least the vast majority of the sales of the relevant product by the parties to and in the [EU] during the relevant periods. The effect of the agreements and practices on prices announced and/or charged to customers and on resale of pulp within the [EU] was therefore not only substantial but intended, and was the primary and direct result of the agreements and practices.[38]

The defendants challenged the regulatory jurisdiction of the EU Commission by submitting that 'public international law [...] preclude[d] any claim by the [EU] to regulate conduct restricting competition adopted outside the territory of the [EU] merely by reason of the economic repercussions which that conduct produces within the [EU]'.[39] In other words, the regulatory jurisdiction for a particular set of competition laws to regulate (or govern) the competition law aspects of the cross-border economic activities appeared to be at the heart of this dispute in so far as the law that was to apply and regulate the conduct was key for the outcome of the case.

The defendants further submitted that the application of EU competition law would be 'contrary to public international law in so far as it is in breach of the principle of non-interference'.[40] The CJEU dismissed defendant's submission by taking the view that there was no conflict of competition laws.[41] It was held that:

> There is not, in this case, any contradiction between the conduct required by the United States and that required by the [European Union] since the Webb Pomerene Act merely exempts the conclusion of export cartels from the application of United States anti-trust laws but does not require such cartels to be concluded.[42]

Since EU competition laws regulated the competition law aspects of the defendants' transnational economic activities, they were liable for breach of EU competition law. The PIL problem with this approach is that the outcome of the dispute would be dependent on where the dispute is adjudicated. Should foreign regulatory interests be factored in cases which concern transnational economic activities? What would be the relevant connecting factors?

[38] Ibid [79]. See also: *Wood Pulp* (n 25) [3].
[39] *Wood Pulp* (n 25) [6].
[40] Ibid.
[41] Compare the US approach – *Hartford Fire Insurance Co v California*, 113 S Ct 2891 at 2909–11 (1993).
[42] *Wood Pulp* (n 25) [20].

Advocate General Darmon[43] identified two different aspects of the regulatory jurisdiction and territorial scope of competition laws which he broadly defined as *subjective* and *objective*.[44] If anti-competitive practices that originate in country A have affected markets in country B, then the jurisdiction of the national court in country A would be *subjective* (in so far as, for example, this is the place where the cartel agreement is concluded) and the jurisdiction of the national court in country B would be *objective* (as being the place where the cartel agreement is implemented).[45] The advanced distinction was followed by the CJEU, holding that *the place of implementation* would be the crucial connecting factor:

> 16 [...] the conclusion of an agreement which has had the effect of restricting competition within the common market, consists of conduct made up of two elements, the formation of the agreement, decision or concerted practice and the implementation thereof. If the applicability of prohibitions laid down under competition law were made to depend on the place where the agreement, decision or concerted practice was formed, the result would obviously be to give undertakings an easy means of evading those prohibitions. The decisive factor is therefore the place where it is implemented.
>
> 17 The producers in this case implemented their pricing agreement within the common market. It is immaterial in that respect whether or not they had recourse to subsidiaries, agents, sub-agents, or branches within the Community in order to make their contacts with purchasers within the Community.
>
> 18 Accordingly the [Union's] jurisdiction to apply its competition rules to such conduct is covered by the territoriality principle as universally recognized in public international law.[46]

The validity of the 'implementation' test as an independent test concerning extraterritorial application of EU competition law was acknowledged by the CJEU in the *Intel* case.[47] The *Intel* case[48] provided some useful clarifications, and it also shows how competitors may play an important role in detecting anti-competitive business practices. The complaint was launched by Advanced Micro Devices (AMD). It was alleged that Intel has abused its dominant position[49] on the global market of x86 central processing units (CPUs).[50] In particular, it was alleged that Intel had foreclosed the relevant market by granting fidelity rebates/discounts to its customers which has limited AMD's market access, distorting the process of competition in a global context.[51]

The transnational nature of the economic activities (and indeed the transnational nature of the infringement) in question could easily be deduced not only from the parties' consensus on the issue, but also from the fact that competition law aspects of the relevant business practices have been subject to investigations by the Japan Fair

[43] Opinion of AG Darmon in Joined Cases 89/85, 104/85, 114/85, 116–17/85, and 125–29/85 *Ahlstrom v Commission* (Wood Pulp) EU:C:1988:258.

[44] Ibid [20].

[45] Ibid.

[46] *Wood Pulp* (n 25).

[47] *Intel* – CJEU (n 19).

[48] COMP/C-3 /37.990, *Intel – Commission Decision of relating to a proceeding under Article 82 of the EC Treaty and Article 54 of the EEA Agreement*, D(2009) 3726final – 13 May 2009.

[49] Ibid [912].

[50] Ibid [835–36].

[51] Ibid [1001].

Trade Commission,[52] the Korean Fair Trade Commission[53] and the Federal Trade Commission of the United States of America.[54] Given the fact that the EU Commission imposed a fine of over €1 billion, it is hardly surprising that Intel tried to inter alia challenge the jurisdiction of the EU Commission by questioning the scope of its territorial jurisdiction. Therefore, the scope of the territorial jurisdiction of EU competition law had to be addressed head-on by the General Court of the European Union.

It is noteworthy that Intel's argument concerning the limited territorial scope of EU competition law was supported by the Association for the Competitive Technology (ACT),[55] which was allowed to intervene in the proceedings before the General Court.[56] The main argument was that the EU Commission failed to demonstrate the causal relationship between the anti-competitive conduct and the territorial impact within the European Union which would require implementation within the EU internal market as well as 'effects within the European Union are immediate, substantial, direct and foreseeable'.[57]

The General Court rejected this argument. The judges went on to re-iterate that 'in order to justify the Commission's jurisdiction under public international law, it is sufficient to establish either the qualified effects of the practice in the European Union or that it was implemented in the European Union'.[58] The decision of the General Court was upheld by the Court of Justice of the European Union. The CJEU took the opportunity to acknowledge that a 'qualified effects test allows the application of EU competition law to be justified under public international law when it is foreseeable that the conduct in question will have an immediate and substantial effect in the European Union'.[59]

Therefore, the place where the conduct has produced *qualified effects* would constitute another connecting factor which would impact on the regulatory jurisdiction in cross-border competition law cases. Would the same connecting factors (ie the place of implementation; place where qualified effects are produced) be relied upon in private antitrust proceedings?

B. Private Antitrust Enforcement – Territorial Scope of Competition Law and Scope of the Claim

The Court of Appeal of England and Wales had an opportunity to opine on the territorial scope of EU competition law (ie dealing with aspects in relation to regulatory jurisdiction) in the context of private antitrust damages claims. The judgment in the *LCD Appeals* case[60] is important because many private antitrust damages claims[61] in the

[52] Ibid [31–32].
[53] Ibid [33].
[54] Ibid [34–35].
[55] Case T-286/09, *Intel v Commission*, EU:T:2014:547 [221].
[56] Ibid [39].
[57] Ibid [221].
[58] Ibid [244].
[59] *Intel* – CJEU (n 19) [49].
[60] *The LCD Appeals* (n 4).
[61] eg *Iiyama UK Ltd v Samsung Electronics Co Ltd* [2016] EWHC 1980 (Ch); *Iiyama UK Ltd v Schott AG* [2016] EWHC 1207 (Ch).

UK would often be preceded by regulatory decisions[62] which had established the transnational infringement, addressing the issues concerning the regulatory jurisdiction.[63] A very important aspect of this case was that '[t]he infringement had a global character both from the geographic and product point of view, with the parties generally aiming at increasing and/or maintaining the prices for LCD panels for TV and IT application'.[64] It should be noted that, in this case, the relevant product market was '[t]he [12"] liquid crystal display panel [which] is the main component of thin, flat monitors used for televisions, computers [...]'.[65]

The transnational nature of the infringement was beyond any doubt because it was established by the European Commission that the infringers had a 'joint worldwide market share of around [65–80%] in large LCD panels'.[66] More specifically, the infringers[67] were well-known companies: Samsung Group (Samsung Electronics Co Ltd and Samsung Electronics Taiwan Co Ltd), LPL Group (LG Philips LCD Co, Ltd and LG Philips LCD Taiwan Co, Ltd), AUO Group (AU Optronics Corporation), CMO Group (Chimei InnoLux Corporation), CPT Group (Chunghwa Picture Tubes), HannStar companies. Indeed, the evidence before the regulator demonstrated that:

> The participating undertakings, Samsung, LPL, AUO, CMO, CPT and Hannstar engaged in a *single, complex and continuous cartel infringement* in respect of LCD panels for IT and TV applications by a series of linked and interacting efforts that lasted from 5 October 2001 until February 2006, with the objective of increasing and maintaining prices of LCD panels for IT and TV applications at world-wide and EEA level. Throughout the period of the infringement those companies were competitors and were aware of the arrangements and the decisions taken which were implemented.[68]

The case shows that the scope of the regulatory jurisdiction (ie the scope of the forum's competition laws) may be a difficult issue in both public and private proceedings in cases where the competition law infringement is transnational. Given that regulators would naturally exclusively apply their own competition laws (as long as the cross-border dispute is within the territorial scope of their competition laws), the issues concerning the regulatory jurisdiction of the regulator and the territorial scope of the competition

[62] *LCD – Commission Decision* (n 6); COMP/39437, *TV and Computer Monitor Tubes – Commission Decision of 5.12.2012 addressed to Chunghwa Picture Tubes Co, Ltd – Chunghwa Picture Tubes (Malaysia) Sdn Bhd – CPTF Optronics Co, Ltd – Samsung SDI Co, Ltd – Samsung SDI Germany GmbH – Samsung SDI (Malaysia) Berhad – Koninklijke Philips Electronics NV – LG Electronics, Inc – Technicolor SA – Panasonic Corporation – Toshiba Corporation – MT Picture Display Co, Ltd relating to a proceeding under Article 101 of the Treaty on the Functioning of the European Union and Article 53 of the EEA Agreement* C(2012) 8839 final; COMP/39605, *CRT Glass – Commission Decision relating to a proceeding under Article 101 Treaty on the Functioning of the European Union and Article 53 of the Agreement on the European Economic Area* C(2011) 7436 final.

[63] *LCD – Commission Decision* (n 6) [230–43]; *TV and Computer Monitor Tubes – Commission Decision* (n 62) [585–599].

[64] *LCD – Commission Decision* (n 6) [402].

[65] Ibid [2].

[66] Ibid [51].

[67] Ibid [13–35].

[68] Ibid [283] – emphasis added.

laws would often overlap in public enforcement proceedings.[69] The point was captured in the judgment of the Court of Appeal of England and Wales in *LCD Appeals*:[70]

> Intel concerns the territorial jurisdiction of the Commission, rather than the territorial scope of Article 101 or Article 102. [...] We cannot accept that the territorial scope of the Commission's jurisdiction differs in principle from the territorial scope of the two Articles, except possibly in relation to foreign transactions which the Commission may legitimately take into account when levying fines. Nor are we aware of any authority which draws a distinction for jurisdictional purposes between the two Articles, and we can see no basis for such a distinction since they both contain similar references to the internal market and trade between Member States.[71]

It should be noted that the issues concerning the regulatory jurisdiction and the territorial scope of EU competition law were dealt with in the regulatory decisions.[72] That said, they reappeared in follow-on private antitrust damages claims because the claimants had to demonstrate 'a real prospect of success in claiming that [the relevant competition law provisions] have been infringed, and losses suffered by them as a result'.[73] In other words, the parties had to demonstrate not only that the transnational cartel had qualified effects in the market, but also that the prices were affected by the anti-competitive conduct.

A major issue in *Iiyama UK v Schott*[74] was whether 'the conduct [has] sufficient territorial connection with the EU'.[75] The same issue had to be considered in *Iiyama UK v Samsung Electronics*.[76] In this case, the claimants issued private antitrust damages claims against the various companies from the Samsung Group as well as against LG Display Co Ltd, all being part of the *LCDs* cartel.[77] The defendants sought to strike out the private antitrust damages claims, challenging inter alia the jurisdiction of the English courts. Hence the adjudicatory jurisdiction may often be intertwined with the territorial scope of EU competition laws and regulatory jurisdiction.[78] The strategic nature of the jurisdictional challenge was captured by Mr Justice Morgan, who noted:

> It is important to note that [the non-EU defendants] do not contend that England and Wales is inappropriate because the courts of another EU member state would be more appropriate. It is not said, for example, that [one of the claimants] as a company incorporated in Germany, should sue [the non-EU defendants] in the German courts. What [the defendants in question] appear to say is that the Claimants should sue them in Taiwan or Japan where there was arguably an infringement of Taiwanese or Japanese law. [The relevant defendants] go on to argue that, in fact, a claim based on Taiwanese law or Japanese law would fail as they have a limitation defence to such a claim, which defence would be given effect in Taiwan or Japan.[79]

[69] *The LCD Appeals* (n 4) [91].
[70] Ibid.
[71] Ibid [91] – the emphasis is in the original.
[72] *LCD – Commission Decision* (n 6) [230–243]; *TV and Computer Monitor Tubes – Commission Decision* (n 62) [585–99].
[73] *The LCD Appeals* (n 4) [2].
[74] *Iiyama v Schott* (n 61).
[75] Ibid [150].
[76] *Iiyama v Samsung* (n 61).
[77] *LCD – Commission Decision* (n 6).
[78] *The LCD Appeals* (n 4) [61].
[79] *Iiyarna v Samsung* (n 61) [75].

Since the claimants pleaded that any sale transactions of products which incorporated cartelised components and which occurred outside of the EU, affected the prices in the EU and caused the claimants' loss,[80] the territorial scope of EU competition law was a central issue in this case[81] which would have had major implications about the scope of the private antitrust damages claim (including its value)[82] and defendants' liability.[83] This would in turn impact on the adjudicatory jurisdiction of the English courts because, in order for a claim form to be served out of the jurisdiction, the claimants should satisfy the court that they have 'a good arguable case against the UK-based "anchor" defendants'.[84]

Therefore, the issues concerning the territorial scope of national competition laws (ie the regulatory jurisdiction) would impact on the adjudicatory jurisdiction of the national courts. If the territorial (ie regulatory) scope of EU competition law was broad enough to cover the claims in question, then this would make England and Wales an appropriate forum for the dispute to be determined.[85]

That said, the English judgments rendered by Mr Justice Morgan[86] and Mr Justice Mann[87] appear to show that different views may be taken on the scope of regulatory jurisdiction and, in particular, the territorial scope of competition laws. Although the Court of Appeal of England and Wales appeared to have clarified the issue by holding that the relevant damages claims are within the territorial scope of EU competition law, the issues require renewed attention, post-Brexit. For example, if the defendants were to be successful in establishing that UK competition law was not applicable to the claims, then the injured parties could have still tried to make a case that there was breach of another set of competition laws, but it would be questionable whether England and Wales would be the proper place for the competition law claims to be tried (ie *forum conveniens* and *forum non conveniens* aspects would have to be considered).[88]

C. Conflict of Jurisdictions and Related/Parallel Proceedings

The problems concerning related proceedings in relation to the same transnational competition law infringement could be illustrated by considering the European Commission Decision in *Liquid Crystal Displays* (*LCDs*),[89] the Court of Appeal of England and Wales's judgment in *The LCD Appeals*[90] and the US Court of Appeals' judgment in *Motorola Mobility LLC v AU Optronics Corp*.[91] The issue might be significant

[80] *Iiyama v Schott* (n 61) [105 and 132]. Compare: The defendants' argument – ibid [64 and 108].
[81] Ibid [72].
[82] Ibid [39].
[83] Ibid [73].
[84] *The LCD Appeals* (n 4) [120].
[85] Ibid [132].
[86] *Iiyama v Samsung* (n 61).
[87] *Iiyama v Schott* (n 61).
[88] See: Chapter 7 above.
[89] *LCD – Commission Decision* (n 6). See also: *CRT Glass – Commission Decision* (n 62); *TV and Computer Monitor Tubes – Commission Decision* (n 62).
[90] *The LCD Appeals* (n 4).
[91] *Motorola Mobility LLC v AU Optronics Corp* 775 F 3d 816 (7th Cir 2015).

because, in cases where manufacturers 'fix the prices and limit the supply of LCDs sold in the global market'[92] and infringe various national competition laws across the globe,[93] antitrust damages would have been caused to multiple injured parties.[94]

A PIL mechanism for judicial cooperation in antitrust matters might be necessary to improve the injured parties' access to legal remedies by avoiding a conflict of jurisdictions. The issue is that, if the competition laws of both country A and country B were to regulate the transnational economic activities, there would be a risk of inconsistent outcomes in related private antitrust damages claims unless a PIL mechanism were devised. As noted above, it is suggested for such a PIL mechanism to allow judges to factor in foreign regulatory interests with a view to determining whether the conduct is anti-competitive, drawing a distinction between the aspects concerning adjudicatory jurisdiction and regulatory jurisdiction (ie the territorial scope of competition laws).[95] Devising such a PIL mechanism would be particularly important in cases where the conduct is implemented and/or has generated qualified effects in a number of jurisdictions – countries C, D, E and F – which could be quite common in cross-border cases.[96]

Finding a PIL solution to the problem of 'concurrent jurisdiction'[97] as identified by Advocate General Darmon presupposes an appropriate definition of jurisdiction. The problem is that the distinction between the regulatory jurisdiction and adjudicatory jurisdiction has not been quite articulated in the CJEU jurisprudence. His view is that, given the nature of the EU, which operates within the competencies conferred on it by the EU Member States,[98] it is important to distinguish between 'jurisdiction to prescribe'[99] and 'jurisdiction to enforce'.[100]

> The jurisdiction thus conferred is 'jurisdiction to prescribe', being the power of the State to 'lay down general or individual rules through its legislative, executive or judicial bodies'. […] It cannot be understood as constituting 'jurisdiction to enforce', which is the 'power of a State to give effect to a general rule or an individual decision by means of substantive implementing measures which may include even coercion by the authorities'.[101]

That said, the problem with such a definition is that the distinction between *the jurisdiction to prescribe* and *the jurisdiction to enforce* is blurred. In particular, it is difficult to provide an adequate response to the question 'whether the power to impose a fine

[92] See the Particulars of the Claim [45] cited in *Nokia Corporation v AU Optronics Corporation & Others* [2012] EWHC 731 (Ch) [39].

[93] *LCD – Commission Decision* (n 6); Case T-91/11, *InnoLux Corp v European Commission*, EU:T:2014:92; Case C-231/14 P, *InnoLux Corp v European Commission* EU:C:2015:451. Further investigations appear to conducted by national competition authorities in Japan, South Korea, Taiwan and Canada – see the Particulars of the Claim [47] cited in *Nokia Corporation* (n 92) [39]. Criminal proceedings appear to have been conducted in the US – *US v Hui Hsiung* 758 F 3d 1074 (9th Cir 2014); *US v Hui Hsiung* 778 F 3d 738 (9th Cir 2015).

[94] *AT & T Mobility LLC v AU Optronics Corp* 707 F 3d 1106 (9th Cir 2013); *Motorola Mobility LLC v AU Optronics Corp* 775 F 3d 816 (7th Cir 2015).

[95] M Danov and C Otero, 'Competition Law Enforcement: Private International Law and Access to Effective Legal Remedies in Cross-Border Cases' in Beaumont and Holliday (n 15) 233–46.

[96] Case C-289/04 P *Showa Denko v Commission* EU:C:2006:431 [52–58]; Case C-308/04 P *SGL Carbon v Commission* EU:C:2006:433 [28–34]; Case C-328/05 P *SGL Carbon v Commission* EU:C:2007:277 [24–35].

[97] *Wood Pulp* – AG Darmon (n 43) [35, 43 and 49].

[98] See Article 3(6) and Article 5(2) – The Treaty on European Union.

[99] *Wood Pulp* – AG Darmon (n 43) [28].

[100] Ibid [28].

[101] Ibid [28].

comes within the scope of prescriptive jurisdiction or enforcement jurisdiction'.[102] AG Darmon appears to believe that regulator's power to impose a fine in public-administrative proceedings is within the scope of its prescriptive jurisdiction.[103] However, this is not an entirely convincing view in so far as the fine or any other periodic penalty payment is intended to punish and deter, which has enforcement (rather than) prescriptive connotations. Moreover, AG Darmon's suggestion flies in the face of the subsequently adopted Council Regulation 1/2003 which states that '[c]ompliance with Articles [101 and 102 TFEU] and the fulfilment of the obligations imposed on undertakings and associations of undertakings under this Regulation should be *enforceable by means of fines and periodic penalty payments*'.[104]

More importantly, any fine imposed by the competent regulator will be preceded by public-administrative proceedings in which the defendant's procedural rights (as opposed to substantive rights) and the right to fair trial and hearing will have been respected. For example, the hearing officer will have had to 'safeguard the effective exercise of procedural rights throughout competition proceedings before the Commission for the implementation of Articles 101 and 102 of the Treaty [...]'.[105] The procedural rights (being closely linked with enforcement jurisdiction) are naturally at stake in the course of the enforcement proceedings, which are set to protect the substantive rights as protected by the relevant legal order which has jurisdiction to prescribe.

That said, a closer look at the opinion of AG Darmon clearly shows that the type of jurisdiction he refers to is a regulatory one, which is linked with the question of whether EU competition law should apply to determine if the conduct is anti-competitive. Indeed, he clearly states that 'international law would prohibit the extraterritorial *application of domestic law* where it might give rise to conflicting obligations [...] or provoke conflicts of jurisdiction'.[106] It has been noted that '[j]urisdiction involves the decision of a community to assert legal dominion over an act or actor'[107] which would clearly be so in public-administrative proceedings where the relevant regulators would exclusively apply their own competition laws.

In order to set out PIL mechanisms which improve injured parties' access to legal remedies in cross-border cases, the author will consider how the *aspects concerning regulatory jurisdiction* could be linked with the *aspects concerning the adjudicatory jurisdiction*.[108] Whereas the regulatory jurisdiction would presuppose for the court to ascertain competition laws which should regulate the matter (ie the nature of the conduct which may or may not be anti-competitive), the adjudicatory jurisdiction would be central for the court to hear and determine multiple and related antitrust damages claims which arise out of the same transnational competition law infringement.

[102] Ibid [28].

[103] Ibid [30–31].

[104] Recital 29 of Council Regulation 1/2003 – emphasis added by the author.

[105] 2011/695/: *Decision of the President of the European Commission of 13 October 2011 on the function and terms of reference of the hearing officer in certain competition proceedings Text with EEA relevance* [2011] Official Journal L275/29.

[106] *Wood Pulp* – AG Darmon (n 43) [35, 43 and 49].

[107] PS Berman, *Global Legal Pluralism: A Jurisprudence of Law Beyond Borders* (CUP, Cambridge University Press, 2012) 191.

[108] Danov and Otero (n 95).

This means that potentially multiple competition laws (reflecting foreign regulatory interests) would need to be factored in, with a view to determining whether the conduct is anti-competitive as well as with a view to quantifying the antitrust damages.

In order to promote judicial cooperation, it is important to draw a distinction between the jurisdiction to *regulate* competition law aspects of cross-border economic activities and the jurisdiction to *adjudicate* competition law claims (addressing issues concerning the anti-competitive nature of the conduct, causation and quantification of damages in claims with an international element).[109]

III. The US Approach to Extra-Territorial Application of US Antitrust Law

The US Sherman Act has also been applied extra-territorially to foreign anti-competitive practices which have '"direct and substantial effect" on United States foreign commerce'.[110] The Sherman Act states that:

> Sections 1 to 7 of this title shall not apply to conduct involving trade or commerce (other than import trade or import commerce) with foreign nations unless-
>
> (1) such conduct has a direct, substantial, and reasonably foreseeable effect -
>
> (A) on trade or commerce which is not trade or commerce with foreign nations, or on import trade or import commerce with foreign nations; or
>
> (B) on export trade or export commerce with foreign nations, of a person engaged in such trade or commerce in the United States; and
>
> (2) such effect gives rise to a claim under the provisions of sections 1 to 7 of this title, other than this section.
>
> If sections 1 to 7 of this title apply to such conduct only because of the operation of paragraph (1)(B), then sections 1 to 7 of this title shall apply to such conduct only for injury to export business in the United States.[111]

In *Timberlane Lumer v Bank of America*,[112] the claimants issued proceedings and sought antitrust damages under the Sherman Act. The dispute concerned cross-border competition law claims against multiple defendants who were allegedly engaging in anti-competitive practices, which were set to limit claimants' ability to mill lumber in Honduras with a view to exporting it from Honduras to the US. The Bank's anti-competitive practices allegedly enabled it to continue to exercise decisive influence over the Honduran lumber cross-border export trade, which was dominated by selected individuals financed by the Bank. In other words, the Bank was effectively controlling the exportation of lumber from Honduras to the US. It was alleged that such a business practice was in breach of the US antitrust law. In addition to the anti-competitive claim

[109] Ibid.

[110] *Timberlane Lumber Co v Bank of America* 549 F 2d 597 at 610 (9th Cir 1976). See also: *Continental Ore Co v Union Carbide & Carbon Corp* (1962) 370 US 268; *United States v Aluminum Co of America (Alcoa)* 148 F 2d 416 (2d Cir 1945).

[111] 15 USCA § 6a – emphasis added by the author.

[112] *Timberlane Lumber* (n 110).

under the Sherman Act, there were additional claims for personal 'injuries allegedly suffered in the course of the extended anti-Timberlane drama'.[113]

The central issue in *Timberlane Lumer v Bank of America*[114] was whether the transnational economic activities in questions were 'directly and substantially affecting the foreign commerce of the United States'.[115] This would have made the US antitrust law applicable, which would have rendered the US courts competent to hear and determine the dispute. The example is set to signify the fact that the issue of whether the Sherman Act should apply extra-territorially would have significant implications for the injured parties to establish that there was an antitrust infringement. If the answer to this question was affirmative, then the US antitrust law would regulate the competition law aspects of the relevant cross-border economic activities and the US courts would have adjudicatory jurisdiction. If the Sherman Act was not applicable, then the US courts would not exercise their adjudicatory jurisdiction.

A closer look at the cases shows that various strategies have been deployed by the defendants in *Timberlane*. Some 'defendants have not been served and have not appeared'.[116] Other defendants questioned whether the US courts had subject-matter jurisdiction over the competition law claims. The parties' decisions to avoid service and/or challenge the regulatory jurisdiction (ie the territorial scope of the US antitrust law) appeared to indicate that the US courts having regulatory and adjudicatory jurisdiction would have directly impacted on the outcome of the case. In other words, the claimants' access to legal remedies and the scope of the defendants' liability was dependent on the place of litigation.

The defendants were successful in challenging the jurisdiction. The US District Court dismissed the action because it had no subject-matter jurisdiction. The US Court of Appeals allowed the appeal, returning the case to the District Court for reconsidering the issue of jurisdiction. The senior judges took the opportunity to make the following clarifications concerning extra-territorial application of US antitrust law:

> A tripartite analysis seems to be indicated. [… T]he antitrust laws require in the first instance that there be some effect actual or intended on American foreign commerce before the federal courts may legitimately exercise subject matter jurisdiction under those statutes. Second, a greater showing of burden or restraint may be necessary to demonstrate that the effect is sufficiently large to present a cognizable injury to the plaintiffs and, therefore, a civil violation of the antitrust laws. […]. Third, there is the additional question which is unique to the international setting of whether the interests of, and links to, the United States including the magnitude of the effect on American foreign commerce are sufficiently strong, vis-a-vis those of other nations, to justify an assertion of extraterritorial authority.
>
> […] It is this final issue which is both obscured by undue reliance on the 'substantiality' test and complicated to resolve. An effect on United States commerce, although necessary to the exercise of jurisdiction under the antitrust laws, is alone not a sufficient basis on which to determine whether American authority should be asserted in a given case as a matter of international comity and fairness. In some cases, the application of the direct and substantial test

[113] Ibid 601.
[114] Ibid.
[115] Ibid.
[116] Ibid 601.

> in the international context might open the door too widely by sanctioning jurisdiction over an action when these considerations would indicate dismissal. At other times, it may fail in the other direction, dismissing a case for which comity and fairness do not require forebearance, thus closing the jurisdictional door too tightly for the Sherman Act does reach some restraints which do not have both a direct and substantial effect on the foreign commerce of the United States. A more comprehensive inquiry is necessary. We believe that the *field of conflict of laws presents the proper approach.*[117]

The point about private international law techniques being used to determine jurisdiction in cross-border competition law cases is a very strong one, being at the heart of this book. The approach advanced by the court is that, in complex case where legitimate regulatory interests of third countries are at stake, various comity considerations[118] of the claim need to be considered in individual cases, as a part of the so-called 'jurisdictional rule of reason'[119] test. The importance of advancing an approach which enables national judges to consider whether there is a conflict of national competition policies and laws in individual cross-border competition law cases could hardly be questioned. Indeed, the validity of an appropriate balancing exercise was most recently reiterated by the US Court of Appeals (Second Circuit) in *In Re Vitamin C Antitrust Litigation*, where Circuit Judge Hall held:

> the 'comity balancing test' [...] guiding our analysis of whether to dismiss on international comity grounds include: (1) Degree of conflict with foreign law or policy; (2) Nationality of the parties, locations or principal places of business of corporations; (3) Relative importance of the alleged violation of conduct here as compared with conduct abroad; (4) The extent to which enforcement by either state can be expected to achieve compliance, the availability of a remedy abroad and the pendency of litigation there; (5) Existence of intent to harm or affect American commerce and its foreseeability; (6) Possible effect upon foreign relations if the court exercises jurisdiction and grants relief; (7) If relief is granted, whether a party will be placed in the position of being forced to perform an act illegal in either country or be under conflicting requirements by both countries; (8) Whether the court can make its order effective; (9) Whether an order for relief would be acceptable in this country if made by the foreign nation under similar circumstances; and (10) Whether a treaty with the affected nations has addressed the issue.[120]

The problems with the current approach, which indicates that the issue of regulatory jurisdiction (ie applicable set of competition laws) is closely linked with the adjudicatory jurisdiction of the relevant court, were further exposed and appropriately captured in *Hartford Fire*.[121] The dispute involved the insurance service providers. A number of London reinsurance companies entered into an agreement which had the effect to 'deny insurance consumers in the United States property coverage for seepage and pollution'.[122] This has affected a number of insurance markets in the UK and US.

[117] Ibid 613 – emphasis added.
[118] Ibid.
[119] Ibid 615. See also: *Timberlane Lumber Company v Bank of America* 574 F Supp 1453 at 1465 (DC ND California, 1983).
[120] *In Re Vitamin C Antitrust Litigation* 837 F 3d 175, 184–85 (2nd Cir 2016). See also: *Mannington Mills v Congoleum Corporation* 595 F 2d 1287, 1297–1298 (3rd Cir 1979); *Timberlane Lumber* (n 110) 614.
[121] *Hartford Fire Insurance* (n 41).
[122] *In re Insurance Antitrust Litigation* 938 F 2d 919 at 924 (9th Cir 1991).

The competition law claims were issued by the State of California, representing some other states.

The defendants challenged the jurisdiction of the US courts by relying on the Foreign Trade Antitrust Improvement Act 1982 which states that the Sherman Act should not apply to:

> conduct involving trade or commerce (other than import trade or import commerce) with foreign nations unless—
>
> (1) such conduct has a direct, substantial, and reasonably foreseeable effect—
>
> (A) on trade or commerce which is not trade or commerce with foreign nations, or on import trade or import commerce with foreign nations; or
>
> (B) on export trade or export commerce with foreign nations, of a person engaged in such trade or commerce in the United States. [...][123]

The US Court of Appeals took the view that the *Timberlane* approach would be inevitably affected by the 1982 Act.[124] This means that, in order for a competition law dispute to be within the regulatory scope of the US antitrust act, a claimant bringing a competition law action would have to demonstrate that, in line with the 1982 Act, 'the conduct has "a direct, substantial, and reasonable foreseeable effect" on American commerce'.[125] If the statutory requirement is satisfied, then 'it is only in an unusual case that comity will require abstention from the exercise of jurisdiction'.[126] In this context, the *Timberlane* approach concerning 'jurisdiction rule of reason'[127] would need to be applied. After doing the balancing exercise, the US judges took the view that the US courts should assume jurisdiction. More specifically, it was held that:

> A single factor points toward abstention: the conflict with a long-established British policy towards a venerable British trade, the underwriting of insurance. Every other factor – nationality, likelihood of compliance, the significance of the effects on American commerce, their foreseeability and their purposefulness – points to the appropriateness of exercising jurisdiction. [...] The comity factors of *Timberlane* indicate that the court's jurisdiction of the subject matter that exists must be exercised.[128]

The case reached the US Supreme Court,[129] which re-iterated that 'the Sherman Act applies to foreign conduct that was meant to produce and did in fact produce some substantial effect in the United States'.[130] But how would such an approach work in cross-border cases where multiple national competition laws have legitimate interests to regulate the economic activities which affect their markets? What are the major issues that shape the parties' strategies in cross-border competition law cases under the current legal landscape? It is one thing for a national regulator to promote consumer welfare at

[123] 15 USCA § 6a. Conduct involving trade or commerce with foreign nations.
[124] *Insurance Antitrust Litigation* (n 122) 932.
[125] Ibid.
[126] Ibid.
[127] Ibid.
[128] Ibid 934.
[129] *Hartford Fire Insurance* (n 41).
[130] Ibid 2909.

national/regional level, but it is highly unlikely for national regulators to be concerned with enhancing global welfare.[131]

A problem is that '[t]he effects test by itself is incomplete because it fails to consider other national interests. [...] Nor does it expressly take into account the full nature of the relationship between the actors and [the US]'.[132] In order to mitigate these weaknesses, the US courts are required to consider the so-called 'comity question'[133] which entails due consideration of any political dimensions concerning the legitimate regulatory interests of foreign states. The problem is that the advanced comity approach may limit not only the regulatory jurisdiction, but also the adjudicatory jurisdiction of the US courts, which could in turn adversely affect the injured parties' access to appropriate legal remedies.[134] Before outlining the relevant risks in relation to the injured parties' access to legal remedies, an important question is how a conflict of competition laws is to be defined.

IV. Definition of Conflict of Competition Laws for PIL Purposes

The US Supreme Court's judgment appears to suggest that a major PIL issue, which was identified as key in *Hartford Fire Insurance Co v California*, concerned the question of whether there was a conflict between the US law and UK law.[135] There is a strong case that, due to the different (and potentially conflicting) regulatory interests at stake, there could be advantages for parties to issue proceedings in one jurisdiction rather than another. The injured parties (especially, if they are sophisticated enough with access to finance) could be strategic when deciding if and where to issue proceedings in so far as national courts would be exclusively applying their competition laws when ascertaining whether there is a competition law infringement.

A closer analysis of the parties' strategies in *Hartford Fire Insurance*[136] re-iterates that the issues of adjudicatory and regulatory jurisdiction are often perceived by the parties as being central to the outcome of the case. This meant that, in order for the injured parties to rely on the US antitrust law which was to be applicable to the merits of their competition law dispute, it was crucial for the claimants to establish jurisdiction in the US. The stark differences in the US law and UK law might explain why these preliminary issues were subject to heated debates in the US proceedings.

The issue is that, in the absence of a framework for judicial cooperation in private antitrust cases, the national judges may be predominantly interested in applying their own national competition laws with a view to determining whether there is

[131] O Budzinski, *The Governance of Global Competition: Competence Allocation in International Competition Policy* (Edward Elgar, 2008) 32.

[132] *Timberlane Lumber* (n 110) 611–12.

[133] Ibid 615.

[134] See: section V below.

[135] *Hartford Fire Insurance* (n 41).

[136] *Hartford Fire Insurance v California* (1993) 509 US 764.

a competition law infringement in cases where their national markets are affected, without actively factoring in any legitimate regulatory interests of third countries. Therefore, in *Hartford Fire Insurance Co v California*,[137] the US court was of the opinion that there was no true conflict of competition laws. More specifically, the US Supreme Court held that:

> since the London reinsurers do not argue that British law requires them to act in some fashion prohibited by the law of the United States [...] or claim that their compliance with the laws of both countries is otherwise impossible, we see *no conflict with British law*.[138]

In other words, the defendant could have been compliant with both US law and UK law.[139] That said, the narrow definition of conflict of competition laws given by the US court[140] means that the outcome of the dispute could have been different, if the dispute was to be litigated in the UK.

The link between the adjudicatory jurisdiction and the outcome of the dispute (which is central to injured parties' access to appropriate legal remedies) is equally important in public enforcement proceedings before national regulators. The relevant problems were exposed by the conflicting views which were shared by the European Commission[141] and the US Federal Trade Commission[142] in the *Google (Shopping Comparison)* case. The challenges, which policy-makers appear to face in cross-border cases, concern the identification and implementation of an appropriate mode of governance that enables national courts to factor in different regulatory interests in cross-border competition law cases.

Notoriously, in the *Google* case (regarding shopping comparison search engines), the EU and US regulators appeared to share different views about the competitive (or anti-competitive) nature of the Google conduct. In 2013, the US Federal Trade Commission took the view that there was no competition law infringement, submitting that:

> A key issue for the [Federal Trade] Commission was to determine whether Google changed its search results primarily to exclude actual or potential competitors and inhibit the competitive process, or on the other hand, to improve the quality of its search product and the overall user experience. The totality of the evidence indicates that, in the main, Google adopted the design changes that the Commission investigated to improve the quality of its search results, and that any negative impact on actual or potential competitors was incidental to that purpose. While some of Google's rivals may have lost sales due to an improvement in Google's product, these types of adverse effects on particular competitors from vigorous rivalry are a common byproduct of 'competition on the merits' and the competitive process that the law encourages.[143]

[137] *Hartford Fire Insurance* (n 41).

[138] Ibid, 2910–11 – emphasis added.

[139] *Hartford Fire Insurance* (n 41) 2909–10.

[140] An identical definition appears to be advanced in *Wood Pulp* (n 25) [21]. See section II.A above.

[141] Case AT.39740, *Google Search (Shopping) – Commission Decision of 27.6.2017 relating to proceedings under Article 102 of the Treaty on the Functioning of the European Union and Article 54 of the Agreement on the European Economic Area*, C(2017) 4444 final.

[142] Statement of the Federal Trade Commission Regarding Google's Search Practices In the Matter of Google Inc. FTC File Number 111-0163 – 3 January 2013, https://www.ftc.gov/sites/default/files/documents/public_statements/statement-commission-regarding-googles-search-practices/130103brillgooglesearchstmt.pdf.

[143] Ibid 2.

In other words, the US FTC appeared to take the view that Google's conduct was not anti-competitive or abusive, but it was rather economically justifiable business practice that generated certain qualitative efficiencies in the relevant product market. This might as well have adversely affected the business activities of Google's less efficient rivals. But an entirely different view was taken by the EU Commission,[144] which held that:

> The Commission concludes that the Conduct constitutes an abuse of Google's dominant position in each of the thirteen national markets for general search services where Google either launched the Product Universal or, if the Product Universal was never launched in that market, the Shopping Unit. The Conduct is abusive because it constitutes a practice falling outside the scope of competition on the merits as it: (i) diverts traffic in the sense that it decreases traffic from Google's general search results pages to competing comparison shopping services and increases traffic from Google's general search results pages to Google's own comparison shopping service; and (ii) is capable of having, or likely to have, anti-competitive effects in the national markets for comparison shopping services and general search services.[145]

In view of these findings, the EU Commission imposed a fine of EUR 2 billion. The foregoing examples clearly show how different national judges could entirely legitimately take contradictory views on whether the same type of business practice is competitive or anti-competitive.

The level of variation between the outcomes under the US antitrust laws and the EU competition law – albeit undesirable – can legitimately be justified by the fact that different legal orders may well share different competition law objectives. For example, it is well established that the market access is central to the functioning of the EU internal market. Since the EU Member States have conferred exclusive competence on the EU for the 'establishing of the competition rules necessary for the functioning of the internal market',[146] the market access analysis may well be part of any assessment which aims to determine whether a particular conduct distorts the process of competition within the EU internal market. As the EU Commission acknowledged in the *Google* case,[147] the process of competition will be distorted 'not only where access to the market is made impossible for competitors, but also where the conduct of the dominant undertaking is capable of making that access more difficult, thus causing interference with the structure of competition on the market'.[148]

The diametrically opposed outcomes in the proceedings before the European Commission and in the proceedings before the US FTC appear to fly in the face of the Agreement between the Government of the United States of America and the Commission of the European Communities regarding the application of their competition laws (US/EC Agreement).[149] After all, the bilateral legal framework for co-operation

[144] *Google Search (Shopping) – Commission Decision* (n 141).

[145] Ibid [341].

[146] Article 3(1)(b) TFEU.

[147] *Google Search (Shopping) – Commission Decision* (n 141).

[148] Ibid [339].

[149] Agreement between the Government of the United States of America and the Commission of the European Communities regarding the application of their competition laws (US/EU Agreement) [1995] OJ L95/47. See also: Agreement between the European Communities and the Government of the United States of America on the application of positive comity principles in the enforcement of their competition laws [1998] OJ L173/26.

inter alia aims to achieve '[a]voidance of *conflicts* over enforcement activities'.[150] Article VI of the US/EU Agreement states that:

> Within the framework of its own laws and to the extent compatible with its important interests, each Party will seek, at all stages in its enforcement activities, to take into account the important interests of the other Party. Each Party shall consider important interests of the other Party in decisions as to whether or not to initiate an investigation or proceeding, *the scope of an investigation or proceeding*, the nature of the remedies or penalties sought, and in other ways, as appropriate.

However, a closer look at the provision suggests that, despite the opposing outcomes of the relevant competition law proceedings, there may well not be a conflict over enforcement activities within the meaning of the US/EU Agreement. In *Google Search (Shopping)*,[151] the European Commission has only determined the nature of the conduct within the EU, imposing fines in respect to the relevant anti-competitive practices adversely affecting the EU internal market. Therefore, it is possible that there would be case where, as Mr Justice Roth noted, '[t]here was no question of the Commission requiring Google to cease [its] practice as applied to users in countries outside the EEA'.[152] The judge went on to note that this was so despite the fact that 'Google's conduct was not restricted to the EEA and the consequences elsewhere would clearly have reduced the revenues of [its competitors'] groups and thus their ability to fund activities in the EEA'.[153]

Whilst limiting the scope of the competition law infringement would minimise the risk of a conflict of competition laws, an enforcement gap is bound to widen in the jurisdictions where regulators would have limited resources and/or where judges have limited experience in dealing with these cases. The effective competition law enforcement would be a particularly difficult issue in the 'developing countries, which almost by definition do not have the resources to catch and deter violations that originate below their borders'.[154] The identified problems concerning injured parties' access to appropriate legal remedies in such jurisdictions could be better dealt with by drawing a distinction between adjudicatory jurisdiction and regulatory jurisdiction in cross-border competition law disputes. To this end, the scope of the adjudicatory jurisdiction may be broader than the scope of the regulatory jurisdiction. In other words, judges might be expected to apply several sets of foreign competition laws.

A somewhat broader adjudicatory jurisdiction should enable a competent national court to apply its own competition law as well as to factor in the third countries' legitimately regulatory interests in relation to competition law aspects of the relevant economic activities. In addition, there might be a need for a broader definition of a 'conflict of competition laws' which should promote a new form of judicial cooperation in competition law matters. An analogy could be made with Council Regulation 1215/2012 (Brussels Ia) which, being based on the principle of '[m]utual trust in the administration of justice',[155] is inter alia set to 'ensure that irreconcilable

[150] Article VI of the US/EU Agreement.
[151] *Google Search (Shopping) – Commission Decision* (n 141).
[152] *Unlockd Ltd v Google Ireland Ltd* [2018] EWHC 1363 (Ch) [39].
[153] Ibid [43].
[154] Fox (n 8) 154.
[155] Recital 26 of Brussels Ia.

judgments will not be given'.[156] If a broader definition of conflict of competition laws is adopted, national courts may naturally consider and strike a balance between any relevant regulatory interests.[157] The proposed approach may need to be advanced in a global context because, without a regime for judicial cooperation in a global context, there is a real risk that the injured parties across the globe would not be able to access effective remedies.

V. Adjudicatory Jurisdiction – Access to Legal Remedies

One way to minimise the risk of a conflict of competition laws is to limit the territorial scope of national competition laws by encouraging national courts to invoke comity principles.[158] For example, in order to take account of other nations' legitimate interests, the US courts have become more inclined to decline exercising adjudicatory jurisdiction as well as by restrictively ascertaining their regulatory jurisdiction, relying on the doctrine of comity.

The US Supreme Court judgment in *Empagran*[159] appears to limit the court's regulatory and adjudicatory jurisdiction to the local harm as opposed to the 'foreign harm'.[160] In this case, it was held that, since the anti-competitive price-fixing activities and their implementation were largely foreign, the US courts had no regulatory and adjudicatory jurisdiction. The US Supreme Court appeared to link the adjudicatory jurisdiction with the regulatory jurisdiction by submitting: 'why should American law supplant, for example, Canada's or Great Britain's or Japan's own determination about how best to protect Canadian or British or Japanese customers from anticompetitive conduct engaged in significant part by Canadian or British or Japanese or other foreign companies?'[161]

The judgment has been interpreted as an indication that the US 'Supreme Court is receptive to comity when presented as a tool for statutory construction'.[162] In other words, an approach that allows the courts to factor in various comity considerations when deciding to assume jurisdiction enabled the US courts to dismiss the class action brought by foreign purchasers of vitamins[163] in so far as the foreign anti-competitive conduct had played a central role and the foreign injury was independent of domestic effects.[164] The advantage is that such an approach will reduce the risk of a conflict of competition laws by limiting the jurisdiction of the national courts.

[156] Recital 21 of Brussels Ia.
[157] von Mehren (n 29).
[158] HE Yntema, 'The Comity Doctrine' (1966) 65 *Michigan Law Review* 9.
[159] *F Hoffmann-La Roche Ltd v Empagran* (2004) 542 US 155; 124 SCt 2359 (Sup Ct (US)). See more: M Danov, 'Global Competition Law Framework: A Private International Law Solution Needed' (2016) 12 *Journal of Private International Law* 77–105. See also: HL Buxbaum and R Michaels, 'Jurisdiction and Choice of Law in International Antitrust Law – A US Perspective' in J Basedow, S Francq and L Idot (eds), *International Antitrust Litigation: Conflict of Laws and Coordination* (Oxford, Hart Publishing, 2012) 225.
[160] *Empagran* (n 159) 167.
[161] *Empagran* (n 159) 165; See also E Wind, 'Remedies and Sanctions in Article 82 of the EC Treaty' (2005) *European Competition Law Review* 659, 667. See more: Chapters 10 and 11.
[162] ET Swaine, 'Cooperation, Comity, and Competition Policy: United States' in AT Guzman (ed), *Cooperation, Comity, and Competition Policy* (Oxford University Press, 2011) 3, 13.
[163] See: *Empagran* (n 159) 167.
[164] *Empagran* (n 159) 169.

It is well established that '[t]he doctrine of comity [...] posed in stark simplicity the basic dilemma of conflicts law in modern times to mediate between the pretensions of territorial sovereignty and the needs of international commerce'.[165] The importance of comity principles with a view to considering legitimate regulatory interests of other nations was re-iterated by the US court in *Motorola Mobility LLC v AU Optronics Corp.*[166] In this case, it was held that:

> Finding jurisdiction for the United States to prosecute component price-fixing need not ignore the international comity concerns of foreign governments. No nation has objected to the DOJ's successful prosecution of foreign companies and even citizens of that country in the LCD panel investigation. As the United States notes in its brief, the DOJ seriously considers the views of foreign nations before bringing cases .... [T]he comity considerations with private plaintiffs are quite different. '[P]rivate plaintiffs ... often are unwilling to exercise the degree of self-restraint and consideration of foreign governmental sensibilities generally exercised by the U.S. Government.[167]

The judgment re-affirmed Collins's view that '[c]omity may be a discredited concept in the eyes of the textwriters, but it thrives in the judicial decisions'.[168] The application of the doctrine of comity serves as a good example, showing how public international law and private international law inter-relate[169] in cross-border competition law cases. That said, the problem is that the advanced comity approach does not sufficiently allow for foreign regulatory interests to be positively factored in because, whilst it is neutralising any negative effects of extra-territorial application of national competition laws,[170] it does nothing to actively encourage judges to, for example, give effect to foreign regulatory findings with a view to facilitating injured parties' access to effective legal remedies.

Advancing a positive comity approach would be fairly important because very many national judges in developing countries would not have the resources to enforce their national competition laws and provide effective and appropriate remedies for injured parties there.[171] In this context, it is nonetheless important to set out a definition of the proposed positive comity approach. At the moment, a somewhat limited definition of 'positive comity'[172] is to be found in the Agreement between the Government of the United States of America and the European Communities on the Application of Positive Comity Principles in the Enforcement of their Competition Laws, which stipulates that:

> The competition authorities of a Requesting Party may request the competition authorities of a Requested Party to investigate and, if warranted, to remedy anticompetitive activities

[165] Yntema (n 158).
[166] *Motorola Mobility* (n 91).
[167] *Motorola Mobility* (n 91) 827.
[168] L Collins, 'Comity in modern private international law' in JJ Fawcett (ed) *Reform and Development of Private International Law* (Oxford University Press, 2002) 89, 95.
[169] Mills (n 20) 1–2.
[170] See more: Chapter 10.
[171] PM Horna, 'David & Goliath: How young competition agencies can succeed in fighting cross-border cartels' (2017) *The University of Oxford Centre for Competition Law and Policy*, Working Paper CCLP (L) 45; Fox (n 8).
[172] Agreement between the Government of the United States of America and the European Communities on the Application of Positive Comity Principles in the Enforcement of their Competition Laws, Article III.

> in accordance with the Requested Party's competition laws. Such a request may be made regardless of whether the activities also violate the Requesting Party's competition laws, and regardless of whether the competition authorities of the Requesting Party have commenced or contemplate taking enforcement activities under their own competition laws.[173]

A drawback of this definition is that each of the parties will be relying on and applying its own competition law. In other words, there is no possibility for the relevant regulators to apply (or factor in) foreign regulatory interests.

Although this approach may be appropriate for international cooperation between regulators, the author suggests a broader definition of positive comity for the purposes of judicial cooperation. In particular, it is suggested that the courts of England and Wales go a step further and factor in (or even apply) foreign competition laws (expressing foreign regulatory interests) with a view to advancing a transnational approach to judicial cooperation in related competition law cases that arise out of transnational competition law infringements.[174] As part of this process, it is suggested for the courts to rather assume jurisdiction and factor in positively any foreign regulatory interests (minimising the risk of inconsistent findings in related proceedings), whilst providing private parties with access to effective legal remedies.

In this context, it should be further noted that negative comity might adversely affect certain injured parties' access to legal remedies in cross-border competition law cases. There is a risk that, if an appropriate and well-resourced court were to decline jurisdiction, the injured parties will not be able to attain effective remedies elsewhere. As a result, the enforcement gap will continue to widen in a global context. In other words, negative comity might turn out to be problematic in some cases. There appears to be a trend for regulators to limit the scope of their regulatory jurisdiction (which in turn limits their adjudicatory jurisdiction). This approach appears to be articulated by AG Wahl:

> The wording of Articles 101 and 102 TFEU does not justify the application of EU rules by the Commission with respect to conduct that has no 'qualified' effect in the territory of the European Union. To hold the contrary would also be problematic under the rules of public international law. An over-reach of EU competition rules would risk encroaching upon the sovereign interests of other States and be legally and practically difficult to enforce. [...] It would also considerably increase the overlaps in the jurisdictions of different States or polities and thereby create great uncertainty for undertakings and increased risks of conflicting rules (or judgments) applying to the same conduct. Lastly, but no less importantly, it may raise questions under the principle of good administration: what would be the interest in enforcing EU rules with respect to conduct that has no significant effect in the European Union? Would that be a valid and effective use of the European Union's limited resources?[175]

The opinion of AG Wahl appears to suggest that one of the leading competition law jurisdictions may be very guarded when deciding whether to assume adjudicatory jurisdiction with a view to avoiding jurisdictional conflicts.

[173] Ibid – Article III.

[174] See more: Chapter 10.

[175] Opinion of Advocate General Wahl in Case C-413/14 P *Intel Corporation Inc v European Commission* EU:C:2016:788 [303].

The problem with this approach could be illustrated by making a reference to the US court's judgment in *Motorola Mobility LLC v AU Optronics Corp*.[176] In this case, the US court was reluctant to expand 'the global reach of the Sherman Act, creating friction with many foreign countries and "resent[ment at] the apparent effort of the United States to act as the world's competition police officer [...]"'.[177] The issues are important because, despite the fact that such transnational infringements would have affected the prices and caused antitrust damages, the US courts declined to consider whether a more positive approach to comity could have been advanced.

The issues concerning injured parties' access to effective legal remedies are real because it seems that, according to the Court of Appeal of England and Wales,[178] the US court may even be more reluctant to assume jurisdiction:

> there are profound differences between the competition law of the USA and the competition law of the EU, notably including the availability of treble damages under the Sherman Act 1890. Thus, although US federal law provides the origin of the doctrine of qualified effects, and it now has statutory recognition in the Foreign Trade Antitrust Improvements Act 1982, it by no means follows that the test will be applied in the same way under EU law as it would be applied under US law. In particular, the availability of treble damages for claims which satisfy the requirements of the 1982 Act is clearly a potent factor in favour of a relatively restrictive application of the territorial effect of US competition law.[179]

As noted above,[180] the US approach appears to be even more problematic in cases where the damage has been suffered by multinational groups of companies. The issues were exposed in *Motorola Mobility LLC v AU Optronics Corp*.[181] In this case, 'Motorola [suggested for the US courts to] treat it and all of its foreign subsidiaries as a single integrated enterprise, as if its subsidiaries were divisions rather than foreign corporations'.[182] The US courts declined to advance this approach. The judges engaged with *Illinios Brick v Illinios*[183] and made a distinction between the harm suffered by direct purchasers (ie foreign subsidiaries) and the parent company (ie Motorola). It went on to note the various comity considerations by submitting:

> Motorola's foreign subsidiaries were injured in foreign commerce – in dealings with other foreign companies – and to give Motorola rights to take the place of its foreign companies and sue on their behalf under U.S. antitrust law would be an unjustified interference with the right of foreign nations to regulate their own economies. The foreign subsidiaries can sue under foreign law – are we to presume the inadequacy of the antitrust laws of our foreign allies? Would such a presumption be consistent with international comity, or more concretely with good relations with allied nations in a world in turmoil?[184]

The negative comity considerations are important, but equally important would be the positive comity aspects which are central to improving the injured parties' access to

[176] *Motorola Mobility* (n 91).
[177] Ibid 824.
[178] *The LCD Appeals* (n 4) [105].
[179] Ibid [105].
[180] Chapter 3.
[181] *Motorola Mobility* (n 91).
[182] Ibid 820.
[183] *Illinios Brick v Illinios* 97 St C 2061 (1977).
[184] *Motorola Mobility* (n 91) 825.

effective legal remedies. The problem with this approach is that the scope of the adjudicatory jurisdiction of a national court would be limited to the private antitrust damages caused by the breach of its own national competition law. This will mean that the scope of the adjudicatory jurisdiction will overlap with the scope of competition law (ie the regulatory jurisdiction).[185]

A major issue at present appears to be that once a judge had balanced the various regulatory interests and connecting factors in individual cases, the court would either assume or decline jurisdiction, exclusively applying its own competition laws. At present, the US approach appears to be that one single set of competition laws needs to be identified and applied. It has been submitted that:

> In refashioning our approach to applying U.S. statutory law – here antitrust – the Ninth Circuit split the traditional talismanic 'act of state' doctrine into two branches: political affront to a sovereign and choice of law. If there is a political question involved, the court usually chooses to drop the matter, citing the act of state doctrine. […] If not, we pick up the choice of law analysis to assess *which body of law – U.S. or foreign – should be applied*, in light of the quantity and quality of the parties' contacts.[186]

Similarly, the EU Commission would naturally and exclusively apply EU competition law. There is a strong case that such an approach, which suggests that complex regulatory questions should be avoided and one single set of competition laws should be applied, would work less effectively than is desirable in cross-border competition law cases where a number of national/regional regulatory interests are at risk. It appears to be unsatisfactory for a national court to apply one single set of competition laws in cross-border cases despite the fact that different national competition policies may be at risk.[187]

A broader approach to judicial cooperation and positive comity is needed to factor in other countries' regulatory interests by applying a number of sets of competition laws, without an adjudicator necessarily declining to exercise jurisdiction by invoking the doctrine of comity. The problem with an approach, which limits the regulatory jurisdiction of a regulator to apply its own competition law, is that it is highly likely to lead to related proceedings in relation to the same set of cross-border economic activities across the globe as well as to an enforcement gap in some of the developing countries.[188]

There is a strong case that, in cross-border competition law cases, an enhanced level of administrative and judicial cooperation requires a nuanced approach to the issues of jurisdiction. It is necessary to make an appropriate 'distinction between the adjudicatory jurisdiction [of the courts] to determine a cross-border competition law dispute and the regulatory jurisdiction of the legal order to regulate the competition law aspects of the [transnational] economic activities'.[189] The problem was identified in the dissenting opinion of Mr Justice Scalia:

> It is important to distinguish two distinct questions raised by this petition: whether the District Court had jurisdiction, and whether the Sherman Act reaches the extraterritorial conduct

[185] von Mehren and Trautman (n 2) 1128.
[186] *Timberlane Lumber Company* (n 119) 1464 – emphasis added by the author.
[187] von Mehren (n 29) 353.
[188] Horna (n 171); Fox (n 8).
[189] Danov and Otero (n 95) 236. Compare: The dissenting opinion of Justice Scalia in *Hartford Fire Insurance* (n 41) 2909.

> alleged here. On the first question, I believe that the District Court had subject-matter jurisdiction over the Sherman Act claims against all the defendants (personal jurisdiction is not contested). Respondents asserted nonfrivolous claims under the Sherman Act, and 28 U.S.C. § 1331 vests district courts with subject-matter jurisdiction over cases 'arising under' federal statutes. […]
>
> The second question – the extraterritorial reach of the Sherman Act – has nothing to do with the jurisdiction of the courts. It is a question of substantive law turning on whether, in enacting the Sherman Act, Congress asserted regulatory power over the challenged conduct. […] If a plaintiff fails to prevail on this issue, the court does not dismiss the claim for want of subject-matter jurisdiction – want of power to adjudicate; rather, it decides the claim, ruling on the merits that the plaintiff has failed to state a cause of action under the relevant statute.[190]

The distinction drawn by Mr Justice Scalia is important for systematically addressing jurisdictional issues in cross-border cases. This strengthens the argument that a PIL approach to judicial cooperation should allow for a national court to factor in the legitimate regulatory interests of a number of diverse competition law systems with a view to governing cross-border economic activities.

The issues are more important than ever because the growing number of transnational economic (and digital) activities strongly suggests that, if the issues concerning application of third countries' competition laws are not appropriately considered by the national judges, there is a risk for inconsistent outcomes in private antitrust damages claims arising out of the same transnational competition law infringement.[191] The increasingly dense network of global supply chains requires a new approach (ie positive comity) which strengthens injured parties' rights and which facilitates their access to legal remedies.[192] An appropriate solution might be for foreign competition laws to be factored in private antitrust damages claims in England and Wales. It is well established that 'it is for each State to determine, as a matter of domestic law, the extent to which effect is given to foreign laws and judgments'.[193]

VI. A PIL Solution – Balancing Diverse Regulatory Interests

The higher the level of complexity which characterises a cross-border competition law dispute, the lower the number of jurisdictions where the relevant infringement could be effectively put to an end, with appropriate remedies being awarded to injured parties.[194] This means that the injured parties' access to effective legal remedies would often depend on issuing private antitrust proceedings before national courts in a jurisdiction where there are appropriate procedural mechanisms and expertise in dealing with this type of complex disputes.

[190] *Hartford Fire Insurance* (n 41) at 2917–18.
[191] Chapters 10, 11 and 12.
[192] Yntema (n 158) 32.
[193] Ibid 28.
[194] Horna (n 171); Bradford (n 5) 434.

A PIL solution promoting judicial cooperation may address a set of problems which concern the inter-relation between the increasingly transnational corporate structure (which is necessary to facilitate cross-border economic activities for the multi-national groups of companies) and the ineffective enforcement of national competition laws in some jurisdictions. The point was clearly made by the US Court of Appeals in *Motorola Mobility LLC v AU Optronics Corp*:[195]

> Domestic corporate purchasers are not without remedy when buying component parts from foreign vendors. First, the U.S. parent could buy directly from the foreign vendor and preserve the right to sue as a direct purchaser (while trading off the benefits the company gained from operating through a foreign subsidiary). *Or, if a U.S. parent doesn't think that antitrust laws are sufficiently, or fairly, enforced in a given country, they certainly don't have to set up a subsidiary there* … So, an adverse ruling in Motorola would not eliminate every avenue of damage redress for component price-fixing ….[196]

The US judges appear to be indicating that the effective enforcement of competition law could be an issue in certain countries. More specifically, there is a risk that the injured parties' access to appropriate legal remedies may be a real issue in certain jurisdictions.[197] An approach which, despite acknowledging the potential inadequacy of the available remedies and the ineffectiveness of the enforcement regime in the third countries, allows the courts to decline jurisdiction would adversely affect certain injured parties' access to effective legal remedies.

Nonetheless, it seems clear that, given the fact the competition laws naturally reflect national regulatory interests, public international law aspects and the various comity considerations should rightly be at the heart of the regime for judicial cooperation. That said, it would be more appropriate to rather develop a model of judicial cooperation on the basis of positive comity rather than negative comity. The legal implications of the proposed positive comity approach should be twofold. First, the courts of England and Wales should positively factor in foreign regulatory interests,[198] which presupposes certain PIL mechanism to be advanced. Secondly, the courts of England and Wales should positively facilitate injured parties' access to effective legal remedies. In other words, positive comity should set the scene for a PIL solution that may be used to address the issues relating to access to effective legal remedies.

For example, if national judges were to factor in multiple national competition laws (to determine whether there was a competition law infringement), then the adjudicatory jurisdiction would not predetermine such issues as the existence of a competition law infringement as well as the availability of effective legal remedies and quantification of damages.[199] There is another set of adjudicatory aspects which link the place of the relevant competition law proceedings with the broader *justice* categories in relation to injured parties' access to appropriate legal remedies. The interrelation between the place of adjudication and the injured parties' access to effective legal remedies in complex

[195] *Motorola Mobility* (n 91).
[196] Ibid 827 – emphasis added.
[197] Ibid. See also: Section 10.VI below.
[198] Chapter 10, 11, 12 and 13.
[199] Compare: Article 15 of Rome II.

cross-border disputes, which cause mass harm to a number of different claimants, was reiterated by Lord Briggs, sitting at the UK Supreme court:

> Even if the court concludes [...] that a foreign jurisdiction is the proper place in which the case should be tried, the court may nonetheless permit (or refuse to set aside) service of English proceedings on the foreign defendant if satisfied, by cogent evidence, that there is a real risk that substantial justice will not be obtainable in that foreign jurisdiction.[200]

Although this was not a competition law case, a closer level of judicial co-operation in competition law might build on this approach with a view to facilitating injured parties' access to justice. Indeed, an effective regime for private antitrust enforcement in a global context presupposes a level of cooperation between national judges which should not only reduce the multiplicity of proceedings, but it will also reduce the risk of inconsistent outcomes in related proceedings.[201]

In this book the author would argue that a more pro-active approach (ie positive comity), which builds on the various private international law techniques, needs to be promoted by the UK judges with a view to facilitating injured parties' access to legal remedies in cross-border cases. More specifically, it will be demonstrated that, since competition law cases are raising difficult issues concerning transnational competition law infringements, quantification of damages and requiring an appropriate level of expertise, it is increasingly important for the UK judges to take a lead in setting up a new model for judicial cooperation that improves access to justice in cross-border competition cases. This is needed to address the problems concerning the governance of multiple sets of judicial proceedings in relation to the same set of cross-border economic activities which may be regulated differently by the applicable national competition laws.[202]

An appropriately devised PIL framework in England and Wales should set the scene for a level of judicial cooperation in private antitrust disputes. As part of this process, it will be important to consider the extent to which English judges would draw on foreign decisions, establishing competition law infringements.[203] Since the application of multiple competition laws is intertwined with the territorial scope of national competition laws,[204] some difficult issues, which are at the crossroads of public international law and private international law,[205] need to be addressed. There is a view that it is not the creation of a mechanism of judicial cooperation which is important, but it is rather its implementation:

> Cooperation among competition authorities and courts is not a new phenomenon. In fact, there have been early attempts between states – by way of bilateral agreements – to ensure a common line of action against international cartels and improved coordination regarding mergers across the border. An example of this development is the cooperation agreement between the USA and Germany from the year 1976, [...] though the practical relevance of this covenant remained marginal. Nevertheless, this example reflects the fundamental insight that global competition politics must come into existence against the background of

[200] *Vedanta Resources PLC and another (Appellants) v Lungowe and others* (Respondents) [2019] UKSC 20 [88].

[201] Chapters 10, 11 and 12.

[202] Danov and Otero (n 95).

[203] Chapter 12.

[204] Compare: *The LCD Appeals* (n 4).

[205] Mills (n 20); A Mills, 'Federalism in the European Union and the United States: Subsidiarity, Private Law, and the Conflict of Laws' (2010-1) *University of Pennsylvania Journal of International Law* 369–455.

> an accelerating globalization of competition restrictions, if the national and supranational Competition Enforcement is to be effectively implemented.[206]

In view of the existing diversity which is a characteristic feature of the multiple national competition laws as well as in various enforcement models, a PIL solution to the problems concerning coordination of related competition law proceedings could hardly have an alternative. A major issue which needs to be addressed in this context is: how could the interests of multiple national competition law systems be balanced to create a mechanism for judicial cooperation which enables judges to deal effectively with cross-border infringements and provide redress for injured parties across the globe?

VII. Conclusion – Some Major PIL Issues to be Considered

It was demonstrated that the aspects concerning the regulatory jurisdiction would be intertwined with the aspects relating to the adjudicatory jurisdiction of national courts. Another major PIL issue is that, since competition laws pursue certain fundamental regulatory objectives,[207] expressing the public policy of the forum,[208] competition laws would often classify as mandatory provisions for the PIL purposes.[209] In other words, there is a risk that, in related private antitrust damages claims arising out of the same transnational infringement/s, national judges would often need to apply exclusively their very own national competition laws, in order to deal with the relevant regulatory aspects (ie determining whether the conduct in question is anti-competitive).[210]

In theory, PIL mechanisms should be capable of addressing the major issues concerning the applicable competition laws with a view to determining whether there is a competition law infringement which would have an impact on the regulatory and adjudicatory jurisdiction of national courts.[211] Such a transnational regime for judicial cooperation should reduce the risk of inconsistent outcomes in related claims arising out of transnational infringements, whilst allowing national judges to preserve the inherent characteristics of the diverse competition law systems.[212] The issues are

[206] JP Terhechte, *International Competition Enforcement Law Between Cooperation and Convergence* (Springer, Berlin 2011) 10.

[207] ICN Advocacy Working Group, *Competition Culture Project*, 14th ICN Annual Conference, Sydney, 29 April–1 May 2015, 9, https://www.internationalcompetitionnetwork.org/wp-content/uploads/2018/09/AWG_CompetitionCultureReport2015.pdf.

[208] Recital 1 of Directive 2014/104/EU (n 16); *Eco Swiss* (n 16); *Maxicar* (n 16).

[209] Articles 9 and 21 of Rome I; Articles 16 and 26 of Rome II.

[210] See more: Chapter 10. Article 16 of Rome II; Article 9(2) of Rome I. See O Lando, 'The EEC Convention on the law applicable to contractual obligations' (1987) *Common Market Law Review* 159, 207. See also C Withers, 'Jurisdiction and Applicable Law in Antitrust Tort Claims' (2002) *Journal of Business Law* 250, 270.

[211] Danov (n 159); Danov and Otero (n 95).

[212] Compare: HM Watt, 'European integration, legal diversity and the conflict of laws' (2005) 9 *Edinburgh Law Review* 6, 7. See also: M Lehmann, 'Regulation, global governance and private international law: squaring the triangle' (2020) 16 Journal of Private International Law 1; HM Watt, 'Integration and diversity: The Conflict of Laws as a Regulatory Tool' in F Cafaggi (ed), *The Institutional Framework of European Private Law* (Oxford, OUP, 2006) 107; L Tichy, 'A new role for private international law and procedural law in European Integration? A critical comment' in R Brownsword, H-W Micklitz, L Niglia and S Weatherill (eds), *The Foundations of European Private Law* (Oxford, Hart Publishing, 2011) 393–412; Mills (n 212); D Lasok and PA Stone, *Conflict of Laws in the European Community* (Professional Books Limited, Abingdon 1987) pp 144–145.

important, as noted by Professor Guzman,[213] who had some reservations as to whether a choice-of-law mode could be employed as a potent governance mechanism in cross-border competition law cases arising in a global context. In particular, he noted that:

> choice-of-law rules cannot, without more, address the problems of over- and underregulation. A choice-of-law system that allows for overlapping jurisdiction leaves the problem of overregulation unresolved. A system that assigns jurisdiction to a single state can reduce the problem of overregulation but may exacerbate the problem of underregulation. Nor can a choice-of-law strategy prevent local favouritism and trade-induced distortions of national substantive policies.[214]

Although Professor Guzman refers to a choice-of-law regime, the above statement appears to be made in respect to the allocation of jurisdiction. Admittedly, the issues in relation to jurisdiction and choice-of-law may be intertwined in private antitrust claims. As noted above, a major PIL issue is that it is not only that competition laws would apply extra-territorially, but they might also have a mandatory character,[215] expressing the fundamental public interests of the forum. In other words, a major drawback of the existing PIL regime is that, once the jurisdiction is assumed by a competent national court, the judges would normally apply their own competition laws which would classify as 'overriding mandatory provisions'[216] for PIL purposes.[217] Therefore, the difficulty is that the applicable national competition law regime/s (ie regulatory jurisdiction) would have an impact on the adjudicatory jurisdiction of the forum's jurisdiction to adjudicate,[218] which would in turn pre-determine the set of competition laws that should be applied by a national court when ascertaining whether there is a breach of competition law.

It is well settled that an appropriate '[c]hoice-of-law analysis considers which community's legal norms should apply to a dispute involving members of multiple communities'.[219] However, traditional private international law techniques might not easily be adjusted to apply in competition law cases in which multiple national judges would be predominantly applying their national law and policies (rather than factoring in third countries' competition laws). If the national competition law regimes along with 'legal systems of all States are of equal value and deserve the same appreciation',[220] then the author believes that private international law techniques which draw on the concepts of regulatory jurisdiction and positive comity (having public international law connotations) and adjudicatory jurisdiction (having private international law connotations) may set the scene for judicial cooperation in competition law matters. Advancing appropriate private international law techniques may be important for attaining consistent outcomes in related private antitrust damages claims in a global context.

[213] AT Guzman, 'The case for international antitrust' in RA Epstein and MS Greve (eds), *Competition Laws in Conflict: Antitrust Jurisdiction in the Global Economy* (AEI Press, 2004) 99.

[214] Ibid 116–17. See also: Danov (n 159).

[215] See: Chapter 10 below.

[216] Article 16 of Rome II; Article 9(1) of Rome I. See also: Chapter 11.VIII below.

[217] Lehmann (n 212) 24.

[218] *The LCD Appeals* (n 4) [119–121 and 128–132]. See more: von Mehren and Trautman (n 2) 1128.

[219] Berman (n 107) 191.

[220] T Pfeiffer, *Private International Law* in R Wofrum (ed), *The Max Planck Encyclopedia of Public International Law* Volume VIII (Oxford University Press, 2012) 459, 464.

In spite of the fact that the author is not aware of any case where one national court has applied foreign competition law/s with a view to determining whether there is a competition law infringement, a new approach appears to be signalled by the High Court of England and Wales in *JJH Enterprises Ltd (trading as ValueLicensing) v Microsoft*.[221] In this case which concerned a stand-alone claim for damages, the English court appeared to indicate that the judges might be willing to apply different laws (eg EU competition law) when determining whether there is a regulatory breach.[222] The advantage of this approach is that the broader jurisdiction of the English courts to apply foreign competition laws means that the value of the claim would be higher, which would incentivise the litigation funders to provide finance, facilitating the injured parties' access to legal remedies. Could this approach along with von Mehren's 'multi-state rule'[223] actually provide the basis for an appropriate model for international co-operation in cross-border competition law cases? Could such a rule enable a competent adjudicator to take account of the fact that '[several] states have legitimate interests'[224] by applying multiple competition laws?

[221] *JJH Enterprises Ltd (trading as ValueLicensing) v Microsoft* [2022] EWHC 929 (Comm). Likewise, the US courts appear to be prepared to apply UK competition law in private antitrust damages claims. See Case No: 1377/5/7/20, *Epic Games v Apple and Google* [2021] CAT 4 [137-9].

[222] *ValueLicensing* (n 221).

[223] von Mehren (n 29) 366.

[224] Ibid 366.

10

A Transnational Approach – Public Policy and Mandatory Provisions

I. Introduction – Transnational Approach – Applicable (Competition) Laws

In the previous chapter, it was noted that an increased level of globalisation and a higher number of transnational competition law infringements would necessitate an enhanced level of judicial cooperation through private international mechanisms which potentially enable the English judges to factor in different regulatory interests.[1] A major governance issue is the lack of a mechanism for judicial cooperation with regard to multiple related claims which arise out of the same transnational infringement (causing antitrust damages in multiple jurisdictions), and which are issued in different jurisdictions (indicating that different national competition laws may be applicable). Addressing this issue would be central to the effective private enforcement of competition law in a global context.

II. Challenges – Transnational Infringements and Judicial Cooperation

A transnational approach to judicial cooperation is necessary because there is a risk that national judges would predominately apply their own competition laws (safeguarding their own regulatory interests) which could lead to major inconsistencies in related private antitrust damages claims. Moreover, the judiciary, for example, in certain developing countries,[2] may not be capable of efficiently awarding effective legal remedies for injured parties in complex disputes involving sophisticated multinational companies and hi-tech giants.[3] The issues are important because if there were to be an enforcement

[1] Chapter 8. See also: J Penrose MP, *Power to the people: stronger consumer choice and competition so markets work for the people, not the other way around* – February 2021, 17.

[2] EM Fox, 'Linked-In: Antitrust and the Virtues of a Virtual Network' (2009) *The International Lawyer* 151, 154.

[3] RA Posner, 'Antitrust in the New Economy' (2001) 68 *Antitrust LJ* 925.

gap in a global context then '[e]xternalities can arise both across borders, and among stakeholder groups'.[4] There is a highly persuasive view that:

> Weak enforcement of antitrust rules [...] in one nation may have a negative impact on the profits of foreign based producers whose products are thereby squeezed out of the market. To the extent that these spillover effects are not based on market-clearing effects, but rather driven by strategic behaviour, suboptimal results must be anticipated. To avoid welfare losses and market distortions, such externalities must be corrected through some form of interjurisdictional collective action.[5]

This quotation strongly suggests that judicial cooperation in competition law matters would be important to providing injured parties with access to legal remedies and closing any enforcement gap in a cross-border context. The aspects concerning international cooperation are also reflected in the UK/EU Trade and Cooperation Agreement which states that 'the Parties recognise the importance of cooperation between their respective competition authorities with regard to developments in competition policy and enforcement activities'.[6]

However, the UK/EU Trade and Cooperation Agreement is not broad enough to cover judicial cooperation in competition law matters,[7] which might be a particularly important omission in follow-on private antitrust damages claims. This means that a new approach to judicial cooperation should be advanced with a view to facilitating the injured parties access to legal remedies in related private antitrust damages claims which arise out of the same transnational competition law infringement.

The Brexit developments strongly indicate that the changing political landscape is another major hurdle which needs to be overcome with a view to devising a transnational regime for judicial cooperation in competition law matters. There is a risk that, if there are no effective remedies for injured parties who have sustained damages caused by transnational competition law infringements, certain multinational companies will not be deterred from maximising their profits by deploying conduct which might be distorting the process of competition (eg affecting the prices in multiple jurisdictions).

A problem is that the process of globalisation has not only promoted an ever-increasing number of transnational economic activities, but it has also intensified national populism[8] movements across the globe. The difficult policy choices, which must be made, have been identified by a former EU Commission's Director General for Competition, Mr Philip Lowe. The former Director General took the view that the '[g]lobalisation and increasing competitive pressure will not make [policy-makers'] task easier. We will be asked to explain why competition and not protectionism is crucial to make our industries more competitive'.[9]

[4] B Gabor, *Regulatory Competition in the Internal Market: Comparing Models for Corporate Law, Securities Law and Competition Law* (Cheltenham, Edward Elgar, 2013) 7.

[5] DC Esty and D Geradin, 'Regulatory Co-operation' in DC Esty and D Geradin (eds), *Regulatory Competition and Economic Integration* (Oxford, OUP, 2001) 30, 34. See also: M Danov and F Becker, 'Concluding Remarks on Promoting Regulatory Competition: Issues to be Addressed' in in M Danov, F Becker and P Beaumont (eds), *Cross-border EU Competition Law Actions* (Oxford, Hart Publishing, 2013) 81, 92.

[6] Article 361(1) of the UK/EU Trade and Cooperation Agreement.

[7] Compare: Part Three of the UK/EU Trade and Cooperation Agreement.

[8] R Eatwell and M Goodwin, *National Populism: The Revolt against Liberal Democracy* (Penguin UK, 2018).

[9] P Lowe, Director General Directorate General for Competition European, 'Commission International Cooperation between competition agencies: Achievements and challenges' – *4th Seoul International Competition Forum* at 5, https://ec.europa.eu/competition/speeches/text/sp2005_021_en.pdf.

In order to advance a transnational approach to the issues of applicable (public) competition laws, PIL techniques which are sufficiently flexible need to be considered. This chapter aims to demonstrate that a PIL mechanism – which draws on the principles of positive comity[10] and which allows and encourages the courts of England and Wales to factor in different and legitimate regulatory interests[11] – should set the scene for judicial cooperation in competition law matters in a global context.[12] Such a PIL mechanism is necessary to improve injured parties' access to effective legal remedies in related private antitrust damages claims that arise out of the same anti-competitive conduct that is deployed across the globe.

An added layer of complexity is that, as already noted above,[13] Mr Justice Aikens's judgment in *Provimi*[14] draws a distinction between the applicable (public) competition law issues in relation to the infringement and the (private) laws in relation to tortious (or contractual) issues with a view to quantifying the antitrust damages.[15] Although the regulatory aspects concerning the breach of EU competition law were only briefly dealt with by the High Court of England and Wales in *Provimi*,[16] the issues concerning the territorial scope of competition laws (ie regulatory jurisdiction) were dealt with by the EU Commission in the public enforcement proceedings[17] which preceded the private antitrust damages claims.

More specifically, the EU Commission noted the question of territorial regulatory jurisdiction may be intertwined with the potentially parallel regulatory proceedings abroad:

> (772) [...] The exercise by the United States of America (or any third country) of its (criminal) jurisdiction against cartel behaviour can in no way limit or exclude the Commission's jurisdiction under [EU] competition law.
>
> (773) More importantly, it is in any case untrue that the Commission was intending to sanction it for the same facts as the US courts had. By virtue of the principle of territoriality, Article [101 TFEU] is limited to restrictions of competition in the [internal] market and Article 53 EEA is limited to restrictions of competition in the EEA market. In the same way, the US antitrust authorities only exercise jurisdiction to the extent that the conduct has a direct and intended effect on US commerce.[18]

This quotation reiterates that, in order to safeguard important public interests, competition laws may be enforced in public enforcement proceedings before various national

[10] See: Chapter 9.

[11] AT von Mehren, 'Special Substantive Rules for Multistate Problems: Their role and significance in contemporary choice of law methodology' (1974–1975) 88 *Harvard Law Review* 347.

[12] Esty and Geradin (n 5) 32–40. See also: Danov and Becker (n 5) 92.

[13] Chapter 3.II and Chapter 9 above.

[14] *Provimi Limited v Aventis Animal Nutrition SA and Others* [2003] EWHC 961 (Comm) [25].

[15] Ibid.

[16] *Provimi Limited v Aventis Animal Nutrition SA and Others* [2003] EWHC 961 (Comm).

[17] Case COMP/E-1/37.512, *Vitamins* – Commission Decision of 21 November 2001 relating to a proceeding pursuant to Article 81 of the EC Treaty and Article 53 of the EEA Agreement (Case COMP/E-1/37.512 – Vitamins) (notified under document number C(2001) 3695) (Text with EEA [2003] Official Journal L6/1–89 [772–3].

[18] Case COMP/E-1/37.512, *Vitamins* – Commission Decision of 21 November 2001 relating to a proceeding pursuant to Article 81 of the EC Treaty and Article 53 of the EEA Agreement (Case COMP/E-1/37.512 – Vitamins) (notified under document number C(2001) 3695) (Text with EEA [2003] Official Journal L6/1–89 [772-3].

regulators (ie competition authorities) as well as in private enforcement proceedings before various national courts.[19] Likewise, the judgment of the Court of Appeal of England and Wales in *The LCD Appeals*[20] might be interpreted as suggesting that the classification[21] of a specific act that restricts competition will be central to applying the connecting factors (eg implementation; qualified effects) and determining whether the conduct is within the 'territorial scope'[22] of UK competition law.[23]

The PIL problem is that if national competition laws were to have a mandatory character, the regulatory issues would be dealt with differently, depending on where the proceedings are taking place. The aspects in relation to consistent outcomes in such related disputes are important because, bearing in mind the increasing prominence of global supply chains, the lack of a framework for judicial cooperation strongly indicates that the multiplicity of proceedings in relation to the same infringement would be a major governance issue. This means that a judge may need to determine, in the first place, whether the competition laws at the place of litigation would be classified as 'overriding mandatory rules'. According to Professor Hartley:

> The concept of a mandatory provision is [...] a form of escape mechanism. Mandatory provisions are provisions that have to be applied – despite the fact that they are not part of the normal applicable law – because their application in the particular circumstances of the case is regarded as essential by a particular country for safeguarding its public interests.[24]

The fact that competition law expresses the legitimate concern of a national competition law regime to regulate the competition law aspects of transnational economic activities which have produced certain effects in their territory raises the following questions: how is the relevant act restricting competition to be classified? Does the anti-competitive conduct meet the effects test[25] for the UK competition laws and/or EU competition laws to apply, considering aspects in relation to the regulatory jurisdiction and the territorial scope of the competition law/s?[26]

III. Competition Laws: 'Overriding mandatory provisions'[27] and 'Public Policy'[28]

A very important preliminary issue is whether the competition laws of the jurisdiction where the proceedings are taking place would classify as 'overriding mandatory

[19] Case Numbers 1377/5/7/20 and 1378/5/7/20, *Epic Games v Apple. Alphabet and Google* [2021] CAT 4 [139].

[20] *The LCD Appeals* [2018] EWCA Civ 220.

[21] Chapter 3.

[22] *The LCD Appeals* (n 20) [22].

[23] See: Chapter 9.

[24] T Hartley, 'Public Policy and Mandatory Provisions' in P Beaumont and J Holliday (eds), *A Guide to Global Private International Law* (Oxford, Hart, 2022) 75, 76.

[25] *The LCD Appeals* (n 20); Case C-413/14 P *Intel v Commission*, EU:C:2017:632.

[26] *The LCD Appeals* (n 20) [90–98].

[27] Article 16 of Rome II; Article of 9 of Rome I.

[28] Article 26 of Rome II; Article of 21 of Rome I.

provisions'[29] which should apply 'irrespective of the law otherwise applicable'[30] to the competition law claim/s. If the response to this question is in the affirmative, national courts would normally exercise their regulatory jurisdiction by applying their own competition laws. In other words, if a private antitrust damages claim is within the ambit of the concept of *civil and commercial matters*,[31] then the fact that competition laws are set to regulate the economic activities of undertakings, safeguarding the consumers' welfare and promoting efficiencies means that another set of classification issues concerning the mandatory character of the relevant competition law provisions would arise in the context of Rome I and II.

The classification issues concerning the mandatory nature of competition laws are bound to arise, irrespective of whether the dispute is raising contractual matters (falling within the scope of Article 9 of the Rome I Regulation) and/or non-contractual matters (being within the ambit of Article 16 of the Rome II Regulation). Addressing the aspects concerning the public policy nature of competition laws would be central to advancing a transnational approach to the issues of applicable law in competition law claims arising out of transnational infringements.

It should be noted that the PIL theory distinguishes the competition law provisions which should classify as mandatory (eg prohibiting cartels agreements and/or abuses of dominant positions) from the principles which reflect the national public policy (eg treble damages being in conflict with the British public policy).[32] The mandatory provisions are clearly set out rules which regulate the competition law aspects of economic activities, expressing national public policy.[33] According to Chong:

> The generally accepted dividing line between the two is that public policy operates negatively in that it involves the disapplication of the relevant applicable law, […] while mandatory rules operate positively in that they are superimposed onto the applicable law of the contract.[34]

It seems that in the context of cross-border competition law claims which are issued in the EU, there is a fine line between the overriding mandatory provisions and the public policy because the CJEU jurisprudence strongly indicates that competition law provisions are set to express the national public policy.[35] The EU competition law provisions are often classified as 'fundamental provision[s], which [are] essential for the

[29] Article 16 of Rome II.

[30] Article 16 of Rome II.

[31] See: Chapter 3.

[32] P Nygh, *Autonomy in International Contracts* (Oxford, OUP, 1999) 206–208; A Chong, 'The public policy and mandatory rules of third countries in international contracts' (2006) 2 *Journal of Private International Law* 27, 32–35.

[33] Nygh (n 32) 206; Chong (n 32) 32.

[34] Chong (n 32) 32. See also: J Harris, 'Mandatory rules and public policy under the Rome I Regulation' in F Ferrari and S Leibbe (eds), *Rome I Regulation: The Law Applicable to Contractual Obligations in Europe* (Sellier, Munich 2009) 268, 297–298.

[35] Case C-126/97 *Eco Swiss China Time Ltd v Benetton International NV* EU:C:1999:269 [39]. See also: Recital 1 of Directive 2014/104/EU on certain rules governing actions for damages under national law for infringements of the competition law provisions of the Member States and of the European Union [2014] Official Journal L349/1; Case C-38/98 *Régie nationale des usines Renault SA v Maxicar SpA and Orazio Formento* EU:C:2000:225. See more: HP Meidans, 'Public policy and *ordre public* in the private international law of the EC/EU: Traditional positions of the Member States and modern trends' (2005) 30 *EL Rev* 95; J-P Beraudo, 'Egregious error of law as grounds for setting aside an arbitral award' (2006) 23 *Journal of International Arbitration* 351.

accomplishment of the tasks entrusted to the [EU] and, in particular, for the functioning of the internal market'.[36]

Since the Competition Act 1998 (as well as Articles 101 and 102 TFEU) clearly specifies the anti-competitive conduct which is prohibited, it seems clear that the Chapters 1 and 2 (as well as Articles 101 and 102 TFEU) prohibitions would likely classify as 'overriding mandatory provisions'[37] for the purposes of Rome I and II. Such interpretation would be in line with Article 9(1) of the Rome I Regulation, which provides the following definition:

> Overriding mandatory provisions are provisions the respect for which is regarded as crucial by a country for safeguarding its public interests, such as its political, social or economic organisation, to such an extent that they are applicable to any situation falling within their scope, irrespective of the law otherwise applicable to the contract under this Regulation.[38]

Thus, there are very strong arguments suggesting that the definition of 'overriding mandatory provisions' should cover UK competition law rules.[39] The point can be reinforced by making reference to the Giuliano and Lagarde Report,[40] which indicates that the rules on cartels, competition, restrictive practices and abuse of dominant position would inter alia classify as 'overriding mandatory provisions'.[41] This is indeed reflected in the Antitrust Damages Directive:

> Articles 101 and 102 of the Treaty on the Functioning of the European Union (TFEU) are a matter of public policy and should be applied effectively throughout the Union in order to ensure that competition in the internal market is not distorted.[42]

Post-Brexit, it seems clear that the English judges should also take the view that the prohibitions set out in Chapters 1 and 2 of the 1998 Act will enjoy public policy character. Indeed, the unique public interest in the enforcement of competition law is further reflected in the Enterprise Act 2002, which introduced criminal sanctions for individuals who have engaged in hard-core cartels.[43]

Article 16 of the Rome II Regulation states that '[n]othing in this Regulation shall restrict the application of the provisions of the law of the forum in a situation where they are mandatory irrespective of the law otherwise applicable to the non-contractual obligation'. The rule is identical to the text of Article 9(2) from the Rome I Regulation.[44] Both provisions strongly indicate that UK competition law rules are to be regarded as overriding mandatory provisions for private international law purposes. This means

[36] *Eco Swiss* (n 35) [36]; *Maxicar* (n 35); Recital 1 of Directive 2014/104/EU.

[37] Article 16 of Rome II; Article of 9 of Rome I. See more: S Francq and W Wurmnest, 'International Antitrust Claims under the Rome II Regulation' in J Basedow, S Francq and L Idot (eds), *International Antitrust Litigation: Conflict of Laws and Coordination* (Hart Publishing, Oxford 2012) 91, 114–17.

[38] See more: Harris (n 34) 292–97 and 334–41.

[39] C Withers, 'Jurisdiction and Applicable Law in Antitrust Tort Claims' (2002) *Journal of Business Law* 250, 270.

[40] M Giuliano and P Lagarde, *Report on the Convention on the law applicable to contractual obligations* [1980] Official Journal C 282/1.

[41] Ibid 28.

[42] Recital 1 of Directive 2014/104/EU. Case 172/73 *BRT v SABAM* [1974] ECR 51. See also: Giuliano and Lagarde Report (n 40) p 28.

[43] 'Sections 188–202 provide for a criminal offence for individuals who dishonestly engage in cartel agreements' – Enterprise Act 2002 Explanatory Notes [401]. See more: P Whelan, 'Section 47 of the Enterprise and Regulatory Reform Act 2013: A Flawed Reform of the UK Cartel Offence' (2015) 78(3) *Modern Law Review* 493.

[44] See more: Chapter 11.VIII below.

that the provisions of the competition law of the forum would always apply 'irrespective of the law otherwise applicable to the non-contractual obligation'[45] and 'irrespective of the law otherwise applicable to the contract under th[e Rome I] Regulation.'[46]

A. Foreign Competition Laws – Regulatory Infringements (Scope of Rome II)[47]

A difficult question is whether the UK competition law rules would exclusively apply if the market in another country was also 'directly and substantially affected by the restriction of competition out of which the non-contractual obligation on which the claim is based arises'[48] or should the English judges rather apply foreign competition laws as well. In other words, a fairly complex matter, which is bound to arise in cross-border cases, concerns the question whether a foreign set of competition laws could be applied by the courts of England and Wales or the UK CAT with a view to ascertaining whether there is a competition law infringement.

The response to this question would matter in cases where, for example, the allegedly prohibited anti-competitive conduct has had the effect of restricting competition in the EU as well as in the UK (being a non-EU market where EU competition law no longer applies) and the US. Could/should the courts of England and Wales or the UK CAT also apply EU competition law and/or the US antitrust law? Can the English courts make a conflict-of-laws analysis, in order to decide which set of overriding mandatory provisions should apply in competition cases, where the applicable UK competition law and/or EU competition law and/or the US antitrust law regulate the matter differently? It has been submitted by Withers that:

> it is difficult to discern any compelling policy interest in favour of the application of English and European antitrust laws to disputes involving anti-competitive activities taking place outside Europe, sufficient to justify their treatment as mandatory rules of the forum. It is therefore, suggested that they should not be regarded as imposing on the courts a duty to apply those laws when a choice of law rule selects the antitrust laws of a foreign jurisdiction as applicable to the activity taking place in that jurisdiction.[49]

Although, the above quotation is advanced prior to the adoption of Rome II, one can see the attraction of an approach which allows the English courts to take account of legitimate and foreign regulatory interests when determining whether there is a breach of competition law. However, there might be a problem to advance such an approach under Rome II which – as opposed to Article 9(3) of Rome I – does not expressly allow for the English courts to give effect to the 'the overriding mandatory provisions' of third countries (ie giving effect to foreign competition laws).[50]

[45] Article 16 of Rome II;.
[46] Article 9(2) of Rome I.
[47] See more: Chapter 11.II below.
[48] Article 6(3)(b) of Rome II.
[49] Withers (n 39) 268.
[50] H Mercer, 'Applicable Law in Cross-Border EU Law Actions – Forum Shopping, Mandatory Rules and Public Policy' in Danov, Becker and Beaumont (n 5) 329, 333. See more: Chapter 11.VIII below.

That said, the English courts should not enforce a contract that is in conflict with foreign antitrust laws and whose performance would be in conflict with the antitrust laws at the place where the contract is to be performed.[51] Such an approach is 'based on the principle that it is contrary to the comity of nations that the Court of one country should seek to enforce the performance of something in another country which is forbidden by the law of that country'.[52] The comity considerations would be particularly important to advance a level of judicial cooperation. In particular, drawing on comity considerations, the English courts could factor in foreign competition law which reflects foreign regulatory interests; but this would be only so if the performance of the contract had been in conflict with the foreign competition laws.[53]

However, if the foreign conduct had been legitimate and compliant with the foreign antitrust laws, but had been prohibited by UK competition law, then the wording of Article 9(3) of Rome I appears to suggest that the foreign antitrust law would not be given any effect.[54] In such circumstances, UK competition law should exclusively apply to determine whether the conduct is anti-competitive as long as the implementation and/or qualified effects tests have been satisfied. Should a somewhat broader approach be advanced under Rome II, enabling judges to factor in foreign competition laws, post-Brexit? The editors of *Dicey, Morris & Collins*[55] have submitted that:

> Article 6(3) concerns the determination of the law applicable to non-contractual obligations arising out of a restriction of competition. [... T]he reference in Art.6(3)(a) is to the law of the country where the market is, or is likely to be, affected, without any restrictions on the country whose law is involved, [...] while Recital (22) envisages application of the competition law of any country where the market is, or is likely to be, affected. The possibility is thus opened up of the English courts applying United States' anti-trust law in respect of acts which are characterised as acts restricting free competition, committed in England, which affect the market in the United States, though this may be subject to the public policy exception within Art.16 of the Rome II Regulation.[56]

Although this quotation appears to indicate that the English courts would apply US antitrust law, the editors of *Dicey, Morris & Collins*[57] appear to be citing Article 6(3) of Rome II which could be interpreting as indicating that they are limiting their analysis to 'the law applicable to a non-contractual obligation arising out of a restriction of competition' without making a distinction between the issues concerning the *regulatory breach* and the issues concerning *remedies and quantifications of damages*.[58]

[51] Compare: *R v International Trustee for Bondholders AG* [1937] AC 500, 519 (Lord Wright). See also Nygh (n 32) 224–25; A Briggs, *Agreements on Jurisdiction and Choice of Law* (Oxford, OUP, 2008) 395.

[52] *International Trustee for Bondholders* (n 51) 519 (Lord Wright). See also: L Collins, 'Comity in modern private international law' in JJ Fawcett (ed), *Reform and Development of Private International Law* (OUP, Oxford, 2002) 89, 99.

[53] Harris (n 34) 320–21.

[54] See more: Chapter 11.VIII below.

[55] L Collins and J Harris (eds) *Dicey, Morris and Collins on the Conflict of Laws* 16th edn (London, Sweet & Maxwell, 2022) Rule 244(3).

[56] Ibid [35-066].

[57] Ibid Rule 244(3).

[58] See more: Chapter 11.II below.

Moreover, the fact that the editors of *Dicey, Morris & Collins*[59] make a reference to Recital 22 might suggest that they appear to be predominantly considering the aspects in relation to the 'law applicable to the non-contractual obligations'[60] (which should cover such aspects as heads of damages and quantification of damages) as opposed to the competition laws (or the regulatory regime) which would be applicable to ascertain whether there is any 'restriction of competition'.[61] In this context, it should be noted that the Rome II Regulation appears to distinguish the aspects concerning 'non-contractual obligations'[62] (ie compensatory claims for damages – where the law of any country should apply with regard to causation and quantum) and the 'concept of restriction of competition'[63] which is explicitly defined as follows:

> For the purposes of this Regulation, the concept of restriction of competition should cover prohibitions on agreements between undertakings, decisions by associations of undertakings and concerted practices which have as their object or effect the prevention, restriction or distortion of competition within a Member State or within the internal market, as well as prohibitions on the abuse of a dominant position within a Member State or within the internal market, where such agreements, decisions, concerted practices or abuses are prohibited by *Articles [101 and 102 TFEU] or by the law of a Member State*.[64]

The above quotation makes it clear that EU competition law or the EU Member States' competition laws are to exclusively apply with a view to ascertaining whether the conduct would restrict the process of competition.[65] Since, as noted above, the competition law rules would normally classify as overriding mandatory provisions, safeguarding the public interests of the forum, the reading of Recital 23 along with Article 16 of Rome II seems to indicate that the provisions were set to primarily cover follow-on private antitrust damages claims (in which the competition law infringement would be established by an EU regulator). The deduction could be strengthened by making reference to Rome II, which suggests that there is an obligation for national judges to only apply the overriding mandatory provisions which are set out in 'the law of the forum'.[66]

The problem with Rome II is that it requires EU Member States' judges to determine whether there is a restriction of competition by exclusively applying their own competition law, which include EU competition law rules and which classify as overriding mandatory provisions (as long as the conduct has been implemented or has qualified effect within the jurisdiction).[67] The issue with the Rome II approach is that it would fly in the face of a major PIL principle for national judges to apply the same sets of laws irrespective of where the parties litigate, which is set to enhance certainty and predictability in cross-border disputes.[68]

[59] *Dicey, Morris and Collins* (n 55) – Rule 244(3).
[60] Recital 22 of Rome II.
[61] Recital 23 of Rome II.
[62] Recital 22 of Rome II.
[63] Recital 23 of Rome II.
[64] Recital 23 of Rome II – emphasis added by the author. See more: Francq and Wurmnest (n 33) 100–102.
[65] See more: Chapter 11.II below.
[66] Article 16 of Rome II.
[67] *The LCD Appeals* (n 20).
[68] Compare: Recital 6 of Rome II.

In view of this, post-Brexit, the UK judges might adopt a different approach by classifying the concept of restriction of competition as encompassing a breach of foreign competition laws (eg US antitrust law; EU competition law in cases where Articles 101 and 102 TFEU are no longer directly applicable in the UK) which might inter alia have implications for the value of the claim. Although the wording of Article 16 (when read along with Recital 23) of Rome II is somewhat restrictive, it does not preclude the English judges from applying the competition laws of other countries, post-Brexit, by broadly interpreting 'the concept of restriction of competition'.[69]

Given the fact that the Rome II appears to be drafted to cover only follow-on private antitrust damages which arise in the EU context, there is an argument for the English court to adopt a broader interpretation of the scope of Rome II, post-Brexit, in the context of stand-alone competition law actions. In *ValueLicensing v Mircosoft*,[70] Mr Justice Picken signalled that the English courts may be prepared to apply EU competition law (factoring foreign regulatory interests) in stand-alone claims which concern conduct that covers a post-Brexit period of time. In particular, the High Court of England and Wales held that:

> for events giving rise to damage from the start of the infringement (2016 at the latest) to the end of the Brexit transition period, ValueLicensing's claims are governed by English law, which in that period included Articles 101 and 102 of the TFEU, as well as the corresponding EEA rules. *As for the post-Brexit period, ValueLicensing's claims are governed by the laws of the countries where the market was (or was likely to be) affected through the application of Article 6(3)(a) of Rome II, namely the markets, and therefore the laws, of the UK and the EU and EEA member states.*[71]

Therefore, in the spirit of international cooperation, an 'internationalist'[72] approach to classification of *restriction of competition* may allow for the English courts to factor in foreign competition laws, expressing foreign regulatory interests.[73] More importantly, if the courts of England and Wales were to deal with these issues differently (and apply Rome II broadly to cover competition law restrictions), then the English courts may apply different laws (eg EU competition law) when determining whether there is a regulatory breach. Indeed, there is a view that the 'court should not […] have any qualms of applying foreign […] antitrust […] rules'.[74] The regulatory issues and the related classification aspects will become even more important in a post-*Brexit* context with a view to ascertaining the applicable set of public competition laws.

There is a strong argument that – given the public policy character[75] of national competition law provisions (and their mandatory nature in particular) – a PIL approach which requires a competent national court to exclusively rely on 'a single governing [competition] law for resolution of multistate disputes'[76] may not appropriately work in

[69] Recital 23 of Rome II. See more: Chapter 11.II.
[70] Compare: *JJH Enterprises Ltd (trading as ValueLicensing) v Microsoft* [2022] EWHC 929 (Comm) [44].
[71] Ibid [44] – emphasis added by the author.
[72] *Raiffeisen Zentralbank Osterreich AG v Five Star Trading LLC and others* [2001] EWCA Civ 68 [26].
[73] See: Chapter 11.II below.
[74] M Lehmann, 'Regulation, global governance and private international law: squaring the triangle' (2020) 16 *Journal of Private International Law* 1, 20.
[75] *Eco Swiss* (n 35) [36]; *Maxicar* (n 35); Recital 1 of Directive 2014/104/EU.
[76] von Mehren (n 11) 353.

cross-border cases. This would be particularly so with regard to transnational competition law infringements which would distort competition and cause antitrust damages in multiple jurisdictions.[77]

B. 'Public Policy of the Forum'[78] – Remedies and Liability in Private Antitrust Damages Claims

It is well established that in cases where foreign laws were to apply to tortious competition law claims falling within the scope of Rome II 'the provisions of that foreign law [should] apply, subject only to the public policy exception'.[79] This is clearly reflected in Article 26 of Rome II which states that: 'The application of a provision of the law of any country specified by this Regulation may be refused only if such application is manifestly incompatible with the public policy (*ordre public*) of the forum'.

An important question is whether an English court or the UK CAT might award exemplary damages when applying foreign law under Rome II. Although Schedule 8 of the Competition Act 1998 now states that '[a] court or the Tribunal may not award exemplary damages in competition proceedings',[80] some other jurisdictions might award exemplary or punitive damages.[81] The response to the question of whether English courts may apply foreign laws which award exemplary damages pre-supposes for the English judges to consider the legal implications of Recital 32, which states that:

> the application of a provision of the law designated by this Regulation which would have the effect of causing non-compensatory exemplary or punitive damages of an excessive nature to be awarded may, depending on the circumstances of the case and the legal order of the Member State of the court seised, be regarded as being contrary to the public policy (*ordre public*) of the forum.

Professor Hay has noted that 'Recital 32 […] acknowledges the aversion of many states against punitive damages and expressly authorizes the refusal to award them under the law otherwise applicable under the Regulation'.[82] The author[83] has taken the view that, since the exemplary damages would be 'additional to an award which fully compensates the claimant for his loss, and which are intended to punish and deter',[84] exemplary or punitive damages should naturally classify as excessive for the purposes of the Rome II Regulation. In other words, it has been argued that Article 26 and Recital 32 of Rome II

[77] See more: Chapter 11.II below.

[78] Article 26 of Rome II; Article 21 of Rome I.

[79] Case Numbers 1240/5/7/15 and 1244/5/7/15, *Deutsche Bahn AG and Others v MasterCard Inc* [2016] CAT 14 [50].

[80] See also: Competition Act 1998 s 47C(9)(b). Compare: Case Number 1178/5/7/11, *2 Travel Group Plc (In Liquidation) v Cardiff City Transport Services Ltd* [2012] CAT 19.

[81] Case C-295/04 *Vincenzo Manfredi v Lloyd Adriatico Assicurazioni SpA EU:C:2006:461* [93] and [99].

[82] P Hay, 'The Development of the public policy barrier to judgment recognition within the European Community' (2007) *The European Legal Forum* 289, 293.

[83] M Danov, *Jurisdiction and Judgments in Relation to EU Competition Law Claims* (Oxford, Hart Publishing, 2010).

[84] *Devenish Nutrition Ltd v Sanofi-Aventis SA* [2007] EWHC 2394 (Ch) [14].

would cumulatively enable the English courts to refuse, on the grounds of public policy, to award exemplary damages, which may classify as excessive in England.[85]

Somewhat more nuanced and rather flexible views have been expressed by Professors Beaumont and Tang, who have rightly reiterated that Recital 32 does not 'categorise all exemplary or punitive damages as being contrary to public policy but only "excessive" damages in those categories'.[86] A level of flexibility should enable the English court to apply foreign law and award exemplary damages in cases where the compensatory damages were 'inadequate to punish [the defendant] for his outrageous conduct, to mark […] disapproval of such conduct and deter him from repeating it […]'[87] as well as to factor in any foreign legitimate regulatory interests which might indicate that exemplary damages should not classify as being excessive. Having a somewhat more flexible approach, which is a rather transnational one, is indeed important because there is a risk that a refusal to apply the foreign antitrust laws that set out appropriate and effective legal remedies may 'defeat the policy involved in following the foreign substantive law'.[88]

But it is entirely different question whether the proposed approach could allow English courts go a step further and award multiple damages under US antitrust law, if applicable under the Rome II Regulation. The Protection of Trading Interests Act 1980 along with Recital 32 of Rome II may indicate that, on the grounds of public policy, an English court may refuse to award treble damages in cases where the US antitrust law is applicable.[89] Since Section 5 of the 1980 Act restricts enforcement of overseas judgments awarding multiple damages, the prevailing opinion[90] is that 'in England a court applying US law has no power to order the payment of triple damages—a power provided under US antitrust legislation'.[91] In other words, an English court cannot apply a US antitrust law which awards treble damages[92] because such a remedy would be against the English public policy,[93] flying in the face of the Protection of Trading Interests Act 1980.[94]

That said, there is a view that an arbitral tribunal sitting in England might apply the Sherman Act, awarding treble damages; such an arbitral award might potentially be enforceable in the US.[95] Post-Brexit, English judges could, through PIL mechanisms, gradually start devising a form of transnational competition law which may with time

[85] See more: M Danov, 'Awarding exemplary (or punitive) antitrust damages in EC competition cases with an international element – the Rome II Regulation and the Commission's White Paper on damages' (2008) 29 *ECLR* 430, 432–33.

[86] PR Beaumont and Z Tang, 'Classification of Delictual Damages – *Harding v Wealands* and the Rome II Regulation' (2008) 12 *Edinburgh Law Review* 131, 136.

[87] *Rookes v Barnard* [1964] AC 1129, 1228 (Lord Devlin). See more: V Wilcox, 'Punitive damages in England' in H Koziol and V Wilcox (eds), *Punitive Damages: Common Law and Civil Law Perspectives* (Springer, Wien/New York 2009) 7, 26–28.

[88] WW Cook, '"Substance" and "procedure" in the conflict of laws' (1932–1933) 42 *Yale Law Journal* 333, 344.

[89] CGJ Morse, 'Torts in private international law: a new statutory framework' (1996) 45 *ICLQ* 888, 895; A Dickinson, *The Rome II Regulation: The Law Applicable to Non-contractual Obligations* (Oxford, OUP, 2008) [6.33 and 14.21–14.23].

[90] Morse (n 89) 895; Dickinson (n 89) [6.33 and 14.21–14.23].

[91] N Blackaby, C Partasides and A Redfern, *Redfern and Hunter on International Arbitration* 6th edn (Oxford, OUP, 2015) [9.45].

[92] Mercer (n 50) 336.

[93] See: Chapter 11 below. See also: Morse (n 89) 895; Dickinson (n 89) [6.33 and 14.21–14.23].

[94] Danov (n 85) 432.

[95] *Redfern and Hunter on International Arbitration* (n 91) [9.45]. Danov (n 83) 247–248.

allow for a level of judicial cooperation that could set the scene for 'transnational public policy'[96] and a transnational private antitrust enforcement regime. In view of this, there are good reasons for suggesting that the Protection of Trading Interests Act 1980 should be revised (if not repealed). The 1980 Act seems to assume that the punitive (or exemplary) damages are always excessive within the meaning of Recital 32. There might be important public policy considerations which may justify a foreign regulatory regime awarding treble damages. Professor Visscher has noted:

> Victims who claim damages in essence serve the social goal of deterrence. However, starting a lawsuit entails costs, which are privately borne. This might lead to too few lawsuits being brought. Increasing the expected damages of victims by awarding punitive damages may solve this problem.[97]

A transnational approach to the issues of applicable law should respect foreign regulators' policy choices in cases where the anti-competitive conduct had anti-competitive effects in the US, causing antitrust damages there.[98] Certain analogies might be drawn with arbitration, which is often perceived as a truly transnational mode of governance[99] that fosters the use of 'transnational commercial law'.[100] Should the 1980 Act be repealed?[101]

IV. Transnational Approach to Establishing a Regulatory Breach

The author has previously[102] argued that a private international law[103] mode of governance should be used to appropriately coordinate related (parallel or subsequent) competition law proceedings in a global context.[104] Since 'in a world with extraterritorial application of antitrust laws, the most restrictive antitrust laws will govern business behaviour',[105] a transnational approach to issues of applicable law is necessary to minimise the risk. The point may be strengthened further by making reference to the literature on global law[106] which indicates that private international law could be used as

[96] M Renner, 'Private Justice, Public Policy: The Constitutionalization of International Commercial Arbitration' in W Mattli and T Dietz (eds), *International Arbitration & Global Governance: Contending Theories and Evidence* (Oxford, OUP, 2014) 117, 130.

[97] LT Visscher, 'Economic analysis of punitive damages' in Koziol and Wilcox (n 87) 220, 224–25.

[98] Compare: *F Hoffmann-La Roche Ltd v Empagran* (2004) 542 US 155 at 165; 124 SCt 2359 (Sup Ct (US)).

[99] Mattli and Dietz (n 96).

[100] J Karton, 'International Arbitration Culture and Global Governance' in Mattli and Dietz (n 96) 79.

[101] See more: Chapter 12.

[102] M Danov, 'Global Competition Law Framework: A Private International Law Solution Needed' (2016) 12 *Journal of Private International Law* 77–105.

[103] AT Guzman, 'The case for international antitrust' in RA Epstein and MS Greve (eds,) *Competition Laws in Conflict: Antitrust Jurisdiction in the Global Economy* (AEI Press, 2004) 99, 116.

[104] A-M Slaughter, *A New World Order* (Princeton University Press, 2004) 16.

[105] JO McGinnis, 'The political economy of international antitrust harmonization' in Epstein and Greve (n 103) 126, 127. E Elhauge and D Geradin, *Global Competition Law and Economics* 2nd edn (Oxford, Hart Publishing, 2011) 1137–38.

[106] Lehmann (n 74); N Walker, *Intimations of Global Law* (Cambridge University Press 2014) 107–114.

a mode of governance in respect of 'increasingly dense and intricate relations between different regulatory regimes'.[107]

A transnational approach is particularly important to address the complex issues concerning the multiplicity of related claims that arise out of the same transnational infringement and which may be governed by multiple national competition laws which would normally express the public interests of the forum. Given the existing level of diversity between national competition policies and objectives,[108] effectively functioning national judicial systems, which cooperate with one another, are central to providing effective remedies for injured parties in a global context.[109] It is unsatisfactory that establishing jurisdiction in one country rather than another would make a difference to whether the cross-border economic activities are competitive (ie legitimate) or anti-competitive (ie illegal).

The issues are indeed important because, as already noted, there may often be a conflict of competition laws in a global context in so far as the regional/national competition law policy objectives may vary[110] and competition law rules themselves may differ.[111] If multiple national courts, which were competent to exercise their adjudicatory jurisdiction, were to determine whether there was a competition law infringement by exclusively applying their own competition laws, the outcome of a competition law dispute would depend on where the proceedings were initiated as well as on the ability/resources of the national judges to award remedies in cases where the conduct is in conflict with their national competition laws. In other words, if recourse to a single national set of competition laws is made, there is risk that inconsistent outcomes would be reached in related private antitrust damages claims that arise out of the same transnational competition law infringements and adversely affect consumers and business in several jurisdictions.

One way to advance a transnational approach to judicial cooperation is to widen the scope of Rome II.[112] In particular, post-Brexit, the courts of England and Wales could/should adopt a broader definition of restriction of competition for the purposes of the retained Rome II to reflect the fact that restrictions of competition would affect markets[113] in a number of countries. A stand-alone claim for antitrust damages would be raising an issue about the regulatory breach (ie UK competition law; EU competition law; US antitrust law) which would be intertwined with the issues concerning 'territorial scope'[114] of the relevant competition laws (ie posing issues about the scope of the regulatory jurisdiction).

In cases where there is a transnational competition law infringement, since the markets would be affected in a number of jurisdictions, Article 6(3)(a) of Rome II should allow the

[107] Walker (n 106) 108–109. See also: H Muir-Watt. 'Private International Law beyond the Schism' (2011) 2 *Transnational legal theory* 347; J Bonhoff and A Meuwese, 'The Meta-regulation of Transnational Private Regulation' (2011) *Journal of Law and Society* 138.

[108] Chapter 9.

[109] AM Mateus, 'Competition and Development: Towards an Institutional Foundation for Competition Enforcement' (2010) *World Competition* 275, 296. See also: S Djankov, R La Porta, F Lopez-de-Silanes and A Shleifer, 'Courts' (2003) 118 *Quarterly Journal of Economics* 453.

[110] H Klodt, 'Conflicts and conflict resolution in international anti-trust: Do we need international competition rules?' (2005) *The World Economy* 877, 882.

[111] Ibid.

[112] See more: Chapter 11.II below.

[113] Compare: Article 6(3) of Rome II.

[114] *The LCD Appeals* (n 20) [62].

English courts to apply the competition law of each country where the market is affected. As part of this process, they may factor in 'the laws of all the countries concerned [which may be] be applied on a distributive basis, applying what is known as "Mosaikbetrachtung" in German law'.[115] Hence there is an argument for the concept of restriction of competition to be broadly defined, covering any set of competition laws. This should enable the English courts to advance a transnational approach to dispute resolution in competition law matters by applying multiple sets of national competition laws, in order to determine whether there is a restriction of competition law in appropriate cases.

The classification issues would be even more important in a global context because any claim for antitrust damages would have some specific features. There would be questions about the nature of the anti-competitive conduct (eg price-fixing; excessive prices) as well as questions about how the markets and/or prices have been affected.[116] On that basis, the affected markets and competition laws will be ascertained. It is to be seen whether an English court would go a step further and apply/factor in foreign competition laws.

Alternatively, as has been already noted elsewhere,[117] a transnational approach to the issues of applicable law might require national judges to make a 'recourse to special substantive rules which would seek to adjust, on a basis of equality, the views of all legitimately concerned jurisdictions'.[118] The proposed approach was developed by relying on von Mehren's proposed 'multi-state rule'[119] which he advanced as an appropriate mode of governance approximately 50 years ago. A major feature of this truly transnational approach is that '[t]he multi-state rule proposed, unlike a domestic-rule solution, thus recognizes that [several] states have legitimate interests in the situation'.[120] This should enable national courts to strike a balance between multiple competition law regimes and factor in any foreign legitimate regulatory interests which may be at stake in cross-border competition law cases.

A somewhat similar approach[121] appeared to be suggested by Lord Justice Thorpe with regard to cross-border matrimonial cases. The analogy between competition law and family law is relevant to the extent that the English courts would normally exclusively apply English law in matrimonial disputes. In order to allow for foreign law to be factored in by the English courts in matrimonial disputes with an international element, the following transnational approach was suggested:

> the judge should give due weight to the marital property regime into which the parties freely entered. This is not to apply foreign law, nor is it to give effect to a contract foreign to English tradition. It is, in my judgment, *a legitimate exercise of the very wide discretion that is conferred on the judges to achieve fairness between the parties* [...].[122]

[115] See Commission (EC), 'Proposal for a Regulation of the European Parliament and the Council on the law applicable to non-contractual obligations' COM (2003) 427 final.

[116] See more: Chapter 11.

[117] Danov (n 102).

[118] von Mehren (n 11) 366.

[119] Ibid.

[120] Ibid 366.

[121] M Danov and P Beaumont, 'Measuring the Effectiveness of the EU Civil Justice Framework: Theoretical and Methodological Challenges' (2015/2016) 17 *Yearbook of Private International Law* 151–180.

[122] *Katrin Radmacher (formerly Grantino) v Nicolas Joseph Jean Granatino* [2009] EWCA Civ 649 [53] emphasis added by the author.

In spite of the fact that the UK Supreme Court did not uphold Lord Thorpe's approach,[123] the author[124] believes that there are advantages for such a transnational approach to be advanced with regard to cross-border competition law cases, post-Brexit.

The following examples (which are modelled on von Mehren's analysis of choice of law theories)[125] might be indicative as to how a 'multi-state rule'[126] could be developed in cross-border competition law cases. In particular, if a loyalty discount was permissible in State A, whilst being prohibited in State B,[127] a transnational approach would provide a workable solution which factors in conflicting regulatory interests. A balance needs to be struck because the regulatory interest of State B (prohibiting the conduct) would not be given effect if the laws of State A were exclusively applied. Similarly, if the laws of State B are exclusively applied, then the regulatory interests of State A (that exempts the conduct in so far as 'its procompetitive consequences likely outweigh its anticompetitive effects')[128] would be adversely affected. A transnational approach should enable an adjudicator to factor in 'both states' [regulatory interests], compromising differences on the basis of the relative strength of each legal order's claim to regulate'.[129]

A transnational approach may apply differently in cases concerning export cartels. Such practices would adversely affect the process of competition in States B and C (ie the importing nations) without having any adverse consequences in State A (ie the exporting nation). Given the legitimate interests of the importing nations, a balance should be struck between the laws of States B and C. The laws of the importing nations will have a stronger claim to regulate the competition law aspects of the cross-border economic activities. On the contrary, the laws of the exporting nation should not apply irrespective of whether the dispute is litigated.

Therefore, a transnational approach to judicial cooperation is necessary for English judges to be able to factor in the legitimate regulatory interests of all states whose markets may be affected and whose competition law regimes share different views on the anti-competitive nature of the conduct. Using PIL mechanisms to strike an appropriate balance between diverse national competition law regimes (which express legitimate national regulatory interests) is essential to any regime for judicial cooperation. In other words, the proposed approach, if advanced by the English courts, post-Brexit, should set the foundation of a framework for judicial cooperation.

Therefore, there are good reasons for suggesting that a new mode of governance, incorporating a private international law solution, which minimises the inconsistent outcomes in related competition law claims arising out of the same transnational infringement, would be needed to appropriately govern cross-border competition law proceedings. A new and flexible mode of governance would be particularly important

[123] *Radmacher (formerly Granatino) v Granatino* [2010] UKSC 42 [108]. See more: Danov and Beaumont (n 121).

[124] Danov (n 102).

[125] von Mehren (n 11) 353 and 366.

[126] Ibid 366.

[127] *Virgin Atlantic Airways v British Airways* 257 F 3d 256 (2001), United States Court of Appeals, Second Circuit; Case T-219/99, *British Airways v Commission of the European Communities* [2003] ECR II-5925. See also: Elhauge and Geradin (n 105) 1137–38.

[128] Elhauge and Geradin (n 105) 1138.

[129] von Mehren (n 11) 366.

in cross-border competition law cases where a balance often needs to be struck between different regulatory interests. An appropriate level of judicial cooperation in competition law matters should enable injured parties to access effective legal remedies, which should also be fair for infringers in cross-border competition law proceedings.

V. Factoring Foreign Regulatory Interests

There is a very strong case for advancing a transnational approach to pursue private antitrust enforcement objectives in a global context. The common law system should provide British judges with sufficiently flexibility to advance a transnational approach to applicable competition laws in cross-border cases.

As part of this process, the issues concerning the effects of foreign regulatory proceedings on English private antitrust damages proceedings should be considered with regard to transnational competition law infringements which are subject to foreign regulatory proceedings. For example, on 11 May 2021, Dr Rachael Kent in her capacity of 'proposed class representative ("PCR")',[130] issued collective redress proceeding on behalf of approximately 20 million consumers against Apple.[131] The alleged competition law infringement concerned abusive (exclusionary and exploitative) practices which appeared to be implemented by Apple, which enjoyed 'a dominant (or monopoly) position by virtue of operating a closed system for iOS devices'.[132] Given the transnational nature of the alleged conduct, the UK Competition Appeal Tribunal made the following observations:

> the PCR brought to our attention a number of other claims and regulatory actions or investigations involving the commission charged by Apple through the App Store. These include:
>
> (1) A Competition and Markets Authority ("CMA") investigation into Apple's conduct in relation to the distribution of iOS apps.
> (2) A CMA market study into mobile ecosystems in the UK.
> (3) An investigation by the Dutch Authority for Consumers & Markets into the market for App Store services on iOS for dating app providers.
> (4) A review by the Korea Fair Trade Commission of compliance by Apple with legislation which prohibits Apple from compelling developers to use its payment system.
> (5) Investigations by the Russian Federal Antimonopoly Service, the Japan Trade Commission and the Competition Commission of India into various restrictions imposed by Apple on developers in relation to tools for app development and payment for apps.
> (6) A number of private actions in courts in the United States, China and the Netherlands, including one case in the USA (*Epic Games, Inc. v Apple Inc., Case No. 4:20-cv-05640-YGR*) which has resulted in a final judgment.[133]

[130] Case No: 1403/7/7/21, *Dr Rachael Kent v Apple Inc. Apple Distribution Int'l Ltd* [2022] CAT 28 [1].
[131] Case No: 1403/7/7/21, *Dr Rachael Kent v Apple Inc. Apple Distribution Int'l Ltd* – Reasoned Order of the President (Service out of the jurisdiction), dated 26th May 2021 [6].
[132] *Dr Rachael Kent* (n 130) [12].
[133] Ibid [14].

This quotation strongly indicates that the multiplicity of proceedings that are related to the same transnational conduct deployed by a dominant undertaking may be a major issue which is likely to be recurring in cases involving hi-tech giants. The EU experience with privately enforcing EU competition law in a number of EU Member States clearly shows that an institutional framework, which aims to facilitate private antitrust enforcement, needs to systematically address the issues concerning the effect of any related proceedings that are related to the same transnational competition law infringements.[134]

Since EU competition laws may be enforced in public proceedings before the regulators as well as in private proceedings, the interrelation between private and public enforcement has been on the legislative agenda in the EU.[135] Pre-Brexit, a notable feature of the private antitrust litigation in England and Wales was that a relatively high proportion of the damages claims were brought on a follow-on basis, being preceded by decisions of the EU Commission, establishing the EU competition law infringements. For example, the collective redress proceedings in *Merricks v MasterCard*[136] were preceded by the Decision of the European Commission of December 2007;[137] the collective redress proceedings in *UK Trucks Claim Ltd v Stellantis and Road Haulage Association Ltd v MAN SE*[138] followed on from the EU Commission's Decisions in relation to the *Trucks* cartel.[139]

Post-Brexit, it would be important for English judges to consider the extent to which foreign regulatory interests should be factored in national court proceedings. Two major questions are bound to arise in cross-border competition law cases: should foreign regulators be allowed to submit any observations in court proceedings where the application of the foreign competition law is at stake? Should any foreign regulatory findings of competition law infringements be given any effects in legal proceedings in England and Wales? Both issues appeared to be reflected in Regulation 1/2003.[140] Although the EU approach could not be followed in a global context, it is still worth considering how EU solutions to these problems could be adjusted with a view to devising PIL mechanisms which set the scene for judicial cooperation in competition law matters.

[134] R Nazzinni, *Competition Enforcement and Procedure* 2nd edn (Oxford, OUP, 2016) pp 3–18. See also: Commission Notice on the co-operation between the Commission and the courts of the EU Member States in the application of Articles 81 and 82 EC.

[135] Commission Work Programme 2012, COM(2011) 777 final at 3.

[136] Case No: 1266/7/7/16, *Walter Hugh Merricks CBE v MasterCard Inc* [2022] CAT 13. See also: Case Nos: 1517/11/7/22 (UM) and 1266/7/7/16, *The Merchant Interchange Fee Umbrella Proceedings* [2022] CAT 31.

[137] Case COMP/34.579 – MasterCard, Case COMP/36.518 – EuroCommerce, Case COMP/38.580 – Commercial Cards, *Non-Confidential Version of the Commission Decision relating to a proceeding under Article 81 of the EC Treaty and Article 53 of the EEA Agreement*, December 2007.

[138] Case Nos: 1282/7/7/18 and 1289/7/7/18, *UK Trucks Claim Ltd v Stellantis and Road Haulage Association Ltd v MAN SE & Ors* [2022] CAT 25.

[139] Case AT.39824, *Trucks – Commission Decision relating to a proceeding under Article 101 of the Treaty on the Functioning of the European Union (the Treaty) and Article 53 of the EEA Agreement* – 19.7.2016, C(2016) 4673 final; Case AT.39824, *Trucks – Commission Decision relating to a proceeding under Article 101 of the Treaty on the Functioning of the European Union and Article 53 of the EEA Agreement* – 27.9.2017, C(2017) 6467 final.

[140] See Articles 15 and 16 of Council Regulation 1/2003. See also: Commission Notice on the co-operation between the Commission and the courts of the EU Member States in the application of Articles [101 and 102 TFEU] [2004] Official Journal C101/04.

A. Foreign Regulator's Intervention in National Court Proceedings

One way for national courts to factor in foreign regulatory interests is for regulators to assist the court by submitting observations.[141] The possibility for the courts to do so appears to be deduced from the US Supreme Court's judgment in *Hartford Fire*[142] where the judge noted that '[t]he London reinsurers contend that applying the Act to their conduct would conflict significantly with British law, and *the British Government, appearing before us as amicus curiae*, concurs'.[143] A somewhat similar approach appeared to be advanced in the EU through a specifically designed legislative mechanism for cooperation between the regulators within the EU and the EU Member States, with Regulation 1/2003 stating that:

> Competition authorities of the Member States, acting on their own initiative, may submit written observations to the national courts of their Member State on issues relating to the application of Article [101 and 102 TFEU]. With the permission of the court in question, they may also submit oral observations to the national courts of their Member State. Where the coherent application of Article [101 and 102 TFEU] so requires, the Commission, acting on its own initiative, may submit written observations to courts of the Member States. With the permission of the court in question, it may also make oral observations.
>
> For the purpose of the preparation of their observations only, the competition authorities of the Member States and the Commission may request the relevant court of the Member State to transmit or ensure the transmission to them of any documents necessary for the assessment of the case.[144]

In other words, this provision enables regulators, without becoming a party, to be involved in the national court proceedings by submitting (written and/or oral) observations which should assist a national court to safeguard their regulatory interests. This would in turn ensure that the relevant competition law provisions are consistently applied by various national courts which may have the adjudicatory jurisdiction to hear competition law claims. Such a form of cooperation might be necessary for the competent national courts to avoid 'errors in the interpretation'.[145]

The importance of a mechanism which enables foreign regulators to intervene in private antitrust enforcement proceedings before the English courts could be further deduced from the Court of Appeal of England and Wales's judgment in *MasterCard*.[146] In this case, Lord Justice Flaux 'granted the Commission permission to intervene in the appeals pursuant to article 15(3) of Regulation 1/2003 […]. He also allowed the

[141] Article 15(3) of Council Regulation 1/2003.
[142] *Hartford Fire Insurance Co v California*, 113 S Ct 2891 (1993).
[143] Ibid 2910 – the emphasis added by the author.
[144] Article 15(3) of Council Regulation 1/2003.
[145] European Commission's Written Observations of 21 February 2018 in the Court of Appeal of England and Wales – *MasterCard v Sainsbury's* [18–30], https://ec.europa.eu/competition/court/visa_mastercard_commission_observation1_en.pdf. See also: European Commission's Written Observations on Article 101(3) Issues Dated 6 April 2018 in the Court of Appeal of England and Wales – *MasterCard v Sainsbury's*, https://ec.europa.eu/competition/court/visa_mastercard_commission_observation2_en.pdf.
[146] *Sainsbury's v MasterCard* [2018] EWCA Civ 1536.

Commission to make oral submissions at the hearing'.[147] This enabled the court to take account of the views expressed by the EU regulator. It might be perceived as a good example[148] that demonstrates that a level of cooperation may be necessary in cases where foreign regulatory interests are at stake. This would be particularly so in cases where a foreign regulator had already opined on the anti-competitive nature of the conduct as well as where regulatory proceedings are pending in another jurisdiction.

That said, a national court should not be bound by a foreign regulator's submission. The point could be strengthened by the US court judgment in *Animal Science Products v Hebei Welcome*,[149] with the judge holding that:

> When foreign law is relevant to a case instituted in a federal court, and the foreign government whose law is in contention submits an official statement on the meaning and interpretation of its domestic law, may the federal court look beyond that official statement? The Court of Appeals for the Second Circuit answered generally 'no,' ruling that federal courts are 'bound to defer' to a foreign government's construction of its own law, whenever that construction is 'reasonable.' In re Vitamin C Antitrust Litigation, 837 F.3d 175, 189 (2016).
>
> [...] We hold otherwise. A federal court should accord respectful consideration to a foreign government's submission, but is not bound to accord conclusive effect to the foreign government's statements. Instead, Federal Rule of Civil Procedure 44.1 instructs that, in determining foreign law, 'the court may consider any relevant material or source TTT whether or not submitted by a party.' As '[t]he court's determination must be treated as a ruling on a question of law,' Fed. Rule Civ. Proc. 44.1, the court 'may engage in its own research and consider any relevant material thus found,' Advisory Committee's 1966 Note on Fed. Rule Civ. Proc. 44.1, 28 U.S.C. App., p. 892 [...]. Because the Second Circuit ordered dismissal of this case on the ground that the foreign government's statements could not be gainsaid, we vacate that court's judgment and remand the case for further consideration.[150]

Hence, an approach which enables an interested national regulator to make submissions in proceedings before another country's court could be play an important role with a view to promoting international co-operation in cross-border competition law cases.

B. Effects of Foreign Regulatory Decisions – Learning from the EU Experience

Pre-Brexit, the effect of Article 16 of Regulation 1/2003 was to impose a duty for the English courts to avoid judgments which are incompatible with decisions of the EU Commission which are (or are about to be) rendered.[151] It may be advantageous for the English courts as well as for private parties that they may not need to wait for the EU regulator to render a final regulatory decision, post-Brexit. But what would be the

[147] Ibid [36].

[148] See more examples: Commission observations to National Courts (Amicus curiae observations, Article 15(3)).

[149] *Animal Science Products v Hebei Welcome* 138 S Ct 1865 at 1869–70 (2018).

[150] Ibid.

[151] *Interpreneur Pub Company v Crehan* [2006] UKHL 38 [64–66]; Case C-344/98 *Masterfoods Ltd v HB Ice Cream Ltd* EU:C:2000:689 [51–2]. See also: Commission Notice on the co-operation between the Commission and the courts of the EU Member States in the application of Articles 81 and 82 EC [2004] C101/54 [12]. See more: Chapter 8.

effects of foreign regulatory decisions/findings in private antitrust damages claims before the courts of England and Wales?

Pre-Brexit, the legal effects of the European Commission's decision on the addressees could not be questioned in cases where 'the meaning of the operative part of that decision [is] unambiguous'[152] and the EU regulator's findings and ruling were subsequently confirmed by the EU courts.[153] Although there was no doubt that a regulator's decision finding an EU would be binding for its addressees,[154] there were issues about the parts of the regulator's decision which were binding.[155] In *BritNed Development v ABB*,[156] Mr Justice Marcus Smith included a separated section entitled 'the law regarding the bindingness of decisions',[157] where the court upheld the binding nature of the relevant article which formed part of the actual Commission's decision (ie *dispositif*). The High Court judge made a distinction between two types of recitals. One set of recitals would lay down 'the essential basis'[158] of the regulator's decision. These recitals, along with the relevant Commission's decision findings, are considered to be binding for the national courts.[159]

Difficulties would arise in cases where a regulator's decision is 'annulled or invalidated',[160] and any annulment (full or partial) might have an impact on any pending damages actions before the national courts. For example, in the *Airfreight* case,[161] a Commission's decision established that a number of air carriers had participated in unlawful business practices that were prohibited by Article 101 TFEU.[162] The Commission decision in question was issued in November 2010.[163] However, in December 2015 (ie approximately five years after the decision of the European Commission was rendered), the European Union General Court annulled the decision because there were inconsistencies between the recitals (setting out the Commission's reasoning) and the *dispositif* (ie the operative part of the regulator's decision).[164]

One problem, which was identified in the White Paper,[165] posed the question of whether an injured party could rely on a decision of one Member State's regulator and

[152] Case T-9/11, *Air Canada v Commission*, EU:T:2015:994 [40]. See also: Case T-61/99, *Adriatica di Navigazione SpA v Commission*, EU:T:2003:335 [43].

[153] *The Secretary of State for Health v Servier Laboratories* [2019] EWCA Civ 1096 [27 and 28]. Case T-474/04, *Pergan Hilfsstoffe für industrielle Prozesse v Commission*, EU:T:2007:306 [73].

[154] Article 288(3) TFEU. See also: *BritNed Development v ABB* [2018] EWHC 2616 (Ch) [67.1].

[155] Case T-138/89, *NBV and NVB v Commission*, EU:T:1992:95 [31]. Compare: *Royal Mail Group v DAF Trucks* [2020] CAT 7 [68]; *BritNed* (n 154).

[156] *BritNed* (n 154).

[157] Ibid [67].

[158] Ibid [67.6.b]. Case C-164/02, *Netherlands v Commission*, EU:C:2004:54 [21]. See also: *Royal Mail Group v DAF Trucks* [2020] CAT 7 [40].

[159] Ibid [67.6.b]. See also: Article 58A of the UK Competition Act 1998; Article 16 of Council Regulation 1/2003.

[160] *Air Canada* (n 152) [40].

[161] Case COMP/39258, *Airfreight – Commission Decision of 9.11.2010 relating to a proceeding under Article 101 of the Treaty on the Functioning of the European Union Article 53 of the EEA Agreement and Article 8 of the Agreement between the European Community and the Swiss Confederation on Air Transport Case*, C(2010) 7694 final.

[162] Ibid.

[163] Ibid.

[164] *Air Canada* (n 152).

[165] White Paper on Damages actions for breach of the EC antitrust rules COM(2008) 165 final [2.3]. M Danov, 'EU Competition Law Enforcement: Is Brussels I suited to dealing with all the challenges?' (2012) 61 *International and Comparative Law Quarterly* 27–54.

seek antitrust damages in follow-on (or hybrid) claims in another Member State's court. The issues are complex: since the territorial jurisdiction of a national regulator would be limited, their decisions may have no binding effect in other Member States' courts that are outside the territory of their regulatory jurisdiction.[166]

There are competing policy considerations which need to be considered with a view to advancing a transnational approach to judicial cooperation. On the one hand, injured parties' access to legal remedies may be impeded by an ineffective regime for judicial cooperation which does not ascertain the extent to which foreign regulator's findings could be relied upon by national courts dealing with private antitrust damages claims arising out of the same business practice or conduct. On the other hand, the effects of foreign regulatory findings should not be overstated. Some settlements decisions which are rendered in the course of regulatory proceedings may well establish that there is a liability for breach of competition law, without containing much (if any) information which may be relied upon by the injured parties in follow-on damages claims. This point was put forward in *AB Volvo v Ryder*[167] by Lady Justice Rose, holding that:

> There are already many advantages for a settling addressee as compared with the addressee of a contested decision facing a follow-on damages claim, in addition to the reduction in the fine and the savings in their own legal costs and management time. The brevity of the decision in many cases creates an obstacle for future damages claimants because there is less detail about the infringement and much less information about the effects of the cartel on prices. Although cartel cases are always 'object' infringement cases so that the Commission does not need to establish effect for the purposes of infringement, there is often useful material in a contested decision about the effect of the cartel in the context of justifying the amount of the fine.[168]

The above quotation strongly indicates that private international law rules concerning jurisdiction and choice-of-law would have a very important role to play with a view to ascertaining the cartel-induced overcharge in cross-border cases, which would be central to quantifying damages in follow-on antitrust damages claims.

Nonetheless, the extent to which foreign regulatory decisions could be relied upon in private antitrust proceedings before English courts would have major implications for the effective resolution of cross-border competition law disputes before the English courts. Ideally, these issues need to be dealt with by a PIL framework that promotes a level of judicial cooperation, but in the meantime might a soft approach to judicial cooperation be advanced in a global context?

The question whether private antitrust damages claimants could rely on 'infringement findings of the South Korean and Taiwanese antitrust authorities',[169] for example, would be bound to arise in private antitrust damages claims before the English courts, post-Brexit.

[166] White Paper on Modernisation of the Rules implementing Articles 85 and 86 of the EC Treaty, Commission Programme 99/027 [60]. See WPJ Wils, *Principles of European Antitrust Enforcement* (Hart Publishing, 2005) pp 116–118; AP Komninos, *EC Private Antitrust Enforcement: Decentralised Application of EC Competition Law by National Courts* (Hart Publishing, 2008) 77; S Brammer, *Co-operation between National Competition Agencies in the Enforcement of EC Competition Law* (Hart Publishing, 2009) 426–436. See also: *Ryanair Limited v Esso Italiana Srl* [2013] EWCA Civ 1450 [5 and 8].

[167] *AB Volvo v Ryder Ltd* [2020] EWCA Civ 1475.

[168] Ibid [83].

[169] Case No: 1382/7/7/21, *Consumers' Association v Qualcomm Inc* [2022] CAT 20 [25].

There is an argument that the UK might learn from the EU experience and address this question. In the pre-Brexit era, a Directive to ensure that an EU Member State finding an EU competition law infringement, if relied upon in court proceedings in another Member State court, would constitute 'at least *prima facie* evidence that an infringement of competition law has occurred'.[170] There is an argument that a similar approach might be advanced in the UK with regard to various regulatory findings, post-Brexit.[171]

VI. Aspects Concerning Remedies – Transnational Infringements

A number of national laws may be applicable with regard to the issues concerning the causation and quantification of damages,[172] but these rules would not necessarily classify as being overriding mandatory provisions. It is not only that the substantive laws could be different in cross-border competition law disputes, but also, once an infringement had been established, the available remedies would be different. For example, it is well established that multiple damages may be regarded by some national policy-makers as an appropriate and effective remedy for breach of its competition laws. The well-known problems concerning the US treble damages and the UK Protection of Trading Interests Act 1980[173] are yet another indication that a flexible solution is needed.

Another example, which exposes the level of variation regarding legal remedies, is *Microsoft*.[174] In this case, it was established that Microsoft abused its dominant position by supplying the Microsoft Windows operating system along with Windows Media Player.[175] However, the US regulator has made some notable and critical remarks with regard to the legal remedies imposed by the EU regulator, with the US Assistant Attorney General for Antitrust stating that:[176]

> Imposing antitrust liability on the basis of product enhancements and imposing 'code removal' remedies may produce unintended consequences. Sound antitrust policy must avoid chilling innovation and competition even by 'dominant' companies. A contrary approach risks protecting competitors, not competition, in ways that may ultimately harm innovation and the consumers that benefit from it. It is significant that the U.S. district court considered and rejected a similar remedy in the U.S. litigation.

[170] Article 9(2) of Directive 2014/104/EU.

[171] See more: Chapter 12.

[172] Article 6(3) of Rome II.

[173] Morse (n 89) 895; Dickinson (n 89) [6.33]. Danov (n 83) 177–78. Compare *Empagran* (98) at 165–66. Visscher (n 97). Compare: Recital 32 of the Rome II Regulation; The Protection of Trading Interests Act 1980, Office of Fair Trading, *Response to the European Commission's Green Paper, Damages actions for breach of the EC antitrust rules* (2006) OFT 844. Case Number: 1178/5/7/11, *2 Travel Group Plc (In Liquidation) v Cardiff City Transport Services Ltd* [2012] CAT 19 [485]. Compare: *Devenish* (n 84) [18]; Case Number: 1166/5/7/10, *Albion Water Ltd v DWR Cymru Cyfyngedig* [2013] CAT 6.

[174] Case COMP/C-3/37.792 *Microsoft* – Commission Decision of 24.03.2004 relating to a proceeding under Article 82 of the EC Treaty C(2004) 900 final; Case T-201/04, *Microsoft Corp v Commission of the European Communities* [2007] ECR II-3619.

[175] Article 2 of the Commission Decision.

[176] Press Release, US Department of Justice, Assistant Attorney General for Antitrust, R. Hewitt Pate, Issues Statement on the EC's Decision in its Microsoft Investigation, https://www.justice.gov/archive/opa/pr/2004/March/04_at_184.htm.

> While the imposition of a civil fine is a customary and accepted aspect of EC antitrust enforcement, it is unfortunate that the largest antitrust fine ever levied will now be imposed in a case of unilateral competitive conduct, the most ambiguous and controversial area of antitrust enforcement. For this fine to surpass even the fines levied against members of the most notorious price fixing cartels may send an unfortunate message about the appropriate hierarchy of enforcement priorities.
>
> With respect to the EC's 'interoperability' remedy, which requires Microsoft to license technologies used by Microsoft server software to communicate with other Microsoft software on a network, there is considerably more overlap with the United States' approach. Like the U.S. decree, the EC decision appears to focus on providing competing software developers with the opportunity to build products that communicate and interoperate with Windows-based PCs. The details of the EC's requirements on this point remain to be seen, and we look forward to examining them.[177]

This quotation captures the fact that, even when the national regulators recognise that a unilateral conduct is anti-competitive, different legal remedies may be seen as appropriate and effective by various regulatory regimes.[178] It seems that PIL mechanisms might allow for national courts to award effective and timely remedies, considering the interests of the parties and various regulatory interests which may be at stake in in a global context.

More importantly, the evolving nature of competition law infringements and any allegedly anti-competitive conduct in a global context poses questions about the ability of some national judges to effectively deal with complex cross-border competition law cases, without relying on a regime for judicial cooperation. In particular, the development of the technologies and various global platforms such as Google[179] and Facebook[180] create new challenges for national judges.[181] A case for comprehensive reform was made by the German Monopoly Commission,[182] holding that:

> **579**. The special characteristics of multi-sided platforms constitute a challenge for **competition policy**. The fundamental contexts and the complexity of multi-sided platforms need to be taken into consideration by competition authorities and courts when assessing specific

[177] Ibid. See also: K Heyer, 'A world of uncertainty: Economics and the globalization of antitrust' (2005) *Antitrust Law Journal* 375.

[178] O Budzinski, *The Governance of Global Competition: Competence Allocation in International Competition Policy* (Edward Elgar, 2008) 45.

[179] AT.39740 – *Google Search (Shopping), Commission Decision of 27.6.2017 relating to proceedings under Article 102 of the Treaty on the Functioning of the European Union and Article 54 of the Agreement on the European Economic Area*, C(2017) 4444 final. See also: P Akman, 'The Theory of Abuse in Google Search: A Positive and Normative Assessment under EU Competition Law' (2017) *University of Illinois Journal of Law, Technology & Policy* 301; P Akman, 'A Preliminary Assessment of The European Commission's Google Search Decision' (2017) 1(3) *Competition Policy International – Antitrust Chronicle*, 7–11; K Stylianou, 'Exclusion in Digital Markets' (2018) 2 *Michigan Telecommunications and Technology Law Review* 181; M Eben, 'Fining Google: a missed opportunity for legal certainty?' (2018) 14 *European Competition Journal* 129.

[180] G Sivinski, A Okuliar & L Kjolbye, 'Is big data a big deal? A competition law approach to big data' (2017) 13 *European Competition Journal* 199–227; C Ducuing, 'When competition law and data protection law embrace: the German Competition Authority investigates Facebook' – 9 January 2018 https://www.law.kuleuven.be/citip/blog/when-competition-law-and-data-protection-law-embrace-the-german-competition-authority-investigates-facebook/. See also: Digital Markets, Competition and Consumers Bill.

[181] Posner (n 3).

[182] German Monopolies Commission, 'Competition policy: The challenge of digital markets' – Special Report No 68 of 1 June 2015, https://www.monopolkommission.de/images/PDF/SG/s68_fulltext_eng.pdf.

> cases under competition law. It is important to include all sides of a platform in the analysis, and to capture both direct and indirect network effects in terms of their economic significance. The assessment of the competitive situation on multi-sided platforms requires an overall view to be taken in which greater importance is to be attributed to other factors than market shares, such as network effects, the availability of user data and the dynamic nature of the market observed.[183]

Indeed, the dynamic nature of the digital markets and digital platforms indicates that transnational competition law infringement would be common. There is a risk[184] that, whilst such highly complex cross-border competition law disputes are resolved, the harm caused to the market structure, business and consumers may be irreversible if no timely and effective legal remedies are awarded to injured parties.[185] In view of that, it seems that, despite the long-lasting proceedings before the EU regulator and the subsequent appeal, the '[r]ivals have filed claims against Google in national courts to recover compensation for the alleged abuse'.[186]

A PIL solution may be used to improve injured parties' access to legal remedies (striking a balance between the interests of the parties in the light of divergent regulatory regimes) as well as to fill in the enforcement gap in a global context. The latter point could be strengthened by making reference to *Motorola Mobility LLC v AU Optronics Corp*.[187] In this case, the US Court of Appeals held that:

> […] If Motorola's foreign subsidiaries have been injured by violations of the antitrust laws of the countries in which they are domiciled, they have remedies; if the remedies are inadequate, or if the countries don't have or don't enforce antitrust laws, these are consequences that Motorola committed to accept by deciding to create subsidiaries that would be governed by the laws of those countries. (An important, and highly relevant, application of the concept of 'antitrust standing' is the indirect-purchaser doctrine of the *Illinois Brick* case […]).[188]

In spite of the fact that the US Court of Appeals identified the difficulties for injured parties in certain jurisdictions, Circuit Judge Posner appeared to suggest the Motorola subsidiaries should rather seek remedies from the relevant regulators/adjudicators at the places where they are incorporated in their capacity of being direct purchasers there. Given the global nature of the economic activities and the impetus for free trade, it does not appear to be a satisfactory solution to decline jurisdiction by saying that a company should have not set its subsidiaries in jurisdictions where competition laws are not effectively enforced.

The English courts could address these issues as part of the 'substantial justice'[189] considerations which would be central to determining whether the UK CAT is the proper place for the claim to be heard and determined.[190]

[183] Ibid [579] – emphasis in the original.

[184] M Danov and S Dnes, 'Cross-border EU competition law actions: new evidence from England and Wales' in Danov, Becker and Beaumont (n 5) 33–59.

[185] R Toplensky and M Acton, 'Google antitrust remedy delivers few changes for rivals', *Financial Times*, 27 October 2017.

[186] Ibid. See more: Chapter 8.

[187] *Motorola Mobility LLC v AU Optronics Corp* 775 F 3d 816 (7th Cir 2015).

[188] Ibid 820–21.

[189] *Vedanta Resources PLC and another v Lungowe and others* [2019] UKSC 20 [89]. See also: Section 9.VI above.

[190] *Spiliada Maritime v Cansulex* [1987] AC 460 at 482 (HL).

VII. Concluding Remarks

Post-Brexit, a PIL solution might be important to systematically deal with the issues in relation to foreign regulator's findings which may be as important for injured parties' access to legal remedies as the recognition of the foreign court judgments in relation to competition law claims.[191] The issues concerning coordination of related private antitrust enforcements are important because the judicial cooperation in antitrust disputes may be intertwined with important regulatory aspects that are closely connected with the public interests of the forum which may vary in different jurisdictions.[192] It is to be determined how the PIL concept of 'conflicts justice',[193] which has been considered in cross-border cases as being 'a peculiar brand of justice that is readily satisfied by the application of the law most closely connected with a particular transaction',[194] should be developed to allow for multiple regulatory interests[195] and multiple substantive laws[196] to be factored in.

There is an argument for the English courts and the UK CAT to advance a transnational approach in relation to applicable laws in cross-border competition law cases where a number of national competition laws may be at stake.[197] In order to accommodate different policy choices, a transnational approach to issues of applicable law should provide for a higher level of flexibility that might allow national judges to balance conflicting regulatory interests.[198] Hence, given that 'the world economy already operates as a global system',[199] PIL has a very important role to play in promoting judicial cooperation, striking a balance between various regulatory interests whilst providing effective remedies for injured parties.

Advancing such a transnational approach may be central to ensuring that the decisions establishing competition law infringements and providing effective legal remedies for injured parties in cross-border cases are duly recognised and enforced across the globe.[200] One way to achieve a greater level of cooperation and consistency is to adjust von Mehren's 'special substantive rules for multistate problems',[201] so that it applies to transnational competition law infringements which, by definition, would pre-suppose for multiple regulatory interests to be balanced.

[191] Chapter 12.
[192] A Bradford et al, 'Competition Law Gone Global: Introducing the Comparative Competition Law and Enforcement Datasets' (2019) 16 *Journal of Empirical Legal Studies* 411.
[193] G Kegel, *Internationales Privatrecht* 6th edn (1987) 186–87, 193 cited in FK Juenger, *Choice of Law and Multistate Justice* (Dordrecht, Martinus Hijhoff Publishers, 1993) 69.
[194] Juenger (n 193) 69.
[195] von Mehren (n 11).
[196] J Fitchen, 'Choice of law in international claims based on restriction of competition: Art 6(3) of the Rome II Regulation' (2009) 5 *Journal of Private International Law* 337, 357–58.
[197] Chapter 8.
[198] Chapters 11 and 12.
[199] Renner (n 96) 134.
[200] Preliminary Document No 2 of December 2018, *Twenty-Second Session Recognition and Enforcement of Foreign Judgments* 18 June – 2 July 2019, The Hague; See more: M Danov and C Otero, 'Competition Law Enforcement: Private International Law and Access to Effective Legal Remedies in Cross-Border Cases' in P Beaumont and J Holliday (eds) *Guide to Global Private International Law* (Oxford, Hart Publishing, 2022).
[201] A von Mehren (n 11).

Another way for the UK courts to advance a transnational approach to the issues of applicable law is to broadly interpret Rome II[202] to cover not only private laws that should apply with regard to non-contractual obligations arising out of competition law infringements, but also the applicable (public) competition laws which should be used to determine whether there is a regulatory breach in cases 'where the market is, or is likely to be, affected'[203] in more than one country. The proposed approach should allow the English courts to take a lead in advancing a regime for judicial cooperation in competition law matters that is necessary to provide redress for multiple injured parties who had suffered loss which is caused by transnational competition law infringements that have distorted the process of competition in different jurisdictions.

Therefore, the author argues that appropriately devised PIL mechanisms should set the scene for judicial cooperation that enables judges to factor in the regulatory interests of multiple legal orders. This should be important for the courts of England and Wales to ensure that the risk concerning inconsistent outcomes in related private antitrust damages claims arising out of the same transnational competition law infringement/s would be minimised. There is an argument for the English courts to allow foreign regulators, whose competition laws are at stake, to intervene in private antitrust enforcement proceedings.[204] More importantly, if foreign regulatory interests are factored in, then it is more likely for the English courts' judgments in relation to competition law claims to be recognised and enforced abroad. To this end, it will be important to consider the extent to which foreign regulatory decisions should be given any effect in related proceedings before the English courts.[205]

[202] Chapter 11.II below.

[203] Article 6(3)(a) – Rome I.

[204] Compare: Article 15(3) of Regulation 1/2003.

[205] Compare: Article 16 of Regulation 1/2003; Article 9(2) of the EU Antitrust Damages Directive. See more: Chapter 12.

11

Applicable Law – Rome II and Some Rome I Aspects of Cross-Border Competition Law Claims

I. Introduction – Applicable Law – Competition Law Claims

As already noted above,[1] a private antitrust damages claim would classify as being tortious for PIL purposes. This means that a private antitrust damages claim should be within the ambit of Rome II which is set to ascertain the law of a country that is to apply 'to a non-contractual obligation arising out of a restriction of competition'.[2]

In the previous chapter it was noted that, post-Brexit, there is an argument for the English courts to expand the scope of Rome II, so that they can factor in foreign regulatory interests which should set the scene for a transnational approach to the issues of applicable competition law in cross-border cases. In this chapter, the author will first consider the original scope of Rome II, as reflected in its recitals. On that basis, the argument that its scope should expand in the UK, post-Brexit, will be reinforced.[3] The issues are important because there is a risk that, as noted in the previous chapter, anti-competitive conduct of multinational groups of companies may distort the process of competition in a number of jurisdictions, affecting the products/services' prices and causing harm to multiple injured parties (consumers;[4] rivals;[5] large purchasers;[6] SMEs)[7] across the globe.

Secondly, once a private antitrust damages claim has been classified as being within the scope of Rome II, the national judges would need to apply the relevant connecting factors and ascertain the law applicable to determine whether there is a competition law infringement, as well as to govern the issues concerning causation and quantification

[1] See: Chapter 3.

[2] Article 6(3)(a) of Rome II.

[3] See: Chapter 10.

[4] eg Case No: 1382/7/7/21 *Consumers' Association v Qualcomm Inc* [2022] CAT 20; Case No: 1403/7/7/21, *Dr Rachael Kent v Apple Inc. Apple Distribution Int'l Ltd* [2022] CAT 28; Case No: 1408/7/7/21 *Elizabeth Helen Coll v Alphabet Inc. and Others* [2022] CAT 39; Case No: 1433/7/7/22, *Dr Liza Lovdahl Gormsen v Meta Platforms Inc, Meta Platforms Ireland Ltd, Facebook UK Ltd* – Reasoned Order, dated 15 March 2022.

[5] Case Nos: 1377/5/7/20 and 1378/5/7/20, *Epic Games v Apple. Alphabet and Google* [2021] CAT 4.

[6] Case Nos: 1284-1290/5/7/18 (T), *Royal Mail Group Ltd v DAF Trucks Ltd* [2021] CAT 10.

[7] Case Nos: 1517/11/7/22 (UM) and 1266/7/7/16, *The Merchant Interchange Fee Umbrella Proceedings* [2022] CAT 31.

of damages. The issues must be addressed head-on by policy-makers because many competition law infringements would last for extended periods of time and cause harm to multiple injured parties, indicating that the aggregate damages – which might be in the billions – may be difficult to quantify.[8] This means that substantive law issues (eg the availability of the pass-on defence; 'broad axe'[9] approach to quantification of damages; application of an appropriate 'methodology')[10] may be intertwined with certain procedural issues (eg standard of proof; access to 'sufficient data').[11] This seems to suggest that the issues concerning the applicable law and its scope may impact on the injured parties' access to legal remedies.[12]

II. '[T]he concept of a non-contractual obligation'[13] and 'the concept of restriction of competition'[14]

As noted above,[15] Recital 23 appears to adopt a somewhat limited definition of 'the concept of restriction of competition' by referring to acts prohibited by Articles 101 and 102 TFEU or by the laws of EU Member States which may be reflects the limited territorial scope of EU competition laws and the EU Member States' competition laws.

The analysis of the distinction between 'the concept of a non-contractual obligation'[16] and 'the concept of restriction of competition'[17] was somewhat blurred in the private international law literature.[18] The question nonetheless requires renewed attention post-Brexit, not least because, whilst Recital 23 does not explicitly state that the restriction of competition would cover anti-competitive conduct that distorts competition in a non-EU country that does not form part from the EU internal market, the UK courts would be primarily concerned with acts which restrict competition in the UK (which is now a non-EU country). On that basis, it is a relatively safe assumption that the scope of the concept of 'restriction of competition' for the purposes of Rome II would be different in the UK in comparison with the scope of the same concept when

[8] *Mastercard Incorporated and others v Walter Hugh Merricks CBE* [2020] UKSC 51.
[9] Ibid [51].
[10] Ibid [32].
[11] Ibid [32].
[12] Article 15 of Rome II. See Chapter 11.VII below.
[13] Recital 11 of Rome II.
[14] Recital 23 of Rome II.
[15] Chapter 10.III.A above.
[16] Recital 11 of Rome II.
[17] Recital 23 of Rome II.
[18] S Francq and W Wurmnest, 'International Antitrust Claims under the Rome II Regulation' in J Basedow, S Francq and L Idot (eds), *International Antitrust Litigation: Conflict of Laws and Coordination* (Hart Publishing, Oxford, 2012) 91, 100. Compare: A Dickinson, *The Rome II Regulation: The Law Applicable to Non-contractual Obligations* (Oxford, OUP, 2008) [6.32–33]; ER Pineau, 'Conflict of laws comes to the rescue of competition law: the new Rome II Regulation' (2009) 5 *Journal of Private International Law* 311, 318–20; J Fitchen, 'Choice of law in international claims based on restriction of competition: Art 6(3) of the Rome II Regulation' (2009) 5 *Journal of Private International Law* 337, 352; R Plender and M Wilderspin, *The European Private International Law of Obligations* 5th edn (London, Sweet & Maxwell, 2020) [20-042].

interpreted in the EU. In the latter context (ie pre-Brexit), Professor Dickinson took the view that:

> It is unclear whether the definition in Recital (23) is exhaustive or whether Art 6(3) is also capable of encompassing similar conduct that is prohibited by the anti-trust legislation of a non-Member State of the European Community.[…] As the Regulation has universal application under Art 3,[…] there seems no reason in principle why it should not.[…] The alternatives, which appear less satisfactory, would be to fit claims to enforce the competition laws of a non-Member State into Art 6(1) or to leave them to be regulated by the general rule for tort/delict in Art 4.[19]

The quotation identifies the issues and the existing level of uncertainty, but Professor Dickinson does not appear to fully address the identified issues. This may be explained by the fact that, pre-Brexit, the question was somewhat less important in practice because most of the cross-border competition law infringements were normally established by the EU Commission.[20] Such transnational infringements would, by definition, be in relation to Articles 101 and 102 TFEU, which were part of English law. It is well settled that, pre-Brexit, Articles 101 and 102 TFEU were 'a direct source of rights and duties'[21] for individuals and businesses across the EU (including the UK), and EU competition law formed part of English law as well as the laws of all EU Member States,[22] which meant the national courts (including the English courts) were obliged to safeguard the rights conferred onto private parties[23] by, for example, awarding compensatory damages for breach of EU competition law.

In other words, it seems that, pre-Brexit, the question about the scope of the concept of 'restriction of competition' for the purposes of Rome II was rather academic. The issues had a little practical relevance in so far as a significant proportion of the private antitrust damages claims were issued on a follow-on basis,[24] which meant that any aspects relating to the restriction of competition were already dealt with in a prior set of regulatory proceedings. Indeed, a significant proportion of the private antitrust damages claims that were issued before the English courts were preceded by decisions of the EU Commission, establishing that the defendants' conduct restricted competition.[25] The findings of the EU Commission were binding for the UK courts.[26]

Nevertheless, Professor Dickinson's argument for the 'universal application'[27] of Rome II, supporting a wider interpretation of the concept of restriction of competition, is important and it has been put forward by a number of other academics.[28]

[19] Dickinson (n 18) [6.33].

[20] M Danov and S Dnes, 'Cross-border EU competition law actions: new evidence from England and Wales' in M Danov, F Becker and P Beaumont (eds), *Cross-Border EU Competition Law Actions* (Oxford, Hart Publishing, 2013) 33–59.

[21] Case C-106/77 *Amministrazione delle Finanze dello Stato v Simmenthal SpA* EU:C:1978:49 [15].

[22] Case C-26/62 *Van Gend en Loos v Administratie der Belastingen* EU:C:1963:1, 12.

[23] Ibid 13.

[24] Danov and Dnes (n 20) 33–59.

[25] Pineau (n 8) 314; Fitchen (n 18). See more: Danov and Dnes (n 20).

[26] Article 16 of Council Regulation; *Royal Mail Group v DAF Trucks* [2020] CAT 7. See more: Chapter 10.

[27] Dickinson (n 18) [6.33]. See also: Article 3 of Rome II.

[28] Fitchen (n 18) 353; Plender and Wilderspin (n 18) [20-042].

There is a suggestion that, despite its wording, Recital 23 was not purposively set to limit the scope of Article 6(3) of Rome II, but it was 'drafted loosely in the sense that it states that the restriction of competition concept "should cover" [only certain infringements]'.[29] Indeed, another highly influential view was put forward by Plender KC and Wilderspin who note that:

> Recital 23 merely provides that the concept of restriction of competition 'covers' such prohibitions: it does not purport to contain an exclusive definition. In the second place, from a factual point of view, particular conduct may be constitutive of a restriction of competition wherever it takes place. Thus, if the Union legislature had intended to restrict the scope of art.6(3) in such a way that would be so clearly contrary both to the natural meaning of the words and to the basic principle of 'universal application' of the Regulation, [...] one would have expected it to say so clearly. In fact, the language of art.6(3)(a) itself suggests that its scope is not so restricted since the choice of law rule that it contains designates as applicable law 'the law of the country' (as opposed to 'Member State') where the market is affected. Thus, the ambiguous and arguably restrictive wording in Recital 23, the purpose of which is only to explain the reasons behind the rule contained in art.6(3), cannot prevail over the clear wording of that article.[30]

That said, the focus of Article 6(3) is on 'the law applicable to [the] non-contractual obligation'[31] as opposed to the law applicable to the 'restriction of competition'[32] which gives rise to the non-contractual obligation.[33] Since the emphasis of Article 6(3) is on the former concept, it seems more convincing that the principle of universal application should only apply to 'the concept of a non-contractual obligation'.[34] For example, EU competition law would apply to determine whether an anti-competitive act, which is committed in England (eg London banks may be manipulating the foreign exchange rates), is anti-competitive.[35] Since the conduct affects the markets in the United States[36] as well as in other non-EU jurisdictions, the principle of universal application should apply with regard to the issues concerning the quantification of damages, which means that any foreign laws, where damage occurs, may be applicable in this respect. This would particularly be so if some of the foreign claimants were to opt into the English proceedings[37] or if some of them were to issue proceedings in England and Wales, subject to the issues of public policy (eg Recital 32)[38] or subject to Article 6(3)(b) of Rome II.[39]

[29] Fitchen (n 18) 352.
[30] Plender and Wilderspin (n 18) [20-042].
[31] Article 6(3)(a) read together with Recitals 11 and 22 of Rome II.
[32] Article 6(3)(a) read together with Recital 23 of Rome II.
[33] Francq and Wurmnest (n 18) 100. Compare: Pineau (n 8) 320.
[34] Recital 11 of Rome II.
[35] Case AT.40135, *FOREX (Three Way Banana Split) – Commission Decision relating to a proceeding under Article 101 of the Treaty on the Functioning of the European Union and Article 53 of the EEA Agreement* – 16.5.2019, C(2019) 3631 final; CASE AT.40135 *FOREX (Essex Express) – Commission Decision relating to a proceeding under Article 101 of the Treaty on the Functioning of the European Union and Article 53 of the EEA Agreement* – 16.5.2019, C(2019) 3621 final.
[36] Case No 13-cv-7789, *In re Foreign Exchange Benchmark Rates Antitrust Litigation*, http://www.fxantitrustsettlement.com/.
[37] Case Nos: 1329/7/7/19 and 1336/7/7/19, *Michael O'Higgins FX Class Representative Limited v Barclays Bank* [2022] CAT 16 [2022] CAT 16.
[38] See: Chapter 10.III.B above.
[39] See: Section VI below.

The point has been nicely captured by Professors Francq and Wurmnest:

> A closer look at Article 6(3) Rome II [...] reveals that this conflict rule was perhaps not conceived as having the same broad reach as other provisions of the Regulation. Article 6(3) Rome II only applies if there is a 'non-contractual obligation arising out of a restriction of competition'. Recital 23 Rome II provides a definition of what a restriction of competition under Article 6(3) Rome II is. It refers to practices which produce a distortion of competition 'within a Member State or within the internal market' and which are prohibited under Articles 101, 102 TFEU or under the law of a Member State. The wording of Recital 23 Rome II seems to suggest that Article 6(3) Rome II is limited to situations which produce a distortion of competition within the EU and can only command the application of either EU law (Articles 101, 102 TFEU) or the law of a Member State because the affected market is necessarily located within the EU.[40]

In view of the above analysis, there is support for an argument that encourages judges to draw a distinction between 'the concept of a non-contractual obligation'[41] and 'the concept of restriction of competition'[42] for the purposes of Rome II. Notwithstanding, as noted in the previous chapter,[43] there is a strong argument for 'the concept of restriction of competition'[44] within the meaning of Article 6(3) of Rome II to be broadly interpreted, post-Brexit, covering anti-competitive conduct which is in conflict with foreign competition law provisions.

Although Article 16 of Rome II appears to indicate the English courts would be required to apply only the *overriding mandatory provisions of the forum* (ie UK competition law)[45] they should be encouraged to advance a transnational approach to judicial cooperation and factor in foreign regulatory interests. As noted above,[46] the judgment of Mr Justice Picken in *ValueLicensing v Microsoft*[47] appears to suggest that the English judges, relying on Article 6(3) of Rome II, are willing to apply EU competition law, post-Brexit, in cases (where it was not directly applicable in the UK).

There is an argument for a broad interpretation of Rome II along the lines suggested by Professor Dickinson, Professor Fitchen, Plender KC and Wilderspin to be advanced in the UK, post-Brexit. A broader interpretation should have important legal implications for the scope of the English courts' jurisdiction to award damages in stand-alone claims in relation to transnational competition law infringements that would naturally cause antitrust harm/damages in multiple jurisdictions (where foreign competition laws would apply). In some of these cases, there could even be a foreign regulatory decision which, despite the fact that it is not binding for the UK courts, could have established a competition law infringement.[48]

[40] Francq and Wurmnest (n 18) 100.
[41] Recital 11 of Rome II.
[42] Recital 23 of Rome II.
[43] Chapter 10.III.A above.
[44] Recital 23 of Rome II.
[45] See: Chapter 10.III above.
[46] See: Chapter 10 above.
[47] *JJH Enterprises Ltd (trading as ValueLicensing) v Microsoft* [2022] EWHC 929 (Comm) [44].
[48] See: Chapter 12.

III. Classification – Private Antitrust Damages Claims[49]

As already noted above,[50] there would be complex classification issues which would arise in cross-border competition law cases.[51] More specifically, there would broadly be two sets of issues that would need to be addressed in a private antitrust damages claim arising out of a transnational competition law infringement. First, it would be necessary for the national courts to determine whether there is a competition law infringement by applying the relevant (public) competition law and/or by relying on a regulatory decision which is binding in the UK. Secondly, for the choice of law purposes, it would be crucial for the judges to ascertain where the direct antitrust 'damage occurred – irrespective of the country or countries in which the indirect consequences of that event occur'.[52] In the latter context, it should be reiterated that ascertaining where the direct antitrust damage occurred pre-supposes for the national judges to classify the restriction of competition that would cause antitrust damages.[53]

A rather pragmatic approach to the issue of classification appears to be advanced by the CAT in its judgment in *Westover Ltd v Mastercard*.[54] In this case, it was necessary for the CAT to give a judgment on a preliminary issue concerning the applicable law, which was important for the Tribunal to ascertain the law that should apply to the issues concerning the limitation periods.[55] As part of this dispute, the CAT addressed 'a difficult issue on the proper interpretation and application of Regulation 864/2007 on the law applicable to non-contractual obligations ("Rome II")'.[56] Although the issue in question was preliminary, it was important for the outcome as the various limitation periods would impact differently on the defendants' liability for antitrust damages. There was a set of questions concerning the classification of the relevant restriction of competition which gave rise to the non-contractual obligation for the purposes of Article 6(3) of Rome II. In order to address them, the CAT systematically set out several issues which had to be considered under Rome II. It was held that:

> In applying Art 6(3)(b), we think it is necessary to address three questions:
> a) what is the non-contractual obligation on which the claim is based;
> b) what is the restriction of competition out of which that obligation arises; [...] and
> c) does that restriction of competition directly and substantially affect the market in the country of the forum?[57]

Although the Tribunal did not explicitly approach this preliminary dispute as raising classification issues for the purposes of Rome II, a closer analysis of the judgment along with the wording of Article 6(3) strongly indicates that the court has impliedly addressed the relevant classification issues. More specifically, the above set of questions

[49] See: Chapter 3.
[50] See: Chapter 3.III.B and Chapter 10 above.
[51] J Fitchen, 'The Applicable Law in Cross-Border Competition Law Actions and Article 6(3) of Regulation 864/2007' in Danov, Becker and Beaumont (n 20) 306–308.
[52] Article 4(1) – Rome II.
[53] See: Chapter 3.
[54] Case Nos: 1349-1350/5/7/20 (T) and 1383-1384/5/7/21 (T), *Westover Ltd v Mastercard* [2021] CAT 12.
[55] See: Section VII below.
[56] *Westover* (n 54) [3].
[57] Ibid [53].

strongly indicates that the alleged restrictions of competition would need to be properly and systematically classified for the court to ascertain if and where the market is affected (eg the prices raised/inflated). In other words, classifying specific restrictions of competition law would enable the court to ascertain where the market is affected, which in turn might lead to different sets of applicable laws. Thus the UK CAT held that:

> 58. […] As regards Italian domestic [multilateral interchange fees 'MIFs'], we consider that the restriction of competition out of which liability in respect of those MIFs arises (or on which the claims in respect of those MIFs rely) is the collusive arrangement to set those positive MIFs. Those Italian MIFs directly and substantially affected the acquiring market in Italy. It cannot be suggested that the setting of the Italian domestic MIFs affected the acquiring market in the UK, still less that it did so directly and substantially. Accordingly, in our judgment the law governing the claims relying on the Italian domestic MIFs is determined by Art 6(3)(a) and is Italian law. Art 6(3)(b) has no application.
>
> 59. The two cross-border MIFs, i.e. the intra-EEA MIF and the inter-regional MIF, can be considered together. The restrictions of competition out of which the liability in respect of those MIFs arises (or on which the claims in respect of those MIFs rely) are the collusive arrangements to set those MIFs at positive levels. Both of those MIFs directly and substantially affected the acquiring market in Italy but the arrangement setting those positive MIFs also directly and substantially affected the acquiring market in the UK, since single rates were set, by the same process, which applied in both the UK and Italy, for those categories of transaction. Accordingly, in our judgment the claims for damages resulting from those MIFs fall within the scope of Art 6(3)(b) and the Italian claimants are entitled to choose to have their claims in the CAT governed by English law.[58]

In other words, on the basis of an analysis of the Tribunal's judgment in *Westover Ltd v Mastercard*,[59] a three-step test with regard to classification under Article 6(3) of the Rome II could be advanced. First, the non-contractual obligation (eg tortious liability for breach of competition law) should be clearly set out. Secondly, the specific act/s restricting competition must be classified (eg setting out domestic or non-domestic MIF; price fixing; access refusal). Thirdly, the direct damage caused by the act restricting competition must be classified (ie effects on prices – an illegal 'overcharge'[60] and/or 'lost sales').[61] On that basis, the tribunal would need to ascertain the market/s which would be affected.[62]

IV. Direct Damage – 'the law of the country where the market is … affected'[63]

In order to ascertain the 'country where the market is […] affected' under Article 6(3)(a) of Rome II, the court might consider whether the anti-competitive conduct had an effect on the prices and/or sales in the country (or the countries) in question.

[58] Ibid [58 and 59].
[59] Ibid.
[60] Case No: 1241/5/7/15 (T), *Sainsbury's Supermarkets v MasterCard* [2016] CAT 11 [13.4–5].
[61] Ibid [13.4 and 13.6].
[62] See more: Chapter 3.II above. Compare: Fitchen (n 18) 346–47.
[63] Article 6(3)(a) of Rome II.

The purpose of carrying out a systematic classification in relation to competition law is to enable judges to ascertain where the direct damage occurred (ie where the market is affected) with a view to ascertaining the applicable law. It is well established that, in a private antitrust damages claim, 'the claimant must prove not only that the relevant [provision] has been broken, but also that the breach in question has caused him a relevant loss'.[64] In the latter context, it is well established that '[o]vercharge and pass-on are the two key elements'[65] which will impact on the outcome of a private antitrust damages claim. This means that ascertaining the applicable law may be central for the national judges to deal with the substantive law aspects in relation to causation and quantification of damages in private antitrust damages claims.

In this section, the *country where the market is affected* will be examined as being a major connecting factor which is used to ascertain the applicable law in cross-border competition law cases. The endorsement of the above connecting factor has been criticised as being far too complex, which would naturally generate a level of legal uncertainty and would inevitably increase the litigation costs.[66] In support of such an argument, Professor Dickinson states that:

> The requirement for individual litigants, and their legal advisers, to undertake legal-economic analysis [...] in order to determine the law applicable to a non-contractual obligation is one of the least satisfactory aspects of the Rome II Regulation, and seems likely significantly to increase costs in cases of this kind.[67]

The author feels that this criticism is, to some extent at least, unjustified. It makes sense for the national judges to build on the approach developed by regulators rather than to invent an entirely new and different approach to the issues concerning applicable law in follow-on competition law claims (which is more likely to generate fresh uncertainty and increase the litigation costs). This approach appears to be working so far because the practice appears to show that Article 6(3) of Rome II does not seem to be generating a huge volume of preliminary disputes on choice-of-law issues (as opposed to preliminary disputes in relation to jurisdiction issues).[68]

More importantly, using the same economic concepts (as the ones used by the regulator) should enable judges and parties to rely on the relevant case law and market analyses which have already been systematically advanced by various regulators.[69] Nevertheless, it should be noted that, for choice-of-law purposes, the connecting factor – 'the country where the market is affected' – is different from the concept of 'relevant geographic market' for the purposes of determining whether the undertakings have market power[70] and/or whether there is a regulatory breach (ie whether

[64] *Devenish Nutrition Ltd v Sanofi-Aventis SA* [2007] EWHC 2394 a'ffd *Devenish Nutrition Ltd v Sanofi-Aventis SA* [2008] EWCA Civ 1086.

[65] J Lawrence and A Morfey, 'Tactical Manoeuvres in UK Cartel Damages Litigation' in Danov, Becker and Beaumont (n 20) 149, 154.

[66] Fitchen (n 18) 346–47; M Helner, 'Unfair Competition and acts restricting free competition – a commentary on Article 6 of the Rome II Regulation' (2007) 9 *Yearbook of Private International Law* 50, 59; Dickinson (n 18) [6.64]; Plender and Wilderspin (n 18) [20-057].

[67] Dickinson (n 18) [6.64].

[68] See: Chapters 3, 4, 5 and 6.

[69] See: Helner (n 66) 60; Plender and Wilderspin (n 18) [20-057].

[70] Francq and Wurmnest (n 18) 121. See *the FT403 & 415 Guidance*. See also: L Kaplow, 'Why (Ever) Define Markets? (2010) 124 *Harvard Law Review* 437.

the conduct is anti-competitive).[71] For example, even though the relevant geographical market in the *Trucks* cartel was defined to cover the entire European Economic Area,[72] the scope of the claim in the UK collective redress proceedings was much narrower.[73]

In spite of the fact that the relevant concepts (ie relevant geographical market; affected market) would not necessarily overlap, the Rome II approach for the special PIL rules to ascertain the country where the direct antitrust damage occurred in cross-border competition cases is justifiably retained and it should be developed further by the English judges, post-Brexit. More importantly, since Article 6(3)(a) of Rome II is intended to be a 'clarification'[74] of the general rule which is set out in Article 4(1) of Rome II, it is highly persuasive to argue that – in competition law cases – the direct antitrust damage would occur at the country where the market is affected.[75] The legislative intention appears to be for this connecting factor – 'the country where the market is affected' (being the place where the direct antitrust damage occurred) – to be systematically used to ascertain the law which should be relied upon to determine liability, causation and quantum in a private antitrust damages claim arising out of competition law infringements with an international element. The rationale for this approach appears to be set out in Recital 16 which states that:

> A connection with the country where the direct damage occurred (*lex loci damni*) strikes a fair balance between the interests of the person claimed to be liable and the person sustaining the damage, and also reflects the modern approach to civil liability and the development of systems of strict liability.[76]

In other words, a strong feature of Rome II is that the connecting factor – 'the country where the market is affected' – appears to align certain concepts (eg restriction of competition; affected markets) which are used by regulators when applying the relevant competition law provisions with the rules concerning the governing law in follow-on antitrust damages claims.

The advantages of this approach could be demonstrated by making reference to the *Trucks* cartel.[77] If the truck manufacturers' arrangements to exchange information about prices were to be 'restricting price competition',[78] then such a restriction of competition would in turn affect the truck prices in the UK (as well as in many other jurisdictions). More specifically, if 'the potential cartel overcharge [were to be fixed] at 25%',[79] then – given the cartelists' volume of commerce in the UK – the damage which may have been sustained in the UK could be significant. This example is set to reiterate

[71] See also: Fitchen (n 18) 363. Compare: Francq and Wurmnest (n 18) 120–22; Helner (n 66) 60; Dickinson (n 18) [6.63–64].

[72] Case AT.39824, *Trucks – Commission Decision relating to a proceeding under Article 101 of the Treaty on the Functioning of the European Union (the Treaty) and Article 53 of the EEA Agreement* – 19.7.2016, C(2016) 4673 final [61].

[73] Case Nos: 1282/7/7/18 and 1289/7/7/18, *UK Trucks Claim Ltd v Stellantis and Road Haulage Association Ltd v MAN SE & Ors* [2022] CAT 25 [176, 177 & 178]. See more below.

[74] Recital 21 of Rome II.

[75] See also: Helner (n 66) 51. Dickinson (n 18) [6.11-3].

[76] Recital 16 of Rome II.

[77] *Trucks – Commission Decision* (n 72).

[78] Ibid [81].

[79] *Road Haulage Association* (n 73) [164]. Compare: Case Nos: 1284/5/7/18 (T) and 1290/5/7/18 (T) *Royal Mail Group Ltd v DAF Trucks Ltd and others* [2023] CAT 6 [838].

that the connecting factor – 'the country where the market is affected' – would involve an enquiry which seeks to ascertain whether there was a sufficient degree of probability that the actual (or alleged) anti-competitive conduct had an actual effect on the market (eg raising prices)[80] in the country in question.[81]

Article 6(3)(b) has been criticised because '[i]ssues of directness and passing-on may potentially interact with Article 6(3)(b)'s condition precedent concerning direct and substantial effects when this is pleaded to the court'.[82] In spite of the criticism, it seems to this author that the question of whether the claimed antitrust damage has been passed-on does not arise at the stage when the judges ascertain where the direct antitrust damage occurred[83] (which is where the market is affected)[84] for the purposes of Rome II.[85] The availability of pass-on would depend on the applicable law. Indeed, aspects concerning causation and quantification (which may be dependent on the availability of the pass-on defence) would only be dealt with by the national court after the applicable law had been identified.[86]

Therefore, another strong feature of the Rome II approach is that the question about the place where the direct antitrust damage has occurred is closely connected with an analysis which determines the effects of a particular restrictive conduct, for example, on the prices and/or the volume of sales. Although there appear to be certain similarities with classifying damage for the purposes of Rome II and para 3.1(9)(a) of PD 6B,[87] there is a notable difference in so far as the antitrust damage must be direct for the purposes of Rome II (whilst indirect damage may suffice for the English courts to assume jurisdiction). According to Lord Justice Lloyd-Jones:

> Although [Rome II] draws a distinction between direct and indirect damage, the Rome II Regulation is concerned with choice of law not with jurisdiction. The two issues are distinct and are not analogous. There can only be one applicable law, whereas under both the Brussels system and under our domestic rules there can be more than one appropriate jurisdiction.[88]

The UK approach of adopting a broader definition for damages for the purposes of para 3.1 of PD 6B and to follow the EU model, having a narrower definition for choice-of-law purposes, is indeed welcome.[89] After all, an English court having international jurisdiction to award antitrust damages that had been sustained in several jurisdictions may reasonably be expected to apply foreign laws with a view to quantifying damages sustained in other jurisdictions.

[80] *AB Volvo v Ryder Ltd* [2020] EWCA Civ 1475 [83]; *NTN Corp v Stellantis NV* [2022] EWCA Civ 16 [25].

[81] Compare: the 'may affect' test defining the jurisdictional reach of Articles 81 and 82 EC. See Commission (EC) 'The effect on trade concept contained in Articles 81 and 82 of the Treaty' (Guidelines) [2004] OJ C101/81 [23].

[82] Fitchen (n 132) 368.

[83] See Recital 16 of Rome II and Article 4(1) of Rome II. See more: Fitchen (n 132) 367.

[84] See Recital 21 of Rome II.

[85] A somewhat different opinion has been expressed by Fitchen (n 132) 368–69.

[86] See more: A Komninos, *EC Private Antitrust Enforcement: Decentralised Application of EC Competition Law by National Courts* (Oxford, Hart Publishing, 2008) 199–202.

[87] See Chapter 4.V.A above.

[88] *Four Seasons Holdings Incorporated v Brownlie* [2021] UKSC 45 [46].

[89] Compare: Dickinson (n 18) [6.14]; Fitchen (n 18) 367.

V. Article 6(3)(a) of Rome II

The foregoing analysis strongly suggests that Rome II is drafted in a way which enables the judges to ascertain the applicable law with regard to the 'necessary elements of the tort'[90] of breach of competition. In particular, Article 6(3)(a) states that: 'The law applicable to a non-contractual obligation arising out of a restriction of competition shall be the law of the country where the market is, or is likely to be, affected'. The provision signifies the fact that damages should result from a competition law infringement (ie regulatory breach) which restricts competition. The wording 'arising out of' should reflect the requirement for 'a causal link between the infringement and the damages'[91] which would be the most common 'non-contractual obligation' which the injured parties will seek to enforce by bringing a private antitrust damages claim. The Rome II requirement is for the sustained private antitrust damages to have been caused by the specified regulatory breach.[92]

Given that the right to antitrust damages is the major non-contractual obligation for the purposes of Rome II,[93] it will be important for judges to ascertain where the direct antitrust damage occurred. This is a central point in the analysis of Article 6(3)(a) of Rome II. Since, as Professor Fitchen[94] has rightly noted, '[n]o definition of such "direct damage" is attempted',[95] the judges should determine, on a case-by-case basis, the country (or the countries) where the market is affected. As part of this process, the national judges should – for the choice-of-law purposes – ascertain *where the specific and restrictive/anti-competitive conduct* has affected the volume of sales and/or prices.[96] Indeed, the CJEU has taken the view that the place where the market is affected would be the place where the antitrust damages occurred.[97]

That said, it is difficult to see how a definition of 'direct damage' could have been provided in Article 6(3)(a) of Rome II. The place where the market is affected would be a question of fact. For example, the CJEU considered the response to this question in a follow-on private antitrust claim in *Tibor-Trans*.[98] The private antitrust damages claim was preceded by a decision of the EU Commission which established that DAF Trucks, along with a number of other cartelists, had agreed upon certain price-fixing arrangements that were in conflict with Article 101 TFEU.[99] Although the claim was issued against DAF Trucks (being one of the addressees of the Commission decision), the claimant, Tibor-Trans, was not buying directly from the defendant, but they were

[90] *Michael O'Higgins* (n 37) [172].

[91] Case No: 1298/5/7/18, *Achilles Information Ltd v Network Rail Infrastructure Ltd* [2016] CAT 11 [5.2]. See also: Case No: 1106/5/7/08 *Enron Coal Services Limited v English Welsh & Scottish Railway Limited* [2009] CAT 36 [88].

[92] Ibid [169] citing *BritNed Development Ltd v ABB AB* [2018] EWHC 2616 (Ch) ('*BritNed*') [10] aff'd *BritNed Development Ltd v ABB AB* [2019] EWCA Civ 1840.

[93] *Unlockd v Google* [2018] EWHC 1363 (Ch) [40].

[94] Fitchen (n 18).

[95] Ibid [367].

[96] *AB Volvo* (n 80) [83]; *Stellantis* (n 80) [25].

[97] Case C-27/17 *AB 'flyLAL-Lithuanian Airlines' v Starptautiskā lidosta 'Rīga' VAS and 'Air Baltic Corporation' AS* EU:C:2018:533 [40-41].

[98] Case C-451/18 *Tibor-Trans Fuvarozó és Kereskedelmi Kft v DAF Trucks NV* EU:C:2019:635.

[99] *Trucks – Commission Decision* (n 72).

rather getting their supplies from their Hungarian dealership. This posed the question whether direct private antitrust damage occurred in Hungary (ie the market where the prices were inflated). The CJEU took the view that:

> As regards the nature of the damage alleged, it should be noted that it is not merely a financial consequence of the damage that could have been suffered by direct purchasers, such as Hungarian vehicle dealerships, and which could have consisted of a loss of sales following the price increase. By contrast, the damage alleged in the case in the main proceedings results essentially from the additional costs incurred because of artificially high prices and, therefore, appears to be the immediate consequence of an infringement pursuant to Article 101 TFEU and thus constitutes direct damage which, in principle, provides a basis for the jurisdiction of the courts of the Member State in which it occurred.
>
> […]
>
> [I]n an action for compensation for damage caused by an infringement of Article 101 TFEU, consisting, inter alia, of collusive arrangements on pricing and gross price increases for trucks, [an important connecting factor would be] the place where the market which is affected by that infringement is located, that is to say, the place where the market prices were distorted and in which the victim claims to have suffered that damage […].[100]

This is in line with the practice of the English courts, which appears to indicate that the direct antitrust damage would occur (or the market will be affected) at the place where the sales were lost or where the overcharge was paid (ie the goods were sold or the services were provided at an inflated price).[101]

As noted above, Article 6(3)(a) should work reasonably well in follow-on damages claims. Since the conduct which classifies as 'restriction of competition' within the meaning of Rome II, and which amounts to a competition law infringement (ie regulatory breach), is often established by a regulator (eg the UK CMA or the EU Commission), the parties' pleadings and judges' analysis of the relevant effects on the market may be informed by the regulatory findings.

However, it should be noted there is a stark difference between a regulator's findings of a competition law infringement[102] (which is the central issue in public enforcement proceedings)[103] and 'the effects of the cartel on prices'[104] (which is the major issue that needs to be addressed in a follow-on claim for damages). It is highly unlikely for a regulatory decision to make any 'findings about the actual effects of the cartel on the market in question. For instance, there [would be] no finding that the cartel succeeded in raising prices by "x"% above the competitive level'.[105] That said, this is not a problem which may be cured by PIL mechanisms; it is rather due to the institutional architecture and the enforcement pattern in the EU.[106]

[100] *Tibor-Trans* (n 98) [31 and 37].
[101] *Apple v Qualcomm* [2018] EWHC 1188 (Pat) [98-99]. See also: *flyLAL-Lithunian Airlines* (n 97) [40–41].
[102] *AB Volvo* (n 80) [83].
[103] *Enron Coal Services Ltd (In Liquidation) v English Welsh & Scottish Railway Ltd* [2011] EWCA Civ 2.
[104] *AB Volvo* (n 80) [83].
[105] *Stellantis* (n 80) [25].
[106] M Danov and F Becker, 'Governance Aspects of Cross-Border EU Competition Law Actions: Theoretical and Practical Challenges' (2014) 10 *Journal of Private International Law* 359–401; *Enron* (n 103); WPJ Wils, 'The relationship between public antitrust enforcement and private actions for damages' (2009) 32 *World Competition* 3.

Moreover, since the scope of the relevant geographical market for the purposes of establishing a restriction by a regulator (and the EU Commission in particular) may cover more than one national market,[107] Article 6(3)(a) of Rome II enables a national court to apply the law of each country where the market is affected. More specifically, there is a possibility that 'the laws of all the countries concerned will have to be applied on a distributive basis, applying what is known as "Mosaikbetrachtung" in German law'.[108] The 'mosaic principle' has been criticised by Professor Dickinson,[109] who made the following observations:

> [A] thorough analysis will in many cases lead to the conclusion that the geographical area of the affected market covers the territory of more than one country, or even an entire free trade area (such as the EC/EEA). As a result, subject to the Art 6(3)(b) escape clause, the Regulation will require the application of the law of each of the countries in which the affected market is located on a distributive basis, the so-called Mosaikbetrachtung or 'mosaic view' approach. [...] This approach is [...] complex and unsatisfactory [....] The requirement, at least in the English courts, to plead and prove each applicable foreign law will further drive costs up in cases of this kind. Having regard to these factors, it would be unsurprising if Member State courts adopted a less technical approach in defining the geographic area of the relevant market more restrictively for these purposes, being more willing to accept that (for example) national preferences or linguistic differences support the conclusion that a national market should be distinguished from that in neighbouring areas.[110]

The difficulties in applying foreign laws are notorious, but there is no risk for the courts to restrictively define a relevant market; it is more a question of what the scope of the private damages claims should/would be. A narrower scope of claim would be a sensible strategy for claimants to manage any of the risks identified by Professor Dickinson, reducing the level of complexity and costs. If the claimant were successful with such a claim, the remainder could well settle at lower cost; which may be one way for claimants to manage such risks. This was indeed the approach adopted by the UK CAT in the *Trucks* collective proceedings, where the following observations were made:

> to include what on the RHA's evidence is a limited number of foreign trucks, even allowing for the fact that the number might grow if a CPO is granted, would very significantly complicate the proceedings. Claims for damages arising from such sales are likely to involve questions of foreign law, and given the range of countries therefore a large number of foreign laws, each relevant to only a tiny proportion of the total claim.[...] Further, the relevant markets on which those sales or leases took place may well be national markets and thus different from each other.[...] Although Dr Davis thought that it may be possible to include factors relevant to specific non-UK countries in the framework of his proposed methodology, he acknowledged that if a country-by-country analysis was required, that would not be feasible unless the number of PCMs from each country substantially increased.
>
> [...]

[107] *Trucks – Commission Decision* (n 72) [61].

[108] See Commission (EC), 'Proposal for a Regulation of the European Parliament and the Council on the law applicable to non-contractual obligations' COM (2003) 427 final.

[109] Dickinson (n 18) [6.64].

[110] Ibid [6.64].

> Having regard in particular to the costs and benefit involved and the need for a fair and efficient resolution of the common issues, in our judgment it is not suitable to include claims for non-UK trucks within the class.[111]

That said, a closer look at the above quotation seems to suggest that the parties and the UK CAT tried to avoid any disproportionate delay and complexities surrounding the application of over 11 sets of foreign laws in relation to a very small number of trucks (ie 697 trucks) which were purchased abroad.[112] The parties' approach appears to be in line with Professor Fitchen's suggestion that there was a risk for some claimants, who are faced with a higher level of complexity, which may be driven by the application of the 'mosaic principle', to rather 'decline to proceed with parts of [their competition law] claim'.[113]

However, one could only wonder why the claimants in Trucks collective redress proceedings did not rely on Article 6(3)(b) of Rome II. Given the volume of commerce in the UK and the fact that a number of defendants were domiciled within the jurisdiction,[114] this could have definitely been a case where 'the market in the United Kingdom is amongst those directly and substantially affected'.[115] On that basis, the law of the forum could have been applicable to all parts of their claim. Might Article 6(3)(b) of Rome II be a more appropriate solution in such cases?

VI. Article 6(3)(b) of Rome II

As noted above, it is well established that '[t]he special rule in Article 6 is not an exception to the general rule in Article 4(1) but rather a clarification of it',[116] which should apply in private antitrust damages claims. The relationship between Article 6(3)*(a)* and 6(3)*(b)* of Rome II is not set out in the recitals. The prevailing view appears to be that Article 6(3)(a) of Rome II would be the 'general rule',[117] with Article 6(3)(b) being regarded as the 'exception'.[118] Such an interpretation appears to draw analogy with how the relationship between Article 4(1) and Article 4(2) is set out in Recital 18 of Rome II. On that basis, one may go a step further to take the view that the exception should be narrowly interpreted, indicating that Article 6(3)(b) of Rome II should only apply in limited number of competition law 'cases where the market is, or is likely to be, affected in more than one country'[119] and where all the other requirements are satisfied.

[111] *Road Haulage Association* (n 73) [177 and 180].
[112] Ibid [176, 177 & 178].
[113] Fitchen (n 18) 358. See also: Dickinson (n 18) [6.64].
[114] Case No: 1289/7/7/18 *Road Haulage Association Limited v Man SE and Others* – Order of the President (Service out of the jurisdiction) – 24 July 2018 [3 and 4].
[115] Article 6(3)(b) of Rome II.
[116] Recital 21 of Rome II. Francq and Wurmnest (n 18) 98.
[117] Pineau (n 8) 318. See also: J Fitchen (n 18) 355, 357 and 364.
[118] Compare: Pineau (n 8) 318; Fitchen (n 18) 355. Professor Fitchen sometimes refers to Article 6(3)(b) as a special rule (ie 357), but more often he refers to it as an exception to Art 6(3)(a) (ie 353, 355, 356, 357, 358, 364, 365 and 366).
[119] Recital 22 of Rome.

That said, the practice under Rome II appears to suggest that Article 6(3)(b) may not be an exception as such; but it may have rather been set to deal with some specific competition law claims which arise out of transnational competition law infringements. There are two specific features of such claims that Article 6(3)(b) appears to be set to address. First, a transnational competition law infringement, by definition, will distort the process of competition in a number of jurisdictions. Secondly, the provision of Article 6(3)(b) would particularly be relevant for a specific category of injured parties who would have had sustained significant antitrust damages in a number of jurisdictions. These might often be relatively sophisticated claimants with access to finance. More specifically, Article 6(3)(b) states that:

> When the market is, or is likely to be, affected in more than one country, the person seeking compensation for damage who sues in [~~the court of the domicile of the defendant~~] *a court in a part of the United Kingdom*, may instead choose to base his or her claim on the law of the court seised, provided that the market in [~~that Member State~~] *the United Kingdom* is amongst those directly and substantially affected by the restriction of competition out of which the non-contractual obligation on which the claim is based arises; where the claimant sues, in accordance with the applicable rules on jurisdiction, more than one defendant in that court, he or she can only choose to base his or her claim on the law of that court if the restriction of competition on which the claim against each of these defendants relies directly and substantially affects also the market in the [~~Member State of that court~~] *United Kingdom*.[120]

The wording of Article 6(3)(b) of Rome II indicates that the provision is rather set to apply only in those claims which are issued before courts in a country where the market is 'amongst those directly and substantially affected'. This reiterates that such private antitrust damages claims would be issued against a special category of defendants (ie infringing undertakings) that would normally have a significant market power in a number of jurisdictions; otherwise they would not be capable of directly and significantly affecting markets in multiple jurisdictions. This poses the question of what the rationale behind Article 6(3)(b) is. The answer to this question would be important for the provision to be purposively interpreted.[121]

A. Rationale – Article 6(3)(b)

Although there is no intention for Article 6(3)(b) to apply in all cases where a restriction of competition affects markets in several countries, the *purpose* of the provision is to enable 'the claimant [...] in certain circumstances to choose to base his or her claim on *the law of the court seised*'.[122] The provision should be purposively interpreted to improve the injured parties' access to justice in highly complex cases against sophisticated defendants.[123] This deduction could be strengthened by the wording of the provision which imposes a requirement for the market in the Member State in question

[120] The Law Applicable to Contractual Obligations and Non-Contractual Obligations (Amendment etc.) (EU Exit) Regulations 2019 s 11(4) – the amendments are emphasised by the author.
[121] Case C-283/81 *Srl CILFIT and Lanificio di Gavardo SpA v Ministry of Health* EU:C:1982:335 [20].
[122] Recital 22 of Rome II – emphasis added by the author.
[123] Recital 14 of Rome II. See also *CILFIT* (n 121) [20]. Compare: Francq and Wurmnest (n 18) 101–102.

to be among those 'directly and substantially' affected by a transnational competition law infringement.

The facilitative nature of the provision appears to be further reflected in the fact that there is no requirement for the market in the UK to be the most affected; nor is there a requirement for the UK market to be the only one which is directly and substantially affected. It is sufficient for the claimants to demonstrate that 'the market in the United Kingdom is amongst those directly and substantially affected' within the meaning of Article 6(3)(b) of Rome II. The points concerning the facilitative nature of Article 6(3)(b) of Rome II were set out in *Westover Ltd v Mastercard*[124] where the following observations were put forward:

> [W]hat if the relevant geographic markets are national and, as is not uncommon, the cartelists do not sell directly into those markets but operate through local subsidiaries? Then the merchant's purchases in X are made from companies in X owned by, say, A, B and C; and its purchases in Y are made from companies in Y owned by, say, B, C and D (since A does not operate in Y); and its purchases in Z are made from companies in Z owned by A, B and D (since C does not operate in Z). The prices charged by those local subsidiaries are inflated by reason of the cartel but it is axiomatic that the merchant can claim against their parent companies, i.e. the cartelists (and any decision of the Commission would be addressed to the parent companies that made the price-fixing agreement). The effect of the cartel was to restrict competition as between the suppliers in national market X, which was distinct from the competition as between the different suppliers in national market Y, which in turn was distinct from the competition as between the different suppliers in national market Z. If the defendants' basic contention was correct, although the merchant would be able to bring a single set of proceedings claiming all its loss against A, B, C and D in the court of a country where one of them is domiciled, that claim would be governed by different laws according to where it suffered damage. In our judgment, that is the consequence which would otherwise apply under Art 6(3)(a) but which Art 6(3)(b) is designed to avoid.[125]

The above quotation sets the facilitative features of Article 6(3)(b) of Rome II. There are indeed significant advantages for claimants in follow-on claims that arise out of a transnational competition law infringement that has been established by the EU Commission. With this in mind, it should be noted that the UK legislator has made three amendments to the original text of Article 6(3)(b) of Rome II. The minor modifications are simply reflecting the fact that the UK is no longer part of the European Union as well as the fact that the Brussels Ia/Lugano regime, which advances the defendant's domicile[126] as a general rule that allocates jurisdiction within the EU/EEA, is no longer applicable in the UK.

Whilst Article 6(3)(b) of Rome II (EU version) requires 'the person seeking compensation for damage [to sue] in the court of the domicile of the defendant', it is sufficient for such a claimant to bring their claim before a court in a part of the UK, irrespective of what the basis for jurisdiction is, under Article 6(3)(b) of Rome II (UK version). This is a welcome development because it was difficult to see why a claimant could not rely on Article 6(3)(b) of Rome II (EU version), if they were to issue their competition law claim under Articles 7(2) of Brussels Ia rather than Article 4 or Article 8(1) of Brussels Ia.

[124] *Westover* (n 54).
[125] Ibid [57].
[126] Article 4(1) – Brussels Ia; Article 2(1) – Lugano.

Since the English jurisdictional rules contain a requirement for the courts to determine whether England and Wales is an appropriate forum for the competition law claim to be issued,[127] the UK version of Article 6(3)(b) of Rome II seems to be better focused on the direct and substantial effects, removing the requirements for the basis for jurisdiction in so far as the appropriateness of the forum will be scrutinised under the CPR or UK CAT rules at the jurisdictional stage. That said, the fact that the EU policy-makers linked the possibility of the parties to rely on Article 6(3)(b) of Rome II with the basis of jurisdiction meant that Article 8(1) of Brussels Ia became an attractive jurisdictional rule which enabled sophisticated claimants to issue proceedings against the two or more infringing undertakings.

There are, at least, two major aspects of the PIL framework which indicate that strategic parties – who have suffered significant damages in multiple jurisdictions – could/should be selective when deciding where to issue their private antitrust damages claims. First, the scope of the jurisdiction of the courts at the place where the damage occurred under Article 7(2) of Brussels Ia would be limited to the local harm.[128] However, the territorial scope of the courts' jurisdiction under Article 8(1) of Brussels Ia would not be limited, which is more in line with the spirit of Article 6(3)(b) of Rome II, enabling strategic claimants to bring their claim before the court of their choice.

Secondly, since many of the infringing undertakings are groups of companies having subsidiaries across the EU, the strategic claimants will have the choice of suing all defendants in any Member State in which one of the subsidiaries is domiciled. An added benefit for such defendants is that they will also have the 'law of the court seised' applicable to all the claims (concerning antitrust damages that were sustained in other countries)[129] as long as the market of that Member State is 'amongst those directly and substantially affected'.[130] The implications for the strategic decisions of the parties could be deduced from Lawrence and Morfey's analysis[131] of the High Court of England and Wales in *Provimi*.[132] In particular, they thought that:

> This judgment opened the door to litigation being brought in England against a number of defendants on the basis of an English anchor defendant which was merely a subsidiary of one of the addressees of a Commission decision, in circumstances where a subsidiary neither played a direct role in the cartel nor had knowledge of it.
>
> The claimant tactic of relying on an English subsidiary to establish jurisdiction in England appears to have been cemented in the *Cooper Tire* litigation.[133]

This means that, as part of the forum selection process, sophisticated parties might consider various procedural rules (including evidence, disclosure, costs and access to finance)[134] as well as substantive law rules that were to apply under Article 6(3)(b) of

[127] See: Chapters 4, 5, 6 and 7.
[128] See: Chapter 4 above.
[129] See also: Helner (n 66) 64.
[130] CDC – AG [73–75]. See J Fitchen, 'The Applicable Law in Cross-Border Competition Law Actions and Article 6(3) of Regulation 864/2007' in Danov, Becker and Beaumont (n 20) 297.
[131] Lawrence and Morfey (n 65).
[132] *Provimi Limited v Aventis Animal Nutrition SA and Others* [2003] EWHC 961 (Comm).
[133] Lawrence and Morfey (n 65) 150.
[134] Ibid 149.

Rome II, which 'is important for claimants seeking certainty and simplicity'.[135] In other words, the provision may inter alia continue to promote a level of adjudicatory/regulatory competition.[136] This would be particularly so in follow-on damages claims.

However, more complex issues would arise in stand-alone cases where different competition laws are at stake. If the English courts were to exclusively apply UK competition law to determine whether there was a transnational competition law infringement, without factoring in foreign regulatory interests, then this would undermine any mechanism for judicial cooperation in competition law matters. Should the English courts decide to advance a transnational approach to judicial cooperation in cross-border competition law cases, then Article 6(3)(a) of Rome might be the more appropriate provision, which should enable the British judges to factor in foreign regulatory interests.[137]

B. The Market – 'Directly and Substantially Affected'[138]

It is beyond any doubt that the connecting factor, 'the country where the market is affected', which is the place where the direct antitrust damage occurs, would be relevant in relation to Article 6(3)(b) of Rome II[139] in so far as the aspects concerning effects in the market would still need to be considered. That said, in order for Article 6(3)(b) of Rome II to be invoked, the effect on the prices (which are paid by the claimant/s) or the sales (which are lost by them) must be *direct* and *substantial*.

Professor Dickinson[140] has pointed out that the EU Commission had originally proposed the following guidance for the national courts to rely upon with a view to determining whether the market is 'directly and substantially' affected:

> When determining whether or not a restriction of competition affects a market directly and substantially, in particular the prices, outputs, innovation or the variety of products on that market, due regard must be given to the position and the importance of the undertakings involved on the market for the products concerned.[141]

Although the EU Commission proposal does not feature in the final version of Rome II, it could be expected that the question of whether the market in the UK is 'directly and substantially' affected should involve a factual assessment. This is less to do with the amount of the relevant overcharge, but it is more to do with the 'volume of commerce'[142] of the infringing undertakings in the UK, which should have direct and substantial effects in the UK market (potentially affecting multiple injured parties in the UK). The stronger the market position of the infringing undertaking/s and the higher their

[135] H Mercer, 'Applicable Law in Cross-Border EU Law Actions – Forum Shopping, Mandatory Rules and Public Policy' in Danov, Becker and Beaumont (n 20) 329, 332.

[136] Danov, Becker and Beaumont (n 20).

[137] Chapter 10 above.

[138] Article 6(3)(b) of Rome II.

[139] Sections IV and V above.

[140] Dickinson (n 18) [6.71].

[141] Commission document SPI (2007) 42 [3.5.2007] 9, cited in Dickinson (n 18) [6.71].

[142] Case No: 1266/7/7/16 *Merricks v MasterCard* [2017] CAT 16 [29–31].

volume of commerce in the UK, the more likely it is for the anti-competitive conduct to be capable of having a direct and substantial effect in the UK.[143]

Article 6(3)(a) of Rome II should apply in competition cases where the markets in several countries are affected, but the conditions of Article 6(3)(b) of Rome II are not satisfied. The high threshold for the parties to rely on Article 6(3)(b) is set to ensure that the law of the court seised would only exclusively apply in cases where the UK market is 'directly and substantially' affected. Indeed, the fact that many cross-border competition law infringements would cause damages to multiple injured parties in many jurisdictions indicates that any PIL rule which allows for the law of the court seised should go along with an adequate 'deterrent to forum shoppers'.[144] The issue of 'forum shopping' would arise in a case where a claimant is 'by-passing his natural forum and bringing his action in some alien forum which would give him relief or benefits which would not be available to him in his natural forum'.[145] There are at least two major caveats to using this definition in cross-border competition law cases. First, one single natural forum may be difficult to identify with regard to competition law claims arising out of transnational economic activities that may be in conflict with multiple competition laws.[146] In other words, the transnational nature of certain competition law infringements would mean that there could be multiple natural forums.[147]

Secondly, whilst policy-makers would normally try to deter forum shopping,[148] the sophisticated parties would naturally endeavour to legitimately gain procedural or substantive advantages as well as to gain even access to funding and/or more experienced legal teams by issuing proceedings in one jurisdiction rather than another.[149] Given the growing number of national policies and given that the rationale of Article 6(3)(b) of Rome II may well be to improve the injured parties' access to justice in competition law, sophisticated claimants may well take legitimate advantage of the applicable procedural and/or substantive laws in a particular jurisdiction. Indeed, it has been submitted that '[t]he unavoidable consequence, even if perhaps unintended, is that [EU] law fosters (and some may even say blesses) forum shopping search of the rule which endows the claimant with the highest damages award for the breach of a given competition rule or rules'.[150]

More importantly, policy-makers may reasonably promote regulatory/adjudicatory competition between different jurisdictions, which should provide claimants with a choice of where to bring their competition law claim arising out of transnational competition law infringements.[151] For example, a private antitrust claimant who intends to sue infringing defendants (which are transnational groups of companies) may have a legitimate choice

[143] Compare: Commission Guidelines (n 142) [45].

[144] Mercer (n 135) 330–332. Dickinson (n 18) [6.71]. See more A Bell, *Forum Shopping and Venue in Transnational Litigation* (Oxford, OUP, 2003) 39.

[145] *Boys v Chaplin* [1971] AC 356, 401 (Lord Pearson); J Fawcett, 'Forum shopping—some questions answered' (1984) 35 *Northern Ireland Law Quarterly* 141.

[146] *Dr Rachael Kent* (n 4) [14]. See more: Chapter 7.

[147] See: Chapters 3, 4, 5 and 6.

[148] See more: AG Slater, 'Forum Non Conveniens: A View from the Shop Floor' (1988) 104 *LQR* 554, 561–62. See also M Monti, 'Competition Law Reform', speech made at the CBI Conference on Competition Law Reform London, June 12, https://ec.europa.eu/competition/speeches/text/sp2000_008_en.html.

[149] Danov and Dnes (n 20).

[150] Pineau (n 8) 327–28. Mercer (n 135) 330–32.

[151] Danov, Becker and Beaumont (n 20).

to exercise when deciding where to issue their competition law claims.[152] As part of this process, the claimant might reasonably consider such aspects as the binding nature of regulatory findings; experience of any specialised judges; disclosure rules; availability of litigation funding and costs; opt-out collective redress proceedings.[153]

Nonetheless, the English courts should be alert and aim to deter forum shopping in competition law cases where a strategic claimant issues proceedings in England and/or another jurisdiction, in order to delay the resolution of the dispute and/or to adversely affect the settlement negotiations.[154] For example, a pre-emptive action may be issued before courts which notoriously take longer before a final decision is rendered, which may impact on the settlement dynamics.[155]

Finally, it should be noted that Rome II takes account of the fact that in competition law cases the defendants (ie infringing undertakings) would normally enjoy market (and bargaining) power, whilst many of the injured parties – SMEs and consumers in particular – would be in a weaker position in comparison to various multinational companies that enjoy a significant market power (if not a dominant position). This is reflected in Article 6(4) of Rome II which states that: 'The law applicable under [Article 6(3)(a) and (b) of Rome II] may not be derogated from by an agreement pursuant to Article 14'.[156] This rule, which is set to limit parties' freedom of choice with regard to the relevant private antitrust damages claims, is just another reflection of the same policy.[157]

The absolute prohibition for parties to choose the law governing the substantive law aspects of their private antitrust damages has been criticised by some commentators.[158] Professor Fitchen goes further to make a case for reviewing the Rome II Regulation, so as to allow the parties to make a restricted choice of law subject to requirements 'prevent[ing] the evasion of […] mandatory rules'.[159] However, it seems to this author that such a liberal proposal should not be supported. It would hardly seem an appropriate policy choice to permit a dominant undertaking to include a choice-of-law provision that does not allow a claimant to rely on a rebuttable presumption of harm[160] or to choose a set of applicable laws which do not use a *broad-brush approach*[161] to assessment of damages. It should be noted that Article 6(4) is not only meant to ensure that mandatory provisions are not evaded, but also to secure that any undertaking enjoying market power would not be allowed to make it excessively

[152] See: Chapter 7.

[153] Danov and Dnes (n 20); M Danov, 'Cross-Border Litigation in England and Wales: Pre-Brexit Data and Post-Brexit Implications' (2018) 25 *Maastricht Journal of European and Comparative Law* 139–67; M Danov), 'Cross-Border Litigation: Evaluating the Brexit impact – A Socio-Legal Model for Data Analysis' (2020) 27 *Maastricht Journal of European and Comparative Law* 199–229.

[154] Fawcett (n 145) 144.

[155] *Cooper Tire & Rubber Company Europe Ltd & Others* [2010] EWCA Civ 864 [54–55]. See more: Chapter 7.

[156] Article 6(4) of Rome II.

[157] Th M de Boer, 'Party autonomy and its limitations in the Rome II Regulation' (2007) *Yearbook of Private International Law* 19, 24–25.

[158] T Petch, 'The Rome II Regulation: an update: part 2' (2006) 21 *Journal of International Banking Law and Regulation* 509, 511; Fitchen (n 18) 344–46. Compare Pineau (n 8) 327.

[159] Fitchen (n 18) 346.

[160] Article 17(2) of Directive 2014/104/EU.

[161] See: Section II above.

difficult for injured parties to access effective remedies by relying on appropriately drafted choice-of-law clauses.

VII. Scope – Applicable Law

The importance of the distinction between issues which classify as procedural and substantive could be further deduced from the High Court[162] and Court of Appeal[163] judgments in *Wall v Mutuelle De Poitiers Assurance*, where it was submitted that the outcome of the dispute may be different in cases where, even if the substantive rules are identical, the national courts apply different sets of procedural and evidential rules.[164]

The Rome II rules also reflect the distinction between the aspects in relation to access to legal remedies – being classified as procedural within the meaning of Article 1(3) of Rome II and the aspects in relation to the entitlement of legal remedies – being classified as substantive law issues within the meaning of Article 15 of Rome II.[165] More specifically, Article 1(3) states that the Rome II 'Regulation shall not apply to evidence and procedure, without prejudice to Articles 21 and 22'. Whilst Article 21 of Rome II aims to deal with issues concerning formal validity of unilateral acts, Article 22 contains an important exception which might be relevant in some competition law cases in so far as it states that '[the law governing a non-contractual obligation under this Regulation shall apply to the extent that, in matters of noncontractual obligations, it contains rules which raise presumptions of law or determine the burden of proof'.

The fact that Directive 2014/104/EU[166] aims to harmonise certain procedural rules (eg disclosure of evidence)[167] as well as certain substantive law rules (eg pass-on; joint and several liability) is yet another acknowledgment that procedural and substantive law issues are intertwined in cross-border competition law cases. This point could be strengthened further, if Article 22 of Rome II is read along with Article 17(2) of Directive 2014/104/EU which states that '[i]t shall be presumed that cartel infringements cause harm'. Ascertaining the scope of applicable substantive law would add a layer of complexity, not the least because the evidential matters will be raising substantive and procedural issues which 'cannot be relegated to clear cut categories'[168] in competition cases.[169] The deduction could be strengthened by considering the issues in relation to the burden of proof and standard of proof in competition cases.[170] Regulation 1/2003 clearly stipulates that the burden of proving an infringement 'rests on the party [...]

[162] *Steven John Kilfoy Wall v Mutuelle De Poitiers Assurance* [2013] EWHC 53 (QB).
[163] *Steven John Kilfoy Wall v Mutuelle De Poitiers Assurance* [2014] EWCA Civ 138.
[164] Ibid [43–44]. See more: Chapter 2 above.
[165] See more: M Danov 'Data Analysis: Important Issues to be Considered in a Cross-Border Context' in P Beaumont et al, (eds), *Cross-Border Litigation in Europe* (Oxford, Hart Publishing, 2017) 475.
[166] See J Fitchen, 'Private Enforcement of Competition Law' in Beaumont et al (n 165) 671, 676–84.
[167] Article 6 of Directive 2014/104/EU.
[168] S Szaszy, 'The basic connecting factor in international cases in the domain of civil procedure' (1966) 15 *ICLQ* 436, 455.
[169] R Garnett, 'Substance and Procedure' in P Beaumont and J Holliday (eds) *Guide to Global Private International Law* (Oxford, Hart Publishing, 2022) 119, 124–25.
[170] Ibid.

alleging [it]',[171] but it does not set the standard of proof.[172] The distinction could be deduced from Recital 5 of the Regulation which states that:

> this Regulation affects neither national rules on the standard of proof nor obligations of competition authorities and courts of the Member States to ascertain the relevant facts of a case, provided that such rules and obligations are compatible with general principles of [EU] law.

The fact that Article 22 of Rome II says nothing about the standard of proof (as opposed to the burden of proof) should be interpreted as indicating that the matter should classify as procedural, which falls within Article 1(3) of Rome II (being outside of the scope of Rome II).

The issues may be very important in cross-border competition law cases because the aspects concerning substance and procedure might be even more closely knitted when it comes to quantification of damages in such disputes. It should be noted that Article 15 of Rome II aims to set out the scope of applicable national law, which would be relevant for quantification of damages, by stating that:

> The law applicable to non-contractual obligations under [the Rome II] Regulation shall govern in particular:
>
> (a) the basis and extent of liability, including the determination of persons who may be held liable for acts performed by them;
> (b) the grounds for exemption from liability, any limitation of liability and any division of liability;
> (c) the existence, the nature and the assessment of damage or the remedy claimed;
> (d) within the limits of powers conferred on the court by its procedural law, the measures which a court may take to prevent or terminate injury or damage or to ensure the provision of compensation;
> (e) the question whether a right to claim damages or a remedy may be transferred, including by inheritance;
> (f) persons entitled to compensation for damage sustained personally;
> (g) liability for the acts of another person;
> (h) the manner in which an obligation may be extinguished and rules of prescription and limitation, including rules relating to the commencement, interruption and suspension of a period of prescription or limitation.[173]

The text of this provision leaves no doubt that the law which is ascertained under Article 6(3)(b) of Rome II would have an important role to play when it comes to issues of causation and quantification of damages.

That said, the point about the fine line between the substantive law matters (which are governed by Rome II) and the procedural aspects (which are governed by the law of the court seised) was captured by the Court of Appeal of England and Wales in *NTN v Stellantis NV*,[174] where the court dealt with the claimants' strike-out application in relation to the defendants' defence that the loss was mitigated by the claimants. In this case,

[171] See: Article 2 of Regulation 1/2003.
[172] J Faull and A Nikpay, *The EC Law of Competition* 2nd edn (Oxford, OUP, 2007) 95.
[173] Article 15 of Rome II.
[174] *Stellantis* (n 80).

the Court of Appeal had to deal with two questions: a substantive law question concerning the issues of causation in relation to mitigation in competition law claims issued by a direct purchaser who might have partly passed through the cartel-induced overcharge, and a procedural question about the relevant standard of proof for the issue to proceed to trial.[175]

In response to the first question it was held that 'there has to be a sufficient causal nexus or connection between the steps that a defendant says a claimant took by way of mitigation (the off-setting) and the overcharge'.[176] More importantly, the court went on to capture how closely the substantive law and procedural aspects may be knitted in competition cases by holding that:

> [T]he second question which is the evidential standard that the CAT (or a court) must apply to determine whether a pleading is to be allowed to proceed to trial. There is a connection with the outcome of the first question since if all that is required is a broad brush and theoretical averment, devoid of fact or particularisation about the causative link, that the claimant *did* mitigate by off-setting, then it might be quite difficult to strike out a pleading, irrespective of the standard to be applied.[177]

This quotation suggests that the distinction between the substantive law matters and the procedural issues may be even more difficult to draw in competition law cases where the national courts may be expected 'to quantify the harm suffered on the basis of approximate best estimates'.[178] In England and Wales, the quantification exercise may be based on a '"broad axe" or "broad brush" principle'[179] which 'is applicable where the claimant has suffered loss as a result of the defendant's culpable conduct but there is a lack of evidence as to the amount of such loss'.[180] This is set to ensure that 'the court will not allow an unreasonable insistence on precision to defeat the justice of compensating a claimant for infringement of his rights'.[181]

More importantly, the UK Supreme Court has noted the correlation between the degree of precision required when quantifying damages and the aspects concerning access to justice in competition law cases by holding that:

> Justice is not achieved if a claimant receives less or more than its actual loss. But in applying the principle the court must also have regard to another principle, enshrined in the overriding objective of the Civil Procedure Rules, that legal disputes should be dealt with at a proportionate cost. The court and the parties may have to forgo precision, even where it is possible, if the cost of achieving that precision is disproportionate, and rely on estimates. The common law takes a pragmatic view of the degree of certainty with which damages must be pleaded and proved.[182]

[175] Ibid [16].
[176] Ibid [17].
[177] Ibid [22]. See also: Section 4.IV above.
[178] Commission Staff Working Document, *Practical Guide Quantifying Harm in Actions for Damages based on Breaches of Article 101 or 102 of the Treaty on the Functioning of the European Union (Accompanying the Communication from the Commission on quantifying harm in actions for damages based on breaches of Article 101 or 102 of the Treaty on the Functioning of the European Union)* SWD(2013) 205 [4].
[179] *Merricks* (n 8) [51].
[180] *Sainsbury's Supermarkets Ltd v MasterCard Incorporated* [2018] EWCA 1536 (Civ) [331]. See also: *Sainsbury's Supermarkets Ltd v MasterCard Incorporated* [2020] UKSC 24 [76].
[181] *ASDA Stores Ltd v Mastercard Incorporated* [2017] EWHC 93 (Comm) [306] cited in *Merricks* (n 8) [51].
[182] *Sainsbury's* – UKSC (n 180) [217].

A major hurdle is that the substantive aspects concerning the quantification of damages on a *broad-axe* basis may be intertwined with the gaps of data and lack of sufficient evidence (ie procedural matters). This means that it will be important for a national competition law regime to appropriately set out the balance between these procedural issues and the substantive law matters, in order to improve access to justice in competition law cases. In cross-border cases, this means that, despite the level of harmonisation within the EU, there would still be advantages for parties to issue their proceedings in one jurisdiction rather than another.

In addition, it should be added that various substantive laws (including divergent limitation periods which would have a direct impact on assessment of damages and parties' entitlement to remedies) could well need to be legitimately considered by a party who wants to strategically issue their claim under Article 6(3)(b) of Rome II. The relevant issues could be deduced from the CAT judgment in *Sainsbury's Supermarkets v MasterCard*[183] where it was held that:

> We note that it was common ground that, under the Scots law on limitation, Sainsbury's is permitted to claim for transactions taking place in Scotland only for a period of 5 years (not 6 years, as is the case for England and Wales). The figures we have used take account of these different limitation periods in England and Wales, and in Scotland.[184]

Indeed, it is well established that the aspects concerning the limitation periods may have major implications for the outcome of the dispute, which is why they have been subject to heated debates between the parties in private antitrust damages claims. The important issues were set out by Lawrence and Morfey[185] who appeared to suggest that these aspects may have an impact on the settlement dynamics in some cases.[186]

Given the importance of the issue, the matter subsequently has recently reached the Court of Appeal of England and Wales in *DSG Retail v MasterCard*[187] and *Gemalto v Infineon Technologies*.[188] In the first case Lord Justice Vos reiterated that, in some competition law cases, an important question would be 'whether the claimants could "with reasonable diligence have discovered" the concealment of "any fact relevant to" the claimants' right of action'.[189] In *Gemalto*,[190] Lord Justice Vos went further to set out '[t]he applicable test to determine when time begins to run in a case where any fact relevant to the claimant's right of action has been deliberately concealed by the defendant'.[191] In particular the Master of the Rolls held that:

> [T]he position after [*Test Claimants in the Franked Investment Group Litigation v HMRC* [2020] UKSC 47] is that the proviso to section 32(1) [of the Limitation Act 1980] has to be construed consistently as between mistake and deliberate concealment cases. Time begins to run in a deliberate concealment case when the claimant recognises that it has a worthwhile claim. In a case of this kind, a worthwhile claim arises when a reasonable person could have

[183] *Sainsbury's* – CAT (n 60).
[184] Ibid [428].
[185] Lawrence and Morfey (n 65) 152–54.
[186] Ibid 154.
[187] *DSG Retail Ltd and Dixons Retail Group Ltd v MasterCard Inc* [2020] EWCA Civ 671.
[188] *Gemalto Holding BV v Infineon Technologies AG* [2022] EWCA Civ 782.
[189] *DSG Retail* (n 187) [3].
[190] *Gemalto Holding* (n 188) 782.
[191] Ibid [39–53].

> a reasonable belief that there had been a cartel. The claimant can embark on the preliminaries to the issue of a writ (and therefore the limitation has begun) once it knows that there may have been a cartel and the identity of the participants, without knowing chapter and verse about the details. It would not, however, know that it had a worthwhile claim if a claim pleaded on the basis of the details it knew would be struck out.[192]

Although this quotation sets out the position under English law, it is possible for different national courts to apply different tests when determining when the limitation claim begins to run for a specific private antitrust damages claim.

Further difficulties are bound to arise in cases where a transnational competition law infringement occurred in a number of different jurisdictions over a prolonged period of time. For example, in *Deutsche Bahn v MasterCard*,[193] the issues concerning assessment of antitrust damages were far more complex because, in this case, the '[c]laimants [we]re some 1,300 retailers, comprising 7 corporate groups who operate in 18 European countries (17 EEA countries and Switzerland)'.[194] The claims in *Deutsche Bahn* were partly follow-on and partly *hybrid* stand-alone.[195] The problem was that, given the fact that the damages were claimed for an extended period of time, the English courts had to rely on three different PIL regimes with a view to identifying the applicable laws. First, Article 6(3) of the Rome II Regulation had to be applied for the damage which occurred 'from 11 January 2009 to date [of the judgment]'.[196] Secondly, the Private International Law (Miscellaneous Provisions) Act 1995 was to be applied for the period from 1 May 1996 to 10 January 2009.[197] Thirdly, the English common law (including the rule of double actionability) was to be applied with regard to damage which occurred between 22 May 1992 and 30 April 1996.[198]

Another important aspect, which would impact on the outcome and litigants' access to remedies, is the passing-on defence. The existence of the pass-on defence may or may not be closely connected with the standing of indirect purchasers to seek redress. Both issues were addressed by the EU Commission in EU Directive 2014/104, which states that 'Member States shall ensure that the defendant in an action for damages can invoke as a defence against a claim for damages the fact that the claimant passed on the whole or part of the overcharge resulting from the infringement of competition law'.[199] The issues are important because the Directive clearly states that anyone who has suffered harm caused by a competition law infringement has the right to be 'able to claim and obtain full compensation for that harm'.[200]

A different approach is adopted in the US. In particular, the passing-on defence cannot be invoked by defendants in the US.[201] Moreover, it is well established that

[192] Ibid [53].
[193] *Deutsche Bahn AG & Others v MasterCard Incorporated* [2018] EWHC 412 (Ch).
[194] Ibid [1].
[195] Ibid.
[196] Ibid [12 and 21–27].
[197] Ibid [12 and 125].
[198] Ibid [12 and 154].
[199] See: Article 13 of the Directive on antitrust damages actions.
[200] See: Article 3 of the Directive on antitrust damages actions. But, 'overcompensation' is not part of the 'full compensation' under the Directive. (See Article 3(3).) Commission Staff Working Paper, Annex to the Green Paper on damages actions for breach of the EC antitrust rules SEC(2005) 1732 paras 1–3.
[201] *Hanover Shoe v United Shoe Machinery*, 392 US 481 (1968).

indirect purchasers would not have standing to bring a claim in the US.[202] A somewhat different approach is advanced by the Supreme Court of Canada in *Pro-Sys Consultants v Microsoft Corporation*.[203] The Canadian court held that: '[a]lthough the passing-on *defence* is unavailable as a matter of restitution law, it does not follow that indirect purchasers should be foreclosed from claiming losses passed on to them'.[204]

The foregoing examples strongly indicate that it may not be easy to draw a distinction between the parties' entitlement to legal remedies (ie quantification of damages) and the parties' access to legal remedies (ie the issues concerning the standard of proof) in cross-border competition law cases.[205] Setting up a regime for judicial cooperation in competition law presupposes for all these aspects to be systematically considered with a view to improving the injured parties' access to legal remedies.

VIII. Contractual Classification of Competition Law Claims

As noted above,[206] competition law claims may either classify as tortious or contractual. Particularly difficult classification issues would arise in cases that arise out of contractual relationships involving undertakings that enjoy dominant positions[207] or that involve undertakings that might be cartel members. Such undertakings may be entering into various contractual arrangements that contain certain anti-competitive terms.

The Rome I Regulation would apply to ascertain which set of competition laws as well as which contract laws should be applied by the English judges to determine whether the contract is compliant with competition law and, if not, whether the contract as a whole (or only the anti-competitive terms) should be invalidated.[208] Although Article 3(1) of Rome I adopts as a basic principle that 'the contract shall be governed by the law chosen by the parties', Article 3(3) of Rome I states that:

> Where all other elements relevant to the situation at the time of the choice are located in a country other than the country whose law has been chosen, the choice of the parties shall not prejudice the application of provisions of the law of that other country which cannot be derogated from by agreement.

As noted above,[209] since competition laws would reflect the national public policy,[210] they should not only classify as 'overriding mandatory provisions' within the meaning of Article 9(1) of Rome I, but they would also be regarded as 'provisions […] which cannot be derogated from by agreement' within the meaning of Article 3 of Rome I.

[202] *Illinois Brick v Illinois* 431 US 720 (1977) 730–31.
[203] *Pro-Sys Consultants v Microsoft Corporation* [2013] SCC 57 (CanLII).
[204] Ibid [60].
[205] See: Chapter 2 above. See more: Garnett (n 169); A Scott, 'Substance and procedure and choice of law in torts' (2007) *Lloyd's Maritime and Commercial Law Quarterly* 44; M Illmer, 'Neutrality matters—some thoughts about the Rome Regulations and the so-called dichotomy of substance and procedure in European private international law' (2009) *Civil Justice Quarterly* 237.
[206] See: Chapters 2 and 5 above.
[207] eg *Unlockd* (n 93).
[208] See: Articles 10 and 12(1)(e) of the Rome I Regulation.
[209] See: Chapter 10.
[210] Recital 1 of Directive 2014/104/EU. Case 172/73 *BRT v SABAM* [1974] ECR 51. See also: Giuliano and Lagarde Report (n 8) p 28.

The rationale of this rule is to limit the parties' freedom to choose the competition laws which are to govern the validity of their agreement in cases where all the elements of the contract are connected with the UK at the time when the choice is made.[211]

That said, the parties will be free to choose the applicable law that is to govern the parts of the contract that are not restricting competition.[212] Such a deduction can be strengthened by the last sentence of Article 3(1) of Rome I, which stipulates that: 'By their choice the parties can select the law applicable to the whole or a part only of the contract'. The issues are important because, even the contract were to contain certain anti-competitive terms, an entirely different question is how the anti-competitive terms would affect the remaining contractual arrangements between the parties.[213] The aspects concerning '[t]he question of severance'[214] were indeed set out by the English court in *English Welsh & Scottish Railway v E. On* where Mr Justice Field held that:

> Where terms are void at common law for being in restraint of trade or by reason of [Article 101 TFEU] and the Chapter I prohibition, the courts apply the doctrine of severance to determine if the offending terms can be severed from the contract leaving the residue to continue to operate as an enforceable contract; see eg *Crehan v Courage Limited; Byrne v Inntreprenneur Beer Supply Co Ltd* [1999] EuLR 834 at 896E-901A. In my judgement, exactly the same approach applies where a term or terms of a contract are void by reason of being in breach of [Article 102 TFEU] and the Chapter II prohibition. It is thus not a question of whether the contract is frustrated but whether the test for severance as formulated in the cases has been satisfied.
>
> The Court of Appeal in *Crehan v Courage* rehearsed various formulations of the severance test propounded over the years without identifying which if any was to be preferred. These included: (i) whether the invalid restraint formed the whole or substantially the whole consideration for the promise; (ii) whether the contract would be so changed in its character as not to be the sort of contract that the parties intended to enter at all; (iii) whether what was unenforceable was part of the main purpose and substance, or whether the deletion altered entirely the scope and intention of the agreement or, on the contrary, left the rest of the agreement a reasonable arrangement between the parties; (iv) whether it would disappoint the main purposes of one of the main parties; and (v) whether the agreement was in substance an agreement for an invalid restraint.[215]

This quotation captures the complex questions that are to be dealt with by the court with a view to applying the law governing the contract (which may be chosen by the parties) and with a view to determining whether the contract as whole should be invalidated and how the principles of severance should apply in individual cases.[216]

Nonetheless, it should be noted that any party subject to a contract, which restricts competition, may raise concerns about the anti-competitive nature of the other

[211] JJ Fawcett, 'Evasion of law and mandatory rules in private international law' (1990) 49 *CLJ* 44; O Lando, 'The EEC Convention on the law applicable to contractual obligations' (1987) 24 *CML Rev* 159, 181.

[212] eg Case C-56/65 *Société Technique Minière (LTM) v Maschinenbau Ulm GmbH (MBU)* EU:C:1966:38; Case C-319/82 *Société de Vente de Ciments et Bétons de l'Est SA v Kerpen & Kerpen GmbH und Co KG* [1983] EU:C:1983:374 [12].

[213] R Whish and D Bailey, *Competition Law* 10th edn (Oxford, OUP, 2021) 344–45.

[214] *Courage Ltd v Crehan (No.1)* [1999] ECC 455 [154].

[215] *English Welsh & Scottish Railway Ltd v E. On UK plc* [2007] EWHC 599 (Comm) [27–28].

[216] See: Article 12(1)(e) of the Rome I Regulation. See also: Komninos (n 86) 156–57; Whish and Bailey (n 213) 344–45.

contracting party's conduct. If and when a contracting party realises that they are (or they have been) subject to contracts restricting competition, they might stop performing their contract and/or issue competition law claims, seeking a declaration that certain contractual terms are in conflict with competition law and thus void.[217] Such competition law claims would classify as contractual, irrespective of whether they are raised as main claims or counterclaims.[218]

As noted above,[219] Article 9(2) of the Rome I Regulation leaves beyond any doubt that UK competition law rules are to be regarded as overriding mandatory provisions, which means that they should apply irrespective of the law chosen by the parties. More importantly for the purposes of this book, it should be noted that an interesting feature of Rome I is that it includes Article 9(3), which states that:

> Effect may be given to the overriding mandatory provisions of the law of the country where the obligations arising out of the contract have to be or have been performed, in so far as those overriding mandatory provisions render the performance of the contract unlawful. In considering whether to give effect to those provisions, regard shall be had to their nature and purpose and to the consequences of their application or non-application.

This provision enables the English judges to apply foreign competition laws, safeguarding foreign regulatory interests in cases where the contract is in conflict with competition law at the place of performance of the contract. However, two caveats should be made. First, it is not quite clear whether English judges could factor in foreign regulatory interests, if the contract only includes a contractual *term* which is anti-competitive at the place of performance, without invalidating the whole contract.[220] Secondly, it seems clear that foreign regulatory interests will not be factored in (at all), if the performance of the contract were to be in conflict with UK competition law. This would be so irrespective of the fact that, for example, the contract and its performance could be entirely legitimate and compatible with the foreign antitrust laws.[221] In such circumstances, UK competition law should exclusively apply to determine whether the conduct is anti-competitive.[222] This is not a satisfactory solution. A truly transnational approach would presuppose for all legitimate regulatory interests to be factored in, as far as possible.[223]

IX. Concluding Remarks

A purposive interpretation of Rome II appears to indicate that a distinction should be drawn between 'the concept of a non-contractual obligation'[224] and 'the concept

[217] *The Football Association Premier League Ltd v QC Leisure & ors* [2008] EWHC 44 (Ch) [17].
[218] See: Chapter 5.
[219] See more: Chapter 10.
[220] M Lehmann, 'Regulation, global governance and private international law: squaring the triangle' (2020) 16 *Journal of Private International Law* 1, 16.
[221] Ibid.
[222] *The LCD Appeals* [2018] EWCA Civ 220.
[223] See more: Chapter 10.
[224] Recital 11 of Rome II.

of restriction of competition',[225] with the principle of universal application not being relevant with regard to the latter.[226] The deduction could be strengthened by making reference to Recital 1, which states that:

> The [European Union] has set itself the objective of maintaining and developing an area of freedom, security and justice. For the progressive establishment of such an area, the [European Union] is to adopt measures relating to *judicial cooperation in civil matters with a cross-border impact to the extent necessary for the proper functioning of the internal market.*

Indeed, one reason for the EU policy-makers to adopt a somewhat narrow definition of 'the concept of restriction of competition'[227] may be found in the fact that the EU objectives in the area of civil justice are somewhat limited to the 'establish[ment] of an internal market',[228] with the EU competition law being central to 'the functioning of the internal market'.[229]

It is equally important to note that, traditionally, the EU regulators would determine whether the conduct restricts competition (ie the regulatory infringement, by exclusively applying EU competition laws) and the national courts would deal with follow-on private antitrust damages claims (ie non-contractual obligations).[230] Indeed, an argument for a narrow interpretation could be reinforced by noting that Rome II (as opposed to Rome I)[231] does not explicitly allow for national judges to apply foreign overriding mandatory rules (which reflect foreign regulatory interests) to be considered.

That said, there is a strong argument for the views of Professor Dickinson, Professor Fitchen, Plender KC and Wilderspin to be followed by the English courts in stand-alone cases (and in follow-on claims with stand-alone elements) in the post-Brexit era. In order for the English courts to take a lead in advancing a soft law mechanism for judicial cooperation in competition law matters, they should be encouraged to broadly interpret the concept of restriction of competition for the purposes of Rome II, which is to continue to apply in the UK.[232] The English judges should, nonetheless, be careful with advancing this approach because it would have major implications for the application of Article 6(3)(a) and (b) of Rome II in stand-alone claims. If the UK CAT were to rely on Article 6(3)(b) of Rome II in such cases, then UK competition law would apply to determine whether the conduct restricts competition – without factoring foreign regulatory interests. This may adversely affect the willingness of foreign courts to recognise and enforce the judgment.[233]

In stand-alone claims, Article 6(3)(a) of Rome II would be the more appropriate (albeit rather complex) solution, which would put the English courts in a good position to balance different public interests in cross-border competition law claims that appear

[225] Recital 23 of Rome II.
[226] Pineau (n 8) 320.
[227] Recital 23 of Rome II.
[228] Article 3(3) of the Treaty on European Union.
[229] Article 3(1)(b) of Treaty on the Functioning of the European Union.
[230] *Enron* (n 103) [149].
[231] Article 9(3) of Rome I.
[232] *ValueLicensing* (n 47) [44].
[233] See: Chapter 12 below.

to be issued in England. More importantly, setting out a regime which enables the English courts to factor in multiple regulatory interests would be important, not least because there is an increasingly growing number of stand-alone claims[234] that are issued before the UK Competition Appeal Tribunal. That said, a broader interpretation of the concept of restriction of competition presupposes for the English court to consider how foreign regulatory interests could/should be most appropriately factored in.[235]

[234] *Dr Liza Lovdahl Gormsen* (n 4) [17]. See also: *Dr Rachael Kent* (n 4) [6]; Case No: 1408/7/7/21, *Elizabeth Helen Coll v Alphabet Inc* – Reasoned order of the President – Service out of the jurisdiction – 29 September 2021 [11].

[235] See: Chapters 10 and 12.

12

Recognition and Enforcement of Foreign Judgments in Relation to Competition Law Claims

I. Introduction

Once a national court had determined the issues concerning the existence of a competition law infringement (or competition law infringements) by applying the relevant set/s of substantive competition laws as well as having dealt with the issues concerning the causation and quantification of damages, the parties' effective access to legal remedies might depend on the enforceability of the judgment in the country where the defendants' assets are located.

The aspects concerning the recognition and enforcement of foreign judgments have been extensively discussed in the private international law literature, with the academic writers taking different perspectives on the relevant issues by considering the common law,[1] EU[2] and even global[3] approaches. Since the competition law infringements would cause harm to multiple injured parties in different countries, the wide bases for the assumption of jurisdiction under the English CPR/UK CAT rules (and the wide bases for the allocation of jurisdiction under the Brussels I Regulation) mean that *related* and *parallel* proceedings in relation to the same transnational competition law infringement would be bound to arise.[4] This means that the rules for the recognition and enforcement of judgments may be important for English judges to avoid inconsistent outcomes in related competition claims arising out of transnational competition law infringements.[5]

[1] eg A Arzandeh, 'Reformulating the common law rules on the recognition and enforcement of foreign judgments' (2019) 39 *Legal Studies* 56; J Harris, 'Recognition of Foreign Judgments at Common Law – The Anti-Suit Injunction Link' (1997) 17 *Oxford Journal of Legal Studies* 477; A Briggs, 'Which Foreign Judgments Should We Recognise Today?' (1987) *International and Comparative Law Quarterly* 240.

[2] P Beaumont and L Walker, 'Recognition and enforcement of judgments in civil and commercial matters in the Brussels I Recast and some lessons from it and the recent Hague Conventions for the Hague Judgments Project' (2015) 11 *Journal of Private International Law* 31; P Hovaguimian, 'The enforcement of foreign judgments under Brussels I bis: false alarms and real concerns' (2015) 11 *Journal of Private International Law* 212.

[3] P Beaumont and J Holliday (eds), *Guide to Global Private International Law* (Oxford, Hart Publishing, 2022).

[4] Case Nos: 1517/11/7/22 (UM) and 1266/7/7/16, *UK Trucks Claim Ltd v Stellantis and Road Haulage Association Ltd v MAN SE & Ors* [2022] CAT 25 [5–6].

[5] JJ Fawcett, 'General Report' in JJ Fawcett (ed), *Declining Jurisdiction in Private International Law – Reports to the XIVth Congress of the International Academy of Comparative Law, Athens, August 1994* (Oxford, OUP, 1995) 1, 41. See more: Section IV below.

It will be demonstrated that a mechanism for judicial cooperation may be central to improving injured parties' access to justice in such cases.

The problem is that there is no special convention to address the specific issues which arise with regard to the recognition and enforcement of judgments in relation to competition law claims in a global context. It should be reiterated that the recognition and enforcement of foreign judgments in relation to competition law is an area where Brexit has made an impact in so far as – subject to the provisions of the UK/EU Withdrawal Agreement – Brussels Ia/Lugano judgments may no longer be registered in England and Wales. In other words, the Brussels Ia regime, which is set 'to ensure rapid and simple recognition and enforcement of judgments [in civil and commercial matters] given in a Member State',[6] only applies within the EU and EEA area. That said, the Brussels Ia/Lugano regime does not specifically deal with the judgments in relation to competition law claims which, it will be demonstrated below, raises some specific concerns.

The importance of the issues in relation to the recognition and enforcements of judgments in a global context was reflected in the 2019 Hague Convention on the Recognition and Enforcement of Foreign Judgments in Civil or Commercial Matters. The Preamble of the latter Convention appeared to suggest that facilitating the recognition and enforcement of foreign judgments would contribute to improving the injured parties' access to legal remedies, with the relevant Contracting Parties explicitly stating that:

> Desiring to *promote effective access to justice* for all and to facilitate rule-based multilateral trade and investment, and mobility, through judicial co-operation,
>
> Believing that such co-operation can be enhanced through the creation of a *uniform set of core rules on recognition and enforcement of foreign judgments in civil or commercial matters*, to facilitate the effective recognition and enforcement of such judgments.[7]

There has been a very persuasive suggestion for the UK to join the 2019 Hague Judgments Convention.[8] The UK has recently opened a consultation which 'seeks views on whether the UK should sign and ratify Hague 2019'.[9] That said, the problem is that the 2019 Hague Convention is yet to enter into force and, more importantly for the purposes of this book, Article 2(1)(p) indicates that the 2019 'Convention shall not apply to […] anti-trust (competition) matters' except to anti-competitive agreements/concerted practices which restrict competition. Another major limitation of the 2019 Convention is that it will only apply to the extent the anti-competitive 'conduct and its effect both occurred in the State of origin'.[10]

[6] See: Recital 4 from Brussels Ia. See more: P Beaumont, 'Abolition of Exequatur under the Brussels I Regulation as it Affects EU Competition Law' in M Danov, F Becker and P Beaumont (eds), *Cross-border EU Competition Law Actions* (Oxford, Hart Publishing, 2013) 371.

[7] Convention of 2 July 2019 on the Recognition and Enforcement of Foreign Judgments in Civil or Commercial Matters – emphasis added by the author.

[8] P Beaumont, 'Some reflections on the way ahead for UK private international law after Brexit' (2021) 17 *Journal of Private International Law* 1, 4–5.

[9] UK Ministry of Justice, *Open consultation – Hague Convention of 2 July 2019 on the Recognition and Enforcement of Foreign Judgments in Civil or Commercial Matters (Hague 2019)*, published 15 December 2022, https://www.gov.uk/government/consultations/hague-convention-of-2-july-2019-on-the-recognition-and-enforcement-of-foreign-judgments-in-civil-or-commercial-matters-hague-2019.

[10] Article 2(1)(p) of the Convention of 2 July 2019 on the Recognition and Enforcement of Foreign Judgments in Civil or Commercial Matters. See more Chapter 3.II.

The fact that the EU PIL Regulations no longer apply in the UK, along with the limitations of the 2019 Hague Convention, strongly indicate that the issues concerning the recognition and enforcement of judgments in relation to competition law claims require renewed attention, post-Brexit. However, one may object to this by noting that the issues concerning the recognition and enforcement of foreign judgments in relation to competition law should not be overstated for two main reasons. First, most of the private antitrust disputes would amicably settle in England and Wales.[11] Secondly, since London is a global business centre, the English judgments in relation to competition claims would likely be enforceable, not least because many defendants (who would normally be large multinational companies) will be doing business in England and Wales. Alternatively, such defendants might be having assets in this jurisdiction and/or another jurisdiction where the rendered English judgment would be recognised and enforced.[12]

Nonetheless, there is a risk that, if foreign judgments in relation to competition law claims were not to be recognised and enforced in England and Wales, this would impact on the settlement dynamics[13] which might – in turn – diminish the attractiveness of the English judgments. Hence, the issues concerning the recognition and enforcement of judgments in relation to competition law claims are important and need to be addressed.

The aim of this chapter is to outline the issues which must be considered. The major principles concerning the recognition and enforcement of foreign judgments in England and Wales will be very briefly reviewed, which should set the scene for the chapter to consider the specific aspects in relation to the recognition and enforcement of judgments in relation to competition law claims. In particular, the public policy nature of competition law will be considered, along with the issues concerning the enforcement of foreign judgments misapplying or disregarding UK competition law. The specific issues of estoppel and abuse of process will be duly highlighted as well. Finally, some of the specific comity considerations will be considered along with the Protection of Trading Interests Act.

II. Major Principles

The editors of *Dicey, Morris & Collins on the Conflict of Laws* draw a distinction between the recognition of foreign judgments and their enforcement.[14] The recognition is not only a prerequisite for the enforcement of a foreign judgment in England and Wales, but

[11] M Danov and S Dnes, 'Cross-Border EU Litigation: New Evidence from England and Wales' in Danov, Becker and Beaumont (n 6) 33; B Rodger, 'Private enforcement of competition law, the hidden story: competition litigation settlements in the United Kingdom, 2000–2005' (2008) 29 *European Competition Law Review* 96; B Rodger, 'Private enforcement of competition law, the hidden story: Part II: competition litigation settlements in the United Kingdom, 2008–2012' (2015) 8 *GCLR* 89.

[12] M Danov, 'Cross-Border Litigation: Evaluating the Brexit impact – A Socio-Legal Model for Data Analysis' (2020) 27 *Maastricht Journal of European and Comparative Law* 199.

[13] M Danov, 'Cross-Border Litigation in England and Wales: Pre-Brexit Data and Post-Brexit Implications' (2018) 25 *Maastricht Journal of European and Comparative Law* 139.

[14] L Collins and J Harris (eds) *Dicey, Morris and Collins on the Conflict of Laws* 16th edn (London, Sweet & Maxwell, 2022) Rule 45 [14-002].

it is also necessary for a foreign judgment in relation to competition law claims to have a '*preclusive* effect [...] in subsequent proceedings in England'.[15] The distinction has also been reflected in the UK Supreme Court judgment in *Clarke v Fennoscandia*[16] where Lord Rodger held that:

> [Counsel for the Appellants] emphasised that the issue raised by the conclusions for the declarators could and should be broken down. The first issue was whether the orders and judgments should be recognised by the Court of Session. Only if the court decided that they should be recognised would the second issue, of enforcement, arise. Adopting the characteristically lucid account by Professor Briggs in his book on *The Conflict of Laws* (2002), p 115, counsel submitted that recognition meant 'treating the claim which was adjudicated as having been determined once and for all.' If the foreign judgment was recognised, the matter was then *res judicata*, and the losing party would be barred from contradicting it in subsequent proceedings in the Scottish court. The Scottish court would then proceed to consider whether the foreign judgment could be enforced. I note that the division into recognition and enforcement is already reflected, of course, in the heading to Chapter 62 of the Court of Session Rules, 'Recognition, Registration and Enforcement of Foreign Judgments etc.'
>
> [...]
>
> My Lords, I am happy to accept that, in the words of Professor Briggs, 'the logic of the law is that recognition is the necessary primary concern ...': *The Conflict of Laws*, p 116. I also accept that recognising a judgment entails the court treating the relevant claim as having been determined once and for all by the foreign court.[17]

It is well established that foreign judgments in relation to competition law claims would have a *res judicata* effect in England and Wales only after they had been duly recognised.[18] Although an application for registration[19] of foreign judgment may be made under Section 4B of the Civil Jurisdiction and Judgments Act 1982, this is now only relevant with regard to the '[r]egistration and enforcement of judgments under the 2005 Hague Convention'.[20] As already noted,[21] the competition law matters are not within the scope of the 2005 Hague Convention.

The rules concerning the 'applications for registration'[22] are set out in the Civil Procedure Rules, pt 74. First, these rules would be particularly relevant with regard to the '[e]nforcement in the United Kingdom of judgments obtained in superior courts in other British dominions'[23] under the Administration of Justice Act 1920. Secondly, the rules of the Foreign Judgments (Reciprocal Enforcement) Act 1933 would be relevant in cases where there are bilateral arrangements. It appears that '[o]f non-Commonwealth countries, only Austria,[...] Belgium,[...] Germany,[...] France,[...] Israel,[...]

[15] P Barnett, *Res Judicata, Estoppel and Foreign Judgments: The preclusive effects of foreign judgments in private international law* (Oxford, OUP, 2001) [2.04] – emphasis in the original.

[16] *Clarke v Fennoscandia Ltd & others* [2007] UKHL 56.

[17] Ibid [18 and 21].

[18] Barnett (n 15) [2.01 and 2.17].

[19] CPR 74.10.

[20] Civil Jurisdiction and Judgments Act 1982, s 4B.

[21] See: Chapter 3.

[22] CPR 74.3.

[23] Administration of Justice Act 1920, s 9 of pt II.

Italy,[...] the Netherlands,[...] Norway,[...] and Suriname[...] have so far come within the Act for general purposes'.[24]

In addition, it should be noted that Schedule 4 of the Enterprise Act 2002 provides special rules for the registration and enforcement of decisions rendered by the UK Competition Appeal Tribunal, with Section 2 stating that:

> "If a decision of the Tribunal is registered in England and Wales in accordance with rules of court or any practice direction—
>
> a) payment of damages which are awarded by the decision;
> b) costs or expenses awarded by the decision; and
> c) any direction given as a result of the decision,
>
> may be enforced by the High Court as if the damages, costs or expenses were an amount due in pursuance of a judgment or order of the High Court, or as if the direction were an order of the High Court.

It is well established that, in cases where there is no statutory regime in place to allow for registration of foreign judgments in England, '[a] judgment creditor seeking to enforce a foreign judgment in England at common law cannot do so by direct execution of the judgment. It must bring an action on the foreign judgment'.[25] As part of the recognition and enforcement process, the English courts, in principle, should verify whether the foreign judgment was rendered by 'a court of competent jurisdiction'[26] and whether the 'judgment is final and conclusive',[27] dealing with the 'merits'[28] by 'adjudicat[ing] upon [any competition law] issue raised in the cause of action to which the particular set of facts give rise'.[29]

It is widely accepted that there are two alternative bases (ie presence in the jurisdiction; and submission) for jurisdiction on which the foreign court should derive its jurisdiction for it to be considered competent.[30] This has been reflected in *Adams v Cape Industries*[31] which is considered as 'the leading modern authority'[32] and where Mr Justice Scott held:

> It is important, to my mind, to keep clear and distinct the two alternative bases upon which the jurisdiction of a foreign court over a defendant may be established. *Jurisdiction on the ground of presence in the foreign country is based on territoriality.* Consent on the part of the defendant is not necessary and is irrelevant. On the other hand, *jurisdiction on the ground of voluntary submission or of an agreement to submit is based upon consent.* An actual consent is, in principle, necessary.[33]

[24] *Dicey, Morris and Collins* (n 14) Rule 57 [14-180] (citations omitted).
[25] Ibid [14-012].
[26] *Schibsby v Westenholz and Others* (1870–71) LR 6 QB 155, 159. See also: *Godard and Another v Gray and Another* (1870–71) LR 6 QB 139, 148. Compare: Article 45(3) of Brussels Ia which states that 'the jurisdiction of the court of origin may not be reviewed'.
[27] *Schibsby* (n 26) 157.
[28] *D S V Silo-und Verwaltungsgesellschaft mbH v Owners of The Sennar and 13 Other Ships ('Sennar (No 2)')* [1985] 1 WLR 490, 494.
[29] Ibid.
[30] Arzandeh (n 1) 59.
[31] *Adams and Others v Cape Industries Plc and Another* [1990] Ch 433.
[32] *Dicey, Morris and Collins* (n 14) Rule 45 [14-002].
[33] *Adams* (n 31) 458 (emphases added by the author).

The aspects concerning the preclusive effects of foreign judgments in relation to competition law claims would be particularly important in so far as multiple claims, which arise out of the same transnational competition law infringements and which involve the same parties, may be issued in different jurisdictions.

Since there are no specific rules on recognition and enforcement of foreign judgments in relation to competition law claims, the common law rules and principles would be equally applicable in such cases.[34] The problem is that, whilst private antitrust damages arising out of transnational competition law infringements are a relatively new phenomenon, '[t]he relevant modern-day principles in this area have been in existence since the 1870 cases of *Godard v Grey*,[…] and *Schibsby v Westenholz*'.[35] A number of academics have suggested that the current English court's approach is far too restrictive and it is high time for it to be reformed.[36] Considering the transnational nature of cross-border trade along with the immense and continuous technological developments, it seems clear that the present English approach in relation to the recognition and enforcement of judgments is somewhat outdated and needs to be modernised.[37]

The author believes there is a strong case that, drawing on the judgments of the Supreme Court of Canada in *Morguard Investments Ltd v De Savoye*[38] and *Beals v Saldanha*,[39] the 'notion of comity'[40] should provide a more appropriate foundation for promoting judicial cooperation in competition law matters.[41] For the purposes of this chapter, the definition of comity will be derived from the US Supreme Court judgment in *Hilton v Guyot*,[42] which was also cited by the Canadian Supreme Court in *Morguard Investments Ltd v De Savoye*.[43] In particular, the US Supreme Court noted that:

> No law has any effect, of its own force, beyond the limits of the sovereignty from which its authority is derived. The extent to which the law of one nation, as put in force within its territory, whether by executive order, by legislative act, or by judicial decree, shall be allowed to operate within the dominion of another nation, depends upon what our greatest jurists have been content to call 'the comity of nations.' Although the phrase has been often criticised, no satisfactory substitute has been suggested.
>
> 'Comity,' in the legal sense, is neither a matter of absolute obligation, on the one hand, nor of mere courtesy and good will, upon the other. But it is the recognition which one nation allows within its territory to the legislative, executive or judicial acts of another nation, having due regard both to international duty and convenience, and to the rights of its own citizens, or of other persons who are under the protection of its laws.[44]

[34] H L Ho, 'Policies underlying the enforcement of foreign commercial judgments' (1997) 46 *ICLQ* 443.
[35] Arzandeh (n 1) 57 (citations omitted). See also: *Godard* (n 26); *Schibsby* (n 26).
[36] eg Arzandeh (n 1); Harris (n 1); Briggs (n 1).
[37] *Morguard Investments Ltd. v De Savoye* [1990] 3 SCR 1077 [33 and 34].
[38] Ibid.
[39] *Beals v Saldanha* [2003] SCC 72.
[40] *Adams* (n 31) 552.
[41] L Collins, 'Comity in Modern Private International Law' in JJ Fawcett (ed), *Reform and Development of Private International Law – Essays in Honour of Sir Peter North* (Oxford, OUP, 2002) 89. Compare: J Walker, 'The great Canadian comity experiment continues' (2004) 120 LQR 365.
[42] *Hilton v Guyot* 16 S.Ct. 139 (1895).
[43] *Morguard Investments* (n 37) [31].
[44] *Hilton* (n 42) 163–4.

Given the important public policy considerations in the enforcement of competition law, the principle of comity[45] should suggest that a broader approach to determining whether a foreign court is competent to hear and determine a competition law claim. Indeed, the English judges could still consider whether the enforcement would be against English public policy which would inter alia include UK competition law. There are indeed some specific issues which need to be considered with regard to the recognition and enforcement of judgments in relation to competition law claims.

III. The 'Notion of Comity'[46] and Public Policy Nature of Competition Laws

It is well established that an English court would not be entitled to review the merits of a substantive law dispute which had been heard and determined by a foreign court.[47] There is a 'general proposition […] that when you bring an action on a foreign judgment, you cannot go into the merits, which have been tried in the foreign court'.[48] Likewise, Article 52 of the Brussels Ia Regulation holds that '[u]nder no circumstances may a judgment given in a Member State be reviewed as to its substance in the Member State addressed'.[49] The principle of *mutual trust* provides the rationale behind the EU approach. In particular, it has been submitted that:

> Mutual trust in the administration of justice in the Union justifies the principle that judgments given in a Member State should be recognised in all Member States without the need for any special procedure. In addition, the aim of making cross-border litigation less time-consuming and costly justifies the abolition of the declaration of enforceability prior to enforcement in the Member State addressed. As a result, a judgment given by the courts of a Member State should be treated as if it had been given in the Member State addressed.[50]

The principle for there to be 'no review of the merits of the judgment in the requested State' is further reflected in the 2019 Hague Judgments Convention. Although the UK is longer part of the Brussels Ia/Lugano regime, there is an argument for a similar approach to continue to apply with regard to the recognition and enforcement of foreign judgments in relation to competition law claims. This should reflect the 'notion of comity'[51] which would be important to ensure that foreign judgments would have effects and

[45] *Adams* (n 31) 552. Compare: *S Schibsby* (n 26). See also: *Dicey, Morris and Collins* (n 14) [14-007–14-008]. See: Chapter 12.III below.

[46] *Adams* (n 31) 552.

[47] *Godard* (n 26) 148.

[48] *Vadala v Lawes* [1890] 25 QBD 310, 316 (Lindley LJ). See also *Ellis v McHenry* [1870–71] LR 6 CP 228 (Court of Common Pleas) 238–39.

[49] See more: Case C-7/98 *Krombach v Bamberski* EU:C:2000:164 [36]. See also: *Report on the Convention on jurisdiction and the enforcement of judgments in civil and commercial matters (Signed at Brussels, 27 September 1968)* by Mr P Jenard ('Jenard Report') [1979] OJ C59/1, 46.

[50] Recital 26 of Brussels Ia.

[51] *Adams* (n 31) 552.

the same issues would not be re-litigated as part of the recognition and enforcement process.[52]

Indeed, given that transnational competition law infringements would affect multiple injured parties in different jurisdictions, and many competition law rules would be expressing the public interests of the forum, there is an argument for the courts of England and Wales to advance an approach which could set the scene for judicial cooperation in competition law matters around the 'notion of comity'.[53] Certain analogies could be drawn with the approach advanced by the judgment of the Canadian Supreme Court in *Morguard Investments Ltd v De Savoye*.[54] In this case, the following observations were put forward:

> the content of comity must be adjusted in the light of a changing world order. The approach adopted by the English courts in the 19th century may well have seemed suitable to Great Britain's situation at the time. One can understand the difficulty in which a defendant in England would find himself in defending an action initiated in a far corner of the world in the then state of travel and communications. The *Symon* case [[1908] 1 K.B. 302] where the action arose in Western Australia against a defendant in England, affords a good illustration. The approach of course demands that one forget the difficulties of the plaintiff in bringing an action against a defendant who has moved to a distant land. However, this may not have been perceived as too serious a difficulty by English courts at a time when it was predominantly Englishmen who carried on enterprises in faraway lands. As well, there was an exaggerated concern about the quality of justice that might be meted out to British residents abroad: see Lord Reid in *Re The Atlantic Star; The Atlantic Star v. The Bona Spes*, [1974] A.C. 436, [1973] 2 W.L.R. 795, [1973] 2 All E.R. 175 at 181 (H.L.).
>
> The world has changed since the above rules were developed in 19th-century England. Modern means of travel and communications have made many of these 19th-century concerns appear parochial. The business community operates in a world economy, and we correctly speak of a 'world community' even in the face of decentralized political and legal power. Accommodating the flow of wealth, skills and people across state lines has now become imperative.[55]

Although this quotation is made in an intra-federal context, an argument can be made for facilitating the recognition and enforcement of judgments in relation to competition law claims on the grounds of comity.[56] The issues are important because, as noted above,[57] there is no adequate mechanism to avoid *parallel* and *related* proceedings in relation to the same competition infringement at present. More importantly, the fact that competition laws safeguard important public policy interests, and the lack of a transnational mechanism to encourage judges to factor in foreign regulatory interests, strongly indicates that the national courts would often be reluctant to stay their proceedings.[58]

[52] *Henderson v Henderson* (1843) 3 Hare 100, 115; *Israel Discount Bank of New York v Hadjipateras* [1984] 1 WLR 137, 144. Compare *Adams* (n 31). See also: N Andrews, *English Civil Procedure – Fundamentals of the New Civil Justice System* (Oxford, OUP, 2003) 952.

[53] *Adams* (n 31) 552.

[54] *Morguard Investments* (n 37).

[55] *Morguard Investments* (n 37) [33–34].

[56] *Adams* (n 31) 455–56, 513, 528, 553.

[57] See: Chapter 7.

[58] Chapters 10 and 11.

This in turn suggests that addressing the issues concerning the recognition and enforcement of foreign judgments could be central to dealing with the issues with regard to related claims that arise out of the same transnational infringement and which are issued before different courts.[59]

The support for the advancement of an approach that enables the national courts to recognise foreign judgments in relation to competition law claims on the grounds of comity and reciprocity in a global context could be further sustained by making a reference to the judgment of the Canadian Supreme Court in *Beals v Saldanha*:[60]

> International comity and the prevalence of international cross-border transactions and movement call for a modernization of private international law. The principles set out in Morguard, [...], can and should be extended beyond the recognition of interprovincial judgments, even though their application may give rise to different considerations internationally. [...]
>
> In light of the principles of international comity, [a] discussion of reciprocity is also equally applicable to judgments made by courts outside Canada. In the absence of a different statutory approach, it is reasonable that a domestic court recognize and enforce a foreign judgment where the foreign court assumed jurisdiction on the same basis as the domestic court would, for example, on the basis of a 'real and substantial connection' test.[61]

The proposed approach, however, has been condemned by Professor Walker.[62] In particular, she criticised the Canadian courts' policy choice to unilaterally advance such an approach, without 'recalibrat[ing] defences to foreign judgments'.[63] That said, the author feels that no such recalibration would be necessary for the English courts to start to systematically recognise and enforce foreign judgments in relation to competition law claims on the grounds of comity, because the unique public interest[64] in the enforcement of competition law would allow an English court to deny recognition of a foreign judgment which is in conflict with UK competition law. In other words, the public policy exception could be an additional defence[65] which may be invoked in competition law cases and which means that no recalibration of the defences to the recognition and enforcement of foreign judgments in relation to competition law claims is necessary.

A. Public Policy Nature – Competition Laws

There are two aspects[66] which need to be considered in the context of the recognition and enforcement of foreign judgments in relation to competition law claims. On the one hand (as noted above), it is well settled that the merits of a competition law dispute could not be reviewed even in cases where it was evident on the face of the foreign

[59] Fawcett (n 5) 41. See more: Section IV below.
[60] *Beals* (n 39).
[61] *Beals* (n 39) [28–29].
[62] Walker (n 41).
[63] Ibid 365.
[64] Chapters 9 and 10.
[65] Beaumont (n 6) 371.
[66] Compare: *Vadala* (n 48) 316–17.

judgment that the adjudicating court had misinterpreted or misapplied English law. Mr Justice Blackburn held that:

> Still the fact remains that we can see on the face of the proceedings that the foreign tribunal has made a mistake on the construction of an English contract, which is a question of English law; and that, in consequence of that mistake, judgment has been given for an amount probably greater than, or, at all events, different from that for which it would have been given if the tribunal had been correctly informed what construction the English contract bore according to English law.[67]

On the other hand, the public policy ground for refusing the recognition and enforcement of foreign judgments would be a major exception[68] which, in cross-border competition law claims, parties might try to invoke under the English common law rules. A public policy exception is also provided in the Brussels Ia regulation as well as in the 2019 Hague Judgments. Under the Brussels Ia regulation, 'the recognition of a judgment shall be refused […] if such recognition is *manifestly contrary to public policy (ordre public)* in the Member State addressed'.[69] A somewhat identical rule appears to feature in the 2019 Hague Judgments which states that '[r]ecognition or enforcement may be refused if […] recognition or enforcement would be *manifestly incompatible with the public policy* of the requested State'.[70] It appears to be universally accepted that the recognition and enforcement of foreign judgments in relation to competition law claims may be refused on the ground of public policy.[71]

The public policy exception could allow the English courts to review the merits, as part of the recognition and enforcement process, with a view to determining whether the foreign judgments are compatible with UK competition law. Although there is no English authority which directly addresses these issues with regard to foreign judgments in relation to competition law claims, analogies could be drawn with the cases where the public policy exception had been invoked due to fraud. For example, in *Vadala v Lawes*,[72] Lord Justice Lindley set out the following principles:

> There are two rules relating to these matters which have to be borne in mind, and the joint operation of which gives rise to the difficulty. First of all, there is the rule which is perfectly well established and well known, that a party to an action can impeach the judgment in it for fraud. Whether it is the judgment of an English Court or of a foreign Court does not matter; using general language, that is a general proposition unconditional and undisputed. Another general proposition which, speaking in equally general language, is perfectly well settled, is, that when you bring an action on a foreign judgment, you cannot go into the merits which have been tried in the foreign Court. But you have to combine those two rules and apply them in the case where you cannot go into the alleged fraud without going into the merits.
>
> Which rule is to prevail? […] That point was raised directly in the case of *Alouloff v. Oppenheimer* […] The fraud practised on the Court, or alleged to have been practised on the

[67] *Godard* (n 26) 148.

[68] See more: C-J Pointon, 'The EEC Convention on the recognition and enforcement of civil and commercial judgments, and its applications for English law' (1975) 2 *Legal Issues of European Integration* 1, 47–48.

[69] Article 45(1)(a) of Brussels Ia – emphasis added by the author.

[70] Article 7(1)(c) of the Hague 2019 Judgments Convention – emphasis added by the author.

[71] *Vadala* (n 48).

[72] Ibid.

> Court, was the misleading of the Court by evidence known by the plaintiff to be false. That was the whole fraud. The question of fact, whether what the plaintiff had said in the Court below was or was not false, was the very question of fact that had been adjudicated on in the foreign Court; and, notwithstanding that was so, when the Court came to consider how the two rules, to which I have alluded, could be worked together, they said: 'Well, if that foreign judgment was obtained fraudulently, and if it is necessary, in order to prove that fraud, to re-try the merits, you are entitled to do so according to the law of this country'.[73]

The deduction that the public policy exception could be invoked with regard to the recognition and enforcement of foreign judgments in relation to competition claims[74] could be strengthened by making reference to the CJEU jurisprudence. In *Eco Swiss*,[75] the CJEU held that competition law rules are to 'be regarded as a matter of public policy within the meaning of the New York Convention'.[76] The ruling was followed for the purposes of the recognition and enforcement under the Brussels Ia Regulation.[77]

There is a strong argument that this *public policy* classification of UK competition law would be advanced in the UK for the purposes of the recognition and enforcement of judgments, post-Brexit. Indeed, there are at least two reasons indicating that UK competition law should be regarded as a matter of public policy for the purposes of recognition and enforcement of foreign judgments in England and Wales. First, the importance for the autonomy of the UK (and the EU) to pursue 'legitimate public policy objectives',[78] which are central to the functioning of the UK internal market (as well as for the functioning of the EU internal market),[79] has been reflected in the UK/EU Trade and Cooperation Agreement. Secondly, competition law is not only enforced in private antitrust enforcement before the English courts or the UK Competition Appeal Tribunal, but it is also enforced in public enforcement proceedings before the Competition and Markets Authority, which reflects the importance of the public policy interests which the regulators should safeguard.[80]

Since competition laws would reflect the 'public policy' of the forum, the English judges might be entitled to consider, as part of the recognition and enforcement process, whether a foreign judgment is in conflict with UK competition law, which would reflect the UK public policy. If Lord Justice Lindley's approach[81] were to be followed, by analogy, with regard to the recognition and enforcement of foreign judgments in relation

[73] Ibid 316–17.

[74] eg Case C-126/97 *Eco Swiss China Time Ltd v Benetton International NV* EU:C:1999:269; Case C-38/98 *Régie nationale des usines Renault SA v Maxicar SpA and Orazio Formento* EU:C:2000:225.

[75] *Eco Swiss* (n 74).

[76] Ibid [39].

[77] *Maxicar* (n 74). See also: Case C-38/98 *Régie nationale des usines Renault SA v Maxicar SpA and Orazio Formento* EU:C:1999:97 [58] (AG Alber). Compare: Case C-145/86 *Hoffmann v Krieg* EU:C:1987:358 [16] (AG Darmon).

[78] Article 359(3) of Trade and Cooperation Agreement between the United Kingdom of Great Britain and Northern Ireland, of the one part, and the European Union and the European Atomic Energy Community, of the other part.

[79] Article 3(1)(b) of the Treaty on the Functioning of the European Union. See more: J Drexl, 'Competition law as part of the European Constitution' in A von Bogdandy and J Bast (eds), *Principles of European Constitutional Law* 2nd edn (Oxford and Munich, Hart Publishing and Verlag C H Beck, 2009) 659, 662–69.

[80] Case C-126/97 *Eco Swiss China Time Ltd v Benetton International NV* EU:C:1999:97 – Opinion of AG Saggio [36-38]. See also: J Penrose MP, *Power to the people: stronger consumer choice and competition so markets work for the people, not the other way around* – February 2021. See more: Chapter 10.

[81] *Vadala* (n 48) 316–17.

to competition law claims, then the central question would be: to what extent would English judges be entitled to review a foreign judgment and determine whether a foreign judgment is in conflict with UK competition law which forms part of the UK public policy? The response to this question is closely connected with the issues concerning the scope of review in cases where the foreign court has not given due regard to UK competition law.

B. Public Policy Defence

Given the fact that UK competition law expresses fundamental public interests, it is a relatively safe assumption that the public policy defence could well be invoked against the recognition of a foreign judgment in relation to competition law claims. One of the most common issues that the English court might need to determine in this context concerns the question of whether foreign judgments' recognition and/or enforcement would be contrary UK competition law. In particular, the following question may arise: would an English judge be entitled to review the merits and refuse the recognition and enforcement of a foreign judgment on the ground of public policy, if they could 'see [...] that the foreign tribunal ha[d] made a mistake on the construction'[82] of UK competition law? Would the scope of review be the same or different in cases 'where the foreign Court ha[d] knowingly and perversely disregarded'[83] UK competition law?

The issues have been dealt with by the Court of Justice of the European Union[84] and thoroughly discussed in the EU context, prior to Brexit.[85] That said, it should be reiterated that, post-Brexit, the Brussels Ia/Lugano regime no longer applies in the UK, which means that the scope of review of foreign judgments that are allegedly in conflict with competition law, would be different. Nonetheless, the relevant CJEU jurisprudence would be briefly examined. A public policy defence was invoked, in *Renault v Maxicar*,[86] against the enforcement of a French judgment in Italy. In this case, it was inter alia alleged that there was a substantive error in the application of competition laws.[87] In particular, the French court had established that there was a breach of the claimant's intellectual property rights. They went further to award damages, which were to be paid by an Italian company.

The Italian company argued that the French judgment should not be enforced in Italy. It was alleged that the recognition and enforcement was contrary to public policy because the French court wrongly applied competition laws which expressed fundamental public interests.[88] The Court of Justice held that:

> The court of the State in which enforcement is sought cannot, without undermining the aim of the [Brussels Ia/Lugano regime], refuse recognition of a decision emanating from another [EU Member] State solely on the ground that it considers that national or [EU competition]

[82] *Godard* (n 26) 148.
[83] Ibid 149.
[84] *Maxicar* (n 74).
[85] Beaumont (n 6).
[86] *Maxicar* (n 74).
[87] Ibid [25, 32 and 33].
[88] See: Article 45(1)(a) of the Brussels Ia Regulation.

law was misapplied in that decision. On the contrary, it must be considered whether, in such cases, the system of legal remedies in each [EU Member] State, together with the preliminary ruling procedure provided for in Article [267 TFEU], affords a sufficient guarantee to individuals.

Since an error of law such as that alleged in the main proceedings does not constitute a manifest breach of a rule of law regarded as essential in the legal order of the State in which enforcement is sought, the reply to the third question must be that [Article 45(1)(a) of Brussels Ia] must be interpreted as meaning that a judgment of a court or tribunal of a [Member] State recognising the existence of an intellectual property right in body parts for cars, and conferring on the holder of that right protection by enabling him to prevent third parties trading in another [EU Member] State from manufacturing, selling, transporting, importing or exporting in that [EU Member] State such body parts, cannot be considered to be contrary to public policy.[89]

In other words, the CJEU made a distinction between a misapplication of competition law and a manifest error in the application of competition law. It seems that an EU Member State court would be entitled to refuse the recognition of a foreign judgment, as being 'manifestly contrary to public policy',[90] only in cases where the adjudicating court had manifestly disregarded or manifestly misapplied competition law.[91] In this context, it has been submitted the 'misapplication of a public policy rule, from which parties cannot derogate, does not lead necessarily to a judgment contrary to public policy as to its enforcement in another Member State'.[92]

The *Renault* approach, which appears to be somewhat restrictively and narrowly interpreting the public policy exception, may be justified by the objective of the Brussels I/Lugano regime, which aims to facilitate the recognition and enforcement of judgments rendered by other EU Member States' courts as well as by the fact that there are a number of appropriate mechanisms (eg Article 267 TFEU; Articles 15 and 16 of Regulation 1/2003) which are set ensure that EU competition law is properly applied by the EU Member States judges.[93]

However, since the English judges are no longer expected to attain the Brussels Ia/Lugano objectives and since none of the above-mentioned mechanisms are applicable in the UK, a different approach – which allows the English courts to have a greater degree of discretion with regard to judgments rendered by EU and non-EU courts – may be advanced by the English courts, post-Brexit. According to Collier,[94] public policy should not be treated differently from fraud because 'the real justification for refusing to enforce a judgment where there was fraud [...] is surely that to enforce them is contrary to public policy'.[95]

Public policy should allow the English courts to examine whether a foreign judgment is in conflict with competition law. Although there appears to be no authority directly addressing these issues with regard to judgments in relation to competition law

[89] *Maxicar* (n 74) [33 and 34].
[90] Article 45(1)(a) of the Brussels Ia Regulation.
[91] *Maxicar* (n 74) [33 and 34].
[92] J-P Beraudo, 'Egregious error of law as grounds for setting aside an arbitral award' (2006) 23 *Journal of International Arbitration* 351, 360–61.
[93] Ibid [34].
[94] JG Collier, 'Public policy and foreign judgments – undue influence – a difficult answer to a simple problem' (1984) 43 *CLJ* 47, 49.
[95] Ibid.

claims, *Rousillon v Rousillon*[96] might be perceived as being somewhat indicative as to how the public policy exception could be invoked. In this case, the English court had to inter alia determine whether a French judgment – in which the adjudicating court had to consider a covenant in restraint of trade[97] – should be enforced in England and Wales. Mr Justice Fry, obiter, made the following observations:

> [Counsel for the Claimants] has insisted that, even if the contract was void by the law of England as against public policy, yet, inasmuch as the contract was made in France, it must be good here, because the law of France knows no such principle as that by which unreasonable contracts in restraint of trade are held to be void in this country. It appears to me, however, plain on general principles that this Court will not enforce a contract against the public policy of this country, wherever it may be made. It seems to me almost absurd to suppose that the Courts of this country should enforce a contract which they consider to be against public policy simply because, it happens to have been made somewhere else.[98]

There are two aspects which could, by analogy, be relevant in competition law cases. First, an English court should be entitled to review whether a foreign judgment is in conflict with UK competition law that has a public policy character in the UK. This would be so even in cases where the question of whether the conduct is compliant with a foreign set of competition laws was before the foreign court.[99] Secondly, it seems that – irrespective of the applicable substantive laws – UK competition law should always apply to ensure that any anti-competitive conduct, which has qualified effects in the UK,[100] would not be implemented by refusing to recognise and enforce any foreign judgment that is in conflict with UK competition law. Such a deduction could be questioned. In particular, Collier[101] has submitted:

> [I]n *Rousillon* the plaintiff brought two actions: (a) on the contract, (b) on a French judgment thereon. Fry J.'s remarks were made in the context of (a), and he did not repeat them when refusing to enforce the judgment, which he did solely because the French court had no jurisdiction. Admittedly, Astbury J. in Re *Macartney* [1921] Ch.D. 522 said that Fry J.'s remarks applied 'directly to the non-enforceability of foreign judgments founded on contracts contrary to public policy,' but this only suggests that he had not read *Rousillon* properly. Nor, it seems, did the Court of Appeal in *Hadjipateras*.[102]

Collier has correctly noted that Mr Justice Fry's statement is made with regard to the claim for an injunction that was sought on the basis of the same contract on which the foreign judgment was rendered. It is also precise to say that the recognition and enforcement of the foreign judgment was denied because the foreign court had not had jurisdiction, but it should likewise be stated that the contract in question was not contrary to English public policy. In other words, the English courts could not have relied on the public policy exception to refuse the recognition of the foreign judgment, which is why the point was obiter.

[96] *Rousillon v Rousillon* (1880) 14 Ch D 351.
[97] Ibid 363–69.
[98] Ibid 369.
[99] Compare: *Syal v Heyward* [1948] 2 KB 443, 448–49.
[100] *The LCD Appeals* [2018] EWCA Civ 220. See also: A Mills, *The Confluence of Public and Private International Law* (Cambridge, CUP, 2009) 259.
[101] Collier (n 94).
[102] Ibid 48.

In view of this, one might suggest that, in *Re Macartney*,[103] Mr Justice Astbury appeared to have properly interpreted *Rousillon*. More specifically, Mr Justice Astbury appeared to take the view that, if a particular contract/conduct was in conflict with the UK public policy, then a foreign judgment that was set to enforce the contract/conduct in question should be unenforceable.[104] His deduction could be strengthened by noting that 'recognition describes the general process by which an English court determines whether a foreign decision is entitled to legal operation or effect in England'.[105] In doing so, the English court has a discretionary power to refuse the recognition of a foreign judgment 'on the grounds of inconsistency with [UK] public policy'[106] and in particular to refuse the recognition of a judgment that is in conflict with UK competition law.

In exercising their discretion, the courts of England and Wales might need to consider two aspects. On the one hand, the literature suggests that, '[a]s public policy regulations [and competition laws in particular] are very numerous in many states, an award which ignores them or misapplies them is not *ipso facto* contrary to public policy'.[107] On the other hand, the public policy nature of UK competition law should enable the English judges to refuse the recognition and enforcement of a foreign judgment that is based on a contract (or any conduct) that is *prima facie* anti-competitive. This will be especially true in cases involving hard-core restrictions on competition that are implemented in the UK. This deduction could be reinforced by referring to Pt 6 of the Enterprise Act 2002 which imposed criminal responsibility for any individual who commits a cartel offence.

Thus, it is unlikely that the English court would enforce a foreign judgment based on an agreement which manifestly misapplies or disregards UK competition law. If an English court were to consider whether a foreign judgment in relation to competition law should be denied the recognition and enforcement, the judges should 'review [its] legality'[108] with a view to safeguarding the legitimate interest in the enforcement of UK competition law which often applies extra-territorially.[109] As part of this process, the English should consider the extent to which due regard to UK competition law was given by the foreign court.[110] If the foreign judgment was rendered in manifest disregard of UK competition law and there is evidence that the foreign judgment enforces an agreement/conduct that would be anti-competitive, there are strong arguments suggesting that an English court should be entitled to hold that it is against English public policy to recognise a foreign decision.

The problem is that, if the evidence in question had been before the foreign court, the issue will be *res judicata* and new evidence may be required.[111] That said, a specific

[103] *Re Macartney* [1921] 1 ChD 522 (Ch D).
[104] Ibid 528. Compare: Collier (n 94) 48.
[105] Barnett (n 15) [2.03].
[106] Mills (n 100) 257.
[107] Beraudo (n 92) 361.
[108] *Eco Swiss* – AG Saggio (n 80) [42].
[109] *The LCD Appeals* (n 100).
[110] *Eco Swiss* – AG Saggio (n 80) [38].
[111] Although this conclusion is drawn by drawing an analogy with D Gordon, 'Fraud or new evidence as grounds for actions to set aside judgments' (1961) 77 *LQR* 358, 361 which is a rather out-of-date opinion, it seems to the author that similar consideration should be applied in competition law cases where there is new evidence indicating a competition law infringement.

feature of competition law disputes is that multiple regulators may be investigating the allegedly anti-competitive conduct. Given their enforcement activities, there is a potential for previously unavailable evidence of anti-competitive conduct to come to light at the recognition and enforcement stage. A 'new evidence' requirement would be easily satisfied in cases, where – after the foreign judgment was rendered – the UK CMA (or another regulator) had taken the view that the conduct is anti-competitive. If the recognition and enforcement of a foreign judgment is irreconcilable with UK CMA's decision establishing a competition law infringement, the recognition and enforcement would be denied.

If there was a foreign regulator's decision (establishing such an infringement) and the decision was not before the adjudicating court, then the foreign regulatory decision must be viewed as persuasive prima facie evidence that the court with original jurisdiction had misapplied competition law.[112] If it was established that UK competition law was manifestly misapplied or manifestly disregarded by the foreign court, then the English court should deny recognition and enforcement of a foreign judgment as being in conflict with English public policy.

IV. Multiplicity of Proceedings – Issues of Estoppel and Abuse of Process

The transnational nature of competition law infringements and the multiple related proceedings strongly indicate that there are some specific issues which need to be examined in cross-border competition law cases. In the multiple sets of related proceedings against the same infringing undertaking/s, the judges would need to determine whether there is a competition law infringement as well as to ascertain certain common issues in relation to causation and quantifications of damages. The issues are important because, in private international law literature, it is well settled that:

> If [multiple] sets of proceedings [arising out of the same transnational competition law infringements] are allowed to continue, the risk of irreconcilable judgments can be dealt with by the use of the doctrine of *res judicata*, provided that the conditions for the operation of this doctrine are met. However, this does nothing to stop the expense and inconvenience to the parties of parallel proceedings in the period leading up to the grant of judgment necessary for *res judicata*.[113]

There is a real risk that the various national judges who are dealing with multiple claims which arise out of the same competition law infringement will not consistently address the common issues that concern various elements: for example, whether the conduct is anti-competitive, or aspects in relation to the quantification of damages – 'volume of commerce',[114] 'overcharge percentages'[115] and the 'level of pass-through',[116] which may

[112] *Innterpreneur Pub Company v Crehan* [2006] UKHL 38 [64–66, 69]. See more: M Danov, *Jurisdiction and Judgments in Relation to EU Competition Law Claims* (Oxford, Hart Publishing, 2010) 195–200.

[113] Fawcett (n 5) 41.

[114] Case No: 1266/7/7/16, *Merricks v MasterCard Inc* [2017] CAT 16 [29–30].

[115] Ibid [31–38].

[116] Ibid [39–44].

be raising issues of fact and which may have an impact on the outcome of the dispute. In this context, it is well settled that:

> A *res judicata* is a decision pronounced by a judicial or other tribunal with jurisdiction over the cause of action and the parties, which disposes once and for all of the fundamental matters decided, so that, except on appeal, they cannot be re-litigated between persons bound by the judgment. A judgment *in personam* binds the parties and their privies [...].[117]

If there were foreign judgments dealing with these issues, would the infringing undertakings be 'estopped'[118] from contesting the issues which had been determined abroad? The rationale of any estoppel mechanism is to ensure that the same cause of action and/or the same issue/s, which had been dealt with by a foreign court in a competition law dispute between the same parties, will not be re-litigated.[119] The PIL jurisprudence draws a distinction between a 'cause of action estoppel' and 'issue estoppel'.[120] According to Viscount Dilhorne:

> In *Thoday* v. *Thoday* [1964] P. 181, 197 Diplock L.J., as he then was, said that there were two species of estoppel per rem judicatam. The first, which he called 'cause of action estoppel,' was that which prevents a party to an action from asserting or denying, as against the other party, the existence of a particular cause of action, the non-existence or existence of which has been determined by a court of competent jurisdiction in previous litigation between the same parties. The second, which my noble and learned friend called 'issue estoppel,' arises where in previous litigation one of the matters in issue between the parties has already been decided by a competent court.[121]

The above quotation strongly indicates that it is not only that the competition law issues must be 'identical',[122] but also 'the parties to the [foreign] judicial decision or their privies [must be] the same persons as the parties to the [English] proceedings in which the estoppel is raised or their privies'.[123] These requirements would be difficult to satisfy in competition law claims that may even be arising out of the same transnational competition law infringement in so far as it is likely that the injured parties (eg consumer; SMEs) in the different jurisdictions would not be identical; but even if the parties were identical the facts might well be different in the different jurisdictions. This means that the 'risk of re-litigating' similar issues between the same parties or identical issues between different parties would be very high in such cases. The difficulties could be deduced from the UK Competition Appeal Tribunal judgment in *Dune Group Ltd v MasterCard*[124] where the Tribunal held:

> As is well known, the outcome of a trial is usually only binding on the actual parties to the trial. [... G]iven the significant number and variety of current and potential claimants and the range and complexity of the issues involved, we are concerned that the risk of re-litigating similar or identical issues in non-lead claims is unacceptably high.[125]

[117] KR Handley, *Spence, Bower and Handley, Res Judicata* 4th edn (London, LexisNexis, 2009) p 1.
[118] *House of Spring Gardens Ltd. v Waite* [1991] 1 QB 241, 250.
[119] Barnett (n 15) [5.02].
[120] *Black-Clawson Int'l v Papoerwerke Waldhof-Aschaffebburg AG* [1975] AC 591.
[121] Ibid 619.
[122] *Dicey, Morris and Collins* (n 14) Rule 46 [14-036].
[123] *Carl Zeiss Stiftung Appellants v Rayner & Keeler Ltd. and Others* [1967] 1 AC 853, 935.
[124] *Dune Group Ltd v MasterCard* [2022] CAT 14.
[125] Ibid [21].

An added layer of complexity in cross-border competition law cases is that multiple claims would be issued by different injured parties in various jurisdictions against different subsidiaries that may form part of the same infringing undertaking/s. Although it is well established that different subsidiaries, along with parent company, would be jointly and severally liable for breach of competition law,[126] the question '[w]hether joint tortfeasors have a sufficient privity of interest that might lead to the application of *res judicata* is not the subject of clear authority'.[127]

There are specific issues that have been briefly discussed in the EU context,[128] but they require renewed and systematic analysis, post-Brexit. Transnational competition law infringements involving joint tortfeasors would pose complex questions with regard to the recognition and enforcement of judgments in relation to competition law claims in England and Wales. It seems that the 'rules as to parties and privies apply to foreign decisions *in personam*'.[129] Also, as noted in *Cooper Tire*, 'Section 6 of the Law Reform (Married Women and Tortfeasors) Act 1935 and Sections 3 and 4 of the Civil Liability (Contribution) Act 1978' may be relevant in England. If the local subsidiary was not party to the proceedings abroad that were issued against a foreign subsidiary and the parent company abroad, then any finding that the parent company had committed a competition law infringement might not preclude the local subsidiary from contesting the infringement.[130] Therefore the problem is that, since different injured parties may be issuing damages claims against different subsidiaries (forming part of the same infringing undertaking/s), there are real issues that indicate that the estoppel requirements would be very difficult to satisfy with regard to judgments in relation to competition law claims which would normally be issued by different injured parties (ie claimants) who would be suing for damages sustained in multiple jurisdictions.

Could the concept of 'abuse of process [be] an exceptional remedy'?[131] More specifically, if a foreign court (and/or even a foreign regulator) were to determine that several infringing undertakings (which consist of multiple subsidiaries) had been fixing prices or shared markets, would it be regarded as 'abuse of process'[132] for the infringing undertaking/s to contend that they had not deployed the conduct that was determined to be anti-competitive? The difficulties in relying on the concept of 'abuse of process' with regard to multiple related claims before the UK CAT have been set out as follows:

> Abuse of process may be appropriately relied upon following decisions in any lead cases to prevent non-lead claimants or defendants from seeking to relitigate common issues determined in those lead cases. However, it is an exceptional remedy. One party's reliance on an

[126] *JJH Enterprises Ltd (trading as ValueLicensing) v Microsoft* [2022] EWHC 929 (Comm) [40, 49 and 64]; Case C-882/19 *Sumal v Mercedes Benz Trucks España* EU:C:2021:800.

[127] *Cooper Tire & Rubber Company v Shell Chemicals UK Limited* [2009] EWHC 2609 [80].

[128] Ibid 79. M Danov and F Becker, 'Introduction: Preclusive Effects of Foreign Judgments/Settlements across Europe' in Danov, Becker and Beaumont (n 6) 365.

[129] *Spence, Bower and Handley, Res Judicata* (n 117) 127. See also: *Carl-Zeiss (No 2)* [1967] 1 AC 853.

[130] Compare Case 1077/5/7/07, *Emerson Electric Co v Morgan Crucible Company PLC and Ors* [2011] CAT 4; *Emerson Electric Co v Morgan Crucible Company PLC and Ors* [2012] EWCA Civ 1559.
See the transcript of the hearing before the CAT, pp 2–3 and 41.

[131] *Dune Group* (n 124) [24].

[132] *Royal Mail Group v DAF Trucks* [2020] CAT 7 [141].

> abuse of process argument is likely to invite a response that *different legal or factual issues are involved in the subsequent case, or that new evidence is available and ought to be heard.*[133]

The issues concerning various questions of fact and law would be multiplied in competition law cases where the prior set of proceedings had taken place in another jurisdiction. There would indeed be difficult questions that must be addressed by national judges with a view to ascertaining whether there is a competition law infringement as well as with a view to dealing with issues of quantification. In particular, the English courts might be 'cautious'[134] because the substantive laws (including competition laws, which reflect the national public policy)[135] may well be different. In addition, English judges may not be 'familiar with modes of procedure in many foreign countries',[136] which might impact on the outcome of the disputes.[137] The issues, which were complex enough prior to Brexit in cases where the EU Commission findings of infringement were binding for the UK courts,[138] would be exacerbated in cases where the parties rely on different foreign regulators' findings.[139]

Pre-Brexit, some difficult issues concerning the concept of 'abuse process' were dealt with in *Royal Mail Group v DAF Trucks*.[140] In this case, the private damages claims in England and Wales were preceded by public-administrative proceedings before the European Commission. The EU regulator took the view that there was a competition law infringement. An important aspect was that the Commission's decision was rendered after the parties had actively engaged in settlements discussions under Article 10a of Commission Regulation No 773/2004.[141] In spite of the fact that all the defendants were addressees of the European Commission's decisions, there was an important preliminary issue concerning the bindingness of the recitals that led to the Commission's decision.[142]

The claimants appeared to believe that all the recitals concerning the 'description of the conduct',[143] 'legal assessment'[144] and 'remedies'[145] were binding.[146] The defendants' position was more nuanced. One of the defendants, DAF, took the view that, in these particular proceedings, Article 1 of the Commission's decision was binding along with the recitals, which would be helpful for interpreting Article 1.[147] The other defendants argued that 'the recitals were binding insofar as they constituted the essential basis of

[133] *Dune Group* (n 124) [24] – emphasis added by the author.
[134] *Carl Zeiss* (n 123) 918.
[135] See below.
[136] *Carl Zeiss* (n 123) 918.
[137] *Steven John Kilfoy Wall v Mutuelle De Poitiers Assurance* [2013] EWHC 53 (QB) [2]. See more: Chapter 2 above.
[138] Article 16 of Regulation 1/2003.
[139] eg Case No: 1382/7/7/21, *Consumers' Association v Qualcomm Inc* [2022] CAT 20.
[140] *Royal Mail Group* (n 132).
[141] Ibid [2].
[142] Ibid [21].
[143] See: Section 3 – Recitals 46-63 – Case AT.39824, *Trucks – Commission Decision of 19.7.2016 relating to a proceeding under Article 101 of the Treaty on the Functioning of the European Union (the Treaty) and Article 53 of the EEA Agreement*, C(2016) 4673 final.
[144] See: Section 4 – Recitals 64-88 – *Trucks – Commission Decision of 19.7.2016* (n 143).
[145] See: Section 7 – Recitals 101-136 – *Trucks – Commission Decision of 19.7.2016* (n 143).
[146] *Royal Mail Group* (n 132) [22].
[147] Ibid.

what is stated in the operative part, and that on this basis only a few of the findings in the recitals were binding'.[148]

The claimants submitted that the argument on this particular issue may constitute *abuse of process*, not least because it was explicitly stated that 'the facts as outlined in this Decision have been accepted by MAN, Daimler, Iveco, Volvo and DAF [...] in the settlement procedure'.[149] The CAT noted the potentially controversial strategies advanced by the defendants by submitting that:

> the defendants' contention that they can admit a fact to the Commission for the purpose of obtaining those benefits in the Decision but then not admit the same fact for the purpose of resisting a consequent damages claim based on the Decision, simply begs the question whether the latter conduct constitutes an abuse.[150]

The CAT went on and specified the principle which need to be systematically considered with a view to determining whether the parties' strategies amount to 'abuse of process'.[151] More specifically, the court made it clear that '[i]t is an abuse of process for a defendant simply to deny or not admit facts set out in a recital relied on by a claimant'.[152] The regulator's findings may still be looked into by the court.[153] However, in order to make a case for this, the defendant should rely on some fresh evidence;[154] or they should demonstrate that there are some inconsistencies with a relevant 'underlying document'.[155] It would also be possible for the defendant to question the claimant's allegations which go beyond what has been established in the recitals of the Commission's decision as long as such defendants do not completely deny the findings that are specified in the relevant recitals.[156]

Post-Brexit, the question would be somewhat different: to extent should parties be entitled to re-argue (or question) the foreign court's/regulator's findings of fact in cases where there is no longer a requirement for the UK court to follow the foreign regulatory decisions, establishing an infringement? Although a regulatory decision would only be enforceable within the territory on which the regulator in question operates,[157] the author believes that – in a view of the transnational nature of competition law infringements – a foreign regulatory decision might contain important information about the conduct of the infringing undertaking/s. That said, a foreign regulatory

[148] Ibid.
[149] Recitals 3 – *Trucks – Commission Decision of 19.7.2016* (n 143).
[150] *Royal Mail Group* (n 132) [130].
[151] Ibid [141].
[152] Ibid [141.1].
[153] Ibid [141.2].
[154] Ibid [141.4].
[155] Ibid [141.3].
[156] Ibid [141.5]. See also: CMS Law-Now, 'Competition Appeal Tribunal rules on binding nature of European Commission infringement decisions in follow-on damages claims', https://www.cms-lawnow.com/ealerts/2020/03/competition-appeal-tribunal-rules-on-binding-nature-of-european-commission-infringement?cc_lang=en.
[157] White Paper on Modernisation of the Rules implementing Articles 85 and 86 of the EC Treaty, Commission Programme 99/027 [60]. See A Komninos, *EC Private Antitrust Enforcement: Decentralised Application of EC Competition Law by National Courts* (Oxford, Hart Publishing, 2008) 77; S Brammer, *Co-operation between National Competition Agencies in the Enforcement of EC Competition Law* (Oxford, Hart Publishing, 2009) 426–36.

decision is unlikely to classify as a judgment[158] for the purposes of the English Civil Procedure Rules, which provide the following definition:

> 'judgment' means, subject to any other enactment, any judgment given by a foreign court or tribunal, whatever the judgment may be called, and includes
> (i) a decree;
> (ii) an order;
> (iii) a decision;
> (iv) a writ of execution or a writ of control; and
> (v) the determination of costs by an officer of the court'.[159]

Although the author has argued in the past that foreign regulatory decisions should be regarded as 'judgments' for recognition and enforcement purposes under the Brussels Ia Regulation, such an approach did not find sufficient support among the drafters of the 2019 Hague Judgments Convention.[160] In spite of the fact that the EU legislator, it seems, originally considered the adoption of a rule to the effect that a Member State court cannot take a decision which is irreconcilable with a final decision, finding a competition law infringement and being rendered by a national competition authority within the European Competition Network,[161] the final solution appeared to be more flexible. The Antitrust Damages Directive states that:

> Member States shall ensure that where a final decision [establishing an EU competition law infringement] is taken in another Member State, that final decision may, in accordance with national law, be presented before their national courts as at least prima facie evidence that an infringement of competition law has occurred and, as appropriate, may be assessed along with any other evidence adduced by the parties.[162]

As noted in chapter 10, an alternative approach may be for foreign regulatory decision to be regarded as prima facie evidence of the conduct, post-Brexit. The proposed approach for cooperation, which is somewhat aligned with the EU model, should allow for foreign regulatory interests to be factored in, whilst ensuring that the opposing party should be allowed to rely on 'counter evidence negativing the existence of'[163] the anti-competitive conduct and/or the effects of the conduct in the UK market. In other words, since the foreign regulators would naturally apply different national laws, it is proposed for the English courts to regard the foreign regulatory decision as prima facie evidence of the defendant's conduct (which would be a question of fact) rather than being evidence that the conduct is anti-competitive which presupposes for the English courts to consider the effects of the conduct in the UK market, applying the UK competition law (as well as in some other markets, if another competition law was applicable).

[158] Preliminary Document No 2 of December 2018 – Cara North, 'The possible exclusion of anti-trust matters from the Convention as reflected in Article 2(1)(p) of the 2018 draft Convention' presented at *Twenty-Second Session Recognition and Enforcement of Foreign Judgments*, 18 June–2 July 2019, The Hague [15].

[159] CPR 74.2(c).

[160] Preliminary Document No 2 of December 2018 (n 158) [15].

[161] White Paper on Damages Actions for Breach of the EC antitrust rules COM(2008) 165 final [2.3].

[162] Article 9(2) of the Antitrust Damages Directive.

[163] Compare: *Godard* (n 26) 150.

There are two additional advantages of the proposed approach. First, the English court would no longer need to stay their proceedings with a view avoiding the risk of irreconcilable decision which may be reached by the EU Commission.[164] In other words, the UK jurisprudence may impact on the EU jurisprudence and vice versa. Secondly, the proposed approach would neutralise the risk of giving any effect to an infringement decision rendered by a foreign regulator – who might be combining the function of a party to competition law proceedings and a judge[165] – undermining the right to a fair trial and hearing (ie raising due process concerns).[166] Therefore, the proposed approach should further safeguard the defendant's right to a fair trial as well as upholding the independence of English courts. This should enable the English courts to advance a truly transnational approach to international cooperation.

V. The 'Notion of Comity'[167] and the Protection of Trading Interests Act[168]

In October 2015, as discussed above,[169] Section 47B of the Competition Act 1998 introduced a collective redress regime which may operate on an *opt-out* basis[170] exclusively for claimants that are domiciled in the UK[171] as well as on an *opt-in* basis[172] for claimants that are UK and non-UK domiciled.[173] These developments indicate that there is a renewed interest in the response to the question whether an English court will recognise and enforce a US judgment rendered in antitrust class actions which operate on an *opt-out* basis. Although the author is not aware of any English authority addressing this question head-on, Professor Briggs has submitted that:

> A judgment in class action proceedings in the United States cannot be recognised as against a person who was offered membership of the class, or who was even regarded by the American

[164] Article 16 of Regulation 1/2003. See also: Case C-234/89 *Stergios Delimitis v Henninger Bräu AG* EU:C:1991:91; Case C-344/98 *Masterfoods Ltd v HB Ice Cream Ltd* EU:C:2000:689 [51–2]; *Crehan* (n 112) [64–66].

[165] WPJ Wils, *Principles of European Antitrust Enforcement* (Oxford, Hart Publishing, 2005) 88.

[166] *Adams* (n 31) 561–72. Compare: The EU approach – Article 47(2) of the Charter of Fundamental Rights; Article 6(1) ECHR; *Krombach* (n 49) [39–45]. *Le Compte v Belgium* (1982) 4 EHRR 1. See also: Wils (n 165) 46–47; IS Forrester, 'Due process in EC competition cases: A distinguished institution with flawed procedures' (2009) 34 EL Rev 817, 821.

[167] *Adams* (n 31) 552.

[168] K Huntley, 'The Protection of Trading Interests Act 1980: Some jurisdictional aspects of enforcement of antitrust laws' (1981) 30 *ICLQ* 213; DL Jones, 'Protection of Trading Interests Act 1980' (1981) 40 *Civil Law Journal* 41; AV Lowe, 'Blocking extraterritorial jurisdiction: the British Protection of Trading Interests Act, 1980' (1981) 75 *American Journal of International Law* 257; MA Blythe, 'The extraterritorial impact of the anti-trust laws: Protecting British Trading Interests' (1983) 31 *American Journal of Comparative Law* 99; L Collins, 'Blocking and Clawback Statutes: The United Kingdom Approach' (1986) *Journal of Business Law* 372 and 452; P Torremans and JJ Fawcett, *Cheshire, North & Fawcett: Private International Law* 15th edn (Oxford, OUP, 2017) 553–55.

[169] Chapter 5.

[170] Competition Act 1998 s 47B(11).

[171] Competition Act 1998 s 47B(11)(b).

[172] Competition Act 1998 s 47B(10).

[173] Compare: Competition Act 1998 s 47B(11)(b). See more: R Mulheron, 'Asserting personal jurisdiction over non-resident class members: comparative insights for the United Kingdom' (2019) 15 *Journal of Private International Law* 445.

> court as a member of that class, if he did nothing which English law sees as a submission or consent to the jurisdiction of the American court.[174]

This is a very persuasive view which appears to indicate that, traditionally, a major difficulty with the recognition and enforcement of judgments in relation to class antitrust actions that are initiated abroad on an *opt-out* basis is that there would be multiple claimants who may not have explicitly consented to the jurisdiction of the foreign court.[175] That said, the fact that the UK has now felt that there was a policy interest for UK policy-makers to introduce a collective redress procedural mechanism, which operates on an opt-out basis, strongly suggests that the UK attitude to the recognition of foreign class action judgments should change, which should in turn strengthen the judicial cooperation in competition law matters between the UK and US on the basis of comity principles.[176]

Therefore, there are strong arguments that, if a claimant had been given adequate notice to join a foreign class action and they did not opt out of the collective redress proceedings, a final US class action judgment should be recognised in England.[177] That said, in order for the UK to take a lead in promoting such cooperation, the Protection of Trading Interests Act 1980 should be repealed. The adoption of the 1980 Act, which empowered the UK Secretary of State to implement certain measures with a view to protecting UK trading interests, exposed the issues concerning the judicial cooperation in competition law matters. In particular, Section 1 stated that:

> If it appears to the Secretary of State—
>
> a) that measures have been or are proposed to be taken by or under the law of any overseas country for regulating or controlling international trade; and
>
> b) that those measures, in so far as they apply or would apply to things done or to be done outside the territorial jurisdiction of that country by persons carrying on business in the United Kingdom, are damaging or threaten to damage the trading interests of the United Kingdom,
>
> the Secretary of State may by order direct that this section shall apply to those measures either generally or in their application to such cases as may be specified in the order.

Although the purpose of the 1980 Act was to inter alia minimise (or even neutralise) any effects of the US antitrust legislation which would apply extra-territorially in the UK,[178] it is now well established that UK competition law would itself apply extra-territorially.[179]

Should the 1980 Act be repealed? It is true that the 1980 Act has not extensively been used, but its adoption has probably *discouraged* other nations from exercising

[174] A Briggs, *Agreements on Jurisdiction and Choice of Law* (Oxford, OUP, 2008) 349–50.

[175] Ibid 345.

[176] Compare: Agreement between the Government of the United States of America and the Commission of the European Communities Regarding the Application of their Competition Laws (1991) 30 *International Legal Materials* 1491.

[177] JCL Dixon, 'The *res judicata* effect of a US class action settlement' (1997) 46 *ICLQ* 134, 150–51. See also: *Greg Currie v McDonald's* [2005] 7 CPC (6th) 60, 250 DLR (4th) 224, 195 OAC 244, 74 OR (3d) 321 (Ontario Court of Appeal) [42]–[43].

[178] See: *British Airways Board v Laker Airways* [1985] AC 58, 89–90 (Lord Diplock). See also s 5(2)b and 5(4) of the 1980 Act.

[179] *The LCD Appeals* (n 100).

adjudicatory jurisdiction applying their competition laws which might in turn impact on some injured parties' access to remedies in cases involving multinational companies. As noted above, from a private international law perspective, an appropriate consideration of various 'reasons of international comity (that is, good relations among nations)'[180] have become an important part of the US jurisprudence in cross-border competition law disputes. The importance of the comity principles for US courts as part of the court's discretion to exercise its adjudication and regulatory jurisdiction was reflected in *Hoffmann-La Roche Ltd v Empagran*, where the US Supreme Court held that:

> While applying America's antitrust laws to foreign conduct can interfere with a foreign nation's ability to regulate its own commercial affairs, courts have long held such application nonetheless reasonable, and hence consistent with prescriptive comity principles, insofar as the laws reflect a legislative effort to redress domestic antitrust injury caused by foreign anti-competitive conduct.[181]

There are two deductions to be drawn from this quotation. First, it is beyond doubt that the comity considerations should be more systematically deployed to deal with a conflict of competition laws. Secondly, there are major developments in the UK law that strongly indicate that the 1980 Act is outdated.

As part of this process, the UK public policy that denies recognition of foreign judgments awarding multiple damages in antitrust claims should also be reviewed. It is well settled that Section 5(1) and (2) of the 1980 Act provides that an English court shall not recognise and enforce a judgment for multiple damages.[182] The effect of this provision can be easily illustrated by taking as an example the judgment of the Court of Appeal of England and Wales in *Eliades & Ors v Lewis*,[183] where it was held that:

> [T]he robust and sensible approach to s.5 of the 1980 Act [...] is not to treat the multiple damages element of the judgment as definitive of, or 'infecting', its character as a whole, but to read s.5(1) as precluding proceedings for recovery at common law only to the extent that the judgment sought to be enforced is for an amount arrived at by multiplying a sum assessed as compensation for the loss or damage sustained by the person in whose favour the judgment was given.[184]

Although this appears to be a fair approach, there are at least two issues that strongly indicate that applying a similar approach in antitrust disputes would not be compatible with the comity principles. First, a real issue is that 'the prohibition on enforcement does not depend on whether the overseas court applied its anti-trust laws extra-territorially'.[185] For example, Section 5 would allow the English judges to deny the recognition and enforcement of a US judgment irrespective of the fact that the anti-competitive conduct was implemented in the US, and affected the US market only,[186] and irrespective of the

[180] *Motorola Mobility LLC v AU Optronics Corp* 775 F 3d 816 at 818 (7th Cir 2015).
[181] *F Hoffmann-La Roche Ltd v Empagran* 124 S Ct 2359 at 2361 (2004 Sup Ct (US).
[182] According to s 5(3), 'a judgment for multiple damages means a judgment for an amount arrived at by doubling, trebling or otherwise multiplying a sum assessed as compensation for the loss or damage sustained by the person in whose favour the judgment is given'.
[183] *Eliades & Ors v Lewis* [2003] EWCA Civ 1758.
[184] Ibid [53].
[185] *Cheshire, North & Fawcett* (n 168) 555.
[186] *British Airways Board v Laker Airways* [1984] QB 142, 162.

fact that, in a similar situation, an English court would have assumed jurisdiction and applied UK competition laws, which will also have had extra-territorial application.[187]

Secondly, if the anti-competitive conduct has 'directly and substantially affected'[188] the US market, the foreign legislator may well have envisaged that multiple damages should be awarded with a view to pursuing important and legitimate public policy objectives. Indeed, Professor Visscher has submitted that:

> Victims who claim damages in essence serve the social goal of deterrence. However, starting a lawsuit entails costs, which are privately borne. This might lead to too few lawsuits being brought. Increasing the expected damages of victims by awarding punitive damages may solve this problem.[189]

Although Schedule 8 of the 1998 Act now states that '[a] court or the Tribunal may not award exemplary damages in competition proceedings',[190] the Competition Appeal Tribunal in an earlier judgment, rendered in the *Cardiff City Transport*[191] case, took the view that that 'exemplary damages can in theory be awarded where there is an intentional breach of the law ie the defendant acts knowing that what he does constitutes an infringement of competition law and intending that infringement',[192] and went on to award such damages.[193] This strongly indicates that various policy choices by different regulators may reasonably be made. Therefore, it is difficult to see why an English court should continue to refuse the recognition of an award of multiple damages in competition law cases which are 'only connected in a very limited way'[194] with the UK in so far as the conduct affected the market in the other country.

VI. Conclusion

The PIL literature[195] suggests that the lack of a global framework, which allows for claims arising out of the same transnational infringements to be centralised before an *appropriate forum*, means issues concerning the recognition and enforcement of judgments in relation to competition law claims would be an important part of any regime for judicial cooperation. This deduction could be strengthened by noting that, given the important public policy interests in enforcing national competition laws, judges might often be reluctant to stay their proceedings.

[187] Blythe (n 168) 123. See also: *The LCD Appeals* (n 100).

[188] Article 6(3)(b) of Rome II.

[189] LT Visscher, 'Economic analysis of punitive damages' in H Koziol and V Wilcox (eds), *Punitive Damages: Common Law and Civil Law Perspectives* (Springer, Vienna/New York, 2009) 220, 224–25.

[190] See also: Competition Act 1998 s 47C(9)(b). Compare: Case Number: 1178/5/7/11, *2 Travel Group Plc (In Liquidation) v Cardiff City Transport Services Ltd* [2012] CAT 19.

[191] Case Number: 1178/5/7/11, *2 Travel Group Plc (In Liquidation) v Cardiff City Transport Services Ltd* [2012] CAT 19.

[192] Ibid 485.

[193] M Danov and F Becker 'Introduction: The Importance of Damages in a Cross-Border Context' in Law' in Danov, Becker and Beaumont (n 6) 291.

[194] Mills (n 100) 259.

[195] Fawcett (n 5) 41. See more: Section IV below.

There is an argument for the English courts to advance an approach which could set the scene for judicial cooperation in competition law matters around the 'notion of comity'.[196] On that basis, English courts should recognise foreign judgments on the grounds of comity and reciprocity in a global context, drawing certain analogies with the practice of the Canadian Supreme Court.[197] Also, in order to minimise the risk of inconsistent outcomes in relation to competition law claims arising out of transnational competition law infringements, any foreign regulatory decisions may be regarded as prima facie evidence of the conduct.

In line with the arguments which have been put forward in chapters 3 and 4, it is further suggested for a multinational group of companies that engages in anti-competitive conduct to be regarded as being present within the jurisdiction as long as it has a wholly-owned subsidiary that is present in the jurisdiction and it has used the subsidiary in question to implement the anti-competitive conduct there. This means that such a multinational group of companies could be regarded as being present in the jurisdiction, aligning the classification of concept of single undertaking[198] for competition law purposes with the classification for private international law purposes.

Although the merits of the competition law dispute should not be reviewed as part of the recognition and enforcement process, the public policy nature of competition law strongly indicates that an English court should be entitled to review whether a foreign judgment is in conflict with UK competition law, which has a public policy nature in England. For example, if the recognition and enforcement of a foreign judgment is irreconcilable with the UK CMA's decision establishing a competition law infringement, the recognition and enforcement would certainly be denied.

Finally, there is a strong argument that, post-Brexit, the UK should repeal the 1980 Act and promote judicial cooperation in with US on the principles of comity. Indeed, the UK competition law policy in relation to opt-out collective redress claims and extra-territorial application appears to have been aligned with the US policies, which the 1980 Act was set to discourage.

[196] *Adams* (n 31) 552.

[197] *Beals* (n 39). See also: *Morguard Investments* (n 37).

[198] Opinion of Mr Advocate General Warner in Case C-6/73 *Istituto Chemioterapico Italiano and Commercial Solvents v Commission* EU:C:1974:5 at 263 cited in *Adams v Cape Industries Plc* [1990] Ch 433, 475.

13

Conclusion – Implementing a PIL Regime to Promote Judicial Cooperation

This book demonstrates that private international law (PIL) rules have a major role to play in setting up an effective regime for judicial cooperation that enables national courts to deal with related private antitrust damages claims arising out of transnational competition law infringements in a global context. The PIL issues are important because many of these competition law infringements will restrict competition and cause antitrust damages to many injured parties (ie consumers; small and large businesses) in multiple jurisdictions. Since many of the infringing undertakings would be multinational groups of companies – enjoying market power and having subsidiaries across the globe, there would be multiple national courts that would have adjudicatory jurisdiction to hear and determine related private antitrust damages claims with an international element.

Indeed, the wide bases for the assumption of jurisdiction[1] strongly indicate that related private antitrust damages claims, which arise out of the same transnational competition law infringement, may be issued before different national courts. The fact that competition laws are set to safeguard important public interests of the forum strongly indicates that many national courts would be reluctant to stay (or decline) their legal proceedings.[2] The complex PIL issues, which are intertwined with the aspects concerning the regulatory/adjudicatory jurisdiction, appear to signify the need for judicial cooperation in competition law matters. In other words, a major PIL problem is that there would be multiple related claims which are connected to the same allegedly anticompetitive conduct and which would be issued before different national courts.[3] With this in mind, an important PIL question is: how to minimise the inconsistent outcomes in related competition law claims, which arise out of the same transnational competition law infringement and which are issued before different national courts?

Since there is no international convention which is set to promote judicial cooperation and govern related court proceedings arising out of the same transnational competition law infringement/s in a global context, there is a strong argument for the English courts to take a lead in advancing a model for judicial cooperation by gaining advantage of the fact that London is a global centre for dispute resolution.[4]

[1] Chapters 4, 5 and 6.
[2] Chapter 7, 8, 9 and 10.
[3] Chapters 7 and 8.
[4] Chapters 8, 9, 10 and 11.

The proposed transnational approach to judicial cooperation should enable the English judges to factor in foreign competition laws, expressing foreign regulatory interests.[5] If the English court were to factor foreign legitimate interests by inter alia giving effect to foreign competition laws,[6] then they could go a step further and award damages, for example, for breach of EU competition law in cases where it does not directly apply in the UK (ie post-Brexit).

Given the important role which London plays as a business and financial centre, a soft law approach to judicial cooperation in antitrust matters might be developed by building on the reputation of English judges and legal practitioners. A transnational network of legal practitioners, representing claimants and defendants in related claims arising out of the same transnational competition law infringement could cooperate and exchange information which would be informing their pleadings; whilst updating the court about the progress of any related (private and public) proceedings in other jurisdictions. It is well established that 'transnational networks occupy centre stage in competition law, which is attentive to (and suspicious of) informal alliances or spontaneous congruence of market behaviour'.[7]

In line with the governance literature such networks could be formed on a case-by-case basis, setting out the issues which need to be dealt with in related claims arising out of the same transnational infringements. That said, the UK CAT judgment in *Michael O'Higgins FX Class Representative v Barclays Bank, Phillip Evans v Barclays Bank*[8] might be interpreted as indicating that any such form of informal cooperation should be carefully approached in so far as it may have both advantages and disadvantages.[9] In this book, the author has suggested for a series of rather flexible PIL solutions to be advanced by the English judges, which along with various ad hoc transnational networks of legal practitioners in relation to related damages claims arising out of specific anti-competitive conduct may set the scene for a soft form of judicial cooperation, which should improve injured parties access to legal remedies.

I. Theoretical Framework – PIL and Access to Legal Remedies

An analysis of the case law was important to consider the relationship between the PIL rules allocating jurisdiction[10] and the PIL rules ascertaining applicable competition laws[11] which will both impact on the English courts' decision to decline (or assume) jurisdiction as well as on the recognition and the enforcement of judgments in relation

[5] AT von Mehren, 'Special Substantive Rules for Multistate Problems: Their role and significance in contemporary choice of law methodology' (1974–1975) 88 *Harvard Law Review* 347.

[6] Chapters 10, 11 and 12.

[7] H Muir-Watt, 'Governing Networks: A Global Challenge for Private International Law' (2015) *Maastricht Journal of European and Comparative Law* 352, 357.

[8] Case numbers 1329/7/7/19 and 1336/7/7/19 *Michael O'Higgins FX Class Representative Ltd v Barclays Bank Plc and Others, Mr Phillip Evans v Barclays Bank Plc and Others* [2022] CAT 16.

[9] Ibid [329]. See more: Section IV below.

[10] Chapters 3–7.

[11] Chapters 9–11.

to competition law claims in England and Wales.[12] In order to analyse the relevant case law and identify the PIL issues which need to be addressed with a view to improving the injured parties' access to justice, some theoretical principles were set out in Chapter 2.

It was demonstrated that there are several major PIL aspects in relation to access to justice which are to be examined as part of the proposed theoretical model. The first key element concerns the applicable (public) competition law/s[13] and substantive (private) law/s)[14] which would impact on the parties' entitlement to legal remedies in cross-border cases. The second key element of the theoretical model concerns the PIL rules which are determining jurisdiction, avoiding parallel and related proceedings. These aspects should be careful considered in light of the relevant case law.

On the basis of the current case law analyses the author has tried to identify the PIL issues which could create obstacles to the resolution of cross-border competition law disputes at present and which – if properly addressed – could improve injured parties' access to legal remedies.[15] An analysis of the interplay between the PIL issues and the access of injured parties to effective legal remedies in competition law cases appears central to identifying the weaknesses of the current PIL framework and starting to consider any soft law solutions along with any long term solution (if an international convention were ever to be adopted). The objective is to identify the important PIL the issues that need to be addressed with a view to improving the injured parties' access to legal remedies in cross-border competition law actions.

Therefore, an important contribution of this book is that it sets out a theoretical model which enables the author to analyse the relevant case law with a view to identifying the PIL issues that need to be dealt with as a priority to attain a level of consistency as well as with a view to setting out possible solutions that need to be advanced to minimise the inconsistencies in relation to private antitrust damages that arise out of transnational infringements. In other words, the case law analysis enables the author to identify the relevant PIL issues which could impact on the injured parties' access to justice with a view to proposing a pragmatic model for judicial cooperation in competition law matters (which might need to be empirically tested).

II. The Role of PIL in Improving Access to Justice

Theoretically, there is a strong argument that PIL techniques should be systematically used with a view to attaining a level of judicial cooperation in related private antitrust damages claims which arise out of transnational competition law infringements. The author believes that PIL mechanisms would be central to enhancing the effectiveness of national private enforcement regimes in a global context. Nonetheless, Professor Terhechte takes the view that:

> Today cooperation between the responsible administrative bodies at the international level mainly takes place in the classical forms, i.e., the administrative assistances that is partly

[12] Chapters 12.
[13] Chapters 9–10.
[14] Chapter 11.
[15] Chapter 2.

> laid down in individual international agreements. [...] From a 'dogmatic' point of view one frequently deals with questions concerning 'classical' international administrative law, which acts to some extent as the counterpart of private international law in solving traditional questions of collision.[16]

This is an interesting observation, which appears to indicate that international administrative law might be used to address PIL issues. The problem is that the EU Commission (or any regulator for that matter) would not apply foreign competition laws. The regulator's bias to always apply their own competition law means that the applicable set of competition laws would depend on the place of the competition law proceedings.

This may be perceived as a problem which a PIL mechanism for judicial cooperation should endeavour to address by encouraging the English judges to factor in to foreign regulatory interests. The fact that multiple private antitrust damages claims, which arise out of the same transnational competition law infringements, could be issued in different jurisdictions strongly indicates that that an appropriate PIL mechanism would be necessary to ensure consistent outcomes in such claims. It is well established that the coordination of conflicting competition laws[17] would naturally be a hard core PIL question, which is dealt with by the PIL theory that is advanced by Currie:[18]

> The central problem of conflict of laws may be defined, then, as that of determining the appropriate rule of decision when the interests of two or more states are in conflict – in other words, of determining which interest shall yield. The problem would not exist if this were one world, with an all-powerful central government. It would not exist (though other problems of 'conflict of laws' would) if the independent sovereignties in the real world had identical laws. So long, however, as we have diversity of laws, we shall have conflicts of interests among states. Hence, unless something is done, the administration of private law where more than one state is concerned will be affected with disuniformity and uncertainty. To avoid this result by all reasonable means is certainly a laudable objective; but how? Not by establishing a single government; even if such a thing were remotely thinkable as a practical possibility, we attribute positive values to the principle of self-determination for localities and groups. The attainment of uniformity among diverse states is, to put it mildly, a long-range undertaking.[19]

Currie's work captures well the issues which PIL is set to deal with. This is particularly the case for the diverse set of competition laws which aim to safeguard countries' legitimate regulatory interests. The extra-territorial application of competition law rules – taken together with the public policy character[20] of competition laws which are considered as 'overriding mandatory provisions of the law of the forum'[21] for PIL purposes – means that the national judges would naturally apply the competition laws of the forum in cross-border cases. In other words, it is perceived that the more effective

[16] JP Terhechte, *International Competition Enforcement Law Between Cooperation and Convergence* (Springer, Berlin 2011) 17.

[17] eg J Basedow, S Francq and L Idot (eds), *International Antitrust Litigation: Conflict of Laws and Coordination* (Oxford, Hart Publishing, 2012).

[18] B Currie, 'Notes on Methods and Objectives in the Conflict of Laws' in B Currie, *Selected Essays on the Conflict of Laws* (Duke University Press, Durham 1963) 177.

[19] Ibid 178–79.

[20] Recital 1 of the EU Antitrust Damages Directive. See also: Case C-126/97, *Eco Swiss China Time v Benetton International ('Eco Swiss')* [1999] ECR I-3055; Case 38/98, *Renault v Maxicar* [2000] ECR I-2973.

[21] Article 9(2) of Rome I; Article 16 Rome II. See more: Chapter 10.

the national private antitrust enforcement regime is, the higher the level of protection of the national regulatory interest.

As a result, there would be significant hurdles to judicial cooperation in related private antitrust damages claims arising out of the same transnational competition law infringement. The issues appear to be identified in Currie's work:

> Lawyers and judges are ordinarily schooled in their own domestic law. Day in and day out they think, advise, and argue and dispose of cases in terms of that law. They develop familiarity with its provisions and sometimes expertness and even insights concerning it. They are prone, at least according to a widely held belief, to overlook the significance of foreign facts and to proceed in accordance with local law in many instances in which attention to the foreign law would have produced a different result. [...] The intrusion of foreign law is an unsettling departure from routine, involving even under ideal conditions some encounter with the unfamiliar, some departure from usual procedures, some additional burden; and there are situations in which the degree of unfamiliarity and the burden of understanding can become oppressive. To say that there is a strong presumption favoring the application of the law of the forum until good cause is shown why it should not be applied is to give prescriptive form to an observation of behavior that has something in common with Newton's laws of inertia.[22]

In other words, the problem is that, since each country would naturally be most interested in enforcing its own competition law (safeguarding its national interests), the inconsistent outcomes in related competition law claims that arise out of the same transnational competition law infringement would be a recurrent issue unless an appropriate regime for judicial cooperation is advanced. Given the cross-border nature of competition law infringements, PIL could be used to limit the regulatory scope of national competition laws, whilst aiming to ensure foreign competition laws and legitimate regulatory interests are factored in by the court which has adjudicatory jurisdiction.[23]

A PIL solution which encourages national courts to apply foreign laws, giving effects to foreign regulatory decisions,[24] may have no alternative in a global context.[25] According to the PIL theory advanced by Currie, '[f]oreign law would be applied only when the court has determined that the foreign state has a legitimate interest in the application of its law to the case at bar and that the forum has none'.[26] Although the PIL research appears to show that foreign law as long as it would make a difference to the outcome of the dispute would generally be pleaded in cross-border cases in England and Wales,[27] this is not quite common as far as public competition law is concerned. There are, however, cases where the application of foreign competition laws (ie the issues concerning the relevant regulatory jurisdiction) are considered by the national court to determine whether there is a conflict of competition laws[28] and assume (or decline[29]

[22] B Currie, 'On the displacement of the law of the forum' in Currie (n 18) 3, 9.

[23] M Danov, 'Global Competition Law Framework: A Private International Law Solution Needed' (2016) 12 *Journal of Private International Law* 77; von Mehren (n 5).

[24] Compare: Article 16 of Council Regulation 1/2003; Article 9 from the EU Antitrust Damages Directive.

[25] Chapter 10, 11 and 12.

[26] Currie (n 18) 184.

[27] P Beaumont et al, 'Great Britain Final Report' in P Beaumont et al (eds), *Cross-Border Litigation in Europe* (Oxford, Hart Publishing, 2017).

[28] eg *Hartford Fire Insurance Co v California*, 113 S Ct 2891 (1993).

[29] eg *F Hoffmann-La Roche Ltd v Empagran* (2004) 542 US 155, 165 (Sup Ct (US)).

to exercise) the adjudicatory jurisdiction. A different PIL approach is needed for the English judges to apply UK competition laws, but also to factor in foreign competition laws, expressing foreign regulatory interests.

An additional problem is that any conflict of competition laws is closely connected with the effective governance of multiple claims in relation to the same anti-competitive conduct. The regulatory jurisdiction is closely connected with the question about the competition laws which are to be applied with a view to determining whether there is a transnational competition law infringement.[30] The fact that the competition laws may be applied by national regulators in public-administrative proceedings (where one of the parties would be a competition authority) as well as by national courts in private antitrust enforcement (involving private parties) is a particularly complex issue, which is sometimes overlooked by PIL scholars as well as by PIL mechanisms (including the Brussels Ia Regulation).[31]

A PIL solution is necessary to address the problems of regulatory jurisdiction and territorial scope of national laws which arise in cases where multiple competition laws are at stake in a global context. Addressing the issue of regulatory jurisdiction is not an easy task because, whilst PIL theory might suggest that some 'rules of conduct [which should inter alia cover the competition law rules, regulating the conduct of undertakings that enjoy market power would] appl[y] only to conduct in the territorial limits of the state',[32] competition laws would often apply extra-territorially.[33]

The PIL issues are important and must be addressed head-on because, even if there is a level of international cooperation between regulators,[34] PIL mechanisms would still be necessary with regard to related private antitrust damages claims which would arise in relation to various transnational competition law infringements (which had been established by regulators). Moreover, PIL mechanisms would still be necessary to ensure that any foreign regulatory findings are given due regard (or effect) to in private antitrust enforcement proceedings before the English courts.[35] In other words, there is a strong argument that a level of judicial cooperation is necessary to improve the injured parties' access to legal remedies. What are the main challenges that are to be addressed in a global context?

III. Global Governance – Desirable and Attainable Level of Judicial Cooperation

The foregoing theoretical model appears to suggest that private international law solutions are necessary to improve access to legal remedies in cross-border competition law cases. There are a number of challenges which need to be addressed through a

[30] See: Chapter 9.

[31] M Danov, 'EU Competition Law Enforcement: Is Brussels I suited to dealing with all the challenges?' (2012) 61 *International and Comparative Law Quarterly* 27–54.

[32] Currie (n 18) 69.

[33] Chapter 9.

[34] Chapter 1.

[35] See: Chapter 12.

PIL instrument which is *to be agreed at a global level*[36] or, alternatively, through soft PIL mechanisms for judicial cooperation in competition law matters (which may be advanced by English judges).

The book aims to devise a pragmatic model for judicial cooperation. An important aspect which is addressed, in this respect, concerns not only what the desired level of judicial cooperation in competition law matters is, but also what the attainable level of judicial cooperation is – considering the global governance aspects and the diverse regulatory interests at stake.[37] Although the literature suggests that a level of 'hierarchy, in which states transfer [adjudicatory] authority to dominant [national courts] for certain limited purposes',[38] the public policy interests in enforcing national competition law might suggest that some national courts are unlikely to decline jurisdiction in cases where the competition law has qualified effects within the jurisdiction.[39]

A specific convention which provides for a level of judicial cooperation in competition law matters may be desirable,[40] but recent developments suggest that such a convention would be extremely difficult to agree upon. For example, the fact the 2019 Hague Judgments Convention included a major exception in relation to competition law matters appears to demonstrate how difficult it might be for the international community to attain a level of judicial cooperation in this area.[41] More importantly, the Brexit developments strongly indicate that the political risks might need to be considered as well. In a global context, there is a risk that ineffective enforcement of competition laws considered along with the process of thc globalisation may raise issues about the rising national populism waves.[42] This means that:

> Today the world economy is as open as it has ever been, and the most important challenge it faces is not lack of openness but lack of legitimacy. The traditional approach to trade deal-making that concentrates on exchanging market access is no longer appropriate. The rules that need to be developed are those that emphasize fairness, address concerns of social dumping, and enhance policy space in both developed and developing nations.[43]

A major governance challenge is how, without a formal convention which promotes judicial cooperation in competition law matters, national judges could be encouraged to factor in foreign regulatory interests as well as to draw on foreign regulatory or judicial findings, which is central to governing the risks of inconsistent outcome in related proceedings.

[36] M Danov and C Otero, 'Competition Law Enforcement: Private International Law and Access to Effective Legal Remedies in Cross-Border Cases' in P Beaumont and J Holliday (eds) *Guide to Global Private International Law* (Oxford, Hart Publishing, 2022).

[37] Chapter 7, 8 and 9.

[38] M Kahler and DA Lake, 'Economic integration and global governance: Why so little supranationalism?' in W Mattli and N Woods (eds), *The Politics of Global Regulation* (Princeton University Press, 2009) 242.

[39] Chapters 7–9.

[40] Danov and Otero (n 36).

[41] Chapters 3 and 12. See more: Danov and Otero (n 36).

[42] D Rodrik, 'Populism and the economics of globalization' (2018) *Journal of International Business Policy* 1, 17, https://drodrik.scholar.harvard.edu/files/dani-rodrik/files/populism_and_the_economics_of_globalization.pdf.

[43] Ibid.

A PIL mechanism that is sufficiently flexible to accommodate the different regulatory interests of the developing and developed countries may be used to minimise the inconsistent outcomes with regard to related private antitrust damages claims issued in different jurisdictions. Such a PIL mechanism could be successfully employed to facilitate injured parties' access to effective legal remedies in cross-border competition law cases. Nonetheless, a somewhat sceptical view has been put forward by Professor Stephan, who argues:

> Three reasons occur to me why, in a contemporary world, international implementation of competition law is limited and weak: The present international system lacks the institutional capacity to implement real cooperation; cooperation requires difficult political choices, not merely technical competences; and there is no consensus about the object of cooperation across a broad range of economic sectors.[44]

The quotation appears to suggest that it is likely than any mode of governance in relation to private antitrust enforcement in a global context should 'be built upon national regulatory systems, certainly for foreseeable future'.[45] Moreover, the Brussels Ia/Lugano regime demonstrates that – even if certain countries were to agree upon a PIL mechanism which deals with the issues of jurisdiction, recognition and enforcement of judgments in civil and commercial matters – this might not be sufficiently suited to deal with the problems arising in cross-border competition law cases.

There is a strong argument that a more flexible approach, which relies on an appropriate set of PIL solutions, is central to the effective private enforcement of multiple national competition laws that are to be applied by different national courts in related competition law claims. As noted above, an appropriate PIL regime which allows for multiple and foreign legitimate regulatory concerns to be factored in by English judges would be central to devising an appropriate framework for judicial cooperation that links the aspects concerning the regulatory jurisdiction with the aspects concerning the adjudicatory jurisdiction, which is concerned with facilitating the injured parties' access to legal remedies.

The author's view is that, given the diverse legal traditions and national competition laws, English judges might endeavour to promote an enhanced level of judicial cooperation between different national courts by factoring in foreign regulatory interests when dealing with private antitrust damages that arise out of transnational infringements. In other words, a well thought-through PIL practice in the UK, factoring in the legitimate interests of concerned states to regulate competition law aspects of the relevant cross-border economic activities,[46] should spread good practice and set the scene for other forms of judicial cooperation. In addition to this, some soft law measures and flexible PIL rules may be relied upon to promote a level of judicial cooperation in competition law matters which should aim to reduce the inconsistencies in relation to outcome in related competition law arising out of the same transnational infringement. What are the specific PIL issues that would need to be addressed, in order to enhance the effective

[44] PB Stephan, 'The problem with cooperation' in AT Guzman (ed), *Cooperation, Comity, and Competition Policy* (Oxford University Press, 2011) 217, 218.

[45] DK Tarullo, 'Competition policy for global markets' (1999) *Journal of International Economic Law* 445, 455.

[46] Chapters 9, 10 and 11.

functioning of national enforcement regimes and improve injured parties' access to legal remedies in cross-border competition law cases?

IV. The Specific PIL Issues and Problems to be Addressed

Given the territorial scope of national competition laws, some of the specific issues which need to be systematically addressed in cross-border cases concern: classification;[47] regulatory jurisdiction;[48] adjudicatory jurisdiction;[49] parallel and related proceedings;[50] applicable competition laws;[51] recognition and enforcement of foreign judgments or giving due regard to foreign regulatory decisions establishing transnational competition law infringements.[52]

A. Classification Issues – Private Antitrust Damages Claims

Related private antitrust damages claims arising out of the same transnational competition law infringement would potentially raise numerous preliminary issues concerning classification. Addressing the classification issues may be important for national judges to determine the scope of their adjudicatory jurisdiction as well as to ascertain the applicable sets of competition laws or any other applicable laws which should apply with regard to issues of causation and quantification of damages.[53]

There are specific classification issues that would arise in cases where the infringements have been committed by transnational groups of companies which, for example, need to be classified for the jurisdictional purposes. The classification of a group of companies for jurisdictional purposes may be important for the courts to determine whether the infringing undertaking as whole (which would often be a multinational group of companies) is present in the jurisdiction for the purposes of the Civil Procedure Rules.[54] Likewise, in the Brussels Ia context, the courts would need to address the classification issue with a view to determining whether such a group of companies should be classified as an 'association of [...] legal persons' within the meaning of Article 63(1) of Brussels Ia.[55] If the courts were to do so, then the domicile of such an association would need to be ascertained.

Another set of classification issues would arise in relation to competition law claims arising out of contracts. It is often necessary for infringing undertakings, which engage in anticompetitive business practices/conduct (eg charging excessive prices), to enter

[47] Chapter 3.
[48] Chapters 9 and 10.
[49] Chapters 4, 5 and 6.
[50] Chapters 7 and 8.
[51] Chapters 10 and 11.
[52] Chapter 12.
[53] Chapter 11.
[54] Chapters 4 and 6.
[55] Chapter 4.

into contractual arrangements with their customers. Specific classification issues would arise with regard to competition law claims which arise out of such contracts.[56] In order to address the classification issues, the courts need to systematically consider the act restricting competition along with specific contractual terms/arrangements and the desired remedies.[57]

The lack of common transnational principles with regard to major issues concerning classification in cross-border competition law disputes means that, if the English courts were to systematically address those classification issues, they could take a lead in advancing an 'internationalist'[58] approach to classification in a global context.

B. Jurisdiction

The Brussels Ia/Lugano regime is a multilateral framework for judicial cooperation which is based on 'mutual trust in the administration of justice in the [European] Union'.[59] It is set to provide certain grounds for allocation of jurisdiction in civil and commercial matters which are broadly defined to cover private antitrust damages claims. Brussels Ia aims to provide its jurisdictional ground on the basis of 'close connection between the court and the action or in order to facilitate the sound administration of justice'.[60] There is no requirement for the court to be the 'proper place in which to bring the claim'.[61]

The issue is that, as noted before,[62] the Brussels Ia/Lugano regime is not suited to allocate jurisdiction in competition law claims. The view could be strengthened by the Opinion of Advocate General Jääskinen in *Cartel Damage Claims (CDC)*.[63] The problem with the application of Brussels Ia in competition law claims is twofold. First, the connecting factor – 'the place where the damage occurred'[64] – is narrowly interpreted to allocate jurisdiction to the courts where the *direct damage* occurred.[65] More importantly, the jurisdiction of the court at that place is limited to the local harm. This is problematic because antitrust damages may be sustained by multiple injured parties in different jurisdictions which would inevitably lead to related proceedings. Secondly, in the majority of the competition law cases, the place where the competition law infringement was committed would be difficult to ascertain.[66]

In view of that and given the fact that many tortious competition law claims would be issued against groups of companies, Article 8(1) of Brussels Ia has turned out to be a

[56] Chapter 5.
[57] Chapter 5.
[58] *Raiffeisen Zentralbank Osterreich AG v Five Star Trading LLC and others* [2001] EWCA Civ 68 [26].
[59] Recital 26 of Brussels Ia.
[60] Recital 16 of Brussels Ia.
[61] The Competition Appeal Tribunal Rules 2015 r 31(3).
[62] M Danov, *Jurisdiction and Judgments in Relation to EU Competition Law Claims* (Oxford, Hart Publishing, 2010).
[63] See the Opinion of Advocate General Jääskinen – Case C-352/13 *Cartel Damage Claims (CDC) Hydrogen Peroxide SA v Evonik Degussa GmbH* EU:C:2014:2443 [8].
[64] Case C-21/76 *Handelskwekerij G J Bier BV v Mines de potasse d'Alsace SA* EU:C:1976:166 [19].
[65] Chapter 4.
[66] See: Chapter 4.V.B. Compare: Case 1329/7/7/19, *Michael O'Higgins FX Class Representative Limited v Barclays Bank* – Order of the President (Service out of the jurisdiction) – 16 August 2019 [2].

major provision for allocation of jurisdiction within the EU.[67] In particular, the English High Court judgment in *Provimi*[68] allowed claimants to issue proceedings against a local subsidiary which could strategically be identified as the anchor defendant for the purposes of Article 8(1) of Brussels Ia. After establishing jurisdiction against the local subsidiary in their preferred jurisdiction, the claimants sought to join the parent companies with a view to centralising litigation there.[69]

Post-Brexit, the UK may adopt a rather different approach in relation to the assumption of jurisdiction in competition law claims arising out of transnational competition law infringements. On the one hand, there would be some similarities. For example, the place where the damage was sustained[70] (or occurred) or where the market was affected[71] as well as the place where the act restricting competition was committed[72] (ie giving rise to antitrust damages) would depend on the specific nature of the 'carte[l arrangements which have] international effects'[73] and/or 'international abuses of a dominant position'[74] which presupposes for the acts restricting the competition and their potential effects to be classified, so that the relevant jurisdictional and choice-of-law rules could swiftly be applied.

On the other hand, it is welcome that the UK Supreme Court has already adopted a broad definition of *damage* for the purposes of para 3.1(9) of PD 6B, which should cover direct and indirect damage.[75] This should not only address the weaknesses of the Brussels Ia regime, but it should also allow the English courts to establish that there is sufficient territorial connection between the competition law infringement and England in cases were indirect damage has been sustained in England.[76] More importantly, the English court would also have jurisdiction to award compensatory damages in relation to the loss which the claimants have sustained in other jurisdictions, provided that 'some significant [antitrust] damage has been sustained in England'.[77]

Likewise, there is a strong argument that Section 15B of the Civil Jurisdiction and Judgments Act 1982 – which is modelled on Section 4 of Brussels Ia – should be interpreted broadly to cover collective redress claims for damages issued on behalf of consumers.[78] The deduction could be strengthened by the UK CAT's reasoned order in *Dr Liza Lovdahl Gormsen v Meta Platforms.*[79] Although it makes sense for the interpretation of the Brussels Ia regime to be aligned with the collective redress mechanisms

[67] Chapters 7 and 11.

[68] *Provimi Limited v Aventis Animal Nutrition SA and Others* [2003] EWHC 961 (Comm).

[69] See more: Chapter 6.

[70] Chapter 4.

[71] Chapter 11.

[72] Chapter 4.

[73] Communication From the Commission to the Council, *Towards an International Framework of Competition Rules*, COM(96) 284 final at p 3.

[74] Ibid.

[75] *FS Cairo v Lady Brownlie* [2021] UKSC 45 [51 & 81].

[76] Case No: 1382/7/7/21, *Consumers' Association v Qualcomm Inc* – Reasoned Order of the President (Service out of the jurisdiction), 15 March 2021 [5].

[77] *Metall und Rohstoff AG v Donaldson Lufkin & Jenrette Inc and Another* [1990] 1 QB 391, 437. *Lady Brownlie* (n 75) [51].

[78] Chapters 5 and 6.

[79] Case No: 1433/7/7/22, *Dr Liza Lovdahl Gormsen v Meta Platforms Inc, Meta Platforms Ireland Ltd, Facebook UK Ltd* – Reasoned Order, dated 15 March 2022 [5, 9 and 10].

which are devised by the EU and EU Member States,[80] Section 15B of the 1982 Act should rather be interpreted in line with the UK objective to improve the UK consumers' access to legal remedies in competition law cases.[81] Thus, Section 15B of the 1982 Act should be interpreted along with Section 47B(11) of the 1998 Act. Both provisions could cumulatively suggest that the UK consumer's domicile will be an important connecting factor. In order to substantiate the argument for a broad interpretation of Section 15B of the 1982 Act to cover collective redress proceedings, 'further consideration should be given to the use of third party funding as a last resort means of providing access to justice'.[82] The proposed approach should allow for collective competition law claims to be issued on behalf of consumers on an opt-out basis, which may be important for litigation funders to provide financial assistance with the litigation costs, facilitating injured parties' access to legal remedies.[83]

It is to be hoped that the specific issues concerning the classification of multinational groups would be addressed by the English courts in due course. Although the initial indication[84] is that, post-Brexit, the *Provimi*[85] approach would be followed under the CPR, an alternative approach which could be developed is to classify the parent company and its local subsidiary as a single economic unit for private international law purposes.[86] If the local subsidiary were to classify as a branch for jurisdictional purposes, then a claim form could be served on the multinational group of companies within the jurisdiction. On that basis, the claim form could be served without permission being required.[87] Of course, any such order for service of a claim form will be made 'without prejudice to the rights of [the defendants] to apply pursuant to Rule 34 of the Tribunal Rules to dispute the Tribunal's jurisdiction'[88] on *forum non conveniens* grounds.[89]

A different (and rather broad) approach to the issues of classification and assumption of jurisdiction under English law (as opposed to the one advanced under Brussels Ia) could be justified by the fundamentally different basis for the assumption of jurisdiction in England and Wales in comparison with the one advanced under the EU private international law rules.[90] In particular, there are three separate requirements that should be satisfied in this context. First, the claimant should be able to substantiate its competition

[80] F Rielaender, 'Aligning the Brussels Regime with the Representative Actions Directive' (2022) 71 *ICLQ* 107–138; A Pato, *Jurisdiction and Cross-Border Collective Redress: a European Private International Law Perspective* (Oxford, Hart Publishing, 2019) 153–55.

[81] Competition Act 1998 Section 47B(11)(b).

[82] Recommendation 13 – M Napier, P Hurst, R Musgrove and J Peysner, *Improved Access to Justice – Funding Options & Proportionate Costs Report & Recommendations* at 12, https://www.judiciary.uk/wp-content/uploads/JCO/Documents/CJC/Publications/CJC+papers/CJC+Improved+access+to+Justice+-Funding+options+and+proportionate+costs.pdf.

[83] See: Chapter 6.

[84] *JJH Enterprises Ltd (trading as ValueLicensing) v Microsoft* [2022] EWHC 929 (Comm).

[85] *Provimi* (n 68).

[86] See: Chapter 7 above.

[87] Paragraph 1A of PD 6B.

[88] *Dr Liza Lovdahl Gormsen* (n 79) [10]. See also: Case No: 1440/7/7/22 *Clare Mary Joan Spottiswoode CBE v Nexans France SAS Nexans SA and Others* – Reasoned Order of the President – Service out of the jurisdiction – 19 August 2022 [2].

[89] Chapter 7.

[90] *Lady Brownlie* (n 75) [55].

claim, with the required standard of proof being 'reasonable prospect of success'.[91] Secondly, if the UK CAT 'proceedings are to be treated as taking place in England and Wales',[92] a claimant has to make a good arguable case that its competition law claim is within one of the gateways set out in para 3.1 of PD 6B.[93] Thirdly, the English courts or 'the Tribunal shall not give permission for service out of the jurisdiction unless satisfied that [England and Wales or] the Tribunal is the proper place in which to bring the claim'.[94]

C. Applicable Law and Judicial Cooperation

The wide bases for the assumption of jurisdiction under English law[95] as well as for the allocation of jurisdiction under Brussels Ia[96] indicates that governance of related competition law claims, which are issued before different national courts, is a key governance challenge.

A major principle is that national competition laws regulate national markets, which in turn means the scope of the relevant competition laws, whose, is territorial. This is reflected in this book which refers to the concept of the regulatory jurisdiction as being important to set out the limits of the national jurisdiction to regulate the competition law aspects of various transnational economic activities.[97] This is inter alia set to 'limit […] conflicts by placing objective restraints on the regulatory authority of states'.[98]

However, the public international law solution does not appear to work well in private antitrust damages claims that arise out of transnational competition law infringements, indicating that multiple sets of competition laws are to apply extra-territorially. The book contains several chapters[99] which suggest that the judicial cooperation through PIL mechanisms in competition law matters would be much needed to attain a somewhat consistent outcome in related claims, which would in turn be important for improving injured parties' access to legal remedies in cross-border competition law cases. There are a number of major PIL issues that need to be addressed with regard to related and parallel proceedings which may arise in different (developed and developing) countries.

In some competition law claims, the related and parallel proceedings would mean that, unless foreign competition laws are factored in, multiple national courts would apply different competition laws (which enjoy mandatory character)[100] depending on where the proceedings are taking place. In order to provide a PIL solution, it is

[91] Civil Procedure Rules 6.37(1)(b); Competition Appeal Tribunal Rules 2015 r 31(2)(b).
[92] Competition Appeal Tribunal Rules 2015 r 31(2)(c).
[93] Ibid. See also: Civil Procedure Rules 6.37(1)(a).
[94] Competition Appeal Tribunal Rules 2015 r 31(3); Civil Procedure Rules 6.37(3).
[95] Chapters 4, 5 and 6.
[96] Chapters 4, 5 and 6.
[97] Chapters 9 and 10.
[98] A Mills, *The Confluence of Public and Private International Law: Justice, Pluralism, Subsidiarity in the International Constitutional Ordering of Private Law* (Cambridge, CUP, 2009) 236.
[99] Chapters 7, 8, 9, 10 and 12.
[100] Chapter 10.

suggested for 'the concept of restriction of competition'[101] in the UK version of Rome II to be broadly interpreted to cover infringements of foreign competition laws, which may be factored in by the English courts. As noted above, this approach would reflect the positive comity principles which should set the scene for an enhanced level of judicial cooperation in competition law matters.

The proposed PIL solution should allow for Article 6(3)(a) of Rome II to be relied on in stand-alone claims in which foreign competition laws are at stake. This approach should put the English courts in a good position to balance foreign regulatory interests in cross-border competition law claims. Another way to achieve a similar result would be for von Mehren's 'special substantive rules for multistate problems'[102] to be adjusted to provide even more flexibility for English judges to decide the extent to which the legitimate foreign regulatory interests should be factored in.[103] In other words, advancing such PIL solutions would enable a national court that has adjudicatory jurisdiction to factor in, or even apply, foreign competition laws (expressing foreign regulatory interests) along with its own competition laws.

A level of judicial cooperation would inter alia presuppose the aspects concerning the inter-relationship between regulatory proceedings in one jurisdiction and court proceedings in another to be an issue which should be thoroughly considered.[104] As part of this process, the judges would need to consider what the effects of foreign regulatory findings would be on private antitrust claims issued before the English courts.[105] It is suggested that, if the comity principles were to be relied upon by the English judges to ascertain applicable competition laws, it would make sense for the English courts to go a step further and rely on the 'notion of comity'[106] with a view to recognising and enforcing foreign judgments in relation to competition law claims.[107] Also, in order to minimise the risk of inconsistent outcomes in relation to competition law claims arising out of transnational competition law infringements, any foreign regulatory decisions may be regarded as prima facie evidence of the conduct.

In other competition law claims, the English judges would need to consider whether an infringing undertaking should be estopped from re-litigating certain issues (eg the nature of conduct; cartel arrangements) which had been determined abroad. In other words, the judges would need to determine whether a foreign judgment against the same infringing undertakings would have any effects in England and Wales.[108] A level of judicial cooperation in this respect should enable the national judges to effectively and efficiently deal with various preliminary issues, which may inevitably impact on the outcome of many cross-border competition law disputes. Addressing systematically these issues may be important for judges and policy-makers to minimise the length of the relevant proceedings, which should reduce costs and improve access to justice.

[101] Recital 23 of Rome II.
[102] von Mehren (n 5).
[103] Chapter 11.
[104] eg Article 16 of Council Regulation 1/2003.
[105] Chapters 11 and 12.
[106] *Adams v Cape Industries Plc* [1990] Ch 433, 552.
[107] Chapter 12. Compare: *Beals v Saldanha* [2003] SCC 72. See also: *Morguard Investments Ltd v De Savoye* [1990] 3 SCR 1077.
[108] Chapter 12.

There is a strong argument that the aspects concerning judicial cooperation in competition law matters need to be thoroughly discussed, post-Brexit, because – whilst the European Union would sometimes be considered as 'the most advanced and successful example of voluntary international co-operation in history'[109] – the UK was one of the most advanced and successful competition law jurisdictions which formed part of the European Union.[110] In particular, the Brexit negotiations[111] demonstrated that it was important for the UK and the EU to 'have the regulatory freedom to respond to new and emerging challenges'[112] in the area of competition law. This means that any mechanism for judicial cooperation needs to factor in the fact that the competition laws would potentially diverge.

Given the regulatory function of competition laws,[113] it is highly likely that there would be multiple competition laws which should apply in cases where transnational competition law infringements adversely affect the process of competition and consumers' welfare in a number of countries. A PIL approach to judicial cooperation should enable English judges to apply the competition laws of other countries that have legitimate concerns to regulate the competition law aspects of the relevant cross-border economic activities. This should ensure that an appropriate balance is struck between the different (but legitimate) regulatory interests.

V. Global Cities and Transnational Networks of Law Firms

The lack of an international convention that effectively deals with any related competition law claims that arise out of the same transnational competition law infringement means that an alternative approach must be considered. It should be noted that, in a broader context, Guzman[114] has taken the view that '[t]here are three forms of cooperation that could be implemented with regard to competition policy – information sharing, agreement on choice of law, and cooperation in terms of substantive rules'.[115] These issues are very important, but – when it comes to private antitrust enforcement – they are intertwined with the issues concerning jurisdiction[116] (including parallel and related proceedings)[117] and local effects (if any) of foreign judgments (or regulatory findings).[118]

[109] A Moravcsik, 'Preferences, Power and Institutions in 21st-century Europe' (2018) 56 *Journal of Common Market Studies* 1648, 1670.

[110] European Commission's Staff Working Document, *Executive Summary of the Impact Assessment* SWD(2013) 204 final [7].

[111] HM Government, 'The Future Relationship with the EU The UK's Approach to Negotiations' CP211 – February 2020 [68]; EU Directives for the Negotiation of a New Partnership with the United Kingdom of Great Britain and Northern Ireland, Brussels, 25 February 2020 [96].

[112] HM Government, 'The Future Relationship with the EU The UK's Approach to Negotiations' CP211 – February 2020 [67].

[113] A Shleifer, 'Understanding Regulation' (2005) 11 *European Financial Management*, 439. See more: Chapters 9 and 10.

[114] A Guzman, 'Competition law and cooperation: possible strategies' in AT Guzman (ed), *Cooperation, Comity, and Competition Policy* (Oxford University Press, 2011) 345.

[115] Ibid 356.

[116] Chapters 4, 5 and 6.

[117] Chapters 7, 8 and 9.

[118] Chapter 12.

This book demonstrates that advancing an appropriate model for judicial cooperation, which is set to minimise the risk of inconsistent outcomes in related competition law claims, would be central to the effective private enforcement of national competition laws in a global context, whilst ensuring that English judgments would be recognised and enforced abroad, which would in turn improve injured parties' access to legal remedies.

It is further suggested that transnational networks of legal practitioners and law firms which are based in such global cities as London might be important to ensure that, at the very least, the English courts (as well as any foreign courts) are aware about the developments with regard to related claims which are pending in the various jurisdictions. Indeed, if one considers the sociological aspects of globalisation,[119] it becomes obvious that the global cities (as London is) will continue to play an increasingly important role, which is central to governing transnational economic activities and the functioning of the global economy. Sassen[120] has noted that:

> The most powerful of the new geographies of centrality at the global level bind the major international financial and business centers: New York, London, Tokyo, Paris, Frankfurt, Zurich, Amsterdam, Los Angeles, Toronto, Sydney, and Hong Kong, among others. But this geography now also includes cities such as Bangkok, Taipei, Sao Paulo, and Mexico City. The intensity of transactions among these cities, particularly in the financial markets, trade in services, and investment, has increased sharply, and so have the orders of magnitude involved [….] Alongside these new global and regional networks of cities is a vast territory that has become increasingly peripheral and increasingly excluded from the major economic processes that are seen as fueling economic growth in the global economy[121]

The fact that certain global cities have emerged as important financial and business centres is another aspect of globalisation which needs to be taken into account with a view to implementing an appropriate mode of judicial cooperation in competition law matters.

Therefore, if the global cities are playing such an important role with a view to servicing the global economy, then it makes sense to go a step further and suggest that some of the law firms and the courts in these cities should be playing a central role in improving injured parties' access to legal remedies in private antitrust damages claims arising out of transnational infringements. Such an approach might find support in the global literature, which appears to indicate that:

> the global economy needs to be produced, reproduced, serviced, and financed. It is not simply a heightening of interdependence or a function of the power of multinational corporations and financial markets. Rather, it takes a vast array of highly complex functions to ensure its existence. These have become so specialised that they can no longer be contained in the functions of corporate headquarters. Global cities are strategic sites for the production of these specialized functions to run and coordinate the global economy.[122]

Therefore, a new approach to judicial cooperation may rather be developed in the global cities where some major international law firms have their offices. The UK CAT along

[119] S Sassen, *A Sociology of Globalization* (WW Norton & Company, London, 2007) 111.
[120] Ibid.
[121] Ibid 111–12.
[122] Ibid 73.

with the law firms in London might take advantage of London's role as a global business/financial centre with a view to advancing a soft law mechanism for judicial cooperation in competition law matters. For example, the courts and the legal practitioners in some global cities (eg London) could play a more prominent role in acting for parties in different sets of proceedings, ensuring that the relevant issues are identified and addressed somewhat consistently in light of the applicable laws and principles, whilst giving due regard to foreign regulatory/judicial findings.

Therefore, transnational networks of law firms may set the scene for a higher level of judicial cooperation in related private antitrust damages claims that arise out of the same set of transnational competition law infringements. If the foreign regulatory/court proceedings were to inform the parties' pleadings, this should facilitate courts' decision-making in so far as the pleadings would provide 'some plausible factual foundation for the application of the broad economic theory',[123] which would be central for the courts to effectively and efficiently deal with these cases, whilst attaining a level of consistency in a cross-border context.

That said, the CAT forewarned that this form of cooperation may have also drawbacks which need to be carefully considered. In particular, the following observations were put forward:

> The O'Higgins [proposed class representative] sought to suggest that Scott+Scott's involvement in similar litigation in the United States was a real advantage. We lay on one side the fact that Hausfeld was also involved in that litigation – albeit in what appears to be a more junior role than Scott+Scott. We consider that involvement in 'similar' litigation in another jurisdiction might involve as many pitfalls as advantages. This is a different jurisdiction, and there is a danger in becoming a prisoner of thinking that worked or might have worked before another court in another jurisdiction.[124]

Further research might be necessary to consider how the disadvantages may be minimised and advantages maximised. The issues are important because it seems that, despite the potential drawbacks, the CAT was briefed by Scott+Scott about the 'recent developments in the US foreign exchange litigation'.[125] Hence, transnational networks of the international law firms, which act for claimants and defendants in private antitrust damages claims, could set the scene for judicial cooperation in private antitrust matters. This cooperation could be facilitated by the domestic PIL rules which allocate adjudicatory jurisdiction, whilst factoring in foreign regulatory interests and minimising the inconsistencies in related proceedings and ensuring that any rendered judgment would be recognised and enforced abroad.

The proposed rather theoretical model for judicial cooperation must be empirically tested in a cross-border context, which should allow for this to be turned into a pragmatic model for judicial cooperation in competition law matters.

[123] *Royal Mail Group Ltd v DAF Trucks Ltd & Other, BT Group Plc & Others v DAF Trucks Ltd & Others* [2021] CAT 10 [43].

[124] *Michael O'Higgins* (n 8) [329].

[125] Ibid – see the list of witness statements at 249.

INDEX

www.ingramcontent.com/pod-product-compliance
Ingram Content Group UK Ltd.
Pitfield, Milton Keynes, MK11 3LW, UK
UKHW020906190926
475560UK00010B/303

9 781509 918669